COLLEGE MEN
AND MASCULINITIES

COLLEGE MEN
AND MASCULINITIES

Theory, Research, and Implications for Practice

Shaun R. Harper and Frank Harris III,

Editors

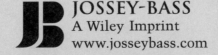

JOSSEY-BASS
A Wiley Imprint
www.josseybass.com

Published by Jossey-Bass
A Wiley Imprint
989 Market Street, San Francisco, CA 94103-1741—www.josseybass.com

Jossey-Bass books and products are available through most bookstores. To contact Jossey-Bass directly call our Customer Care Department within the U.S. at 800-956-7739, outside the U.S. at 317-572-3986, or fax 317-572-4002.

Jossey-Bass also publishes its books in a variety of electronic formats. Some content that appears in print may not be available in electronic books.

Credits begin on p. 583.

Library of Congress Cataloging-in-Publication Data
College men and masculinities : theory, research, and implications for practice / Shaun R. Harper and Frank Harris III, Editors.
    p. cm.
  Includes bibliographical references and index.
  ISBN 978-0-470-44842-7 (pbk.)
  1. Male college students—Psychology. 2. Male college students—Attitudes. 3. Men—Socialization. 4. Gay college students. 5. Masculinity. 6. Gender identity. I. Harper, Shaun R., 1975– II. Harris, Frank, 1975–
  LB2377.C65 2010
  378.1'9821—dc22

2009043624

Printed in the United States of America

FIRST EDITION

PB Printing 10 9 8 7 6 5 4 3 2 1

Contents

■   PART TWO
SEXUALITIES AND SEXUAL ORIENTATIONS   101

The Jossey-Bass
Higher and Adult Education Series

List of Figures and Tables

FIGURES

TABLES

To Emanuel Harper, Jr.,
the grandfather whose imprint on my manhood is everlasting
— SRH

To Wilbert L. Tillman,
whose love and inspiration I will forever appreciate
– FH III

Preface

The Boy Crisis: At Every Level of Education, They're Falling Behind. What to Do? (*Newsweek,* January 30, 2006)

College Gap Widens: 57% Are Women (*USA Today,* October 19, 2005)

The Gender Gap: How Much Does Higher Education Matter to Black Males? (*Black Issues in Higher Education,* May 10, 2001)

The New Gender Divide: At Colleges, Women Are Leaving Men in the Dust (*New York Times,* July 9, 2006)

UCLA Study Reveals Growing Gender Gap Among Hispanic College Students (*Diverse Issues in Higher Education,* October 16, 2008)

Why Black Men Struggle to Finish College (*Essence,* March 30, 2009)

The list of alarming headlines regarding the trouble with men on college and university campuses seems endless. At this point, little else remains to be done to inform the American public that there is a gender gap in college enrollments and baccalaureate degree attainment. For sure, postsecondary faculty and administrators have become intimately acquainted with the problems through news stories, an increased emphasis on men's issues at national education conferences, and firsthand observations of gender shifts in classroom engagement, student organization leadership, and participation in enriching educational experiences such as study abroad programs. At most institutions, there is also visual proof that something is not quite right with the guys. Take for instance the huge photograph that appeared on the front page of the January 26, 2007 edition of the *Chronicle of Higher Education*. Shown is a lone White male student in a college classroom with women seated all around him—they're smiling, he appears aloof. The picture was accompanied by a bold, attention-grabbing headline: "The Case of the Missing Men." Those who have somehow failed to notice all the recent headlines and are less familiar with these trends may ask, "How big is this problem and when did it start?"

According to data from the U.S. Department of Education, men were 52% of undergraduates in 1976. At that time they barely remained in the majority, a position held by male collegians throughout most of American history. But interestingly, they slipped behind their female peers in just four years; 52.3% of bachelor's degree seekers in 1980 were women. Given that the gender gap in college enrollments is a 30-year-old problem, why is it getting so much attention now? And besides, Black women have outnumbered their same-race male counterparts at Black Colleges since the 1950s. So why is this suddenly a big deal on those campuses? Perhaps it is because the student who has become increasingly missing from the college campus is someone's son, brother, friend, former teammate, or future co-parent. The effects of their dwindling presence in higher education are finally being felt in middle class and financially affluent White families, not just among minority and lower income groups.

With women comprising 56.9% of undergraduate enrollments in 2008, the panic about what's going on with men seems warranted. At present, women outnumber men across all racial groups in American higher education. However, the gap is most pronounced between Black students, with women outnumbering their male counterparts by 28% (the comparative gap for White undergraduates is 11.2%). Thus, the media attention placed on Black male collegians is indisputably important, though we argue in Chapter 1 of this book that the emphasis is often misplaced. Also of concern are gaps in degree attainment. For example, in 2007 men earned only 37.8% of all associate's degrees; 38.9% of bachelor's degrees awarded to Latinos; 28.6% of master's degrees awarded to Blacks; and 38.6% of doctorates awarded to Native Americans. These numbers make clear that educational intervention is urgently needed.

Our focus on the magnitude of the gender gap in enrollments and degree attainment ends here. We devote no more attention to it beyond this point, nor do we revisit the stack of media reminders that amplifies men's problematic postsecondary participation. Instead, this book offers explanatory insights into the undercurrents of issues reported in the news, trends observed in campus judicial affairs offices, and the complex (sometimes tumultuous) developmental journeys of college men. Our aim here is not to reduce the rightful sense of sudden public concern regarding how many men make it to and through higher education. However, our stance is this: The most pressing problems affecting male student outcomes would persist regardless of how many or how few are enrolled. Attempts to close the gender gap will continually fail if those enacting such efforts possess an insufficient understanding of who men are and the social conditions under which their masculinities are manufactured.

■ MEN'S LIVES IN COLLEGE

This book was inspired by another produced by two brilliant sociologists and leading men's studies scholars, Michael Kimmel and Michael Messner. Now in its eighth edition, *Men's Lives* is an anthology of exceptional scholarship published about men across the lifespan, not just during the college years. Consistently in each edition, the editors masterfully bring together a collection of "greatest hits" that provide insights into the social construction of masculinities, variable ways in which men perform gender, and the lived experiences of men as gendered beings. Kimmel and Messner state the following in their introduction to the eighth edition: "This is a book about men. But unlike other books about men, which line countless library shelves, this is a book about *men as men*."

Similarly, *College Men and Masculinities* is a book about *men as men* in the context of postsecondary education. In the tradition of the wildly popular book produced by those whom we regard as role models, ours is a collection of theory and research that helps explain much of what gets reported about male undergraduates in the news, in meetings of campus administrators, and at professional conferences. Because so little has been written about *men as men* in the higher education and student affairs literature (this is a problem on which we elaborate in Chapter 1), we have amassed a compendium featuring *some* of the best perspectives on male undergraduates published in the fields of sociology and gender studies, psychology, health, and anthropology. Contained in the sections and chapters that follow is a multidimensional view of men's lives in college—heterosexual men, men of color, gay men, fraternity men, men with disabilities, White men, bisexual men, community college men, and intercollegiate sportsmen are all represented in this book.

The terms "male" and "man" are used interchangeably throughout this volume. However, we acknowledge that *male* is a biological concept, whereas *man* encompasses the social meanings that are culturally defined as masculine and associated with traditionally male sex roles. Also understood is that sex is determined biologically and gender is socially constructed. Most of what we have chosen to include here is concerned with the latter. Notwithstanding, we deliberately chose a dual-pronged title. It is about both college men *and* their masculinities. Hence, a few contributions are neither written from social constructionist viewpoints nor focused on masculinities—they are simply about men.

The book is organized into six sections, each containing four to five contributions authored by some of the most prolific and widely cited scholars in education and the other aforementioned fields of study. The sections begin with a preface in which we describe the issues explored therein and briefly introduce the chapters that follow. At the end of each section is a set of implications for educational practice—programmatic efforts that postsecondary educators and administrators can employ to improve outcomes, reduce destructive behaviors and health risks, and facilitate the development of healthy identities among male undergraduates. We view the inclusion of practical implications as one of the most distinctive and useful attributes of this book. We were careful, though, to avoid being too prescriptive in our approach, as we recognize how campus cultures and localized gendered norms regulate the implementation of educational interventions. Therefore, we caution readers against viewing our recommendations as quick fix, "just add water" solutions to problems that play themselves out differently depending on context.

■ ACKNOWLEDGMENTS

We begin by thanking the two Michaels (Messner and Kimmel) for their various editions of *Men's Lives*. It was the first book we read as we joined Jason Laker, Tracy Davis, Chuck Eberly, Rachel Wagner, Brian Reed, Ryan Barone, and Keith Edwards on the journey to bring men's studies to higher education and student affairs. *Men's Lives* compelled the two of us to embark upon an interdisciplinary search for theoretically rich, methodologically sound, and socially important scholarship pertaining to college men. Honestly, without a model produced by two researchers outside our field, *College Men and Masculinities* in its present form probably would have never been conceived—at least not by us. Along with Messner and Kimmel, we wish to salute other architects of the men's studies and profeminist men's movements in the social sciences, college student affairs, and beyond. Their efforts made possible the availability of most that is published in this book. Appreciation is also expressed to our faculty colleagues and administrators on campuses across the country who are working in serious ways to enroll, engage, develop, retain, graduate, and prepare college men for productive participation in a socially honorable democracy. Especially laudable are Estela Mara Bensimon, George D. Kuh, Michael L. Jackson, Lori S. White, Marilee Bresciani, Fred McFarlane, Caren Sax, Marjorie Olney, James T. Minor, Darnell C. Cole, Andrew C. Porter, Sylvia Hurtado, Mitchell J. Chang, Stephen John Quaye,

Samuel D. Museus, Lori D. Patton, Ontario S. Wooden, David J. Johns, Margaret Sallee, Jaime Lester, Adrianna Kezar, Amanuel Gebru, and Gwendolyn Jordan Dungy, whose support for us is only superseded by more important commitments (i.e., student success, educational effectiveness, and social justice).

We both are privileged to have cultivated meaningful professional relationships with highly regarded scholars and administrators who know much about college men and exhibit extraordinary care for their well-being. Several of them graciously agreed to serve as members of the advisory board for this project. Their expertise led to the identification of over 130 books, journal articles, and book chapters that we read and considered for inclusion. Who knew so much had been published elsewhere about college men? This book has benefitted from having an advisory board that includes yet extends beyond the disciplinary borders of higher education as a field of study. Indeed, we are indebted to these 26 friends and colleagues for their amazingly helpful suggestions and feedback. Our sincerest gratitude also belongs to April Yee, Shizz H-H, Tryan L. McMickens, Kimberly A. Truong, Laura Struve, and Christopher B. Newman for their assistance with the technical assembly of this book. In addition, Harper is indebted to Cory Buckner, Shareef Ross McDonald, Collin Williams, Joshua Bennett, Marshawn Wolley, Brian A. Burt, Paul A. Young, De'Javieur Speller, Julian Curry, Trey Cotten, Andrew H. Nichols, and his other male mentees (past and present) whose undergraduate experiences enriched the development of his expertise on college men. Harris also acknowledges his partner, Amie, and their two children, Olivia Maddison and Anderson Joseph, and his mom, Sheila Duckworth, for loving him, believing in him, and allowing him to be the man in their lives.

Lastly, we wish to honor a dozen of the most significant men in our lives: Ryan J. Davis, Shon Fuller, William Emanuel Harper, Frank Harris, Jr., Frank Harris, Sr., Shawn K. Hill, Brien R. Kelley, Brandon E. Martin, Adewale Oyemade, Philip Rodgers, Hayward White, Jr., and Hayward White III. These are the men who support us, laugh with us, collaborate with us on the creation of memorable moments, accept us for who we are, simultaneously challenge and affirm our masculinities in productive ways, and afford us a refreshing view of the variable manifestations of manhood. They also love us and allow us to love them back. We are better men because we have these 12 men and numerous important others in our lives.

Shaun R. Harper
Philadelphia, Pennsylvania
Frank Harris III
San Diego, California

About the Editors

Shaun R. Harper is assistant professor of higher education at the University of Pennsylvania. He also holds a faculty appointment in the Center for Africana Studies at Penn. His research focuses on racism and gender inequities in higher education, Black male college access and achievement, the effects of college environments on student behaviors and outcomes, and gains associated with educationally purposeful student engagement. In September 2007, Harper was featured on the cover of *Diverse Issues in Higher Education* for his National Black Male College Achievement Study, the largest-ever empirical research study of Black undergraduate men. He has published seven books and more than 50 peer-reviewed journal articles, book chapters, and other academic publications. *The Journal of Higher Education*, *Journal of College Student Development*, *Teachers College Record*, *Men & Masculinities*, *Journal of Men's Studies*, *American Behavioral Scientist*, and several other well-regarded journals have published his research. In addition, Harper has delivered over 30 keynote addresses and presented more than 100 research papers, workshops, and symposia at higher education and student affairs conferences since 2004. His professional honors include the 2004 NASPA Melvene Hardee Dissertation of the Year Award, the 2005 ACPA *Annuit Coeptis* Award for early career contributions, the 2008 Outstanding Contribution to Research Award from the National Association of Academic Advisors for Athletics, the 2008 Early Career Award from the Association for the Study of Higher Education, and the 2010 NASPA Outstanding Contribution to Research Award. Harper has prior administrative experience in student activities, sorority and fraternity affairs, graduate admissions, and academic program administration. His Ph.D. in higher education administration is from Indiana University.

■■

Frank Harris III is assistant professor of postsecondary educational leadership and student affairs at San Diego State University. His research is broadly focused on student development in higher education and explores questions related to the social construction of gender and race on college campuses, college men and masculinities, and racial/ethnic disparities in college student outcomes. His scholarship has been published in the *Journal of College Student Development, Journal of Men's Studies, NASPA Journal, New Directions for Student Services, About Campus*, and a range of other journals and edited books. In 2007, Harris received two Dissertation of the Year awards from the American Educational Research Association (Division J) and the Association for Student Judicial Affairs. In 2008, he was recognized by the American College Personnel Association's Standing Committee for Men with its Outstanding Research Award. Harris was program chair for the 2008 Conference on College Men, co-sponsored by NASPA and ACPA. In addition, he has served as Region 6 chair for the NASPA Men and Masculinities Knowledge Community. Before joining the faculty at San Diego State, Harris spent nearly 10 years as a student affairs educator and college administrator. He earned an Ed.D. in higher education from the University of Southern California, Rossier School of Education.

Advisory Board

Harry Brod, Professor of Philosophy and Religion, University of Northern Iowa

Michael J. Cuyjet, Associate Professor of Education, University of Louisville

James Earl Davis, Professor of Education, Temple University

Tracy L. Davis, Professor, College Student Personnel Program, Western Illinois University

Keith Edwards, Director of Campus Life, Macalaster College

Nancy J. Evans, Professor of Higher Education, Iowa State University

Luoluo Hong, Vice Chancellor for Student Affairs, University of Hawaii-Hilo

Mary F. Howard-Hamilton, Professor of Higher Education, Indiana State University

Robin Hughes, Editor, *Journal for the Study of Athletes and Education,* Assistant Professor of Higher Education, Indiana University

Jerlando F. L. Jackson, Associate Professor of Higher Education, University of Wisconsin

Jackson Katz, Co-Founder, *Mentors in Violence Prevention*

Michael Kaufman, Founder, *The White Ribbon Campaign*

Michael S. Kimmel, Editor, *Men & Masculinities,* Professor of Sociology, State University of New York at Stony Brook

Jason A. Laker, Associate Vice Principal and Dean of Student Affairs, Queen's College

Bryant T. Marks, Assistant Professor of Psychology, Morehouse College

COLLEGE MEN
AND MASCULINITIES

CHAPTER 1

Beyond the Model Gender Majority Myth

Responding Equitably to the Developmental Needs and Challenges of College Men

Shaun R. Harper and Frank Harris III

> *Too often, though, we treat men as if they have no gender.*
> KIMMEL & MESSNER, 2010

In May 2009, Elizabeth Redden, a reporter for *Inside Higher Ed*, wrote a news story titled, "Lost Men on Campus." She began by briefly describing some contemporary issues facing college men, such as their lower rates of enrollment, persistence, and graduation in comparison to college women; their relative disengagement in enriching educational experiences and campus leadership positions; and their overrepresentation among campus judicial offenders. The remainder of the article was devoted to the Second National Conference on College Men, which had been recently co-sponsored by two student affairs professional associations and hosted at the University of Pennsylvania. Reportedly, educators and administrators from postsecondary institutions across the United States and Canada gathered to devise a set of educational strategies in response to the alarming status of male undergraduates. Highlighted in the story were conference presenters whose research linked various problems concerning college men to troubled masculinities and gender identity development. Perhaps more fascinating than Redden's article were the comments posted in response to it—nearly 100 within the first week.

Almost instantly, anonymous persons offered virtual commentary regarding the magnitude, sociocultural origins, political underpinnings, and implications of the gender gap in college. Remarks ranged from expressions of sympathy for men's loss of power in society to reminders of the permanence of patriarchy and its harmful effects on both women and men. Some attempted to share solutions based on anecdotal observations, and a few others critiqued the research cited in the news story. One responder proposed that women be allowed to carry guns on campus to defend themselves against male rapists; another suggested the politically correct ethos of American higher education is responsible for the disengagement of White male heterosexuals. "I'm a rising senior in high school. I'm not overly terrified by the loss of men at college campuses. All that means to me is a greater selection of hot chicks," one student wrote. In another post, attendees at the Conference on College Men were condemned for failing to recognize their own complicity in the cyclical reproduction of problematic educational outcomes among male students. These are just some of the many viewpoints written in response to the article.

We were disturbed by the apparent "either/or" bent to the online discussion—*either* equity for women *or* a stronger focus on men's issues, but very little advocacy for both. Although anonymous screen names were sometimes used, numerous posts were obviously gendered, with men on one side of the debate and women and pro-feminists (some of whom may have been men) on the other. This made us wonder, why not both? Why was there such a robust debate about who was disadvantaged more on college and university campuses? It was interesting that several posters also expressed that focusing on a male student's gender identity is considerably less important than other efforts to curb his destructive behaviors and reduce negative consequences of his actions. An emphasis on masculinities is really about "fixing" heterosexual White men, some felt. And others argued that gender studies courses and related programming are a waste of time and institutional resources, as they merely exacerbate political correctness and favor women at the expense of male students.

In this chapter, we unpack several issues reflected in comments on the *Inside Higher Ed* story. Specifically, our aim is to explain why there is such resistance to moving beyond singular notions of gender, beginning with historical insights into the privileged position of undergraduate men throughout the lifespan of American higher education. We then show how gender has been mishandled in recently published higher education and student affairs scholarship, and differentiate studies *of* men from those *about* men as men. This is followed by our observations of flawed assumptions regarding the universality of male privilege in college, which we have termed the "Model Gender Majority Myth." The chapter concludes with a call for greater participation of faculty and administrators in the developmental journeys of male undergraduates, as well as a more positive disposition toward the study of college men.

■ HIGHER EDUCATION: A MASCULINE HISTORY

Historian Frederick Rudolph noted: "Given the conditions of American life, it was inevitable that the college classroom should one day be blessed with the charms of femininity and graced by the presence of aspiring American womanhood. But it would take time" (1990, p. 306). He goes on to tell how a young woman was deemed fully qualified for admission to Yale in 1783 but was denied on the basis of her sex. Rudolph explains that women were viewed as being intellectually inferior and unworthy of education—their place was perceivably in the home. Hence, from the founding of Harvard in 1636 until 205 years later when Oberlin College awarded the first bachelor's degree to a woman, previously established men's colleges in the United States refused to become coeducational. Rudolph further reports that fewer than six of these institutions enrolled women prior to the start of the American Civil War. Consequently, for more than two centuries, masculine norms and gendered ideologies that privileged men were woven into the structural character of colleges and universities. These would not be easily changed.

In her book, *In the Company of Educated Women*, Barbara Miller Solomon writes about female academies and seminaries that eventually led to the founding of women's colleges in the mid-1850s. Solomon maintains that early feminists preferred coeducation, as they viewed women's colleges as "second best." In some instances, coordinate or annex female institutions were founded next to men's colleges that resisted coeducational instruction (for example, Radcliffe to Harvard and Barnard to Columbia). Accordingly, Radcliffe women were not awarded Harvard degrees until 1965, and Columbia did not admit female undergraduates until 1983. It was mostly during periods of war, when college-aged men were in shorter supply, that many coeducational institutions allowed more women to enroll (Eisenmann, 2007; Rudolph, 1990). Although women's access to higher education increased in the latter half of the 1800s, still just about half of all institutions remained single-sex at the turn of the century. That American higher education has excluded women longer than it has included them certainly weakens current concerns regarding the declining presence of men on campus. Also noteworthy is that the majority of colleges and universities in the United States have never achieved gender equity—the quest for it has indeed remained elusive.

In addition to restricting women's participation, Solomon (1985) also notes the historical absence of female faculty and the masculine-dominated curricula at coeducational institutions. Eisenmann (2007) discovered that despite their increased presence at U.S. postsecondary institutions during and immediately after World War II, women were viewed as "incidental students" and few policies and practices were developed to respond to their needs. Since their entry into a dual-gender version of higher education, women have been forced to contend with sexism, sexual harassment, and egregious acts of differential treatment that often cause them to question their intellectual competence and develop lower career aspirations than their male peers.

Dorothy Holland and Margaret Eisenhart's book, *Educated in Romance,* is based on a comparative study of undergraduate women attending two universities, one predominantly White and the other historically Black. Most of the students they followed from college into adulthood were extraordinarily bright and possessed high post-baccalaureate career aspirations upon entering the two institutions. But unfortunately, Holland and Eisenhart found that less than one-third of the women actualized such expectations. "Most had ended up with intense involvements in heterosexual relationships, marginalized career identities, and inferior preparation for their likely roles as future breadwinners," the authors report (p. 4).

Holland and Eisenhart (1990) describe a duo of campus cultures that amplified romance, reinforced traditional gender roles, and compelled women to invest much care into how attractive they were perceived by male students (prospective husbands). Similar findings emerged in Jacqueline Fleming's (1984) study of undergraduates, which included 1,514 Black women and 1,077 Black men. In her acclaimed book, *Blacks in College*, Fleming furnishes data on the emotional pain, social isolation, and competence anxieties that Black women felt on the eight predominantly White campuses she studied. Moreover, she offers this conclusion about gender at the seven Historically Black Colleges and Universities (HBCUs):

> It seems that when there are men around who are flexing their assertive muscles, there is no room for Black women to do the same. This basic pattern of women failing to translate their academic gains into good career development holds true in most of the Black Colleges studied. (p. 145)

Consistent with Fleming's findings regarding the subordination of women at HBCUs, Gasman's (2007) historiography shows how the experiences and contributions of women at these institutions have been consistently ignored in the higher education literature.

Jay, an anonymous person who contributed to the *Inside Higher Ed* post-article discussion, maintained: "Men are now damned at the university. We must instead conform to Women's Studies." Honestly, given the historical exclusion of women and the constant reinscription of masculine norms into the cultural fabric of most coeducational colleges and universities, it makes sense to us that some would care less about the current dilemmas facing college men. In fact, those who resist any attempt to shift gendered programming and curricula from women to men are wise for so doing, as American higher education has long proven itself incapable of responding simultaneously and separately to the needs of both women and men. Those who ask, "What will a focus on college men mean for enduring efforts to ensure the fair, respectful, and equitable treatment of women," should be labeled gender realists, not skeptics. Although our focus in this chapter is on men, our greater plea is for the closing of gendered outcomes gaps in postsecondary education. We simply want to make clear that men have gender too. Thus, the ongoing quest for gender equity should also be inclusive of them and responsive to their challenges.

■ INTRODUCING THE OTHER HALF OF GENDER

In their book, *The Other Half of Gender,* Ian Bannon and Maria Correia make clear how gender has long remained synonymous with women. That is, gender-related public policies and programmatic efforts are rarely inclusive of men. The male side of gender is acknowledged mostly in conversations regarding men's roles in eliminating the oppression and subordination of women, Bannon and Correia assert. Otherwise, any emphasis on men as gendered beings is thought to be in opposition to important efforts to achieve equity for women. The one-sided mishandling of gender occurs in most social spaces, including college and university campuses. For instance, student activities, resources, and courses offered on "gender" are almost always about rape and sexual assault, empowering and protecting the rights of women, and illuminating consciousness of women's experiences around the world. Though each is undeniably essential, they are examples of how gender is misused as a substitute for women. For sure, we are not arguing for a reduction in or the elimination of women's courses and initiatives; in fact, we feel there should be more. But we are advocating a two-sided treatment of gender for two important reasons: (1) It needs to be more widely understood that men have gender too; and (2) because gender is relational, the status of women cannot be improved without a corresponding emphasis on tending to the social forces that misshape men's attitudes and behaviors and helping them develop productive masculinities (Bannon & Correia, 2006; Connell, 2005).

Recent media facilitation with the troubled status of male undergraduates has not been accompanied by a sufficient emphasis on better understanding and responding productively to their developmental needs. This is certainly evidenced in the higher education and student affairs literature. The subtitle of Sharon Gmelch's (1998) book, *Gender on Campus: Issues for College Women,* is reflective of how several scholars have ascribed gender to only one group of college students. For example, the 2003 edited book, *Gendered Futures in Higher Education,* included only one chapter on men—it was titled, "The Gender of Violence on Campus." Similarly, chapters published in Jaime Lester's (2008) volume on gender at community colleges were overwhelmingly focused on women's needs, experiences, and issues. Moreover, most articles in student affairs journals that are supposedly about "gender" are almost always studies of women or statistical documentations of gender differences. Little higher education research, most of it recent, has been published on college men as men. Besides *College Men and Masculinities,* only two books (Byrne, 2006; Cuyjet, 2006) and two *New Directions for Student Services* monographs (Cuyjet, 1997; Kellom, 2004) have been published about male undergraduates; three of these four publications were focused specifically on African American men.

In our view, the most balanced consideration of gender (at least in recent years) is Linda Sax's 2008 book, *The Gender Gap in College.* In it she presents four decades of survey data on differences between male and female undergraduates, giving reasonably equal consideration to both. Sax's study furnishes an impressive supply of statistical proof on how gender variably affects students' identities, values, experiences, and outcomes. On some measures men were more advantaged, whereas on others women scored bigger gains. Thus, she submits that postsecondary educators and administrators should be equally concerned about the anxiety and low self-esteem issues faced by women as well as the increasing academic disengagement of men, along with other developmental and experiential differences found. Despite its laudable consideration of the duality of gender, Sax's book is based on a study *of* women and men, yet leaves much to be understood *about* them.

■ STUDENT DEVELOPMENT THEORY: STUDIES OF MEN—NOT AS MEN

Some fellow higher education and student development researchers may take issue with claims made in the previous section about the absence of men in gender studies. "Aren't most foundational studies of college students based on men," one might ask? As Nancy J. Evans and her colleagues note in the second edition of *Student Development in College,* several theories taught in graduate programs that prepare college and university administrators were derived from predominantly or exclusively male samples (for example, Erikson, 1968; Kohlberg, 1971; Levinson, 1978; and Perry, 1970). Hence, there is a widely held view that much is already known about men in the postsecondary domain. This is problematic in at least three ways. First, it ignores important demographic characteristics of the men upon whom these theories are based—most were White, heterosexual, young, and middle class. Because men of color, gay and bisexual men, and male students from lower-income backgrounds were excluded, the universality of these theories is extremely limited. Second, most theories are based on men from prior generations. As Kimmel (2008) notes, contemporary cohorts of college men are drastically different from those who were enrolled in the 1960s and 1970s. Although more recent theories have been formulated on women's development in college (for example, Belenky, Clinchy, Goldberger, & Tarule, 1997; Jones & McEwen, 2000; and Josselson, 1987), significantly fewer have been offered on men over the past 30 years.

The third and perhaps most noteworthy problem with the view of men as the foundational basis of the student development literature is that the studies were indeed based on men, but they were not explicitly concerned with gender (Davis & Laker, 2004). Classic studies with all-male samples are not necessarily synonymous with men's studies. The latter hinges on questions asked, particularly the pursuit of insights into various aspects of a male student's lived experiences as a gendered being. In more recent years, sociologists and psychologists have endeavored to gain more sophisticated understandings of men as men—the social construction of their masculinities, how environments shape their attitudes and behaviors, conflicts that ensue as they struggle to fulfill hegemonic conceptions of manhood, and so on (Connell, 2005). Few such studies have been undertaken by higher education researchers (i.e., Edwards & Jones, 2009; Harris III, 2008). We further explain in the next section how these theoretical misconceptions and the one-sided study of gender contribute to the routine disregard of male undergraduates in higher education and student affairs practice.

■ THE MODEL GENDER MAJORITY MYTH

Because male students have historically comprised the majority in American higher education and the structures of most colleges and universities (curricula, pedagogy, policies, staffing and leadership practices, etc.) remain largely based on norms established by men, gender-related initiatives over the past 40 years have been justifiably geared toward women. Such important work, however, has led to the manufacturing of a major erroneous assumption: that everything is just fine with college men. The basis and perpetuation of this misconception reminds us of a popular and unfortunate fallacy concerning another population in U.S. schools and colleges: Asian Americans.

Museus and Kiang (2009) describe the infamous "Model Minority Myth" that has misshaped public opinion about Asian Americans. Accordingly, this myth causes educators and others to wrongfully mistreat persons from various Asian backgrounds as a monolithic group. Since *some* Asian Americans have historically outperformed others in school, are gifted in mathematics and science, and are exceptional standardized test takers, *all* Asian American students are often thought to possess these talents and are expected to achieve accordingly. Such stereotypes are universally imposed on Asian Americans, despite their socioeconomic, cultural, linguistic, and intellectual differences. Museus and Kiang summarize five common misconceptions associated with the Model Minority Myth: (1) Asian Americans are all the same; (2) Asian Americans are not really racial minorities; (3) Asian Americans do not encounter major challenges because of their race; (4) Asian Americans do not require resources and support; and (5) college degree completion is equivalent to success.

In a similar fashion, we offer five flawed assumptions about college men: (1) Every male student benefits similarly from gender privilege; (2) gender initiatives need not include men unless they are focused on reducing violence and sexual assault against women; (3) undergraduate men do not encounter harmful stereotypes, social and academic challenges, and differential treatment in college environments because of their gender; (4) male students do not require gender-specific resources and support; and (5) historical dominance and structural determinism ensure success for the overwhelming majority of contemporary college men. We have termed this the Model Gender Majority Myth.

"The institutional structure advantages men and always has," several respondents to the *Inside Higher Ed* article argued. As such, equitable outcomes are presumed to be automatically conferred to the male student collective, despite stark differences within it. Most coeducational institutions have been contaminated by this reasoning. Consequently, too few efforts are enacted to respond to what media and institutional researchers report about the problematic status of male undergraduates. Campus leaders commonly fail to connect data from health centers, student engagement surveys, and judicial affairs offices with men's troubled gender identities and their obvious need for help. Furthermore, challenges faced by male subgroups, such as men with disabilities or those who work more than 20 hours per week off campus, are overshadowed by their presumed gender privilege. These are just some of the detrimental byproducts associated with the Model Gender Majority Myth.

■ HELP NEEDED IN GUYLAND

> Guyland is the world in which young men live. It is both a stage of life, a liminal un-defined time span between adolescence and adulthood that can often stretch for a decade or more, and a place, or, rather, a bunch of places where guys gather to be guys with each other, unhassled by the demands of parents, girlfriends, jobs, kids, and the other nuisances of adult life. (p. 4)

In his 2008 book, *Guyland: The Perilous World Where Boys Become Men,* Michael Kimmel takes readers on a journey from adolescence into adulthood. Based on interviews with over 400 young men (many of whom were college students or recent graduates), the book offers powerfully rich details about who these men are, how they struggle to negotiate manhood with themselves and their peers, why so many seem to wander aimlessly through their teenage years and twenties, and what their social interactions entail and signify. Guyland is a complex social sphere governed by a perceivably rigid set of behavioral and attitudinal regulations, which Kimmel refers to as "the Guy Code." For sure, those who fail to adhere to it bear the burden of ridicule and other penalties imposed by their peers (especially other men); yet those who abide by the code often feel like frauds.

After reading *Guyland,* we have never been surer of this: it is not a place that any young man should be expected to successfully navigate on his own. Our position on this is informed by four of Kimmel's provocative statements (p. 4):

1. Guyland becomes the arena in which young men so relentlessly seem to act out, seem to take the greatest risks, and do some of the stupidest things.
2. Directionless and often clueless, they rely increasingly on their peers to usher them into adulthood and validate their masculinity.
3. They feel incomplete and insecure, terrified that they will fail as grownups, that they will be exposed as fraudulent men.
4. Guyland is a volatile stage, when one has access to all the tools of adulthood with few of the moral and familial constraints that urge sober conformity. These 'almost men' struggle to live up to a definition of masculinity they feel they had no part in creating, and yet from which they feel powerless to escape.

These guys are enrolled at every postsecondary institution in America—they need help! Colleges and universities pay hundreds of professionals thousands of dollars each to help students mediate challenges encountered during their persistence through the undergraduate years. One college student posted this remark in response to the *Inside Higher Ed* news story: "Student affairs airheads teaching classes on masculinity. If that isn't a vision of hell I don't know what is." Acknowledging this perspective, we augment our previous declaration: college men need help from well-informed administrators and educators who recognize them as gendered beings, are familiar with their complex developmental needs, actually take time to talk with them about their conflict-laden voyages toward becoming better men, and are committed to equitably eradicating experiential and outcomes disparities between them and their female counterparts.

The stakes in Guyland are enormously consequential. Albeit in different ways, both women and men are harmed when an institution makes a one-sided investment into pursuing gender equity (Davis & Laker, 2004; Davis & Wagner, 2005). A man who graduates from college without having benefitted from a well-guided exploration of his gender identity is likely to find himself stranded on a destructive pathway of confusion and self-doubt. His stifled emotional maturity, bad health habits, undisrupted sexist viewpoints, and insufficient preparation for meaningful employment will not only negatively affect him but also other men and women he encounters during and after college (including spouses, partners, and colleagues). Those who work at colleges and universities have a professional responsibility to aid women and men alike in productively resolving identity conflicts and transitioning into a version of adulthood where patriarchy, sexism, homophobia, misogyny, misandry, sexual harassment, and all forms of abuse and oppression ends with them. We doubt that a 20-year-old person who is treated as though he has no gender will achieve all this on his own.

■ REPLICATING THE GOOD IN COLLEGE MEN

They are drunken, promiscuous, academically disengaged lovers of pornography, sports, and video games who rape women, physically assault each other, vandalize buildings on campus, and dangerously risk their lives pledging sexist, racially exclusive, homophobic fraternities. This view of male undergraduates was not only conveyed in several comments on the *Inside Higher Ed* article but are also reflective of what is generally reported about them in the higher education and social science literature. Although it is true that a fraction of young men engage in some of the dumbest, most alarming acts imaginable, not all are as destructive as the headlines and journal article abstracts lead us to believe. The institutional action we have advocated throughout this chapter is likely to be met with enormous resistance by those who possess only one view of college men. That is, some may understandably argue that trying to fix those who are not mature enough to behave sensibly in college is a waste of institutional resources. Our reaction to this is threefold.

First, once an institution admits a student and accepts payment for his enrollment, its agents (faculty, staff, and administrators) have a serious responsibility to aid in his development. Instead of "fixing" him, we prefer to align such efforts with those long recommended by student development theorists (i.e., Nevitt Sanford, who emphasized challenge and support) and routinely promoted by student affairs professional associations (i.e., the American College Personnel Association, whose core values include "development of the total student"). Second, we strongly agree with other scholars (namely Davis & Laker, 2004; Davis & Wagner, 2005) that an increase in gender-specific services and educational interventions crafted specially for college men will lead to a dramatic decrease in their self-mistreatment, excessive alcohol consumption, abuse of women, and other acts associated with misguided masculinities. We comfortably predict that the continued one-sided mistreatment of gender in higher education will sustain the very worst in college men, which concurrently and cyclically yields negative effects for them and their female peers. Concerning this, we believe it to be educationally irresponsible to continue doing what we have done over the past several years.

Our final reaction is concerning the stereotypical, unfairly popularized view of college men. Like Kimmel (2008), we fully acknowledge that young men in their teens and twenties at times behave stupidly and without good judgment. But what about those who don't—student leaders who are productively engaged on campus, make good grades, achieve healthy masculine identities, act responsibly and with honor, and respect women and themselves? Who are they and what can they teach us? Unfortunately, little is known about undergraduate men who act in these ways and embody such positive attributes. We know they exist, yet they are rarely consulted as models upon whom effective educational interventions should be based.

Although continuing to explore the social undercurrents and enablers of men's misbehavior and bad habits in college environments is important, so too is the pursuit of instructive insights based on student success. For example, researchers (Fries-Britt, 1997; Harper, 2009) have called attention to the deficit-orientation of most published scholarship and public discourse regarding African American male under-graduates. "In the research literature, there has been little attention given to solving educational problems for African American males, but more emphasis placed on documenting it" (Jackson & Moore III, 2008, p. 848). This fetish with the amplification of negative outcomes among these students has been counterbalanced with recent contributions that reveal how they productively negotiate masculinities within their same-race male peer groups (Harper, 2004); how they manage to succeed on HBCU campuses despite their academic underpreparedness (Palmer & Young, 2009); strategies they employ to gain access to social capital and exclusive information networks (Harper, 2008a); factors that lead to their persistence at community colleges (Hagedorn, Maxwell, & Hampton, 2002), as well as through baccalaureate degree attainment at four-year institutions (Warde, 2008); and enablers of their simultaneous achievement in academics and intercollegiate athletics (Martin & Harris III, 2006). Desperately needed are more studies such as these. Likewise, whereas Nuwer (1999) and Jones (2004) expose hazing as one of the grimiest aspects of the college fraternity, other scholars (i.e., Harper, 2008; Harper & Harris III, 2006; Kimbrough, 1995) reveal positive behaviors that are reinforced in modern day Greek-letter men's organizations; unfortunately, the latter is consistently overshadowed by the former.

To meet their developmental needs, educators and administrators must move beyond a singular view of college men. Identifying the good in them and seeking to replicate those traits in their same-sex peers should be the center of gender programming and educational interventions designed to reverse problematic outcomes among male undergraduates. One student who is trapped in the darkest corner of Guyland may be rescued through what has been learned from his buddy who somehow managed to escape its harmful trappings. Those of us who care authentically about gender in the postsecondary context need to better understand how some men develop into mature adults who responsibly enter society as healthy citizens, ethical leaders and professionals, principled parents, and unwavering agents for social justice.

■ CONCLUSION

Maintaining our composure while reading the *Inside Higher Ed* posts was difficult, but writing this chapter proved to be even harder. Frustrating for us was the zero-sum perspective articulated in several of the online posts—a common and unfortunate misconception that equity for one automatically disadvantages the other. Although we disagree with this point of view, revisiting the history of American higher education helped us better understand from where it comes. As we noted previously, most colleges and universities in the United States have done a poor job of simultaneously and equitably educating women and men. Why should we expect educators and administrators who work within predominantly masculine institutional structures to suddenly get better at closing gendered experiential and outcomes gaps between women and men when doing so has not occurred over the 374-year lifespan of postsecondary education in this country? Our answer is this: as long as students, regardless of their gender, come to us with developmental needs, educational goals, and tuition dollars in hand, we should expect no less of those who are entrusted with their success. Moreover, the U.S. Department of Education projects 2,375,000 associate's and bachelor's degrees will be awarded this year (2010); 40.9% of them will be earned by men. To send nearly one million college-educated men into the world with troubled masculinities, underdeveloped gender identities, and erroneous assumptions concerning women and other men with whom they co-occupy society makes contemporary institutions of higher education one of the guiltiest culprits in the perpetual maintenance of patriarchy, sexism, and homophobia in America.

REFERENCES

Bannon, I., & Correia, M. (Eds.). (2006). *The other half of gender: Men's issues in development*. Washington, DC: The World Bank.

Belenky, M. F., Clinchy, B. M., Goldberger, N. R., & Tarule, J. M. (1997). *Women's ways of knowing: The development of self, voice, and mind*. New York: Basic Books.

Byrne, D. N. (Ed.). (2006). *Models of success: Supporting achievement and the retention of Black males at HBCUs*. New York: Thurgood Marshall College Fund.

Connell, R. W. (2005). *Masculinities* (2nd ed.). Berkeley: University of California Press.

Cuyjet, M. J. (Ed.). (1997). *Helping African American men succeed in college*. New Directions for Student Services (No. 80). San Francisco: Jossey-Bass.

Cuyjet, M. J. (Ed.). (2006). *African American men in college*. San Francisco: Jossey-Bass.

Davis, T. L., & Laker, J. A. (2004). Connecting men to academic and student affairs programs and services. In G. E. Kellom (Ed.), *Developing effective programs and services for college men*. New Directions for Student Services (No. 107, pp. 47–57). San Francisco: Jossey-Bass.

Davis, T. L., & Wagner, R. (2005). Increasing men's development of social justice attitudes and actions. In R. D. Reason, E. M. Broido, T. L. Davis, & N. J. Evans (Eds.), *Developing social justice allies*. New Directions for Student Services (No. 110, pp. 29–41). San Francisco: Jossey-Bass.

Edwards, K. E., & Jones, S. R. (2009). "Putting my man face on": A grounded theory of college men's gender identity development. *Journal of College Student Development, 50*(2), 210–228.

Eisenmann, L. (2007). *Higher education for women in post-war America, 1945–1965*. Baltimore: Johns Hopkins University Press.

Erikson, E. H. (1968). *Identity: Youth and crisis*. New York: Norton.

Evans, N. J., Forney, D. S., Guido, F. M., Patton, L. D., & Renn, K. A. (2010). *Student development in college: Theory, research, and practice* (2nd ed.). San Francisco: Jossey-Bass.

Fries-Britt, S. L. (1997). Identifying and supporting gifted African American men. In M. J. Cuyjet (Eds.), *Helping African American men succeed in college*. New Directions for Student Services (No. 80, 65–78). San Francisco: Jossey-Bass.

Gasman, M. (2007). Swept under the rug? A historiography of gender and Black Colleges. *American Educational Research Journal, 44*(4), 760–805.

Gmelch, S. B. (1998). *Gender on campus: Issues for college women*. New Brunswick, NJ: Rutgers University Press.

Hagedorn, L. S., Maxwell, W., & Hampton, P. (2002). Correlates of retention for African-American males in community colleges. *Journal of College Student Retention, 3*(3), 243–263.

Harper, S. R. (2004). The measure of a man: Conceptualizations of masculinity among high-achieving African American male college students. *Berkeley Journal of Sociology, 48*(1), 89–107.

Harper, S. R. (2008a). Realizing the intended outcomes of *Brown*: High-achieving African American male undergraduates and social capital. *American Behavioral Scientist, 51*(7), 1029–1052.

Harper, S. R. (2008b). The effects of sorority and fraternity membership on class participation and African American student engagement in predominantly White classroom environments. *College Student Affairs Journal, 27*(1), 94–115.

Harper, S. R. (2009). Niggers no more: A critical race counternarrative on Black male student achievement at predominantly white colleges and universities. *International Journal of Qualitative Studies in Education, 22*(6), 697–712.

Harper, S. R., & Harris III, F. (2006). The role of Black fraternities in the African American male undergraduate experience. In M. J. Cuyjet (Ed.), *African American men in college* (pp. 128–153). San Francisco: Jossey-Bass.

Harris III, F. (2008). Deconstructing masculinity: A qualitative study of college men's masculine conceptualizations and gender performance. *NASPA Journal, 45*(4), 453–474.

Holland, D. C., & Eisenhart, M. A. (1990). *Educated in romance: Women, achievement, and college culture*. Chicago, IL: University of Chicago Press.

Jackson, J.F.L., & Moore III, J. L. (2008). The African American male crisis in education: A popular media infatuation or needed public policy response? *American Behavioral Scientist, 51*(7), 847–853.

Jones, R. L. (2004). *Black haze: Violence, sacrifice, and manhood in Black Greek-letter fraternities*. Albany: State University of New York Press.

Josselson, R. (1987). *Finding herself: Pathways to identity development in women*. San Francisco: Jossey-Bass.

Jones, S. R., & McEwen, M. K. (2000). A conceptual model of multiple dimensions of identity. *Journal of College Student Development, 41*(4), 405–414.

Kellom, G. E. (Ed.). (2004). *Developing effective programs and services for college men*. New Directions for Student Services (No. 107). San Francisco: Jossey-Bass.

Kimbrough, W. M. (1995). Self-assessment, participation, and value of leadership skills, activities, and experiences for Black students relative to their membership in historically Black fraternities and sororities. *Journal of Negro Education, 64*, 63–74.

Kimmel, M. S. (2008). *Guyland: The perilous world where boys become men*. New York: HarperCollins.

Kimmel, M. S., & Messner, M. A. (Eds.). (2010). *Men's lives* (8th ed.). Boston: Allyn & Bacon.

Kohlberg, L. (1971). *Stages of moral development as a basis for moral education*. Cambridge, MA: Harvard University Center for Moral Education.

Lester, L. (Ed.). (2008). *Gendered perspectives on community colleges*. New Directions for Community Colleges (No. 142). San Francisco: Jossey-Bass.

Levinson, D. (1978). *The seasons of a man's life*. New York: Knopf.

Martin, B. E., & Harris III, F. (2006). Exploring productive conceptions of masculinities: Lessons learned from academically-driven African American male student-athletes. *Journal of Men's Studies, 14*(3), 359 –378.

Museus, S. D., & Kiang, P. N. (2009). Deconstructing the model minority myth and how it contributes to the invisible minority reality in higher education research. In S. D. Museus (Ed.), *Conducting research on Asian Americans in higher education*. New Directions for Institutional Research (No. 142, pp. 5–15). San Francisco: Jossey-Bass.

Nuwer, H. (1999). *Wrongs of passage: Fraternities, sororities, hazing, and binge drinking*. Bloomington: Indiana University Press.

Palmer, R. T., & Young, E. M. (2009). Determined to succeed: Salient factors that foster academic success for academically underprepared Black males at a Black College. *Journal of College Student Retention, 10*(4), 465–482.

Perry, W. G. (1970). *Forms of intellectual and ethical development in the college years: A scheme*. Troy, MO: Holt, Rinehart, & Winston.

Redden, E. (2009, May 22). Lost men on campus. *Inside Higher Ed*. Retrieved August 19, 2009, from http://www.insidehighered.com/news/2009/05/22/men

Ropers-Huilman, B. (Ed.). (2003). *Gendered futures in higher education: Critical perspectives for change*. Albany: State University of New York Press.

Rudolph, F. (1990). *The American college & university: A history*. Athens: University of Georgia Press.

Sax, L. J. (2008). *The gender gap in college: Maximizing the developmental potential of women and men.* San Francisco: Jossey-Bass.

Solomon, B. M. (1985). *In the company of educated women: A history of women and higher education in America.* New Haven, CT: Yale University Press.

U.S. Department of Education. (2009). *Digest of education statistics, 2008.* Washington DC: Institute of Education Sciences, National Center for Education Statistics.

Warde, B. (2008). Staying the course: Narratives of African American males who have completed a baccalaureate degree. *Journal of African American Studies, 12*(1), 59 –72.

PART ONE

IDENTITY DEVELOPMENT AND GENDER SOCIALIZATION: INTRODUCTION

The notion that masculinity is a socially constructed concept has been a central argument in the recent discourse on college men and masculinities. To say that masculinity is a socially constructed concept is to assert that it is a performed identity—that is, one is not born knowing how to express masculinities according to socially prescribed expectations but rather learns to do so through social messages and interactions that are reinforced beginning in childhood and persisting through adulthood. A central message that is conveyed throughout this process is that boys should not "act like girls" and should avoid behaviors that are socially constructed as feminine. These lessons about masculinities are reinforced in nearly all of boys' social interactions—with adults, with other children, in schools, in youth activities, and so forth. Boys also learn that there are rewards (e.g., praise, acceptance, validation) that are associated with performing masculinities according to socially prescribed expectations. Likewise, there are consequences (e.g., shame, alienation, reprimands) for violating these expectations.

The social construction of masculinities is not a new concept. Informed by the work of feminist theorists, this concept was popularized in the late 1970s and early 1980s by men's studies scholars, notably Harry Brod, R. W. Connell, Michael Kaufman, Michael Kimmel, Michael Messner, James Messerschmidt, Joseph Pleck, and Don Sabo. But only recently have higher education scholars and student affairs educators begun to approach their research and practice relating to college men from a social constructionist perspective and view college men as "gendered beings" (Kimmel & Messner, 2009). As we noted in Chapter 1 of this book, theories and perspectives that formed the foundation of student affairs as a profession are based, almost exclusively, on research that prioritized the experiences of men (Evans, Forney, Guido, Patton, & Renn, 2010). However, gender was not a construct that was purposefully explored in this research. Consequently, such studies offer very little insight into the experiences of college men as gendered beings.

Identity development is, as a social process, influenced largely by people's interactions with others. Thus, understanding the development of college men requires examining their experiences from a social constructionist perspective. Recent studies on the gender identity development of college men (e.g., Edwards & Jones, 2009; Harris, 2008) have concluded that masculinities have noticeable influences on the ways in which men experience college—namely, in the decisions they make about friendships, how they choose to spend their time outside of class, the choices they make about careers and majors, and how they engage in sexual and romantic relationships.

The chapters in Part One highlight key issues, processes, and challenges related to gender socialization and identity development among college men. In doing so, at least three key questions are raised and explored: (1) What are the culturally dominant norms, meanings, and expectations of masculinities in America; (2) how do men come to learn and internalize these meanings and expectations; and (3) what are the consequences for men when they embrace them, either knowingly or unknowingly?

Chapter 2, written by Michael S. Kimmel, is a theoretical discussion of masculinity as a socially constructed identity. Kimmel foregrounds several fundamental components of masculinities. One key argument Kimmel advances in this chapter is that men both police and validate the gender performance of other men. Therefore, although it is widely assumed that men perform masculinities to attract the attention of women, it is ultimately other men who are the targets of men's masculine performance. Kimmel also discusses the "paradox of masculinity." This concept suggests that, despite having a disproportionate amount of social power (in comparison to women), men often feel powerless because they are taught that in order to be "real men" they must be tough, fearless, powerful, wealthy, sexually attractive, and successful (among other things) at all times. Of course, this is an expectation that cannot be realized by the overwhelming majority of men, especially those who are low income, ethnic minority, physically disabled, and non-heterosexual (to name a few). This disconnect between what men are socialized to believe about masculinities and what they actually experience as men leads to a host of risky and destructive behaviors to hide insecurities and fears of not measuring up to what others expect of them as men. One way of expressing masculinities is to assume dominance and control over others. Thus, sexism, homophobia, racism, and other oppressive acts are used by men to gain or recapture a sense of manhood. Lastly, Kimmel acknowledges that because gender intersects with other identities (race/ethnicity, social class, age, ability, sexual orientation, etc.), a hierarchy of masculinities exists. In other words, some masculinities are socially constructed as more privileged or dominant than others. Situated at the top of the masculine hierarchy are White, affluent, heterosexual, and able-bodied men, whereas ethnic minority, non-heterosexual, working-class, and physically disabled men are less privileged and valued.

Whereas Michael Kimmel deconstructs masculinity as a socially constructed identity, the three remaining chapters in Part One illuminate the consequences of performing masculinities according to culturally defined expectations—not only for men themselves but also for the people who are important in their lives and the communities in which they interact. Chapter 3, written by James M. O'Neil, Barbara J. Helms, Robert K. Gable, Laurence David, and Lawrence S. Wrightsman, is a groundbreaking piece that offers several important concepts for examining and theorizing about social constructions of masculinities and how they manifest in college contexts. They were among the first to propose men's "fear of femininity" as an empirically proven phenomenon to explain a host of gender-related conflicts and patterns that are typical among men, including homophobia, a decreased capacity for intimacy, increased anxiety, depression, and poor help-seeking. Building on the work of O'Neil et al. and that of early identity development scholars, in Chapter 4, Tracy L. Davis examines how college men cope with culturally defined notions and expectations of what it means to be a man. One of the most compelling findings from Davis's study is that college men both recognized and valued the need for self-expressions that lie outside the boundaries of what has been socially constructed as masculine, yet fears and concerns about being perceived as feminine or gay made it difficult for the participants to embrace the psychoemotional aspects of their identities.

That "previous research has neglected to explore identities and development among male students at community colleges" is a noteworthy critique of the published research on college men and masculinities that is offered by Frank Harris III and Shaun R. Harper in Chapter 5. In response to this gap in the published research, Harris and Harper endeavor to move the discourse surrounding men enrolled at community colleges beyond simply reporting rates and disparities in enrollment, persistence, and graduation by infusing perspectives relating to gender and masculinities into this discussion. Harris and Harper profile four community college men who represent diverse backgrounds and experiences and are challenged by gender-related conflicts. This chapter will be of particular interest to community college educators who work with college men in that the authors propose strategies to support the identity development and success of men who are challenged by issues much like the four men who are profiled in the chapter. Harris and Harper conclude their discussion by calling for more research on masculinities as they manifest in community college contexts.

In the last chapter in Part One, James R. Mahalik, Glenn E. Good, and Matt Englar-Carlson explore the consequences of masculinities from a counseling and therapy perspective. Like O'Neil and his colleagues, Mahalik, Good, and Englar-Carlson also propose a set of patterns or "scripts" that capture the gender conflicts that manifest as a result of socially constructed masculinities. Each script highlights specific aspects of masculinities, such as physical violence, aggressiveness, homophobia, and sexual promiscuity. A key takeaway point from this chapter is that although masculinity is a socially constructed concept that encompasses shared meanings and assumptions about gender, some conceptualizations of masculinities will present more strongly with some men than others. Thus, those who work with men in counseling and advising capacities must recognize which socially prescribed messages are most salient for the individual they are treating or working with.

Taken as a whole, these chapters confirm the ways in which narrow and rigid norms that govern gender performance for men limit their ability to be fully human and realize their full potential. Unfortunately, these consequences manifest strongly on college campuses via several gendered trends and outcomes. For example, recent reports conclude that men are underrepresented among college students who enroll, persist, and graduate from college; participate in campus service and leadership activities; and seek help at campus health and counseling centers (Kellom, 2004; Sax, 2008). Despite being a quantitative minority on most campuses, men are overrepresented among students who commit acts of violence, perpetrate sexual assaults, and abuse drugs and alcohol while enrolled in college.

The consequences that are associated with performing masculinities according to culturally defined expectations are well documented. Yet the same narrow patterns of socially appropriate masculine performance have persisted relatively undisrupted for decades (if not centuries), which begs the question: "What, if any, positive functions do traditional social constructions serve in the lives of men?" This question remains largely unexplored in the discourse on college men and masculinities. Yet this seems to be an important starting point for educators who aim to help men develop healthy and conflict-free gender identities. The overwhelming majority of the scholarship on masculinities assumes a negative or deficit perspective, which may leave some educators wondering, "What does 'good' masculinity look like and how can we help students achieve it?" James Mahalik and his colleagues suggest that traditional expectations of performing masculinities may be associated with some productive behaviors, such as an increased capacity for problem solving, calmness during crisis, and the tendency to sacrifice one's personal needs in order to meet the needs of others. Chapter 22 by Shaun R. Harper in Part Five of this volume also considers productive conceptualizations that were observed among a group of African American male college achievers. Beyond the insights offered by these studies, we know little about the positive aspects of masculinities for college men.

REFERENCES

Edwards, K. E., & Jones, S. R. (2009). "Putting my man face on": A grounded theory of college men's gender identity development. *Journal of College Student Development, 50* (2), 210–228.

Evans, N. J., Forney, D. S., Guido, F. M, Patton, L. D., & Renn, K. A. (2010). *Student development in college: Theory, research, and practice* (2nd ed). San Francisco: Jossey-Bass.

Harris III, F. (2008). Deconstructing masculinity: A qualitative study of college men's masculine conceptualizations and gender performance. *NASPA Journal, 45* (4), 453–474.

Kellom, G. E. (Ed.). (2004). *Developing effective programs and services for college men.* New Directions for Student Services no. 107. San Francisco: Jossey-Bass.

Kimmel, M. S., & Messner, M. A. (Eds.). (2009). *Men's lives* (8th ed). Boston: Allyn & Bacon.

Sax, L. J. (2008). *The gender gap in college: Maximizing the developmental potential of women and men.* San Francisco: Jossey-Bass.

CHAPTER 2

Masculinity as Homophobia

Fear, Shame, and Silence in the Construction of Gender Identity

Michael S. Kimmel

W e think of manhood as eternal, a timeless essence that resides deep in the heart of every man. We think of manhood as a thing, a quality that one either has or doesn't have. We think of manhood as innate, residing in the particular biological composition of the human male, the result of androgens or the possession of a penis. We think of manhood as a transcendent tangible property that each man must manifest in the world; the reward presented with great ceremony to a young novice by his elder for having successfully completed an arduous initiation ritual. In the words of poet Robert Bly (1990), "the structure at the bottom of the male psyche is still as firm as it was twenty thousand years ago" (p. 230).

This idea that manhood is socially constructed and historically shifting should not be understood as a loss, that something is being taken away from men.

In fact, it gives us something extraordinarily valuable—agency, the capacity to act. It gives us a sense of historical possibilities to replace the despondent resignation that invariably attends timeless ahistorical essentialisms. Our behaviors are not simply "just human nature," because "boys will be boys." From the materials we find around us in our culture—other people, ideas, objects—we actively create our worlds, our identities. Men, both individually and collectively, can change.

■ MASCULINITY AS A HOMOSOCIAL ENACTMENT

Other men: We are under the constant careful scrutiny of other men. Other men watch us, rank us, grant our acceptance into the realm of manhood. Manhood is demonstrated for other men's approval. It is other men who evaluate the performance. Literary critic David Leverenz (1991) argues that "ideologies of manhood have functioned primarily in relation to the gaze of male peers and male authority" (769). Think of how men boast to one another of their accomplishments—from their latest sexual conquest to the size of the fish they caught—and how we constantly parade the markers of manhood—wealth, power, status, sexy women—in front of other men, desperate for their approval.

That men prove their manhood in the eyes of other men is both a consequence of sexism and one of its chief props. "Women have, in men's minds, such a low place on the social ladder of this country that it's useless to define yourself in terms of a woman," noted playwright David Mamet.

"What men need is men's approval." Women become a kind of currency that men use to improve their ranking on the masculine social scale. (Even those moments of heroic conquest of women carry, I believe, a current of homosocial evaluation.) Masculinity is a *homosocial* enactment. We test ourselves, perform heroic feats, take enormous risks, all because we want other men to grant us our manhood.

Masculinity as a homosocial enactment is fraught with danger, with the risk of failure, and with intense relentless competition. "Every man you meet has a rating or an estimate of himself which he never loses or forgets," wrote Kenneth Wayne (1912) in his popular turn-of-the-century advice book. "A man has

his own rating, and instantly he lays it alongside of the other man" (18). Almost a century later, another man remarked to psychologist Sam Osherson (1992) that "[b]y the time you're an adult, it's easy to think you're always in competition with men, for the attention of women, in sports, at work" (291).

Homophobia is a central organizing principle of our cultural definition of manhood. Homophobia is more than the irrational fear of gay men, more than the fear that we might be perceived as gay. "The word 'faggot' has nothing to do with homosexual experience or even with fears of homosexuals," writes David Leverenz. "It comes out of the depths of manhood: a label of ultimate contempt for anyone who seems sissy, untough, uncool" (1986, 455). Homophobia is the fear that other men will unmask us, emasculate us, reveal to us and the world that we do not measure up, that we are not real men. We are afraid to let other men see that fear. Fear makes us ashamed, because the recognition of fear in ourselves is proof to ourselves that we are not as manly as we pretend, that we are, like the young man in a poem by Yeats, "one that ruffles in a manly pose for all his timid heart." Our fear is the fear of humiliation. We are ashamed to be afraid.

Shame leads to silence—the silence that keeps other people believing that we actually approve of the things that are done to women, to minorities, to gays and lesbians in our culture. The frightened silence as we scurry past a woman being hassled by men on the street. That furtive silence when men make sexist or racist jokes in a bar. That clammy-handed silence when guys in the office make gay-bashing jokes. Our fears are the sources of our silences, and men's silence is what keeps the system running. This might help to explain why women often complain that their male friends or partners are often so understanding when they are alone and yet laugh at sexist jokes or even make those jokes themselves when they are out with a group.

The fear of being seen as a sissy dominates the cultural definitions of manhood. It starts so early. "Boys among boys are ashamed to be unmanly," wrote one educator in 1871 (cited in Rotundo 1993, 264). I have a standing bet with a friend that I can walk onto any playground in America where six-year-old boys are happily playing and by asking one question, I can provoke a fight. That question is simple: "Who's a sissy around here?" Once posed, the challenge is made. One of two things is likely to happen. One boy will accuse another of being a sissy, to which that boy will respond that he is not a sissy, that the first boy is. They may have to fight it out to see who's lying. Or a whole group of boys will surround one boy and all shout, "He is! He is!" That boy will either burst into tears and run home crying, disgraced, or he will have to take on several boys at once, to prove that he's not a sissy. (And what will his father or older brothers tell him if he chooses to run home crying?) It will be some time before he regains any sense of self-respect.

Violence is often the single most evident marker of manhood. Rather it is the willingness to fight, the desire to fight. The origin of our expression that one "has a chip on one's shoulder" lies in the practice of an adolescent boy in the country or small town at the turn of the century, who would literally walk around with a chip of wood balanced on his shoulder—a signal of his readiness to fight with anyone who would take the initiative of knocking the chip off (see Gorer 1964, 38; Mead 1965).

As adolescents, we learn that our peers are a kind of gender police, constantly threatening to unmask us as feminine, as sissies. One of the favorite tricks when I was an adolescent was to ask a boy to look at his fingernails. If he held his palm toward his face and curled his fingers back to see them, he passed the test. He'd looked at his nails "like a man." But if he held the back of his hand away from his face, and looked at his fingernails with arm outstretched, he was immediately ridiculed as a sissy.

As young men we are constantly riding those gender boundaries, checking the fences we have constructed on the perimeter, making sure that nothing even remotely feminine might show through. The possibilities of being unmasked are everywhere. Even the most seemingly insignificant thing can pose a threat or activate that haunting terror. On the day the students in my course "Sociology of Men and Masculinities" were scheduled to discuss homophobia and male-male friendships, one student provided a touching illustration. Noting that it was a beautiful day, the first day of spring after a brutal northeast winter, he decided to wear shorts to class. "I had this really nice pair of new Madras shorts," he commented. "But then I thought to myself, these shorts have lavender and pink in them. Today's class topic is homophobia. Maybe today is not the best day to wear these shorts."

Our efforts to maintain a manly front cover everything we do. What we wear. How we talk. How we walk. What we eat. Every mannerism, every movement contains a coded gender language. Think, for example, of how you would answer the question: How do you "know" if a man is homosexual? When I ask this question in classes or workshops, respondents invariably provide a pretty standard list of stereotypically effeminate behaviors. He walks a certain way, talks a certain way, acts a certain way. He's very emotional; he shows his feelings. One woman commented that she "knows" a man is gay if he really cares about her; another said she knows he's gay if he shows no interest in her, if he leaves her alone.

Now alter the question and imagine what heterosexual men do to make sure no one could possibly get the "wrong idea" about them. Responses typically refer to the original stereotypes, this time as a set of negative rules about behavior. Never dress that way. Never talk or walk that way. Never show your feelings or get emotional. Always be prepared to demonstrate sexual interest in women that you meet, so it is impossible for any woman to get the wrong idea about you.

In this sense, homophobia, the fear of being perceived as gay, as not a real man, keeps men exaggerating all the traditional rules of masculinity, including sexual predation with women. Homophobia and sexism go hand in hand.

The stakes of perceived sissydom are enormous—sometimes matters of life and death. We take enormous risks to prove our manhood, exposing ourselves disproportionately to health risks, workplace hazards, and stress-related illnesses. Men commit suicide three times as often as women.... In one survey, women and men were asked what they were most afraid of. Women responded that they were most afraid of being raped and murdered. Men responded that they were most afraid of being laughed at (Noble 1992, 105–6).

■ HOMOPHOBIA AS A CAUSE OF SEXISM, HETEROSEXISM, AND RACISM

Homophobia is intimately interwoven with both sexism and racism. The fear—sometimes conscious, sometimes not—that others might perceive us as homosexual propels men to enact all manner of exaggerated masculine behaviors and attitudes to make sure that no one could possibly get the wrong idea about us. One of the centerpieces of that exaggerated masculinity is putting women down, both by excluding them from the public sphere and by the quotidian put-downs in speech and behaviors that organize the daily life of the American man. Women and gay men become the "other" against which heterosexual men project their identities, against whom they stack the decks so as to compete in a situation in which they will always win, so that by suppressing them, men can stake a claim for their own manhood. Women threaten emasculation by representing the home, workplace, and familial responsibility, the negation of fun. Gay men have historically played the role of the consummate sissy in the American popular mind because homosexuality is seen as an inversion of normal gender development. There have been other "others." Through American history, various groups have represented the sissy, the non-men against whom American men played out their definitions of manhood, often with vicious results. In fact, the changing groups provide an interesting lesson in American historical development.

At the turn of the 19th century, it was Europeans and children who provided the contrast for American men. The "true American was vigorous, manly, and direct, not effete and corrupt like the supposed Europeans," writes Rupert Wilkinson (1986). "He was plain rather than ornamented, rugged rather than luxury seeking, a liberty loving common man or natural gentleman rather than an aristocratic oppressor or servile minion" (96). The "real man" of the early nineteenth century was neither noble nor serf. By the middle of the century, black slaves had replaced the effete nobleman.

Slaves were seen as dependent, helpless men, incapable of defending their women and children, and therefore less than manly. Native Americans were cast as foolish and naïve children, so they could be infantilized as the "Red Children of the Great White Father" and therefore excluded from full manhood.

By the end of the century, new European immigrants were also added to the list of the unreal men, especially the Irish and Italians, who were seen as too passionate and emotionally volatile to remain controlled sturdy oaks, and Jews, who were seen as too bookishly effete and too physically puny to truly measure up. In the mid-twentieth century, it was also Asians—first the Japanese during the Second World War, and more recently, the Vietnamese during the Vietnam War—who have served as unmanly templates against which American men have hurled their gendered rage. Asian men were seen as small, soft, and effeminate—hardly men at all.

Such a list of "hyphenated" Americans—Italian-, Jewish-, Irish-, African-, Native-, Asian-, gay— composes the majority of American men. So manhood is only possible for a distinct minority, and the definition has been constructed to prevent the others from achieving it. Interestingly, this emasculation of one's enemies has a flip side—and one that is equally gendered. These very groups that have historically been cast as less than manly were also, often simultaneously, cast as hypermasculine, as sexually aggressive, violent rapacious beasts, against whom "civilized" men must take a decisive stand and thereby rescue civilization. Thus black men were depicted as rampaging sexual beasts, women as carnivorously carnal, gay men as sexually insatiable, southern European men as sexually predatory and voracious, and Asian men as vicious and cruel torturers who were immorally disinterested in life itself, willing to sacrifice their entire people for their whims. But whether one saw these groups as effeminate sissies or as brutal uncivilized savages, the terms with which they were perceived were gendered. These groups become the "others," the screens against which traditional conceptions of manhood were developed.

Being seen as unmanly is a fear that propels American men to deny manhood to others, as a way of proving the unprovable—that one is fully manly. Masculinity becomes a defense against the perceived threat of humiliation in the eyes of other men, enacted through a "sequence of postures"—things we might say, or do, or even think, that, if we thought carefully about them, would make us ashamed of ourselves (Savran 1992, 16). After all, how many of us have made homophobic or sexist remarks, or told racist jokes, or made lewd comments to women on the street? How many of us have translated those ideas and those words into actions, by physically attacking gay men, or forcing or cajoling a woman to have sex even though she didn't really want to because it was important to score?

■ POWER AND POWERLESSNESS IN THE LIVES OF MEN

I have argued that homophobia, men's fear of other men, is the animating condition of the dominant definition of masculinity in America, that the reigning definition of masculinity is a defensive effort to prevent being emasculated. In our efforts to suppress or overcome those fears, the dominant culture exacts a tremendous price from those deemed less than fully manly: women, gay men, nonnative-born men, men of color. This perspective may help clarify a paradox in men's lives, a paradox in which men have virtually all the power and yet do not feel powerful (see Kaufman 1993).

Manhood is equated with power—over women, over other men. Everywhere we look, we see the institutional expression of that power—in state and national legislatures, on the boards of directors of every major U.S. corporation or law firm, and in every school and hospital administration. Women have long understood this, and feminist women have spent the past three decades challenging both the public and the private expressions of men's power and acknowledging their fear of men. Feminism as a set of theories both explains women's fear of men and empowers women to confront it both publicly and privately. Feminist women have theorized that masculinity is about the drive for domination, the drive for power, for conquest.

This feminist definition of masculinity as the drive for power is theorized from women's point of view. It is how women experience masculinity. But it assumes a symmetry between the public and the private that does not conform to men's experiences. Feminists observe that women, as a group, do not hold power in our society. They also observe that individually, they, as women, do not feel powerful. They feel afraid, vulnerable. Their observation of the social reality and their individual experiences are therefore symmetrical. Feminism also observes that men, as a group, are in power. Thus, with the same symmetry, feminism has tended to assume that individually men must feel powerful.

This is why the feminist critique of masculinity often falls on deaf ears with men. When confronted with the analysis that men have all the power, many men react incredulously. "What do you mean, men have all the power?" they ask. "What are you talking about? My wife bosses me around. My kids boss me around. My boss bosses me around. I have no power at all! I'm completely powerless!"

Men's feelings are not the feelings of the powerful, but of those who see themselves as powerless. These are the feelings that come inevitably from the discontinuity between the social and the psychological, between the aggregate analysis that reveals how men are in power as a group and the psychological fact that they do not feel powerful as individuals. They are the feelings of men

who were raised to believe themselves entitled to feel that power, but do not feel it. No wonder many men are frustrated and angry. This may explain the recent popularity of those workshops and retreats designed to help men to claim their "inner" power, their "deep manhood," or their "warrior within."

The dimension of power is now reinserted into men's experience not only as the product of individual experience but also as the product of relations with other men. In this sense, men's experience of powerlessness is *real*—the men actually feel it and certainly act on it—but it is not *true,* that is, it does not accurately describe their condition. In contrast to women's lives, men's lives are structured around relationships of power and men's differential access to power, as well as the differential access to that power of men as a group. Our imperfect analysis of our own situation leads us to believe that we men need more power, rather than leading us to support feminists' efforts to rearrange power relationships along more equitable lines.

Philosopher Hannah Arendt (1970) fully understood this contradictory experience of social and individual power:

> Power corresponds to the human ability not just to act but to act in concert. Power is never the property of an individual; it belongs to a group and remains in existence only so long as the group keeps together. When we say of somebody that he is "in power" we actually refer to his being empowered by a certain number of people to act in their

name. The moment the group, from which the power originated to begin with . . . disappears, "his power" also vanishes. (p. 44)

Why, then, do American men feel so powerless? Part of the answer is because we've constructed the rules of manhood so that only the tiniest fraction of men come to believe that they are the biggest of wheels, the sturdiest of oaks, the most virulent repudiators of femininity, the most daring and aggressive. We've managed to disempower the overwhelming majority of American men by other means—such as discriminating on the basis of race, class, ethnicity, age, or sexual preference.

Masculinist retreats to retrieve deep, wounded, masculinity are but one of the ways in which American men currently struggle with their fears and their shame. Unfortunately, at the very moment that they work to break down the isolation that governs men's lives, as they enable men to express those fears and that shame, they ignore the social power that men continue to exert over women and the privileges from which they (as the middle-aged, middle-class white men who largely make up these retreats) continue to benefit—regardless of their experiences as wounded victims of oppressive male socialization.

Others still rehearse the politics of exclusion, as if by clearing away the playing field of secure gender identity of any that we deem less than manly—women, gay men, nonnative-born men, men of color—middle-class, straight, white men can reground their sense of themselves without those haunting fears and that deep shame that they are unmanly and will be exposed by other men. This is the manhood of racism, of sexism, of homophobia. It is the manhood that is so chronically insecure that it trembles at the idea of lifting the ban on gays in the military, that is so threatened by women in the workplace that women become the targets of sexual harassment, that is so deeply frightened of equality that it must ensure that the playing field of male competition remains stacked against all newcomers to the game.

Exclusion and escape have been the dominant methods American men have used to keep their fears of humiliation at bay. The fear of emasculation by other men, of being humiliated, of being seen as a sissy, is the leitmotif in my reading of the history of American manhood. Masculinity has become a relentless test by which we prove to other men, to women, and ultimately to ourselves, that we have successfully mastered the part. The restlessness that men feel today is nothing new in American history; we have been anxious and restless for almost two centuries. Neither exclusion nor escape has ever brought us the relief we've sought, and there is no reason to think that either will solve our problems now. Peace of mind, relief from gender struggle, will come only from a politics of inclusion, not exclusion, from standing up for equality and justice, and not by running away.

REFERENCES

Arendt, H. (1970). *On Revolution*. New York: Viking.

Bly, R. (1990). *Iron John: A Book about Men*. Reading, Mass.: Addison–Wesley.

Gorer, G. (1964). *The American People: A Study in National Character*. New York: Norton.

Kaufman, M. (1993). *Cracking the Armour: Power and Pain in the Lives of Men*. Toronto: Viking Canada.

Leverenz, D. (1986). "Manhood, Humiliation and Public Life: Some Stories." *Southwest Review* 71, Fall.

Leverenz, D. (1991). "The Last Real Man in America: From Natty Bumppo to Batman." *American Literary Review* 3.

Mead, M. (1965). *And Keep Your Powder Dry*. New York: William Morrow.

Noble, V. (1992). "A Helping Hand from the Guys." In K. L. Hagan, ed., *Women Respond to the Men's Movement*. San Francisco: HarperCollins.

Osherson, S. (1992). *Wrestling with Love: How Men Struggle with Intimacy, with Women, Children, Parents, and Each Other*. New York: Fawcett.

Rotundo, E. A. (1993). *American Manhood: Transformations in Masculinity from the Revolution to the Modern Era*. New York: Basic Books.

Savran, D. (1992). *Communists, Cowboys and Queers: The Politics of Masculinity in the Work of Arthur Miller and Tennessee Williams*. Minneapolis: University of Minnesota Press.

Wayne, K. (1912). *Building the Young Man*. Chicago: A. C. McClurg.

Wilkinson, R. (1986). *American Tough: The Tough-Guy Tradition and American Character*. New York: Harper and Row.

CHAPTER 3

Gender-Role Conflict Scale

College Men's Fear of Femininity

James M. O'Neil, Barbara J. Helms, Robert K. Gable,
Laurence David, and Lawrence S. Wrightsman

The negative effects of socialized gender role continues to be an area of scientific inquiry. These negative effects have been described as gender- or sex role conflict and sex role strain (Garnets & Pleck, 1979; O'Neil, 1981a,b, 1982; Pleck, 1981). For purposes of this research, the terms gender-role conflict and strain and sex role conflict and strain are used synonymously throughout the manuscript. Gender-role conflict is a psychological state where gender roles have negative consequences or impact on a person or others. The ultimate outcome of this conflict is the restriction of the person's ability to actualize their human potential or the restriction of some else's potential. Sex role strain has also been described as an intrapsychic process that can lead to a poor psychological adjustment, particularly low self-esteem (Garnets & Pleck, 1979).

A recent sex role strain (SRS) paradigm (Pleck, 1981) provides additional understanding of the negative effects of socialized gender roles. This paradigm enumerates ten propositions indicating that gender roles produce conflict and strain for both sexes. Pleck's paradigm indicates that: (1) violation of gender roles can lead to negative psychological consequences, (2) certain gender-role characteristics are psychologically dysfunctional, (3) both sexes experience strain and conflict because of gender roles. Furthermore, these assumptions are based on two theories of sex role strain: self-role discrepancy theory and socialized dysfunctional characteristics theory. The former theory suggests that individuals suffer negative consequences when they fail to live up to sex roles. The latter theory suggests that because of sex roles, individuals are socialized to have personality characteristics that are dysfunctional. Pleck's sex role strain paradigm provides a theoretical base to empirically study gender-role conflict in men's and women's lives.

Men's gender-role conflicts have been topics of discussion for some time in the popular literature (Farrell, 1974; Fasteau, 1974; Nichols, 1975; Pleck & Sawyer, 1974). Conceptual analysis of men's problems have also emerged in the professional literature (David & Brannon, 1976; Doyle, 1983; O'Neil, 1981a, 1982; Pleck & Pleck, 1980; Scher, 1981; Skovholt, Gormally, Schauble, & Davis, 1980; Solomon & Levy, 1982). Additionally, three case studies of men's conflict have been reported in the literature (Komarovsky, 1976; Levinson, Darrow, Klein, Levinson, & McKee, 1978; Vaillant, 1974). There have been few empirical studies documenting men's conflict around socialized gender roles. This lack of empirical research on gender-role conflict delays scientific understanding of how gender roles produce conflict in men's lives.

One impediment to assessing men's gender-role conflict has been few unifying constructs that capture its factors and patterns. One unifying theme of gender-role conflict has been hypothesized as men's fear of femininity (David & Brannon, 1976; Farrell, 1974; O'Neil, 1981b,c, 1982). The fear of femininity is defined as a strong, negative emotion associated with stereotypic feminine values, attitudes, and behaviors. These emotional reactions are learned primarily in early childhood when gender identity is being formed by parents, peers, and societal values. Men's fear of their feminine sides and women have been noted in the theoretical literature for many years (Boehm, 1930; Hays, 1964; Horney, 1967; Jung, 1953, 1954; Lederer, 1968; Menninger, 1970). Most of these analyses of men's fears about femininity have a psychodynamic foundation. Jung's archetype in men, the animal, is a well-known concept about men's difficulty integrating their feminine sides. Reviews of mythology (Lederer, 1968; Johnson, 1977) provide even more substantial evidence that threats and fears of femininity have existed over the centuries. More recently, Levinson et al. (1978), in their case study of men, found that men (1) neglected or repressed the feminine sides of self, or (2) regarded those parts of themselves as feminine as being dangerous. Men's fear about their femininity has direct relevance to patterns of gender-role conflict and strain.

Patterns of gender-role conflict and strain associated with the fear of femininity have been described in the literature (David & Brannon, 1976; O'Neil, 1981a,b, 1982; O'Neil, Helms, Gable, David, & Wrightsman, 1985). Figure 3.1 shows a model of gender-role conflict and strain that includes the following six patterns: (1) restrictive emotionality, (2) homophobia, (3) socialized control, power, and competition, (4) restrictive

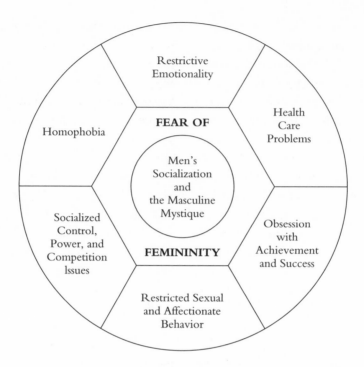

Figure 3.1. Six Patterns of Gender-Role Conflict and Strain Emanating from Men's Socialization and Their Fear of Femininity.

Reprinted with kind permission of Springer Science and Business Media from: *Men in Transition: Theory and Therapy* (p. 7, Figure 1). Edited by Kenneth Solomon and Norman B. Levy. New York: Plenum Press, ©1982

sexual and affectional behavior, (5) obsession with achievement and success and (6) health care problems. The relationship between these gender-role patterns and the fear of femininity has been discussed elsewhere (O'Neil, 1981b, 1982; O'Neil & Fishman, 1985). Foremost to the model is the hypothesis that men's fears of femininity contribute to the six patterns of gender-role conflict found in Figure 3.1.

Another reason for limited research on men's gender-role conflict has been the lack of psychometric instruments to assess it. Other measures of gender-role attributes, orientations, and attitudes have been developed (Bem, 1974; Doyle & Moore, 1978; Spence & Helmreich, 1978; Spence, Helmreich, & Stapp, 1974, 1975). The Personal Attitudes Questionnaire (PAQ; Spence & Helmreich, 1978) and the Bem Sex Role Inventory (BSRI; Bem, 1974) have been developed to assess androgyny or expressiveness-instrumentality. The Attitudes toward Women Scale (AWS; Spence & Helmreich, 1972) assesses the rights and roles of women in society. The Attitudes toward the Male's Role Scale (AMR; Doyle & Moore, 1978) measures attitudes toward the male's sex role in contemporary society.

Currently, there is no instrument to assess men's personal gender-role attitudes, behaviors, and conflict. Research instruments have not been developed because gender roles, and their subsequent strain and conflict, are multifaceted. Gender-role conflict can be conceptualized from four overlapping and complex dimensions: cognitions, affective experience, behaviors, and unconscious experience. Cognitive experience of gender-role conflict is how we think about our gender roles and aspects of masculinity, femininity, and androgyny. Affective experience of gender-role conflict represents our emotional feelings around our gender-role issues. Behavioral aspects of gender-role conflict includes how we act, respond, and interact with ourselves, and others, around gender-role issues. Unconscious aspects of gender roles includes the intrapsychic and repressed aspect of our gender roles beyond our conscious awareness. The multidimensionality of gender-role conflict and men's individual differences provide challenges for assessing it through psychometric instruments.

Three approaches to assessing men's gender-role conflict are apparent from the dimensions described above. First, gender-role conflict can be assessed by asking men about the specific ways they think and feel about their gender-role behaviors. Second, men can report the degree of conflict and comfort in particular gender-role situations. These two approaches provide an analysis of how men see themselves in terms of gender roles, as well as how they might act in

gender-role conflict situations. Thirdly, the assessment of men's gender-role conflict will vary according to the man's personal attributes. For example, men who describe themselves differentially in terms of gender-role characteristics (i.e., expressiveness or instrumentality) may show differential aspects of gender-role conflict.

The purpose of this study is to present initial construct validity data on two scales to measure men's gender-role conflict patterns found in Figure 3.1. Through a series of methodological and statistical procedures, two scales were developed: Gender Role Conflict Scale I and II (GRCS-1 and GRCS-II). One scale assessed men's thought and feelings about their gender-role behaviors, and the other assessed men's degree of conflict and comfort in particular situations.

Cronbach and Meehl (1955) discuss five methods of experimentation to investigate construct validity including factor analysis, test–retest reliability, internal consistency reliability, group differences, and studies of process. This study assessed four of the five above methods by testing three hypotheses. First, it was hypothesized that items from the instrument would cluster into the six gender-role factors found in Figure 3.1. Second, it was hypothesized that these factors and the instrument would demonstrate moderately high reliability and validity. Third, it was hypothesized that subjects with different gender-role orientations, measured by the PAQ, would differ with respect to the degree to which they express patterns of gender-role conflict. Specifically, it was hypothesized that men who describe themselves as expressive, instrumental, or both, would express differential degrees of gender-role conflict. The overall purpose of the research was to gain empirical support for the construct validity and overall reliability of gender-role conflict in men's lives using GRCS-I and II.

■ METHOD

Subjects

Undergraduate men ($N = 527$) at two Midwestern universities enrolled in introductory psychology classes were the subjects. The mean age of the subjects was 19.8 years. Class levels of subjects included 57% freshmen, 27% sophomores, 11% juniors, and 5% seniors. The marital status of subjects indicated 95% single and 5% married.

Procedure

Operational definitions of the six patterns of gender-role conflict shown in Figure 3.1 were developed from previous theoretical literature (O'Neil, 1981a, b, 1982). The six patterns are defined below:

1. *Restrictive emotionality*—having difficulty expressing one's feelings or denying others their rights to emotional expressiveness.
2. *Homophobia*—having fear of homosexuals or fear of being a homosexual including beliefs, myths, and stereotypes about gay people.
3. *Control*—to regulate, restrain, or to have others or situations under one's command. *Power*—to obtain authority, influence, or ascendancy over others. *Competition*—striving against others to win or gain something.
4. *Restricted sexual and affectionate behavior*—having limited ways of expressing one's sexuality and affection to others.
5. *Obsession with achievement and success*—having a disturbing and persistent preoccupation with work, accomplishment and eminence as a means of substantiating and demonstrating value.
6. *Health care problems*—having difficulties maintaining positive health care in terms of diet, exercise, relaxation, stress, and a healthy life style.

From these definitions and the available literature, GRCS-I and GRCS-II were developed. For GRCS-I, 85 items were generated with the following number of items per gender-role pattern in Figure 3.1: (1) restrictive emotionality ($N = 15$), (2) health care problems ($N = 14$), (3) obsession with achievement and success ($N = 16$), (4) restrictive sexual and affectionate behavior ($N = 17$), (5) control, power, and competition ($N = 14$), (6) homophobia ($N = 9$). For GRCS-II, 51 items were generated with the following number of items per gender-role pattern in Figure 3.1: (1) restrictive emotionality ($N = 12$), (2) health care problems ($N = 4$), (3) obsession with achievement and success ($N = 7$), (4) restrictive sexual and affectionate behavior ($N = 6$), (5) control, power, and competition ($N = 15$), (6) homophobia ($N = 7$).

Subjects were given these two scales, along with the PAQ (Spence & Helmreich, 1978). These instruments are described below.

Instrumentation

Gender-Role Conflict Scale I (GRCS-I)

The original scale was an 85-item self-report instrument designed to assess aspects of gender-role conflict described in the literature (O'Neil, 1981a, b, 1982) and in Figure 3.1. Respondents are asked to report the degree to which they agree or disagree about their personal gender-role attitudes, behaviors, and conflicts. Each item provides an assessment of men's conflict by the respondent's self-rating of attitude or behavior previously categorized as gender-role conflict. Respondents are asked to report the degree to which they agree or disagree with statements using a 6-point Likert scale, ranging from *strongly agree* (6) to *strongly disagree* (1). Example items from GRCS-I include "I have difficulty expressing my tender feelings," "I strive to be more successful than others," "Finding time to relax is difficult for me." Each statement expresses a gender-role conflict pattern found in Figure 3.1. Thus, a high score assumes and reflects an expression of gender-role conflict and fear about femininity (O'Neil, 1981b, 1982).

Gender-Role Conflict Scale II (GRCS-II)

The original scale was a 51-item self-report instrument designed to assess situational dimensions of gender-role conflict patterns found in Figure 3.1. This scale asks subjects to report their degree of comfort of conflict in specific gender-role conflict situations. Each item provides an assessment of men's conflict by the respondent's self-rating of conflict or comfort in a concrete gender-related situation. Respondents are asked to rate the degree of comfort or conflict in specific situations using a 4-point Likert scale, ranging from *very much conflict–very uncomfortable* (4) to *no conflict–very comfortable* (1). Example items from GRCS-II include (1) "Your best friend has just lost his job at the factory where you work. He is obviously upset, afraid, and angry but he has these emotions hidden. How comfortable/uncomfortable are you to responding to your friend's intense emotions and fear about unemployment?" (2) "There's a guy you've idolized since grade school. He's three years older than you are. In high school he was the star quarterback, valedictorian, and very active in the Young Methodist Fellowship. Last year he graduated from college. You have just learned he is a homosexual. How much conflict do you feel between your admiration for this person and the fact that he is a homosexual?" Each statement expresses a gender-role conflict pattern found in Figure 3.1. Thus, a high score reflects and assumes an expression of gender-role conflict and fear about femininity (O'Neil, 1981b, 1982).

Personal Attributes Questionnaire (PAQ)

The PAQ (Spence & Helmreich, 1978) measures the psychological dimension of masculinity and femininity. The PAQ is a 24-item self-report instrument consisting of a number of trait descriptions, each set upon a 5-point bipolar scale. These trait descriptions of dispositional properties makes no reference to overt behavior or to the situations in which these dispositions are manifested. Each item describes a characteristic stereotypically believed to differentiate the sexes. The PAQ is divided into three separate scales labeled Masculinity (M), Femininity (F), and Masculinity–Femininity (M-F). In content, the M scale contains socially desirable traits stereotypically more characteristic of males than females and refer to self-assertive, instrumental attributes. The F scale contains socially desirable traits stereotypically more characteristic of females and refer to interpersonally oriented expressive qualities. The M-F scale consists of traits dimensions for which the social desirability ratings were related to gender, the ideal woman falling toward the stereotypically feminine pole and the ideal man toward the stereotypically masculine pole (Spence & Helmreich, 1980). Median split of subjects' PAQ scores produced medians for masculinity (M) and femininity (F) both at 23. These medians were used to classify subjects to masculine (high masculinity, low femininity), feminine (low–high), and androgynous (high-high), or undifferentiated (low-low), gender-role categories. As defined by Spence and Helmreich (1980) the PAQ assesses respondents' self-reported attributes of expressiveness and instrumentality. In this study, the man categorized as "masculine" has instrumental traits but is low on expressive traits. The "feminine" man possesses expressive

traits but is low on instrumental traits. The "androgynous" man is high on both instrumental and expressive traits. Finally, the "undifferentiated" man is low on both instrumental and expressive traits. In short, the PAQ represents men's self-reported attributes of expressiveness and instrumentality. Cronbach's alphas for the short form of the PAQ are .85, .82, and .78 for M, F, and M-F, respectively (Spence & Helmreich, 1978).

Data Analysis

The analysis of the data and construct validity of the GRCS-I and II was determined by the following approaches: item-reduction procedures, factor analysis, reliability data analysis, and multivariate analysis of variance (MANOVA). Each will be described below.

Item-Reduction Procedures

A systematic procedure was utilized to reduce the number of items on the GRCS. The goal of this systematic reduction of items was to obtain the best items and factor structure from the original items. A three-step procedure was employed to decide which items to retain for further analysis. First, all items were submitted to three different raters to assess the degree to which the items were gender related rather than related to other kinds of human conflicts. For GRCS-I, raters assessed the items by indicating on a 1–5 point scale that *item definitely does not relate to men's gender role* (1) to *item definitely does relate to man's gender role* (5). For GRCS-II, raters assessed the items by indicating on a 1–5 point scale, (1) *item definitely relates to human conflict, not male gender role* to (5) *item definitely relates to conflict in male gender roles.* Using an arbitrary 3.5 cut off, all items met the criteria for being assessed as a gender-role related item. Second, all items were excluded that did not meet the criterion of having a standard deviation of at least 1.00; these items were essentially answered the same way by most respondents and hence did not discriminate. Third, each item had to correlate with at least one other item at the .30 level to be retained.

Factor Analysis

Factor analyses, employing both principal components and common factor models, with both orthogonal and oblique rotations, were completed on GRCS-I and II. The goal of these numerous analyses was to determine the best simple structure of observed factors for the items (Rummel, 1970). All items with factor loadings less than .35 were excluded from the scale (Nunnally, 1978) as well as items that had loadings of greater than .30 on two or more factors. Consequently, no item was allowed to cross-load on any other factor in the construction of the scales.

Reliability Data

Internal consistency reliabilities for each scale score were calculated using Cronbach's alpha procedure. Using the described sample, four-week test–retest reliabilities ($N = 17$) for scale scores were calculated for GRCS-I using Pearson product moment correlations. Four-week test–retest reliabilities ($N = 14$) for GRCS-II were calculated from students in an introductory educational psychology class using Pearson product moment correlations.

Multivariate Analysis of Variance

Additional exploratory construct validity evidence was obtained through multivariate analysis of variance (MANOVA). Scale scores were developed by summing the responses to the items defining each factor. MANOVA was performed on derived factors using the PAQ classification for all subjects. Univariate analysis of variance and Tukey post hoc procedures were used to further analyze significant MANOVA findings.

■ RESULTS

Using the item-reduction procedure described above, 37 of the original 85 items met the criteria for inclusion in GRCS-I. Common factor analysis with oblique rotation yielded the most significant factor composition for the GRCS-I. Table 3.1 lists and names four emergent factors as follows: Factor 1— success, power, competition (13 items); Factor 2—restrictive emotionality (10 items); Factor 3—restrictive affectionate behavior between men (8 items); Factor 4—conflicts between work and family relations (6 items). The four factors explained 36% of the total variance.

Assessments of the scales' reliabilities found internal consistency scores using Cronbach's alpha ranged

Table 3.1.   Factor Structure for Gender-Role Conflict Scale I

Items	Factor Loadings
Factor 1 — success, power, competition (13 items)	
1. Moving up the career ladder is important to me.	.64
5. Making money is part of my idea of being a successful man.	.52
8. I sometimes define my personal value by my career success.	.54
12. I evaluate other people's value by their level of achievement and success.	.54
14. I worry about failing and how it affects my doing well as a man.	.45
18. Doing well all the time is important to me.	.43
21. I often feel that I need to be in charge of those around me.	.49
23. Competing with others is the best way to succeed.	.58
24. Winning is a measure of my value and personal worth.	.57
28. I strive to be more successful than others.	.72
32. I am often concerned about how others evaluate my performance at work or school.	.41
34. Being smarter or physically stronger than other men is important to me.	.61
37. I like to feel superior to other people.	.53
Factor 2 — restrictive emotionality (10 items)	
2. I have difficulty telling others I care about them.	.70
6. Strong emotions are difficult for me to understand.	.35
9. Expressing feelings makes me feel open to attack by other people.	.37
13. Talking (about my feelings) during sexual relations is difficult for me.	.52
15. I have difficulty expressing my emotional needs to my partner.	.78
19. I have difficulty expressing my tender feelings.	.76
22. Telling others of my strong feelings is not part of my sexual behavior.	.44
25. I often have trouble finding words that describe how I am feeling.	.41
29. I do not like to show my emotions to other people.	.43
30. Telling my partner my feelings about him/her during sex is difficult for me.	.75
Factor 3 — restrictive affectionate behavior between men (8 items)	
3. Verbally expressing my love to another man is difficult for me.	.50
7. Affection with other men makes me tense.	.69
10. Expressing my emotions to other men is risky.	.58
16. Men who touch other men make me uncomfortable.	.67
20. Hugging other men is difficult for me.	.71
26. I am sometimes hesitant to show my affection to men because of how others might perceive me.	.52

Table 3.1. *(continued)*

Items	Factor Loadings
33. Being very personal with other men makes me feel uncomfortable.	.66
35. Men who are overly friendly to me make me wonder about their sexual preference (men or women).	.48
Factor 4 — conflicts between work and family relations (6 items)	
4. I feel torn between my hectic work schedule and caring for my health.	.45
11. My career, job, or school affects the quality of my leisure or family life.	.65
17. Finding time to relax is difficult for me.	.57
27. My needs to work or study keep me from my family or leisure more than I would like.	.70
31. My work or school often disrupts other parts of my life (home, health, leisure).	.58
36. Overwork, and stress, caused by a need to achieve on the job or in school affects hurts my life.	.46

from .75 to .85. Four-week test–retest reliabilities ($N = 17$) ranged from .72 to .86 for each factor.

For GRCS-II, 16 of the original 51 items met the criteria for inclusion. Principal component analysis with oblique rotations yielded the most meaningful factor composition for GRCS-II. Table 3.2 lists and names four emergent factors for the instrument as follows: Factor 1—success, power, and competition (6 items); Factor 2—homophobia (4 items); Factor 3—lack of emotional response (3 items); Factor 4—public embarrassment from gender-role deviance (3 items). The four factors explained 48% of the total variance.

Assessments of the scale reliabilities found internal consistency scores using Cronbach's alpha ranged from .51 to .76. Four week test–retest reliabilities ($N = 14$) ranged from .79 to .85. Table 3.3 summarizes the factor reliabilities and validity data for both scales.

Tables 3.4 and 3.5 contain the means and standard deviations for the four factors of GRCS-I and GRCS-II according to the PAQ categories. For GRCS-I, multivariate analysis of variance (MANOVA) indicated an overall significant main effect, $F(12, 1535) = 9.87$, $p < .000$. Univariate analysis of variance on the four factors indicated significant differences on three of the four factors. Differences between PAQ categories were found for Factor 1, $F(3, 519) = 7.86$, $p < .000$; Factor 2, $F(3, 522) = 20.43$, $p < .001$; Factor 3, $F(3, 522) = 9.69$, $p < .000$. No significant differences were found for Factor 4.

For GRCS-II, multivariate analysis of variance indicated an overall significant main effect, $F(12, 1541) = 5.53$, $p < .000$. Univariate analysis of variance

Table 3.2. Factor Structure for Gender-Role Conflict Scale II

Items	Factor Loadings
Factor 1 — success, power, competition (6 items)	
3. How much conflict do you feel about your brother's success compared to your own job as a plumber's supply truck driver?	.58
6. How much conflict do you feel between your poor performance and your desired level of performance?	.68
8. How conflicted do you feel that her salary is much higher than yours during a conversation with this new couple you have just met?	.43
13. How conflicted would you feel with your desire to have intercourse and your inability to achieve an erection?	.59
15. How comfortable/uncomfortable do you feel with your lower grades compared to your friends' grades?	.59
16. How conflicted do you feel about your low ranking and that they will be known by your other colleagues?	.73
Factor 2 — homophobia (4 items)	
4. How comfortable/uncomfortable would you feel talking during intermission to this person who is a known homosexual?	.71
7. At the bar you notice that an unknown man is staring at you and then he comes over to introduce himself. How comfortable/uncomfortable would you feel talking to this man?	.67
11. Under these conditions, how conflicted would you feel as a heterosexual male going out with a man thought to be gay?	.67
14. How much conflict do you feel between your admiration for this person and the fact that he is a homosexual?	.82
Factor 3 — lack of emotional response (3 items)	
5. How comfortable/uncomfortable do you feel responding to her sadness, emotions, and tears?	.71
1. How comfortable/uncomfortable are you responding to your friends' intense emotions and fears about employment?	.71
9. Disregarding your sadness of his dying state, how comfortable/uncomfortable are you specifically with your father's expression of love for you?	.63
Factor 4 — public embarrassment from gender-role deviance (3 items)	
2. How comfortable/uncomfortable do you feel with this public display of affection?	.62
10. How comfortable/uncomfortable do you feel carrying a woman's purse in front of people in the restaurant?	.62
12. How conflicted do you feel about what your male coworker might think about your contact and relationship with your intimate friend?	.60

*Each item is preceded by a descriptive situation that ends with the above questions for each factor.

Table 3.3. Factor Composition and Reliability Data for GRCS-I and II

GRCS-I (personal self-report)			
1. Success, power. and competition	13	.85	.84
2. Restrictive emotionality	10	.82	.76
3. Restrictive affectionate behavior between men	8	.83	.86
4. Conflicts between work and family relations	6	.75	.72
GRCS-II (situational self-report)			
1. Success, power, and competition	6	.70	.79
2. Homophobia	4	.76	.78
3. Lack of emotional response	3	.51	.85
4. Public embarrassment from gender-role deviance	3	.59	.83

★Test-retest for GRCS-I was with 17 subjects, whereas test-retest for GRCS-II included 14 subjects.

on the four factors indicated significant differences on three of the four factors. Significant differences between PAQ categories were found for Factor 2, $F(3, 522) = 3.51$, $p < .05$; Factor 3, $F(3, 522) = 13.43$, $p < .000$; Factor 4, $F(3, 522) = 9.67$, $p < .000$. No significant differences were found for Factor 1.

Significant univariate results were followed up with the Tukey procedure at the .05 level. For GRCS-I, instrumental men (masculine) reported significantly higher scores on Factor 1 than feminine, androgynous, or undifferentiated men. For Factor 2, instrumental and expressive men (androgynous) had significantly lower scores than masculine, feminine, or undifferentiated men. Also, men who were neither expressive nor instrumental (undifferentiated) had significantly higher scores on restrictive emotionality than the three other types. For Factor 3, instrumental men (masculine) and men who were neither instrumental nor expressive (undifferentiated) had significantly higher scores than androgynous and feminine types.

For GRCS-II, instrumental men (masculine) had significantly higher scores than expressive men (feminine) on Factor 2. For Factor 3, men who neither were instrumental or expressive (undifferentiated) had significantly higher scores than masculine, feminine, and androgynous men. For Factor 4, men without instrumental or expressive traits (undifferentiated) were significantly higher than both feminine and androgynous men. Finally, instrumental men (masculine) had significantly higher scores than androgynous men on this factor.

■ DISCUSSION

This research tested three hypotheses focused on the construct validity of the GRCS and men's gender-role conflict. The first hypothesis, stating that GRCS-I and GRCS-II items would cluster into the six gender-role patterns, was partially supported. Some of the patterns were clearly evident and two new factors emerged from the factor analysis. Other factors were renamed, combined, and

Table 3.4. Means and Standard Deviations for PAQ Groups and Factors of the GRCS-I[a,b]

		GRCS Factor 1		GRCS Factor 2		GRCS Factor 3		GRCS Factor 4	
PAQ Groups	N	X	SD	X	SD	X	SD	X	SD
Masculine	120	56.68	8.97	30.98	8.08	30.33	7.85	20.87	5.88
Feminine	118	50.28	11.77	29.69	9.24	27.63	7.68	21.25	5.88
Androgynous	129	53.12	10.76	26.33	8.52	27.04	9.22	21.70	6.60
Undifferentiated	160	52.66	9.59	34.09	8.10	31.39	6.87	21.95	5.32

[a]Factor 1, success, power, competition; Factor 2, restrictive emotionality; Factor 3, restrictive affectionate behavior between men; Factor 4, conflicts between work and family relations.
[b]N = 527. High score indicates greater self-concern regarding that attribute.

Table 3.5. Means and Standard Deviations for PAQ Groups and Factors of the GRCS-II[a,b]

		GRCS Factor 1		GRCS Factor 2		GRCS Factor 3		GRCS Factor 4	
PAQ Groups	N	X	SD	X	SD	X	SD	X	SD
Masculine	120	15.64	2.95	1L99	2.82	5.93	1.78	6.73	1.80
Feminine	118	IS.ll	1.18	10.96	2.61	5.44	1.69	6.36	1.89
Androgynous	129	14.88	1.44	11.23	2.89	5.37	1.76	6.04	1.79
Undifferentiated	160	15.60	3.11	11.b5	2.49	6.S2	1.69	7.12	1.67

[a]Factor 1, success, power. competition; Factor 2, homophobia; Factor 3, lack of emotional response; Factor 4, public embarrassment from gender-role deviance.
[b]N = 527. High score indicates greater self-concern regarding that attribute.

one factor (health care problems) did not emerge from the analysis. Overall, eight related patterns of gender-role conflict were identified.

The patterns of control, power, competition and obsession with achievement and success in GRCS-I and GRCS-II (see Figure 3.1) were combined into one factor named "success, power, and competition." The restrictive emotionality pattern was clearly evident in GRCS-I, and a similar pattern, named "lack of emotional response," was evident from GRCS-II. The pattern of restrictive sexual and affectionate behavior was renamed "restrictive affectionate behavior between men" because the items retained reflected only affectional exchanges between men. A separate but related pattern of homophobia was evident in GRCS-II. Two new patterns not hypothesized in Figure 3.1 were named "conflict between work and family relations" and "public embarrassment from gender-role deviance."

In summary, GRCS-I and GRCS-II identified gender-role conflict reflecting men's thoughts, feelings, and behaviors, as well as conflicts in particular gender-role situations. The patterns of success, power, and competition; restrictive emotionality; and lack of emotional response were clearly evident in men's self-report and also in a situational context. The subjects also self-reported restrictive affectionate behavior with other men and homophobia was identified as a situational gender-role conflict issue. Likewise, conflict between work and family relations was self-reported and public embarrassment from gender-role deviance was identified as a situational problem area.

The second hypothesis stating that the derived scales would demonstrate moderately high reliability and validity was supported. Internal consistency reliabilities ranged between .51 to .85 for GRCS-I and GRCS-II, with the reliabilities of the latter scale being somewhat lower than the former. Test–retest reliabilities on each scale ranged between .72 to .86 for the derived dimensions from GRCS-I and II measures. These initial reliability and validity data are adequate for the earlier stages of instrument development. Further research and item development is needed to raise the reliabilities of each scale and add to the construct validity of GRCS-I and GRCS-II.

The third hypothesis, stating that men describing themselves as expressive, instrumental, or both would express differential degrees of gender-role conflict, received strong support. The post hoc analysis indicated numerous differences among the eight observed factors across the four gender types assessed by the PAQ. Men who described themselves as expressive, instrumental, both expressive and instrumental, or neither expressive nor instrumental expressed differential degrees of gender-role conflict. Two patterns of significant results are apparent across the two scales on related factors. First, men reporting neither instrumental or expressive characteristics (undifferentiated) reported significantly higher scores on both restrictive emotionality and lack of emotional response. Second, men reporting themselves as instrumental (masculine) reported significantly higher scores on restrictive affectionate behavior between men and homophobia than did expressive (feminine) men.

These initial results support further research of the GRCS-I and GRCS-II. The present results indicate that further empirical research is needed on both scales. GRCS-I needs to be validated on older adult men across different racial and socioeconomic groups. GRCS-II needs the same validation, but more importantly, more items need to be added to each factor.

For over ten years, the professional literature has made claims that men experience strains and conflict from their socialized gender roles. Much of the evidence documenting this conflict has emanated from theoretical analysis in the professional and popular literature. Only recently has a sex role strain (SRS) paradigm (Pleck, 1981) provided a coherent statement that critically reviews the previous literature and provides direction for research. This paradigm allows researchers to move from theory to empirical assessment of gender-role strain and conflict. Pleck (1981) believed "[t]his is the research agenda for the future, and it carries the promise of more humane and egalitarian scientific study of the sexes" (p. 160).

The present research represents preliminary efforts to move beyond theoretical speculation about gender-role conflict to empirical and construct validation. Overall, the results do provide some empirical support for the sex role strain paradigm in college-aged men. Additional empirical research would allow more authoritative statements on the negative effects of gender-role conflict for men, women, and children.

REFERENCES

Bem, S. L. The measurement of psychological androgyny. *Journal of Consulting and Clinical Psychology*, 1974, *42*, 115–162.

Boehm, F. The femininity-complex in men. *International Journal of Psycho-Analysis*, 1930, *11*, 444–469.

Cronbach, L. J., & Meehl, P. E. Construct validity in psychological tests. *Psychological Bulletin*, 1955, *52*, 281–302.

David, D. S., & Brannon, R. *The forty-nine percent majority: The male sex role*. Reading, Mass.: Addison-Wesley, 1976.

Doyle, J. A. *The male experience*. Dubuque, Ia.: William C. Brown, 1983.

Doyle, J. J., & Moore, R. J. Attitudes toward the male's role scale (AMR): An objective instrument to measure attitudes toward the male's sex role in contemporary society. *JSAS Catalog of Selected Documents in Psychology*, 1978, *8*, 35.

Farrell, W. *The liberated man*. New York: Bantam Books, 1974.

Fasteau, M. F. *The male machine*. New York: McGraw-Hill, 1974.

Garnets, L., & Pleck, J. H. Sex role identity, androgyny, and sex role transcendence: A sex role strain analysis. *Psychology of Women Quarterly*, 1979, *3*, 270–283.

Hays, H. R. *The dangerous sex: The myth of feminine evil*. New York: Pocket Books, 1964.

Horney, K. *Feminine psychology*. New York: W. W. Norton, 1967.

Johnson, R. A. *He: Understanding masculine psychology*. New York: Harper & Row, 1977.

Jung, C. G. Animus and anima. *Collected works* (Vol. 7). New York: Pantheon, 1953.

Jung, C. G. Concerning the archetypes, with special reference to the anima concept. *Collected works* (Vol. 9, Part I). New York: Pantheon, 1954.

Komarovsky, M. *Dilemmas of masculinity: A study of college youth*. New York: W. W. Norton, 1976.

Lederer, W. *The fear of women*. New York: Harcourt, Brace and Jovanovich, 1968.

Levinson, D. J., Darrow, C. H., Klein, E. B., Levinson, M. H. & McKee, B. *The seasons of a man's life*. New York: Ballantine Books, 1978.

Menninger, K. *Love against hate*. New York: Harcourt, Brace and Jovanovich, 1970.

Nichols, J. *Men's liberation: A new definition of masculinity.* New York: Penguin Books, 1975.

Nunnally, J. C. *Psychometric theory* (2nd Ed.). New York: McGraw-Hill, 1978.

O'Neil, J. M. Male sex-role conflicts, sexism, and masculinity: Psychological implications for men, women and the counseling psychologist. *The Counseling Psychologist*, 1981, *9*, 61–80. (a)

O'Neil, J. M. Patterns of gender role conflict and strain: The fear of femininity in men's lives. *The Personal and Guidance Journal*, 1981, *60*, 203–210. (b)

O'Neil, J. M. *A measure of men's fear of femininity: A rationale and initial statement.* Paper presented at the annual convention of the American College Personnel Association (ACPA), Cincinnati, Ohio, March 1981. (c)

O'Neil, J. M. Gender and sex role conflict and strain in men's lives: Implications for psychiatrists, psychologists, and other human service providers. In K. Solomon & N. Levy (Eds.), *Men in transition: Theory and therapy.* New York: Plenum Press, 1982.

O'Neil, J. M., & Fishman, D. Adult men's career transitions and gender role themes. In Z. Liebowitz & D. Lea (Eds.), *Adult career development: Concepts, issues, and practices.* Alexandria, Va.: American Association for Counseling and Development Press, in press.

O'Neil, J. M., Helms, B. A., Gable, R., David, L., & Wrightsman, L. *Data on college men's gender role conflict and strain.* Storrs, Conn.: University of Connecticut, Department of Educational Psychology, 1985. (ERIC Document Reproduction Service No. 248488)

Pleck, E. H., & Pleck, J. *The American man.* Englewood Cliffs, N.J.: Prentice Hall, 1980.

Pleck, J. *The myth of masculinity.* Cambridge, Mass.: The MIT Press, 1981.

Pleck, J. H., & Sawyer, J. *Men and masculinity.* Englewood Cliffs, N.J.: Prentice Hall, 1974.

Rummel, R. J. *Applied factor analysis.* Evanston, Ill.: Northwestern University Press, 1970.

Scher, M. (Ed.). Counseling men [Special Issue]. *Personnel and Guidance Journal*, 1981, *60*(4).

Skovholt, T., Gormally, A., Schauble, P., & Davis, R. *Counseling men.* Monterey, Calif.: Brooks/Cole, 1980.

Solomon, K., & Levy, N. *Men in transition: Theory and therapy.* New York: Plenum Press, 1982.

Spence, J. T., & Helmreich, R. L. The attitudes toward women scale: An objective instrument to measure attitude toward rights and roles of women in contemporary society. *JSAS Catalog of Selected Documents in Psychology*, 1972, *2*, 66.

Spence, J. T., & Helmreich, R. L. *Masculinity and femininity: Their psychological dimensions, correlates, and antecedents.* Austin, Tex.: University of Texas Press, 1978.

Spence, J. T., & Helmreich, R. L. Masculine instrumentality and feminine expressiveness: Their relationship with sex role attitudes and behaviors. *Psychology of Women Quarterly*, 1980, *5*, 147–163.

Spence, J. T., Helmreich, R. L., & Stapp, J. The personal attributes questionnaire: A measure of sex-role stereotypes and masculinity-femininity. *JSAS Catalog of Selected Documents in Psychology*, 1974, *4*, 43.

Spence, J. T., Helmreich, R. L., & Stapp, J. Ratings of self and peers on sex role attributes and their relation to self-esteem and conceptions of masculinity and femininity. *Journal of Personality and Social Psychology*, 1975, *32*, 29–39.

Vaillant, G. E. Natural history of male psychological health. *Archives of General Psychiatry*, 1974, *31*, 15–22.

CHAPTER 4

Voices of Gender Role Conflict

The Social Construction of College Men's Identity

Tracy L. Davis

Gilligan's (1982) landmark self-in-relation theory of women's development inspired important challenges to traditional views of human development and led to the re-evaluation of many of the theories that undergird the practice of student development. Student affairs scholars and practitioners no longer rely solely on theories that have been constructed primarily by and about men. Belenky, Clinchy, Goldberger, and Tarule (1986), for example, developed a conceptual framework that helped student affairs practitioners better understand women's cognitive development. Josselson's (1987, 1996) and Jones's (1997) investigations allow student affairs professionals to hear women's voices in the context of identity development. The findings in these studies demonstrate the need for student affairs practitioners to become familiar with the ways that gender affects development.

Although researchers have begun to investigate how gender affects women's identity development, there has been relatively little written about such impact on the psychosocial development of college men. One reason for this lack of research may be based on a faulty assumption that most traditional scholarship regarding human development has already been about men. At first glance, this assumption seems obvious and well-founded. After all, Gilligan (1982) and others have convincingly argued that developmental research has too often viewed the male sex as representative of humanity. However, as Meth and Pasick (1990) point out:

> Although psychological writing has been androcentric, it has also been gender blind [and] it has assumed a male perspective but has not really explored what it means to be a man any more than what it means to be a woman. (p. vii)

Researchers need, therefore, to more closely examine the development of men through the lenses of gender.

Researchers' understanding of identity formation is commonly attributed to Erikson's (1968) developmental theory. According to Erikson, individuals gain a sense of who they are by confronting a universal sequence of challenges or crises (e.g., trust, intimacy, etc.) throughout their lives. Marcia (1966) operationalized Erikson's original theory and similarly suggested that identity formation is the most important goal of adolescence. Marcia viewed identity development as a process of experiencing a series of crises with one's ascribed childhood identity and subsequently emerging with new commitments. That is, as individuals consider new ideas that are in conflict with earlier conceptions, they weigh possibilities, potentially experiment with alternatives, and eventually choose commitments that become the core of a newly wrought identity. Those successfully transcending crises and making commitments are said to have an achieved identity. Individuals avoiding the process altogether, neither experiencing crises nor making commitments, are in a state of identity diffusion. Individuals may also be somewhere between these two possibilities by either simply maintaining a parentally derived ideology (foreclosed) or by actively experimenting with and resolving identity related questions prior to commitment (moratorium).

Josselson's longitudinal research (1987, 1996), based upon Marcia's framework, investigated women's identity development. Josselson (1987) categorized participants into all four identity statuses and found that women:

> Internalize the central priorities of their mothers as the issues to feel the same or different about. As college-age, late adolescents, these women judge their distance from their families by whether and how much they carry on family religious traditions, whom they choose as friends, what sexual values they adopt, how they dress, whether and when and whom they plan to marry. These were the central points of negotiation in the separation-individuation drama. (p. 172)

For the women in her study, relationships with primary family, partners, children, and friends were what Josselson (1987) called key "anchors" (p. 176) that mediated making new commitments.

Whereas Marcia (1966) found decisions involving occupational choice, religious beliefs, and political ideology to be predictive of overall identity statuses, especially with men, Josselson (1987) and Schenkel and Marcia (1972) each found that crises and commitments in the areas of religion and sexual values to be more indicative of women's identity statuses.

Recent models of identity development have gone beyond these more epigenetic conceptualizations, with their emphasis on cognitive processes of development, to increasingly focus on the dynamic interaction between individuals and the social systems in which they function. Chickering and Reisser (1993), for example, in an update of Chickering's

(1969) work, added a section to the establishing identity chapter entitled "sense of self in a social, historical, and cultural context" (p. 181). In addition, Josselson (1996) recently suggested that identity is "not just a private, individual matter . . . [but] a complex negotiation between the person and society" (p. 31). Similarly, D'Augelli (1994) conceived identity as "the dynamic processes by which an individual emerges from many social exchanges experienced in different contexts over an extended historical period" (p. 324). The construction of identity also depends, therefore, on the cultural, social, and political context in which these processes occur. A recent model offered by Jones and McEwen (2000) reinforces this idea. In their model, sexual orientation, race, culture, class, religion, and gender are identity dimensions that circulate around one's core identity. The salience of a particular dimension to one's core identity depends on changing contexts that include current experiences, family background, sociocultural conditions, career decisions, and life planning. In the current investigation, we examined one of these dimensions-gender-in an attempt to understand how college men internally experience externally defined gender roles.

Gender role conflict is defined as "a psychological state occurring when rigid, sexist, or restrictive gender roles learned thorough socialization, result in personal restriction, devaluation, or violation of others or self" (O'Neil, 1990, p. 25). Numerous studies using a common measure of men's gender role conflict, the Gender Role Conflict Scale (GRCS) (O'Neil,

Helms, Gable, David, & Wrightsman, 1986) resulted in four underlying Factors: Restrictive Emotionality; Success, Power, and Competition; Restrictive Affectionate Behavior Between Men; and Conflict Between Work and Family Relations. In a review of the gender role literature, Thompson, Pleck, and Ferrera (1992) concluded that "gender role conflict provides an important link between societal norms scripting traditional masculinities and an individual's adaptation" (p. 598). Exploring men's gender role conflict, therefore, may provide rich information about college men's identity development.

Gender role conflict has been correlated with higher levels of anxiety and lower capacity for intimacy (Sharpe & Heppner, 1991). In addition, research has found that gender role conflict is related to negative attitudes toward seeking help (Good & Wood, 1995), low self-esteem (Cournoyer & Mahalik, 1995), negative attitudes and intolerance toward homosexuals (Rounds, 1994), depression (Good & Mintz, 1990), and endorsement of a traditional masculine ideology (Good, Braverman, & O'Neil, 1991). Results of these studies illustrate the importance of understanding male gender role conflict and its effects on the healthy development of men.

The purpose of this study was to explore conflicts related to socially constructed gender roles that may impact men's identity development. Given the increasing emphasis on the social construction of identities and the negative impacts that gender role conflict have on men, it seemed critical to examine how college men are coping with culturally defined notions of what it means to be a man. That is, assuming identity develops as one interacts with society and that gender is a central dimension of one's conception of self, it would be helpful to investigate how societal gender role expectations are influencing college men. Although the underlying concepts of identity development and gender role conflict assisted in making sense of the interviews, interpretations were allowed to emerge from the data.

■ METHOD

General identity development models and theories offer descriptions of a wide array of experiences for diverse populations of individuals. To more clearly understand how gender roles influence college men's identity development, unconstrained by current deterministic conceptualizations, I used a constructivist approach (Lincoln & Guba, 1985). The purpose of constructivist inquiry is "to produce depth of understanding about a particular topic or experience" (Manning, 1999, p. 12). The constructivist perspective, based largely on the research of Piaget (1954) and Vygotsky (1978), suggests that knowledge does not and cannot produce representations of an independent reality, but instead is rooted in the perspective of the knower. As such, identity development is not the result of stage development related to maturation; rather, it is understood as a construction

by the individual through social learning and interpretive reorganization. There has been a recent debate about constructivism among those who place more emphasis on the individual cognitive structuring processes and those who emphasize the sociocultural effects of learning. In this study, I assumed a more social constructivist approach with emphasis on (a) the social context in which development occurs and (b) the importance of social interaction and negotiation.

Consistent with the epistemological assumptions of constructivism is the phenomenological methodology employed in this study. Phenomenology addresses experience from the perspective of the individual and is based on the assumption that people have a unique way of making meaning of their experience. That is, for people to understand a phenomenon, they must grasp it from another's perspective.

In addition to constructivist epistemological assumptions and a phenomenological methodology, this investigation is informed by a hermeneutic philosophical position. Hermeneutics is the science of interpretation. According to van Manen (1990), meanings are often hidden and must be brought to the surface through reflection. Hermeneutic phenomenology, thus, can "bring explicitness out of implicitness, to unveil the essence of the lived experience of a few, which allows for insight into the possible lived experience of others" (p. 316).

Consistent with these paradigmatic assumptions, interviews were conducted at Western Illinois University (WIU).

Western Illinois University enrolls approximately 12,000 students, about half of whom are men. WIU is a public regional institution with popular ROTC and law enforcement programs, and high student participation in Greek life and intramurals. WIU is also a politically conservative and rural campus. Interviews were conducted between Spring 2000 and Spring 2001.

Participants

Participants in this study were 10 male undergraduate students who ranged in age from 18 to 21 years old. Five were in their last semester of their senior year, 4 were juniors, and 1 was a sophomore. All participants in this study were White and heterosexual. Three individuals were enrolled in the College of Liberal Arts, two in Business, two in Communications, one in Education, one in Agriculture, and one in Law Enforcement. Each participant was extensively involved in leadership of at least one of the following organizations: Interfraternity Council, Student Alumni Council, University Housing and Dining Services, or the Bureau of Cultural Affairs.

Procedure

Participants were purposefully selected through snowball or chain sampling (Patton, 1990). This approach "identifies cases of interest from people who know people who know people who know what cases are information-rich, that is, good examples for study" (p. 182). These exemplar cases were identified based on the recommendations of student affairs professionals and graduate assistants who work directly with students. The referral contact people were asked to identify students who were reflective about gender or currently struggling with gender-related issues. They were also given a description of gender role conflict and asked if they knew men who might be grappling with socially scripted gender expectations.

Interviews were conducted by a male investigator and three graduate students (one male and two female). Each researcher was skilled at conducting interviews and trained in microcounseling and listening skills. Interviewers were also knowledgeable about gender-related developmental issues in general and men's issues, in particular.

Interviews

Prior to individual interviews, prospective participants were given a description of the study and its methods, a clarification of the commitment required for participation, and an informed consent form describing procedures to ensure confidentiality. After consent was given, participants provided basic demographic information.

Individual interviews were conducted in a private room by one of the four interviewers. According to Lincoln and Guba (1985), interviewing is one strategy for examining an individual's constructions and reconstructions of "persons, events, activities, organizations, feelings, motivations, claims, concerns, and other entities" (p. 268). Interviews lasted between 45 minutes and 70 minutes and were tape-recorded. Following each session, interviewers noted their experience and specifically commented on general impressions of the meeting, their reactions to the participant, and any notable or peculiar aspects of the interview. These journals were included in the data set and used in the analysis.

The interviewers used a set of questions adapted from Josselson's (1996) study of women's identity development. The protocol focused on how participants see themselves, important factors in their lives that shape who they are, how they have changed and what has stimulated that change, how they imagine their future, and what it is like being a man on campus. According to Kavale (1996), "an interview is literally an inter view, an inter-change of views between two persons conversing about a theme of mutual interest" (p. 14). Although the interview protocol was structured, interviewers were given latitude to explore responses in more depth. This open-ended questioning helps to "minimize the imposition of predetermined responses when gathering data" (Patton, 1990, p. 295).

Data Analysis

One of the greatest difficulties I had in analyzing the data was negotiating the Self-Other dynamic. Jones (1997) warns qualitative researchers to check their "own subjectivity and theoretical stance so that decisions are indeed rooted in the research process as it unfolds rather

than in the researchers' own points of view." For me, this meant being aware that I might try to make the interview data fit my preconceptions (Self) rather than allowing the participants (Other) to speak for themselves. I am drawn to the study of gender and men due to my own curiosity about the impact of gender on men's development, but I also have political, social, and cultural views related to this topic. I also clearly have biases associated with my own development as a White, heterosexual, Italian American male. As I read transcripts and listened to participants, for example, I had to intentionally avoid relying on initial intuitive interpretations rooted in my own experience. Negotiating interpretations with other interviewers helped me routinely assess whose story was being told. My own theoretical filter of knowledge, based in developmental gender role conflict and identity theory, also influenced my interpretations. In addition to the fact that these interpretations were subjected to the scrutiny of other members of the research team, I use participants' own language to illustrate our interpretations. These and several strategies listed below are aimed at "working the hyphen" (Fine, 1994, p. 72) in the Self-Other split to try to maintain the integrity of the participants' stories.

The data set for this study consisted of the 10 interviews, which were transcribed verbatim, and the interviewer journals. Following procedures outlined by Coffey and Atkinson (1996), the first step in the analysis was for each investigator to independently read the interview transcripts and mark concepts, words, phrases, or sentences that seemed interesting or important. We then met to compare categories, negotiate and reconcile discrepancies, and develop a set of meaning categories or themes. As the transcripts were read and reread, the meaning categories were refined by analyzing the concepts that the data were organized around, comparing concepts across transcripts, and adding new themes that emerged only after seeing similar concepts in multiple transcripts. As Miles and Huberman (1994) pointed out, this refinement process illustrated critical nuances and generated awareness of previously unnoticed and seemingly unremarkable units of data.

This technique of reexamination (similar to Arminio and Hultgren's description of unloosening and uncovering in this volume) continued throughout the data analysis and interpretation processes. The major themes that emerged from this process were identified, discussed among analysts, and compared to literature related to men's psychosocial development. These themes and comparisons are reported in the following sections.

Trustworthiness of these findings was enhanced through peer debriefing, keeping a methodological journal, and member checking. Lincoln and Guba (1985) defined peer debriefing as "a process of exposing oneself to a disinterested peer in a manner paralleling an analytic session and for the purpose of exploring aspects of the inquiry that might otherwise remain only implicit within the inquirer's mind" (p. 308). The peer debriefer for this study was a doctoral candidate in the University of Iowa College of Education. Lincoln and Guba also maintained that member checks, a process through which participants verify data and the resulting interpretations, are necessary to establish credibility. Participants in this study were given an opportunity to review the categories and summative interpretations for review, clarification, and suggestions. Due to the length of the study, graduation, and in one case, failure to show up for scheduled sessions, only two respondents participated in member checks.

Dependability and confirmability added to the trustworthiness of this study and were assessed through an auditor. According to Lincoln and Guba (1985), dependability can be established as the auditor examines the processes by which the various stages of the study, including analytic techniques, were conducted. The auditor, an advanced doctoral candidate well versed in qualitative methodologies, confirmed that the analytic processes were applicable to this study and that the data analysis strategies were applied consistently. To demonstrate confirmability, a journal of the inquiry process, copies of all taped interviews, notes from interviewer reflections and discussions, and hard copies of all transcripts were maintained.

In addition to peer debriefing, limited member checks, auditor review, and keeping a methodological journal, this study provided information regarding transferability of findings. The standard of transferability is a measure of whether or not the reader is given enough information about the setting to evaluate the extent to which the study's findings might be transferred to other contexts (Lincoln & Guba, 1985). According to Patton (1990), this can be accomplished through "thick description" and solid descriptive data. In this chapter, the context of the investigation is described and readers are given rich descriptions of participants' characteristics, including direct quotes from the interviews.

■ RESULTS

Five themes emerged from the data: the importance of self-expression, code of communication caveats, fear of femininity, confusion about and distancing from masculinity, and a sense of challenge without support.

Importance of Self-Expression

Contrary to the popular image of the inexpressive male, participants felt that self-expression and communication were very important to them. It was clear, however, that being comfortable with self-expression was something recently learned and not a behavior that was routinely practiced earlier in life. For example, one man reflected,

> What I enjoy the most is having good conversations with people, like interacting with people. It's something I really enjoy—especially—this is a really

new thing for me too. I didn't really do it a lot in the past and it's something I'm starting to [do] a little more. I'd say right now that's probably something that I enjoy most.

Moreover, participants rarely mentioned how they communicate with others without indicating some awareness that what they were doing was somehow outside of the boundaries of traditional masculinity. One participant reported:

> It just seems like it's amazing how different men and women are regarding handling stress and things. It's kind of a role confusion for me, because I'm the kind of person that likes to talk it out. It's difficult when you're supposed to keep things in.

Whereas verbal interaction was seen as personally important, the awareness of how others might view expressivity seemed to shape these participants' reflections on their behavior.

Code of Communication Caveats

There were three important caveats that seemed to affect these students' styles and levels of communication. These caveats are related to feelings of safety, worrying about how others will perceive them, and learned, socially appropriate ways of interacting, particularly with other men.

Communication with Women

Men seemed to be able to express themselves more freely with women than with other men. One participant put it this way, "I like to talk to friends. I like to talk and chat—I'll talk about anything, I'm especially a chatterbox with girls [sic]. We'll just sit around and watch TV, we'll discuss like relationships, life, anything." Opening up to women as friends was seen as safer and easier than being vulnerable to other men. Although this appeared to be true with female friends, there was some fear that expressive and relational behavior might be penalized if women were seen as potential partners. According to one man:

> You've got to be jerky to women, I know that. They say they want nice guys but they really don't. The thing that bugs me is that I've always been the ideal husband rather than the ideal boyfriend, which bothers me. They're like, "you're the type of guy I'd like to marry, not the type of guy I'd want to date." I just think it's because I'm too nice.

Messages that these men received from women affected their attitudes about dating. Although communication was less inhibited with female friends than with male friends, it appears to be more affected by sex-typed assumptions with potential female mates.

One-on-One Communication with Other Men

Participants also felt that their style of communication was quite different in groups than it was with one other person.

When these men were with a group of other men, even friends, there was some level of performance associated with their communication. Humorous comments and "putdowns" were the norm. On the other hand, respondents felt able to become more intimate and direct in the context of just one other friend. One man commented:

> Men don't communicate unless they have their secure circle of friends and they can talk with this one guy. I mean they all hang out and drink beer and have a good time, but after everyone leaves, Stan's going to stay behind and we're going to have a great talk. There's always that one guy that stays behind and there's always going to be that connection too.

These students sent a strong message that they were conscious of gendered rules associated with when and how relational communication can occur. Another student talked about limiting what he said during discussions with groups of men until he was confident they were accepting and that he would not have to worry about what they were going to think.

Nonverbal and Side-by-Side Communication

The way that participants communicated affection to other men took a form that could easily be missed or misunderstood. These men talked about indirectly showing affection through both verbal and nonverbal means. One participant, for example, discussed how he relates to his father.

> The way I show affection, like the first thing I do is come in the house and he just grabs a hold of my shoulder, squeezes it a little bit and then I punch him in the stomach a little bit and that's—I mean I've told my dad I love him like maybe four times in my entire life—I mean that's just how we show affection. And that's basically the way I am with all guys too, like if I don't feel like I can punch you, you're not my friend . . . It's like a love tap, you know, that's basically what it amounts to.

When participants did verbally express themselves with other men, they often did so in a "side-by-side," as opposed to a "face-to-face," manner. One student shared that his most memorable bonding experience with his best friend occurred as they sat next to each other and talked about their fears and problems during a long trip in the car. Similarly, other participants discussed taking a trip to a casino or getting together to watch World Wrestling Federation (WWF) as activities that created opportunities to communicate and relate to other men. On the surface, these activities might appear to be anything but relational, but note how two participants described their activity: "One of the big things me and Nick do is play Playstation. We get out of class and we can play for like 8 hours and just—it's kind of like a bonding experience between us." or "Like when I go gambling. It's the trip down and talking with somebody that kind of knows at the same level as what I'm doing, it's sorting things out, you know at the same level as me." These men discussed their connection to and relationship with other men in the context of an activity, but their story was not about the activity itself.

Fear of Femininity

Although participants described ways that they were able to express themselves to other men, some communicated both fear and frustration related to the narrow boundaries of that expression. At the root of this frustration was a fear of being seen as "feminine" or somehow "unmanly." One student said, "You know if at the bar someone bumps into you, you have to be the tough guy. You can't have guys thinking weird things about you, you know you got to prove yourself." Participants also discussed how even seemingly nongendered activities raised questions about how others interpret their sexual orientation. Openness to talking, wearing a lot of cologne, and clothing choices were each actions mentioned by participants that made other people question their sexual orientation. One student, for example, said, "People have thought I am gay. I think it's because I talk, but, I'll sit there and listen too, and I'll put input into other people's problems like friends do or gay guys do." This connection between ostensibly feminine activities and being gay sent a clear message to these students that to avoid certain labels, they had to restrict their behavior.

Confusion About and Distancing from Masculinity

Each participant was asked about what it was like being a man on campus. This question, more than any other, was generally met with a long silence before a response was given. It was as if these men had given very little thought to this part of their identity. Several students replied by saying, "I really don't think about it too much," or, "I really don't pay attention to differences." Students were clear, however, that they did not see themselves as typical of most men. One man said, for example, "I'm not a stereotypical male macho kind of person. I talk about lots of things, and I really value my relationships with people." Participants communicated a general sense of unease with masculinity. They were simultaneously unreflective about what being a guy means and aware that masculinity was something with which they did not want to identify.

Sense of Challenge without Support

For those respondents who did answer the question about what it was like being a man on campus, there was a common theme of feeling left out. Several students mentioned the existence of support services designed specifically for women (e.g., women's center, women's leadership programs) without a corresponding focus on men. One student gave a specific example of feeling challenged, whereas female students were supported.

I know a lot of men because I'm in a lot of math and physics classes and there are not a whole lot of girls [sic] in them. It seems like they get more attention, I don't know why. Our male teachers, it seems like they are more apt to give them help. If we don't get it, it's like "I don't understand how you don't understand this—you should be understanding this." I'm like "OK, fine, I don't understand." Then the girl goes up there and he talks quieter and he's more apt to listen to her. I don't know, it just seems he's more understanding of why a girl would not understand. I don't see why girls and guys are different that way.

■ DISCUSSION

The finding that these men did not often think of themselves in terms of their gender is not surprising. This is consistent with Levine and Cureton's (1998) study, which found that "males were neither as eloquent nor as thoughtful in describing gender differences. In the main, it was simply not on the male radar screen" (p. 111). It is, however, problematic if men do not see themselves as men. If identity development is fostered by experiencing crises and choices, as Marcia (1966) suggested, gender and sex need to at least be a blip on the radar screen before reflective commitment can occur. The lack of gender awareness may also be explained by Jones and McEwen's (2000) multiple identity model. According to this model, privilege and inequality are least visible and least understood by those who are most privileged by cultural systems. Like White people who do not see themselves as having a race (Helms, 1992), these men may not have been conscious of their sex. This may be particularly true within university cultures like WIU, where pro-feminist influences are not as visible as they are on many college campuses.

It was similarly noticeable that these men did not mention anything about their racial identity in the interviews. Existing in a cultural context where their gender and race are not "on the radar screen" is both a privilege and a problem. That is, being in an environment where one's race and gender are routinely affirmed promotes a foreclosed identity where crisis is absent and commitments are not explored. To reach an achieved identity, important aspects of one's identity (such as race, gender, and religion) need to be explored.

Although gender and race identity issues were generally unconsidered, men in this study had a sense that they were not being supported. Consistent with Pollack's (1999) research, this study found that men felt pushed or challenged without sufficient empathy or support. One participant's story about feeling that female students were supported whereas male students were challenged is particularly poignant. Not only is it outside the traditional male role for an individual to express a need for help (Good & Wood, 1995), but also educators may misunderstand this lack of expression as a lack of need. Osherson (1986), moreover,

described the archetypal scene of a distressed little boy crying out for emotional soothing only to experience both the minimizing of his pain and disapproval for showing such unmanly behavior. The common phrase "take it like a man" is an artifact of this deeper cultural script.

This research also illuminates the importance of gender role conflict on college men's identity development. Students described several instances where they were fearful about how other people might interpret their behavior. According to O'Neil (1981), fear of femininity is at the center of men's gender role conflict. In this study, fear manifested itself through stories of homophobia, restricted emotional expression (e.g., no crying), and limits on verbal expression and communication. These heterosexual men were afraid, essentially, that others would view them as feminine, gay, or somehow other than a man. Thus, when others' assumptions about their sexual orientation did not fit with their own sense of self, participants felt a need to alter their behavior. Men's self-expression may be mediated by what this behavior means, or might mean, to other people. In other words, being less expressive had the benefit of helping to avoid labels they wanted to evade. This may also help to explain findings that male students tend to exhibit more homophobic attitudes and perpetrate significantly more hate-motivated assaults than women do (D'Augelli, 1991).

The finding that participants felt restrictions associated with expression is problematic in a number of ways.

First, gender-related limits on men's self-expression have been linked to negative emotional outcomes (Blazina, 2001; Brody, 1996). Second, one of the central findings in this study was that these students clearly felt that self-expression was important to them. The fact that they valued self-expression even though they were aware that this behavior was sometimes penalized illustrates one the tensions causing gender role conflict. In other words, these men wanted to give voice to certain emotions but were acutely cognizant of the parameters in which these feelings could be expressed. The expression of certain feelings or certain behaviors is quite simply outside of what Pollack (1999) calls "the boy code." Not wanting to appear vulnerable to other men, fear of being seen as gay, and wanting to avoid the "just friend—not boyfriend" label all shaped how and what men in this study communicated.

Students also described communication with their male friends in a way that could easily be misunderstood. Stories about playing video games, traveling in a car to go gambling, and watching WWF wrestling were initially overlooked by investigators. When, however, we suspended our assumptions and more carefully listened to the participant's descriptions, it became clear that they were describing these activities in relational terms. Although communication was "side-by-side" and "doing oriented," the stories being told were about relationship building and connection. This finding is similar to Pollack's (1999) investigation into male development which found that "many mothers find that if they engage in action-oriented activities with their sons, their boys began to open up and talk" (p. 101). Although various activities that men do together may appear on the surface to be incongruent with intimacy, the actions may in fact be rooted in forging relationships and building "buddyship."

Interestingly, the interviewers felt that some of these communication patterns were evident during the interviews. The female researchers noted that men were generally more comfortable expressing themselves than the interviewers anticipated. Several men in this study felt that expressing themselves to women was generally easier than talking with men, as long as the women were viewed as friends and not potential partners. This was true about most topics, although female interviewers felt that discussions about sex and relationships were sometimes awkward. The male interviewers felt that the participants were generally very expressive. This may be, in part, due to the one-on-one nature of the interaction. Men in this study mentioned that it was easier to express themselves with just one other male as opposed to groups of men.

Implications for Student Affairs

Results of this study suggest that student affairs professionals need to provide programming and learning interventions aimed at putting gender on the radar screen for men. Just as we need to help White students see themselves as racial beings, we need to facilitate men learning about themselves as men. Helping men become more aware of their gender should help to promote identity development to the extent that unconsidered gender roles are keeping them from making reflective identity commitments. One strategy that I have used with undergraduate men is to show commercial, movie, and sitcom video clips that have gender-related messages. I then follow these clips with questions to focus attention on both how gender roles are constructed and how to become a critical consumer of these messages. The goal is to help students select for themselves who they are and who they want to become.

In addition to the need for student development professionals to facilitate reflection regarding gender identity, participants' stories also suggest that we may need to give college men more support. In a patriarchal culture, men are privileged, but that should not keep us from treating men developmentally. Pollack (1990), for example, challenged us to "be sensitively aware (and less countertransferentially critical) of the particular forms of affiliative needs and capacities shown by men" (p. 318). Student affairs professionals need to be alert to any disposition to rely on sex role expectations in deciding on developmentally appropriate challenges and supports. Similarly, in this study, several men noticed institutional supports for women, but no such safety net or safe harbor for men on campus. It is important to offer direct services to men, as men, on campus.

Student affairs professionals should also understand that certain forms of men's communication might be more relational than we initially realize. Gender-related restrictions regarding verbal expression clearly influenced how men in this study communicated. The students generally preferred one-on-one communication, felt more comfortable communicating with women, and expressed intimacy "side-by-side" or in the context of doing. Certain developmental interventions may, therefore, be more effective outside of the context of groups. For example, resident assistants (RAs) trying to confront a male student may meet less resistance if the confrontation is handled one-on-one.

It is similarly important for male RAs to be aware that men may have a hard time expressing certain feelings to them. Activity-based or "doing" strategies may help facilitate such expression. According to Pollack (1999), the following approaches are critical to facilitating discussion with men: create a safe space, give men time to feel comfortable with expression, seek out and provide alternative pathways for expression (i.e., relate while engaging in action-oriented activities), listen without judging, and give affirmation and affection. Student affairs professionals should consider engaging men in action-oriented activities such as going for a walk or some other "doing" activity in order to get beyond the mask of masculinity.

■ CONCLUSION

Research into women's identity development grew out of a belief that women must be understood within the context of their role expectations and restrictions. To understand men's identity development, student affairs professionals need to explore how men see themselves as men within "the context of the restraints, constraints, and expectations of the male gender role" (Scher, 1990, p. 325). Identity models that are focused on naturally occurring developmental tasks may tell only a portion of the story. Researchers and student affairs practitioners would be well advised to consider models that reflect the idea that identities are also socially constructed (e.g., Jones & McEwen, 2000). Participants in this research clearly articulated conflicts between behaviors that they personally valued (e.g., self-expression) and how they felt others interpreted that behavior. To the extent that people accept scripted gender roles either blindly or due to perceived sanctions for acting outside of these roles, their identity is less self-authored and more socially constructed.

O'Neil's (1981) concept of gender role conflict provides a useful framework for understanding how a man may see himself in the context of culturally transmitted role expectations. Fear of femininity, restricted expression, and restricted affectionate behavior among men were evident in the stories told by students in this study. The themes emerging from these stories suggest ways for student affairs professionals to design developmentally appropriate interventions for men, especially those experiencing gender role conflict.

The findings from this study must be interpreted within the limitations of the phenomenological methodology, participants, and context in which the research was conducted. Consistent with the constructivist tradition, the participants' voices and research team's interpretations are not intended to be representative of all men. Clearly, the fact that the research was based on a nondiverse group of men, especially in terms of important identity dimensions of sexual orientation and race, limits the transferability of findings. Information is given, however, regarding the research context and participant interviews to assist the reader in applying the results.

Future researchers should consider implementing longitudinal qualitative studies to get a sense of the events that promote or inhibit development, how other components of self (e.g., sexual orientation, cultural heritage, etc.) might impact growth, and how identity development progresses over time. It is also important to vary the contexts in which studies are implemented. In addition, more research is clearly necessary for various populations of men, including gay men, men with disabilities, and men from various cultural backgrounds.

REFERENCES

Belenky, M. F., Clinchy, B. M., Goldberger, N. R., & Tarule, J. M. (1986). *Women's ways of knowing*. New York: Basic Books.

Blazina, C. (2001). Analytic psychology and gender role conflict: The development of the fragile masculine self. *Psychotherapy, 38*(1), 50–59.

Brody, L. R. (1996). Gender, emotional expression, and the family. In R. Kavanaugh, B. Zimmerberg-Glick, and S. Fein (Eds.),

Emotion: Interdisciplinary Perspectives. Hillsdale, NJ: Lawrence Erlbaum.

Chickering, A. W., (1969). *Education and identity.* San Francisco: Jossey-Bass.

Chickering, A. W., & Reisser, L. (1993). *Education and identity* (2nd ed.). San Francisco: Jossey Bass.

Coffey, A., & Atkinson, P. (1996). *Making sense of qualitative data: Complementary research strategies.* Thousand Oaks, CA: Sage.

Cournoyer, R. J., & Mahalik, J. R. (1995). Cross-sectional study of gender role conflict examining college-aged and middle-aged men. *Journal of Counseling Psychology, 42*(1), 11–19.

D'Augelli, A. R. (1991). Gay men in college: Identity processes and adaptations. *Journal of College Student Development, 32,* 140–146.

D'Augelli, A. R. (1994). Identity development and sexual orientation: Toward a model of lesbian, gay, and bisexual development. In E. J. Trickett, R. J. Watts, & D. Birman (Eds.), *Human diversity: Perspectives on people in context* (pp. 312–333). San Francisco: Jossey-Bass.

Erikson, E. (1968). *Identity, youth, and crisis.* New York: Norton.

Fine, M. (1994). Working the hyphens: Reinventing self and other in qualitative research. In N. R. Denzin & Y. S. Lincoln (Eds.), *Handbook of Qualitative Research* (pp. 70–82). Thousand Oaks, CA: Sage Publications.

Gilligan, C. (1982). *In a different voice.* Cambridge, MA: Harvard University Press.

Good, G. E., Braverman, D., & O'Neil, J. M. (1991). *Gender role conflict: Construct validity and reliability.* Paper presented at the annual meetings of the American Psychological Association, San Francisco, CA.

Good, G. E., & Mintz, L. B. (1990). Gender role conflict and depression in college men: Evidence for compound risk. *Journal of Counseling and Development, 69,* 17–21.

Good, G. E., & Wood, P. K. (1995). Male gender role conflict, depression, and help seeking: Do college men face double jeopardy? *Journal of Counseling & Development, 74*(1), 70–75.

Helms, J. E. (1992). *A race is a nice thing to have: A guide to being a White person or understanding the White persons in your life.* Topeka, KS: Content Communications.

Jones, S. R. (1997). Voices of identity and difference: A qualitative exploration of the multiple dimensions of identity development in women college students. *Journal of College Student Development, 38*(4), 376–385.

Jones, S. R., & McEwen, M. K. (2000). A conceptual model of multiple dimensions of identity. *Journal of College Student Development. 41*(4). 405–414.

Josselson, R. (1987). *Finding herself: Pathways to identity development in women.* San Francisco: Jossey-Bass.

Josselson, R. (1996). *Revising herself: The story of women's identity from college to midlife.* New York: Oxford University Press.

Kavale, S. (1996). *Interviews: An introduction to qualitative research interviewing.* Thousand Oaks, CA: Sage.

Levine, A., & Cureton, J. (1998). *When hope and fear collide.* San Francisco: Jossey-Bass.

Lincoln, Y., & Guba, E. (1985). *Naturalistic inquiry.* Thousand Oaks, CA: Sage.

Manning, K. (1999). *Giving voice to critical campus issues: Qualitative research in student affairs.* Lanham, MD: University Press of America.

Marcia, J. (1966). Development and validation of ego-identity status. *Journal of Personality and Social Psychology, 3,* 551–559.

Meth, R. L., & Pasick, R. S. (1990). *Men in therapy: The challenge of change.* New York: Guilford Press.

Miles, M. B., & Huberman, A. M. (1984). *Qualitative data analysis.* Beverly Hills, CA: Sage.

O'Neil, J. M. (1981). Patterns of gender role conflict and strain: Sexism and fear of femininity in men's lives. *The Personnel and Guidance Journal, 60,* 203–210.

O'Neil, J. M. (1990). Assessing men's gender role conflict. In D. Moore & F. Leafgren (Eds.), *Problem-solving strategies and interventions for men in conflict* (pp. 23–38). Alexandria, VA: American Counseling Association.

O'Neil, J. M., Helms, B, J., Gable, R. K., David, L., & Wrightsman, L. S. (1986). Gender role conflict scale: College men's fear of femininity. *Sex Roles, 14,* 335–350.

Osherson, S. (1986). *Finding our fathers.* New York: Fawcett Columbine.

Patton, M. Q. (1990). *Qualitative evaluation and research methods* (*2nd ed.*). Newbury Park, CA: Sage.

Piaget, J. (1954). *The construction of reality in the child* (M. Cook, Trans.). New York: Basic Books.

Pollack, W. S. (1990). Men's development and psychotherapy: A psychoanalytic perspective. *Psychotherapy, 27,* 316–321.

Pollack, W. S. (1999). *Real boys: Rescuing our sons from the myths of boyhood.* New York: Holt.

Rounds, D. (1994). *Predictors of homosexual intolerance on a college campus: Identity, intimacy, attitudes toward homosexuals and gender role conflict.* Unpublished master's thesis, Department of Psychology, University of Connecticut.

Schenkel, S., & Marcia, J. E. (1972). Attitudes toward premarital intercourse in determining ego identity status in college women. *Journal of Personality, 40*(1), 472–482.

Scher, M. (1990). Effect of gender role incongruities on men's experience as clients in psychotherapy. *Psychotherapy, 27,* 322–326.

Sharpe, M. J., & Heppner, P. P. (1991). Gender, gender-role conflict, and psychological well being in men. *Journal of Counseling Psychology, 38,* 323–330.

Thompson, E. H., Pleck, J. H., & Ferrera, D. L. (1992). Men and masculinities: Scales for masculinity ideology and masculinity-related constructs. *Sex Roles, 27,* 573–607.

van Manen, M. (1990). *Researching the lived experience: Human science for an action sensitive pedagogy.* Albany, NY: SUNY Press.

CHAPTER 5

Masculinities Go to Community College

Understanding Male Identity Socialization and Gender Role Conflict

Frank Harris III and Shaun R. Harper

"The Case of the Missing Men," a front-page news story in the January 26, 2007, issue of the *Chronicle of Higher Education*, focused on gaps in college enrollments between undergraduate men and women. As is the case with most other treatments of gender in the higher education literature, the story highlighted disparities at four-year institutions, leaving readers relatively uninformed about similar trends at community colleges. Also problematic is the insufficient attention given to gender identity development, as well as attitudinal and behavioral expressions among male community college students. Most of what has been published about men at community colleges pertains to how many enroll and actualize the aspirations with which they entered (completing one course for skill acquisition, earning a certificate or associate degree,

or transferring to a four-year institution) and, secondarily, the extent to which they are engaged in educationally purposeful activities. In 2006, men were 41.4 percent of students enrolled at two-year colleges and earned 38.4 percent of associate degrees awarded (U.S. Department of Education, 2007).

Although gendered attainment disparities exist across all racial groups, the gap is widest among black students, with black women earning 68.6 percent of associate degrees. Analyses of data from the Community College Survey of Student Engagement (2006) revealed that women put forth more academic effort and spend more time studying, reading, doing homework, and participating in other class-related activities. Furthermore, black male respondents to the survey were less likely than their same-race female counterparts to discuss ideas or readings with others outside class, use the Internet for academic work and research, or spend significant amounts of time studying. Thirty-one percent of black men were uncertain of their plans to return to college the next term, compared to 24 percent of black women. These engagement data, absent of social context to explain gender differences, are hardly useful for educators who endeavor to enhance male student outcomes, increase their participation in enriching educational experiences, and ultimately improve their persistence toward associate's degree attainment and transfer rates to four-year institutions.

Disparities in enrollment, attainment, and engagement constitute most of what is known about men at community colleges and therefore make the exploration of gendered questions necessary: What prior gender socialization experiences do men bring with them to college? How do variable masculinities and identity conflicts affect male students' attitudes and behaviors on campus? And what sociocultural factors explain gender differences in engagement and retention within community colleges? These questions have been explored theoretically and empirically using samples of male undergraduates at four-year institutions (Davis, 2002; Harper, 2004; Harper, Harris, and Mmeje, 2005; Harris, 2006), but not at community colleges.

Informed by perspectives from sociology, men's studies, and education, this chapter devotes attention to some of the challenges and experiences of men at community colleges. Our exclusive reliance on published literature pertaining to male students at four-year institutions is attributable to the dearth of research exploring men at community colleges. Notwithstanding, we examine how these students are socialized and how various dimensions of their identities intersect, regardless of postsecondary educational context (meaning, two-year or four-year).

■ MANHOOD MESSAGES: FROM BOYHOOD TO COLLEGE

This section provides insights into the precollege sociocultural factors that contribute to the behavioral trends that are common among male students in college contexts. We consider some of the published literature on boyhood, adolescence, and masculinities. Several socializing agents are identified by researchers as key influences on boys' and young men's precollege gender socialization. Families, male peer groups, and schools are consistently cited as having the most significant and lasting effects on the development of masculine identities for boys (Harper, Harris, and Mmeje, 2005; Kimmel and Messner, 2007; Kimmel, Hearn, and Connell, 2005). These influences are discussed in further detail below.

Parents and Familial Influences

The traditional American family structure facilitates the gender socialization of children (Kimmel and Messner, 2007). This process entails teaching and reinforcing norms and expectations of gendered behavior, which are respectively characterized as masculine and feminine for boys and girls. Children learn the expectations of gender performance for boys and girls (and subsequently men and women) by way of the direct and implicit messages they receive from their parents, as well as through observation and imitation of their parents' gendered behaviors and interactions (MacNaughton, 2006). Children learn throughout their development that domestic duties are culturally associated with women and femininities. Conversely, men and masculinities are associated with duties that represent physical rigor, strength, and power.

The interactions that characterize father-son relationships are especially critical during the process of gender socialization. The ways in which a father shapes his son's gender identity is informed by his own conceptualization of gender. More often than not, fathers' perceptions of masculinities are heavily influenced by traditional, socially constructed expectations. As such, Harper (2004) maintained that "no father wants his son to grow up being a 'pussy,' 'sissy,' 'punk,' or 'softy'—terms commonly associated with boys who fail to live up to the traditional standards of masculinities in America" (p. 92).

Fathers' expectations are reinforced through their daily interactions with their sons and reflected in the toys they purchase, the games they teach their sons, and the strategies they employ for punishing and rewarding gender performance. Fathers are also chiefly responsible for getting their sons involved in sports,

martial arts, and other socializing activities that are popular among boys. These activities, coupled with the pressure from fathers to perform gender along stereotypical norms, lead boys to internalize the masculine values of competitiveness, toughness, and aggressiveness. Since these activities and interactions often take place in male-dominated spaces, boys also learn the language and lessons of patriarchy and male privilege (Griffin, 1998).

Male Peer Groups

Male peers also have profound influences on boys' gender identities. Interactions with male peers reinforce the early lessons about gender and masculinities that are learned primarily in the home. Harris (1998) contended that the influence of male peers on gender performance among boys is more intense than parental influences. Similarly, Pollack (2000) described a boy code, which restricts emotional expression among boys. Boys consider being called a "girl," "sissy," or "fag" highly insulting. Therefore, many boys conform to the expectations of their peers by engaging in behaviors and expressing attitudes that are contradictory to what they deem appropriate and desirable in order to avoid these characterizations.

Participating in sports also weighs heavily in peer interactions among boys. Sports provide contexts for boys to establish status by way of physical dominance and competitiveness (Griffin, 1998). Martin and Harris (2006) suggested that boys who can run the fastest, throw the farthest, and hit the hardest are positioned at the top of the hierarchy within their peer groups. Conversely, boys who are not gifted athletically and those who are uncomfortable interacting in male-dominated spaces struggle to gain the acceptance of their peers; they are often the targets of teasing and bullying. Gilbert and Gilbert (1998) noted that boys' peer interactions are shaped by their athletic prowess in school settings too.

Schools as Venues for Socialization

Masculinizing practices, as characterized by Swain (2005), are heavily situated in traditional American school settings. Gender-related lessons and messages that are consumed by boys in schools are remarkably consistent with those reinforced within families and peer groups. Scholars consistently note that the tasks that lead to academic success do not complement the activities in which boys engage to achieve a masculine identity. Swain described the relationship between achieving a masculine identity and attending to schoolwork as fundamentally incompatible, given the processes of gender socialization for boys. For boys, learning and studying are equated with femininity.

Establishing a masculine identity becomes especially difficult in middle and high school contexts in which sports and heterosexuality emerge as important indicators of masculinities. The most popular boys are those who are perceived to be cool, which is defined in large part by a young man's athleticism and his heterosexual desirability. Teenage boys who establish reputations for engaging in sexual relationships with girls are considered among the coolest by their peers (Davis and Jordan, 1994). Thus, increasing their popularity and masculine statuses becomes an incentive for boys to pursue sex with girls and share the details of these acts with their peers. Consequently sex and girls are often the subjects of highly charged sexist behaviors and conversations among male teens. There is intense pressure to engage in these conversations; those who choose not to do so are viewed with suspicion by peers.

The patterns of interactions among middle and high school boys also persist into postsecondary settings. Ludeman (2004) asserted, "If the male socialization process indeed shapes or restricts the emotional skills and development of boys and men, then it seems likely that the demands of the college environment will create challenges for men related to their relationships and experiences on the college campus" (pp. 79–80). Ludeman's remarks facilitate our transition to the next section of this chapter, which considers the ways in which traditional patterns of male socialization conflict with men's development and success in college.

■ MASCULINITIES IN CONFLICT DURING COLLEGE

Scholars who have explored undergraduate men in their research have not focused their analyses on men enrolled at community colleges. Therefore, little is known about the gender-related developmental challenges with which these men must contend. This discussion of masculinities in conflict during college is, by default, informed by the published research on college men who attend four-year institutions.

Higher education researchers have linked healthy psychosocial development with the achievement of important outcomes in college (Chickering and Reisser, 1993; Evans, Forney, and Guido-DiBrito, 1998). Engaging in campus activities and organizations, cultivating meaningful friendships and interpersonal relationships, and seeking help when necessary are some indicators of healthy psychosocial development for college students. College men are often reluctant to exhibit these behaviors because they are traditionally defined as feminine and conflict with lessons learned about masculinity prior to college (Harper, Harris, and Mmeje, 2005; Ludeman, 2004). Moreover, men's adherence to unproductive masculine conceptions such as sexism, homophobia, violence, and anti–intellectualism are often requisite for their access to male peer groups. As is the case in high school, men who openly reject these conceptions risk being alienated or having their masculinities questioned by their male peers (Kimmel, 1996; Messner, 2001). When examined critically, the incongruence between the behaviors that are linked empirically to student development and success in college and those that constitute the performance of traditional masculinities are evident.

■ MALE GENDER ROLE CONFLICT

Male gender role conflict (MGRC) is an empirically grounded phenomenon that helps to make sense of the gender and identity-related challenges with which college men must contend. O'Neil (1981) characterized MGRC as a negative consequence of the discrepancies between men's authentic selves and the idealized, socially constructed images that are culturally associated with masculinity. When men are unable to perform masculinity, they are likely to view themselves as less masculine and assume others will do the same. MGRC is also directly related to men's fears of being perceived as feminine (O'Neil, 1981). Femininity, when exhibited by men, is associated with being gay and therefore encourages homophobia and hypermasculinity among men. Young men are socialized at very early ages to strategically avoid values, attitudes, and behaviors that are socially constructed as feminine or gay. Thus, the detrimental effects of MGRC are not surprising.

The consequences of MGRC on development and outcomes for college men are noteworthy. Several behavioral patterns that are associated with MGRC are reportedly prevalent among men in college. Restricted emotionality relates to men's difficulty or unwillingness to express their feelings, their refusal to display emotional vulnerability, and their disdain for male femininity. This pattern stems from the belief that disclosing feelings, emotions, and vulnerabilities is an indication of weakness and therefore should not be exhibited by men (O'Neil, 1981). Seeking help through counseling and other means of emotional expressiveness is also inconsistent with restricted emotionality. In college contexts, men who have internalized restricted emotionality can be overwhelmed by failure, setbacks, and frustrations (O'Neil, 1981). Once internalized, these feelings surface through acts of aggressiveness and, in extreme cases, physical violence. O'Neil also found that restricted emotionality discourages genuine interpersonal closeness between men. This may explain why college men often limit their interactions with male peers to stereotypically masculine norms (Ludeman, 2004).

Socialized control, power, and competition is a second pattern of MGRC that informs this discussion of college men. Whereas restricted emotionality denotes men's control over their feelings and emotions, this pattern relates to men's desires to regulate the situations and the people in their lives (O'Neil, 1981). The pattern describes a man's tendencies to compete with and show superiority over other men in order to assert his masculinities. Key sites for power and competition among college men are sexual relationships with women, status within exclusively male peer groups, and the accumulation of material possessions. When college men are unsuccessful in securing the power and control within these and similar contexts, they often rely on other, usually destructive, strategies for doing so. For instance, O'Neil (1981) posited that socialized power and control are achieved

through homophobia within male peer groups. "Homophobia," O'Neil writes, "is a device of social control to maintain traditional male behavior appropriate to social situations and to control all men, not just [gay men]" (p. 208).

Finally, men's obsession with achievement and success has also been identified as a behavioral pattern of MGRC that provides insights into behaviors and outcomes for college men. Men are socialized to embrace the breadwinner role in the home. Thus, many college men pursue postsecondary degrees for access to high-paying jobs and careers, and thereby facilitate their fulfillment of this expectation. This pattern also partially explains why men have traditionally been overrepresented among students pursuing degrees in business, engineering, and other technical disciplines. Fears of failure and intense pressure to succeed are two consequences accompanying men's obsession with achievement and success (O'Neil, 1981). College men who fall into this behavioral pattern are predisposed to physical and emotional stress and reliance on food, alcohol, and drugs to sooth anxieties.

■ IDENTITY CONFLICTS AMONG FOUR COMMUNITY COLLEGE MALE STUDENTS

In this section, we present the profiles of four racially different men enrolled in community colleges. Each student is confronting a unique set of challenges relating to his masculine identity. These profiles illustrate the concepts and conflicts discussed in the chapter.

The Working White Mechanic

Adam came from a working-class background. While pursuing an associate degree in business, he simultaneously worked part time as a mechanic in order to make ends meet. Adam was a former high school all-American football player. In fact, he had expected to earn an athletic scholarship to attend a major university with a high-profile football program, but in the summer prior to his senior year of high school, he was in a motorcycle accident and suffered severe head and leg injuries, which ended his athletic career. The accident and subsequent injuries left Adam angry and depressed, and they marked the beginning of a downward spiral.

Adam did not have grades and test scores that would earn him admission to a four-year institution without an athletic scholarship. Therefore, he pursued other career options that did not require a degree. To cope, he began abusing alcohol, having risky sex (which led him to fatherhood at age nineteen), and occasionally engaging in violent altercations with others. In his third semester of community college, Adam encountered a host of challenges. He struggled academically and found it difficult to fit in with the "smart kids," as he often referred to his classmates. His girlfriend suggested that he talk with his professors, join a study group, or consult a tutor at the college's academic support center. Adam

refused for fear that his classmates and professor would view him as incapable. "They already think I'm stupid and don't belong there. I am not going to kiss their asses to pass a class!" he exclaimed.

Adam also found it difficult to accept the opportunity costs he had to endure in order to attend college. Prior to enrolling, he worked sixty hours a week and earned enough income to allow his girlfriend to stay at home and take care of their two children. Suddenly Adam had to reduce his work hours by half to make time for classes and studying. Consequently, his girlfriend took a part-time job to supplement their income. Adam recently asked a friend, "What kind of man has two kids and quits working so he can go and read poetry at some damn college?"

The Struggling Asian Help Seeker

Jimmy grew up in a traditional Vietnamese family in which education and high academic achievement were constantly emphasized. He has two older brothers, both of whom graduated with honors from top universities. His issues stemmed primarily from the pressure he felt to follow his father's professional footsteps. Jimmy's father expected him to earn an accounting degree and assume ownership of the family business. But Jimmy wanted to be a writer, which had become a source of tension between him and his father. In his second semester of college, Jimmy began to struggle academically and suffered from undiagnosed depression. He also had not established any meaningful friendships in college, in sharp contrast to his high school years when he was highly engaged in clubs and regularly enjoyed social interactions with his friends. An academic adviser offered access to tutors, counseling, and other sources of support, and she encouraged him to consider changing his major. However, Jimmy refused to take advantage of these options, fearing they would be met with his father's disapproval.

The Latino Homeboy

Erik had always enjoyed school and was a good student until his freshman year of high school, when he began hanging out with a group of young men who had a bad influence on him. They regularly skipped school, spent significant amounts of time pursuing sex with girls, and were occasionally involved in minor illegal activities. At times Erik tried to pull away from the group and get on the right path. However, the other questioned his loyalty and manhood. Somehow Erik managed to complete high school, but he decided not to participate in graduation for fear of his friends' reaction. In fact, one year had passed before Erik disclosed to them that he earned his high school diploma.

A critical moment occurred in Erik's life that motivated him to reconsider his future and recapture some of his promise and potential: His father became terminally ill. Realizing that in his father's absence he would need to care for his mother and two young sisters, Erik decided to enroll in community college to pursue a vocational certificate and an associate's degree. His friends from high school offered a perspective on his decision: "School is for girls and sissies. If you need to support your family, be a man and go out and get a real job." Despite this advice, he lived at home with his mother and siblings, commuted to campus each day, and decided not to work so he could concentrate on school. Erik's performance in college classes was satisfactory; however, he often questioned his decision to return to school and wondered if he should have gotten a full-time job.

The Closeted Black Gay Achiever

Toreé graduated from high school with an academic record that would have easily gained him admission to a four-year institution. He chose to spend his first two years at a community college to relieve his family of some of the financial burden of paying for college. Toreé came from a tightly knit family with strong religious values. In fact, his closest male friends were those he had met in church as a youngster. The significant roles that family and religion played in Toreé's life and identity were profound.

During his time in community college, Toreé established a reputation as an outstanding student and a respected campus leader. He served as president of the student government and was well known by many of his peers. On the surface, he appeared to be enjoying a healthy and fulfilling college student experience. However, no one around him knew that Toreé was incredibly conflicted. As a junior in high school, Toreé discovered his attraction to other men and started engaging in sexual experiences and relationships with boyfriends. Toreé worried that disclosing his sexual orientation would change the way he was perceived on campus. Moreover, he was certain that his family would disown him if they learned he was gay. Over the years, he had heard his father make strong homophobic remarks about gay and lesbian persons. Also, given his religious background, Toreé was concerned that his sexual orientation would bring shame to his family. Overcommitment was a strategy he employed to cope with the stress and anxiety. The community college had only a handful of student clubs, and Toreé was involved in nearly all of them. Of course, he was applauded for his high level of service and commitment. But in spite the success and status he enjoyed in college, Toreé became increasingly depressed and unhappy.

A CONCLUSION ON CONFLICT AMONG COMMUNITY COLLEGE MEN

Though racially different, Adam, Jimmy, Erik, and Toreé had one thing in common: each experienced conflicts related to his masculine identity while enrolled in community college. These four men's stories are more common than atypical, which makes understanding the unique issues and gendered experiences

of college men urgently important. For example, two gender-related challenges were prominent in Adam's profile. First, he had clearly internalized the breadwinner role that men are often socialized to embrace. He viewed his decision to enroll in community college as a violation of this prevalent masculine norm, especially considering that his girlfriend had to share the responsibility of earning the income necessary to provide for their family. Second, much of the success Adam experienced during his adolescent years came by way of his participation in sports. Thus, returning to school required him to learn new skills and develop his intellectual competence. These new growth and learning processes resulted in increased anxiety, feelings of inadequacy, and frustration.

Taken as a whole, Adam's behaviors were consistent with the restricted emotionality and socialized power and control patterns of MGRC. Sources of support that validated his new identity as a student would have eased his college transition. Also, connecting Adam with a male faculty or staff mentor could have been helpful. Supporting Adam through his challenges may have provided an opportunity to identify other men on campus who had recently returned to school and were balancing academic demands with caring for their families and working off campus. Finally, Adam may have benefited from career advising. Given his past involvement and success in athletics, pursuing a career in coaching, athletics administration, sports medicine, or a related field may have elicited more enthusiasm for college.

Getting reconnected to sports also could have offered therapeutic benefits for Adam by providing some closure on the unexpected termination of his football career. Similarly thoughtful approaches should be used to understand and help resolve identity conflicts with students like Jimmy, Erik, Toreé, and other men with conflicted identities at community colleges. We offer the following potentially promising suggestions:

- Encourage male students to reconsider their negative perceptions of help seeking.
- Provide opportunities for critical reflection on masculinity through journaling, course readings, analyzing popular media, and other assignments (Davis and Laker, 2004).
- Increase male students' participation in campus activities and programs that facilitate healthy identity development and lead to productive outcomes.
- Provide opportunities for bonding by way of facilitated discussion groups and other activities that are popular among male students.
- Collect campus-level data (interviews, focus groups, and surveys for example) from male students to assess their gender-specific needs.
- Organize a committee of student affairs administrators, counselors, faculty members, coaches, and student leaders to provide proactive campuswide leadership in addressing issues concerning male students.

One question remains: How do masculinities in community college contexts differ from those in four-year institutions? The paucity of published literature that provides insights into the gender-related experiences of community college men makes this question difficult to answer. While this chapter serves as a first step toward understanding community college men, additional inquiries that consider their unique challenges and experiences are urgently necessary. Studies that show ways in which community college campus contexts both facilitate and hinder gender identity development for male students are especially needed.

REFERENCES

"The Case of the Missing Men." *Chronicle of Higher Education*, Jan. 26, 2007, p. A1.

Chickering, A. W., and Reisser, L. *Education and Identity*. (2nd ed). San Francisco: Jossey-Bass, 1993.

Community College Survey of Student Engagement. *Act on Fact: Using Data to Improve Student Success, 2006 Findings*. Austin: University of Texas, 2006.

Davis, J. E., and Jordan, W. J. "The Effects of School Context, Structure, and Experience on African American Males in Middle and High School." *Journal of Negro Education*, 1994, *63*, 570–587.

Davis, T. "Voices of Gender Role Conflict: The Social Construction of College Men's Identity." *Journal of College Student Development*, 2002, *43*(4), 508–521.

Davis, T., and Laker, J. "Connecting Men to Academic and Student Affairs Programs and Services." In G. Kellom (ed.), *Developing Effective Programs and Services for College*

Men New Directions for Student Services, no. 107. San Francisco: Jossey-Bass, 2004.

Evans, N. J., Forney, D. S., and Guido-DiBrito, F. *Student Development in College: Theory, Research, and Practice.* San Francisco: Jossey-Bass, 1998.

Gilbert, R., and Gilbert, P. *Masculinity Goes to School.* New York: Routledge, 1998.

Griffin, P. *Strong Women, Deep Closets: Lesbians and Homophobia in Sports.* Champaign, Ill.: Human Kinetics, 1998.

Harper, S. R. "The Measure of a Man: Conceptualizations of Masculinity among High-Achieving African American Male College Students." *Berkeley Journal of Sociology*, 2004, *48*(1), 89–107.

Harper, S. R., Harris III, F., and Mmeje, K. "A Theoretical Model to Explain the Overrepresentation of College Men among Campus Judicial Offenders: Implications for Campus Administrators." *NASPA Journal*, 2005, *42*(4), 565–588.

Harris III, F. "The Role of Pre-College Socialization in the Meanings College Men Make of Masculinities." Paper presented at the Association for the Study of Higher Education annual meeting, Anaheim, Calif., Nov. 2006.

Harris, J. R. *The Nature Assumption: Why Children Turn Out the Way They Do.* London: Bloomsbury, 1998.

Kimmel, M. S. *Manhood in America: A Cultural History.* New York: Free Press, 1996.

Kimmel, M. S., Hearn, J., and Connell, R. W. (eds.). *Handbook of Studies on Men and Masculinities.* Thousand Oaks, Calif.: Sage, 2005.

Kimmel, M. S., and Messner, M. A. (eds.). *Men's Lives.* (7th ed). Needham Heights, Mass.: Allyn and Bacon, 2007.

Ludeman, R. B. "Arrested Emotional Development: Connecting College Men, Emotions, and Misconduct." In G. Kellom (ed.), *Developing Effective Programs and Services for College Men.* New Directions for Student Services, no. 107. San Francisco: Jossey-Bass, 2004.

MacNaughton, G. "Constructing Gender in Early-Years Education." In C. Skelton, B. Francis, and L. Smulyan (eds.), *The Sage Handbook of Gender and Education.* Thousand Oaks, Calif.: Sage, 2006.

Martin, B. E., and Harris III, F. "Examining Productive Conceptions of Masculinities: Lessons Learned from Academically Driven African American Male Student-Athletes." *Journal of Men's Studies*, 2006, *14*(3), 359–378.

Messner, M. A. "Friendship, Intimacy, and Sexuality." In S. M. Whitehead and F. J. Barrett (eds.), *The Masculinities Reader.* Malden, Mass.: Blackwell, 2001.

O'Neil, J. M. "Patterns of Gender Role Conflict and Strain: Sexism and Fear of Femininity in Men's Lives." *Personnel and Guidance Journal*, 1981, *60*, 203–210.

Pollack, W. S. *Real Boys' Voices.* New York: Random House, 2000.

Swain, J. "Masculinities in Education." In M. Kimmel, J. Hearn, and R. W. Connell (eds.), *Handbook of Studies on Men and Masculinities.* Thousand Oaks, Calif.: Sage, 2005.

U.S. Department of Education. *Digest of Education Statistics, 2006.* Washington, D.C.: National Center for Education Statistics, 2007.

CHAPTER 6

Masculinity Scripts, Presenting Concerns, and Help Seeking

Implications for Practice and Training

James R. Mahalik, Glenn E. Good, and Matt Englar-Carlson

Ask almost any practitioner and you will inevitably hear that working with men presents special challenges. A therapist may wonder, "How can I be effective with men when it seems many are reluctant to be in therapy, uncomfortable with the process of disclosure, and quick to avoid emotional exploration?" Others ask, "How do I work with presenting issues such as emotional restriction, interpersonal isolation and conflict, workaholism, or substance abuse that many men bring to therapy?" All seem to sense that masculinity plays a role in affecting men's experience of therapy, but they wonder how they can address these gender issues in their work with men.

In response to the need to work more effectively with men and integrate an important part of men's experiences (i.e., their masculine selves) into the therapeutic work, a great deal has been written and discussed recently regarding therapy with men (see Brooks & Good, 2001). This work addresses a broad range of therapeutic concerns, including group therapy with men (Andronico, 2001), working with boys and adolescent males (Horne & Kiselica, 1999), treatment strategies with traditional men (Brooks, 1998), new theoretical models for working with men (Good, Gilbert, & Scher, 1990), and integrating masculine socialization issues into existing theoretical frameworks (Mahalik, 1999a, 1999b).

Although research on therapeutic issues and masculinity has been limited to questions of how masculinity relates to presenting issues and attitudes toward therapy, findings from these studies identify a critical dynamic that must be addressed by psychologists—namely, elements of masculinity appear to contribute both to men's psychological distress and to their reluctance to get help for those stressors. The purpose of this chapter is to examine this research and make suggestions on ways in which men's gendered lives can be incorporated into therapeutic work with men.

■ MASCULINITY AND PRESENTING PROBLEMS

To apply research findings from the masculinity literature to practice and training, one has to sort through a literature that seems to reach different conclusions. For example, some research reports that men are less likely than women to be diagnosed with anxiety and depression-related disorders (e.g., Sachs-Ericsson & Ciarlo, 2000). We might thus conclude that masculinity is associated with greater psychological well-being. However, when we learn that women are more likely to recognize and label nonspecific feelings of distress as an emotional problem (Kessler, Brown, & Boman, 1981) and that men have higher rates for the total prevalence of mental disorders when substance abuse and antisocial behaviors are considered (e.g., Bland, Orn, & Hewman, 1988), the earlier conclusion appears unfounded.

There is also a body of literature, mostly using the Bem Sex Role Inventory (BSRI), that reports "masculinity" to be related to better psychological functioning (e.g., Long, 1986; O'Heron & Orlofsky, 1990). However, these findings need to be reinterpreted given the evidence that masculinity, as measured by the BSRI, is an instrumental personality trait that shows "little or no relationship to global self-images of masculinity" (Spence & Helmreich, 1981, p. 365). Thus, it would be more correct to conclude that this body of research demonstrates that having an instrumental personality trait, rather than being masculine, is associated with greater psychological well-being.

It is also challenging to understand masculinity's relationship to presenting concerns when we recognize that certain masculine ideologies (i.e., culturally based scripts for males) should be associated with positive functioning. For example, men who enact more traditional masculine ideologies may have strengths in such areas as problem solving, logical thinking, appropriate risk taking, and assertive behavior (Levant, 1995). However, to date, research has not examined whether these psychological benefits are connected to masculine ideologies. Instead, research finds that the more men endorse traditional masculinity ideologies, the more they experience a host of presenting issues, including poorer self-esteem (Cournoyer & Mahalik, 1995), problems with interpersonal intimacy (Fischer & Good, 1997; Sharpe & Heppner, 1991), greater depression and anxiety (Cournoyer & Mahalik, 1995; Good & Mintz, 1990; Sharpe & Heppner, 1991), abuse of substances (Blazina & Watkins, 1996), problems with interpersonal violence (Franchina, Eisler, & Moore, 2001), greater biomedical concerns (Watkins, Eisler, Carpenter, Schechtman, & Fisher, 1991), as well as greater overall psychological distress (Good et al., 1995; Hayes & Mahalik, 2000). Thus, although our intention is not to be antimasculine, and many other psychological benefits may be identified that are associated with masculine ideologies, the current research literature is very consistent that men's endorsement of certain masculine ideologies is associated with a range of presenting problems.

To organize our presentation and discussion of these findings, we think it important to translate the research into descriptions of masculine behaviors that clinicians might better recognize when working with men. To do so, we describe an array of masculine "scripts" that are tied to presenting issues likely to show up when working clinically with men. In doing so, we recognize that some scripts may be important for some men but not for others. We also believe, consistent with interpersonal theory (e.g., Kiesler, 1983), that all of the scripts may be adaptive for men if they are flexibly enacted. However, our purpose in discussing each script is to help clinicians make connections between how masculinity may be connected to the issues that men present when coming to counseling and therapy. To further the exploration of these scripts, we also provide brief case examples to highlight how these masculinity scripts may appear in clinical settings.

Strong-and-Silent Script

Being viewed as unemotional is central to the "strong-and-silent" masculine script (e.g., Brannon, 1976). Enacting this script helps boys and men to live up to masculine role expectations through being stoic and in control of one's feelings; however, the longer term adverse consequences of emotional restriction for men are becoming increasingly apparent. For example, Levant (1998) initiated the theoretical discussion of the problem of "alexithymia" (meaning "without words for emotions") as a potential result of masculine socialization. And although alexithymia has not been found to demonstrate a consistent sex-based pattern (Mallinckrodt, King, & Coble, 1998), men's restricted emotionality has been consistently connected to greater levels of alexithymia (Fischer & Good, 1997; Shepard, 1994), as well as to increased paranoia and psychoticism (Good, Robertson, Fitzgerald, Stevens, & Bartels, 1996), fear of intimacy (Cournoyer & Mahalik, 1995; Fischer & Good, 1997; Good et al., 1995), higher levels of depression (Cournoyer & Mahalik, 1995; Good & Mintz, 1990; Good et al., 1996), greater hostile–submissive personality styles (Mahalik, 2000), and higher levels of anxiety, anger, and personality styles similar to those of substance abusers (Blazina & Watkins, 1996).

"Raymond," a 70–year-old retired engineer, came to therapy only to accompany his wife, who was suffering from depression compounded by the recent diagnosis of a progressive debilitating disease. During the collection of background information, his wife indicated that their only child had been killed in a tragic accident at age 7. At that point in their lives, Raymond had said, "I don't want to talk about it!" and spent the next 3 decades of his life trying to "be strong and not talk"—eventually avoiding discussion of any important aspect of his life with anyone. Not surprisingly, he too was deeply depressed, isolated, and afraid to feel anything.

Tough-Guy Script

Closely related to the strong-and-silent masculine gender role script are those messages associated with being a "tough guy." For example, when boys learn to be tough, they too frequently do so by suppressing emotions potentially associated with vulnerability. These coping styles often "have dysfunctional health consequences for many men and for those with whom they come into contact" (Eisler, 1995, p. 208). For example, if a man is unable to express openly his honest emotions of sadness and grief, he is likely to turn to alternate (and less healthy) coping mechanisms, such as substance abuse. Indeed, men are three times more likely than women to die from alcohol-related ailments (Doyle, 1996); 39% of men have some level of psychological dependency on alcohol in their lifetime (Lemle & Mishkind, 1989).

Other tough-guy messages that relate to presenting issues include prescriptions that men must be aggressive, fearless, and invulnerable. As with repression of emotions, aggressiveness and attempts to be fearless can contribute to health problems and premature death. Often, the extent to which a man is considered masculine is defined by his willingness to engage in extreme behaviors that attest to his supposed indestructibility. In this vein, men are far more likely than women to take risks while driving motor vehicles—for example, men are involved in fatal crashes three times more often than women (Li, 1998).

"Jake," a 28-year-old ex-marine employed in a blue-collar profession, lifted weights, drank excessively, and got violent when drunk. He very reluctantly accompanied his wife into marital therapy. In the course of marital therapy, it became apparent that Jake's tough-guy facade was his attempt to cover the deep insecurity he felt about several aspects of his life. He was especially fearful that his wife would leave him for another man who made more money or was a better lover.

"Give-'em-Hell" Script

Research finds that men disproportionately perpetrate, and are the victims of, most forms of violence (Uniform Crime Report, 1997). Violence becomes part of the socialization of men early in life when they are encouraged to fight in order to "build character" and keep from being bullied (Levant & Pollack, 1995). Later on, men may belong to groups that are primarily male (e.g., the military, college fraternities) in which a certain amount of violent peer hazing is considered an acceptable way of initiating men into an exclusive "club."

Violence also plays an especially prominent role in the world of organized sports, which is an important socialization environment for many males.

Sports such as boxing and wrestling directly encourage male violence against other males. Additionally, coaches' support of violence in practices and games may lead to an admiration of violence (Pollack, 1998). For example, in their study of hockey games, Weinstein, Smith, and Weisenthal (1995) found that fist fights, more than playing or skating skills, were seen as indicating greater competence by both teammates and coaches. Thus, boys and men may learn that violence is, at least to some extent, a socially acceptable way to behave and work out problems, and they may not learn to separate aggression and violence that occur within the context of a sporting event from aggression and violence against others outside of the sports arena. Violence and aggression may also be avenues through which some boys and men compensate for uncomfortable feelings such as shame and hurt (Bergman, 1995). Therefore, instead of recognizing, understanding, and coping with their hurt or scared feelings, males may externalize their distress by "taking it out on others."

Research finds that men who conform to violence norms are more likely to experience greater psychological distress in the form of somatic complaints and irritability (Mahalik et al., 2003). This study also found that men's conformity to violence norms was associated with being in trouble with the law, having "blackouts" while drinking, and preferring inequitable social relationships (e.g., where men have power over women).

Research also documents that men's endorsement of traditional masculinity has been related to violence against their partners. Specifically, findings indicate that men who endorsed traditional masculine roles were more likely to have committed actual physical abuse against their female dating partners or wives (Bernard, Bernard, & Bernard, 1985; Prince & Arias, 1984; Telch & Lindquist, 1984; Vass & Gold, 1995), to have attitudes supportive of husbands' violence against their wives (Finn, 1986), as well as to respond with greater anger to women's negative feedback (Vass & Gold, 1995).

An explanation for these research findings is that some men may be very averse to losing power or control to a woman (Dutton & Browning, 1988). Abusive behavior may therefore become one way for these men to restore their sense of power and control. Thus, violence may be a way in which men try to gain a sense of control when interpersonal experiences (e.g., conflict with partner, loss of a job, parenting difficulties) threaten their control and sense of power.

"PJ," a 22-year-old who was in court-mandated counseling following an assault conviction, told the counselor, "Nobody 'disses' [disrespects] me or my brothers [members of his gang] and gets away with it! I don't start fights, but I'm not afraid to finish them!" He said his older brothers taught him to fight so that others would not view him as a "punk" who gets pushed around. In addition to being in and out of trouble with the law from age 12, he described experiencing a lot of pent-up emotions and a chronically upset stomach.

Playboy Script

Sexuality is a normal component of human development. However, a variety of societal messages and traumatic experiences can deflect young men's sexual development onto problematic trajectories. Boys often learn to suppress the extent to which they allow themselves to care for and connect with others. This suppression may lead to nonrelational sex, which is a tendency to experience sex primarily as lust, without any requirements for relational intimacy or emotional attachment. Hence, when sexuality enters their lives, it is often of an unconnected and nonrelational nature (Good & Sherrod, 1997; Levant, 1997). Many observers have pointed out the various ways in which playboy attitudes are harmful to others. For example, in conforming to playboy norms, men tend to be more hostile, to prefer inequitable social relationships (Mahalik et al., 2003), as well as to support rape myths (Locke, 2001). However, an important trend in research is finding that this value system is also quite harmful to men themselves. For example, although for some men engaging in nonrelational sex may be a useful stage of exploration during their life's journey, for others it becomes a problematic, self-perpetuating stage from which they have difficulty progressing (e.g., Brooks, 1998; Good & Sherrod, 1997). Men's fear of vulnerability and

shame lead to a fear of intimacy in sexual relations. Thus, men may come to believe that the "slam-bam-thank-you-ma'am" form of sexuality is safer for them (Brooks, 1998) even though little communication or caring is shared and the risk of exposure to a variety of sexually transmitted diseases is high.

"Ted's" mother provided comfort but was ineffective in protecting him and his brother from his physically abusive father, who suffered from combat-related posttraumatic stress disorder. Ted learned early in school that other males respected him more when he was "successful" in having sexual relations with women. Ted grasped onto a sense of power, control, and mastery that he had not experienced during his childhood by seducing numerous women. Not until his second marriage began to crumble in his 40s did he begin to question the formula that "sexual conquest = self-esteem."

Homophobic Script

For the majority of people who have a dualistic way of viewing the world (Perry, 1970), the corollary of being traditionally masculine is to avoid any features associated with femininity or homosexuality. In this vein, characteristics that are potentially associated with homosexuality, such as any intimate connection with other men, must be avoided in oneself and disdained in others.

Research supports that this script is related to men's well-being in various ways. For example, men who restrict affectionate behavior with other men tend to employ more immature psychological defenses, such as projection and turning against the object (Mahalik, Cournoyer, DeFranc, Cherry, & Napolitano, 1998), and report greater paranoia, psychoticism, and feelings of personal inadequacy (Good et al., 1996). Indeed, recent research reports that heterosexual men react more negatively to homosexual men when the former feel less masculine (Gramzow, 2002). These notions of paranoia, turning against the (threatening) object, and regaining a sense of being masculine appear to be exemplified by the murderers of Matthew Shepard (an unimposing gay man in Wyoming).

This type of violence may be an example of the difficulty men have coping with feelings of same-sex attraction when homophobia is so prevalent in U.S. society. For example, recent research reports that men who had higher levels of homophobia experienced greater sexual arousal when watching homosexual pornography compared with men who had lower levels of homophobia (Adams, Wright, & Lohr, 1996). Thus, homophobia may be a way in which men try to gain a sense of control when feelings of attraction to other men create anxiety for them.

"Richard," a successful 50-year-old car salesman, was a "man's man." He had a clear sense of right and wrong and was "in charge" of his family. When Tom, Richard's bright, handsome, popular, musical, and athletic 18-year-old son, informed Richard that he was dating other guys, Richard erupted in rage, disowned him, and put him out of the house.

Winner Script

An extremely important masculine script in American culture is that of being competitive and successful (David & Brannon, 1976). Although competition is often fun and an important aspect of sports activities, competition in the workplace is thought to be a significant source of stress that contributes to elevated blood pressure and other cardiovascular health problems for men (Good, Sherrod, & Dillon, 2000). For example, men have twice the age-adjusted death rate from heart disease as women (National Center for Health Statistics, 1992), with 48% of men who die suddenly of coronary heart disease having had no previous symptoms (American Heart Association, 1998).

"Type A" behavior, which has been consistently linked to coronary health problems, includes characteristics such as impatience, high drive for achievement, hostility, high need for control, competitiveness, and inability or unwillingness to express oneself. Many of these qualities are valued as ideals of American masculinity having to do with success and being a "winner" (O'Neil, Good, & Holmes, 1995). Supporting this connection to masculinity is the finding that Type A behavior has been associated directly with masculine gender role stress in working adults (Watkins, Eisler, Carpenter, Schechtman, & Fisher, 1991), which has been linked to serious health problems in men (Eisler, 1995).

In terms of psychosocial implications, men who endorse success, power, and competition display more controlling and rigid interpersonal

behavior (Mahalik, 2000), more immature psychological defenses (Mahalik,
Cournoyer, DeFranc, Cherry, & Napolitano, 1998), and more paranoia (Good
et al., 1996). Also, research examining
men's conformity to winning norms
finds that it is related to greater hostility
and being socially uncomfortable
(Mahalik et al., 2003).

"Paul," an 18-year-old high school
senior and athlete, described his con-
flictual relationship with his parents as a
win–lose competition. He said, "If I am
going to lose a [verbal] fight with them,
then I want to make sure that they lose
something and hurt too!" Instead of
viewing relationship problems as being
worked out through compromise, Paul
viewed his relationships with his parents,
teammates, and girlfriend as power
struggles that have clear winners and
losers.

Independent Script

Recent advances in relational psychology
theories have promoted the notion that
young boys typically experience "forced
disidentification" from their mothers too
early in their development (Bergman,
1995; Pollack, 1998), which can create
problems with attachment relationships
(Chodorow, 1978). Although research
finds that males are no more likely than
females to develop maladaptive attachment styles (Kiselica, 2001b), research
does demonstrate a connection between
traditional masculine gender roles and
parental attachment and separation.
Specifically, as males were more rigid

in enacting masculine ideologies (i.e.,
had greater gender role conflict) and
more stressed from failing to live up to
masculine ideals (i.e., had greater gender
role stress), they reported less attachment
to, and more psychological separation
from, parental relationships (Blazina &
Watkins, 2000; DeFranc & Mahalik,
2002; Fischer & Good, 1998). Thus,
because poorer parental attachment
interferes with affective self-regulation,
leaving the individual vulnerable to
stress and at risk for compulsive self-
sufficiency (Ainsworth, 1989; Bowlby,
1969), hyperindependence in men
may signal being uncomfortable with
"attaching" to others or with needing
assistance from others, including their
partners, health care professionals, or
when seriously injured or ill. Supportive
of this is research that finds men's
conformity to self-reliance norms
related both to greater psychological
distress (specifically to greater depression,
anxiety, irritability, intrusive thoughts,
and social discomfort) as well as to less
willingness to seek psychological help
(Mahalik et al., 2003).

"John," a 44-year-old computer
programmer, experienced intense periods of anxiety and loneliness. Heterosexual, but never married, he wondered why
he has always found something wrong
with the women he has dated. His most
common complaint was that the women
he has become involved with get "too
clingy after awhile." He began almost
every session by saying, "I don't know if
I really need to be here," and then talked
about how he would only need one or

two more sessions and he would be ready to quit therapy and set out on his own.

■ RESPONDING TO MEN'S MASCULINITY SCRIPTS

It seems clear that living out certain masculinity scripts can be tied to many stressors for men and the important others in their lives. Even armed with this knowledge, however, clinicians are still likely to be wondering how they should address masculinity issues effectively in their work with men. We suggest the following strategies as potentially useful. First, determine what the salient masculinity scripts are for a particular client. For one client, being emotionally controlled (i.e., "strong and silent") may feel central to his masculine self, but for another it may be that being successful and competitive (i.e., "winner") or not taking any "crap" (i.e., "give 'em hell") is most important. Although these scripts may be related to each other, we believe it is a mistake to focus on masculinity in a global way when working with clients, as men's individual constructions of masculinity are likely to focus on some normative messages but not on others (Mahalik et al., 2003).

Second, identify the positive functions these scripts serve for the client. For example, being strong and silent may be an effective strategy for a man at work, as others view him as steady in a crisis. Being a tough risk-taker may have helped him advance in his career or

gain peer acceptance. Being aggressive or even violent may help him feel he can keep himself from being taken advantage of, or bullied, by others. Being sexually promiscuous may be exciting and a way to make himself feel desirable. Being homophobic might help him feel less anxious about peer rejection. His accomplishments through competition are likely to help him feel a sense of worth. And being self-reliant is likely to help him feel capable and not dependent on others for what he needs.

Beyond the specific benefits that a particular masculinity script may have for the client, conforming to traditional masculinity scripts also offers clear guidance about how one is supposed to act in society (Mahalik et al., 2003). This is no small benefit, as the process of identity development is often a difficult one. As such, conformity to gender role norms helps establish an identity for the individual who is wrestling with this stage of development. For example, being a tough guy or a "big wheel" are ready-made identities for men, and they provide individuals with clear priorities and ways of being that are likely to be useful.

After the client has had the opportunity to explore how these masculinity scripts have value for him, the client can be moved to examine some of the costs in relation to his presenting concerns that were highlighted in the review of the research discussed earlier. For example, the strong-and-silent script may disconnect the client from important others and contribute to his feelings of isolation.

Being a tough guy may lead him to neglect himself or push himself in ways that hurt his health. Giving others "hell" may lead to trouble with the law or to family members' leaving him. Being a playboy may prevent him from real intimacy in his life and may hurt a partner to whom he is committed. Ensuring that others do not think he is homosexual may prevent any real connection to other men, whether family members or male friends, and may lead to self-loathing if he feels any same-sex attraction. Being a winner may cause physical stress as well as interpersonal alienation from always having to compete and beat others; and standing alone may lead to interpersonal isolation and feelings of hopelessness if one is unable to handle things by oneself.

Although our review and examples may be a place for therapists to start when anticipating the costs that such masculinity scripts may incur for their male clients, we are really suggesting that therapists help male clients identify costs by exploring their emotional and physical health in all of their work, family, and leisure relationships. For example, a client may talk about feeling competitive at work, but does he also compete with family members, and how does all of this affect his experiences of stress? The client is aware of being emotionally disconnected from his partner or children and wants to improve these relationships, but does he view these as the only potentially intimate relationships he can have? Although he has discussed blowing up and "giving hell" to coworkers, are his wife and children also afraid of him,

and do other important people in his life steer clear of him?

Having gone through these previous steps, the therapist can now help the client become more flexible in the enactment of masculine scripts that are causing distress for him. For example, maybe the strong-and-silent script is effective at work, but it makes family members feel disconnected from the client. More flexibility in this script might include leaving his workplace relationships as they are but trying to open up more with his partner, family, and/or close friends. For another client, more flexibility with the winner script might mean simply competing with a fewer number of people. For another, it might mean learning new interpersonal skills beyond "kicking butt" or "blowing up" at people. As these more flexible outcomes would be specific to individual clients, identifying all of them is beyond the scope of this chapter. However, by identifying the salient masculinity scripts, understanding the positive role they play, and comprehensively documenting their costs, therapists and their male clients are more likely to understand what changes need to be made, and clients are more likely to be motivated to make those changes.

MASCULINITY AND PSYCHOLOGICAL HELP SEEKING

In addition to identifying strategies for working with men in therapy, clinicians need to be aware of how masculinity scripts may affect men's help seeking. From a socialization perspective, many of the tasks associated with help seeking, such as relying on others, admitting that one needs help, or recognizing and labeling an emotional problem, are at odds with the masculinity scripts identified and discussed above. Supportive of this thinking, research indicates that masculine gender role conflict is consistently inversely related to men's willingness to seek psychological help. Examining specific elements of gender role conflict, Good, Dell, and Mintz (1989) reported that men who endorse restrictive emotionality and affectionate behavior between men were reluctant to seek psychological help. Similarly, Robertson and Fitzgerald (1992) reported that success/power/competition and restrictive emotionality were correlated with negative attitudes toward psychological help seeking. If these findings are interpreted through the lens of our review, their results indicate that the strong-and-silent, winner, and homophobic scripts are connected to less willingness to seek psychological help.

These results suggest that internalized gender roles may create barriers to help seeking for men, particularly if help seeking involves violating important masculine gender roles. For example, seeking help often implies dependence, vulnerability, or even submission to someone with more power (such as a physician), and if men succumb to illnesses, they may be threatened by feelings of helplessness and loss of power—feelings that directly contradict societal pressures demanding

their independence and invulnerability (Pollack, 1998; Sutkin & Good, 1987).

Of particular importance to beginning the therapeutic process are male clients' reactions to emotional expression. Specifically, male clients may expect that they will be encouraged, or even demanded, to use affective language and explore the emotional context of their life experiences. Because of the inhibition against strong emotional expression valued in North American culture (Bronstein, 1984), men may believe that feelings are unnecessary and better left unexplored, particularly if they feel comfortable and more skilled in rational problem solving. Thus, men who are ambivalent about experiencing or expressing emotions may be more likely to avoid or terminate counseling as the work becomes focused on feelings.

As treatment fears appear to be different from negative attitudes toward seeking help (Englar-Carlson, Vandiver, & Keat, 2002), we believe it is also helpful to understand treatment fearfulness in men. Specifically, Kushner and Sher (1991) considered the decision to seek help to be motivated in part by a conflict between approach tendencies (e.g., mental distress, transition in life, pressures from others) and avoidance tendencies (e.g., fear of stigma, cost, time commitments, access to services). From this perspective, although men experience mental distress, they may also experience specific treatment fears around image concerns (i.e., fears of being judged negatively by oneself or others for seeking treatment; Deane &

Chamberlain, 1994; Komiya, Good, & Sherrod, 2000) and coercion concerns (i.e., fears about being pushed to think, do, or say things related to their problems in a new way).

Related to men's image concerns is a perceived "gender specific" stigma that men may associate with breaching the dictates of the masculine gender role that goes beyond the general negative societal reaction toward those who seek psychological help (Sibicky & Dovidio, 1986). In this case, the stigma of not living up to a masculine image likely interferes with asking for psychological help, particularly when asking for help is related to a salient (i.e., ego-central) masculine script (see Addis & Mahalik, 2003). For example, men who live out the winner script likely fear the stigma associated with being a "loser" that seeking therapy might bring. Men who live out the strong-and-silent, tough-guy, and give-'em-hell scripts likely fear the stigma associated with weakness; and men who live out the independent script are likely to fear the stigma associated with being dependent.

When considering men's fear of treatment, we think this same analysis may be applied to a fear of coercion. For example, men who live out the strong-and-silent script may fear being coerced into being weak and emotional in therapy. Men who live out the homophobic script may fear appearing passive; and if working with a male therapist or in group therapy with other men, such men may fear being coerced into intimacy with other men. Men who endorse

the independent script may fear being coerced into being dependent in therapy, or in their lives, as a result of therapy.

Given these issues, we recommend that clinicians first work to identify the expectations that male clients have of the therapeutic process and either correct those that are erroneous or change the structure of therapy to be more congruent for a given male client. For example, if the client believes that the therapist is going to make him talk about things he does not want to talk about, the therapist can provide more accurate information about the therapeutic process (e.g., reassuring him that he is the one who is ultimately in charge of what gets talked about in therapy).

Second, psychologists might find ways to change the context of the help-seeking environment for men. To this end, Addis and Mahalik (2003) propose a model of men's help seeking that uses social psychological theory to integrate the masculinity research with social constructionist and feminist analyses of masculinity. They recommend contextual changes to help-seeking environments, such as providing greater opportunities for reciprocity (e.g., with other group members), increasing the perception of normativeness for particular problems (e.g., depression), training professional helpers to recognize the ego-centrality of certain problems (e.g., unemployment for men who view their family role primarily as "provider"), and creating alternative, nontraditional forums more congruent with masculine socialization (e.g., psychoeducational classes in work settings; see also Kiselica's, 2001a, suggestions for making the therapeutic environment more male-friendly by using shorter sessions or doing therapy outside of the office, for example).

In these ways, clinicians can anticipate stigma and treatment fearfulness, and then take concrete steps to help male clients feel more comfortable. By doing so, clinicians have a greater chance to work on difficult issues with male clients who may be ambivalent toward the traditional therapeutic process than if they do not do so and the male client takes control of the therapeutic process by leaving it.

■ IMPLICATIONS FOR TRAINING

Because men's socialization into masculine roles contributes both to clients' presenting problems as well as to their negative attitudes and fears about counseling, we believe that the guidelines developed for multicultural counseling proficiency (American Psychological Association, 1990) and principles concerning psychotherapy with women (see Fitzgerald & Nutt, 1986) offer important considerations regarding training psychologists to work with men. Specifically, the principles developed for multicultural counseling proficiency and psychotherapy with women incorporate a sociocultural context into recommendations for training and practice that we believe are equally important to include when training psychologists to work

with men. Using this same sociocultural perspective, we suggest that training address a number of issues when preparing psychologists to work with men:

1. It is important that psychologists be knowledgeable about masculine socialization. Specifically, we recommend that psychologists have knowledge about the cultural, racial, political, historical, and economic contexts that influence masculine socialization experiences. Given the research findings reviewed previously, psychologists who develop awareness of how these socialization experiences may constrain men's lives and affect their well-being are likely to be more effective in working clinically with men. Training programs could also design curricula to increase students' knowledge about the way in which masculine socialization contributes to personality formation, vocational choices, and the manifestation of psychological stressors.

2. Psychologists should strive to recognize the interface between an individual's experiences of masculine socialization and his thoughts, behaviors, and feelings regarding getting help. Therapists would do well to assess and understand the help-seeking process that male clients experience in terms of their masculine selves and their expectations and concerns about seeking psychological help. Greater understanding and anticipation of how masculinity issues, including help-seeking norms in the client's male peer groups, interact with experiences of seeking help can lead

to initial therapeutic encounters that respect the experiences of men while exploring what may be unrealistic fears and expectations male clients may be holding (e.g., that a client may lose control of himself or that the therapist will try to turn him into a "sensitive male"). Asking such questions as "What parts about talking to a therapist or coming for therapy make you feel uneasy or skeptical?" can identify reactions to help seeking that are tied to fear of stigma, coercion, emotional expression, or other issues that may interact with the client's masculine identity. By giving corrective information about the realities of the therapeutic process (e.g., "you are the one who decides what to talk about" or "you decide what changes to make or not make in your life"), male clients are less likely to have unrealistic fears of the therapeutic process.

3. Psychologists should incorporate a gender role analysis into their work with men. This would help clinicians and clients to better understand the contribution that masculine socialization may be making to men's presenting issues. This could be done by exploring the experiences that contributed to their masculine socialization. For example, the clinician can explore with the client by saying, "You talk about believing that men aren't supposed to show feelings. What are some of the experiences you've had that taught you that lesson?" In a similar way, clinicians could help clients connect earlier socialization experiences with current stressors. For example, "Given what you say about

your father's emphasis on winning, I wonder how you felt when you didn't get that promotion?" Such exploration with male clients can help them better understand the connection between their masculine socialization and current psychological stressors. Such insight should lead to therapeutic goals coming from the client to loosen some of the constraints associated with those experiences and messages.

4. Psychologists should become aware of, and continually review, their own values and biases and the effects these have on their male clients. At the heart of the clinical bias literature is the idea that psychotherapists' clinical judgments, and their in-session behavior with clients, are influenced by the stereotypes that clinicians hold about specific populations to which clients may belong. Describing how this may occur for both male and female therapists, Mintz and O'Neil (1990) emphasized that because therapists undergo the same gender role socialization as do their clients, therapists' attitudes and behaviors related to gender role are likely to influence the process of assessing, diagnosing, and treating clients who enact traditional or nontraditional gender roles. Supportive of this thinking is research that has found that experienced male therapists who were traditional in their gender roles rated a nontraditional male client as having a poorer prognosis than a traditional male client (Wisch & Mahalik, 1999). Also, these therapists reported that they liked the nontraditional male client less, were less comfortable

with him, had less empathy for him, and were less willing to see him. Conversely, nontraditional male therapists rated the traditional male as having a poorer prognosis than the nontraditional male and reported that they liked him less, were less comfortable with him, had less empathy for him, and were less willing to see him. Although female therapists were not examined in this study, it is not unreasonable to expect that their own values and biases connected to their traditional or nontraditional gender roles will likely interact with their male clients' gender roles.

■ CAVEATS AND CONCLUSIONS

Although the body of research that we have reviewed documents the linkages between traditional masculinity scripts, psychological distress, and negative attitudes toward getting psychological treatment, a number of positive features associated with traditional conceptions of masculinity bear repeating from the first section of this chapter. Specifically, men holding more traditional conceptions of masculinity may have strengths in such areas as problem solving, logical thinking, risk taking, expressing anger, and assertiveness that are important skills for living and may be especially beneficial in times of crisis (Levant, 1995). Examples of how these positive aspects of more traditional masculinity ideologies may be manifested include the ability to remain calm and problem-focused in

times of crisis, to subsume personal needs to the greater duty of protecting, and to provide for one's family or country through personal sacrifice.

These same skills may also be strengths that men who hold more traditional conceptions of masculinity bring to therapy. For example, problem-solving skills and a willingness to take risks in one's interpersonal life (e.g., to make changes in one's life or to try new behaviors—such as sharing feelings—that might be uncomfortable or awkward at first) are likely to affect positively the counseling process and the client's well-being. However, research on masculinity and therapy has not yet examined strengths that men who conform to traditional masculine norms may bring to therapy, nor has it evaluated the effectiveness of any of these clinical strategies or models proposed as effective in working with men.

Nevertheless, research on masculinity and therapy has identified an important irony associated with how elements of masculinity contribute to men's psychological distress as well as to their reluctance to seek help for psychological problems. These findings highlight the need for clinicians to better understand masculine socialization, to make efforts to explore the linkages between masculine scripts and men's presenting problems in their work with men, and to anticipate men's possible ambivalence to seeking help by finding ways to make the therapeutic experience more comfortable and effective. Our suggestion to the field is that programs begin training psychologists to attend to the sociocultural context of men in the same way in which we have already recognized how the sociocultural context shapes the experiences of persons of color and women.

REFERENCES

Adams, H. E., Wright, L. W., & Lohr, B. A. (1996). Is homophobia associated with homosexual arousal? *Journal of Abnormal Psychology, 105,* 440–445.

Addis, M. E., & Mahalik, J. R. (2003). Men, masculinity, and the contexts of help-seeking. *American Psychologist, 58,* 5–14.

Ainsworth, M.D.S. (1989). Attachment beyond infancy. *American Psychologist, 44,* 709–716.

American Heart Association. (1998). Cardiovascular disease. *1998 Heart and Stroke Statistical Update.* Dallas, TX: Author.

American Psychological Association. (1990). *Guidelines for providers of psychological services to ethnic, linguistic, and culturally diverse populations.* Washington, DC: Author.

Andronico, M. (2001). Mythopoetic and weekend retreats to facilitate men's growth. In G. R. Brooks & G. E. Good (Eds.), *The new handbook of psychotherapy and counseling with men: A comprehensive guide to settings, problems, and treatment approaches* (Vol. 2, pp. 664–682). San Francisco: Jossey-Bass.

Bergman, S. J. (1995). Men's psychological development: A relational perspective. In R. F. Levant & W. S. Pollack (Eds.), *The new psychology of men* (pp. 68–90). New York: Basic Books.

Bernard, J., Bernard, S., & Bernard, M. (1985). Courtship violence and sex typing. *Family Relations, 34,* 573–576.

Bland, R. C., Orn, H., & Hewman, S. C. (1988). Lifetime prevalence of psychiatric disorders in Edmonton. *Acta Psychiatrica Scandinavica, 77,* 24–32.

Blazina, C., & Watkins, C. E., Jr. (1996). Masculine gender role conflict: Effects on college men's psychological well-being, chemical substance usage, and attitudes toward help-seeking. *Journal of Counseling Psychology, 43,* 461–465.

Blazina, C., & Watkins, C. E., Jr. (2000). Separation/individuation, parental attachment, and male gender role conflict: Attitudes toward the feminine and the fragile masculine self. *Psychology of Men and Masculinity, 1,* 126–132.

Bowlby, J. (1969). *Attachment and loss.* New York: Basic Books.

Brannon, R. (1976). The male sex role: Our culture's blueprint for manhood, what it's done for us lately. In D. David & R. Brannon (Eds.), *The forty-nine percent majority: The male sex role* (pp. 1–45). Reading, MA: Addison-Wesley.

Bronstein, P. (1984). Promoting healthy emotional development in children. *Journal of Primary Prevention, 5,* 110 .

Brooks, G. R. (1998). *A new psychotherapy for traditional men.* San Francisco: Jossey-Bass.

Brooks, G. R., & Good, G. E. (Eds.). (2001). *The new handbook of psychotherapy and counseling with men: A comprehensive guide to settings, problems, and treatment approaches* (Vols. 1–2). San Francisco: Jossey-Bass.

Chodorow, N. (1978). *The reproduction of mothering*. Berkeley: University of California Press.

Cournoyer, R. J., & Mahalik, J. R. (1995). Cross-sectional study of gender role conflict examining college-aged and middle-aged men. *Journal of Counseling Psychology, 42,* 11–19.

David, D. S., & Brannon, R. (1976). *The forty-nine percent majority: The male sex role*. Reading, MA: Addison-Wesley.

Deane, F. P., & Chamberlain, K. (1994). Treatment fearfulness and distress as predictors of professional psychological help-seeking. *British Journal of Guidance and Counselling, 22,* 207–217.

DeFranc, W., & Mahalik, J. R. (2002). Masculine gender role conflict and stress in relation to parental attachment and separation. *Psychology of Men and Masculinity, 3,* 51–60.

Doyle, R. (1996). Deaths caused by alcohol. *Scientific American, 275,* 30–31.

Dutton, D. B., & Browning, J. J. (1988). Concern for power, fear of intimacy, and aversive stimuli for wife assault. In G. Hotaling, D. Finkelhor, J. T. Kirkpatrick, & M. A. Straus (Eds.), *Family abuse and its consequences: New directions in research* (pp. 163–175). Newbury Park, CA: Sage.

Eisler, R. M. (1995). The relationship between masculine gender role stress and men's health risk: The validation of the construct. In R. F. Levant & W. S. Pollack (Eds.), *A new psychology of men* (pp. 207–225). New York: Basic Books.

Englar-Carlson, M., Vandiver, B. J., & Keat, D. B. (2002). *Gender role conflict, treatment fearfulness and help-seeking in white college men*. Manuscript submitted for publication.

Finn, J. (1986). The relationship between sex role attitudes and attitudes supporting marital violence. *Sex Roles, 14,* 235–244.

Fischer, A. R., & Good, G. E. (1997). Masculine gender roles, recognition of emotions, and interpersonal intimacy. *Psychotherapy, 34,* 160–170.

Fischer, A. R., & Good, G. E. (1998). Perceptions of parent–child relationships and masculine role conflicts of college men. *Journal of Counseling Psychology, 45,* 346–352.

Fitzgerald, L. F., & Nutt, R. (1986). The Division 17 principles concerning the counseling/psychotherapy of women: Rationale and implementation. *Counseling Psychologist, 14,* 180–216.

Franchina, J. J., Eisler, R. M., & Moore, T. M. (2001). Masculine gender role stress and intimate abuse: Effects of masculine gender relevance of dating situations and female threat on men's attributions and affective responses. *Psychology of Men and Masculinity, 2,* 34–41.

Good, G. E., Dell, D. M., & Mintz, L. B. (1989). Male role and gender role conflict: Relations to help-seeking in men. *Journal of Counseling Psychology, 36,* 295–300.

Good, G. E., Gilbert, L. A., & Scher, M. (1990). Gender Aware Therapy: A synthesis of feminist therapy and knowledge about gender. *Journal of Counseling and Development, 68,* 376–380.

Good, G. E., & Mintz, L. B. (1990). Gender role conflict and depression in college men: Evidence for compounded risk. *Journal of Counseling & Development, 69,* 17–21.

Good, G. E., Robertson, J. M., Fitzgerald, L. F., Stevens, M. A., & Bartels, K. M.

(1996). The relation between masculine role conflict and psychological distress in male university counseling center clients. *Journal of Counseling & Development, 75,* 44–49.

Good, G. E., Robertson, J. M., O'Neil, J. M., Fitzgerald, L. F., DeBord, K. A., Stevens, M., et al. (1995). Male gender role conflict: Psychometric properties and relations to distress. *Journal of Counseling Psychology, 42,* 3–10.

Good, G. E., & Sherrod, N. (1997). Men's resolution of non-relational sex across the lifespan. In R. Levant & G. Brooks (Eds.), *Men and sex: New psychological perspectives* (pp. 182–204). New York: Wiley.

Good, G. E., Sherrod, N., & Dillon, M. (2000). Masculine gender role stressors and men's health. In R. Eisler & M. Hersen (Eds.), *Handbook of gender, culture, and health* (pp. 63–81). Mahwah, NJ: Erlbaum.

Gramzow, R. H. (2002, February). *Self and social attitudes: Predicting and manipulating attitudes toward homosexuals.* Poster session presented at the meeting of the Society for Personality and Social Psychology, Savannah, GA.

Hayes, J. A., & Mahalik, J. R. (2000). Gender role conflict and psychological distress in male counseling center clients. *Psychology of Men and Masculinity, 1,* 116–125.

Horne A. M., & Kiselica, M. S. (1999). *Handbook of counseling boys and adolescent males: A practitioner's guide.* Thousand Oaks, CA: Sage.

Kessler, R. C., Brown, R. L., & Boman, C. L. (1981). Sex differences in psychiatric help-seeking: Evidence from four large-scale surveys. *Journal of Health and Social Behavior, 22,* 49–64.

Kiesler, D. J. (1983). The 1982 interpersonal circle: A taxonomy for complementarity in human transactions. *Psychological Review, 90,* 185–214.

Kiselica, M. (2001a, August). *Are males really emotional mummies? What do the data indicate?* Symposium conducted at the 109th Annual Convention of the American Psychological Association, San Francisco.

Kiselica, M. (2001b). A male-friendly therapeutic process with school-age boys. In G. R. Brooks & G. E. Good (Eds.), *The new handbook of psychotherapy and counseling with men: A comprehensive guide to settings, problems, and treatment approaches* (Vol. 1, pp. 43–58). San Francisco: Jossey-Bass.

Komiya, N., Good, G. E., & Sherrod, N. B. (2000). Emotional openness as predictor of college students' attitudes toward seeking psychological help. *Journal of Counseling Psychology, 33,* 148–154.

Kushner, M. G., & Sher, K. J. (1991). The relation of treatment fearfulness and psychological service utilization: An overview. *Professional Psychology: Research and Practice, 22,* 196–203.

Lemle, R., & Mishkind, M. E. (1989). Alcohol and masculinity. *Journal of Substance Abuse Treatment, 6,* 213–222.

Levant, R. F. (1995). Toward the reconstruction of masculinity. In R. F. Levant & W. S. Pollack (Eds.), *A new psychology of men* (pp. 229–251). New York: Basic Books.

Levant, R. F. (1997). Nonrelational sexuality in men. In R. Levant & G. Brooks (Eds.), *Men and sex: New psychological perspectives* (pp. 9–27). New York: Wiley.

Levant, R. F. (1998). Desperately seeking language: Understanding, assessing, and treating normative male alexithymia. In W. S. Pollack & R. F. Levant (Eds.), *New psychotherapy for men* (pp. 35–56). New York: Wiley.

Levant, R. F., & Pollack, W. S. (Eds.). (1995). *A new psychology of men*. New York: Basic Books.

Li, G. (1998). Are female drivers safer? An application of the decomposition method. *Epidemiology, 9*, 379–384.

Locke, B. D. (2001, August). Investigation of men's conformity to masculine norms and their self-reported sexually aggressive behaviors and attitudes. In James Mahalik (Chair), *Research on conformity to masculine norms: Examining perennial questions in the new psychology of men*. Symposium conducted at the 109th Annual Convention of the American Psychological Association, San Francisco.

Long, V. O. (1986). Relationship of masculinity to self-esteem and self-acceptance in female professionals, college students, clients, and victims of domestic violence. *Journal of Consulting and Clinical Psychology, 54*, 323–327.

Mahalik, J. R. (1999a). Incorporating a gender role strain perspective in assessing and treating men's cognitive distortions. *Professional Psychology: Research and Practice, 30*, 333–340.

Mahalik, J. R. (1999b). Men's gender role socialization: Effect on presenting problems and experiences in psychotherapy. *Progress: Family Systems Research and Therapy, 3*, 13–18.

Mahalik, J. R. (2000). Men's gender role conflict as predictors of self-ratings on the Interpersonal Circle. *Journal of Social and Clinical Psychology, 19*, 276–292.

Mahalik, J. R., Cournoyer, R. J., DeFranc, W., Cherry, M., & Napolitano, J. M. (1998). Men's gender role conflict and use of psychological defenses. *Journal of Counseling Psychology, 45*, 247–255.

Mahalik, J. R., Locke, B., Ludlow, L., Diemer, M., Scott, R.P.J., Gottfried, M., & Freitas, G. (2003). Development of the Conformity to Masculine Norms Inventory. *Psychology of Men and Masculinity, 4*, 3–25.

Mallinckrodt, B., King, J. L., & Coble, H. M. (1998). Family dysfunction, alexithymia, and client attachment to therapist. *Journal of Counseling Psychology, 45*, 497–504.

Mintz, L. B., & O'Neil, J. M. (1990). Gender roles, sex, and the process of psychotherapy: Many questions and few answers. *Journal of Counseling & Development, 68*, 381–387.

National Center for Health Statistics. (1992). *Advance report on final mortality statistics, 1992*. Hyattsville, MD: U.S. Department of Health and Human Services.

O'Heron, C. A., & Orlofsky, J. L. (1990). Stereotypic and nonstereotypic sex role trait and behavior orientations, gender identity, and psychological adjustment. *Journal of Personality and Social Psychology, 58*, 134–143.

O'Neil, J. M., Good, G. E., & Holmes, S. (1995). Fifteen years of theory and research on men's gender role conflict: New paradigms for empirical research. In R. F. Levant & W. S. Pollack (Eds.), *A new psychology of men* (pp. 164–206). New York: Basic Books.

Perry, W. G., Jr. (1970). *Forms of intellectual and ethical development in the college years: A scheme*. New York: Holt, Rinehart & Winston.

Pollack, W. (1998). *Real boys: Rescuing our sons from the myths of boyhood.* New York: Random House.

Prince, J. E., & Arias, I. (1984). The role of perceived control and the desirability of control among abusive and nonabusive husbands. *American Journal of Family Therapy, 22,* 126–134.

Robertson, J., & Fitzgerald, L. F. (1992). Overcoming the masculine mystique: Preferences for alternative forms of assistance among men who avoid counseling. *Journal of Counseling Psychology, 39,* 240–246.

Sachs-Ericsson, N., & Ciarlo, J. A. (2000). Gender, social roles, and mental health: An epidemiological perspective. *Sex Roles, 43,* 605–628.

Sharpe, M. J., & Heppner, P. P. (1991). Gender role, gender-role conflict, and psychological well being in men. *Journal of Counseling Psychology, 39,* 240–246.

Shepard, D. S. (1994. August). *Male gender role conflict and expression of depression.* Paper presented at the 102nd Annual Convention of the American Psychological Association, Los Angeles.

Sibicky, M., & Dovidio, J. F. (1986). Stigma of psychological therapy: Stereotypes, interpersonal reactions, and the self-fulfilling prophecy. *Journal of Counseling Psychology, 47,* 138–143.

Spence, J. T., & Helmreich, R. L. (1981). Androgyny versus gender schema: A comment on Bem's gender schema theory. *Psychological Review, 88,* 365–368.

Sutkin, L. C., & Good, G. (1987). Therapy with men in health-care settings. In M. Scher, M. Stevens, G. Good, & G. A. Eichenfield (Eds.), *Handbook of counseling and psychotherapy with men* (pp. 372–387). Thousand Oaks, CA: Sage.

Telch, C. F., & Lindquist, C. U. (1984). Violent versus non-violent couples: A comparison of patterns. *Psychotherapy, 21,* 242–248.

Uniform crime report. (1997). Washington, DC: U.S. Federal Bureau of Investigations, U.S. Department of Justice.

Vass, J. S., & Gold, S. R. (1995). Effects of feedback on emotion in hypermasculine males. *Violence and Victims, 10,* 217–226.

Watkins, P. L., Eisler, R. M., Carpenter, L., Schechtman, K. B., & Fisher, E. B. (1991). Psychosocial and physiological correlates of male gender role stress among employed adults. *Behavioral Medicine, 17,* 86–90.

Weinstein, M. D., Smith, M. D., & Weisenthal, D. L. (1995). Masculinity and hockey violence. *Sex Roles, 33,* 831–847.

Wisch, A., & Mahalik, J. R. (1999). Male therapists' clinical bias: Influence of client gender roles and therapist gender role conflict. *Journal of Counseling Psychology, 46,* 51–60.

Identity Development and Gender Socialization

Implications for Educational Practice

U pon reading the chapters in Part One, one question that may come to mind is, "How can college educators, particularly those working in student affairs, disrupt long-standing patterns of male gender socialization and support men in recognizing and appreciating their authentic selves?" The typical response on most campuses is to treat male misbehavior and related issues strictly as judicial matters. However, addressing the underlying sociocultural factors that lead to these behaviors is also necessary. Based on the salient themes and findings that resonate across the five chapters in Part One, we offer several implications related to the identity development and gender socialization of college men.

The chapters in Part One have important implications for educators who are responsible for developing programs and interventions to facilitate identity development and student success for college men. A necessary outcome of any program or intervention for college men is to help them recognize the range of options for expressing masculinities. This will be an especially powerful outcome for men who have never felt comfortable embracing socially prescribed male gender roles. Equally important is providing opportunities for men to continually reflect upon their identities and the ways in which gender influences their interpersonal relationships and experiences. In Chapter 4, Tracy L. Davis argues that it is important for men to recognize themselves as gendered beings, as doing so facilitates growth and identity development. College educators can help men achieve this developmental milestone by providing opportunities for critical reflection through one-on-one and facilitated group discussions about masculinities, readings, service projects, and campus activities. For example, we have found the following questions very effective in facilitating reflection and dialogue about gender and masculinities among men: "What does being a man mean to you?" and "What are some of the things you do to express yourself as a man?"

These chapters also have implications for graduate education, training, and professional development in student affairs. Given the key issues that are raised in the chapters and the potential impact on students and the campus community, providing ongoing opportunities for professional development for student affairs educators to build their capacities to address gender-related issues among men on their campuses seems warranted and worthwhile. This may be even more important for entry-level professionals, particularly those working in residential education and judicial affairs roles, as they are often the professional staff who spend the most time with students and are perhaps best positioned to recognize and reach out to men who are challenged by gender-related conflicts. Student affairs department directors and senior officers may find the chapters by Michael S. Kimmel (Chapter 2) and Tracy L. Davis (Chapter 4) useful in raising awareness and facilitating discussion within their units of trends, challenges, and outcomes among men on their campuses. These discussions can be contextualized with data from the office of judicial affairs or the department of public safety. Inviting faculty colleagues whose research focuses on the social construction of gender to lead a series of conversations throughout the division may also be a potentially effective strategy. One tangible outcome of these discussions can be a comprehensive action plan for helping men deal with the effects of male gender role conflict, thus reducing incidents of male misbehavior and increasing male student engagement and success.

Educators who earn degrees in student affairs preparation programs are rarely exposed to theories and concepts related to the social construction of masculinities because these issues have not been a part of the traditional student affairs graduate program curriculum. Moreover, as we discussed earlier, classic theories of college student development that serve as the foundation of the profession offer little insight into masculinities on college campuses. Therefore, faculty teaching in student affairs preparation programs might consider incorporating the frameworks presented in Chapter 3 by James M. O'Neil et al. and Chapter 6 by James R. Mahalik et al. into their courses to introduce students to the social construction of masculinities and male gender role conflict. Even more important is for students to learn to use these frameworks to guide their practice in working with college men. Case studies and role-playing exercises requiring students to (1) identify salient gender-related issues, (2) make sense of these issues using the frameworks, and (3) propose appropriate action steps are effective learning activities that focus on the practical application of these frameworks.

Lastly, because student affairs educators experience processes of gender socialization similar to those experienced by their students, it is reasonable to assume that they too have internalized culturally defined beliefs about masculinities. As a result, some educators may unknowingly reinforce socially prescribed expectations of masculinities among their male students. Therefore, it is critical that educators become aware and continually reflect upon their own biases and assumptions about masculinities and their impact on their interactions with male students. Davis in Chapter 4 and Mahalik et al. in Chapter 6 warn practitioners to not allow "sex role expectations" to guide their work with men.

PART TWO

SEXUALITIES AND SEXUAL ORIENTATIONS: INTRODUCTION

In 2008, two University of Nebraska wrestlers were kicked off the team for their performances on a pornographic website frequented mostly by men who are sexually attracted to other men. Although they agreed to be featured masturbating on a gay site, both students claimed to be heterosexual. Reportedly, their sole motive was money and a free trip to Los Angeles. Upon learning of the wrestlers' nude video appearances, officials in the athletics department cited as grounds for dismissal a violation of the National Intercollegiate Athletic Association's (NCAA) policy that prohibits student-athletes from receiving money to promote their individual images. Despite this, the two wrestlers told an ESPN reporter they felt they did nothing wrong, especially in comparison to other student-athletes who had been protected and pardoned by the university for countless institutional and NCAA policy indiscretions—fighting, gambling, marijuana possession, theft and property destruction, underage drinking, and drunk driving were among the examples given. Hence, the two wrestlers felt they had been unfairly banned from the sports program. "I could have got in a fight. I could have got a DUI. I'd still be wrestling for that team," one student told the reporter. But both believed they were held to a more punitive standard because the university was embarrassed that two of its male student-athletes did gay porn.

This case raises a number of issues about how sexualities and sexual orientations are treated on college campuses, not just in athletics departments. First, college students—women and men alike—engage in sexual choice-making, often without the benefit of structured opportunities for dialogue. As is the case in other sectors of the American public, topics concerning sex are often deemed taboo on college and university campuses. Although this is a period of profound sexual experimentation for many students, decisions about the parameters of one's sexuality tend to be self-constructed in the absence of guided sense making. At best, educational efforts are typically confined to campaigns about condom use and preventing the spread of sexually transmitted infections. And most conversations about sex are initiated by peers and remain between friends. Although they may have been generally apprised of the NCAA's amateurism policy, it is possible that no one ever told the two Nebraska wrestlers that it was against the rules to accept payment for appearing on a pornographic website. Might their positions on the wrestling team been secured had these two student-athletes not been compensated? Was it the payment or the porn that ultimately led to their dismissal?

A more important question is this: How often are undergraduates provided venues through which to critically weigh the consequences of their sexual decisions? Given the now hundreds of college students who have appeared in the famed *Girls Gone Wild* and *Guys Gone Wild* videos—as well as on other websites and films that involve nudity, public drunkenness, and other behaviors that could later engender professional penalty—it is clear that educators and administrators do too little. Another byproduct of the silence governing sexualities on campus is the reinscription of heterosexuality. Despite their willingness to perform for what they knew would be media consumed almost exclusively by other men, the two wrestlers said they were straight. But how could they be so sure? Was it because they had always been told they were heterosexual (or at least were expected to be)? Or could not having had any previous sexual encounters with other men led to such assurance? Unnecessary for debate are these two male students' sexual orientations. But our point here is related to the socialization experiences described in Part One of this book. Rarely are undergraduates offered structured occasions to talk through pre-college messages they receive about sex and sexual orientations. Consequently, assumptions they have about themselves and others go unexamined. Put differently, it is entirely possible for a student to persist through college without having a structured opportunity to process his sexual identity with peers or a college counselor. Many do not even know to ask the question, "How do I know for sure I am straight?"

Also reflected in the Nebraska story is the differential treatment of students who are gay or bisexual, as well as those whose heterosexuality is questionable. The wrestlers cited numerous cases in which their teammates and other student-athletes were protected by the athletics department, in spite of criminal wrongdoings and NCAA policy violations. They believed it was the perceivably disgraceful appearance of two male athletes on a gay website that garnered tougher punishment for them. As Patrick Dilley notes in Chapter 7, gay male students, especially those who publicly disclose their sexual orientations, tend to experience college environments in ways similar to what the wrestlers described. That is, they are constantly burdened by the question of whether they would be treated differently if they were heterosexual. Dilley also problematizes the binary of sexual orientation as either in or out of the closet, and gay or straight. Consistent with this perspective, some who read the case of the wrestlers might say, "Given how comfortable they seemed appearing naked on a gay pornographic site, surely they must be gay." Not necessarily. Dilley's chapter rightfully complicates existing theoretical models that were created to explore how college environments shape students' sexual identities. Combining historical and qualitative research methods with queer theory approaches, he provides evidence of six different ways non-heterosexual men have identified in college from the 1940s to the present and explains distinctive elements that comprise each identity type.

The two suspended student-athletes at the University of Nebraska were both White; the situation is likely to have been even more complex had they been African Americans. In Chapter 8, Jamie Washington and Vernon A. Wall write about the challenges that normally ensue when race and sexual orientation converge for African American gay male students. Their synthesis of the literature is situated both within and beyond the boundaries of higher education. Considered are contextual, familial, and cultural factors that make the coming out process especially tumultuous for gay male students who are also African American. Among them is the burden of prioritizing one identity over the other, the insufficient supply of same-race gay role models, and conflicts with religious perspectives on homosexuality. Ideal for these students would be the availability of counter spaces in which peer support is readily available, such as the gay fraternities that King-To Yueng, Mindy Stombler, and Reneé Wharton write about in Chapter 9. The authors illustrate how gay fraternity members challenged their stigmatized status within heteronormative fraternity systems on their campuses yet reproduced hegemonic masculinities within their chapters. Absent from their reappropriated meaning of fraternity was a disruption of longstanding gendered norms, especially the social construction of women as "other" and the necessity of gender exclusivity.

Given that their performances merely entailed unaccompanied masturbation, the Nebraska wrestlers did not view being videotaped for a gay website as gay—it was not the same as penetration or sexual engagement with another man. In some ways, these views are consistent with those expressed by heterosexual male participants in a study conducted at Universidad de Puerto Rico by David Pérez-Jiménez, Ineke Cunningham, Irma Serrano-García, and Blanca Ortiz-Torres. In Chapter 10, they tell how Puerto Rican men they interviewed largely viewed sex as involving some form of penetration. The authors connect this to the participants' views of gender roles (which overwhelmingly positioned women as subordinate) and contextual influences (namely media, family, peers, and religion) on the social construction of sexualities. These are examples of perspectives that several college men bring to campus that often go unexplored outside of women's and gender studies courses. Necessary in Puerto Rico, the United States, and other places are interventions that help reshape men's conceptions of gender roles, sex, and sexual orientations.

The last chapter in Part Two, Chapter 11 by Aleksandar Štulhofer, Vesna Buško, and Ivan Landripet, focuses on the effects of pornography on Croatian college men's sexual socialization and sexual satisfaction. The authors explored men's early (starting at age 14) and present use of pornography, frequency of masturbation, sexual boredom, acceptance of sex myths, and sexual compulsiveness. Perhaps their most salient finding is that not all pornography is the same, nor are the effects on college men universal. Negative effects were primarily isolated to those who preferred paraphilic sexually explicit content (for example, sadomasochism, bestiality, and violent/coercive sex). The authors argue the importance of helping young men become critical consumers of pornographic materials, as so doing can help expand men's capacity for intimacy and alter their notions of partner roles (especially women) in sexual relationships. Taken together, Chapter 11 and the University of Nebraska case make clear the following: Many young men consume, and some even participate in the production of, pornographic materials before and during college, which shape meanings they make of sexual encounters, boundaries, and relationships.

CHAPTER 7

Which Way Out?

A Typology of Non-Heterosexual Male Collegiate Identities

Patrick Dilley

Although numerous studies over the latter half of the twentieth century examined the identities and development of students during their collegiate experiences (as summarized in Evans, Forney & Guido-DiBrito, 1998; and Pascarella & Terenzini, 1991), surprisingly few have focused specifically on students who were not heterosexual. Only within the past 15 years have major studies of identities of non-heterosexual youth been published (D'Augelli, 1994; D'Augelli & Patterson, 1995; Herdt & Boxer, 1993; Savin-Williams, 1990, 1998); a smaller number of studies specifically looks at non-heterosexual college students (Dilley, 2002b; Evans & D'Augelli, 1996; Love, 1999; Rhoads, 1994, 1997).

Most investigations of this student population have focused on three related elements affecting aspects of particular non-heterosexual identities. First, much of the research posits a static binary identity (in or out, gay or straight), drawn from contemporary student populations. Second, this research places a primacy on the social climates of postsecondary institutions for non-heterosexual students but often does not examine those climates historically. Finally, related to campus climates is the collegiate experience of gays' and lesbians' processes of admitting to self and others one's non-heterosexual orientation ("coming out") (Cohen & Savin-Williams, 1996; D'Augelli, 1989a, 1989b, 1994; D'Augelli & Rose, 1990; Evans & Broido, 1999; Evans & D'Augelli, 1996; Love, 1997, 1999; Rhoads, 1995). A few researchers (particularly Cohen & Savin-Williams, 1996; D'Augelli, 1991, 1994; Rhoads, 1994, 1997; Savin-Williams, 1990, 1998) examined how these climates and experiences might affect individual identities.

A reader of this research could easily-and perhaps rightly-come to believe that there exists a singular "positive" or "healthy" gay identity that is attained progressively, with particular emphasis on coming out publicly (or, at least, in increasingly public stages). Theories of how college affects students' identities and how their identities develop (such as Astin, 1993; Chickering, 1969; Chickering & Reisser, 1993; Thomas & Chickering, 1984) imply that almost everyone in a given campus population (or sub-population) progresses along specific paths, toward more complete ideation of identity or fulfillment of potential. The primacy of coming out reflects (or begins to create) in understandings of non-heterosexual identity a very specific identity in particular relation to heterosexual identity; if all goes well, those students undergoing the process become progressively more committed to and public about a "gay" identity for themselves. In this regard, models of gay student development mirror those designed to reflect heterosexual student identity development.

Despite attempts to reframe understandings of student sexual identity in higher education research (including D'Augelli, 1994; Dilley, 2002b; Rhoads, 1994; and Savin-Williams, 1999), most conceptualizations of gay student identity development do not move beyond the normative presumptions of heterosexual models. Other researchers have presumed a fixed non-heterosexual identity fitting within the binary distinction between "normal" and heterosexual, and "different" or homosexual; one is either heterosexual or one is gay. Various stages or points of self-realization center on how and to whom to proclaim this difference. In this view, students (straight or not) develop from one identity (or understanding of their lives and relation to society) to another. But the path is singular, the outcome unquestioned, and that outcome unquestionably either achieved or not.

These colleagues calling for a reconceptualization of collegiate non-heterosexuality appear to me to be struggling with how to define the population and its experiences in ways that are understandable (and relatable) to heterosexual models. Yet, in building bridges between the normative heterosexual and the "queer" non-heterosexual, what we often do not convey is the multiplicity of non-heterosexual identities: the experiences and qualities of which do not match the "gay" student identity nor, perhaps, the experience of "coming out" in the ways previously explicated.

The pervasive traditional thinking depicts only one form of identity, one that is very particular, public, and easily positioned within the binary of straight or gay, normal or deviant. But as I shall show in this chapter, multiple non-heterosexual male collegiate identities exist. I use the term *non-heterosexual* purposefully both to draw attention to the binary nature of how sexual identity has been conceptualized and to include particular, diverse identities that are not heterosexual yet not necessarily conforming to *gay* or even *queer*.

Queer approaches to understanding and representing non-heterosexual identity (Chauncey, 1994; Dilley, 2002b; Mendelsohn, 1999) question those presumptions, paths, and identities in relation to the norms of heterosexuality and non-heterosexuality. In this chapter, I take this queered perspective to examine and explain the collegiate lives I have researched-both those that fit the traditional models and those that do not. I first outline the method and analyses comprising my qualitative, historical study. Then, in the Findings section, I delineate six identity types, providing evidence of different ways non-heterosexual college men identified in college from the 1940s to the present. Next, I summarize the distinctive elements that comprise each of these six types. Finally, I conclude with observations about how the six types complicate existing notions of identity development and non-heterosexual identity.

■ METHOD

Participants

For this study, I interviewed 57 men who were college undergraduates between 1945 and 1999. The participants' years of attendance were not concentrated in any single period of time but rather represented fairly equally each year of the 55-year period. The men attended over 50 different institutions (some attended more than one institution to complete their undergraduate education), located in 22 states across the U.S. The schools include public and private, religiously-affiliated and state-supported, smaller liberal-arts institutions and larger research universities. Racial diversity was less stratified:

48 of the respondents were Caucasian, two Hispanic, one Asian-American, one African-American, and five of international origin.

Procedure

The respondents were solicited primarily through direct contact with key informants from academic, alumni, and/or social groups (chiefly graduate/faculty/staff groups at the University of Southern California and the University of California at Irvine), as well as from non-heterosexual social clubs (particularly the Phoenix, Arizona, chapter of Primetimers, a national organization for senior gay men), academic conferences, and establishments catering to non-heterosexual males. I also placed requests for participants in local publications with audiences matching the target population and postsecondary institutions' gay/lesbian/bisexual student and/or alumni electronic mailing lists. From those initial informants, I employed "snowball" or "network" techniques of recruiting interview respondents (Glesne & Peshken, 1992; Merriam, 1998). Snowballing, coupled with the response from initial respondents in the Los Angeles and Phoenix areas, helped me narrow the focus of the in-person interviews to those two metropolitan areas.

Interviews

I primarily conducted in-person interviews privately, one-on-one. Six couples were interviewed together, and in addition, I conducted one small focus group of three friends. The interviews were semistructured, in-depth, biographical interviews (Denzin, 1989; Johnson, 2002; Kvale, 1996; Warren, 2002) designed to elicit each respondent's educational life history.

In the interviews, I used a variety of question styles. Most often I employed a recursive questioning technique to address sensitive, potentially confusing, or distant events, approaching the topics through a number of redundant questions and varied vantage points to probe a respondent's memories of his collegiate experience, his concepts (both past and present) of his identity and sexuality, and his analysis of the meanings and/or importance of each. To do so, I adapted the traditional phenomenological, three-pronged series of interviews (Seidman, 1998) into a single interview event. Within the interviews, I adopted a life-history or life-story approach (Atkinson, 1998, 2002; Denzin, 1989) to better understand (and later, to convey) changes that the individual felt concerning his ideation of himself and his collegiate experiences. This style allowed me to adopt both the respondent validation and constant-comparative (Glaser & Strauss, 1967; Strauss & Corbin, 1990, 1994) techniques: not only was I repeating respondents' terms and stories back to them for confirmation (and at times clarification), I also compared their beginning ideas and ideations about their identity with apparent changes (evident from their responses) that occurred during college (or, for a very few, soon after college). Further, I compared the respondents' ideations with those of other interview subjects, theories of gay and/or student development, and/or other published research, as well as their previously stated personal recollections and analyses. Each of these styles of eliciting data works within Garmezy's (1974) retrospective method of data collection.

Given the comfort, interest, and experiences of the individual respondents, the in-person interviews often deviated from the protocol, but they always focused on the men's self-concepts, concepts of sexuality, and college memories. Our meetings lasted between 45 minutes and 3 hours, depending upon the number of respondents being interviewed at the time, their time available for the interview, and the depth of our conversations. I tape recorded the interviews for later transcription. I also took field notes during and drafted interview summaries immediately following the interviews.

The remaining six interviews were conducted via electronic mail and consisted of three sets of questions posed to the informants. For those, I edited the interview protocol to two sets of questions (Goldman-Segall, 1995; Mann & Stewart, 2002). After receiving the respondents' second set of answers, I conducted a brief content analysis and followed up on their first two sets of responses in the third and final collection of questions. That set of questions included inquiries of veracity as well as questions chosen to probe for deeper, more analytical responses to the first sets of questions, utilizing recursive and comparative/contrast techniques.

Data Analysis

I utilized a pragmatic approach through-out my analysis of the data, drawing from a number of analytic strategies, including constant-comparative (Glaser & Strauss, 1967), typographic (Lofland & Lofland, 1995), and narrative (Clandinin & Connelly, 2000). I also blended queer theory (Dilley, 1999; Jagose, 1996) and queer historiography (Bravmann, 1997; cf. Chauncey, 1994; Dilley, 2002b; Howard, 1999) into my examinations of the men's lives, particularly in how their sensibilities related to normative concepts of both heterosexual and non-heterosexual identities. In addition, the typological format of representation allowed me to represent collective patterns of individuals' lives.

As another non-heterosexual man, I was viewed by the respondents as an "insider" who shared many of the same formative questions of self-identity as the respondents; this helped to increase their levels of comfort and insight, since neither the respondents nor I had to confront layers of difference between us because of differing social norms (Coffey, 1999; Denzin, 1989; Glesne & Peshkin, 1992; Merriam, 1998; Warren, 2002). I feel this identification engendered a sense of trust and openness in the re-sponses of most of the men, causing them to feel less inhibited and less likely to "reinterpret" their experiences or ideas into a heterosexual context. To further safeguard for veracity of the respondents' narratives and experiences, I invited the respondents in this project to provide a "member check" (Kushner & Norris, 1980–1981; Lincoln & Guba, 1985) by reviewing and commenting on the first draft of the manuscript of the data on a non-public website.

Using retrospective data collection methods requires one to address two issues of truthfulness: Did the data provided by the respondents actually happen or occur as the researcher presented it (*veracity*)? Second, did the respondents' analyses, as well as the researcher's, represent truth-fully the data (*validity*)? Menneer (1978) proffered guidelines for assessing memory-based data:

- Is the subject matter sensitive to time errors?
- If so, will the errors be important to the study?
- Can erroneous data be corrected by comparing it to data from other existing sources?
- Can other, more mechanical (i.e., less human) methods be used to collect the data?

In planning this project, I deter-mined that the understanding of changes in non-heterosexual male identities in the latter half of the twentieth century was not highly dependent upon respondents' perceptions of single events; as Gandara (1995) pointed out, "there is considerable evidence that the reporting of general attitudes and factual information is rela-tively stable over time" (1995, p. 20). Consequently, I examined, through the culmination of experiences, patterns of ideas about the respondents' self-identity. The project was consequently less vulnerable to distortion of respondents' experiences in college, for the interview questions could be answered with reference to events over time rather than to specific instances. Moreover, the typological model appears less susceptible to such distortions, as it based upon how a number of individuals experience the same kinds of events, emotions, or ideations, creating patterns of identity; by design, such patterns would not exist if multiple men did not have similar (and thus verifiable) experiences and meanings.

■ FINDINGS

Identity is much researched and discussed in higher education, but it is rarely defined. I found that, operationally, I could define identity for non-heterosexual men in the U.S. over the latter part of the twentieth century as comprised of three elements: *senses,* or what an individual felt or perceived about himself and his contexts; *experiences,* or what and/or how he behaved or acted; and *sensibilities,* or the meanings he ascribed to himself and his life concerning his senses and experiences, in juxtaposition to what he perceived as the normative values of the contexts of which he was a part. How an individual sensed himself and his world, behaved in different contexts, and created meaning of his life comprised the differences between the types which might best describe his collegiate identity. For some collegians in this study, identity was as much a matter of unbecoming as it was of becoming, a queer twilight time between what was considered "normal" for

heterosexuals and what was often considered "normal" for non-heterosexuals.

As Table 7.1 displays, these considerations framed the individual's concept of his identity. To understand what these men thought they could "be" as students and then "become" in their lives, we must understand both concepts of normality and the relation of those concepts to the lives of these men. No singular, monolithic "gay" identity existed, or exists, for U.S. college students; rather, several forms of understanding, of sensibilities, are evident. I have mapped six, although certainly more might exist.

The six identities were formed historically not only in juxtaposition to the concept of heterosexuality (or a heterosexual identity) but also in relation to the other forms of non-heterosexual identity. The identities appeared in particular contexts of social change, and the participants conveyed that they understood their identities in relation to the changing concepts of what it meant to be a non-heterosexual. Just as homosexuality depends upon the concept of heterosexuality for its definition, so too the notion of gay needs homosexual as a contrast, and queer requires the concepts of all three to be understood. I will explore the six types in their apparent chronological sequence.

Homosexual

Some men knew at relatively early ages that their feelings of difference placed them in a category juxtaposed to "straight." In the words of one student from the early 1950s, "I knew I was gay,

Table 7.1. Non-Heterosexual Male Collegiate Male Identity Typology—Late Twentieth Century

Years Most Evident	Identity Type
1940s to Late 1960s	*Homosexual*—acknowledged feelings/attractions, but did not necessarily tell others; sex and identity viewed as a very private matter. Engaged in clandestine socialization with other non-heterosexuals, if at all.
Late 1960s to Present	*Gay*—publicly acknowledged/announced feelings/attractions; often involved within institutional systems to create change. Publicly socialized with other non-heterosexuals.
Late 1980s to Present	*Queer*—very publicly deployed identity, in opposition to normative ("straight") culture; often tried to change mores and social systems.
1940s to Present	*Closeted*—recognized feelings/attractions to other males, and acknowledged to self the meanings of those feelings and attractions. Did not tell many others of his feelings (if anyone at all). Tried to avoid social contexts that might reveal his feelings/attractions.
1940s to Present	*"Normal"*—identified as heterosexual ("just like everyone else"); homosexual activity did not have an effect upon self-identity, and the dissonance between self-concept and deeds was not recognized.
1940s to Present	*Parallel*—identified and experienced as "straight" (non-homosexual) while within those situations and contexts, and as non-heterosexual in non-straight situations and contexts. The cognitive and emotional dissonance, if experienced at all, was compartmentalized, so long as the two worlds were kept separate.

always would be . . . [but thought] there aren't many people like me. At the time, it was harder for me to study, to plan for my life." In the mid-century, their ideations of how they could live, their relations to other people (both straight and non-straight), and their personal goals were constricted by their perceptions of others' concepts of sexuality. *Homosexual* collegians could find others whose feelings and experiences mirrored theirs, and with whom they could socialize more freely but not necessarily openly. Private gatherings and parties were the main form of socialization, and if sex were found, it was usually quick, anonymous, and secret.

The consequences for transgressing these boundaries—being too open sexually, socializing too frequently with homosexuals "known" by straight authorities—could be dire. Expulsions from college were not uncommon, nor were the possibilities of arrest or humiliation through publicity (Dilley, 2002b; Loughery, 1998; Sears, 1997). In almost all cases, homosexual collegians considered their sexuality not something publicly displayed or discussed, at most relevant (or revelatory) only to close friends (but rarely to family). In the words of an undergraduate in the early 1980s, "I had a very limited number of friends, certainly nobody I could talk to. I was so na1ve, I didn't even know that a community existed, that social places existed, that there were books about gay people." Sexual identity was "a private, personal matter." Homosexual identities were juxtaposed to the public lives and emotions of heterosexuals; homosexuals not only were opposite in their sexual affections but also in their ability to enact (vocally or physically) those identities. The identity of the typical homosexual male student was formed as much by his desires as it was by the dissonance he experienced between those desires and the cultural norms he perceived. It was the intent, the emotional investment, of the desire to have sex with another man that primarily determined his homosexual identity. As Duchess stated,

> I guess back then, especially consider-
> ing being nineteen, twenty years old,
> I think more than anything it was about
> the sex. It was the fact that I could have
> sex with another guy. But I don't want
> to say that was what it was all about.
> I couldn't fathom the idea that two men
> could live together like a married cou-
> ple, like a heterosexual couple.

Duchess's sexuality "was an attach-ment to my life. My life didn't revolve around it. I think I still identified with having a heterosexual existence: work, professionally; the way I lived, socialized. Even when I was out with someone I liked, I became very straight-passing." That sense of isolation felt by homosexual-type collegians gave way to one of socialization for gay-type men.

Gay

By the late 1960s and early 1970s, the concepts of what it meant to be non-heterosexual had changed: the women's movement, the anti-war movement, the hippie movement, and a growing critique of what was "normal" prompted some collegians to question the social compo-nents of sexuality. While the "free to be you and me" attitude could promote a concept of pan-sexuality (an idea of sex not based upon a person's—or the desired person's—gender), it was soon overshad-owed by a redefinition of the duality of sexuality. *Gay* replaced the term *homo-sexual,* both politically and ideologically. No longer was hiding one's sexual feel-ings the option of choice for many men.

A gay identity connoted an open social life with others who felt similar sexual attractions; implicit in the term *gay,* too, was a willingness to identify publicly in solidarity with others with the same identity. For some gay students, the integration of sexual orientation into their identity fostered a need to become involved in the local community; others brought their sexual identity to the fore of their campus experience, through work in collegiate organizations and/or political movements.

The concepts of self-identity and life goals transformed accordingly. The recollections of James's first years in col-lege are indicative:

> I was attracted to my roommate. I was
> attracted to a lot of guys, and I just
> didn't know how to deal with it.

But...the second year, 1969–70,
I tried to organize a men's group. I put
an ad on the opinion board, saying
"This is not necessarily to deal with
homosexuality but to deal with us as
men." It was subconsciously a way of
my wanting to come out.

Not all gay students necessarily associated with gay students in gay student
organizations, however. Tim had started
to come out prior to matriculation, in
the early 1980s, while in high school. But
in college he did not participate in campus gay activities, although he had attempted to become a part of his campus's
gay student organization:

> I did try to [join] the gay and lesbian
> student union, or whatever it was called.
> The first year, when I was trying to
> meet people or figure stuff out, I went
> to that a couple of times. I found that
> really cliquish and not welcoming.
> I think I went maybe twice and didn't
> go back, because it was very insular.

Despite the opportunity to become
socially involved with other non-
heterosexuals on campus, Tim felt his
sense of self did not mesh with those of
students comprising the campus student
organization. Nonetheless, other elements of Tim's identity fit strongly
within the gay type. Tim had a boyfriend
with whom he lived, off and on campus,
during college:

> I guess I felt like the relationship with
> my boyfriend made me feel connected

[to college life] in some way. [Our
relationship] didn't feel like it was
anything that needed to be named,
in some sort of special and different
way. We were constantly around each
other. Sharing the dorm room, it was
like all the mutual free time, we were
together. In the Art Department, it
wasn't a problem or an issue. I think I
did a couple of paintings where that
[homosexuality] was part of the painting
or part of the subject matter, so I didn't
feel like that was a big issue there.

Gene, who attended college in the
early 1990s, became more involved primarily only with other gay students:

> Somehow I lost touch with straight
> friends, the straight scene, so to speak. If
> we'd bump into each other in the school
> cafeteria and stuff, we'd sit together and
> talk, but I don't think we'd be buddy-
> buddy friends. I had so much work to
> do, a work-study job, manage my per-
> sonal things, so my social time was really
> limited, and I could not separate that
> between gay friends and straight friends.
> I had to combine everything into one,
> so gay friends seemed like the most
> practical way of utilizing my limited
> social hours for the maximum capacity.

Gay students understood their identity as a social one, not constructed in
medical models of pathology as *homosexual* was (cf. Greenberg, 1988; Katz,
1995; Tierney & Dilley, 1998). Consequently, their interactions with peers and

institutions differed from those of homosexual students or closeted collegians. Gay students' ideology was twofold. First, sexuality—in all of its permeations, including those not considered "normal"—was viewed as a more central (and visible) part of social life and thus far more "normal" than previously understood. Second, just as "other" sexualities were to be included in the spectrum of "normal" life, so too should gays be a part of regular social functions, whether as a part of the existing system (university governance, the curriculum, campus statements and missions) or separate (yet equal) functions that mirrored heterosexual (or "straight") functions (student organizations and gay dances being the two most obvious). These ideas brought larger numbers of non-heterosexual men to participate in public life on campus.

Queer

By the 1970s, a distinctly different identity, *queer,* became apparent. This identity was formed not just in juxtaposition to heterosexual concepts and culture, but also in relation to the concept of *gay. Queer* is something different from both the norm of straight culture and the norm of gay culture (although the concept had more in common with the latter than the former). Queer students tended not simply to join campus or community organizations, but instead attempted to subvert or to reinvent the structures of those very institutions. Whereas gay students working for change on a college campus might become involved in university or college governance, student politics, or campus

activities, queer students might form groups to protest many of those very elements of campus life or might plan events that highlighted the social stigmatization they felt in a non-homosexual environment. In the late 1980s and early 1990s, queer became not only a marker of difference from normal but also a political and social rallying cry.

Jimmy was an undergraduate and graduate student in the 1970s. "From 1970 to 1976, I very consistently (and usually adamantly) identified as a gay man." That identification, however, did not align Jimmy with other non-heterosexual students on campus:

> I watched other gay people fleeing from me! I was so outrageously out as a freshman in college that most of the local gay community actively avoided me for guilt by association. There were a few brave souls who allowed their queerness to me (though there was only one who would be seen with me outside the safety of the Art Department halls). With my Betty Grable hairdo (though sometimes I did Carmen Miranda, replete with fruit and bobbles inserted in carefully coifed curls), gold lamé tank tops, and elephant bells that looked like some prom queen's formal, it was hard to miss me on campus. I didn't have to go out looking—I was a walking billboard for queerness.

Jimmy's sensibility—the meanings he made from his experiences and feelings—was queer, despite the fact that the term and concept for queer were not labeled as such until at least a decade after his collegiate experiences. This identity put Jimmy in conflict with both hetero-sexual and non-heterosexual students and identities: "I believe that my outward queerness during my undergraduate years was a real turn-off to most men and especially those in the closet."

Rad was an undergrad in the late 1990s who questioned the normative social markers of sexuality, a signifier of queer identity. He was a resident advisor, a columnist for his school paper, and an officer in his campus's gay and lesbian stu-dent organization. He too offered visible evidence of his questioning of the social norms of identity representation. "I had really funky colored hair and [body] piercings." He deployed his identity by being open about his sexual identity in classes, both to students as faculty. "I was very involved in the gay group on campus, the newspaper, the mentoring program through the counseling center, trying to work full-time between two jobs, taking a full load of classes." He viewed his sexuality and sexual identity as central to his learning activities:

> I was getting more [involved] on the gay activism front, and it just occurred to me that my teaching assistant was talking about marriage or something, and it was just completely assumed that we were all straight. It really hit me as bizarre. That's when I started raising my hand. I would ask, *Well, what about gay and lesbian relationships?*

Rad also deployed his identity to create change in his position in residence life:

I ended up being the only out gay R.A. that year. I had a big rainbow flag hang-ing from my campus window. I told [my residents], "I'm gay, and I'm active in these groups on campus." I made it more of an example of what they could do to be active on campus. I wanted to set an example of being a positive, out role model, and I think I did that.

Part of Rad's queer sensibility is re-flected in his desire for visibility, as well as in his aspiration to work with other stu-dent constituencies for programming and campus change:

> The first year I was involved, gay life on campus was . . . not visible, I think. Other than [National Coming Out Week] I don't remember ever seeing or being a part of anything that was public or offering visibility for the gay community. Compared to the way things are now, I think it's changed, not dramatically, but I think for the better. I was amazed at the amount of support from other student groups. We were always pushing for that. When I was more active, my freshman and sophomore years, we would go to the black student assembly and the Hispanic students' functions. So I guess it's finally coming about, more equality in the student groups.

Queer collegians, like their homo-sexual and gay peers, envisioned their lives in opposition to heterosexuals'. But whereas homosexuals saw themselves as differing from straight people only in terms of their sexual activity (which was viewed as a private matter), queer students positioned their differences publicly; this differentiated their queer identity from *homosexual* and *gay*. Their sexuality was seen less as a variation of the norm and more as an agitator to the notions of normality. Where gay students strove to fit into the accepted campus formats and components of student government, organizations, and politics, queer students were more likely to buck the system, as well as to challenge the acceptance of those norms through actions and appearances.

Closeted

For the prior three types, coming out publicly—whether the students did so or not—was an act with great social and psychological power. But while some collegians were cautiously open about their sexuality during college, others feared the social disapprobation more than the isolation necessary to avoid society's stings of denigration. The term "living in the closet" served as a metaphor for denying, suppressing, or hiding one's non-heterosexual feelings or activities (Signorile, 1993; Tierney, 1997). Closeted collegians felt distanced from both heterosexual and non-heterosexual classmates, despite their efforts at joining social and living organizations. Some dated and even married women to prove (or to disprove) their sexuality to themselves and peers. Still others found sex, or at least symbolic substitutes, in the most conspicuous and seemingly heterosexual places. But the men in this type, who spent their college years evading, avoiding, or lying about their sexuality, were living, in the words of an undergraduate in the late 1970s, a life "on the fringes."

Some closeted students did not reveal themselves for fear of being arrested, expelled from college, or forced to undergo therapy (Dilley, 2002a, 2002b); for others, the impetus was more internal than instrumental. Rick, who matriculated in 1958, recalled:

> My recollection of [myself] is someone who was withdrawn, not real frightened but not real sure of himself. Did my sexual orientation affect [my self-confidence and collegiate performance]? I suppose so, looking back. I was always so afraid that someone would find out, that I never really wanted to reveal my whole persona, sit down and chat with somebody about it. I was just having to learn to deal with that as well. Probably the worst thing you could be, when I was in college, was gay. It was frowned upon. It was barely talked about, if it were talked about at all. The gay man of that time was a Clifton Webb–type, a fussy interior decorator or hairdresser. We didn't have a benchmark by which to go from.
>
> I had a couple of gay experiences when I was in high school, with friends who were also in high school. Not a serious thing, but just a physical kind of thing, just an exchange of physical-ness. I had that, but when I went to college, I put that away in locked chest. I never looked, never did anything. Now, if the opportunity had come up, I might have, but I was very careful.

I always knew what I was, but I put this away in a closet. What I didn't do is important. I never married because of that. I did not want to hurt someone else because I couldn't face up to who I was. Definitely I had an identity.

But that identity was of a person divorced from his senses of emotion, desire, and community.

Juan, an undergrad in the mid-1980s, provided another example of the closeted collegiate identity. "I knew I was attracted to men. . . . I had never acted on the feelings in high school, but I knew subconsciously they were there." The one gay person whom Juan knew, a friend of his brother, advised him, "'You don't want to be gay. It's, like, the worst thing. You don't want to do it.' It was really hard for him to be gay, horrible. I think that pushed me back. [because] he encouraged me to be straight."

Like other former students in this study, Juan found another, more accepted climate on campus to enjoy being with men. "I joined a fraternity. I think I joined because I wanted the social outlets of it. Over the years I've come to realize that I joined the Greek system to prove to myself that I wasn't gay. My being a fraternity member would alleviate anyone's doubts, if they thought I was gay."

The fraternity environment, though, allowed him eventually to experience furtive sexual encounters with one of his fraternity brothers. The first time it happened, in Juan's senior year, "It was great; it was like, Oh my gosh. I wasn't scared; we weren't nervous. We stayed together that night. I got up early the next morning, because it was his room. I snuck out and went back to my room. And we never talked about it. It was this awkwardness between us." Despite the awkwardness and the need to keep their activities secret, Juan and his fraternity brother did have sex a few more times throughout the rest of the year:

> Alcohol was always involved. We never really talked about it. It just happened, then we moved on and continued our distance as we always did, because we didn't hang out in the same circles. In some ways I did [want to spend more time with him], because I wanted to explore this more, but I also didn't want to, because I didn't want other people in the house to think something was weird.

"Normal"

Concurrent with these identity types, a number of collegiate men defied the norms of both the straight and the non-straight cultures. They did not identify socially, personally, or politically as gay, homosexual, or queer; indeed, they did not seem to undergo the process of "finding" or "establishing" an identity, the "unbecoming" that many of their non-heterosexual peers experienced, an act that those who are non-homosexual (or not a member of other minorities) often never experience. Yet at the same time as they were not questioning their identities, these men were engaging in homo-sex, often quite frequently. While they were not denying to themselves that they enjoyed the sex, it had no correlation to whom they were, to how they viewed themselves in relation to their (straight) peers; indeed, many of these peers were their sexual partners. At the time, these men found no dissonance between their actions and their "selves": they were "just like everybody else"; they were *"normal."* These categories move even further away from the binary master categories of *heterosexual* and *homosexual,* blurring the lines of demarcation while conversely corroborating those classifications as well. This paradox is evidence of the diversity in collegiate non-heterosexual identification, a diversity that is lacking in the identity development theories currently existing for students and gay men.

For some students, collegiate life, like that of earlier education, was dominated by peer pressure to conform, to be "just like all the other guys." The pressure was not to be so conscripted to a limited role in campus life: an effeminate gay; "catty, backstabbing, bitchiness"; a weak queer. In the words of an undergraduate in the 1970s:

> Homosexual did not equal normal—and I wanted more than anything to be normal—regular—one of the guys. Being gay or homosexual back then was still filled with the negative stereotypes of the limp-wristed, effeminate, lisping hairdresser. I wasn't that, so I decided I couldn't be homosexual or gay. My homosexuality back then was just about sex, nothing more.

Sexuality for "normal"-type students, at least in terms of a social identity, was neatly divorced from sexual activity. One could have sexual thoughts about other males, even engage in sexual activity with them (which many "normal" guys did, frequently), but such actions did not necessarily have any bearing upon one's identity. A 1980s undergraduate summarized the experience:

> I never really considered [my sexuality]. I mean I remember having sexual thoughts about men as far back as eighth grade. And in high school they were there constantly. But I just never considered being gay. I think the main reason for this (besides my natural inclination to suppress it) was because I literally did not know one gay person. Or, you know what I mean, anyone identifying himself as gay. I mean growing up I thought maybe, just maybe Liberace and Jim Nabors (as so many said) were gay. And I didn't identify with them *at all.* Nor did I want to . . . It was just an insult really.

On the other hand, "normal" students had no concept of themselves as "other" or bad; in some senses, their identity integrated all of their behaviors into a fairly cohesive whole. The importance of being "just like everyone else," however, prevented the "normal" students' sensibilities from incorporating the fact that their senses and experiences did not match the presumed (and promoted) norm of heterosexual identity (which was based upon a lack of homosexual desire and/or activity). These men were not in denial; instead, it would be more accurate to view their collegiate identities as distinct. They clearly acknowledged—and even acted upon—the behavioral aspects of homosexuality, considered those activities in relation to their perceived ideas of non-heterosexual identity, and rejected the notion that they were anything but "just like everybody else." Their sexuality had no bearing upon their social identity (presented to others) or personal identity (as understood by themselves at the time).

These young men could not fathom an identity as anything other than that of their friends and peers. This concept of self-identity framed the collegiate activities and sensibilities for "normal" guys. Instead of finding (or creating) a meaning of their homosexual behavior based upon difference from heterosexual-identifying peers, "normal" students viewed their sexual actions as having no bearing upon how they self identified nor upon their social, academic, or extra-curricular activities. Ralph, who attended college in the late 1940s and early 1950s, expressed this view:

> I never had any feelings like that [guilt over sexual activity] at all. My feelings were, anything that was beautiful, I loved it, and I didn't give a damn what anyone thought about it. [But] I didn't want to get caught at all, because it would just be too much. What I would do was to sneak around and do things.

I would sneak in the bathroom and play around under the stalls, you know. In the library, [there were] those big study tables. We'd sit and put our feet in the other person's crotch, under the table. I had several different guys that we would sit across from each other, so we could play footsie under the table. They were guys in my classes. Some of them were in the religious groups I was in. But we never talked about it.

> My college experiences definitely lead me into the idea that I was going to have a family and that I was going to stay married all of my life and all that, and have children (which I did; I had five). But sex, although it was very prominent in my life, never figured in my plans. I never planned for the sexual part of my life; I just figured that would come naturally.

Chris was a college student and fraternity member in the 1980s. "Within my fraternity, my closest five or six friends were also gay but had not called themselves that yet. In high school I was the school queer; the other guys were very astute at figuring out what I liked, even though I had a girlfriend and things like that. I didn't have to deal with a lot of that in college, because I had a safety net of my gay friends who did not know they were gay, either." Despite not talking about homosexuality, he did experience it. "I first started off, in college, in bookstores, because that was my experience in high school. And then learning the bathroom system; the undergrad bathroom was the meeting point for all of that. I just kind of happened upon that one time at the library. And then reading the bathroom walls, figuring out where everyone else went. There was a whole system and a mechanic to the whole thing: where to go to meet someone, where to then go to have sex with that person, where the hot guys hung out."

Chris applied the same standards to both Greek life and tearoom sex:

> [The bathrooms] were the whole system; that's where we [fraternity men] all went. The funny thing is, it was a title thing as well. Just like a girl dating a Beta at school was considered really cool, if you were able to do a Beta in the bathrooms you were a very cool bathroom guy. There were people that I'd have sex with more than once; there was never a schedule to it, but more than once. There were some guys that I only saw once and never saw [there] again. But I would see them later on [elsewhere on campus] with their fraternity letters on.

> It was important for people to know I was Greek. My goal was to get other fraternity guys. That was my element of fun. And really, that game and that community became my group. I mean, we never spoke, of course, but I at least knew that there were other people out there who were young, attractive and hot, who also liked doing the same things I did.

Those things included frequenting straight bars with fraternity friends, dating girls, and becoming engaged. "I was not gay but I did gay things. So the behavior was gay, not necessarily the essence. I had my regular life and my sex life. There was no conflict within me at all." At the time, Chris considered his life in college "pretty normal."

Normal, as Greg, another respondent, pointed out, is an unconsidered position, a concept so self-evident that to even question its qualities is to call into question one's own normality: "When you're straight, you normally don't have terminology about your sexual identity; you just kind of associate that you're just like everyone else. I thought of myself exactly like everybody else." Each of the "normal" respondents made it clear that the terminology, the concepts, of non-heterosexual identity were available. In each case, though, the markers of identification were not necessarily sexual activity but social roles ascribed and decried by heterosexual peers.

Parallel

In contrast to the integration of homosexual activities into their sensibilities and concurrent lack of consideration of meaning of those acts to one's self-concept experienced by the "normal" students, other male collegians keenly felt the disjuncture of the homo- and the hetero-experiences. For these men who exemplified the *parallel* type, the undergraduate years were a combination of distinctly different sets of cultures, acquaintances, and behaviors. By day (usually, but not always so, though), these collegians attended class, worked on or off campus, spent time with friends from school, or participated in home or family life. But by night (usually, but not always confined to those hours), they engaged in different behaviors. They led "this secret, shadow life," cruising bars, parks, or other sexualized spaces, looking for male sexual partners; they took great pains to ensure their anonymity (at least as far as beyond those sexualized settings). Unlike Chris's sensibility, these men did not think of their lives as normal nor see their behavior mirrored in their peers; unlike Greg, they considered their sexual activity as sex, and not simply fooling around or reaching an orgasm. These parallel collegians ensured that the two social milieus in which they were maneuvering never converged. In the words on one student from the late 1940s, "I felt I was leading two lives"; another student from the 1970s stated, "My life became separated into sort of parallel lives." For most of these men, being a public non-heterosexual man (be that called *gay, queer,* or *homosexual)* was not something that was a part of campus life; it was an aspect of off-campus life. When the two worlds intersected, the student would feel uncomfortable in both student/straight and citizen/sexual roles: as one said, "The two worlds, I knew, couldn't mix." This discomfort fostered in these men barriers between not only the two cultures but also their emotions and the people they knew in each culture. Dennis attended college during the late 1960s and early 1970s.

> Socially, I would hang out with a crowd, so I wouldn't be attached with any particular person. During the week I would study my head off. I didn't have time

to do anything socially. But predominately on the weekends I had my own little private life. On Friday after class, I would get on the bus . . . and go into the city. And [I] would cruise the train station to find some old man to spend the weekend with. Now, when I say "old man," I was seventeen, he was probably thirty, you know? I'd find some older business guy on the way home from work, [who would] pick me up in the men's room in the train station. And I'd spend the weekend with him.

On campus, Dennis lived a very different kind of life.

> I think a lot of people suspected, but I was not out, and no one knew. I did not share these feelings with anyone except the strangers I would meet and get to know, off campus and in the city. Even once I met other people on campus who were gay, there was nothing sexual about that. Sexuality was expressed with older men. Older men were outside of my way of life. Even if I ran into a younger man outside of that [in the city], that was too close to my real life.

Dennis's reflection upon his identity—then and now—reflects the distinctions both in definitions of commonly unconsidered terms of identity and in how male non-heterosexual collegians could distinguish between different forms of non-heterosexuality.

> I would say I was gay [in college], but differently than I use that word today. Gay, meaning my sexuality, ruled my

every movement, thought and interaction with people. I was either trying to flaunt it to those I wanted to know, or to hide it from those I didn't. But not like I would say today *gay,* meaning a whole complete person who is gay. Most academic situations, I would try to hide it. That was a conscious effort. But the minute I got away from that, in my own time, I was using it to my best ability to get what I wanted: sex. I was very preoccupied with sex. Lots of things, lots of achievements that I may have made or would have liked to have made, I didn't, because they took time away from what I saw was my personal life, or my sexual life. And it came first.

Pete joined a fraternity when he transferred from a two-year to a four-year institution. Like Dennis, he kept his homo-socialization separate from his campus activities:

> I definitely knew I was gay, and I was having relationships with other men. But I did not do that my first semester in the fraternity. I was incredibly busy. The first semester I was completely immersed in the fraternity. That was my first and second semesters. I was an officer, and I took that responsibility seriously. Then I started going downtown to the bars and stuff, and I decided that was a better life for me, personally.

For over a year Pete lied to his fraternity brothers to conceal that he was spending the night—and more and more of them—with male sexual partners. Eventually he

left the fraternity, without coming out to the membership:

> I just think that [gay socialization] was more of who I was. I was having sex, and I decided I was done with the fraternity scene. I didn't want to have that experience my whole undergraduate life. Essentially, I saw something I wanted to do more. And that was to be downtown and experience the gay life fully, to be in the clubs, to dance, meeting and making a new network of people, local people. The two groups, I knew, couldn't mix. I couldn't bring my gay friends I was meeting in the clubs to meet the people in the fraternity house, nor the other way around.

◼ DISTINGUISHING BETWEEN TYPES

Specific differences between the types of non-heterosexual male collegiate identity are evident within six key areas of sense, experience, or sensibility. More might exist, but within this study, the six primary domains I have found relevant to the understanding of identity of nonheterosexual college males are: experiences within campus environments; involvement (or not) with student organizations; involvement (for some) in fraternity life; sexual experiences; consideration of a concept of peer "normality"; and the display and handling of emotions. These differences are summarized in Table 7.2. Each domain reflects specific influences upon non-heterosexual identity for the

Table 7.2. Elements of Distinction Between Non-Heterosexual Collegiate Identity Types

Campus Environments. The constraints and the opportunities of particular physical and social campus environments did impact non-heterosexual identity—both positively and negatively.

Gay Student Organizations. The formation of a gay student organization on campus provided some benefits to some non-heterosexual collegians, but simply having such an organization was not enough to provide social and/or developmental opportunities needed for positive identity development.

Fraternity Life. A sense of "common background and instant rapport" that enriched interpersonal relationships—albeit usually in non-overtly sexual ways—was a theme in the life stories of members of Greek-letter organizations.

Sexual Activity. Sexual activity was very important in the identity development of non-heterosexual male college students, more so than represented in either student identity development models or gay identity development models.

The Goals of Being "Normal." Being "normal"—or at least considered by others as such—was an early goal of many students who later identified as non-heterosexual.

Emotional Attractions. While the physical act of sex with another man might be seen as a clear sign of not being heterosexual, often emotional attractions to other men were the first indications to non-heterosexual men of their difference.

collegiate males in this study. Table 7.3 depicts how those influences differed across the types; the differences are key to distinguishing between the types.

Campus Environments

The constraints and the opportunities of particular campus environments impacted non-heterosexual identity—positively and negatively. Men seeking other men—for sex, for companionship, for identification with others who are like themselves—found ways to do so in every campus community. In the 1940s, Walter knew of a "gay cruising area in a park," as well as private social gatherings in faculty members' homes. Tim and his boyfriend shared a dorm room as an openly gay couple. Chris and Ralph found sex in the public spaces of campus, while Juan found sex in his fraternity house with a fraternity

brother. Jim attempted to form a men's discussion group using his campus opinion board to find others who were "like" him.

The importance of these experiences for these men is more than just being in a context with other adolescents who might share their inclinations (although that certainly happened, as many of the respondents' conveyed), for through the experiences, the men discovered another aspect or quality against which to compare themselves and their identities. Clearly, from the narratives, over the last half of the twentieth century non-heterosexual students found more opportunity for social (not necessarily sexual) gatherings on college campuses in the United States. A number of respondents reported being a part of—either socially or as an active member—gay and lesbian student organizations, and historical reflections from

Table 7.3.   Elements of Distinctions Across Identity Types

	Campus Environments	Student Organizations	Fraternity Life
Homosexual	Felt oppressed by campus	Rarely; participated in social events, if at all	If a member, usually not out to other Greek members
Gay	Challenged campus oppression; viewed campus as site for social inclusion	Formed student organizations and participated in existing campus activities	If a member, usually not out to other Greek members
Closeted	Felt oppressed through campus institutions	Did not join or participate in social activities	If a member, usually not out to other Greek members
Queer	Saw campus as site of public disruption for contesting social norms	Involved more in loose-knit social action groups, rather than traditional or gay student groups	Viewed as repressive, normalizing constructs
"Normal"	Campus viewed as nonpoliticized in public, but often very sexual in private or semi-public campus locales	Usually not involved in gay student or community organizations, as these students did not identify as non-heterosexual	Members often experienced homo-affectional and occasional homosexual experience with other fraternity members
Parallel	Campus seen only as a heterosexual (and homosex-less) environment	Usually not involved in non-heterosexual campus or community organizations	If involved in Greek system, separated sex from Greek life; might experience homo-affections for other Greek members

	Sex	"Normality"	Emotions
Homosexual	A private matter, even if conducted in semi-public places	Did not consider themselves normal	Did not display emotions publicly
Gay	Viewed sex as less a private matter and more as a human right	Viewed themselves as virtually normal, differing only in gender of sexual partner and society's perceptions of them	Posited and displayed emotions in public, but not usually confrontationally

Table 7.3. (*continued*)

	Campus Environments	Student Organizations	Fraternity Life
Closeted	Rarely experienced, if at all	Tried to appear normal (i.e., heterosexual)	Felt homo-affections but did not reveal them to others
Queer	Publicly deployed sexuality, to demonstrate social stigmatization	Normality seen as oppressive and opposite of queer	Emotions deployed in public to disrupt social norms
"Normal"	Viewed homo-sex as normal activity, not as signifying homosexuality (or gay or queer) as an identity	Viewed themselves as normal; experienced a disjuncture between homosexual acts and homosexual identity	Often no emotions involved in homo-sex relations; emotions often involved in hetero-sex relations
Parallel	Homo-sex seen as separate from hetero-sex	Heterosexual aspects seen as normal, homosexual aspects as not	Experienced a disjuncture between homo-affections and self-identity

non-members indicated a direct, positive attitudinal and climatic impact of such groups upon campuses.

Gay Student Organizations

Gay student organizations operating on campus provided some benefits to some respondents, but this alone was not enough to provide the myriad social and/or developmental opportunities needed for positive identity development. Older respondents, having attended college before court rulings in the 1970s allowed non-heterosexual student organizations the right to assemble on campus, frequently mentioned their desire to have had such a group on campus. The creation of the organizations and the concurrent resulting interpersonal and personal development

for non-heterosexual students provided opportunities for growth named on traditional student development models that, possibly, these collegians would not have had. Non-heterosexual students involved in non-heterosexual campus organizations found some new friends and relationships; the majority reported having, on the whole, negative experiences with the student organizations, although the involvement in campus student organizations for some (Duchess and Rad, for example) did facilitate relationships, friendships, and development along the tenets of traditional student development theories.

Gay student groups, by themselves, did not mitigate social stigmatization for non-heterosexual students; some students, such as Tim, found such organizations "cliquish" and "very insular." Tim's encounter with gay campus organizations pointed out an incongruity in these organizations that many non-heterosexual men described: a conflict between personal goals (usually for socialization) and political goals (usually for inclusion of and equity for non-heterosexual students). On the other hand, Rad, a queer type, wanted to be active in efforts at social (political, yet still personal) change in the non-heterosexual student activities and organization at University of Southern California. He, too, found his time with the organization less than fulfilling; in his view, the efforts were not as "visible" or integrated with the other aspects of student life as he would have hoped them to be.

Whatever their motives for wanting to become part of the campus organizations for non-heterosexuals, clearly the students in this study did not find fulfillment of their needs or goals through such organizations. In this sense, their abilities to connect socially with other non-heterosexuals was as limited as that expressed by this student from the 1980s:

> I didn't really meet any other gay people in college—I mean there were other gay people I met, but it wasn't openly discussed (besides the gossip/speculation of other dorm members), so I didn't know they were gay. It wasn't like now, where sexuality brings a certain common background and instant (if not lasting) rapport.

Fraternity Life

A sense of "common background and instant rapport" that enriched interpersonal relationships—albeit usually in non-overtly sexual ways—was a theme in life stories of certain collegiate non-heterosexuals: members of Greek-letter fraternities. Indeed, fraternity life greatly influenced the homo-emotional experiences of several respondents in this study. Juan found his fraternity brothers a source of companionship and friendship. Chris also reported that being a fraternity member provided a sense of "fitting in" on campus; Pete echoed this and added that he viewed Greek-letter life as an opportunity to be "very socially active," a personal goal for his collegiate experience after leaving community college.

Interestingly, the respondents involved in non-heterosexual student organizations often reported alienation and isolation within those groups, while those who were members of Greek-letter fraternities found camaraderie and friendship within those organizations (albeit while not publicly acknowledging their sexuality). This runs counter to the intuitive belief of the older non-heterosexuals in the study (as well as my own belief) that involvement in campus organizations would create better environments for establishing identities with non-heterosexual peers. I also caution that, despite the data presented in this chapter, not all respondents in Greek-letter organizations had positive experiences. While these analyses of the benefits of Greek life and its related social world are not novel, they are most striking when coming from non-heterosexual men.

Sexual Activity

Perhaps not surprisingly, and confirming prior studies (Savin-Williams, 1999; Howard, 1999; Sadownick, 1996), sexual activity was quite important to the respondents' concepts of their identity. The meanings, however, of those sexual acts upon their identity were not necessarily tied to the self-concept of a non-heterosexual identity; for some, the distinctions between heterosexual and non-heterosexual were not created by sexual activity but in social roles and identifications. The "normal" type men provide a clear example of students engaging in homosexual activity without necessarily thinking of themselves as anything other than heterosexual.

In many instances, the subcultural, clandestine activities engaged in by non-heterosexuals influenced how those non-heterosexuals pictured their identities, both personally and as members of a campus. Gathering large numbers of post-adolescent males onto campuses with public "private" facilities fostered many opportunities to explore the physical side of non-heterosexual identities. As Chris stated about being at the University of Illinois in the 1980s:

> It was just a perfect situation for me to find the type of sex I enjoyed at the time, without feeling any guilt. There's a lot of people who are jealous of my college experiences, because I had so much sex in college, and the type of sex and the type of guy I had sex with. U of I definitely enabled that, definitely allowed that to happen.

Sex was crucial to the respondents, both in terms of their eventual understanding of their identity and in much of their collegiate lives. One student indicated sex "was important. At the beginning, I needed to know whether I was really gay. Then, it became an affirmation of self-worth." Some students hid from situations where they might be physically attracted to men, while others sought it out. Others engaged in activities with a great number of sexual partners, while others had no sexual activity during college. A few collegians believed that their sexuality was central to their identity, while others thought it was a "private, personal matter." "It was not intended to become a way of life, merely sidelines and detours. It was just something I did; it just wasn't me."

In contrast to this view, sexual activity was viewed by most of the respondents—particularly by those whose narratives I included as representative of the types—as important, even if they did not identify as an "other" type (say, *gay* or *homosexual)*. In the words of Greg, "Once I found the sex part, it all made sense." Indeed, many of the respondents reported engaging in numerous sexual encounters and activities, even in repressive environments and contexts. For most of the respondents, sex was always available in college, if not on campus then close by (in what surely was never intended to be classified as "town and gown" relationships). But whether they were running from it or toward it, sex was a dominant concept affecting self-understanding (knowing one's self) and, consequently, self-identity (presenting one's self).

The degree of importance of sexual activity, however, varied. To some non-heterosexual men, particularly those who were closeted or leading parallel lives, the impact and importance of the sex was relegated to a non-existent role in their identity: "My homosexuality back then was just about sex, nothing more." Another student classified as "normal" summarized his contemporary views of homo-sex: "In college, being gay meant just having sex with another guy." It certainly did not create a sense of identity for him.

But for men in the study who do not fit into the "closeted" or "homosexual" types, particularly those who attended college after the early 1970s, sex played a more primal role in their daily lives and in their self-concepts of identity. Many of them engaged in sexual activity at quite young ages; such early sexual activity has only recently begun to be addressed by gay identity development theorists (Savin-Williams, 1998) and has not been discussed at all by student identity development theorists. "Having sex with boys was not the same as being gay" (Savin-Williams, 1998, p. 56). This is certainly the case for the students classified as "normal," but some collegians who

engaged in sex prior to college (or high school) made a direct connection between their (homo-) sexual behavior and their identity. As Tim's story conveyed, he felt different from his high school and college peers "maybe because I lost my virginity at a very early age." In Cliff's estimation, sex opened up ways of not only understanding himself but also allowed him "to become a good [theater set] designer." Another respondent agreed on the importance of sex upon his understanding of his identity: "Yes! It was exploring and learning what sex was. It was a novelty. It was exciting. My first top, bottom, three-way, hustler, etc. It was all uncharted, new experiences. It was mostly fun, but a bit superficial. Something was always lacking; I think it was the romance." For others, like Dennis, romance was sometimes evident, even if an on-going relationship was not desired. In any event, though, sex—the thought of, the search for, the experience of, and the consequences afterwards—profoundly affected the identities of the collegians in this study.

The Goals of Being "Normal"

Sex was not the only objective of non-heterosexual collegians; in their quests for understanding "who" they were—and to whom they were similar—they also hoped to prove that they were like the majority of their peers (be they straight, homosexual, gay, or queer). Being "normal" was a goal of many students who later identified as non-heterosexual. Even if they were engaging in homo-sexual activity, the respondents perceived the identity formation process in relation to the societal norms of the time. That the norms favored heterosexuality and sanctioned against homosexuality was no surprise in the 1940s and 1950s. One e-mail respondent commented:

> Homosexual did not equate normal— and I wanted more than anything to be normal—one of the guys. Being gay or homosexual back then was still filled with the negative stereotypes of the limp-wristed, effeminate, lisping hairdresser. I wasn't that, so I decided I couldn't be a homosexual or gay. There weren't any images of regular homosexual men to refer back then. For a long time—and certainly at that time—I considered the possibility of being homosexual to be a terrible curse—something evil had happened to me—and I was determined that it would go away if I denied it long enough. I wanted to be regular and normal. At that time, the idea that I could be gay and normal was an absurd thought.

This paradox is the essential point of non-heterosexual college identity. One respondent viewed himself as "Normal. All the kids in school were like me. At the same time, the idea that I could be gay and normal was an absurd thought." The process of comparing one's experiences to the (perceived) identities of others was ongoing and extended to other non-heterosexuals as well as heterosexuals. This comparison between self and others, however, did not always bring about acceptance of one's sense of self as different. For many respondents, such comparisons fostered behavior and ideation—at least for a time—that mirrored the closet or parallel types. Here is a telling comment from one collegian: "I was very uncomfortable with the idea and reality of being gay when I was in college. It was a burden then—something to hide." His perception of his sexuality in the absence of sexual activity is also distinguishing. While the physical act of sex with another man might be seen as a clear sign of not being heterosexual, often emotional attractions to other men were the first indications to non-heterosexual men of their difference. He hid his "idea and reality" of being gay, and effected a facade of being "normal."

This identification as "normal" highlights the dilemmas of using gay identity development theories in the way educators use student development theory. Should the student development practitioner program activities and experiences for the "normal" student, or for those in the closet or in denial, that challenge their concepts of their own sexuality, in the hopes of progressing that understanding to more closely align with their sexual impulses or affections? On the other hand, should practitioners not address these issues through programming or advice, thereby perpetuating the feelings that form the closet and facilitate denial?

The issues are made murkier when one considers that, as the narratives corroborate, identity is neither stable nor fixed. How students conceptualized themselves (vis-à-vis their sexuality)—and how they allowed others to conceptualize them—fluctuated during their collegiate years. The parallel types formulated two almost disparate identities, based in relation to what was considered customary for different contexts; some students self-identified as "gay" while exhibiting qualities, behaviors, and sensibilities that are classified by others as "queer"; the homosexual students (like Duchess) made it clear that acting "too gay" was something they avoided, even though, in private, they might want to behave in those fashions.

Such is the untenable position student programmers and advisors find when confronted with counseling non-heterosexual male college students. Rather than progress through orderly stages of development, non-heterosexual male identity is situational, adapted by individuals to suit the needs (and desires) they have to perform (or live) in different contexts. The sense of being "normal, just like all the other kids" changes accordingly, as does the students' individual impressions of what is considered befitting the non-heterosexual identities.

Emotional Attractions

How the respondents managed the expression of their emotions to themselves and to others is a final distinctive element of each type. Tim's relationship with his boyfriend of the time was a given among their friends: "The group of people that I was in perceived us as being a couple. So we were a couple." Dennis, a parallel student, "would hang out with a crowd, so I wouldn't be attached with any particular person. I did not share these feelings with anyone except the strangers I would meet and get to know, off campus and in the city." Chris, a "normal" student, "didn't think that an emotional relationship with a man was possible; I figured that it was all sexual." Chris finally began to define his experience and identity as gay when he developed feelings of affection towards men instead of women. While the (multiple) physical acts of sex with other men might be seen as a clear sign of not being heterosexual, often emotional attractions to other men were the first indications to non-heterosexual men of their identity difference.

■ CONCLUDING OBSERVATIONS

The concepts of identity—along with the interpersonal behaviors and communications that deploy those concepts into practice—for the men in this study are far less static than the existing identity development models (both student and gay) depict. While on the one hand most of the respondents depicted knowing, confidently, that they were truly nonheterosexual, on the other hand they often had difficulty conceiving how they could "be" non-heterosexual while "being" themselves. It is important to remember that the classifications in this typology are neither prescriptive nor proscriptive; individuals might slide between type classifications, based upon their own definitions of their sexuality, the specific actions they undertake, and (in instances) the motives behind both the definitions and the actions. Or perhaps individuals will remain firmly fixed within a particular type.

For non-heterosexual collegians, self-identity was not a process particularly of "unbecoming" straight or of "becoming" gay or queer; rather, their paths to self-identity were (fairly) continuous negotiations of self and other, of straight and non-straight, of activities of varying meanings and meanings with varying activities. Some students moved swiftly from one identity to another and remained fairly secure in their comprehension of their place in campus societies; they might engage in social and interpersonal communications and activities that placed them in opposition to the norms of heterosexuality, or they might remain publicly aligned with the center while trying to understand how they could feel disconnected from that center. Others played (or frayed) at the margins, attempting to calibrate their sense of self with the views of others (both straight and non-straight).

A proponent of stage models could argue that different ideations represented individual stages of progression through identity development; *queer,* for instance, could be a phase of rebellion, an affectation of youth (or desired youth) to attempt to create change while on a "quest" or "journey" towards a normative concept of self-identity. But the data from this study belie the singular outcome (either for gay males or for college students in general) on which existing stage-development models are based. None of the men I studied felt they were "underdeveloped" when they "grew up"; even when they remembered desiring to be more publicly open about their identity or not feeling "like" the other non-heterosexuals they viewed in their historical social context, no one suggested that his development was inherently of a lesser quality than those of other non-heterosexual men.

Specific college environments— social, temporal, and geographic—most certainly impacted both the process (ways and/or manners to self-identify, as depicted as elements of distinction in Table 7.3) and the product (identity as label or term used for self-understanding and presentation to others) of these men. Postsecondary institutions created environments (both positive and negative), provided structures for socialization and organization, gathered together like-minded peers, and offered the idea(l) of not only the prerogative to determine through college experiences whom one was but also, in time, the right to do so openly and publicly. This relationship has deepened within the last half century, as witnessed by the increasing number of respondents who found not only their time in college easier in regards to their sexuality but also encouraging (in ways intentional and not) of their examination of the possibilities of—and opportunities for—not being a heterosexual.

The value of previous developmental theories and models is not nullified by this complexity of identity; those theories and models are, however, limited in their ability to reflect fully non-heterosexual male collegiate identity. As identity is neither fixed nor stable, the types I proffer are not based solely upon the essentializing concept of identity determined by a set "out"-come. Neither is non-heterosexual identity exclusive because of the specific contemporaneous cultures of the individuals (a constructionist view of identity); many forms of being non-heterosexual can exist, understood against the norms of heterosexuality and the concurrent norms of other forms of non-heterosexuality. Not all of the forms need to have "coming out" as an objective.

If student identity development theories reflect a particular progressive process of public proclamation, a progressive element is also evident in some of the stories of the men in this study. That progression of understanding, however, did not occur in college for many respondents, especially those who led parallel or closeted lives and those who, at the time, thought of themselves as "just like everybody else." Coming out was not a "goal" for their concept of identity nor their experience; nonetheless, the identity of members of each type were affected (and perhaps effected) as a result of differed levels and forms of social and campus involvement.

For all intents, these students would not be thought of by most educators on campus as homosexual, gay, or queer. Parallel, closeted, and "normal" students would not typically be found in gay student organizations or campus activities, let alone as participants in political or social functions for campus change. They are hidden populations, experiencing circumstances and constructing meanings of their senses in manners that neither student identity development theories nor gay identity development theories address. The norms that postsecondary educators and practitioners see in visible non-heterosexual populations do not translate to other types of non-heterosexual collegians; neither do the tenets of the stage-models used to depict and understand that visible gay (and/or queer) student identity.

The non-public types of non-heterosexual identity create dilemmas for educators and practitioners who use student development theories. Should we program activities and experiences for the "normal" student, the parallel student, or the closeted student, activities that would challenge their concepts of their own sexuality and identity, in the hopes of progressing that understanding to more closely align their sexual impulses or affections with the more public, dominant identities? On the other hand, should we not address these issues at all in our programming or interventions, thereby perpetuating feelings that keep students from associating with others? What is our level of commitment to respecting the primacy of students' abilities to define their own lives, experiences, and identities? Whatever one's answer is to those questions, understanding the nuances of non-heterosexual collegiate identities will allow researchers to avoid the trap of extrapolating from only the visible elements or actions of a diverse population; further, practitioners might be better prepared to provide more precise interventions and programming for their non-heterosexual students, out or not.

REFERENCES

Astin, A. W. (1993). *What matters in college?: Four critical years revisited.* San Francisco: Jossey-Bass.

Atkinson, R. (1998). *The life story interview.* Qualitative Research Methods Series No. 44. Thousand Oaks, CA: Sage.

Atkinson, R. (2002). The life story interview. In J. F. Gubrium and J. A. Holstein (Eds.), *Handbook of interview research: Context and method* (pp. 121–140). Thousand Oaks, CA: Sage.

Bravmann, S. (1997). *Queerfictions of the past: History, culture, and difference.* Cambridge, England: Cambridge University Press.

Chauncey, G. (1994). *Gay New York: Gender, urban culture, and the making of the gay male world, 1890–1940.* New York: Basic Books.

Chickering, A. W. (1969). *Education and identity.* San Francisco: Jossey-Bass.

Chickering, A. W., & Reisser, L. (1993). *Education and identity* (2nd ed.). San Francisco: Jossey-Bass.

Clandinin, D. J., & Connelly, F. M. (2000). *Narrative inquiry: Experience and story in qualitative research.* San Francisco: Jossey-Bass.

Coffey, A. (1999). *The ethnographic self: Fieldwork and the representation of identity.* Thousand Oaks, CA: Sage.

Cohen, K. M., & Savin-Williams, R. C. (1996). Developmental perspectives on coming out to self and others. In R. C. Savin-Williams & K. M. Cohen (Eds.), *The lives of lesbians, gays, and bisexuals: Children to adults* (pp. 113–151). Fort Worth, TX: Harcourt Brace College.

D'Augelli, A. R. (1989a). Homophobia in a university community: Views of prospective resident assistants. *Journal of College Student Development, 30,* 546–552.

D'Augelli, A. R. (1989b). Lesbians' and gay men's experiences of discrimination and harassment in a university community. *American Journal of Community Psychology, 17*(3), 317–321.

D'Augelli, A. R. (1991). Gay men in college: Identity processes and adaptations. *Journal of College Student Development, 32,* 140–146.

D'Augelli, A. R. (1994). Identity development and sexual orientation: Toward a model of lesbian, gay, and bisexual development. In E. J. Trickett, R. J. Watts, & D. Birman (Eds.), *Human diversity: Perspectives on people in context* (pp. 312–333). San Francisco: Jossey-Bass.

D'Augelli, A. R., & Patterson, C. J. (Eds.). (1995). *Lesbian, gay, and bisexual identities over the lifespan: Psychological perspectives.* New York: Oxford University Press.

D'Augelli, A. R., & Rose, M. L. (1990). Homophobia in a university community: Attitudes and experiences of heterosexual freshmen. *Journal of College Student Development, 31,* 484–491.

Denzin, N. K. (1989). *Interpretive biography.* Qualitative Research Methods Series No. 17. Newbury Park, CA: Sage.

Dilley, P. (1999). Queer theory: Under construction. *International Journal of Qualitative Studies in Education, 12*(5), 457–472.

Dilley, P. (2002a). 20th century postsecondary practices and policies to control gay students. *Review of Higher Education, 25*(4), 409–431.

Dilley, P. (2002b). *Queer man on campus: A history of non-heterosexual men in college, 1945–2000.* New York: RoutledgeFalmer.

Evans, N. J., & Broido, E. M. (1999). Coming out in college residence halls: Negotiation, meaning making, challenges, supports. *Journal of College Student Development, 40*(6), 658–668.

Evans, N. J., & D'Augelli, A. R. (1996). Lesbians, gay men, and bisexual people in college. In R. C. Savin-Williams & K. M. Cohen (Eds.), *The lives of lesbians, gays, and bisexuals: Children to adults* (pp. 201–226). Fort Worth, TX: Harcourt Brace College.

Evans, N. J., Forney, D. S., & Guido-DiBrito, F. (1998). *Student development in college: Theory, research, and practice.* San Francisco: Jossey-Bass.

Gandara, P. (1995). *Over the ivy walls: The educational mobility of low-income Chicanos.* Albany, NY: State University of New York Press.

Garmezy, N. (1974). Children at risk: The search for the antecedents of schizophrenia. Part I, Conceptual modes and research methods. *Schizophrenia Bulletin, 8,* 14–90.

Glaser, B. G., & Strauss, A. L. (1967). *The discovery of grounded theory.* Chicago: Aldine.

Glesne, C., & Peshkin, A. (1992). *Becoming qualitative researchers: An introduction.* White Plains, NY: Longman.

Goldman-Segall, R. (1995). Configurational validity: A proposal for analyzing ethnographic multimedia narratives. *Journal for Educational Multimedia and Hypermedia, 42*(2–3), 163–183.

Greenberg, D. F. (1988). *The construction of homosexuality.* Chicago: University of Chicago Press.

Herdt, G., & Boxer, A. (1993). *Children of Horizons: How gay and lesbian teens are leading a new way out of the closet.* Boston: Beacon Press.

Howard, J. (1999). *Men like that: A southern queer history.* Chicago: University of Chicago Press.

Jagose, A. (1996). *Queer theory: An introduction.* New York: New York University Press.

Johnson, R. (2002). In-depth interviewing. In J. F. Gubrium & J. A. Holstein (Eds.), *Handbook of interview research: Context and method* (pp. 103–120). Thousand Oaks, CA: Sage.

Katz, J. N. (1995). *The invention of heterosexuality.* New York: Dutton.

Kushner, S., & Norris, N. (1980–81). Interpretation, negotiation, and validity in naturalistic research. *Interchange on Educational Policy, 11*(4), 26–36.

Kvale, S. (1996). *Interviews: An introduction to qualitative research interviewing.* Thousand Oaks, CA: Sage.

Lincoln, Y. S., & Guba, E. G. (1985). *Naturalistic inquiry.* Beverly Hills, CA: Sage.

Lofland, J., & Lofland, L. H. (1995). *Analyzing social settings: A guide to qualitative observation and analysis.* Belmont, CA: Wadsworth.

Loughery, J. (1998). *The other side of silence: Men's lives and gay identities: A twentieth-century history.* New York: Henry Holt.

Love, P. G. (1997). Contradictions and paradoxes: Attempting to change the culture of sexual orientation at a small Catholic college. *Review of Higher Education, 20*(4), 381–398.

Love, P. G. (1999). Cultural barriers facing lesbian, gay, bisexual students at a Catholic college. *Journal of Higher Education, 69*(3), 298–323.

Mann, C., & Stewart, F. (2002). Internet interviewing. In J. F. Gubrium & J. A. Holstein (Eds.), *Handbook of interview research: Context and method* (pp. 603–628). Thousand Oaks, CA: Sage.

Mendelsohn, D. (1999). *The elusive embrace: Desire and the riddle of identity.* New York: Alfred A. Knopf.

Menneer, P. (1978). Retrospective data in survey research. *Journal of Marketing Research, 20,* 182–195.

Merriam, S. B. (1998). *Qualitative research and case study applications in education.* San Francisco: Jossey-Bass.

Pascarella, E. T., & Terenzini, P. T. (1991). *How college affects students: Findings and insights from twenty years of research.* San Francisco: Jossey-Bass.

Rhoads, R. A. (1994). *Coming out in college: The struggle for a queer identity.* Westport, CT: Bergin & Garvey.

Rhoads, R. A. (1995). The cultural politics of coming out in college: Experiences of male students. *Review of Higher Education, 19*(1), 1–22.

Rhoads, R. A. (1997). A subcultural study of gay and bisexual college males: Resisting developmental inclinations. *Journal of Higher Education, 68*(4), 460–482.

Sadownick, D. (1996). *Sex between men: An intimate history of the sex lives of gay men postwar to present.* San Francisco: Harper-SanFrancisco.

Savin-Williams, R. C. (1990). *Gay and lesbian youth: Expressions of identity.* New York: Hemisphere.

Savin-Williams, R. C. (1998) . . . . *And then I became gay: Young men's stories.* New York: Routledge.

Sears, J. T. (1997). *Lonely hunters: An oral history of lesbian and gay southern life.* Boulder, CO: Westview Press.

Seidman, 1. (1998). *Interviewing as qualitative research: A guide for researchers in education and the social sciences* (2nd ed.). New York: Teachers College Press.

Signorile, M. (1993). *Queer in America: Sex, the media, and the closets of power.* New York: Random House.

Strauss, A., & Corbin, J. (1990). *Basics of qualitative research: Grounded theory procedures and techniques.* Newbury Park, CA: Sage.

Strauss, A., & Corbin, J. (1994). Grounded theory methodology: An overview. In N. K. Denzin & Y. S. Lincoln (Eds.), *Handbook of qualitative research* (pp. 262–272). Thousand Oaks, CA: Sage.

Thomas, R., & Chickering, A. W. (1984). Education and identity revisited. *Journal of College Student Personnel, 25,* 392–399.

Tierney, W. G. (1997). *Academic outlaws: Queer theory and cultural studies in the academy.* Thousand Oaks, CA: Sage.

Tierney, W. G., & Dilley, P. (1998). Constructing knowledge: Educational research and gay and lesbian studies. In W. F. Pinar (Ed.), *Queer theory in education* (pp. 49–72). Mahwah, NJ: Erlbaum.

Warren, C.A.B. (2002). Qualitative interviewing. In J. F. Gubrium & J. A. Holstein (Eds.), *Handbook of interview research: Context and method* (pp. 83–102). Thousand Oaks, CA: Sage.

CHAPTER 8

African American Gay Men

Another Challenge for the Academy

Jamie Washington and Vernon A. Wall

The topics of same-sex love, homo-sexuality, men who have sex with men, and bisexuality are historically "don't ask, don't tell" in the African American community. Although most African Americans know of a cousin, aunt, uncle, sister, brother, teacher, pastor, choir director, or barber who "messes around" or "has a special friend," these topics are often given little serious attention in dominant culture (heterosexual) conversations. Most of the literature on sexual orientation in America estimates that 10 to 20 percent of the population would identify as gay, lesbian, or bisexual (Human Rights Campaign, 2004; Mondimore, 1996; Kennedy, 1988). If one accepts these numbers, we must consider what this means for African American men in higher education.

In this chapter we address the impact of identity development, religion, finding of role models, and self naming on the experiences of gay and bisexual men of African descent (GBMAD). We explore issues and challenges related to having two subordinated identities and the influence of religion on gay, lesbian, bisexual, transgender (GLBT) issues. We also suggest some possible campus supports and programs. Since there is very little written about the experiences of same-gender loving men of African descent in higher education, we draw from other bodies of literature to inform this writing.

■ UNDERSTANDING OF SEXUAL ORIENTATION IDENTITY DEVELOPMENT FOR GLBT PERSONS

Gay and bisexual men of African descent (GBMAD), like most college students, have very little scholarly understanding of sexuality and sexual orientation. Hence, many GBMAD are carrying the same misinformation and missing information about sexuality as their heterosexual counterparts. Some GBMAD believe

136

they were "born that way"; others believe they are gay because of an absent father or strong mother or sexual assault as a child. There are no conclusive data on the cause of sexual orientation, and the lack of information for persons questioning or exploring their same-sex attraction can contribute greatly to identity confusion and the absence of self-esteem.

A fair amount has been written about homosexual identity formation (Cass, 1979, 1983, 1984; Lee, 1977; Plummer, 1975; Troiden, 1989; Savin-Williams, 1990, 1995, 1998; Fassinger, 1998), but most of these theories were developed based on the experiences of White gay men and later women. Thus the dynamic of another subordinated identity impacting the developmental process is not considered in these models to any great extent, if at all.

That being said, the basis of most of these models is similar. These theories posit a general process of moving from identity confusion, to exploration and comparison, to tolerance, deepening commitment, and acceptance. Although most of these are linear stage models, they do provide a basis for understanding some of the experiences a same-gender loving person may have.

For GBMAD, these models lack the complexity of the race or religion intersection, thus making them only partially useful. Let us look, however, at the four basic stages. In the first stage, usually depicted as one of identity confusion, GBMAD are not only dealing with the confusion as it relates to their attraction to other men, but what that means for them in the context of the Black community, the church, and the eyes of God. Issues that arise at this stage for GBMAD can keep them in denial of their true feelings for years. Without a supportive environment in which to deal with these intersections, these men are at a loss and often remain silent and afraid.

The second stage is that of exploration. In this stage the person is exploring his feelings and attractions through interactions with others. If this person does not have access to a GBMAD community, he is not likely to find safety in the heterosexual African American community, thus leaving him to find his way amidst the racism often present in largely White gay communities.

These spaces can often feel isolating and disconnected for two main reasons. First, in the larger White gay community there is often less space to engage and explore Christian concepts or other strong religious beliefs. Second, the discussion of race is often minimized by a pseudo-understanding of all oppression because of one's status as a sexual minority.

Failure to overcome the challenges faced in the first two stages makes it really difficult for students to move to the last two stages of deepening commitment and identity synthesis. The general frustration and confusion in the first two stages of identity development in GBMAD can cause them to delay "coming out" until after college. Identity synthesis occurs when one's sexual orientation becomes an integral part of one's being. This entire process is informed by the availability of role models and other supports and whether or not they are present and accessible to GBMAD students.

Much of the writing that has been done on racial identity development gives little attention to the impact of sexual orientation on that process (Cross, 1971, 1995; Helms, 1994, 1995). Although this information is quite useful and important on its own, there is an inherent assumption of heterosexuality. The psychosocial developmental process of a subordinated race identity is confounded when you add to it the psychosocial developmental process of a subordinated sexual orientation identity.

Listen to these voices, from interviews with students at the Baltimore Gay Community Center:

Student One

I grew up in this hood in Baltimore. I have lived with Black people all of my life. I went to school with all Black people and I get teased sometimes because I was feminine. When I got ready to go to college I was so glad so I could get away from my neighborhood. People would whisper and call me names sometimes, but those same boys were trying to talk to me when they were by themselves or I was sitting on the steps alone late at night. I guess most people knew I was gay, but didn't talk about it except with my gay friends. When I got to college, with all these White people, I didn't know what to do. I really wanted to party with other gay people, but I couldn't find anybody Black. The White gays were too "queeny" for

me and besides there was few Blacks on campus, especially men. What would they say about me hanging around with White gay people?

Student Two

I went to private school. While I grew up my family still lived in a Black urban area. My school was predominantly White. I was the president of the Black Student Society at my private high school and I was at the top of my class. There were several people who questioned my sexuality but I just let them keep guessing. I fell in love with this wonderful Jewish boy and we kept our secret pretty well. By the time I got to college, because I interacted so well with everyone, I was not interested in hanging out with just Black people. I got seen as snotty, stuck-up, and gay. I made some friends in the gay alliance and started attending their meetings and social functions. This was fine, but I really had a hard time not being as accepted amongst Blacks, especially men.

Student Three

I went to a public school in rural North Carolina. I spent my high school years as the "asexual student leader," participating in clubs and organizations rather than having close personal relationships with my classmates. I was afraid that they would learn of my secret desires for other boys. When I arrived at college, I saw that there was a distinct separation between the African American and the Gay Community. How was I to choose? As a result, I stay in the "invisible middle," becoming involved in campus leadership positions but not connecting with either community. I would attend events in each community but never really stayed around long enough to develop relationships or close friendships.

These three men, all of whom attended predominantly White institutions (PWIs), illustrate some of the identity challenges facing GBMAD. The first two young men came from similar socio-economic backgrounds. However, the influence of private education on Student Two made his experience at college different. Although Student Three came from a higher socioeconomic background, there were some similarities in his words with the thoughts conveyed by the other two. His experiences were informed by his connection or lack of connection to his communities.

Role Models

Finding role models and mentors for college men of African descent is challenging regardless of sexual orientation or gender identity and expression. Many students can go through their entire college experience without significant contact with an African American man in a leadership position, such as a member of the faculty, administration, or staff. Given the pressures that many African American men feel to be everything for everybody, those who identify as GBT are less likely to be willing to take the risk of being "out" and identified as both Black and gay, thus leaving students who are looking for role models at a disadvantage. Students often know who the "suspected" gay faculty or administrators are. The message that is sent by their inability to be "out" is that it's not okay to be gay and professional. Thus, most African American men have only White gay men as examples. This is not to say that mentoring cannot happen across race, gender, and sexual orientation; however, the experience is not the same.

For gay and bisexual men, an unspoken tension exists for both the students and, particularly, the staff or faculty member. Given the assumptions and stereotypes of gays as predators and recruiters, many professionals feel at risk to connect with students for fear of being accused of inappropriate behavior. The other very real risk is that if the student has never had a supportive relationship with an adult African American male, the support could be misinterpreted, putting the faculty or staff member in a difficult situation. One might ask how this is different from a heterosexual person in the same situation with a student. The simple answer is that there is a culture that allows for this dilemma to be dealt with in a fairly open way between heterosexuals. When it is between two persons of the same sex, the dynamics are not as comfortable to address and there are generally no systems in place to support both the faculty or staff person and the student. All of these issues impact how a man comes to see and name himself. Thus, some discussion about naming and labels is warranted.

Labels and Naming

College is a time in which self-identity and the politics that surround identity are often explored. How a man names himself is important. One of the issues facing a man of African descent with a homosexual or bisexual orientation is how he names himself and then how he becomes seen and named by others. Lesbian, gay, and bisexual persons of African descent continue to face the questions "Who are you first?" and "Are you Black first or gay first?"

Constantine-Simms (2001) identified two ways in which self-naming and group affiliation occurs. African American identified gays (AAIG) are those whose primary connection is within the African American community. These men look for opportunities to be fully embraced within the African American community, and they are clear that race is the more salient identity. AAIGs tend to be involved in Black student organizations, attend primarily Black functions, participate in Black religious experiences, and, in some cases, allow ambiguity about their sexual orientation. These men are not as likely to participate in gay organizations or activities without a really strong reason to do so. These men care most about how they are seen in the Black community; how they are seen in the heterosexual White or gay community is not as important to them.

Gay identified African Americans (GIAA) are more connected to their sexual orientation's identity group. This group of men often does not feel welcome in the Black community. They find themselves not as comfortable in discussion around race because of the heterosexist assumptions that often inform those conversations. At PWIs these men may be involved in the Gay Student Alliance or simply attend gay functions. They are likely to be "out" as resident assistants or student leaders, whereas their counterpart AAIGs are more likely to leave their sexual orientation unspoken. These two major categories represent the backdrop for looking at the experiences and issues of GBMAD. The other major factors one must consider are class, religion, and gender identity and expression.

It is very common for GBMAD to not feel attached or connected to the labels of gay or bisexual, because the political and cultural agendas associated with these labels often are more White and middle class than those of the Black community and not as religiously focused. For this reason some GBMAD may not identify with any label; others may name themselves as heterosexuals who "mess around" on the side. Another popular term among GBMAD is same-gender loving; in smaller liberal arts communities some GBMAD also choose the term queer. Although this term is not one traditionally accepted by African American gays and lesbians, there is a population of younger, middle- and upper-class GBMAD who find the term acceptable. What a person names himself is less important than the support he needs to move through the naming and renaming process.

Some men are more comfortable identifying as bisexual, even if they are sexually involved exclusively with men. The label of bisexual is an easier sell in some spaces in the Black community than the identification as gay. This brings us to a discussion of the currently popular term used in Black and Latino communities: DL, or the down low. This term describes gay men who are not "stereotypically gay" and therefore could pass for heterosexual. These men are more often than not involved with women to some extent, and their involvement with men is not shared with their female partners. Unfortunately, men "on the DL" don't often find the space to develop healthy sexual orientation identities. This is not a new issue. There is no research to support that there are currently more men on the DL than at other times in history; however, the Internet has made it easier for these men to find each other. Unfortunately, most of the popular attention that has been paid to the DL phenomenon has been negative. Men on the DL are being blamed for the spread of HIV and AIDS among African American women. This dynamic alone has served only to push these men further into silence. The blame is misplaced. Although each individual has to accept responsibility for what he does, we live in a culture that makes it unsafe for men who are bisexual to tell the truth.

Finally, the construction of masculine and feminine identity is also a factor that impacts how GBMAD see and name themselves. The construction of masculine identity within the Black community, although not as rigid as thirty years ago, is still centered on traditional male stereotypes. "Strong men, according to such stereotypes, do not show their emotions, carry on the family name, are good financial providers, are athletic, are conquerors of women, and are not afraid to fight" (Katz, 2000). These expectations are strongly encouraged and reinforced in some households and communities. The extent to which a man finds his identity connected to these gender expectations will also inform how he identifies.

THE IMPACTS OF CLASS IDENTIFICATION AND CAMPUS COMMUNITY

The dynamics of social and economic class are important to consider as we examine the experience of being a GBMAD. Many GBMAD from poor, working-class backgrounds in urban settings are likely to be more connected to a Black gay community than those from middle-class urban or rural areas. Thus, seeing others like them and being accepted within a Black context may have an impact on how they identify. The urban middle-class or rural Black man may have only experienced a level of acceptance for all of who he is in a White gay context, not ever knowing Black acceptance; this affects how he identifies.

The intersection of race and economic class is an important dynamic to understand when discussing the experiences of GBMAD. As the African American middle class grows and more families move into predominantly White communities and schools, the context of identification shifts. Acceptance into the predominantly White community is often the focus. This behavior of blending into the predominantly White culture is sometimes modeled by parents and other family members, thus adding another level of complexity to the experience of identity development as the young man enters higher education.

For many college students, engaging the topic and dynamics of race are new. Most students come to college underprepared to have honest dialogue about issues of race. This is primarily due to lack of experience in real discussion. Thus the race politics that show up at PWIs are often challenging even for those who have come from integrated experiences. There are many dynamics that impact a person's sense of community in this campus environment. However, most people would agree that a comfortable community is a place in which you feel at home. For many African American gay, bisexual, and transgender men, finding community can be a real challenge. The identity development process described earlier will have a major impact on a person's experience, but one must consider the context and community in which the person is moving through the developmental process.

Students of color quickly learn that they are being given a "race test" by their own community that can have a profound impact on how they move through the social environment at college. Thus, GBMAD may have to think about things in new, unfamiliar ways. Like all students, finding a place where they matter and

can feel at home is important. Navigating a campus climate where race and sexual orientation politics are not aligned is often very challenging for the GBMAD.

Religious Impact

One aspect of the race test often involves religion. Are the GBMAD's religious views, understandings, and practices more traditionally "Black" (that is, born-again Christian fellowship, church attendance every Sunday, gospel music, services of at least two hours, and a fairly fundamentalist view of the Bible) or more "White" (that is, more Christian in a broad sense, room for other belief systems, fairly calm worship experiences, services of no more than an hour, and a less strict adherence to biblical teachings)? To understand the experiences of this population, one must carefully consider the intersection of race, religion, and sexual orientation for GBMAD.

Most GBMAD who attend PWIs face the challenge of needing to choose to connect their race, religious, or sexual orientation communities. Although these are not distinct things, they are often seen as separate. The issue of religion is always present in the Black community. Traditional religions such as Islam and Christianity have a major influence in the Black community, even if individual members do not participate or practice. Given that these two religious traditions in general do not bless same-sex relationships, the extent to which a man is connected to these faith communities can have a major impact on how he identifies. GBMAD who were raised in the traditional Black church are likely to have gotten some messages that it would not be okay to connect to the LGBT community on campus. Men without the strong religious messages may struggle with the dilemma of either connecting with an almost completely White LGBT campus community or connecting with an often homophobic or at least non-embracing and non-affirming African American community. The importance of religious affiliation in the African American community, as long as it is Christian or Islam, is pretty well accepted and entrenched; all others are suspect. However, in the LGBT communities, there is often a silencing of one's religious belief, particularly if it is Christian, given the unsupportive messages that have come from some of the Christian church leadership.

Although more religious denominations—particularly Christian ones—are becoming open and affirming of LGBT persons, most of those denominations are predominantly White. For GBMAD who are used to participating in a traditional Black church, this option is often not sufficient. There are some African American congregations that are open and affirming of same-sex loving persons, but they are hard to find and most people give up the search. The impact of this void cannot be overstated. For many African Americans, the church is their very foundation. For a person who has had the Black church community as home for most of his life, not having that place of support, comfort, and community is a major loss.

For GBMAD at nonpublic HBCUs, the challenge is magnified by the strong religiously based spoken and unspoken rules that inform behavior, values, practice, and the very culture on many of these campuses. Until the mid-1990s, the number of HBCUs with recognized LGBT student organizations could be counted on one hand. Although LGBT students are on these campuses—and often a very visible presence—they have not found institutional and community support to express themselves fully.

An additional impact of religion on GBMAD is the effect of the subtle (or not-so-subtle) message regarding HIV and AIDS in the Black church. For many years, from pulpits all over the country, came the message that AIDS is God's punishment to the homosexual community. Although this message has quieted somewhat, the residual impact has endured. The parents of today's college students and the students themselves have grown up hearing these messages in the church. Very little has been done to address the impact of such a damaging message. As an example, between 1999 and 2004, there was an increase in HIV and AIDS diagnoses among young people between the ages of 18 and 25 (CDC, 2004). Many of these young people suffered in silence because of guilt and shame that they carried as a direct result of the messages about God's punishment. Their level of guilt, shame, and despair often resulted in low self-esteem, deep depression, self-destructive behavior, and even suicide.

Whenever we engage in conversation about sexual orientation, particularly in the African American community, religion will surface. This conversation is never an easy one—hence, most people simply choose not to have it. This conversation must be considered with much patience and care, given the level of conservatism in Black religious communities. There are those who are perfectly content to live with inconsistent and incongruent religious beliefs. Because the Black community is largely Christian or Christian-influenced, interpretation of what the Bible says about homosexuality is where the discussion starts—and, more often than not, comes to a screeching halt.

Those who wish to engage folks on biblical issues should do their homework and be prepared for some disagreement (Boykin, 1996). However, if people are at least willing to have a conversation, there is potential for increased understanding and respect. Much writing has been done on the Bible and homosexuality. Some key writings include Sexuality and the *Black Church: A Womanist Perspective* by Kelly Brown Douglas (1999), *What the Bible Really Says About Homosexuality* by Daniel Helminiak (2000), *The Good Book* by Peter Gomes (1996); there are many others. These are useful resources for gaining a more comprehensive understanding of these issues.

It is important to note that this conversation has been going on for a long time, and it will not end in one setting. Helping students, faculty, staff, community, and, in this situation, family stay engaged is a part of the ongoing challenge for those struggling to reconcile these issues.

■ PROVIDING SUPPORT IN A CHALLENGING ENVIRONMENT

We have talked about identity, community, religion, role models, and naming. All of these dynamics inform the experiences of GBMAD. We would like to offer a few suggestions for creating supportive environments for these students. All faculty, staff, and students need to be prepared to see the LGBT community as more than White and nonreligious, and the Black community as more than heterosexual. This must start with our admissions and recruitment staff and include all who may interact with GBMAD throughout their relationship with the institution. The following suggestions may minimize the division between race and sexual orientation and help to provide support in often challenging environments.

- When sharing opportunities for involvement with new students, mention the LGBT student organization to everyone.
- When students come to campus for the Black student overnight, make sure the LGBT student association is notified and encouraged to participate and serve as a host.

- When selecting and training orientation leaders, prepare them for the diversity in the Black and the gay communities.
- Hire openly gay and lesbian students, faculty, and staff of color who represent their diversity.
- Train resident assistants, program board members, student government representatives, and other organization leaders to think more broadly about the Black and the gay communities.
- Work with the athletic department to identify, at a minimum, one person to whom GBMAD athletes can go for support.
- Work with faith communities to do work that explores and engages sexual orientation issues.
- Work with the LGBT student organization to make sure that during the awareness week or month celebration the diversity of the community is represented.
- Work with the Black Student Union and others planning for Black History month events to include the diversity as it relates to sexual orientation in the program.
- Work with faculty in African American studies, women's studies, and religious, psychology, and LGBT studies to be inclusive of student diversity in the readings, examples, and potential projects.
- Work with the alumni association to identify LGBT persons of color to serve as role models, mentors, and supports for students.

This list is not comprehensive by any means, and there are many other things to be considered before trying to implement a program. This list is designed to generate some thought about ways that we can begin to create a more supportive community for GBMAD.

ADDITIONAL GBMAD TOPICS FOR EXPLORATION

This chapter focused on sexual orientation of African American men, but not all of the various aspects of that topic could be explored in this brief treatment of the subject. Among numerous other issues for GBMAD, the experience of transgender persons in the African American community needs much attention. Although some campuses across the country are developing policies and procedures for addressing issues and concerns for transgender persons, little, if any, of the work has taken into consideration the particular needs of transgender African American men. This is a topic for further research and discussion.

The diversity of ethnicities amongst GBMAD could also use further exploration. Although the experiences of immigrants from Africa and different regions of the Caribbean may be similar in the context of race to that of African Americans, there are culture dynamics that make these experiences very different and, in some cases, even more delicate. These differences should also be explored as programs and trainings are being developed.

■ CONCLUSION

In this chapter we have attempted to focus attention on the impact of sexual orientation on the experiences of men of African descent. We have addressed the issues of racial and sexual orientation identity development and the complexities present when one's racial and sexual orientation identities are historically oppressed. We also discussed the impact of religion on homosexuality for African American men. To achieve real understanding of and support for GBMAD, we must not understate the role of religion in their lives.

Finally, the process of identifying role models and self-naming by African American gay and bisexual men was discussed, and we suggested potential strategies for minimizing challenges and increasing supports for GBMAD. We hope to have demonstrated that for the experiences of GBMAD to reach their full potential, they must be able to find positive role models and safe spaces in the college or university community to explore issues such as naming, dating, sex, religion, and race.

REFERENCES

Boykin, K. (1996). *One more river to cross: Black and gay in America.* New York: Bantam Doubleday Dell.

Cass, V. C. (1979). Homosexuality identity formation: A theoretical model. *Journal of Homosexuality, 4*(3), 219–235.

Cass, V. C. (1983). Homosexual identity: A concept in need of definition. *Journal of Homosexuality, 9*(1–2), 105–126.

Cass, V. C. (1984). Homosexuality identity formation: Testing a theoretical model. *Journal of Sex Research, 20*(2), 105–126.

Centers for Disease Control. (2004). HIV/AIDS Surveillance Report, 2004 (Vol. 15). Atlanta: U.S. Department of Health and Human Services, CDC: 2004–1–46.

Constantine-Simms, D. (2001). *The greatest taboo: Homosexuality in Black communities.* New York: Alyson.

Cross, Jr., W. E., (1971). Toward a psychology of Black liberation: The negro-to-black convergence experience. *Black World, 20*(9), 13–27.

Cross, Jr., W. E. (1995). The psychology of Nigrescence: Revising the Cross model. In J. G. Ponterotto, J. M. Casas, L. A. Suzuki, & C. M. Alexander (Eds.), *Handbook of multicultural counseling.* Thousand Oaks, CA: Sage.

Douglas, K. B. (1999). *Sexuality and the Black church: A womanist perspective* (pp. 93–122). New York: Orbis Books.

Fassinger, R. E. (1998). Lesbian and bisexual identity and student development theory. In R. L. Sanlo (Ed.), *Working with lesbian, gay, bisexual and transgender college students: A handbook for faculty and administrators* (pp. 13–22). Westport, CT: Greenwood Press.

Gomes, P. J. (1996). *The good book: Reading the Bible with mind and heart.* New York: Morrow.

Helminiak, D. A. (2000). *What the Bible really says about homosexuality*. San Francisco: Alamo Square Press.

Helms, J. E. (1994). The conceptualization of ethnic identity and other racial constructs. In E. J. Thicket, R. J. Watts, & D. Birman (Eds.), *Human diversity: Perspectives on people in context* (pp. 285–311). San Francisco: Jossey-Bass.

Helms, J. E. An update of Helms's White and people of color racial identity models. In J. G. Ponterotto, J. M. Casas, L. A. Suzuki, & C. M. Alexander (Eds.), *Handbook of multicultural counseling* (pp. 181–198). Thousand Oaks, CA: 1995.

Human Rights Campaign. (2004). *Annual report*. Washington, DC: HRC 2004, 1–50.

Katz, J. (2000, June 25). Putting blame where it belongs: On men. *Los Angeles Times*. p. M5.

Kennedy, H. U. (1988). *The life work of Karl Heinrich Ulrichs: Pioneer of the modern gay movement*. Boston: Alyson.

Lee, J. A. (1977). Going public: A study in the sociology of homosexuality liberation. *Journal of Homosexuality, 3*(1), 49–78.

Mondimore, F. M. (1996). *A natural history of homosexuality*. Baltimore: Johns Hopkins University Press.

Plummer, K. (1975). *Sexual stigma: An interactionist account*. New York: Routledge.

Savin-Williams, R. C. (1990). *Gay and lesbian youth: Expressions of identity*. New York: Hemisphere.

Savin-Williams, R. C. (1995). Lesbian, gay male, and bisexual adolescents. In A. R. D'Augelli & C.J. Patterson (Eds.), *Lesbian, gay, and bisexual identities over the lifespan: Psychological perspectives* (pp. 165–189). New York: Oxford University Press.

Savin-Williams, R. C. (1998) .... *And then I became gay: Young men's stories*. New York: Routledge.

Troiden, R. R. (1989). The formation of homosexual identities. *Journal of Homosexuality, 17*(12), 43–74.

CHAPTER 9

Making Men in Gay Fraternities

Resisting and Reproducing Multiple Dimensions of Hegemonic Masculinity

King-To Yeung, Mindy Stombler, and Reneé Wharton

"The fraternity makes men." This motto from *Baird's Manual of American College Fraternities* (Robson 1977), a handbook first published in 1879, succinctly summarizes the manifest function of the fraternity system. Researchers have found that fraternities on American campuses produce a particular type of men through the construction of "hegemonic masculinity" (Bird 1996), a set of gender practices valorizing men over women and reinforcing patriarchal legitimacy. This type of masculinity "guarantees (or is taken to guarantee) the dominant position of men and the subordination of women" (Connell 1995, 77).

Emerging consensus in recent research suggests that the brotherhood cherished by fraternity men both produces and reproduces gender inequality and the exploitation of women. Women's exclusion from membership, for example, blocks women from the privileged social networks potentially leading to social mobility (Clawson 1989). Even when women are formally incorporated into fraternities—such as the partial membership available through little sister programs—they are still subject to exploitation (Stombler 1994; Stombler and Martin 1994; Stombler and Padavic 1997). In day-to-day interactions, fraternity men use sexual jokes as a symbolic means to devalue women and, hence, create a privileged bond among men (Lyman 1987), and several studies have found that fraternities construct a "rape culture" (Martin and Hummer 1989; Sanday 1990) that is reinforced by gender segregation in residential arrangements (Boswell and Spade 1996).

College fraternities thus do not stand independently as an institution designed merely for young men to bond. Rather, they are part of a larger gender system, one that is defined by power and conflict between two sets of socially constructed binaries: men/women and masculinity/femininity. These two sets of binaries, moreover, intertwine. For instance, men who do not conform to the hegemonic definition of masculinity— being white, heterosexual, aggressive, dominant, competitive, muscular, class privileged—are equated with women and thus feminized. Following this binary logic, the traditional fraternity institution maintains itself through the exclusion of both women and marginal men who are rejected by the terms of hegemonic masculinity (James 1998; O'Conor 1998).

This chapter examines the effort of a group of marginal gay men to break into the exclusive fraternity institution by adopting the hegemonic model on their own terms. The assumption that fraternity men are heterosexuals is never explicit but always operative in maintaining a fraternity brotherhood (O'Conor 1998). While no formal policy bars gay men from fraternity membership, gay members are often reticent about revealing their sexuality to avoid harassment by other brothers (Windmeyer and Freeman 1998). Even when homoerotic rituals are prevalent in some fraternities, they are merely tools to humiliate pledges and reinforce brothers' heterosexuality, serving as a rite of passage to "real" manhood (James 1998). With the intention to produce men who are not-women and not-feminine, the process of men-making in the traditional model hinges on stigmatizing homosexuality and constructing a particular ideology toward women and femininity. But when gay men organize themselves as fraternities,

to what extent can they challenge or modify the entrenched fraternity culture that is hostile to gay men? Do members of the gay fraternity resist or reproduce hegemonic masculinity in their efforts to redefine the meaning of college fraternities?

We answer these questions by situating gay fraternities in relation to the larger gender system that embeds college fraternities and gives them a hegemonic status. We do not take it for granted that marginal men must necessarily resist hegemonic masculinity. In fact, recent research has shown that marginal men employ different gender strategies to compensate for their stigmatized status, sometimes even enabling them to maintain a dominant position over women (Chen 1999; Duneier 1992; Gerschick and Miller 1994; Kanuha 1999; Majors and Billson 1992; Nonn 2003). Furthermore, we also do not assume that when a hegemonic institution begins to tolerate or incorporate stigmatized elements or categories into its original form, it must abandon its fundamental hegemonic power.

Following these leads, we examine gay fraternities in relation to two dimensions of the hegemonic process. On one hand, we explore how members of gay fraternities negotiated their stigmatized status among other men—that is, within the internal dimension of hegemonic masculinity. On the other hand, we explore the hegemony's external dimension by analyzing how gay brothers, as men, relate to all women (gay or straight). We further examine the connection between these two hegemonic dimensions. We provide evidence showing how these two dimensions are coupled or disjointed.

CONNECTIONS BETWEEN TWO DIMENSIONS

Lacking an inherent meaning, masculinity is always constructed, sometimes implicitly, by a feminine other. In the social processes that reproduce or resist hegemonic masculinity, two sets of relations are important. On one hand, we can look at how some men are marginalized and deemed feminine by dominant men. This "internal hegemony" represents multiple masculinities as differentiated and stratified (Connell 1995; Demetriou 2001). On the other hand, we can examine the global oppression of all women in relation to men of different kinds. This "external hegemony" treats women as an undifferentiated category and as objects of domination. Hegemonic masculinity is therefore not a thing but a structural and cultural consequence resulting in the negotiations and interactions within and between genders.

In R. W. Connell's model of hegemonic masculinity, one set of negotiations precludes the other, because it conceives the relationship between men/women and masculinity/femininity as the locus around which relationships among men developed. Internal hegemony—that is, why some men are marginalized and feminized—is therefore explained by "the overall social relation between men and women, that is, the structure of gender

relations as a whole" (Connell 2000, 31). Following this logic, the relationship between dominant and subordinate men tends to be one dimensional: So long as external hegemony against all women exists, marginal men would always be the internal others stigmatized by dominant men. It also follows that when external hegemony disappears, we would see internal hegemony diminishing as well. Less clear, however, is the other direction of this logic: If the effects of internal hegemony against some men begin to lessen, and if the rigid boundary between dominant and subordinate men begins to fade, to what extent should we expect to see a weakening of external hegemony against women?

In a recent theoretical critique, Demetriou (2001) argues that relationships among men and within masculinities are dialectical and reciprocal. Using the Gramscian notion of hegemony, he argues that hegemonic masculinity equally relies on the manufacturing of "consent" from the marginalized. Demetriou argues that dominant men's incorporation of "gay sensibilities" into consumer culture creates the appearance of an alliance among a diversity of men, producing a sense of legitimacy in the larger gender system. As the dominant men appear to become more feminine, sensitive, and enlightened, "this appropriation of gay elements blurs sexual differences, enables some masculinities to appear less rigid and thus conceals patriarchal domination" (Demetriou 2001, 353). This strategy helps neutralize the feminist critique against hegemonic masculinity, as dominant men create an illusion of gender equality by blurring the boundary between masculinity and femininity. Dismantling these barriers among men, and seemingly reducing internal hegemony does not, however, alleviate external hegemony against all women.

So what is the theoretical connection between the two dimensions of hegemonic masculinity? While Connell (1995, 2000) proposes that external hegemony is a necessary condition for the internal marginalization of some men, we ask how changes in internal hegemony affect relations between men and women, masculinity and femininity. Chen (1999), for example, finds that some Asian men could strike a "hegemonic bargain" by highlighting their hegemonic qualities—athleticism, heterosexuality, or economic power—and downplaying their stigmatized status as a racial minority in a white society. The active involvement of these men in negotiating their marginal status shows that complicity operates as an important mechanism that reproduces hegemonic masculinity in social relations. Thus, external hegemony against women can remain intact even when internal hegemony appears to be weakened.

Whether some men could afford to be complicit depends on their social positions within a matrix of domination (Collins 1991). While some combinations of dominant-subordinate statuses are more coherent in producing complicity with hegemonic masculinity, other combinations may be more contradictory. In Chen's (1999) research, we see that the straight Asian men held a complicit attitude in response to internal hegemony, whereas only the gay Asian man in the study repudiated the white heterosexual masculine culture. The fact that some marginal men can repudiate hegemonic masculinity suggests that we can look at another form of internal negotiation within masculinity: how subordinate men's self-conscious resistance to internal hegemony affects their relations with women. Thus, we are dealing with the flip side of Demetriou's (2001) theoretical challenge. Instead of looking at how dominant men incorporate marginal masculinity as a means to resolve a legitimation crisis posed by feminism, we examine how marginal men's internal resistance transforms or reproduces external hegemony.

Resistance includes the counteractive activities and motives of marginal groups intended to challenge dominant groups. This opposition does not have to be formal, public, or organized to necessarily count (Davis and Fisher 1993; Scott 1985, 1990; Willis 1977). Scott (1990), for example, stresses the importance of everyday transgression to subvert the power structure, even though the real effect on social change may vary (Melucci 1989; cf. Rubin 1996). We take the position that resistance to hegemonic masculinity can take place through attempted resistance, where intentional resisting acts in the form of cultural protests may not be recognized by any "public" but are essential tools for marginalized groups to construct collective identity and subculture (Hollander and Einwohner 2004; Rupp and Taylor 2003; Taylor and

Whittier 1996).[1] How far can subordinate men resist without being co-opted into the overall hegemonic order?

We answer this question by examining men who occupy a contradictory position in the matrix of domination and who try to resist hegemonic masculinity within an institution that exemplifies such hegemony. Gay fraternities offer such a case because of the apparent contradiction they exhibit. On one hand, gay men's forming fraternities represents an organized challenge to a fraternity tradition in which the assertion and construction of hegemonic masculinity is fundamental. On the other hand, adopting an all-male organizational form appears only to reinforce the oppression of women by excluding them based merely on their biological sex. Due to these apparent contradictions, we wondered why young gay men, who presumably were aware of the dominating character of the traditional fraternity system, would adopt and emulate the fraternity model for organizing their college and social life.

■ THE SETTING AND METHOD

Recognizing the lack of venues for young gay men to form meaningful social relationships beyond those of dance clubs or organizations motivated toward political or service goals, a small group of men in Washington D.C. began to recruit the first Delta Lambda Phi (DLP) pledge class in 1986. Their efforts intended to counteract what they saw as the limitation of gay organizations at the time: internal divisions, deviant sexual activities, and lax membership standards (DLP n.d., II-6). The founders of DLP adopted a traditional collegiate fraternity model but stressed the fraternity's openness for "men of all races, color, creed, irrespective of sexual orientation" (DLP n.d., III-8). Twenty-four men were initiated into active brotherhood, and the alpha chapter of DLP was born in 1987. By 1998—the year this research was completed—the fraternity had grown to a nationwide organization with 16 active chapters and four colonies based mostly on numerous state and private universities across the country.[2]

DLP members shared many similarities with members of straight fraternities, such as a commitment to creating intimate and long-lasting social bonds among members, involvement in campus and community life, and a nationwide network of alumni. DLP also modeled itself after the formal structure of collegiate fraternities. All DLP chapters were run by elected officers who occupied formal positions (e.g., president, vice president, secretary, treasurer, sergeant at arms) and committees consisting of active members. Members were divided into cohorts of pledge classes, and standards were implemented to determine whether a pledge brother would be initiated. Furthermore, they constructed big-brother/little-brother relationships based on the differential seniority of members; many brothers we interviewed found these relationships most rewarding.

From the perspective of the brothers, DLP was a real fraternity that welcomed members with a stigmatized identity and alternative lifestyles, as the group fostered an environment where being gay was accepted and embraced. Elsewhere (Yeung and Stombler 2000), we have documented how gay brothers learned to be gay in DLP and how gay fraternities facilitated entry into the larger gay community. In this chapter, we focus on the way DLP members collectively redefined the gendered meaning of "fraternity men."

Data for the chapter came from 42 open-ended, in-depth interviews, two years of participant observation, and extensive archival data. The project was divided into two phases. In the first phase, Stombler conducted participant observation for one year in 1996 in a DLP chapter-in-formation. She gained access through a student organizer who introduced her to all participants. She attended all fraternity chapter meetings, social events, rituals, and community service projects. In addition, she conducted in-depth, face-to-face interviews with fraternity members (all members volunteered to be interviewed). In these interviews, Stombler asked members about the story of their participation, such as how and why they initially got involved, their experiences of participating, their assessment of the organization, and their participation. Interviews were open-ended, and she frequently revised interview questions as she was informed by her data analysis. Stombler also attended a National Gay Fraternity Convention (Diva

Las Vegas) where she observed interaction among members across the nation, interviewed members who responded to her research project announcement, and solicited additional interview volunteers for in-depth phone interviews.

In the second phase, Yeung and Wharton joined the project[3] and interviewed the previously recruited members from various chapters by telephone.[4] We contacted chapter presidents and asked them for a list of additional interview volunteers. In addition, we used the deviant cases sampling technique that involves seeking out respondents who are atypical to a setting such as straight or bisexual men in the case of the gay fraternity (Glaser and Strauss 1967; Martin and Turner 1986). One of the men in our sample identified as heterosexual, while the rest identified as gay. Men of color composed approximately 15 percent of our interview sample. We would describe the vast majority of the sample as middle class. Besides the advisors we interviewed, the men ranged in age from approximately 18 to 35, with most traditionally college aged. Of the interviewed brothers, 5 were members of chapters in the Northeast; 2 in the Southeast; 2 in the Midwest; 10 in the Southwest; and 23 in the West.[5] Interviews—which were tape-recorded and transcribed—averaged two hours. When the emergent concepts became "saturated,"[6] we ended the interview portion of the project.

Yeung and Wharton continued to conduct participant observation in the same local chapter originally observed by Stombler until the chapter decided to seek official inactive status due to poor leadership, which led to a shortage of active members. We then terminated the observation in 1998. Archival data consisted of the official fraternity handbook (shared by the local chapter), Web sites of the national and all local chapters with a presence on the Web, and newspaper and magazine articles identified through Internet and LexisNexis searches (using "Delta Lambda Phi" and "gay fraternity" as common search terms). As participant observation was conducted only in the Southwest, these multiregional archival data provided us with a picture of how chapters operated in a broader national context.

■ NEGOTIATING HEGEMONIC MASCULINITY INTERNALLY

Did adopting a traditional fraternity model necessarily lead to the reproduction of hegemonic masculinity? The group practices of DLP show that there was plenty of space in which gay fraternity brothers could redefine what "fraternity men" meant. At one level, these practices self-consciously deployed notions of femininity within the framework of a traditionally masculine environment. But given the persisting homophobic college environment, DLP members had to constantly renegotiate their status as marginalized men. This section analyzes how DLP members grappled with these challenges.

Performing Femininity

If femininity is stigmatized in the traditional hegemonic fraternity model, it is not because traditional (straight) fraternity members never participate in the enactment of a recognizably feminine representation, such as wearing women's clothing. Rather, what may be called "performing femininity" functions in straight fraternities as a form of humiliation and punishment to members, often as part of hazing during the pledging and initiation process (James 1998). Performing femininity in straight fraternities thus plays an ironic role in the "test of manhood" marking the rite of passage to brotherhood. In informal interactions, straight fraternity members also enact femininity in mockery. Parodying femininity provides opportunities for laughter, perhaps even serving to diffuse the threat of homosexuality (Lyman 1987).

Gay fraternities similarly performed femininity, but their practices had a very different origin. Since acting campy or "queeny" is one of the major cultural markers in American gay communities, DLP members often used demonstrative and flamboyant feminine gender performances as a means to individually and collectively construct their sexual identity and express their queer sensibility.[7] Brothers also embraced a variety of performance practices in everyday interactions, from calling each other "girls" or "girlfriends," to adopting stereotypical queeny mannerisms, to dressing in full drag at fraternity parties.

Instead of viewing these practices as a form of collective punishment, DLP members considered these practices an expression of their identity. Because gay men have been the subject of oppression historically, performing femininity allowed the brothers to "be yourself," even though sometimes this freedom might come in dissonance with the fraternity tradition.

One member recalled that at the first formal rush of the founding chapter, an occasion that traditionally required formal (masculine) attire, a brother appeared in an "impeccably embroidered evening gown" that was "perfect to go along with the tuxedos." While the founder was "beside himself" because he was expecting a black tie party, others were delighted and thought it was great. Not only was this practice not suppressed, according to some brothers; this initial event might have also set the dissident tone for DLP, as members resisted the founder's intention to construct a mainstream masculine fraternity for gay men.

Certainly, not all brothers were interested in performing femininity.[8] Some brothers did not act effeminately unless they were in the company of other brothers; others did not dress up in drag unless they were attending group parties. All of them, however, grew to accept and appreciate these practices much more after they joined DLP. For example, one brother who did not do drag appreciated the courage it took and said, "It takes a fair amount of guts to do it at a party, not where a lot of your brothers are, but to go out on the street and do that. I think people respect that." Some initially

disinterested brothers had also been transformed, as one brother described how another brother just needed a taste of drag to fully accept it: "When he was initially interviewed, they asked him about drag, and he said, 'Oh no, I would never do drag,' but once he got himself into a dress for the talent show we had to put on, oh my god, it's all downhill from there. He just turned into the biggest queen in the world. You know, went out and bought the pumps and everything." Performing femininity thus sometimes served as a means through which members found their "true" selves. The gay fraternities provided a collective environment that joined identity construction with resistance to hegemonic masculinity at the individual level.

Performing femininity was not only an individual subversive behavior; members also organized collective events to raise public visibility. For example, one chapter set up a shopping committee to draw attention to their behavior: "[The shopping committee's] sole purpose is to schedule the next shopping spree. It's a hoot.... You get 5 to 10 queens together; it's a riot. It's a riot.... We all go to Neiman's and...other stores.... Then we go to PayLess or Shoe Rack.... We go in there and see if we can find pumps in everybody's size. That's fun because most of us are not drag queens, but we do it just to cause a stir." Depending on the degree of tolerance on particular campuses, chapters also resisted hegemonic masculinity with different degrees of visibility. In one chapter, members dressed up in full drag to publicize a fraternity party at the school's student center. According to one witness, his DLP brothers "were just all outrageously dressed. They went straight to the middle [of the center] and just had a great time. I was like, Oh my god, I would never have done that. It would scare me too much."

Here we also see a dissonance between how out the chapter intended to be and how comfortable individual members felt about their sexuality's being displayed in public. Since DLP claimed to respect individuality, closeted members were not forced to participate in public events if they did not desire. However, collectively organized (resistance) events often became an opportunity for closeted or semi-closeted members to try out their courage.[9] Overall, at both the individual and the collective levels, performing femininity in DLP served as a means, among others, through which members could discover their selfhood and their sexual identity. It allowed members to explore gender fluidity and reappropriate the meaning of "fraternity men."

Promoting Intimacy Among Men

College fraternities construct their brotherhood through rituals, secrecy, and most important, an ideology that adopts a familial metaphor by emphasizing brothers' lifelong commitment to one another. Hegemonic masculinity often plays a part in forging this sense of solidarity. For example, the fraternity institution historically practiced hazing as a tool to test the manhood of pledging members

and, hence, keeping their loyalty to the group (James 1998). Most of these practices emphasized toughness, competition, and physical or emotional submission of junior brothers to senior brothers (Nuwer 1990). Rejection of femininity and homosexuality was operative in defining fraternity brotherhood (Cancian 1987; Martin and Hummer 1989; Nardi 1992; Swain 2000). The fear of showing weakness and intimate feelings to other brothers, then, is linked to homophobia.

When the DLP men first organized, they confronted a dual challenge as to the kind of brotherhood they should build. They needed to dispel the stereotypical notion, according to both the straight and the gay communities, that DLP was merely a sex club. DLP members also wanted to build a brotherhood that did not have all the "bad elements"—hazing, toughness, emotional detachment, lack of individuality—by which traditional fraternities monitored and enforced brotherhood.

The resolution to these challenges was a gay brotherhood that centered on asexual intimacy. To DLP members, their organization served as a complement to what they perceived as an over-sexualized and alienated gay world (cf. Levine 1998). As one brother pointed out, "I think that there is a gay culture but I don't necessarily believe that there is a gay community. . . . Gay men are very alienated from each other. We go around, we walk around on the streets and see each other, but at the same time, there seems to be a lack of a real—there is just this lack of feeling that we are a community.

There is a substantial amount of rejection of gay men toward each other."

By committing themselves to a fraternity model that idealizes long-lasting bonding relations, DLP brothers were able to solve what they saw as a problem of being gay in America. But again, DLP did not completely adopt the traditional model without modification. Not only did DLP completely reject bonding through hazing (Yeung and Stombler 2000); they also facilitated a safe environment where brothers could share their "fears, hopes, and dreams" with one another in group settings. Brothers did not have to be afraid of expressing themselves at the emotional level, which in the straight fraternity context may be impossible or stigmatized. Essentially, DLP brought qualities that are often associated with femininity back into the development of brotherhood. One DLP man claimed that no other brothers "think you're a wimp if you say what you are feeling." Although "sticking up" for your brothers and "being there when a brother needs you" were still important ideals for DLP brotherhood, they often lacked a hypermasculine connotation in DLP.

Interactional norms and rituals illustrate how DLP challenged the hegemonic understanding of men-to-men relations. The norm of self-disclosure, for example, was encouraged through rituals such as the Lamp of Truth. Designed to strengthen emotional bonds and resolve group conflict through communication, the Lamp of Truth ceremony called for members to speak honestly and openly to the group (when holding a candle in a darkened room). Another ritual designed to promote intimacy also resisted the common notion of toughness or invulnerability, traditionally associated with masculinity:

> In our warm fuzzy exercise, we have a ball of yarn, or we have a warm, fuzzy pillow or something. And then one person starts and throws the pillow at somebody and gives that person a warm fuzzy. Like, "Oh, thank you for helping me out, you're one of the nicest people I've seen." And that person has to throw it to somebody else in the fraternity. We did this like for two hours, until we're all like really comfortable and tired. It's all sappy, and then a box of Kleenex gets passed around. It's like "boo hoo [weeping sound] you're so wonderful to me." You know a big drama, but it's great; it really pulls us all together.

The use of "drama" with props like pillows and Kleenex indicates DLP's efforts to weave cultural motifs from the gay world into its brotherhood, while simultaneously challenging both the straight fraternity brotherhood and what they viewed as the alienated gay world. Below, we analyze how DLP brothers negotiated their marginal status in the presence of other straight fraternities.

The Limits of Resistance

Although DLP members experienced space to negotiate the definition of "fraternity men" in their backstage private settings, their resistance tended to be limited in the frontstage campus public arena, especially when they were in the presence of other fraternities. Public challenge to the fraternity institution was uncommon among DLP chapters. Chapters located on conservative campuses tended to reduce their visibility to "avoid troubles." Most brothers, however, believed that when students learned about their existence, it alone would be a shock. Hence, brothers often thought they could "make a difference" simply by participating in general recruiting events on campus. For example, one fraternity subtly challenged the connection between traditional masculinity and fraternities at a campus recruiting event with a sign on their booth that read, "Do you like Gladiator movies? Then we're the frat for you!" A brother recounted the reactions of the crowd: "People kind of look and do double takes. Then they see the part of the sign that says 'gay, bisexual, whatever.' We're kind of talked about. We're kind of like stereotyped. But we're like, wow, that's the whole point. We just almost like the shock value, I think.... Hopefully we're teaching some people."

The move from backstage to frontstage challenge, however, was not always easy. Facing a hegemonic tradition, DLP would be viewed as illegitimate if it overchallenged the fraternity tradition. However, if too little was done to the hegemonic model, DLP's group identity would become less distinctive compared to other straight fraternities, and it would offer few reasons why gay men should join DLP. In certain situations, therefore, DLP members were forced to deal with

the pressure of respectability through compromise.

Toning down its performances of femininity in public was an example of how the gay fraternity subdued its otherwise subversive actions. While enjoying (or not stigmatizing) these performances within their private space, brothers were aware that to gain acceptance on campus, they should not act like "flaming queens." In an interfraternity function—a volleyball competition with straight fraternities—this concern over feminine mannerisms became a sore spot for some members in a DLP chapter: "The queeny guys sometimes don't want to tone it down, you know? It becomes really uncomfortable... to the more butch guys. I guess it's because [the butch guys] don't mind, but they don't want to be stereotyped as queeny. So when we're in public, it becomes a problem when the queeny guys just go off: 'Girlfriend! Oh he's got a nice ass.' And the straight-acting guys are like: 'Uh-oh... let's tone it down there.' We don't want to draw too much attention to ourselves. We just like to keep a low profile." In social settings where a "reputable image" was called for, brothers collectively pursued a masculine image that they felt was the appropriate or legitimate image of the fraternity.

The pursuit of respectability compromised DLP's resistance to internal hegemony and also could have created conflict between "butch brothers" and "femme brothers"—a challenge to the intimate brotherhood DLP members originally intended to build. What is surprising, however, is that the brothers rarely described (nor did we observe) conflict over the self-image of gay fraternities. It appeared that all brothers, butch or femme, had tacitly agreed to a normalized public representation: When the queeny brothers were asked to tone it down, they usually succumbed to the request with little complaint.

DLP's levels of complicity to the terms of hegemonic masculinity thus varied depending on setting. In one setting, the brothers could "let their hair down" and began to "queen out," but in another, they conformed to hegemonic demands and "straight-acted." Shifting from one mode of interaction to the other reflects DLP's contradictory institutional position, as they simultaneously emulated and challenged a hegemonic institution. We will return to the institutional origin of these contradictions below, but now it suffices to state that DLP brothers' internal challenge to an all-male fraternity institution was partial. They were able to reappropriate the meaning of "fraternity men" primarily through in-group practices, but institutional pressures often contained these challenges within the fraternity's private settings.

■ REINFORCING EXTERNAL HEGEMONY

Not only was DLP's challenge to the traditional fraternity institution partial; it was also selective in how the group drew its membership boundaries. This selectivity is particularly clear when we consider how the gay fraternity drew its membership boundaries. For DLP brothers, a fraternity was, by definition, a place of men; including women as members was simply out of the question. While some kind of membership boundary must be drawn for any collective to operate, DLP posed a specific puzzle for us because the gay fraternities had decisively excluded all women (gay or straight) in their policy but did not prevent any straight men from joining. Although DLP questioned almost every single aspect of the traditional model, they viewed the single-sex policy as something immutable or even sacred to the fraternity institution. We argue that DLP's (gendered) ideological construction facilitated this selectivity. How might a single-sex model serve to reproduce the external dimension of hegemony (against all women), even though this model was upheld by a group of marginal men who actively used performing femininity to challenge the fraternity institution?

Inclusion of All Men

It may appear that DLP was just like any other exclusive traditional fraternity that could not deal with diversity. However, we found that DLP chapters were highly inclusive in many other aspects besides gender. For example, most DLP chapters were ethnically diverse, and in some community-based chapters, men of different ages were included.[10] In terms of the femme-butch distinction, most chapters had a mix of queeny and straight-acting members. Since the brothers believed that gay men were themselves subjects of exclusion in traditional fraternities, they made a conscious effort to become an inclusive fraternity that did not discriminate against differences.[11]

Indeed, DLP did not even exclude straight men, hence the notion of DLP as "a fraternity founded by gay men for all men." Among the two straight men who had joined DLP at the time of our research, neither was treated as a minority token. Not only did the gay brothers express admiration for those straight members who had "balls enough to join a gay fraternity"; they also went out of their way to accommodate the needs of their straight brothers. For instance, on one occasion, the brothers took a straight member to a (heterosexual) strip bar at a national convention on an outing with several other chapters. The gay brothers claimed, "We took him under our wing. We're gonna find him the right woman. You know, we're gonna take care of him. [We're] hunting and searching."

Some brothers saw that the inclusion of straight members into DLP had many benefits. One brother thought that straight membership could bridge the gap between the straight and gay worlds because "part of the reason why homophobia can be so rampant is because there is total misunderstanding of what homosexuality is." Another brother explained that straight members might even help mitigate some of the "bitchiness" and "petty gossips" in an all-gay setting; they could help the gay ones "find out what it is like to be a man." Thus, DLP brothers admitted straight men as a

means to improve the quality of the gay fraternity, perhaps leading it to a better fit into the straight fraternity institution and fulfilling the desire to become "just like another fraternity down the block."[12]

Although the brothers saw exclusion based on sexual orientation as a problem to be corrected, few of those we talked to considered gender a problematic boundary marker. Why think differently about sexuality and not gender? If including straight men enhanced diversity in the fraternity, would not including women who could equally provide the fraternity with diversity, different viewpoints, and the individuality that was valued by the brothers do the same?

Exclusion of All Women

As a collective, DLP brothers made a conscious effort to defend their single-sex model by claiming equality vis-à-vis other straight men, as shown in the following official statement: "In 1992, the Fraternity's governing body decided to remain exclusively male rather than going coed. The reasoning being, if straight men can have a 'traditional' (i.e., non-coed) Greek experience, gay men should be able to have it as well" (www.dlp.org). Consistent with its larger legitimacy project, DLP drew parallel comparisons with straight fraternities that maintained fraternities as an all-male space. DLP assumed that the gay brothers' needs for the "traditional" Greek experience were similar to the needs of straight men.

While accepting straight and bisexual men, albeit in small numbers, members claimed they excluded women to maintain the fraternal form. One brother argued that while gay men and lesbians could bond, "it wouldn't be a fraternity anymore." Another brother concurred: "They [members of the gay, lesbian, bisexual, transgendered (GLBT) community] are thinking that we are being exclusionist. . . . Well of course we are. It's a fraternity. That's the point. It's men dealing with men things." Including women from this perspective meant that DLP would no longer be different from other GLBT organizations. As we discuss later, the construction of a gay brotherhood as a male-only space should be viewed partly as a result of DLP brothers' fear of losing their collective identity vis-à-vis other similar student groups on campus.

The idealized value of male bonding further reinforced biological sex as the distinguished element in a fraternal form. According to one brother, "a bond among men is different than the bond among people." Even though DLP brothers had attempted many ways to redefine what such a bond could mean— for example, it could mean men's sharing their emotional feelings with each other or dressing up in drag together—the brothers clung to an almost sacred ideal wherein fraternal bonding experience is possible only for men. One brother described his bonding experience as "something magical you carry with you always . . . that almost transcends words."

Justification of gender segregation therefore often depends on an entrenched notion of gender differences. The sacred ideal of an all-male brotherhood that DLP embraced relied on a set of ideologies that purports men and women to be essentially different. These ideologies ignore the diversity within the category of women and reduce them into the other.[13] Next, we look at how DLP members evaluated different kinds of women, straight or lesbian, as potential members.

The Ideology of Gender Differences

Although DLP members comfortably performed femininity (at least in certain situations), a strict gender distinction was re-inscribed when brothers rationalized the gender exclusiveness of the fraternal model. Brothers supported these entrenched boundaries through a rigid but vaguely articulated understanding of gender differences in their discourse. As one brother said, "I'm not trying to sound chauvinistic or anything. I just don't think we should allow women to join DLP primarily because men and women are obviously different. Men and women also have different needs and different ideas, and I think that would actually cause more problems than be good because there are [already] so many differences on various levels." Another brother agreed when he stated that he does not have anything against women, "but they just wouldn't fit into that thing that we do, and I, I don't even know if I can even pinpoint what the thing is." The difference brothers often pointed to lacked specificity, often relegated to the notion that "there is a different kind of energy when men are around." Those who did try to pinpoint a specific difference usually relied on essentialized notions, such as this brother who tried to explain why women and men are so different by referencing physical ailments: "The closest thing I am going to come to understanding PMS is really constipation, and I am pretty sure that is not coming real close. Like a woman won't particularly understand having gotten jock itch—those types of things." Although we cannot ascertain whether the brothers held these vague and arbitrary ideas on gender differences before they joined DLP, the adoption of a traditional fraternity model certainly reinforced and made these arbitrary boundaries more rigid.

This rigid conceptualization was made even clearer when the brothers expressed their differences from lesbians, women who were arguably more similar to them (in some ways) than straight men or women. With their shared sexual orientation and experiences as oppressed groups, DLP men could have considered lesbians potential members. However, brothers invoked an even more stereotypical and essentialist narrative, treating lesbians as a unified group with little internal diversity. A few members stated that lesbians in particular, "just don't know what it is like to be a man or a gay man, just as they [the brothers] do not understand what it is like to be a lesbian." The DLP official Web site reinforced this narrative and suggested that potential lesbian members join the DLP-equivalent, a lesbian sorority: "Those who claim that our lesbian

friends, as much as we love and support them as comrades-in-arms, have the same social experience as gay men, are frankly, deluding themselves. Our lesbian friends have the option of pledging our sister sorority, Lambda Delta Lambda." Another brother stated, "I don't know how lesbians work. I don't know how they socialize." Members viewed lesbians as essentially different from gay men. However, rather than perceiving lesbians as weaker or lesser than gay men, one brother narrated a fear of being controlled by lesbians once they were accepted to the gay fraternity: "Lesbians want to be in control of the situation; they will take charge, and they just want to run everything. I think gay men typically want to influence everything. They don't want to do anything, but they want to influence everything. So right there you're going to have a problem with the power dynamic there. You're going to have a group of women who wants to do and be in charge, but not be controlled." Lesbians were thus largely associated with traits typically connected to masculinity. Valuing femininity, as many of the members did, these perceptions of lesbians both offended and intimidated some of the men, as one member claimed: "I'm not crazy about the lesbians because they are bigger than me and can kick my ass." Another argued that not only would lesbians want to play more sports, but "they could probably play sports better than us." Brothers did not express similar fears surrounding the inclusion of straight men. For the most part, DLP members were uncomfortable with women who displayed masculine traits rather than the masculine traits themselves. With few exceptions, brothers did not appear to recognize, as they did with gay men, that there was great variation in how lesbians do gender. They saw lesbians as either butch or femme (predominantly butch), not both or changing, as they saw and did themselves.[14]

DLP members' attitudes toward straight women were slightly different. Perhaps because brothers tended to perceive themselves as more or less gender fluid (as opposed to their conception of lesbians), they expressed a sense of closeness to straight sorority women. Some chapters tried arranging social events with both lesbian organizations and straight sororities, but the gay brothers often reported preferring socials with straight women for the reason that "when we invite a straight sorority, we all distribute ourselves among the girls, and we talk with girls, and we all mingle with girls. I guess we have more common ground." On the surface, it appeared that DLP members and straight sorority women could interact successfully because they shared common interests (femininity, dating men). But when asked about whether they intended to model traditional fraternities and create little sister programs and, if so, whom they would recruit as little sisters, DLP men revealed that part of their attraction to straight women over lesbians had less to do with common interests and more to do with common arrangements of subordination: "I would prefer straight women because the lesbians would try and take over. A straight woman might enjoy being a little sister and attending functions and hanging out, while a lesbian would consider the role subordinate and get tired of it quickly, trying to dominate and manipulate the program. Basically, a straight woman *might understand the role* while a lesbian would not. [To interviewer:] Are you a lesbian? Did I offend you? I see their role as supportive and basically helping out" (emphasis added).

Ultimately, while most members did not want women to be involved in anyway, straight women were seen as more palatable (although they shared neither the gender nor the sexual orientation of the members) because they were seen as sharing similar interests and as entirely less intimidating. Moreover, straight women knew their place.

In sum, exclusionary policy does not reproduce hegemony by itself. After all, any social organization in some way needs to draw certain categorical boundaries if it is to develop a distinct identity. Rather, DLP members justified excluding women (and welcoming straight men) by presenting women as essentially different from men, rejecting masculinity in women, and valorizing men over women. By forming a social organization around these notions about women, DLP inscribed, if not institutionalized, hegemonic masculinity at the collective level. When the fraternity organizational form is legitimized and its gender exclusion legalized, it is readily available for marginal men to adopt. This allows marginal men an opportunity to achieve legitimacy vis-à-vis other men yet reproduce domination over women within the larger order of hegemonic masculinity.

■ RELATIONS WITH OTHER GROUPS

As marginal students in a homophobic college environment, DLP men organized themselves as fraternities to respond to two problems at once. On one hand, the gay fraternity model satisfied some gay men who desired to join the traditionally homophobic institution in an effort to reap the same benefits as other men. On the other hand, the notion of brotherhood—idealized by the very same homophobic tradition—provided a solution for these gay men to form intimate non-erotic relations outside what they perceived was an alienating gay culture. More important, the fraternity model appealed to stigmatized students because it was associated with prestige and legitimacy among peers (Stombler 1994), something that GLBT student groups may not have provided. DLP's group identity thus provided a collective solution to these conflicting relations on campus. Organized as gay and Greek, the brothers had to distinguish themselves from GLBT student groups on one hand and homophobic straight fraternities on the other (Yeung and Stombler 2000).

Although GLBT student groups provided another avenue for gay men to participate in college life, DLP brothers felt that these groups were either "too political" and "businesslike" or filled with sexual tensions, which they believed mirrored a flawed gay culture. In practice, however, the boundary between the gay fraternities and GLBT organizations was quite thin. The two overlapped their activities and politics by sponsoring AIDS events and Pride activities, educating peers on topics such as safer sex, and participating in other gay and lesbian functions. Brothers frankly noted that if DLP included women, "it would become just another GLBT student organization" (ignoring other delineating features such as the use of tradition and ritual, in-group/out-group dynamics, and the construction of quasi-familial relationships). Tightening and fortifying the gender boundary as a criterion of membership further helped DLP resolve a potential identity crisis.

In relation to other straight fraternities, DLP largely remained segregated on campus. Few chapters had fraternity houses, and their links to college administration tended to be weak. While a few chapters did have limited interaction with other fraternities (predominantly university-based chapters), the majority did not. At the time we conducted our research, fewer than 15 percent of the chapters were part of their local Interfraternity Council. This is still the case today although none of the Interfraternity Council–affiliated chapters remain the same. The observed chapter had no access to other fraternities on campus, although they would have gladly accepted genuine invitations. Brothers assessed their own impact on the fraternity system as "limited," often citing lack of participation in their membership base as an obstacle to campus involvement.

Still, even though campus reaction from administrators and newspaper coverage was usually positive, some brothers felt that the straight fraternity system would never welcome them and that trying to "infiltrate" was "a waste of time."

Brothers were also aware of their low prestige on campus, some noting that other fraternities thought of them as a "joke fraternity." On campuses where DLP was actually recognized by other fraternities, brothers recounted isolated incidents where straight fraternities sent their pledges through DLP's rush and pledge process as a form of hazing. Another brother recounted seeing a sign on a straight fraternity's balcony that said "Guys, I can't take the pressure anymore. I'm going to join Delta Lambda Phi." Simply adopting an organizational model—even with the school's recognition—guaranteed no collective access to the resources and prestige accompanying a hegemonic institution. Indeed, DLP ultimately appeared to have retreated from seeking legitimacy altogether by collectively deciding not to seek entrance into the North-American Interfraternity Conference, the major umbrella organization for college fraternities.[15] This decision ultimately prevented DLP from becoming visible as a challenging voice in the traditional fraternity institution.

■ DISCUSSION

Some theorists suggest a tight coupling between internal and external hegemonic masculinity: Hegemonic relations between men and women are preconditions for some men's marginalizing other men (Connell 1995). However, others find increasing detachment, as changes in relations among men do not necessarily reshape hegemony against women (Chen 1999; Demetriou 2001). This chapter shows evidence supporting a detachment perspective. We found that marginalized men persistently perceived women as others, even as they tried to destroy the boundaries between marginalized and dominant men.

In contrast to Demetriou (2001) and Chen (1999), whose arguments imply that men who are incorporated into dominant institutions and culture are complicit, we found that members of gay fraternities tried to change the traditional fraternity model at different levels. With clear intention to reappropriate the meaning of fraternity, DLP brothers drew on elements from gay culture (rather than traditional fraternities), such as performing femininity, and used them to construct a collective identity. They also refused to haze as a tool to achieve group cohesion and fostered an environment where men could establish intimate relationships in other ways. Even though many of these efforts were not shown in public, due to DLP's low visibility on campus, they nonetheless constituted a form of cultural protest, creating an autonomous space where DLP members could contest and redefine the hegemonic meaning of "fraternity men" (Rupp and Taylor 2003; Taylor and Whittier 1996).

Yet even the best intentions do not necessarily produce fruitful outcomes.

DLP's cultural protests were largely backstage. Furthermore, its relative isolation from other fraternities on campus and its decision to not pursue North-American Interfraternity Conference membership limited the reformative outcomes of its efforts. Moreover, despite the many fraternity traditions that DLP gladly challenged, it left the single-sex organizational model intact, justifying biological sex as a criterion of exclusion by a set of loosely connected beliefs about the essential differences between men and women. DLP excluded the other sex but not the other sexuality, as it welcomed straight men. While DLP tolerated straight women as potential companions, it excluded all women (straight or lesbian) from membership. The detachment between the two dimensions of hegemonic masculinity was indicated by the brothers' uncritical view of differences across gender and a heightened demand for recognition of similarities among men.

DLP's gender strategies that separated femininity as a cultural notion, which the brothers had no problem adopting, from women as persons enabled this detachment. Performing femininity was playful and did not require the engagement of women, but it allowed the brothers to contest gendered meaning in a traditional institution. The result was a collective identity and a process of "making men" that was unique to the gay fraternity with little reflection on the hegemonic relationship of men over women.

We can imagine that there are many ways for marginalized men to challenge dominant men; some may happen independently of women's lives in general— as shown in the case of gay fraternities— others may involve serious engagement with women's issues, deconstructing gender, and a critique of the relationship between women and men. A limitation of this study has been our single focus on the gay fraternity. To further understand the relationship between the reproduction of internal and external hegemony, other organizations, such as Men Stopping Violence, should be analyzed. We expect that decidedly feminist organizations would tighten the coupling between resisting internal and resisting external hegemony. As different kinds of men become more similar because of, not in spite of, their engagement with women's lives, we would expect to see a weakening in the external hegemony that reduces women as undifferentiated others.

NOTES

1. We distinguish resisting acts from resisting consciousness that may or may not be actualized in action (Hollander and Einwohner 2004). We consider "repudiation"—the rejection of the "basic assumptions or premises that underlie hegemonic masculinity" (Chen 1999, 603)—a resisting consciousness.

2. A few chapters are community based and thus accept non-college men for active membership. Other chapters are multi-university based. By 2005, the fraternity had gained significant growth with 20 active chapters and 10 colonies.

3. Regardless of the fact that two of us were women, we are confident our respondents were candid in their communication (discussing anything from their frustration with the organization to the details of their private sexual relationships). We spent years with the men in the local chapter, supporting their organization, and were trusted (and presented to others) as allies in a hostile environment. In an effort to both thank and include her, local brothers named Stombler an "honorary brother" and presented her with a formal certificate. The local chapter "vouched" for us at the national convention (often jokingly referring to Stombler as "Michael," a brother who had gone through sex realignment) and assisted us in our recruitment for future phone interviews. Furthermore, the data collected by the male researcher did not significantly differ from the data collected by the female researchers (although a few brothers asked the male researcher if he was gay before sharing sexual stories during interviews). The only difference we noticed was that some respondents sometimes prefaced sexist remarks with "I don't mean to be chauvinistic, but . . . " during phone interviews with one of the women researchers (Williams and Heikes 1993).

4. The respondents either signed consent forms ensuring confidentiality or gave their verbal consent to participating.

5. While our sample was approximately 15 percent men of color, we would estimate that nationally, Delta Lambda Phi (DLP) was at least 20 percent men of color. Stombler had completed participant observation at traditional, predominantly straight fraternities prior to this research. She noted a much more racially and ethnically diverse membership in DLP. This diversity usually reflected that of the local campuses. Thus, racial and ethnic diversity was not uniform across chapters, as this brother from the West Coast described: "At one point, we were a very Hispanic fraternity. Now it's much more of a mix of everything from white, Black, to Asians, to Hispanics. I know some chapters have been predominantly Asian at some time." Another brother from the West claims, "[Our diversity] fluctuates. Right now we are pretty much all white boys."

6. "Saturation" refers to the point in the process of data collection and analysis where incidents of a particular category become repetitive and additional data no longer elaborate on the meaning of the category (Charmaz 1983).

7. These performances were unique in that they were not necessarily traditionally feminine yet drew from feminine reference points. Indeed, the men did not refer to them as camp, but rather as "showing their feminine side." Muñoz (1999) describes camp as "not only a strategy of representation but also as a mode of enacting self against the pressures of the dominant culture's identity-denying protocols" (p. 120) and as style of performance that "relies on humor to examine social and cultural forms" (p. 119).

8. Although we observed a degree of freedom allowing DLP members to express their femininity, we wondered whether DLP had been recruiting feminine men. In contrast, we found that many DLP members were not "queeny" to begin with, and many of them did not act in such a way in their daily lives even after joining.

9. DLP accepted closeted and semicloseted members for several reasons. First, it respected the individual decisions of members to "be who they wanted to be." Second, it needed members. Third, it saw itself as a group that could uniquely support men in the process of coming out.

10. While DLP remained inclusive on the basis of race and ethnicity, its collective identity and practices did not revolve around members' racial or ethnic identities. Unlike research by Stombler and Padavic (1997) that illustrates race-based resistance strategies among fraternity little sisters, this research found that DLP men focused on their similarities as gay men and modeled resistance strategies from the gay movement.

11. For instance, while DLP brothers, like many college students, desired upward mobility, we did not see recruitment efforts that targeted upper-class men. In fact, unlike more elite fraternities, DLP kept its dues and other monetary requests extremely low.

12. We are sure, however, that DLP brothers did not take for granted the issues of exclusion and inclusion as a way to achieve some political and social aspirations (either symbolically or otherwise). While including straight members might help the group enhance its legitimacy in the traditional fraternity system, including women would not.

13. Complicity expressed at the individual and collective levels should be differentiated. While some group members expressed deep sympathy or ambivalence toward gender segregation, they still conformed to or agreed with the gendered policy of the fraternity. This disjunction between individual and group expressions of gender assumptions and values led us to focus on the organizational form that gave rise to the restrictive gender boundary of DLP.

14. In many situations, brothers placed femme lesbians in the same category as straight women. As a result, brothers saw "lipstick lesbians," like straight women, as more submissive and less confrontational than butch lesbians.

15. At the DLP's Diva Las Vegas Conference in 1996, the membership voted to stop pursuing membership in the North-American Interfraternity Conference. While leaders reported that they had been "very well-received," DLP had unique challenges. With fewer men to draw from on individual campuses (gay men or nongay men who wished to affiliate), many chapters were forced to cast a wide net to find potential pledges. Some chapters followed a model where geographically

proximate schools pooled their members to form one multischool chapter. Other brothers formed city-based chapters where members did not have to be students to join. Conforming to the standards of the North-American Interfraternity Conference would have required following a stricter interpretation of fraternity than many DLP members felt they could maintain. Ultimately, this decision limited many local chapters' ability to join their school's Interfraternity Councils (thus limiting their contact with traditional, straight fraternities), as North-American Interfraternity Conference membership was often a prerequisite.

REFERENCES

Bird, Sharon R. 1996. Welcome to the men's club: Homosociality and the maintenance of hegemonic masculinity. *Gender & Society* 10:120–32.

Boswell, A. Ayres, and Joan Z. Spade. 1996. Fraternities and collegiate rape culture: Why are some fraternities more dangerous places for women? *Gender & Society* 10:133–47.

Cancian, Francesca M. 1987. *Love in America: Gender and self-development.* Cambridge, UK: Cambridge University Press.

Charmaz, Kathy. 1983. The grounded theory method: An explication and interpretation. In *Contemporary field research,* edited by R. Emerson. Boston: Little, Brown.

Chen, Anthony S. 1999. Lives at the center of the periphery, lives at the periphery of the center: Chinese American masculinities and

bargaining with hegemony. *Gender & Society* 13:584–607.

Clawson, Mary Ann. 1989. *Constructing brotherhood: Class, gender, and fraternalism.* Princeton, NJ: Princeton University Press.

Collins, Patricia Hill. 1991. *Black feminist thought: Knowledge, consciousness, and the politics of empowerment.* New York: Routledge.

Connell, R. W. 1995. *Masculinities.* Berkeley: University of California Press.

———. 2000. *The men and the boys.* Berkeley: University of California Press.

Davis, Kathy, and Sue Fisher. 1993. Power and the female subject. In *Negotiating at the margins: The gendered discourses of power and resistance,* edited by Sue Fisher and Kathy Davis. New Brunswick, NJ: Rutgers University Press.

Delta Lambda Phi (DLP). n.d. *Chapter handbook.* Archival data.

Demetriou, Demetrakis Z. 2001. Connell's concept of hegemonic masculinity: A critique. *Theory and Society* 30:337–61.

Duneier, Mitchell. 1992. *Slim's table.* Chicago: University of Chicago Press.

Gerschick, Thomas J., and Adam Stephen Miller. 1994. Gender identities at the crossroads of masculinity and physical disability. *Masculinities* 2:34–55.

Glaser, Barney, and Anselm Strauss. 1967. *The discovery of grounded theory.* Chicago: Aldine.

Hollander, Jocelyn A., and Rachel L. Einwohner. 2004. Conceptualizing resistance. *Sociological Forum* 19:533–54.

James, Anthony W. 1998. The defenders of tradition: College social fraternities, race, and gender, 1845–1980. Ph.D. diss., University of Mississippi.

Kanuha, Vailli Kalei. 1999. The social process of "passing" to maintain stigma: Acts of internalized opposition or acts of resistance? *Journal of Sociology and Social Welfare* 26:27–46.

Levine, Martin P. 1998. *Gay macho.* New York: New York University Press.

Lyman, Peter. 1987. The fraternal bond as a joking relationship: A case study of the role of sexist jokes in male group bonding. In *Changing men,* edited by Michael S. Kimmel. Newbury Park, CA: Sage.

Majors, Richard, and Janet Billson. 1992. *Cool pose: The dilemmas of Black manhood in America.* New York: Lexington Books.

Martin, Patricia Yancey, and Robert A. Hummer. 1989. Fraternities and rape on campus. *Gender & Society* 3:457–73.

Martin, Patricia Yancey, and Barry A. Turner. 1986. Ground theory and organizational research. *Journal of Applied Behavioral Science* 22:141–57.

Melucci, Alberto. 1989. *Nomads of the present: Social movements and individual needs in contemporary society.* London: Century Hutchinson.

Muñoz, José Esteban. 1999. *Disidentifications: Queers of color and the performance of politics.* Minneapolis: University of Minnesota Press.

Nardi, Peter M. 1992. Sex, friendship, and gender roles among gay men. In *Men's friendships,* edited by Peter M. Nardi. Newbury Park, CA: Sage.

Nonn, Timothy. 2003. Hitting bottom: Homelessness, poverty, and masculinity. In *Men's lives,* 6th ed., edited by Michael Kimmel and Michael Messner. Boston: Allyn & Bacon.

Nuwer, Hank. 1990. *Broken pledges: The deadly rite of hazing.* Atlanta: Longstreet Press.

O'Conor, Andi. 1998. The cultural logic of gender in college: Heterosexism, homophobia and sexism in campus peer groups. Ph.D. diss., University of Colorado–Boulder.

Robson, J. 1977. *Baird's manual of American college fraternities.* Menasha, WI: The Baird's Manual Foundation.

Rubin, Jeffrey W. 1996. Defining resistance: Contested interpretations of everyday acts. *Studies in Law, Politics, and Society* 15: 237–60.

Rupp, Leila J., and Verta Taylor. 2003. *Drag queens at the 801 Cabaret.* Chicago: University of Chicago Press.

Sanday, Peggy Reeves. 1990. *Fraternity gang rape: Sex, brotherhood, and privilege on campus.* New York: New York University Press.

Scott, James C. 1985. *Weapons of the weak: Everyday forms of peasant resistance.* New Haven, CT: Yale University Press.

———. 1990. *Domination and the art of resistance.* New Haven, CT: Yale University Press.

Stombler, Mindy. 1994. "Buddies" or "slutties": The collective sexual reputation of fraternity little sisters. *Gender & Society* 8: 297–323.

Stombler, Mindy, and Patricia Yancey Martin. 1994. Bringing women in, keeping women down: Fraternity little sister groups. *Journal of Contemporary Ethnography* 23: 150–84.

Stombler, Mindy, and Irene Padavic. 1997. Sister acts: Resisting men's domination in Black and white fraternity little sister programs. *Social Problems* 44:257–75.

Swain, Scott. 2000. Covert intimacy: Closeness in men's friendships. In *The gendered society reader*, edited by Michael S. Kimmel. New York: Oxford University Press.

Taylor, Verta, and Nancy E. Whittier. 1996. Analytical approaches to social movement culture: The culture of the women's movement. In *Social movements and culture*, edited by Hank Johnson and Bert Klandermans. Minneapolis: University of Minnesota Press.

Williams, Christine L., and Joel Heikes. 1993. The importance of researcher's gender in the in depth interview: Evidence from two case studies of male nurses. *Gender & Society* 7:280–91.

Willis, Paul. 1977. *Learning to labor.* Westmead, UK: Saxon House.

Windmeyer, Shane L., and Pamela W. Freeman, eds. 1998. *Out on fraternity row: Personal accounts of being gay in a college fraternity*. New York: Alyson Books.

Yeung, King-To, and Mindy Stombler. 2000. Gay and Greek: The identity paradox of gay fraternities. *Social Problems* 47:134–52.

CHAPTER 10

Construction of Male Sexuality and Gender Roles in Puerto Rican Heterosexual College Students

David Pérez-Jiménez, Ineke Cunningham,
Irma Serrano-García, and Blanca Ortiz-Torres

Historically, issues related to sexuality have been taboo in Latino culture. Puerto Rico is not an exception (Díaz 1998). As a consequence, there are few studies about the influence that social and cultural contexts play in the development of the meanings that people ascribe to gender roles and sexuality. Gender roles relate to a set of norms and beliefs about how men and women must behave and think in a particular culture (Beal 1994; Francoeur et al. 1995; Golombok and Fivush 1994; Howard and Hollander 1997). This set of norms and beliefs is not "natural" or inherited biologically, but rather is socially and culturally defined and constructed through a process of human interaction with surrounding social institutions (Biever et al. 1998; Courtenay 2000b, 2000c; Glenn 1999; Levant 1995;

Ramírez 1993). Institutions such as family, church, school, and mass media exert great influence on the transmission and acquisition of these roles (Kimmel and Levine 1992). In the same manner, masculine ideology dictates the social and behavioral norms that men must abide by. To infringe upon these norms implies suffering the sanctions that society imposes. Analyzing men's gender roles denotes examining the way in which they construct their masculine ideology by using the meanings and values they have socially learned.

Some researchers have offered critical analyses of sexuality and power relations between genders (Jiménez-Muñoz 1994). A study conducted recently with a group of Puerto Rican blue-collar workers revealed that they endorse many hegemonic masculinity traits, such as being hard workers, masculine, respected, courageous, and the main providers for their family (Ramírez et al. 2002). However, this study also revealed that they rejected "negative" traits such as being dominant, aggressive, and insensitive. This could indicate that traditional gender roles assigned to men in Puerto Rican culture are changing. These findings are consistent with studies conducted in the United States where changes in traditional male sex roles (Young 1996), masculine ideology (Gale 2000), and *machismo* (Torres, Solberg, and Carlstrom 2002) have been observed.

We could argue that questioning or rejecting traditional gender roles could be an indicator that a new view of masculinity or a "new psychology of men" is emerging (Levant 1996; Levant and Pollack 1995). Stemming from this view, the assumptions of the preceding *gender role identity paradigm,* which assumed that men have an intrinsic inherent psychological need to develop specific gender traits, attitudes, and interests, are rejected (Pleck, Sonenstein, and Ku 1994). Rather, based on the *gender role strain paradigm,* males act the way they do not because of a psychological need to develop a specific role trait or identity but because of the social norms about masculinity that they acquire through their cultural belief systems and gender ideologies (Levant et al. 2003; Pleck, Sonenstein, and Ku 1993, 1994). "Masculinity ideology" has been proposed as the construct to describe the process by which men internalize society's definition of masculinity (Pleck,

Sonenstein, and Ku 1993, 1994). In this sense, the social constructionist approach views masculinity not as a dimension of personality, but as an ideology, a set of beliefs and expectations about how men should think and behave (Pleck, Sonenstein, and Ku 1993).

Culturally accepted norms regarding masculinity ideology are not static abstract entities outside of the individual's domain but a product of active interactions of men with surrounding institutions (Courtenay 2000b, 2000c). Masculine ideology has been found to vary within groups in a given culture (Levant and Majors 1997; Levant, Majors, and Kelley 1998; Gale 2000), from culture to culture (Abreu 2000; Levant et al. 2003) and even within the same culture over time (Kimmel and Messner 1992). Therefore, the social construction of gender implies a process by which an individual perceives and interprets gender characteristics, behaviors, and expectations, as well as the attributes and parameters that determine gender and its relation to people's anatomy.

Kimmel and Levine (1992, 320) argue that the "cultural construction of masculinity" indicates that men organize the conceptions of themselves as masculine by their willingness to take risks, by their ability to experience pain or discomfort without submitting to it, by their drive to accumulate constantly (i.e., money, power, sex partners, experiences), and by their resolute avoidance of any behavior that might be constructed as "feminine." In addition, men must deny the existence of feelings that can be seen as feminine. Different authors have shown that the norms that rule masculinity contradict efforts toward the prevention of risky sexual practices because they make men more vulnerable and more willing to take risks while ignoring precautions for risk reduction (Campbell 1995; Kimmel and Levine 1992; Levant and Kopecky 1995).

In recent years, it has been well documented that men engage in riskier practices and lifestyles than do women, which makes them more vulnerable to severe chronic illness and premature death (Billy et al. 1993; Courtenay 2000a; Eisler 1995; Helgeson 1995; UN-AIDS 2000; Kimmel and Levine 1992; Levant and Kopecky 1995; Lorber 1997; Stillion 1995; The Panos Institute 1999; Waldron 1995). An extensive literature review conducted recently by Courtenay (2000a, 109) revealed that gender differences exist in behaviors that influence the health and longevity of men and women. This author showed that men are worse off in areas such as health care utilization, preventive care, diet, weight control, physical activity, substance use, risk taking, violence, social support, and employment. He raised an important question based on these findings: "Why are men more likely than women to engage in behaviors that put them at greater risks for disease, injury, and death?" In this chapter, we argue that the answer to this question is directly related to the way men construct their gender roles and sexuality.

With this in mind, we conducted a study to examine how contextual variables influence the construction of male gender roles and sexuality in a group of Puerto Rican male college students. We believe that the ability to make healthy sexual decisions is directly influenced by the way men construct their notions of masculinity—notions which in turn affect their expression of sexuality. Thus, in order to prevent men's unhealthy behaviors, we should consider the social values they are taught and the level of influence that these values exert on the expression of their sexuality.

■ METHOD

Participants

So as to ascertain their opinions concerning gender roles and sexuality, we recruited male university students at the University of Puerto Rico, Río Piedras Campus. We contacted one hundred and fifteen male students averaging twenty-one years of age. Fifty-four percent (54%) of the students were in their freshman year. Fifty-eight percent (58%) stated that they were sexually active, while forty-two percent (42%) indicated they were not. Of those who reported being sexually active, seventy-four percent (74%) reported having sex only with women, eighteen percent (18%) only with men, and the remaining eight percent (8%) with both. Eighty percent (80%) of those sexually active also stated that they practiced safer sex "always" or "sometimes."

We conducted three focus groups with twenty-five of the one hundred and fifteen students. Although most of the students verbally agreed to participate when contacted, many of them did not attend the groups. The first group consisted of sexually active heterosexual men who used condoms during sexual intercourse (G-1; $n = 12$); the second group was made up of sexually active heterosexual men who did not use condoms during sexual intercourse (G-2; $n = 4$); and the third group was composed of heterosexual men who were not sexually active (G-3; $n = 9$). This strategy aimed to create homogeneous groups, which is an important element for focus groups (Carey 1994; Morgan 1997; Stewart and Shamdasani 1998).

Instruments

A brief screening interview was designed consisting of questions about age, year of study, gender, sexual orientation, and sexual practices. This screening was used in the recruitment process to qualify participants according to the characteristics of each group.

We also developed questions to facilitate the focus group discussions. These were classified in the following areas: (1) notions about sexuality, (2) notions about gender roles, (3) notions about sexual practices, and (4) notions about sexual negotiation and safer sex. Participants were asked not to give an opinion of what they thought about the issues under discussion but to express what they thought college students believed.

Procedure

This study was conducted at Río Piedras, the largest campus of the University of Puerto Rico. Students were recruited at different sites on campus and near dormitories. They were approached by another student working as a research assistant and invited to participate in a group discussion with other students of the same gender and approximately the same age. They were informed that they would discuss and share their opinions about their conceptions of university students' gender roles and sexuality. They were informed that this was part of a research project to explore aspects related to the construction of gender roles and sexuality and that the information would be useful in the design of an intervention for the promotion of safer sex practices. If they showed interest, they were given a brief explanation of the objectives of the study and what would be expected of them in the focus groups.

To determine eligibility, the screening interview, which did not request their name, was administered to all candidates to determine their age, year of study, gender, sexual orientation, and sexual activity. Only undergraduates who met group criteria based on their sexual orientation and activity were eligible. They were informed that answers to questions, both during the screening and group process, would be anonymous and confidential.

All students who qualified were invited to participate in a conversation with other male students to share their views regarding gender roles, sexuality, relationships with partners, safer sex, and sexual negotiation. They were told that their general opinions would be discussed and that disclosure of personal/intimate information was not required. They were asked to provide only their first name or nickname during the discussion. They were also informed that group discussions would be audiotaped for later transcription and analysis and that their names would not be associated with their answers. They were given two copies of a consent form, one to be signed and returned to the cofacilitator and the other for their records. The facilitator read the consent form aloud to all groups and asked if there were any questions, after which they were told to sign and return one of the copies.

The facilitator was required to ask a set of compulsory questions in the four areas mentioned above, while other probing questions were optional depending on the lack of response from the group to specific topics in the discussion. Participants were paid ten dollars each for attending the group meeting, which lasted approximately two hours.

Analysis

Conversations in the groups were audiotaped and transcribed, and categories were developed for a content analysis. The following steps were followed: (1) A group consisting of three judges was organized and trained by the project's coordinator. (2) Each judge read and coded each group separately. (3) A meeting was conducted to discuss individual coding. Only those segments all three judges agreed on were included for analysis (Boyatzis 1998; Miller 2001). (4) We used NUD*ISTVivo (v1.3) qualitative software for the data analysis, and we selected those segments that illustrated each category or subcategory, while responding to our research questions. Our results include quotes that were selected during the coding process.

■ RESULTS

In this section, we present qualitative data regarding our categories. We include the frequency of categories that were mentioned more often, followed by quotes that are most illustrative of each one. Every quote will be identified according to the participants' group: G-1=heterosexual men who used condoms during sexual intercourse; G-2=heterosexual men who did not use condoms; G-3=heterosexual men who were not sexually active. However, we are not reporting group comparisons because we did not find differences between the groups. All quotes were translated by Dr. Pérez-Jiménez and Dr. Serrano-García because the group discussions were in Spanish.

Definition of Sexuality

In Table 10.1, we present five categories related to the definition of sexuality. A total of fifty quotes were coded within these categories. There is a fairly generalized belief that sexuality spans a number

Table 10.1. Frequency of Categories Related to the Definition of Sexuality

Category	Frequency	Percent
Sexual relations	17	34
Different sexualities	17	34
Emotions	7	14
Process	6	12
Satisfaction/pleasure	3	6
Total	50	100

of dimensions from sexual intercourse to emotions and interpersonal relations.

Most comments associated sexuality with sexual relations or sexual intercourse. Those students who lacked sexual experience (Group 3) perceive sexuality as directly linked to penetration. One participant in this group commented: "I perceive consummating a sexual act as intercourse. When there is, to be more specific, penetration" (G-3).

Other participants defined sexuality in a broader sense, not only as sexual intercourse. For these students sexuality also meant making love, sharing affection, and the need to love and be loved.

> It's like everything that leads to sexual behavior, not necessarily intercourse. Because it is not necessary for sexual activity. (G-3)

> Sexuality is a very general word which includes everything related to sexual relations or even everything having to do with sex. (G-2)

Many students identified different types of sexuality. Some students established a difference between "having sex"

and "making love." For them, having sex is limited exclusively to the sexual act, while making love involves the other partner's feelings. This type of sexuality is shared with a significant person, with whom a long-term relationship is established and/or is expected to last a lifetime. The goal of this type of relationship is not only physical pleasure; rather it includes the emotional and spiritual (love) dimensions as well. Others indicated that the emotional dimension also entails "sharing each other's needs for affection"(G-1). Other participants made similar comments:

> Regardless of what sexuality one engages in, one tries to satisfy the other person, one does it right. But when one has other feelings, that one is making love which is different to sex, then one really tries, and one doesn't care about oneself, one cares about the person and that she feels well. (G-1)

> It depends on the kind of sexual relationship, because if I'm going to have sex strictly for pleasure, I'm not going to worry about the other person. You understand? Of course I enjoy it, at least personally, I enjoy it, to see someone else enjoy it like I do. (G-1)

In other groups, some students commented:

> When one has a partner and feels more than desire, feels love, sex becomes love and that is feeling. When you do not feel anything, that is just "to come."(G-2)

Most guys have two kinds of girls, the ones that they want to fool around with on weekends and the ones with whom they would like to have a serious relationship. (G-3)

According to these students, men have sex with a person in a casual or temporary relationship with pleasure as their main objective. There is no affective involvement whatsoever, and he does not care if the other person is satisfied or not but rather thinks more about his own sexual satisfaction.

In all groups, they also mentioned that sexuality has an emotional component. For these men, sexuality includes feelings toward oneself and the other person.

Among the other categories, participants mentioned that sexuality is a process in which physical and emotional changes occur.

Sexuality is also related to physiological changes; we were children and now are adults, there are physiological changes. (G-1)

Maybe it has something to do with maturity in the couple's relationship. You are involved in a relationship in which changes have to occur, or you have to please your partner as much as possible, so you can, in some way, stay together so that the feeling in the relationship does not go away. (G-1)

Finally, even though sexuality is still linked to the search for pleasure, this category was mentioned on only three occasions.

In summary, for these students sexuality is a natural human expression and it is directly related to sexual relations, specifically sexual intercourse. They distinguished between two different sexualities, one related to "making love" and one to just "having sex." They identified an emotional component in sexuality. Finally, there were some who believe that sexuality is directly related to the search for pleasure.

Conceptions of Male Gender Roles

In Table 10.2, we present the categories related to the definition of gender roles. A total of six categories were created.

Roles Imposed by Society

As can be seen in Table 10.2, most comments defined gender roles as those rules imposed by society to distinguish men from women:

That is [. . .] the position men and women should assume in society, I think, society makes us assume it. (G-2)

Table 10.2. Frequency of Categories Related to the Definitions of Gender Roles

Category	Frequency	Percent
Roles imposed by society	41	60.3
Behavior of men	12	17.7
Mental and physical capacity of men	10	14.7
Styles of communication	3	4.4
Attitudes toward problems	2	2.9
Total	68	100

What society says each gender should do. (G-3)

Participants in all groups were asked to mention some of the more consolidated and sanctioned male gender roles in Puerto Rican culture (See Table 10.3). All participants reported that society dictates norms from birth about how they should act and even about the way they should think. For example, referring to economic issues, they indicated that society sets norms such as:

Men should work and women should stay home. (G-2)

In relationships, men are supposed to work and earn more money than women. If this does not happen, men tend to think less of themselves. (G-2)

Participants also mentioned a number of socially accepted behaviors that men manifest. One of these behaviors has to do with a double standard regarding the expression of sexuality. One student stated:

If I have sex with ten women I am a superman, a macho man; people praise me. If a woman does the same thing, she's considered a whore. (G-2)

They also argued that men have other responsibilities including initiating the sexual relationship and condom use.

In society many [men] have to start everything. Sometimes, for example, if you like a woman and she likes you, you still have take the initiative; but not always, not always, because some women take the offensive. (G-3)

Men wear it, have it, carry condoms and wear them, men have to protect [. . .](G-2)

Other students commented that men's preference for virgins and women's preference of experienced men are also gender issues.

Table 10.3.   Male Gender Roles Identified by the Participants

Male Gender Roles	
Men bring home the food.	Men should not be as sentimental as women.
Men should be as masculine as possible.	Men come to a halt and think; they don't sit down and start crying.
Men should always fight, but women should not.	Men are more in control.
Men don't cry.	In relationships, men are supposed to work and earn more money than women.
Men should exercise control.	Men have to carry or bring the condoms.
In general, men are dominant.	Being a man means fucking around more and having many women.

It's almost certain that a guy is going to prefer a virgin over a girl who has had various relationships. However, girls always tend to look for a guy that everyone refers to as a supermacho, who has been with every girl that he could get his hands on. (G-2)

Another student shared his experience in terms of the double standard that exists when men's and women's behaviors are evaluated.

I had a girlfriend. And if you decide to go out with the guys on a Friday night instead of going to her house it's okay, but if she does it means that she's looking for another guy. Girls can't go out with their girlfriends because it's viewed as though they are playing the field or are "easy" just because they go out. (G-2)

Overall, participants revealed a negative conception of behaviors that men and women must follow. Some presented alternative or emerging roles. Some examples are:

Men should be allowed to be as sentimental as women. (G-2)

Being a man means to respect women and have only one. (G-3)

In addition, some students criticized the role that women supposedly assume in perpetuating male roles and transmitting certain stereotyped gender roles. One student commented:

We are not in a male chauvinistic society that women are trying to change, but rather

in one that women foster and maintain. It's really rare that you go out with a girl who picks you up, opens and closes the door for you. It is unheard of, for a girl to get up to offer you her seat. (G-1)

Behavior of Men

This category is defined as relating to those behavior characteristics that differentiate men from women. In other words, how men are supposed to behave. Participants related these behavior characteristics to the way men and women dress, communicate and to their attitudes toward situations or problems.

Clothes, communication, and attitudes. To behave like a man is like I don't spend all my type speaking softly like women because this or that. That is not manly behavior. That is effeminate behavior. (G-1)

Mental and Physical Capacity of Men

Other participants commented that the difference between men and women is in their mental capacity and their physical appearance. Regarding their mental capacity some participants believe that women are more mature emotionally and intellectually. In terms of their physical capacity, one participant commented:

This issue of physical capacity I can also interpret it as the women who carries her role is supposed to be delicate, even if she is 6′ tall and this big always, because she tries to look more delicate, and the man tries to look more like the stereotype, stronger. (G-1)

Communication Styles and Attitudes Toward Problems

Some participants commented that men and women have different communication styles and that their attitudes toward problems are also different.

> Men talk a lot of shit, really, pardoning the expression [. . .] what's bad about us is that we're all like this, we do something with a woman, and always someone else will know, what you did, and they'll say it and the women's reputation will be lost. (G-2)

> The attitudes about problems [. . .] if you have a problem, are you going to cry like a woman? Women usually start to cry [. . .] (G-1)

> I'm not saying they all do that, I'm not generalizing, but men stop and think they don't sit down and start crying. (G-1)

Institutions That Influence Our Notions About Sexuality

All participants agreed that gender roles are imposed by society through a series of institutions and in particular contexts. The institution most frequently mentioned with a frequency of thirty-six (36.7%) was the mass media, followed by the family with eighteen (18.4%), and friends and religion with thirteen (13.3%) each (See Table 10.4). The educational system, society overall, and culture were less frequently mentioned.

Mass Media

Most students attacked the mass media, particularly television, for exploiting

Table 10.4. Frequency of Categories of Institutions That Influence Our Notions About Sexuality

Category	Frequency	Percent
Mass media	26	35.6
Family	13	17.8
Friends	12	16.4
Religion	8	11
Education system	6	8.2
Society	5	7
Culture	3	4
Total	73	100

women's bodies as sexual objects, as well as marketing campaigns that use women's bodies to sell products.

> On TV, always, the hero is desired by all women, she ends up with all of them. One wants to be like him, more macho, one does not want to be the studious guy in the library; one wants to be playing around, one says, I want to be like him. (G-2)

> What do they present to sell a product or to host a program? A woman! And, what are they emphasizing about the woman . . . . They don't present them pretty, as a mother; they present a fine-looking woman with a great body. They use deceitful messages. (G-1)

In addition, participants also condemned the mass media for using women "to create the need" to have sex.

> They are always creating a need for sex, sex, sex. And of course, those who do not know what sex is, want to find out. (G-1)

What they are after is the exploitation of that need by bombarding us. It is clear that the need [for sex] exists, but with marketing they aim to exploit it as an addiction. (G-1)

One participant commented that different notions of sexuality and gender roles are transmitted in an unconscious way.

It's like they're talking to you in different ways, to your conscious and unconscious self, so the image of sexuality is always latent or active in some way every day. (G-1)

Family
Participants stated that the above-mentioned institution exercises diverse levels of influence at different moments in their development. For example, all agreed that the primary influence regarding the roles men should assume comes from the family, since they are born and raised in it. Referring to this process one student stated:

It starts with your parents. They put you in front of a television and you start to see advertisements. Then it's your grandparents. When you go to school you have friends. When you start to go into the streets there is another influence. But it starts in the family, then other elements are involved and they transform the vision that you first had. (G-3)

Strong criticism was raised about the indoctrination they received from their families, since it consisted of imposing prohibitions on things that "should not be done." One student stated:

Parents start telling you early on not to touch yourself there. They start nagging about that. (G-3)

Friends
Some students said that friends' influence was most important on their construction of sexuality.

Friends talk to you about sex, even before the family. (G-2)

On the street, you find out about everything, on the street. Then, maybe, when one makes a mistake your family explains things or tells you not to do this; when they see you are on the move. (G-2)

Another student commented that peer pressure is stronger at the university.

You get there a virgin, and you didn't know it was necessary until you get to college and you see everyone [. . .] Then one is motivated to experiment what one hears others are doing. And if you feel someone they say "boy, you have to do it, you have to do it because if you don't [. . .]" (G-3)

Religion
Students also criticized religious doctrine, which they perceived as classifying sexuality as bad, as a taboo that should not be spoken of.

The church as an institution profoundly influences the way that we think and the concepts that we have about sexuality. It's an entity that forces many taboos on us, and it exerts a lot of influence on us at times when we make decisions. (G-2)

According to students, not only does the church influence the ways they interpret sexuality, but it also exerts influence on the sexual practices they engage in.

In church they always tell you that you can't do this and you can't do that; they only give you abstinence as an alternative. But they aren't living in the real world, which is out there and ongoing, and you have to protect yourself somehow. (G-2)

Educational System

According to some of the students, the educational system also plays an important role in transmitting values regarding the expression of sexuality.

In school, they also tell you these are things you can't do more like they don't exist. They try to ignore them, and then when one is older and gets to college, they say "blind men who have never seen, go crazy when they do." (G-2)

One gets here [to college] and sees something totally different, because you don't have the same teachers, or the church. (G-2)

At least, in school there is this taboo that everything is politics. You know

how, in school curricula they foster not talking, because if you do you're promoting sex, you know you're promoting promiscuity. (G-2)

Finally, some students mentioned that society and culture, in general, also play a fundamental role in transmitting values regarding the expression of sexuality.

Institutions That Influence Our Notions About Gender Roles

There are some institutions that not only exert influence on the construction of sexuality, but on the construction of gender roles as well. As in the case of sexuality, the institution most mentioned was the mass media, followed by religion ($n = 4$) and family ($n = 2$). Other institutions were only mentioned once (See Table 10.5).

Mass Media

Participants also believe that the mass media, particularly television, exert a strong influence on the construction of gender roles. One student commented

Table 10.5. Frequency of Categories of Institutions That Influence Our Notions About Gender Roles

Category	Frequency	Percent
Mass media	10	50
Religion	4	20
Family	2	10
Other	4	20
Total	20	100

that television advertisements assume and promote an image of men as strong.

> For those ads with those chicks, "brother" they have to assume that men are strong, that he has a woman, that he's going to get her [. . .] he likes women, he likes sex, and he has to assume that attitude to make those ads, because if they didn't think men were that way, those ads would not exist today. (G-1)

In another group one student commented that *machismo* is transmitted and promoted through television.

> TV promotes machismo a lot. TV, as a mass media, well it presents a film at seven pm when all the children are awake, then the kids come and see that film which promotes gender roles where women are never heroes, you know, women are after men. In the movies, women do not have lead roles where they kill everybody. Women always follow men, you know. Like, ah, women always get the men in trouble too. (G-2)

Religion

Religion was another of the institutions frequently mentioned by students as transmitting moral values about how a man should behave. Some students criticized religion and the Bible for conveying "limited ideologies" by defining God as a man and presenting woman as inferior.

> The Bible; women must obey men. God is a man. God is all-powerful; he is a man. (G-2)

They present God as a man, but for me God is energy without sex or gender. (G-2)

Family

From students' anecdotes, we can assume that gender roles are taught through a process in which social institutions, such as the family, play a fundamental role. The family transmits values that dictate rules of behavior that men and women should follow.

> I always found it amusing that when you visit relatives, there is always an uncle who asks you, "How many girlfriends do you have?" And when you're a kid you say, "I have three girlfriends!" But girls can't have boyfriends. And if they have more than one, they are labeled as whores. It's a very male chauvinistic culture. (G-3)

One student pointed out that one way in which the family inculcates values concerning gender roles has to do with the toys they allow their children to play with.

> In your family [. . .] well, boys can't play with dolls, boys play with cars, and [. . .] girls play with dolls, boys [. . .] with boys, and girls with girls. (G-2)

In summary, these results support the conception of gender roles as those behaviors and ways of thinking that differentiate men from women. To these participants the expression of male sexuality is determined by a process of social interaction with certain social institutions such as mass media, friends, religion, the family, and the educational system. These institutions exert different influences during certain periods of time in the process of human growth and development.

■ DISCUSSION

Our goal in performing this research was to explore contextual variables that influence the construction of male gender roles and sexuality and to evaluate their potential impact on men's risky sexual behaviors. Before we examine contextual variables, however, we must look at the construction of gender roles and sexuality that these participants verbalized.

Our participants still strongly link sexual relationships to penetration. This confirms statements regarding the value of penetration within Latin American culture (Ramírez 1993). It is particularly interesting that men without sexual experiences verbalized this link more frequently. Broadening the definition of sexual experience seems to be linked to practice.

When participants presented a broader definition of sexuality they incorporated emotions and feelings. This was related to the kind of relationship they were engaged in. Sexuality with feeling was linked to stable relationships or those with a long-term future commitment. Sexuality without emotion was strictly linked to pleasure with disregard for the other person. Thus, although participants reject the strict binomial of

sex = penetration, they do maintain a double standard of sexuality which is implicit in the dominant double standard of fidelity. In their conception, if one separates emotion from sexuality one can have casual relationships without violating the validity of the primary relationship. This supports the social construction that men can have multiple partners while women must remain faithful (Campbell 1995; Courtenay 2000a; Mane and Aggleton 2001; UNAIDS 2000).

Regarding gender roles, these men are strongly aware of differences that should exist between men and women. They clearly identify that men are supposed to be in control (dominant, aggressive), that they should not be sentimental, that they carry the burden of economic providers, that they should have many sexual partners, and that they dress and communicate differently. However, the view that these differences are natural or biologically based is absent from their discourse. They strongly believe that these are socially constructed behaviors imposed by different institutions.

This leads us then to the contextual variables they identify as most powerful. The central importance of the mass media was somewhat surprising in a cultural context where the value of family and religion are so frequently stressed (Arismendi and Serrano-García 1997). This emphasis could be the result of two converging factors. On the one hand, although the dominant view of masculinity is very clear in participants' minds evidencing the continued and powerful impact of traditional messages transmitted in the family, church, and schools, it could be argued that the family and the church are not as central in our everyday lives anymore since changes in our socioeconomic conditions have fostered early institutional child care, new roles for women, and a hurried life where going to church is not as important. In terms of church-going itself, results from other studies with university populations show that although students still consider religion important they attend mass and other rituals sparingly (Serrano-García, Torres-Burgos, and Galarza 2001).

The other factors that can explain the importance of mass media arise when we examine participants' responses. Most of the messages they identify with family, school, and church are prohibitions, things one must not do. These messages are transmitted early on thus making them quite pervasive. On the other hand, the mass media is viewed as fostering or promoting behaviors. Images of sex, female voluptuousness, and strong and promiscuous men are presented, urging viewers to be like them or practice similar behaviors. Although participants expressed disagreement with the objectification of women and the "superman" images that are transmitted, overall this mode of socialization fosters exploration, freedom, and the tabooless expression of sexuality. Friends, although less frequently mentioned as influential, serve the same purpose as the mass media. They facilitate communication regarding topics that are usually silenced in family settings and, particularly in college, they provide peer pressure to engage in sexual experiences.

Some of the constructions we have emphasized as well as the contextual factors that influence them have been identified previously as leading to risky sexual behaviors. These include inequitable relations between the genders where men are seen as always having to be in control (Anderson and Umberson 2001), the importance of multiple partners (Mendez, Hulsey, and Archer 2001–02; Remez 2000), the double standards of sexuality and fidelity (Alexander and Fisher 2003; Barash and Lipton 2001; Crawford and Popp 2003; Haavio-Mannila and Kontula 2003), and for youth, the centrality of peer pressure (Donenberg et al. 2003). However, participants' awareness of the social nature of these roles can lead to seeking alternatives that lead to improved relationships between the genders and to safer sexual behaviors. Although sparingly, they mentioned a couple of norms that they would change: allowing men to be sentimental and fostering fidelity to one partner. Conceiving gender and sexuality roles as an imposition can promote an awareness that leads to developing new, nontraditional roles.

This creates an opportunity and a challenge for those of us who wish to foster greater equality between the genders, a broader construction of masculinity and engagement in safe and healthy behaviors. Our results point to various potential interventions. If we know of the importance of the mass media for youth, then this medium should also be used to deconstruct harmful notions and educate about healthier options regarding the expression of sexuality, and more equitable and diverse gender roles. We know that soap operas are already being used as media to carry HIV prevention messages and other venues have been used to carry antismoking or antiviolence campaigns, thus exemplifying what we could do in this realm (Andreasen and Social Marketing Institute 2000; U.S. Department of Health and Human Services 1992).

We also need to focus on the family, church, and school settings which were identified as influential. Interventions directed at changing dominant values and the way in which these are presented could be extremely useful. It would be particularly interesting to explore efforts which integrate the various social domains in which youth interact (e.g., family and friends, child care centers and family).

In conclusion, we believe that although traditional views of masculinity are "alive and well," the socializing institutions in our society are generating contradictory messages that allow youth to grasp the social nature of gender constructions and to challenge them. This also challenges those of us committed to an agenda of changing values, norms, and behaviors about sexuality and gender roles to transcend individual levels of intervention, focusing instead on the mass media, family, friends, the church, and the settings where their influences interact.

REFERENCES

Abreu, J. M. 2000. Ethnic belonging and traditional masculinity ideology among African Americans, European Americans, and Latinos. *Psychology of Men and Masculinity* 1(2): 75–86.

Alexander, M. G., and T. D. Fisher. 2003. Truth and consequences: Using the bogus pipeline to examine sex differences in self-reported sexuality. *Journal of Sex Research* 40(1): 27–35.

Anderson, K. L., and D. Umberson. 2001. Gendering violence: Masculinity and power in men's accounts of domestic violence. *Gender and Society* 15(3): 358–380.

Andreasen, A. R., and Social Marketing Institute. 2000. Interjectors transfer of marketing knowledge. *Handbook of marketing and society*. http://www.socialmarketing.org/papers/intersectorstransfer.html (accessed October 9, 2002).

Arismendi, K., and I. Serrano-García. 1997. *La relación entre la construcción de género y la sexualidad que imparte la doctrina católica y la incidencia de violencia doméstica en un grupo de mujeres puertorriqueñas*. Honor's Thesis for the McNair Program, University of Puerto Rico, Río Piedras Campus.

Barash, D. P., and J. E. Lipton. 2001. *The myth of monogamy: Fidelity and infidelity in animals and people*. New York, NY.: W.H. Freeman/Times Books/Henry Holt and Co.

Beal, C. R. 1994. *Boys and girls: The development of gender roles*. New York, NY: McGraw-Hill.

Biever, J. L., C. de las Fuentes, L. Cashion, and C. Franklin. 1998. The social construction of gender: A comparison of feminist and postmodern approaches. *Counseling Psychology Quarterly* 11(2): 163–179.

Billy, J. O. G., K. Tanfer, W. R. Grady, and D. H. Klepinger. 1993. The sexual behavior of men in the United States. *Family Planning Perspectives* 25(2): 52–60.

Boyatzis, R. E. 1998. *Transforming qualitative information: Thematic analysis and code development.* Thousand Oak, CA: Sage.

Campbell, C. A. 1995. Male gender roles and sexuality: Implications for women's AIDS risk and prevention. *Social Science and Medicine* 41(2): 197–210.

Carey, M. A. 1994. The group effect in focus groups: Planning, implementing, and interpreting focus groups research. In *Critical issues in qualitative research methods*, ed. J. M. Morse, 225–243. Thousand Oaks, CA: Sage.

Courtenay, W. H. 2000a. Behavioral factors associated with disease, injury, and death among men: Evidence and implications for prevention. *The Journal of Men's Studies* 9(1): 81–142.

Courtenay, W. H. 2000b. Constructions of masculinity and their influence on men's well-being: A theory of gender and health. *Social Science and Medicine* 50(10): 1385–1401.

Courtenay, W. H. 2000c. Engendering health: A social constructionist examination of men's health beliefs and behaviors. *Psychology of Men and Masculinity* 1(1): 4–15.

Crawford, M., and D. Popp. 2003. Sexual double standards: A review and methodological critique of two decades of research. *Journal of Sex Research* 40(1): 13–26.

Díaz, R. M. 1998. *Latino gay men and HIV: Culture, sexuality, and risk behavior.* New York, NY: Routledge.

Donenberg, G. R., F. B. Bryant, E. Emerson, H. W. Wilson, and K. E. Pasch. 2003. Tracing the roots of early sexual debut among adolescents in psychiatric care. *Journal of the American Academy of Child and Adolescent Psychiatry* 42(5): 594–608.

Eisler, R. M. 1995. The relationship between masculine gender role stress and men's health risk: The validation of a construct. In *A new psychology of men*, ed. R. F. Levant and W. S. Pollack, 207–225. New York: Basic Books Inc.

Francoeur, R. T., M. Cornog, T. Perper, and N. A. Scherzer. 1995. *The complete dictionary of sexology.* New York: The Continuum Publishing Company.

Gale, S. R. 2000. A phenomenological analysis of masculinity ideologies among college males. *Dissertation Abstracts International* 60 (10-B): 5250.

Glenn, E. N. 1999. The social construction and institutionalization of gender and race. In *Revisioning gender*, ed. M. M. Ferree, J. Lorber, and B. B. Hess, 3–43. Thousand Oaks, CA: Sage.

Golombok, S., and R. Fivush. 1994. *Gender development.* New York, NY: Cambridge University Press.

Haavio-Mannila, E., and O. Kontula. 2003. Single and double sexual standards in Finland, Estonia, and St. Petersburg. *Journal of Sex Research* 40(1): 36–49,

Helgeson, V. S. 1995. Masculinity, men's roles, and coronary heart disease. In *Men's health and illness*, ed. D. Sabo and D. F. Gordon, 68–104. Thousand Oaks, CA: Sage.

Howard, J. A., and J. Hollander. 1997. *Gender situations, gender selves.* Thousand Oaks, CA: Sage.

Jiménez-Muñoz, G. M. 1994. Arráncame la vida!: Masculinidad, poder y los obstáculos al sexo seguro. *Centro* VI(1 and 2): 129–135.

Kimmel, M. S., and M. P. Levine. 1992. Men and AIDS. In *Men's lives*, ed. M. S. Kimmel and M. A. Messner, 318–329. New York: Macmillan Publishing Company.

Kimmel, M. S., and M. A. Messner. 1992. Introduction. In *Men's lives*, ed. M. S. Kimmel and M. A. Messner, 1–11. New York: Macmillan Publishing Company.

Levant, R. F. 1995. Toward the reconstruction of masculinity. In *A new psychology of men*, ed. R. F. Levant and W. S. Pollack, 229–251. New York: Basic Books.

Levant, R. F. 1996. The new psychology of men. *Professional Psychology: Research and Practice* 27(3): 259–265.

Levant, R. F., A. Cuthbert, K. Richmond, A. Sellers, A. Matveev, O. Mitina, et al. 2003. Masculinity ideology among Russian and U.S. young men and women and its relationship to unhealthy lifestyle habits among young Russian men. *Psychology of Men and Masculinity* 4(1): 26–36.

Levant, R. F., and G. Kopecky. 1995. *Masculinity reconstructed: Changing the rules of manhood at work, in relationships, and in family life*. New York: Penguin Group.

Levant, R. F., and R. G. Majors. 1997. Masculinity ideology among African American and European American college women and men. *Journal of Gender, Culture, and Health* 2(1): 33–43.

Levant, R. F., R. G. Majors, and M. L. Kelley. 1998. Masculinity ideology among young African American and European American women and men in different regions of the United States. *Cultural Diversity and Mental Health* 4(3): 227–236.

Levant, R. F., and W. S. Pollack. 1995. Introduction. In *A new psychology of men*, ed. R. F. Levant and W. S. Pollack, 1–8. New York: Basic Books.

Lorber, J. 1997. *Gender and the social construction of illness*. Thousand Oaks, CA: Sage.

Mane, P., and P. Aggleton. 2001. Gender and HIV/AIDS: What do men have to do with it? *Current Sociology* 49(6): 23–37.

Méndez, R. V., T. L. Hulsey, and R. L. Archer. 2001–02. Multiple partners in the age of AIDS: Self consciousness theory and HIV risk behavior. *Current Psychology: Developmental, Learning, Personality, Social* 20(4): 349–62.

Miller, R. L. 2001. Innovation in HIV prevention: Organizational and intervention characteristics affecting program adoption. *American Journal of Community Psychology* 29(4): 621–47.

Morgan, D. L. 1997. *Focus groups as qualitative research*. Thousand Oaks, CA: Sage.

Pleck, J. H., F. L. Sonenstein, and L. C. Ku. 1993. Masculinity ideology: Its impact on adolescent males' heterosexual relationships. *Journal of Social Issues* 49(3): 11–29.

Pleck, J. H., F. L. Sonenstein, and L. C. Ku. 1994. Problem behaviors and masculinity ideology in adolescent males. In *Adolescent problem behaviors: Issues and research*, ed. R. D. Ketterlinus and M. E. Lamb, 165–86. Hillsdale, NJ: Lawrence Erlbaum Associates.

Ramírez, R. L. 1993. *Dime capitán: Reflexiones sobre la masculinidad* Río Piedras, Puerto Rico: Ediciones Huracán, Inc.

Ramírez, R. L., V. I. García-Toro, M. L. Vélez-Galván, and I. Cunningham. 2002.

Masculine identity and sexuality: A study of Puerto Rican blue-collar workers. In *Caribbean masculinities: Working papers*, ed. R. L. Ramírez, V. I. García-Toro, and I. Cunningham, 83–103. San Juan, PR: HIV/AIDS Research and Education Center.

Remez, L. 2000. Range of risky behaviors is tied to risk of multiple partners among teenagers. *Family Planning Perspectives* 32(2): 100–101.

Serrano-García, I., N. Torres-Burgos, and M. Galarza. 2001. Power relations and the prevention of HIV/AIDS: A research intervention with Puerto Rican women. [In Spanish]. In *Models of community psychology for the promotion of health and the prevention of illness in the Americas*, ed. F. Bálcazar, M. Montero and J. R. Newbrough, 111–24. Washington, DC: PAHO.

Stewart, D. W., and P. N. Shamdasani. 1998. Focus group research: Exploratory and discovery. In *Handbook of applied social research methods*, ed. L. Bickman and D. J. Rog, 505–26. Thousand Oaks, CA: Sage.

Stillion, J. M. 1995. Premature death among males. In *Men's health and illness*, ed. D. Sabo and D. F. Gordon, 46–67. Thousand Oaks, CA: Sage.

The Panos Institute. 1999. *AIDS and men: Taking risks or taking responsibility?* London, UK: The Panos Institute and Zed Books.

Torres, J. B., S. H. Solberg, and A. H. Carlstrom. 2002. The myth of sameness among Latino men and their machismo. *American Journal of Orthopsychiatry* 72(2): 163–81.

UNAIDS. 2000. *Men and AIDS—A gender approach*. Geneva, Switzerland: Joint United Nations Programme on HIV/AIDS.

U.S. Department of Health and Human Services in Office of Communications of the National Cancer Institute. 1992. Making health communication programs work: A planner's guide. http://oc.nci.nih.gov/services/HCPW/HOME.HTM (accessed October 6, 2002).

Waldron, I. 1995. Contributions of changing gender differences in behavior and social roles to changing gender differences in mortality. In *Men's health and illness*, ed. D. Sabo and D. F. Gordon, 22–45. Thousand Oaks, CA: Sage.

Young, P. A. 1996. A transgenerational study of sex role norms and development in adult men. *Dissertation Abstracts International* 56(11-B): 6413.

CHAPTER 11

Pornography, Sexual Socialization, and Satisfaction Among Young Men

Aleksandar Štulhofer, Vesna Buško, and Ivan Landripet

The use of pornography in Western culture has been controversial. Since the 1880s, sexually explicit materials (SEM) have been deemed not just morally problematic, but dangerous due to the medical and social hazards its consumption allegedly entails (Abramson & Pinkerton, 1995). While in the 19th century these concerns focused primarily on individual health hazards (the disease model of masturbation), in the second half of the 20th century the emphasis shifted to social harms, ranging from objectification and degradation of women to encouragement of sexual violence (Dines, Jensen, & Russo, 1998; McKee, 2005; Russell, 1997). The research agenda formed around these concerns is known as the standard social science model of studying pornography (Malamuth, 2001).

According to the standard model, exposure to SEM can affect both attitudes and behaviors (Allen, D'Alessio, & Brezgel, 1995; Allen, Emmers, Grebhardt, & Griery, 1995; Barwick, 2003; Davis & Bauserman, 1993; Fisher & Grenier, 1994; Malamuth, Addison, & Koss, 2000). So far, social research in this area has focused on social harms, analyzing potential effects of SEM consumption on the acceptance of rape myths, prevalence and intensity of sexist attitudes, sexual callousness, proclivity to sexual offenses, as well as micro- and macro-dynamics of sexual violence. Although no consensus has been reached over whether SEM cause any of these social problems, this standard approach still carries substantial political weight, especially in the U.S.

Only recently have new suggestions regarding the direction of research on SEM been introduced, arguing for the need to understand the production of sexual meanings, displays, and performative norms in contemporary SEM (Attwood, 2002; Hardy, 2004; Zillmann, 2000).

To a large extent, these claims reflect the new reality of a "pornified" world (Paul, 2005), the one that came into existence through the digital revolution and the Internet (Cooper, McLoughlin, & Campbell, 2000; Binik, 2001; Fisher & Barak, 2001). Available, affordable, and anonymous pornography (especially cyberpornography) has become a part of contemporary lifestyles (Cooper & Griffin-Shelley, 2002; Paul, 2005; Traen, Sorheim Nilsen, & Stigum, 2006). This normalization and mainstreaming of SEM is evident not only at the micro-level, in the ease with which young people talk about pornography and the role it plays in their lives, but also in contemporary art and popular culture (McNair, 2002). Pornography has become an integral part of the contemporary Western culture of permissiveness (Scott, 1998).

Paradoxically, an accelerated rise in the SEM supply and the related increase in SEM exposure among young people—mostly voluntary, but sometimes also involuntary (Flood, 2007; Rideout, 2001; Wolak, Mitchell, & Finkelhor, 2007)—has not been met by adequate scholarly response. According to Zillmann (2000), "next to nothing is known about the consequences of the steadily increasing amount of such exposure" (p. 41). Moreover, recent calls for a more active role of social research focused primarily on presumed harms (Manning, 2006; Paul, 2005), especially when discussing exposure to SEM among young people (Flood, 2007; Thornburgh & Lin, 2002; Ybarra & Mitchell, 2005; Zillmann, 2000). Although a number

of correlation-based studies of young people's SEM use has been recently published (Hald, 2006; Lam & Chan, 2007; Stella, Mazzuco, & Dalla Zuanna, 2004; Ven-Hwei & Ran, 2005; Wallmyr & Welin, 2006; Wolak et al., 2007; Ybarra & Mitchell, 2005), clear understanding of the ways SEM consumption contributes to contemporary construction of adolescent sexuality is still largely missing.

Two possible directions for future research have been recently proposed: a "reconceptualization of harm from exposure to erotica" (Zillmann, 2000, p. 42) that would focus on detrimental relationship-related effects of SEM, and a more broad and sex-positive approach to the myriad of ways SEM can affect the totality of young people's sexuality (Attwood, 2005). To contribute to this emerging new research agenda, we present a model of the effects of early exposure to SEM on sexual satisfaction, based on the sexual scripting theory (Gagnon & Simon, 1973).

■ BEYOND THE STANDARD SOCIAL SCIENCE MODEL: SEXUALLY EXPLICIT MATERIALS, SEXUAL SOCIALIZATION, AND SATISFACTION

The questions that initiated and steered our study were straightforward: does SEM use contribute—and if so, how—to the construction of young people's "internalized working models of . . . sexuality" (Hardy, 2004, p. 16) and, consequently, their sexual satisfaction? We were particularly interested in the interaction between SEM, related fantasies, and real-life experiences, which include partners' desires and demands, as well as the influence of peer readings of pornography. In contrast to the dominant emphasis on social harms, we decided to focus on possible links between SEM use and sexual satisfaction. Apart from a well-known experimental study published in the 1980s, which found that participants of both sexes reported diminished sexual happiness and satisfaction with partner's appearance, sexual curiosity, and sexual performance after being exposed to non-violent SEM during six 1-h weekly sessions (Zillmann & Bryant, 1988), quantitative research studies of the relationship between SEM consumption and sexual satisfaction are sparse. One other study, not available in English, that surveyed habitual SEM users, members of a U.S.-based association of porn enthusiasts, found no effects of SEM on participants' sexual satisfaction (Štulhofer, Matkovic, & Elias, 2004).

When examining the potential impact of SEM exposure among young people, an operative theory of sexual socialization seems necessary. Originally conceived as a social learning approach to human sexuality and never intended to be a comprehensive theory, the sexual scripting perspective has been widely accepted as the social constructionist framework for exploring the process of social organization of sexuality (Frith & Kitzinger, 2001; Simon &

Gagnon, 2003). The scripting approach has also been used in the context of SEM use, but as yet only qualitatively (Attwood, 2002; Hardy, 2004).

According to Gagnon and Simon (1973), the process of sexual socialization occurs through a combination of three sources of influence: intrapersonal, interpersonal, and environmental or sociocultural. Their impact is organized through the formation of sexual scripts, which are specific cognitive schemata or personalized systems for defining sexual reality (Frith & Kitzinger, 2001; Simon & Gagnon, 1986). This everyday heuristic, like cognitive shortcuts, enables and guides sexual decision-making.

Although it could appear that there are as many operational sexual scripts as there are people, the scripting theory views sexuality as social conduct partially determined by historical traditions, culture, and societal norms (Gagnon, 1990; Gagnon & Simon, 1973; Irvine, 2003; Lenton & Bryan, 2005; Simon & Gagnon, 2003). The theory allows for variations and innovations in sexual scripting, but postulates, nonetheless, that only a limited number of scripts are commonly pursued within a certain (sub)culture (Simon & Gagnon, 1999).

In theory, SEM exposure can affect the scripting process via several interrelated routes. Explicit imagery and symbolic normative order presented in SEM may influence one's scripting of their sexual role, as well as cognitive and affective shaping of the perception of partners' sexual role and expectations. The scripting of what constitutes good or "successful" sex may also be influenced by SEM. In such a case, the criteria for evaluation of sexual performance are provided by the way SEM depicts sexual exchange and concomitant pleasure. SEM may also contribute to the scripting of sexiness and cognitive mapping of one's own body. Finally, as argued by many critics of pornography (Dines et al., 1998; McKee, 2005), SEM consumption might affect young people's conceptualization of the linkage among emotions, intimacy, and sexuality, and strengthen power inequality within sexual relationship.

Theoretically expected mediated effects of SEM on sexual satisfaction are schematically presented in Figure 11.1. The model stipulates the role of early SEM exposure in the process of intrapersonal sexual scripting that affects sexual and relationship experiences, which, in turn, shape sexual satisfaction. The choice of sexual satisfaction as the outcome variable was governed by two reasons. In contrast to the usual emphasis on possible risks of SEM use, our intention was to focus on young people's sexual well-being and reframe the discussion about SEM in sex-positive terms. In addition, the satisfaction issue is of substantial (and reinforcing) importance for the process of sexual scripting. Although little is known about the life-course dynamics of

intrapersonal sexual scripts, successful sex therapeutic interventions, based on cognitive restructuring techniques, seem to suggest that the process of sexual scripting may never be finished (Hawton, 1986).

Although not presented in the proposed model, a bidirectional association between sexual scripting and real-life experience should be briefly mentioned. Sexual scripts guide sexual reactions and behaviors (Simon, 1996), but they are also affected by the reality they helped to create. Sexual reality provides material—sexual triumphs and traumas, emotional investments and exchanges, communication and shared meanings—for re-writing intrapersonal sexual scripts. Another fact is the impact of sexual and relationship experiences (through, for example, partner's objection to SEM or their insistence on using pornography for initiating sex) and sexual (dis)satisfaction on the continuity of SEM use. In the latter case, increase in SEM use could be the consequence of sexual frustration and sexual marginality, in which case it would serve as a substitute for real-life sexual activities. Since our model focused on early SEM exposure, these issues were not further explored.

The main purpose of this study was to explore possible links between early SEM exposure and sexual satisfaction.

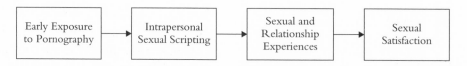

Figure 11.1.   A Theoretical Model of Sexual Socialization Affected by the Early Exposure to SEM.

Two hypotheses were proposed based on the outlined model.

Firstly, effects of early SEM exposure on sexual satisfaction—positive, negative or combined—would be mediated by sexual scripting. In regard to positive effects, our analyses focused on educational benefits or the informational effect of SEM, which was expected to result in a more varied sex life. As for the possible negative effects, we measured relationship intimacy to assess the level of emotional involvement. The indicator of intimacy served as a proxy for sexual callousness (absence of intimacy), which was suggested to increase with SEM use (Manning, 2006; Paul, 2005; Zillmann, 2000). The second hypothesis postulated that SEM genre or a type of pornography used would moderate the impact of early exposure to SEM on sexual satisfaction. It was expected that negative effects would be more likely observed among men with paraphilic SEM preferences.

In the first article from this research project, we reported on mediated effects of SEM use on sexual satisfaction among young women and men (Štulhofer et al., 2007). SEM genre was not included in the analyses. Since negative effects were observed only among young men, in this study we focus exclusively on male participants.

■ METHOD

Participants

An on-line study on SEM use and sexual behavior was recently carried out among young adults in Croatia (Štulhofer et al., 2007). In November 2006, a generic e-mail message was sent to college students' mailing lists at several Croatian universities and a number of electronic forums. It contained a brief explanation of the study, the link to an on-line questionnaire, and a request which asked the recipient to forward the message to their friends and acquaintances of a certain age (18–25).

From November 14 until December 7, 6,443 individuals visited the site. Of those, 4,605 started the questionnaire (71% response rate) and 3,136 completed the task (49% completion rate). After excluding participants of ineligible age (under 18 and over 25), those who did not provide information about their age or sex, those whose answers contained over 10% of missing values, and those who reported not using pornography at any of the three time points assessed (at the age of 14, at the age of 17, and in the last 12 months), the sample was reduced to 2,092. In this chapter, we focused exclusively on men who used pornography at all three-time points and reported the experience of sexual intercourse (n = 650).

The questionnaire application was based on Microsoft ASP.NET version 2 technology. Raw data were recorded as a flat text file, which was later preprocessed into Microsoft Excel compatible format. To ensure anonymity, neither IP address recording nor permanent cookies were used. Only a session cookie, lasting for 20 min from the last access, was used to identify a user session.

The questionnaire consisted of 244 items—including sociodemographic indicators, experience with SEM, attitudes toward SEM, sexual experience, and sex attitudes—and required up to 40 min to complete. The first and lengthier version of the questionnaire was pre-tested on 277 college students to assess reliability and validity of composite variables. The second, shortened version was pre-tested again for comprehensibility and time requirements on a dozen students.

The study was approved by the Ethical Review Board for the Protection of Human Subjects at the Faculty of Humanities and Social Sciences, University of Zagreb.

Measures

The *Sexual Scripts Overlap Scale* (SSOS), a new tool for measuring the linkage between SEM and sexual scripting, was developed by asking two groups of college students (76 young women and men) to make inventories of things/activities/sensations that are (1) important for pornographic depiction of sex and (2) personally important for great sex. The two inventories, the porn script inventory and the "great sex" inventory, were then merged. (If an item was mentioned only once in either list and was judged irrelevant by all members of the research team, it was removed from the final inventory.) In total, the list included 42 items (the complete list of items is provided in the Appendix).

In the first part of the questionnaire, participants were asked to assess the importance of the listed items for "great sex" using a 5-point scale (ranging from 1 = "not important at all" to 5 = "exceptionally important"). At the end of the questionnaire, participants were asked to assess the inventory again, but this time they were asked about each item's importance "for pornographic presentation of sex." The SSOS scores were computed on the paired (the great sex vs. the porn) items by subtracting the second from the first. If, for example, the item "cuddling after sex" was judged as "somewhat important" (3) for good sex life and "completely unimportant" (1) for pornographic presentation of sex, the pair was scored 2. Participant's SSOS score was additive, representing the sum of scores for all 42 pairs of items. Although factor analysis suggested the existence of several subdimensions of the instrument (sexual performance and activity, emotions and communication, physical appearance, bodily features, and power aspects), internal consistency of the total scores proved to be rather high (Cronbach's $\alpha = .91$). The results ranged from 0 to 143 and were normally distributed. The SSOS scores were then reverse recoded, so that higher scores indicated greater overlap between the great sex and the porn script; the mean score was 79 (SD = 21). Keeping in mind that early SEM exposure precedes first sexual experiences, it seems reasonable to assume that higher SSOS scores reflected a stronger influence of pornography on one's personal sexual script.

Early exposure to SEM was measured by one 5-point (1 = every day,

5 = never) indicator assessing frequency of SEM use at the age of 14. The answers were recoded so that higher scores denoted more exposure. The indicator was significantly correlated with the average number of hours per week that participants spent using SEM at the time of the survey (r = .22, p < .001).

Varied Sexual Experience Scale was composed of 11 dichotomous items (yes/no) that measured the range of participant's sexual experience. A variety of sexual activities were assessed, including oral and anal sex, same-sex sex, group sex, role playing, bondage and dominance, sadomasochistic role playing, sex with stranger, and sex in a public place. Affirmative answers were coded 1 and negative (no experience) 0; the higher the score, the more varied or extensive personal sexual experience.

The degree of intimacy in current relationship—or, if currently not in a relationship, in the most recent one—was assessed by five items based on the Miller Social Intimacy Scale (Miller & Lefcourt, 1982). The items measured the degree to which one feels close to a partner, readiness to help the partner when he/she has problems or feels low, the need to open up emotionally to one's partner, to share highly personal information, and to spend time together. Responses were given on a 5-point scale (1 = almost never to 5 = almost always) with higher composite scores denoting higher levels of intimacy. The scale scores computed in the study sample proved to have acceptable internal consistency (Cronbach's α = .79).

Satisfaction with one's sexual life was measured by the modified Snell's Index of Sexual Satisfaction (Snell, Fisher, & Walters, 1993). The original instrument was reduced from five to three Likert-type items to include satisfaction with the way in which one's sexual needs are being met, the degree in which one feels sexually fulfilled, and the appraisal of whether something is presently missing in one's sexual life. The scale ranged from 3 to 15, higher scores indicating higher level of sexual satisfaction, with a mean score of 9.88 (SD = 3.46). Cronbach's α for the scale was .92. Sexual satisfaction was also assessed by a single item indicator ("All things considered, how satisfied are you with your sexual life at present?") with a 7-point scale (1 = fully satisfied to 7 = extremely dissatisfied). The correlation between the sexual satisfaction scale and the single-item indicator was strong (r_s = .77, p < .001).

Sexual boredom was assessed by a brief version of the 18-item Sexual Boredom Scale (Watt & Ewing, 1996). Ten items that loaded highly on the two dimensions of the scale (Sexual Monotony and Sexual Sensation factors) were included in the initial version of the questionnaire used in this study. After pre-test, the scale was further reduced to five items. Responses were recorded on a 5-point scale (from 1 = completely disagree to 5 = completely agree); larger scores reflected being more easily and rapidly bored with sexual routine. Internal consistency of this shortened scale was satisfactory (Cronbach's α = .88).

Myths about Sexuality Scale was comprised of eight 5-point items (1 = completely disagree to 5 = completely agree) that measured agreement with common myths about sexuality, such as "Men are always ready for sex," "In order to be successful, sexual intercourse has to end with orgasm," or "Good sex can save even the worst relationship." Most of the items were clinically encountered sexual myths reported and discussed in a well-known sex therapy manual (Hawton, 1986). Cronbach's α for the scale was .70. The larger the score, the stronger acceptance of sexual myths.

Sexual compulsiveness was assessed with Kalichman's Sexual Compulsiveness Scale (Kalichman & Rompa, 1995), composed of 10 items asking about participant's experience of sexually compulsive behaviors and thoughts, such as: "My desires to have sex have disrupted my daily life," "I sometimes fail to meet my commitments and responsibilities because of my sexual behaviors." All items were anchored on a 5-point scale ranging from "not at all like me" to "exactly like me."1 The scale was found to have satisfactory reliability (α = .87).

Mainstream vs. paraphilic SEM genre dichotomy was based on four dichotomous questions regarding preferred sexually explicit contents ("In the last 12 months, which of the following pornographic genres did you use most often?/Multiple answers are possible./"). The four listed genres were: S & M and B & D, fetishism, bestiality, and violent/coercive sexual activities. Participants who reported preference for one or more of the four types were defined as users of paraphilic SEM. Participants who stated that none of the four genres described their preferred content were coded as mainstream SEM users.

■ RESULTS

As shown in Table 11.1, no significant differences in sociodemographic characteristics were found between mainstream (n = 445) and paraphilic SEM users (n = 205). The majority of participants in both groups were living in a metropolitan setting, had parents with above average education, and reported being in steady relationship. Of the three measures of sexual activity, significant differences were found for two: users of paraphilic SEM reported significantly higher masturbation frequency (χ_2 = 6.82, df = 2, p < .05) and a higher number of lifetime sexual partners (χ_2 = 9.75, df = 3, p < .05).

Next, we compared the patterns of SEM exposure in the two groups (Table 11.2). Median age at first exposure to SEM was 10 years in both groups. As expected, cyberpornography was the most popular form of SEM. Over two thirds of all participants reported the Internet as their primary source of SEM. Significant between-group differences were found in the frequency of SEM use at the age of 14 and the average amount of time spent on SEM. In comparison to mainstream users, paraphilic SEM users were exposed to SEM more often at the age of 14 (χ_2 = 11.69, df = 3,

Table 11.1. Sociodemographic and Sociosexual Characteristics of the Sample by Type of Sexually Explicit Material (SEM) Used

Variables	Users of Mainstream SEM ($n = 445$)		Users of Paraphilic SEM ($n = 205$)		All ($n = 650$)	
	N	%	N	%	N	%
Age						
18–21	170	38.2	92	44.9	262	40.3
22–25	275	61.8	113	55.1	388	57.9
Parents' education						
Both parents without college education	180	40.5	81	39.7	261	40.3
One parent with college education	126	28.4	58	28.4	184	28.4
Both parents with college education	138	31.1	65	31.9	203	31.3
Place of residence at the age of 14						
Metropolitan setting	267	60.1	125	61.0	392	60.4
City	102	23.0	45	22.0	147	22.7
Town	50	11.3	21	10.2	71	10.9
Village	25	5.6	14	6.8	39	6.0
Currently in a relationship						
Yes	279	63.0	128	63.1	407	63.0
No	164	37.0	75	36.9	239	37.0
Sexual partners						
Exclusively of the other sex	365	82.8	154	75.1	519	80.0
Mostly of the other sex	7	1.6	10	4.9	17	2.6
Of both sexes	6	1.4	6	2.9	12	1.8
Mostly of the same sex	8	1.8	4	2.0	12	1.8
Exclusively of the same sex	58	13.1	31	15.1	89	13.7
Lifetime number of sexual partners						
1	119	26.9	37	18.3	156	24.2
2–3	133	30.0	60	29.7	193	29.9
4–7	125	28.2	58	28.7	183	28.4
≥ 8	66	14.9	47	23.3	113	17.5
Frequency of masturbation						
Few times a month or less	67	15.1	16	7.8	83	12.8
Once a week	82	18.4	38	18.5	120	18.5
Few times a week or more	296	66.5	151	73.7	447	68.8

Table 11.2. Differences in SEM Consumption and Patterns of Use Between Users of Mainstream and Paraphilic Contents

	Users of Mainstream SEM		Users of Paraphilic SEM		All	
	N	%	N	%	N	%
Age at first exposure to SEM						
≤11	270	60.8	135	66.2	405	62.5
12	98	22.1	36	17.6	134	20.7
13	46	10.4	25	12.3	71	11.0
≥14	30	6.8	8	3.9	38	5.9
SEM exposure at 14						
Once a month of less	89	20.0	30	14.6	119	18.3
Several times a month	149	33.5	54	26.3	203	31.2
Several times a week	162	36.4	85	41.5	247	38.0
Daily	45	10.1	36	17.6	81	12.5
Main source of SEM						
Internet	307	69.0	153	74.6	460	70.8
VCR, CD and DVD	99	22.2	40	19.5	139	21.4
Cable/satellite TV	22	4.9	9	4.4	31	4.8
Other	17	3.8	3	1.5	20	3.1
Average SEM consumption per week (h)						
0	16	3.6	2	1.0	18	2.8
1	221	50.1	60	29.3	281	43.5
2	83	18.8	53	25.9	136	21.1
3 or more	121	27.4	90	43.9	211	32.7
Frequency of SEM used as an overture to having sex (last 12 months)						
Never	286	64.6	115	56.1	401	61.9
Rarely	102	23.0	59	28.8	161	24.8
Sometimes	46	10.4	23	11.2	69	10.6
Often to always	9	2.0	8	3.9	17	2.6

$p < .01$). Also, at the time of the survey, they consumed pornography more extensively: 44% reported using it three or more hours per week ($\chi_2 = 32.90$, $df = 4$, $p < .001$).

In order to assess adequacy of the main stream vs. paraphilic SEM users distinction, statistical significance of group differences on a number of indicators theoretically associated with SEM genre

Table 11.3. Differences in Sexual Scripts Overlap, Sexual Boredom, Acceptance of Sexual Myths, Viewing Sex as Emotional Experience, and Sexual Compulsiveness Between Users of Mainstream and Paraphilic SEM

	Mainstream SEM Users		Paraphilic SEM Users		Cohen's d
	M	SD	M	SD	
SSOS	77.25	21.33	83.42	21.14	−.29
Sexual boredom	9.45	3.71	11.17	4.10	−.44
Myths about sexuality	20.57	4.48	21.90	5.13	−.28
Sexual compulsiveness	23.41	6.57	25.53	7.65	−.30

preferences was tested. The two groups differed significantly on all four composite indicators (Table 11.3). The paraphilic SEM user group was characterized by a greater overlap between the porn and the "great sex" script (t = −3.13, df = 534, p < .01), a higher level of sexual boredom (t = −3.75, df = 641, p < .001), greater acceptance of sexual myths (t = −3.17, df = 638, p < .01), and higher average score on the sexual compulsiveness scale (t = −3.60, df = 634, p < .001). Effect size calculations pointed to small to medium magnitude of the observed differences (Cohen, 1988).

Our theoretical model assumed an indirect effect of early SEM exposure on sexual satisfaction (Figure 11.1). In addition, we hypothesized a moderating effect of SEM genre. The finding that exposure to SEM at the age of 14 was weakly, but significantly correlated with sexual satisfaction only among paraphilic SEM users (r = −.13, p < .05) substantiated those theoretical expectations. To examine the nature of relationships among the measures of pornography-related sexual socialization, experiences, intimacy, and sexual satisfaction, we performed structural equation modeling using LISREL 8.7 statistical package (Joreskog & Sorbom, 1996). The initial structural model was specified following theoretical expectations and previous findings on gender-moderated relations among the stated constructs (Štulhofer et al., 2007). The analyses were based on covariance matrices of SEM exposure, sex scripts overlap, sexual experiences, relationship intimacy, and sexual satisfaction observables that served as indicators of the five latent variables included in the model. Maximum Likelihood was used as an estimation method. It was hypothesized that the pattern, that is, the strength of the examined relationships, may be different depending on the type of SEM used. Therefore, hypothetical structural models were tested by two-group multi-sample analyses. This approach was used to allow for the direct test of the hypothesized moderating role of the SEM contents.

The two multi-group analyses included the same set of observed and latent variables, as well as the paths to be estimated among them. In the first analysis, it was assumed that all sets of model parameters were invariant over groups (Model 1). Since the same model was set to account for the observed covariances within each group, the pattern of relationships among the studied constructs was not expected to vary with the content of pornographic materials used. In other words, the proof of this model would speak in favor of the null hypothesis stating that there are no moderating effects of SEM type. The second analysis included a less constrained model where the values of structural parameters were allowed to vary between the groups (Model 2). This model assumed a different structure of relationships among the examined constructs between the two groups, pointing to the moderating role of pornographic genre. As the two models were nested, a direct comparison of their fit to the data was possible.

The main results of the analyses of fit regarding the tested structural models are given in Table 11.4; the obtained solutions for the two groups are presented in Figure 11.2a, b.

Reasonably acceptable goodness-of-fit measures were obtained for both models. However, the less constrained Model 2 with freed structural parameters over the groups showed significantly better fit to

the data ($\Delta \chi_2 = 24.47$, $\Delta df = 6$, $p < .001$; Table 11.4) and was used to calculate path and other estimates.

Although somewhat different in absolute values, path coefficients obtained in both groups pointed to the importance of varied sexual experience and relationship intimacy for sexual satisfaction (Figure 11.2a, b). Interestingly, the findings suggested that intimacy might be more important for sexual satisfaction among young men than the range of sexual experience. In both groups, intimacy was significantly predicted by sexual scripting. The lesser the overlap between the porn and the "great sex" script, the greater the intimacy achieved.

The main differences in the parameter estimates obtained for the two groups pertained to the role of early SEM exposure, that is, to the pattern of paths between the exposure, sexual scripting, varied sexual experience, and intimacy. Our results clearly support the hypothesized moderating role of SEM genre preferences on the nature and extent of the effects of early SEM exposure on sexual satisfaction among young men. Early SEM exposure was found to be directly and indirectly associated with the range of sexual experience, but only among paraphilic SEM users. Mediated

Table 11.4. Main Goodness-of-Fit Statistics: Multi-Sample Analyses of the Hypothesized Impact of SEM-Affected Sexual Socialization on Sexual Satisfaction Among the Groups of Mainstream and Paraphilic SEM Users

Model	x^2	df	p	RMSEA	x^2/df	Δx^2	Δdf	p	CFI	GFI
1	46.30	28	.016	.051	1.65				.96	.98/.95
2	29.58	22	.318	.022	1.34	16.72	6	<.001	1	.99/.97

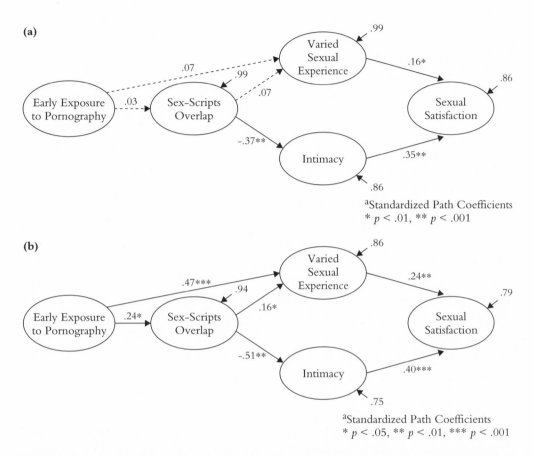

Figure 11.2. Path Diagram of the Hypothesized Impact of SEM-Affected Sexual Socialization on Sexual Satisfaction Among Users of (a) Mainstream Contents (n = 334) and (b) Paraphilic Contents (n = 165).

effect of early SEM exposure on relationship intimacy was also confirmed only in this group.

The hypothesis about mediated impact of pornography on sexual satisfaction was confirmed only in the paraphilic SEM user group. Although both positive and negative effects of SEM were observed, the model parameters obtained for this group suggested that early exposure to SEM may affect later sexual satisfaction primarily by suppressing

intimacy. Since the mediated effects of early SEM exposure were confirmed only in the group of paraphilic SEM users, comparing the strength of the paths between sexual scripting, intimacy, and sexual satisfaction between the two groups can provide some insight into the magnitude of SEM effects. Negative effect of SEM exposure on relationship intimacy appeared small. Although significant, it did not greatly improve our understanding of the determinants of relationship intimacy among men. This conclusion was supported by the lack of significant difference in the average levels of relationship intimacy and sexual satisfaction reported by the two groups of participants.

■ DISCUSSION

In an earlier study, we found both positive and negative mediated effects of SEM on sexual satisfaction, but only among young men (Štulhofer et al., 2007). While the observed positive effects were associated with the range of sexual experiences, the negative effects were related to relationship intimacy. No direct effects of either SEM exposure or sexual scripting on sexual satisfaction were observed in the sample of 915 women and 565 men aged 18–25.

Focusing exclusively on men, the present study extended the previous analyses by introducing the effect of SEM genre and focusing on early SEM exposure. To assess possible influence of SEM use on sexual scripting, we used an original measure of the overlap between the "great sex" and the porn script. Instead of asking participants directly about the effect SEM has on their attitudes toward sex and sexual behavior, as recently done by Hald and Malamuth (2008), we aimed to develop an approach less affected by social desirability. Distinguishing between the preferential use of mainstream and paraphilic SEM, we explored the assumption that the effects of early SEM exposure would not only

be mediated by sexual scripting, but also moderated by a type of preferred SEM.

The finding that paraphilic SEM genre influenced the relationship between other latent variables in our model is hardly surprising. It seems reasonable that the nature of sexually explicit imagery—especially if the exposure preceded first sexual experiences—would have some impact on young people's conceptualization of sex and sexual expectations. SEM can serve as a normative system that provides clues about what sex "really is" and "what it should feel like." Our retrospective study suggested that the interaction between early exposure to SEM and paraphilic SEM preferences should be further explored. The role and mechanism of sexual scripting (associated with early exposure) in the development of paraphilic preferences remain unclear. Is it a vandalized love map (Money, 1986), certain personal characteristics—as suggested by the confluence model (Bogaert, 2001; Malamuth et al., 2000; Malamuth & Huppin, 2005)—or the effect of excitatory habituation that predisposes one to search for nonstandard SEM (Zillmann, 2000)? All three explanatory models could account for the higher frequency of SEM use at 14 among participants in the paraphilic SEM user group, but the cross-sectional nature of our study precludes their testing.

If the confluence model fits the reality, the lack of systematic knowledge of the etiology of paraphilias taken into account, great caution should be exercised when interpreting the finding regarding the effect of paraphilic SEM use on intimacy and sexual satisfaction. It could well be that suppression of intimacy is the consequence of one's native (or consolidated) love map and not of one's exposure to paraphilic SEM. In other words, a specific intrapersonal sexual script might be the cause of interest in specific (paraphilic) SEM and suppression of intimacy. The role of early exposure to SEM in this process remains to be explored.

The concept of sexual scripts overlap proved useful for understanding sexual satisfaction among male SEM users. Regardless of the type of SEM consumed, sexual scripting was found to affect sexual satisfaction through relationship intimacy. A noteworthy finding was that intimacy proved an important ingredient of overall sexual satisfaction among young men. As reported in our previous article, relationship intimacy was an equally strong predictor of male and female sexual satisfaction (Štulhofer et al., 2007). Leaving aside popular stereotypes about gender-specific emotional and sexual needs that are occasionally reinvigorated by "pop" psychology (Potts, 1998), the role of intimacy in male sexual satisfaction points to an interesting question. What are the factors that determine the overlap between the pornographic and the "great sex" script? In addition to SEM consumption and the fact that SEM are based, at least partially, on real sexual experiences and sensations, could it be that some of the overlap between the pornographic and the "great sex" script should be attributed to the contemporary culture of sexual explicitness and self-exposure (McNair, 2002)? The porno-chic trend, which, according to McNair (2002), describes the growing representation of pornography in popular art and culture, seems to point that direction. If so, sexual self-centeredness, defined as problematic for developing or sustaining intimate sexual relationships, could be a by-product of a culture of hyper-individualism (Bauman, 2003; Štulhofer & Miladinov, 2004) rather than the result of much maligned exposure to pornography.

Limitations

Several study limitations should be noted. Our sample was not probabilistic, which makes it impossible to assess how well (or how poorly) it represents the surveyed age group. It should be assumed that the data collection procedure was substantially biased by self-selection, most probably resulting in over-representation of sexually permissive individuals (Wiederman, 1999). This is supported by the fact that parents' education in our sample was well above national average. In addition, although we attempted to minimize the problem by limiting participants' age to 25, it is likely that recall bias was introduced when asking about the early exposure to SEM.

Although the results of structural equation modeling presented in this chapter provided support for our theoretical model, the cross-sectional nature of our study cannot rule out possible existence of other structural models (of different interpretative power) that would fit the data equally well. The study design clearly precludes causal inferences.

Finally, we focused on individual and not couple sexual satisfaction. As highlighted by a recent finding of only a moderate correlation between heterosexual partners' satisfaction (McNulty & Fisher, 2007), our research strategy left unexplored the possibility that exposure to SEM may have a different effect on user's sexual satisfaction in comparison to their partner's.

Conclusion

As our study suggested, there may be important links between early SEM exposure, sexual socialization, and sexual satisfaction—particularly among men with specific SEM preferences. Overall, the observed mediated effects of SEM exposure on sexual satisfaction were either small, as in the case of suppression of intimacy, or marginal, as in the case of the educational effect expressed in a more varied sexual experience. Nevertheless, the importance of comprehensive sex education that would address the issue of contemporary pornography should not be disregarded. Inclusion of contents designed to improve media literacy among young people and help them to critically evaluate pornographic images, as well as the fantasies and fears they produce, could be invaluable to advancing young people's sexual well-being. Neither moralistic accusations, nor uncritical glorification of contemporary pornography can do the job.

Appendix. List of Items Included in the Sexual Scripts Overlap Scale

The "Great Sex" Inventory	The "Porn" Inventory Items (When Different from the "Great Sex" Inventory)
How important for great sex do you personally find:	How important for pornographic depiction of sex do you find:
1 = not at all; 2 = somewhat; 3 = moderately; 4 = a great deal; 5 = exceptionally	
I am always ready for sex	Men are always ready for sex[a]
My partner is always ready to have sex	Women are always ready for sex
Sex that includes a variety of sexual acts	
Free experimenting	
No forbidden activities, no taboos	
It is easy to initiate sex	
Sex is possible in any situation	
Long foreplay	
Threesome (ménage à trois)	
Enacting sexual fantasies	
Long lasting sex	

Oral sex

Anal sex

Use of protection

Partner's sexual pleasure

Romance

Emotions, love

Intimate communication

After-sex cuddling and tenderness

Sex presumes relationship

Tender sex

Partner has a great body   Actors/actresses have great bodies

Partner is beautiful   Actors/actresses are beautiful

Partner is well endowed   Actors/actresses are well endowed

Shaven genital area

Sex that occasionally involves humiliation

Sex that occasionally includes coercion

Ejaculation on partner's face or body

Penetration

Use of sex toys

Sexual role playing

Being constantly horny   Men are constantly horny

Partner is constantly horny   Women are constantly horny

Trust in partner

Commitment

Intense passion

Feeling safe and well-cared for

Spontaneity

Sexual variety

Imagination

Unselfishness

"Pumping" (fast, vigorous and deep
   penetration)

[a]If respondent was male, the item was paired with the first item on the "great sex" inventory list; if respondent was female, the item was paired with the second item on the "great sex" inventory list.

REFERENCES

Abramson, P. R., & Pinkerton, S. D. (1995). *With pleasure: Thoughts on the nature of human sexuality*. New York: Oxford University Press.

Allen, M., D'Alessio, D., & Brezgel, K. (1995). A meta-analysis summarizing the effects of pornography. II. Aggression after exposure. *Human Communication Research*, 22, 258–283.

Allen, M., Emmers, T., Gebhardt, L., & Giery, M. A. (1995). Exposure to pornography and acceptance of rape myths. *Journal of Communication*, 45, 5–26.

Attwood, F. (2002). Reading porn: The paradigm shift in pornography research, *Sexualities*, 5, 91–105.

Attwood, F. (2005). What do people do with porn? Qualitative research into the consumption, use and experience of pornography and other sexually explicit media. *Sexuality & Culture*, 9, 65–86.

Barwick, H. (2003). *A guide to the research into the effects of sexually explicit films and videos*. New Zealand Office of Film and Literature Classification. http://www.censorship.govt.nz/pdfword/research_document_2003.pdf. (Accessed 30 June 2007).

Bauman, Z. (2003). *Liquid love: On the frailty of human bonds*. Cambridge: Polity Press.

Binik, Y. M. (2001). Sexuality and the Internet: Lots of hyp(otheses)—only a little data. *Journal of Sex Research*, 38, 281–282.

Bogaert, A. F. (2001). Personality, individual differences, and preferences for the sexual media. *Archives of Sexual Behavior*, 30, 29–53.

Cohen, J. (1988). *Statistical power analysis for the behavioral sciences*. Hillsdale, NJ: Lawrence Erlbaum.

Cooper, A., & Griffin-Shelley, E. (2002). The Internet: The next sexual revolution. In A. Cooper (Ed.), *Sex and the Internet: A guidebook for clinicians* (pp. 1–15). New York: Brunner-Routledge.

Cooper, A., McLoughlin, I. P., & Campbell, K. M. (2000). Sexuality in cyberspace: Update for the 21st century. *CyberPsychology and Behavior*, 3, 521–536.

Davis, C. M., & Bauserman, R. (1993). Exposure to sexually explicit materials: An attitude change perspective. *Annual Review of Sex Research*, 4, 121–209.

Dines, G., Jensen, R., & Russo, A. (1998). *Pornography: The production and consumption of inequality*. New York: Routledge.

Fisher, W. A., & Barak, A. (2001). Internet pornography: A social psychological perspective on Internet sexuality. *Journal of Sex Research*, 38, 312–325.

Fisher, W. A., & Grenier, G. (1994). Violent pornography, antiwoman thoughts, and antiwoman acts: In search of reliable effects. *Journal of Sex Research*, 31, 23–38.

Flood, M. (2007). Exposure to pornography among youth in Australia. *Journal of Sociology*, 43, 45–60.

Frith, H., & Kitzinger, C. (2001). Reformulating sexual script theory: Developing a discursive psychology of sexual negotiation. *Theory & Psychology*, 11, 209–232.

Gagnon, J. H. (1990). The explicit and implicit use of the scripting perspective in sex research. *Annual Review of Sex Research*, 1, 1–41.

Gagnon, J. H., & Simon, W. (1973). *Sexual conduct.* Chicago: Aldine.

Hald, G. M. (2006). Gender differences in pornography consumption among young heterosexual Danish adults. *Archives of Sexual Behavior*, 35, 577–585.

Hald, G. M., & Malamuth, N. M. (2008). Self-perceived effects of pornography consumption. *Archives of Sexual Behavior*. doi: 10.1007/s10508–007–9212–1.

Hardy, S. (2004). Reading pornography. *Sex Education*, 4, 3–18.

Hawton, K. (1986). *Sex therapy: A practical guide.* Oxford: Oxford University Press.

Irvine, J. M. (2003) Introduction to "Sexual scripts: Origins, influences and changes". *Qualitative Sociology*, 26, 489–490.

Joreskog, K. G., & Sorbom, D. (1996). *LIS-REL 8: User's reference guide.* Chicago: Scientific Software International.

Kalichman, S. C., & Rompa, D. (1995). Sexual sensation seeking and sexual compulsivity scales: Reliability, validity, and predicting HIV risk behaviors. *Journal of Personality Assessment*, 65, 586–602.

Lam, C. B., & Chan, D. (2007). The use of cyberpornography by young men in Hong Kong: Some psychosocial correlates. *Archives of Sexual Behavior*, 36, 588–598.

Lenton, A. P., & Bryan, A. (2005). An affair to remember: The role of sexual scripts in perception of sexual intent. *Personal Relationships*, 12, 483–498.

Malamuth, N. M. (2001). Pornography. In J. Smelser & P. B. Baltes (Eds.), *International encyclopedia of social and behavioral sciences* (Vol. 17, pp. 11816–11821). Amsterdam: Elsevier.

Malamuth, N. M., Addison, T., & Koss, M. (2000). Pornography and sexual aggression: Are there reliable effects and can we understand them? *Annual Review of Sex Research*, 11, 26–95.

Malamuth, N. M., & Huppin, M. (2005). Pornography and teenagers: The importance of individual differences. *Adolescent Medicine Clinics*, 16, 315–326.

Manning, J. C. (2006). The impact of internet pornography on marriage and the family: A review of research. *Sexual Addiction and Compulsivity*, 13, 131–165.

McKee, A. (2005). The objectification of women in mainstream pornographic videos in Australia. *Journal of Sex Research*, 42, 277–290.

McNair, B. (2002). *Striptease culture: Sex, media, and the democratization of desire.* London: Routledge.

McNulty, J. K., & Fisher, T. K. (2007). Gender differences in response to sexual expectancies and changes in sexual frequency: A short term longitudinal study of sexual satisfaction in newly married couples. *Archives of Sexual Behavior.* doi:10.1007/s10508–007–9176–1.

Miller, R. S., & Lefcourt, H. M. (1982). The assessment of social intimacy. *Journal of Personality Assessment*, 46, 514–518.

Money, J. W. (1986) *Lovemaps: Clinical concepts of sexual/erotic health and pathology, paraphilia, and gender transposition in childhood, adolescence, and maturity.* New York: Irvington.

Paul, P. (2005). *Pornified: How pornography is transforming our lives, our relationships, and our families.* New York: Times Books.

Potts, A. (1998). The science/fiction of sex: John Gray's Mars and Venus in the bedroom. *Sexualities*, 1, 153–173.

Rideout, V. (2001). *Generation Rx.com: How young people use the Internet for health information*. Washington, DC: Kaiser Family Foundation. http://www.kff.org/entmedia/20011211a-index.cfm. [Accessed 3 June 2007].

Russell, D. E. H. (1997). Pornography causes harm to women. In M. R. Walsh (Ed.), *Women, men and gender: Ongoing debates* (pp. 158–169). New Haven, CT: Yale University Press.

Scott, J. (1998). Changing attitudes to sexual morality: A crossnational comparison. *Sociology*, 32, 815–845.

Simon, W. (1996). *Postmodern sexualities*. New York: Routledge.

Simon, W., & Gagnon, J. H. (1986). Sexual scripts: Performance and change. *Archives of Sexual Behavior*, 15, 97–120.

Simon, W., & Gagnon, J. H. (1999). Sexual scripts. In P. Aggleton & R. Parker (Eds.), *Culture, society and sexuality: A reader* (pp. 29–38). London: UCL Press.

Simon, W., & Gagnon, J. H. (2003). Sexual scripts: Origins, influences and changes. *Qualitative Sociology*, 26, 491–497.

Snell, W. E., Fisher, T. D., & Walters, A. S. (1993). The multidimensional sexuality questionnaire: An objective self-reported measure of psychological tendencies associated with human sexuality. *Annals of Sex Research*, 6, 27–55.

Stella, R., Mazzuco, S., & Dalla Zuanna, G. (2004). Pornography and sexual behaviour. In G. Dalla Zuanna & C. Crisafulli (Eds.), *Sexual behaviour of Italian students* (pp. 383–407). Messina, Italy: University of Messina.

Štulhofer, A., Landripet, I., Momcilovic, A., Matko, V., Kladaric, P. G., & Busko, V. (2007). Pornography and sexual satisfaction in young women, men: How to conceptualize and measure possible associations. In S. V. Knudsen, L. Lofgren-Martenson, & S. A. Mansson (Eds.), *Youth, gender and pornography* (pp. 66–84). Copenhagen: Danish University Press.

Štulhofer, A., Matkovic, T., & Elias, J. (2004). Pornografija i seksualno zadovoljstvo: Postoje liveze? [*Pornography and sexual satisfaction: Any associations?*]. Zbornik Pravnog fakulteta Sveuclista u Rijeci, 25, 707–720.

Štulhofer, A., & Miladinov, K. (2004) Kraj intimnosti? Suvremenost, globalizacija i intimne veze [The end of intimacy? Contemporaneity, globalization, and intimate relationships]. *Sociologija*, 46, 1–18.

Thornburgh, D., & Lin, H. S. (Eds.). (2002). *Youth, pornography, and the Internet*. Washington, DC: National Academy Press.

Traen, B., Sorheim Nilsen, T., & Stigum, H. (2006). Use of pornography in traditional media and on the Internet in Norway. *Journal of Sex Research*, 43, 245–254.

Ven-Hwei, L., & Ran, W. (2005). Exposure to Internet pornography and Taiwanese adolescents' sexual attitudes and behaviour. *Journal of Broadcasting and Electronic Media*, 49, 1–19.

Wallmyr, G., & Welin, C. (2006). Young people, pornography, and sexuality: Sources and attitudes. *Journal of School Nursing*, 22, 290–295.

Watt, J. D., & Ewing, J. E. (1996). Toward the development and validation of a measure of sexual boredom. *Journal of Sex Research*, 33, 57–66.

Wiederman, M. W. (1999). Volunteer bias in sexuality research using college student participants. *Journal of Sex Research*, 36, 59–66.

Wolak, J., Mitchell, K., & Finkelhor, D. (2007). Unwanted and wanted exposure to online pornography in a national sample of young Internet users. *Pediatrics*, 119, 247–257.

Ybarra, M. L., & Mitchell, K. J. (2005). Exposure to internet pornography among children and adolescents: A national survey. *CyberPsychology and Behavior*, 8, 473–486.

Zillmann, D. (2000). Influence of unrestrained access to erotica on adolescents' and young adults' dispositions toward sexuality. *Journal of Adolescent Health*, 27, 41–44.

Zillmann, D., & Bryant, J. (1988). Pornography's impact on sexual satisfaction. *Journal of Applied Social Psychology*, 18, 438–453.

Sexualities and Sexual Orientations

Implications for Educational Practice

S exualities, understandably, are difficult to talk about in public spaces. More-over, conversations about sex are likely to be controversial at public universities and religiously affiliated postsecondary institutions. However, the five chapters in Part Two suggest that college men could benefit from productive engagement in structured opportunities for dialogue about their sexual orientations, pre-college sex-ual socialization, and views of what constitutes healthy sexual relationships. This could occur, for example, through a programming series offered by the Office of Sorority and Fraternity affairs on campus. More often than not, fraternity members, like other male undergraduates, have sex, indulge in sexual joking and swapping stories with each other about sexual conquests with women, and watch pornography together. Thus, the advisor to the Interfraternity Council (IFC) could work with chapter lead-ers to provide space for men to think critically about their own assumptions and debate alternative viewpoints with peers. In many instances, these conversations al-ready occur within peer groups. However, without proper facilitation, hegemonic and sexist viewpoints are likely to go undisrupted. Similar programming models could be used to engage students who live in all-male residence halls, members of men's student organizations (i.e., Student African American Brotherhood at University of Texas and Men in Power at the University of Chicago), and those who play on men's sports teams.

In addition, professionals who work in first-year experience offices should consider thoughtful ways to integrate sex-related topics into new student orientation sessions. Not doing so erroneously presumes that students will not have sex or watch pornography, that someone has already helped them understand the wide range of sexualities, and that every new student recognizes the consequences of choices such as agreeing to be videotaped for *Guys Gone Wild*. Orientation seems like a logical space in which to engage women and men in important conversations about the various dimensions of sexual exploration that are likely to occur on campus. Beyond informing them of the availability of condoms in the student health center (which is undeniably important and something we advocate), it is also essential to empower students to be reflective about their own sexualities, as opposed to operating under the assumptions with which they entered the institution. This message will be liberating to gay, bisexual, and questioning students, while also enabling heterosexuals to achieve a healthy sense of assurance about their sexual identities. Challenging homophobia and heterosexism should be another aim of the orientation sessions. Like racial and religious diversity, new students should be meaningfully encouraged to at least respect peers with sexual orientations that are different from their own, even if they do not agree. Doing this would be an affirmative step toward enacting the espoused values concerning diversity and inclusiveness found in most college and university mission statements.

It is also necessary to disrupt homophobia in athletics. An August 2009 story in *ESPN: The Magazine* reported that slightly fewer than half of college football players surveyed knew a gay teammate. Ignoring the presence of these students only isolates them, complicates the negotiation of their identities (with self as well as teammates and coaches), and permits the perpetuation of homophobia in intercollegiate sports. Bringing a speaker (perhaps a former student-athlete who is gay), hosting a conversation series, or inviting someone from the Counseling Center to talk with members of sports teams are just some strategies that could be employed.

Also needed on most campuses is increased support for students with intersecting identities (i.e., Latino gay men). LGBT Center staff and others who offer programming and resources aimed at non-heterosexual students should endeavor to be more culturally inclusive. Given that these students are often struggling to multitask the multiple dimensions of their identities (i.e., "Which I am first, gay or Native American?"), it is essential that they find a comfortable space in which to be gay and Native American at the same time without feeling pressure to compromise one for the other. Only offering programs that are supposed to appeal widely to "gay students" is likely to be interpreted as "White gay students" by racial and ethnic minorities. In this same way, culture centers and multicultural affairs offices that sponsor initiatives for students of color need to ensure that topics and content are inclusive of LGBT students and do not reinforce heterosexism.

Lastly, those who interact with gay and bisexual men or work with LGBT student organizations should challenge those students to better align their ongoing quests for equity and inclusiveness with a personal commitment to eradicating the marginalization of other oppressed groups. For example, a White gay male student who desires social justice for himself should be encouraged to critically examine his own treatment of racial minorities and avoid acting in racist ways. Likewise, advisors to predominantly gay fraternities should challenge members to collaborate with campus organizations for women to co-sponsor activities aimed at eliminating sexism and heterosexism.

PART THREE

COLLEGE MEN BEHAVING BADLY: INTRODUCTION

Male misbehavior is a salient theme in the current discourse on college men and masculinities. Therefore, we found it imperative to focus an entire section of this book in full consideration of this phenomenon. The relationships between male gender socialization and a host of beliefs and attitudes that lead to destructive behaviors have been well documented. Acts of violence, sexual assault, and sexual harassment on college campuses are overwhelmingly committed by men. In addition, when compared to women, college men are much more drawn to dangerous activities that threaten their safety and are more likely to abuse drugs and alcohol. The chapters in Part Three offer important insights about why destructive behaviors persist among college men. Specifically, the following questions regarding the nexus between misbehavior and masculinities on college campuses are addressed in these chapters: Why do college men have a greater tendency toward committing acts that are harmful to themselves and others? What do men gain from their participation in activities that violate campus policies and result in

217

judicial sanctions? What sociocultural factors, situated in college contexts, facilitate misbehavior among men?

In Chapter 12, Shaun R. Harper, Frank Harris III and K. C. Mmeje propose a conceptual model to explain why college men are overrepresented among students who are sanctioned for violations of campus behavioral policies. The model comprises six sociocultural constructs that have been linked to male misbehavior in college: pre-college socialization, male gender role conflict, the social construction of masculinities, developing competence and self-efficacy, context-bound gendered social norms, and environmental ethos and corresponding behaviors. Each of these factors, in isolation, offers insights for understanding why men misbehave on college campuses. However, misbehavior is further illuminated when each factor is viewed in relationship to the others. Harper and his colleagues theorize that because the model is comprehensive and captures multiple factors that lead to male misbehavior on college campuses, educators who use it to inform practice will be more effective in reducing incidents of unwanted behavior among college men. They also call for more campus programming and cross-departmental collaboration on gender issues that disproportionately impact college men.

In Chapter 13, Rocco L. Capraro explores what may be perhaps the most pervasive destructive behavior exhibited among men on college campuses, alcohol abuse. Although the use and abuse of alcohol among college men is a well-known and well-documented phenomenon, few published reports on this issue offer much more than statistical analyses of men's drinking behavior and how the consumption patterns of men and differ from those of women. Capraro situates masculinities at the center of his discussion of men's alcohol abuse and argues that men consume alcohol for two related, yet contradictory, reasons—to enact male power and privilege and to cope with feelings of powerlessness that emerge when men fall short of socially constructed expectations of expressing masculinities. What results from this study is a conceptual framework for seeing how alcohol abuse among men is the outcome of their experiences as gendered beings within the cultural context of campus life.

The influence of male peer groups on behavioral norms for men is considered in Chapter 14 by Robert A. Rhoads and Chapter 15 by Luoluo Hong. Both researchers share what they learned about how masculinities are performed on college campuses by observing men's interactions in all-male peer groups. Rhoads uses critical perspectives of culture and power to examine group dynamics and gendered interactions that are situated in college fraternities. Rhoads captured these interactions as a participant-observer during fraternity activities as well as through formal and informal interviews with key informants. Among Rhoads's key findings from this study was that because social status is an important form of capital among fraternities and is earned primarily through members' abilities to attract desirable women, fraternity cultures are oppressive environments for women. Rhoads offers numerous illustrative examples of sexual objectification and subordination of women in ways that served to affirm the masculinities of the chapter members.

It is interesting that Rhoads characterizes the chapter he observed as one of the most progressive fraternities at the institution, which makes his findings even more intriguing. The chapter was one of few on campus that had eliminated hazing from its pledge process. The chapter had also taken leadership on addressing several systemic issues that plagued fraternity cultures, including sexual assault and alcohol abuse. Nevertheless, despite its progressive stance on these issues, chapter members struggled with homophobia and sexism. The conflict Rhoads discovered between what the chapter publicly valued and their actual behavior underscores the pervasiveness of hegemonic masculinities and how deeply embedded they are within culture of college fraternities.

Whereas Rhoads discovered ways that men can influence each other to behave in undesirable ways, the behavioral norms in the male peer group that Hong observed were far more positive and productive. Hong observed men who were engaged in a peer-led education group whose goal was to eliminate men's violence on campus. Given its purpose, the group offered a context for men to deconstruct hegemonic masculinities thereby making their relationships to physical and sexual violence transparent. Recognizing this relationship motivated the participants to engage in action for social change on their campus through outreach and discussions with male peers on masculinities and campus violence. One of the most compelling implications that emerge from Hong's study is that, with appropriate intervention and ongoing support, conceptualizations of masculinities that lead to destructive behaviors can be challenged and renegotiated by men.

There are several common issues that are conveyed across the four chapters in Part Three. Each identifies men's gender socialization prior to college as an explanatory factor for why they are predisposed to destructive and sanctionable behaviors in college. For example, Harper et al. and Hong note that boys spend much of their social time as children and young adolescents engaged in games or activities that prioritize or reward toughness and physical aggression—behaviors that are regularly observed among men on college campuses. In addition, during the process of early childhood gender socialization, adults often passively accept misbehavior among boys or dismiss it as a natural part of growth and development. Given these and other similar practices in the gender socialization of boys, many men arrive to college campus having learned to view aggression, rule-breaking, and violence as appropriate ways to express masculinities or simply as what men are expected to do. This assumption is reinforced when men observe other men on campus violate campus policies and receive affirmation from male peers. In addition, rebellion is also viewed as a desirable characteristic among men. Therefore, the likelihood of being caught and sanctioned for violating campus policy may not be enough incentive to dissuade men from engaging in misbehavior. This is one of several reasons that destructive behaviors are often more prevalent among men than they are among women on college campuses.

Another shared assumption across the chapters in Part Three relates to the relationship between destructive behaviors and restricted emotionality among men. Through the aforementioned process of gender socialization, men learn that expressing fear, pain, vulnerability, empathy, and other emotions (aside from anger) is a violation of male gendered norms, which puts them at risk of having their status as men questioned and leaves few productive alternatives for men to express emotion. On college campuses most students at some point become overwhelmed by pressures relating to coursework, friendships, relationships, personal setbacks, and career decisions, to name a few. Thus, the need for men to express emotions beyond those that are socially constructed as masculine is not surprising. However, men who embrace narrow conceptualizations of masculinities may express their emotions through destructive behaviors or violence directed either towards property or other people.

Context-bound social norms and the impact on the expression of masculinities on college campuses are discussed in each of the four chapters. The authors argue that college men, especially those who spend a substantial amount of time engaged in male-dominated subgroups, work hard to ensure that their gendered behavior is aligned with the identity and values of the group. Consequently, some men suppress personal values that contradict group norms. Similarly, Rhoads stated that self-selection plays a role in that individuals seek membership in groups that share their personal values, which are in turn affirmed and reinforced within the group context. Regardless of how men find their way into all-male peer groups, the key point here is that their interpretation of group norms influence the strategies they will rely upon to perform gender in these settings. Men who interact frequently in groups that reward destructive behaviors will embrace them in order to protect their status and credibility within the group—even if they deem these behaviors undesirable.

CHAPTER 12

A Theoretical Model to Explain the Overrepresentation of College Men Among Campus Judicial Offenders

Implications for Campus Administrators

Shaun R. Harper, Frank Harris III, and
Kenechukwu (K. C.) Mmeje

In his classic text, *The American College and University,* historian Frederick Rudolph (1990) cites numerous incidences of student misconduct and discipline throughout the lifespan of higher education. For instance, he describes the introduction of a disciplinary sanction at Harvard in 1718, where "a bad boy was made to kneel at the feet of his tutor, who proceeded to smack him sharply on the ear" (p. 27). Reportedly, incivility and disruptions have long ensued on most campuses, especially those with residence halls. Physical brawls, food fights, property destruction, underage drinking, arson, stoning, and even stabbing were among the early examples of student misconduct. Most institutions responded by developing strict conduct codes

and articulating the consequences of inappropriate behavior. Over time, some institutions, including Harvard, relaxed their disciplinary codes and took a more developmental approach to sanctioning student offenders. In an address to the faculty, former Harvard President Jared Sparks (as cited in Rudolph, 1990) pleaded, "Oh gentlemen, let the boys alone" (p. 107). It is interesting to note that most of the offenses described throughout Rudolph's book were overwhelmingly committed by male students—a trend that still persists on most contemporary college and university campuses.

Limited theoretical insight has been offered into the reasons why college men violate rules and commit acts that lead to disciplinary consequences. Van Kuren

221

and Creamer (1989) noted that existing studies of student judicial issues were disproportionately focused on demographic and personality characteristics of offenders, not on the underlying causes of misbehavior. Dannells (1997) offers some characteristics of those who commit judicial offenses: "Most students who become involved in campus discipline difficulties are men, and most often they are younger, usually in their freshman and sophomore year" (p. 25). These male offenders, he notes, typically live on campus, are more likely to violate policies than are students who have positive feelings toward the institution, and are usually engaged in alcohol use or abuse at the time of the incident. Beyond this, little else is known about why college men engage in inappropriate acts, especially those that lead to judicial sanctions on their campuses. Moreover, the need for additional scholarship on the development and experiences of college men is consistently advocated throughout Kellom's (2004) *New Directions for Student Services* edited volume, *Developing Effective Programs and Services for College Men.*

In response to the call for additional inquiry on college men in general and judicial offenders in particular, a theoretical model that explains the disproportionate representation of male students in campus judicial processes is proposed in this chapter. Specifically, the impetus and underlying drivers of misbehavior, aggression, violence, and rule-breaking are explained. The model is based on a synthesis of existing literature and theories from sociology, psychology, men's studies, and education. Biological and heredity explanations for male misbehavior are not offered in this chapter, as the existing published research on masculinity almost exclusively considers these behaviors through a social constructivist lens. This perspective relates closely to the new psychology of men proposed by Levant (1996). "The new psychology of men views gender roles not as biological or even social givens, but as psychologically and socially constructed entities that bring certain advantages and disadvantages and, most importantly, can change" (p. 259). Social constructivism is later described in greater detail.

Following a detailed description of the theoretical model are practical implications for campus judicial affairs officers and student affairs administrators who are interested in minimizing violence and disruptive behaviors among college men. Before proceeding with the presentation of the theoretical model, it should be noted that not all behavioral expressions of masculinity are negative. Given that only a limited number of scholars have investigated positive aspects of masculinities (e.g., Harper, 2004; Mirande, 2004) and that this chapter focuses exclusively on judicial offenders, much of the literature and theoretical perspectives reviewed herein, appropriately by default, illuminate negative male behaviors.

■ PRESENTATION OF THE THEORETICAL MODEL

An interdisciplinary synthesis of existing literature and theories resulted in the identification of the following six variables that help explain male over-representation among campus judicial offenders: (1) precollege socialization, (2) male gender role conflict, (3) the social construction of masculinities, (4) the development of competence and self-efficacy, (5) context-bound gendered social norms, and (6) environmental ethos and corresponding behaviors. Each theoretical construct of the model in Figure 12.1, along with its specific relationship to misbehavior among college men, is described in this section; interactions among the six variables are discussed later in the chapter.

Precollege Socialization

The behaviors that men bring to college are often shaped by prior school experiences and home environments in which certain acts are deemed excusable and typical of boys. In many cases, parents, K–12 teachers, and school administrators socialize boys and girls differently by posing an uncommon set of rules, sanctions, and standards regarding acceptable behavior. These socialization experiences begin at birth. One classic example of this was found in Smith and Lloyd's (1978) study, which involved 32 mothers and a bald infant. When the baby was dressed as a girl, the mothers spoke to 'her' differently; handled 'her' more affectionately; and selected softer toys for 'her,' such as dolls. A few days later, the exact same bald baby was dressed as a boy, but the same women treated 'him' completely different. For example, they selected a toy hammer for 'him' to play with instead of a soft stuffed animal or doll. Oftentimes, the toys that parents select for boys promote ruggedness, toughness, and violence. In fact, Askew and Ross (1988) maintain:

> Girls are even encouraged to buy "My First Sink," and a "head" on which they

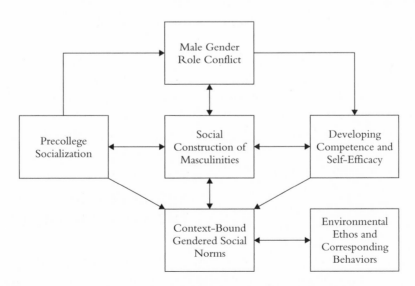

Figure 12.1. Theoretical Model of Misbehavior Among College Men.

can practice putting [on] make-up and putting in curlers. Boys, on the other hand, quite predictably are shown playing with games, cars, mechanical toys, or space monsters. Most of these are toys taken straight from violent cartoons. The main aim of playing with the toy is to battle it out with an opponent. (p. 7)

These toys and games, as well as the violent cartoons with which they are affiliated, are often infused with boys' definitions of self as they take on the characteristics of monsters, wrestlers, racecar drivers, and other physically active animated characters. These attributes are prominently displayed in their behaviors at home and in school, especially when other boys are present.

According to Gilbert and Gilbert (1998) and Head (1999), parents and teachers are more forgiving of behavioral problems among boys and accept the fact that "boys will be boys." Similarly, Harper (2004) asserts that parents "communicate messages of power, toughness, and competitiveness to their young sons. No father wants his son to grow up being a 'pussy,' 'sissy,' 'punk,' or 'softy'— terms commonly associated with boys and men who fail to live up to the traditional standards of masculinity" (p. 92). Gilbert and Gilbert also found that interests in combat, wrestling, and active play interferes with male students' abilities to concentrate in school and take their teachers (who are mostly female) seriously, which often results in classroom disruptions. Interestingly, boys are over four times more likely

than girls in K-12 schools to be referred to the principal's office for disciplinary infractions, suspended, or subjected to corporal punishment (Gregory, 1996; Skiba, Michael, Nardo, & Peterson, 2002). Despite this, boys are still socialized to believe that they are to be rough, tough, and rugged, even if it means getting into trouble at school (Mac an Ghaill, 1996).

College men who attended primary and secondary schools where male disruption and weak sanctions were the norm bring their prior socialization experiences to the postsecondary learning environment. Thus, some may presume that occasionally disobeying rules (without committing acts that are punishable in criminal court) is simply "what boys do" at school, and subsequently in college. Thus, some male undergraduates, to varying degrees, willingly disregard campus policies and risk being subjected to judicial sanctioning. Sudden freedom from parents and living on one's own only intensifies this problem.

Hong (2000) suggests there is a critical link between male students, socialization, and violence. College men bring aspects of prior socialization assumptions surrounding active play to the postsecondary setting. For example, they are more likely than their female counterparts to play with "toys" that are deemed unsafe and in violation of university policies. College men are more likely to be caught in possession of dangerous items (e.g., BB guns, firecrackers, paintball guns, knives) that violate university weapons policies. Despite knowing that these items constitute a policy violation and may result in severe sanctioning, some male undergraduates still choose to engage in play that involves their coveted toys. These toys, coupled with popular violent video games, enable male students to exert toughness, roughness, and perceivably harmless simulations of violence.

Male Gender Role Conflict

Conflict generally occurs when rigid and restrictive gender roles that are learned and reinforced during early socialization experiences result in personal restraint, devaluation, or violation of one's self or others (O'Neil, 1990). Male gender role conflict is a more specific concept that is used to describe the negative consequences associated with men's tendencies to conform to narrow socially constructed masculine roles (Good & Wood, 1995; O'Neil & Nadeau, 2004). Societal messages repeatedly indicate that men should become breadwinners for and protectors of their families, high-performers in competitive sports, and leaders and executives in the places at which they work (Harper, 2004). Failure to live up to these standards often results in conflict. Men's *fear of femininity* is also central to O'Neil's (1990) theory of male gender role conflict. This fear is described as "a strong, negative emotion associated with stereotypic feminine values, attitudes, and behaviors learned primarily in early childhood when gender identity is being formed by parents, peers, and societal values" (O'Neil, Helms, Gable, David, & Wrightsman, 1986, p. 337). Other researchers have

linked male gender role conflict with the unhealthy attitudes and risky behaviors exhibited by some college men, including violence, sexual assault and harassment, poor help-seeking tendencies, substance abuse, and homophobia (e.g., Davis, 2002; Good & Wood, 1995; Ludeman, 2004). The propensity of these conflicts among college men indisputably contributes to their overrepresentation in campus judicial systems.

Male gender role conflict usually elicits a variety of emotional responses. Unfortunately, many undergraduate men are both unable and unwilling to productively unpack their emotions, and therefore resort to violent and aggressive behavior as a form of expression. For instance, a student may choose to release anger and frustration caused by romantic rejection through vandalizing a university building or destroying another student's property. This helps explain why college men commit the majority of vandalism and property destruction on college and university campuses.

Davis's (2002) study provides an assessment of socially prescribed gender roles among college men. Five key themes emerged in his qualitative study of ten White, traditional-aged male undergraduates. The *importance of self expression* is the first theme. Therein the participants described the conflicts that existed between their desires to express their authentic selves and the social constraints that limited their doing so. The second theme, *code of communication caveats,* is comprised of the following three sub-themes: (1) communication with women, (2) one-on-one communication with other men, and (3) nonverbal and side-by-side communication. Here, participants reflected upon the physical and interpersonal dynamics that characterized interactions with their same-sex peers, including the normality of humorous put-downs and jokes when groups of men interacted socially.

The third theme in Davis's study, *fear of femininity,* highlights the anxiety and frustration participants felt due to the narrow and traditional gendered boundaries that governed their self-expression with other men. A key observation within this theme is that nongendered activities (e.g., openness to talking, wearing a lot of cologne, and styles of dress) potentially raised questions about men's sexual orientations. *Confusion about and distancing from masculinity,* the fourth theme, relates to the participants' general sense of discomfort in identifying with masculinity, combined with their lack of critical thought and reflection on the issue. Davis posits: "They were simultaneously unreflective about what being a guy means and aware that masculinity was something with which they did not want to identify" (p. 516). Finally, a *sense of challenge without support* was identified as the fifth theme. The participants expressed a general feeling of being neglected, primarily because there were no gender-specific support services available to men that paralleled campus resources offered for women.

On a college or university campus, male gender role conflict plays itself out as men seek to compensate for certain perceived inadequacies or attempt to interact with their same-sex peers in ways that are void of emotion and closeness. Public displays of hypermasculinity, sexism, homophobia, and other exaggerated behaviors that are stereotypically male are among the manifestations of such conflict (O'Neil et al., 1986). It is important to note that gender role conflict theory suggests outward attempts to conform to narrow societal expectations of behavior are often incongruent with genuine internal desires to behave differently.

Social Construction of Masculinities

An examination of the overrepresentation of undergraduate men in campus judicial processes must consider the influence of typical patterns of masculine identity formation. Social constructivism, which is guided primarily in the work of Vygotsky (1978), provides an appropriate framework for understanding that learning is cultural, not just internal and individualistic. Accordingly, direct interactions with others and overall engagement in society provides context and stimuli for the juxtaposition of learned behaviors. Certain cultures tend to exist among boys and men. Thus, social constructivists would argue that traditional male behavior and attitudes such as violence, preoccupation with physical prowess, and masculine aggressiveness are *learned* behaviors that are produced and reinforced in social institutions and through cultural interactions (Connell, 1993; Kimmel, Hearn, & Connell, 2005;

Kimmel & Messner, 2004; Levant, 1996; Pleck, 1981; Pollack, 2000). Male peer groups, sports, and popular culture are the three primary social institutions in which masculinity is constructed.

Homosocial peer interactions often include fellowship, camaraderie, validation, homophobia, and unhealthy expressions of masculinity (Kimmell, 1996). Homophobia is not only the discomfort of interacting with gay men or the fear of being mistaken as gay by one's peers. Kimmell explains that homophobia also includes anxiety about not measuring up to peer-approved standards of what it means to be "a real man" (p. 8). Though many are, not all behavioral manifestations of homophobia are intentional. Pressure to be perceived as masculine by peers and self causes some men to subconsciously exhibit homophobic masculine behaviors (Messner, 2001). Moreover, Connell (1993) asserts that men of all ages and ethnicities are often forced to "negotiate" their masculinities with other men—meaning their manhood must be approved and validated by their same-sex peers. Morrison and Eardley's (1985) assertions illuminate what most published literature reports on socially produced learned behaviors among males:

> Boys grow up to be wary of each other. We are taught to compete with one another at school, and to struggle to prove ourselves outside it, on the street, the playground and the sports field. Later we fight for status over sexual prowess, or money, or physical strength or technical know-how. We fear to admit our weaknesses to one another, to admit our failures, our vulnerability, and we fear being called a 'sissy' or a 'softy.' The pressure is on to act tough. We fear humiliation or exclusion, or ultimately the violence of other boys if we fail to conform. (p. 19)

Morrison and Eardley also note that sports are popular vehicles for male-to-male competition. "Sports figure strongly into what it means to be cool and it is crucial to [boys'] need to be part of a social group" (Gilbert & Gilbert, 1998, p. 63). Participation in sports serves a critical role in reinforcing socially constructed traditional masculine behaviors. For instance, sports allow for meaningful interaction between adolescent and adult males—usually in the absence of women. It is through this interaction that boys internalize customary male language and are acculturated to traditional male attitudes such as homophobia and the sexual objectification of women. Also, the locker room serves as both a physical and symbolic setting for this type of interaction, as male locker room jokes in high school and college are almost always about degrading women (Messner, 1992). Once internalized, these socially constructed masculine misperceptions and their corresponding behaviors are continually reinforced through social institutions and interactions, and they become a core component of the male identity.

In addition to sports-related interactions, male peer groups produce, model, police, and reinforce socially constructed masculine behaviors in other ways. Theorists frequently identify a "masculine code" (Davis, 2001; Ferguson, 2004) or a "boy code" (Pollack, 2000) that serve to reinforce socially constructed masculine behaviors among male peers. Conformity to the norm by appearing as "one of the boys" is a strategy employed within male peer groups to protect oneself from teasing or subordination (Swain, 2005). Carol Gilligan's (1982) theory suggests that empathy, emotional expression, humility, and moral reasoning are perceived as feminine traits by most men; and are grossly inconsistent with the aforementioned codes of most male peer groups. This may partially explain why some college men publicly embrace the sexist, homophobic, or violent behaviors exhibited by their peers, even when they are privately inconsistent with their own personal values and beliefs.

Furthermore, popular culture as depicted through television, film, and magazines presents media images of masculinity that serve both comparative and aspirational purposes for everyday men. Most popular images of men strive to differentiate them from women (McKay, Mikosza, & Hutchins, 2005). Thus, portrayals of men as authoritative, powerful, tough, defiant, and sexually aggressive are commonplace in popular culture. Images of high-profile male athletes are often constructed in this regard. Finally, scholars have linked socially constructed images of masculinity in popular culture to the disproportionate rates of sexual assault (Katz, 1995), violence (Hong, 2000), and

alcohol and tobacco use (Capraro, 2000; Courtenay, 2004) among college men.

"Male violence represents the darkest feature of masculinity" (Brooks & Silverstein, 1995, p. 282). That college men are grossly overrepresented among the perpetrators and victims of physical assault on college and university campuses warrants serious attention. Though often male-on-male, violent acts are also committed against female students by their male counterparts. Alcohol, in more cases than not, plays a role in these occurrences (Boswell & Spade, 1996), as drinking engenders feelings of power and sexual aggression within some men (Capraro, 2000). College men engage in this type of abusive behavior to earn the approval and respect of their same-sex peers. Most male-on-male fights escalate from verbal disputes to physical altercations. Reportedly, men are more likely to resort to physical violence as a means of resolving disputes (Gilligan, 1982). Fighting allows them to demonstrate their toughness, assert dominance over another individual, and earn the approval of their male peers; whereas alternative conflict resolution is associated with weakness, another socially constructed misperception.

Developing Competence and Self-Efficacy

Chickering (1969) and Chickering and Reisser's (1993) work presented hypotheses regarding the relationships between college experiences and environments and the psychosocial identity development of students. Those hypotheses have been tested in numerous college-impact and student development studies throughout the past 30 years (Evans, Forney, & Guido-DiBrito, 1998). Chickering's theory includes seven vectors that contribute to identity formation, one of which is developing competence. This vector focuses on a student's perceived sense of competence regarding a certain task or goal. Chickering and Reisser suggest that competence is often developed in three areas: intellectual competence, physical and manual skills, and interpersonal competence. The third area relates most closely to the proposed theoretical model in this chapter. Accordingly, a sense of interpersonal competence is developed when one is able to successfully negotiate and build affirming relationships with peers. Furthermore, the ability to communicate effectively with others leads to greater feelings of approval and acceptance. Thus, in order to develop higher degrees of interpersonal competence, college men often feel the need to engage in socially desirable behaviors that will presumably win the approval of their same-sex peers, even if these acts violate campus rules.

Some college men resort to a variety of unhealthy behaviors in their attempts to build interpersonal competence. For instance, a 17-year old freshman may strive for interpersonal competence by demonstrating to his male peers that he can consume large quantities of alcohol. The same rationale may explain why some male students commit sexual assault. In accordance with traditional conceptualizations of masculinity, men gain approval from their same-sex peers by engaging in sexual activity with multiple female partners (Harper, 2004). A male college student may strive for interpersonal competence by showing his peers how capable he is of having sex with any attractive woman he desires, even if the sexual contact is nonconsensual.

Similar to the development of interpersonal competence, social interactions, acceptance, and peer influences have been shown to influence self-efficacy. Bandura's (1977, 1991, 1997) self-efficacy theory is based on an individual's perception of his or her abilities and competencies in performing various tasks. These perceptions are typically informed by previous experiences and the positive reinforcement provided by various actors in the individual's environment. The theory also posits that recognition of competence leads to improved performance, increased motivation to repeat the task, and the development of higher related goals, even if the task is destructive in nature. Consistent with the "I can do it" spirit of self-efficacy is an assumption that "I can get away with it, like I did before," a belief typically held among repeat judicial offenders who were not previously caught or sanctioned. Peers sometime endorse and validate rule-breaking behaviors, which tends to be the case among college men, especially those who live on all male residence hall floors and in fraternity houses (Kuh & Arnold, 1993).

Bandura (1991) suggests that students sometimes learn "vicariously" through their peers and benchmark their abilities against other students in their campus communities, especially those with whom they have much in common. Vicarious learning, Bandura maintains, requires both modeling and observation. That is, one must model a certain behavior or act that is observed by the vicarious learner. The observer also learns the outcomes, benefits, and consequences associated with the behavior or act. Such vicarious observations lead students to believe that if their peers can accomplish a certain task (or get away with a certain offense), they should be able to as well. If comparable competence cannot be demonstrated, some college men look for other ways to prove their manhood, skill, and power; or their frustration is released through violent, aggressive, and antisocial behaviors.

Context-Bound Gendered Social Norms

This variable of the model concerns itself with gendered norms in the context of a particular college or university campus, as opposed to society at large. Social norms theory states that a student's behavior is influenced by misperceptions of the attitudes and/or behaviors of his or her peers (Berkowitz, 2003). The original application of the theory by Berkowitz and Perkins (1986) involved a study that analyzed patterns of student alcohol use. A key finding was that college students often overestimate the extent to which their peers are engaged in and supportive of irresponsible drinking behaviors. In addition, they also found that students often modified their own consumption levels based on this overestimation. Thus, students drank more than they personally desired primarily because they perceived their peers to be engaged in more drinking than was actually true.

Regarding social norms, Berkowitz (2004) presents three types of misperceptions. *Pluralistic ignorance,* the most commonly held misperception, occurs when the majority of individuals erroneously assume that their attitudes and/or behaviors are inconsistent with those of their peers, when they are in fact consistent. This misperception operates by encouraging individuals to suppress healthy attitudes and behaviors that are believed to be contradictory to the norm and to encourage unhealthy attitudes and behaviors that are falsely perceived as normative. For example, a common phenomenon among most male subgroups is to engage in sexist and homophobic joking. College men who are uncomfortable with this behavior rarely confront their peers for fear that their opinion represents the minority. *False consensus,* the second misperception, encourages an individual to incorrectly assume that there is more peer adherence to the way one thinks and acts than is actually the case (Berkowitz, 2004). This misperception functions by reinforcing an individual's belief that his or her own problematic attitudes or behaviors are normative and appropriate when they are not. An example offered by Berkowitz is that of the heavy drinker who is personally motivated to binge drink because he believes his peers are engaging in the same behavior, which enables him to justify his own heavy drinking.

Finally, the third misperception is *false uniqueness*, which occurs when individuals with minority attitudes or behaviors assume the difference between themselves and the majority population is greater than what is actually the case. Berkowitz offers the example of abstainers who underestimate the prevalence of abstinence among their peers. One common effect is that individuals holding this misperception self-select out of participation in the larger community, believing that their attitudes or behaviors will be deemed unpopular by the majority. Suls and Green (2003) found that alcohol-related social norms have a stronger effect on men than on women. In addition, fraternities, athletic teams, and other influential campus subgroups play a greater role in shaping the social norms of a campus (Berkowitz, 2004).

Environmental Ethos and Corresponding Behaviors

Lewin's (1936) Interactionist Perspective provides insight into the nexus between student behaviors and the campus environment. Translated, the equation $B = f(P \times E)$ means behavior (B) is a function (f) of the interaction ($\times$) of person (P) and environment (E). This theoretical perspective serves as a guide for understanding how individual students' backgrounds and characteristics, coupled with environmental factors,

affect their behaviors in college. Evans et al. (1998) offer the following:

> Student development theories help describe the 'person' aspect of Lewin's equation ... however, we must not neglect the 'environment' side of the equation, for it is environments, in the form of physical surroundings, organizational structures, and human aggregates that present the experiences that either retard or facilitate development. (p. 25)

A campus with a rowdy fraternity community, a big-time sports culture, and a weak judicial affairs office that rarely imposes strict sanctions on offenders will likely incite destructive behaviors among those who come to the environment already socialized to deem such behaviors excusable. Similarly, the ethos of a fraternity house may cause certain members to behave in ways they would not have even considered if they were in a different environment with a different cast of characters.

■ INTERACTIONS AMONG VARIABLES

Though described separately in the previous section, each construct of the model interacts with another to explain the overrepresentation of college men among campus judicial offenders. The precollege socialization experiences that men bring to a campus inform their assumptions regarding appropriate gender roles and behaviors. Although childhood and high school peers were not discussed as part of the precollege socialization variable, men come to college having been influenced (to varying degrees) by the three agents that tend to have the most authority in the social construction of their masculine identities: peers, parents, and popular culture, including sports. Precollege socialization experiences also affect the establishment and communication of gendered norms within the context of a particular campus. The point here is that students' past experiences and previous orientations to manhood play a major role in deciding gendered norms and facilitating the misperceptions that often ensue on a college or university campus.

Male gender role conflict also affects the social construction of masculine identities, as peers and media images help shape students' understanding of what tasks, behaviors, and attitudes are appropriately male. One's ability to resolve these conflicts results in the development of competence and high levels of self-efficacy, even if conflict resolution is achieved through peer-approved misbehavior. Unsuccessful resolution can also affect interpersonal competence and self-efficacy, as frustrated male students seek other ways to prove their manhood and skill. This is complicated by socially constructed messages about what it is men should be able to do. Campus norms are also shaped by the competencies of its actors. Specifically, messages about the skills that male students should possess become part of the norms for a campus, and misperceptions about

exactly how many men on the campus possess those skills are often exaggerated.

It is important to acknowledge that four of the six variables influence and are influenced by the social construction of masculinities. The centrality of this construct in the model is consistent with most of the men's studies literature. Reportedly, social institutions and social interactions continually influence the ways in which society and men themselves view masculine-appropriate behaviors, skills men ought to possess, and the normative rules that should govern men when they interact in various contexts. Furthermore, these perceptions inform the ways parents, K–12 teachers, and various others socialize young boys, which becomes cyclical as boys become consumers and agents of popular culture who enroll in college and later become fathers themselves. Gendered social norms are wrought by external messages that are brought to the campus context by male students whose masculine identities have already been socially constructed and will continue to be negotiated throughout their matriculation at the institution. The gendered social norms of a campus ultimately affect environmental ethos that yield certain behaviors among men and women.

■ PRACTICAL IMPLICATIONS

In an attempt to curb the overrepresentation of men in campus judicial processes, colleges and universities must develop programmatic interventions that are designed to redefine traditional male behavior. These efforts should provide opportunities for male students to express themselves and explore their perceptions of manhood, while simultaneously exposing them to positive examples of masculinity. Gehring (2001) argues, "The disciplinary process on campuses has been too procedural and mirrors an adversarial proceeding that precludes student development" (p. 466). To this end, developmental approaches to addressing male misbehavior on college and university campuses are offered in this section. These practical recommendations are informed by the theories presented throughout this chapter, as well as Davis and Laker's (2004) framework for designing services for college men.

New student orientation continues to be a prime opportunity to prepare students for their undergraduate experiences by providing valuable information and resources. Because many students come to college with perceptions rooted in popular culture, it is essential that they are given a more accurate description of environmental realities upon arrival to campus. A "men's only" orientation session led by juniors and seniors would afford incoming students the opportunity to engage peers in candid discussions about their preconceived notions of what it means to be a man in general, and a male collegian at that particular institution specifically. Allowing experienced same-sex students to challenge these assumptions and provide actual accounts of the college experience will aid incoming

students in shaping accurate and realistic perceptions of the college environment.

Student affairs professionals should also make a conscious effort to showcase individual students and organizations that represent positive masculine behaviors and attitudes. The benefit of highlighting positive behavior is two-fold: (1) It rewards the individual or group exhibiting desired and productive behaviors, and (2) it exposes conflicted students to healthy role models. If campuses fail to provide positive role models and examples of healthy behaviors, students will resort to traditional stereotypes and misperceptions of manhood, which often incite acts that violate university policies.

Campus counseling centers should also consider approaches that focus on building healthy masculinities among college men. Private, individualized sessions as well as small group therapy may help male students unpack their identity issues and eliminate misperceptions of pluralistic ignorance, false consensus, and false uniqueness. Ludeman (2004) advocates a small group counseling approach with male judicial offenders led by a judicial affairs officer. The focus of these sessions should not be punitive, but instead developmental, he maintains. Similar to women's centers that exist on several college and university campuses across the country, administrators should also consider investing resources into the establishment of men's centers. These centers could provide support, information, and programming on masculinity, violence reduction, the prevention of sexual assault, healthy peer interactions, and sexual orientation, as well as offer an empowering venue for the cultivation of male friendships. If resources are not available to start this type of center, perhaps multicultural affairs offices could expand their purposes to include programming on gender, including men's issues.

Exploring strategies for reducing the overrepresentation of men in college judicial processes would be an exercise in futility without properly giving attention to undergraduate fraternity chapters, especially those with houses on or nearby campus. Greek-letter organizations continue to be among the most popular choices for out-of-class involvement among college men, and fraternity houses continue to be venues in which members are socialized toward certain behavioral norms (i.e., drinking). Administrators must collaborate with fraternity leaders to design and implement programs that minimize destructive behaviors and policy infractions. These initiatives should be incorporated into annual fraternity retreats and new member orientations. Advisors and administrators should find creative methods to reward fraternity chapters that experience a decrease in campus judicial violations.

Campuses alone cannot change the way male students conceptualize masculinity—student affairs professionals and other administrators must enlist the assistance of parents in this endeavor. Much of male students' masculine identity socialization stems from the promotion and reinforcement of traditional models of masculinity, which often occur

at home. Student affairs professionals can assist parents in expanding their own conceptualizations of what it means to be a man and alter the messages they communicate to their college-going sons. Male students are more likely to modify their perceptions of masculinity if they are receiving consistent messages from their parents and the institution. Parents' orientation would be an ideal venue in which to introduce this topic, and perhaps a special brochure designed specifically for parents of male students might be effective.

Institutions should dedicate adequate human and financial resources to programmatic interventions designed to reduce the frequency with which male students violate university policies. These resources should not only be used to provide activities and programs, but also to train staff and faculty on effective ways to challenge and support male students. Additionally, administrators should conduct annual comprehensive analyses of campus judicial trends and disaggregate these data by gender. The information gathered will illuminate patterns in male policy violations, and may also inform future programmatic interventions. Sanctions issued for common male infractions (i.e., alcohol policy violations, physical assault, vandalism, and sexual assault) should be reviewed on a regular basis to ascertain the effectiveness of interventions. Judicial sanctions and corresponding developmental initiatives should educate students about the consequences of their behaviors; deter them from repeating the same infractions in the future; and assist them in resolving issues that may have caused the unwanted behavior, including male gender role conflict and masculine identity issues surrounding competence.

■ CONCLUSION

Many scholars have written about the quantitative overrepresentation of men among perpetrators and victims of violence and destructive behaviors (e.g., Brooks & Silverstein, 1995; Dannells, 1997; Hong, 2000; Ludeman, 2004; Pollack, 2000). The theoretical model proposed in this chapter attempts to explain the overrepresentation of college men among campus judicial offenders. Grounded in several different theories from multiple academic disciplines, the model needs to be tested among contemporary college men to confirm its accuracy, completeness, and applicability to diverse populations (e.g., different racial/ethnic minority male subgroups, gay and bisexual men, and male students with physical disabilities). In addition, a study based on various constructs of the model in which data are collected from male judicial offenders to determine the gendered and environmental causes of misbehavior would be instructive.

College and university administrators and faculty aspire to create safe learning environments that facilitate students' intellectual and psychosocial development. Addressing the overrepresentation of college men among judicial offenders is clearly consistent with this

goal. By understanding the interaction between the variables comprising the theoretical model presented herein, student affairs professionals will be better equipped to not only address the aggressive and sometimes violent behaviors that men exhibit, but also support male students in their total development. Ultimately, this will reduce the frequency of alcohol-related incidents, physical and sexual assaults, and other unwanted behaviors that are disproportionately committed by male students on college campuses, and lead to a campus environment in which healthy, nondestructive masculine identities are formed.

REFERENCES

Askew, S., & Ross, C. (1988). *Boys don't cry: Boys and sexism in education*. Philadelphia: Open University Press.

Bandura, A. (1977). Self-efficacy: Toward a unifying theory of behavioral change. *Psychological Review, 84*, 191–215.

Bandura, A. (1991). Social cognitive theory of moral thought and action. In W. M. Kurtines & J. L. Gerwitz (Eds.), *Handbook of moral behavior and development* (pp. 45–103). Hillsdale, NJ: Earlbaum.

Bandura, A. (1997). *Self efficacy: The exercise of control*. New York: W. H. Freeman.

Berkowitz, A. D. (2003). Applications of social norms theory to other health and social justice issues. In H. W. Perkins (Ed), *The social norms approach to preventing school and college age substance abuse: A handbook for educators, counselors, clinicians*. San Francisco: Jossey-Bass.

Berkowitz, A. D. (2004). An overview of the social norms approach. In L. Lederman & L. Stewart (Eds.), *Changing the culture of college drinking: A socially situated health communication campaign.* Cresskill, NJ: Hampton Press.

Berkowitz, A. D., & Perkins, H. W. (1986). Resident advisers as role models: A comparison of drinking patterns of resident advisers and their peers. *Journal of College Student Personnel, 27*, 146–153.

Boswell, A. A., & Spade, J. Z. (1996). Fraternities and collegiate rape culture: Why are some fraternities more dangerous places for women? *Gender & Society, 10*(2), 133–147.

Brooks, G. R., & Silverstein, L. B. (1995). Understanding the dark side of masculinity: An interactive systems model. In R. Levant & W. Pollack (Eds.), *A new psychology of men* (pp. 280–336). New York: Basic Books.

Capraro, R. L. (2000). Why college men drink: Alcohol, adventure, and the paradox of masculinity. *Journal of American College Health, 48*, 307–315.

Chickering, A. W. (1969). *Education and identity.* San Francisco: Jossey-Bass.

Chickering, A. W., & Reisser, L. (1993). *Education and identity* (2nd ed.). San Francisco: Jossey-Bass.

Connell, R. W. (1993). Disruptions: Improper masculinities. In L. Weis & M. Fine (Eds.), *Beyond silenced voices* (pp. 191–208). Albany, NY: State University of New York Press.

Courtenay, W. H. (2004). Best practices for improving college men's health. In G. E. Kellom (Eds.), *Developing effective programs and services for college men. New Directions for Student Services* (No. 107, pp. 59–74). San Francisco: Jossey-Bass.

Dannells, M. (1997). *From discipline to development: Rethinking student conduct in higher education. ASHE-ERIC Higher Education Report* (Vol. 25, No. 2). Washington, DC: The George Washington University Graduate School of Education and Human Development.

Davis, J. E. (2001). Black boys at school: Negotiating masculinities and race. In R. Majors (Ed.), *Educating our Black children: New directions and radical approaches* (pp. 169–182). New York: RoutledgeFalmer.

Davis, T. (2002). Voices of gender role conflict: The social construction of college men's identity. *Journal of College Student Development, 43*(4), 508–521.

Davis, T., & Laker, J. A. (2004). Connecting men to academic and student affairs programs and services. In G. E. Kellom (Ed.), *Developing effective programs and services for college men. New Directions for Student Services* (No. 107, pp. 47–58). San Francisco: Jossey-Bass.

Evans, N. J., Forney, D. S., & Guido-DiBrito, F. (1998). *Student development in college: Theory, research, and practice.* San Francisco: Jossey-Bass.

Ferguson, A. (2004). Making a name for yourself: Transgressive acts and gender performance. In M. Kimmel & M. Messner (Eds.), *Men's lives* (6th ed.). Boston: Allyn & Bacon.

Gehring, D.D. (2001). The objectives of student discipline and the process that's due: Are they compatible? *NASPA Journal, 38*(4), 466–481.

Gilbert, R., & Gilbert, P. (1998). *Masculinity goes to school.* New York: Routledge.

Gilligan, C. (1982). *In a different voice: Psychological theory and women's development.*

Cambridge, MA: Harvard University Press.

Good, G. E., & Wood, P. K. (1995). Male gender role conflict, depression, and help seeking: Do college men face double jeopardy? *Journal of Counseling & Development, 74*, 70–75.

Gregory, J. F. (1996). The crime of punishment: Racial and gender disparities in the use of corporal punishment in U.S. public schools. *Journal of Negro Education, 64*, 454–462.

Harper, S. R. (2004). The measure of a man: Conceptualizations of masculinity among high-achieving African American male college students. *Berkeley Journal of Sociology, 48*(1), 89–107.

Head, J. (1999). *Understanding the boys: Issues of behaviour and achievement.* London: Falmer.

Hong, L. (2000). Toward a transformed approach to prevention: Breaking the link between masculinity and violence. *Journal of American College Health, 48*, 269–282.

Katz, J. (1995). Reconstructing masculinity in the locker room: The Mentors in Violence Prevention Project. *Harvard Educational Review, 65*(2), 163–174.

Kellom, G. E. (Ed.). (2004). *Developing effective programs and services for college men. New Directions for Student Services* (No. 107). San Francisco: Jossey-Bass.

Kimmell, M. (1996). *Manhood in America: A cultural history.* New York: Free Press.

Kimmel, M. S., & Messner, M. A. (Eds.). (2004). *Men's lives* (6th ed.). Boston: Allyn & Bacon.

Kimmel, M. S., Hearn, J., & Connell, R. W. (Eds.). (2005). *Handbook of studies on men and masculinities.* Thousand Oaks, CA: Sage.

Kuh, G. D., & Arnold, J. C. (1993). Liquid bonding: A cultural analysis of the role of alcohol in fraternity pledgeship. *Journal of College Student Development, 34*, 327–334.

Levant, R. F. (1996). The new psychology of men. *Professional Psychology: Research and Practice, 27*(3), 259–265.

Lewin, K. (1936). *Principles of topological psychology.* New York: McGraw-Hill.

Ludeman, R. B. (2004). Arrested emotional development: Connecting college men, emotions, and misconduct. In G.E. Kellom (Ed.), *Developing effective programs for college men. New Directions for Student Services* (No. 107, pp. 75–86). San Francisco: Jossey-Bass.

Mac an Ghaill, M. (1996). "What about the boys?" Schooling, class, and crisis masculinity. *Sociological Review, 44*(3) 381–197.

McKay, J., Mikosza, J., & Hutchins, B. (2005). "Gentlemen, the lunchbox has landed": Representations of masculinities and men's bodies in the popular media. In M. Kimmel, J. Hearn, & R. W. Connell (Eds.), *Handbook of studies on men & masculinities* (pp. 270–288). Thousand Oaks, CA: Sage.

Messner, M.A. (1992). *Power at play: Sports and the problem of masculinity.* Boston: Beacon Press.

Messner, M.A. (2001). Friendship, intimacy, and sexuality. In S. M. Whitehead & F. J. Barrett (Eds.), *The masculinities reader* (pp. 253–265). Malden, MA: Blackwell.

Mirande, A. (2004). "Macho": Contemporary conceptions. In M. Kimmel & M. Messner (Eds.), *Men's lives* (6th ed., pp. 28–38). Boston: Allyn & Bacon.

Morrison, P., & Eardley, T. (1985). *About men.* Philadelphia: Open University Press.

O'Neil, J. M. (1990). Assessing men's gender role conflict. In D. Moore & F. Leafgren

(Eds.), *Men in conflict: Problem solving strategies and interventions* (pp. 23–38). Alexandria, VA: American Counseling Association.

O'Neil, J. M., Helms, B. J., Gable, R. K., David, L., & Wrightsman, L. S. (1986). Gender role conflict scale: College men's fear of femininity. *Sex Roles, 14*(5/6), 335–350.

O'Neil, J. M., & Nadeau, R. A. (2004). Men's gender-role conflict, defense mechanisms, and self-protective defensive strategies. In M. Harway & J. M. O'Neil (Eds.), What causes men's violence against women? (pp. 89–116). Thousand Oaks, CA: Sage.

Pleck, J. H. (1981). *The myth of masculinity.* Cambridge, MA: MIT Press.

Pollack, W. S. (2000). *Real boys' voices.* New York: Random House.

Rudolph, F. (1990). *The American college and university: A history.* Athens, GA: The University of Georgia Press.

Smith, C., & Lloyd, B. B. (1978). Maternal behavior and perceived sex of infant. *Child Development, 49,* 1263–1265.

Skiba, R. J., Michael, R. S., Nardo, A. C., & Peterson, R. L. (2002). The color of discipline: The sources of racial and gender disproportionality in school punishment. *The Urban Review, 34*(4), 317–342.

Suls, J., & Green, P. (2003). Pluralistic ignorance and college student perceptions of gender-specific alcohol norms. *Health Psychology, 22*(5), 479–486.

Swain, J. (2005). Masculinities in education. In M. Kimmel, J. Hearn, & R.W. Connell (Eds.), *Handbook of studies on men & masculinities* (pp. 213–229). Thousand Oaks, CA: Sage.

Van Kuren, N. E., & Creamer, D. G. (1989). The conceptualization and testing of a causal model of college student disciplinary status. *Journal of College Student Development, 30,* 257–265.

Vygotsky, L. S. (1978). *Mind and society: The development of higher psychological processes.* Cambridge, MA: Harvard University Press.

CHAPTER 13

Why College Men Drink

Alcohol, Adventure, and the Paradox of Masculinity

Rocco L. Capraro

And you drink this burning liquor like your life. Your life which you drink like an eau-de-vie.
APOLLINAIRE, 1971

Though terror speaks to life and death and distress makes of the world a vale of tears, yet shame strikes deepest into the heart of man.
TOMKINS, 1991

Given the magnitude of the negative consequences of some college men's drinking—for themselves and for those around them—on campuses across the nation (Perkins, 1992), college health professionals and alcohol prevention educators might well wonder: "Why do college men drink?" Because most college men drink in unproblematic ways and only to be sociable (Berkowitz & Perkins, 1987), those men who drink in a way that is likely to be harmful to themselves or others are actually the central focus of this chapter—that is, those men "for whom drinking has become a central activity in their way of life" (Fingarette, 1989, p. 100).

Writing from a men's health studies perspective, I articulate what is necessarily only a tentative answer to the question of men's problem drinking by offering a model for conceptualizing the complex connections between college men and alcohol. Men's health studies, a subfield of men's studies, describes and analyzes men's experience of health, injury, morbidity, and mortality in the context of masculinity (Brod, 1987; Sabo & Gordon, 1995). I also suggest an answer to the companion question that immediately presents itself to us: "What can we do about it?"

Part 1 of this chapter discusses the connections between alcohol, men, and masculinity generally; Part 2, the cultural and developmental aspects of men in a college setting; and Part 3, conceptual and programmatic responses to the men's problem drinking. In general, I conclude that when college men drink, they are simply being men in college: That is the best context for understanding why they drink. I further conclude, in what is perhaps my central insight in this chapter, that college men's drinking appears to be profoundly paradoxical in a way that seems to replicate a larger paradox of masculinity itself: that men's alcohol use is related to both men's power and men's powerlessness. Stated most succinctly, my interpretation of a variety of evidence suggests that many college men may be drinking not only to enact male privilege but also to help them negotiate the emotional hazards of being a man in the contemporary American college.

■ ALCOHOL AND MASCULINITY

Drinking as a Male Domain

If we want to understand why college men drink, then we might embed drinking and college in masculinity and ask in what ways each might be seen as a specific male experience (Brod, 1987). When we look for connections between drinking, men, and masculinity, we observe that the most prominent feature on the social landscape of drinking is that drinking is a "male domain" (Perkins, 1992, p. 6). By male domain, I suggest that drinking is male dominated, male identified, and male centered (Johnson, 1997).

Men outnumber women in virtually every category of drinking behavior used in research for comparison—prevalence,

consumption, frequency of drinking and intoxication, incidence of heavy and problem drinking, alcohol abuse and dependence, and alcoholism (Berkowitz & Perkins, 1987; Lemle & Mishkind, 1989; McCreary, Newcomb, & Sadave, 1999; Wechsler, Deutsch, & Dowdell, 1995; Courtenay, In Press). Although most college men and women say they drink to be sociable, men are more likely than women to say they drink for escapism or to get drunk (Berkowitz & Perkins, 1987, p. 125).

These findings hold true for the categories of age, ethnicity, geographic region, religion, education, income, and marital status (Lemle & Mishkind, 1989). Although there has been some speculation that changing gender roles may be narrowing the gap between women and men vis-à-vis alcohol, discussed by scholars as the convergence hypothesis, research tends to reject that proposition (Perkins, 1992).

In a classic and often-cited article, Lemle and Miskind (1989) asked, "Why should it be that males drink and abuse alcohol in such magnitude and in such marked contrast to females?" Citing empirical research that placed men mostly in the company of other men in the life course of their drinking, they suggested that drinking was a symbol of masculinity and speculated that men may drink to be manly (Lmele & Mishkind, 1989, p. 215). They found little or no empirical evidence to support many of the theoretical possibilities they discussed, particularly for any theories concerned with men's abusive drinking, yet they remained intrigued with the idea that men were affirming their manliness by drinking.

More recently, McCreary et al. (1999) ask what specific aspects of the male gender role correlate with alcohol involvement. In addition to the personality traits of instrumentality and expressiveness, they explore the traits of traditional male-role attitudes and masculine gender-role stress. For their research, traditional male role attitudes represent a "series of beliefs and assumptions that men should be in high-status positions in society, act in physically and emotionally toughened ways, and avoid anything stereotypically feminine." Masculine gender-role stress is a term used to "describe the stress resulting from a man's belief that he is unable to meet society's demands of what is expected from men or the male role or from having to respond to a situation in a feminine-typed manner" (McCreary, 1999, p. 111–112).

McCreary et al. (1999) identify traditional male-role attitudes as the one aspect of the male gender role they studied that predicts alcohol use among men. Alcohol use itself correlates with alcohol problems. However, masculine gender-role stress, while statistically unrelated to alcohol use, does predict alcohol problems for men (p. 121). In short, this study suggests that, from the point of view of masculinity or culture of manhood as a factor among many others, men qua men might arrive at alcohol problems by two routes: one route starts at traditional male-role attitudes, passes through alcohol use, and ends in alcohol problems; another route starts at masculine gender-role stress and ends directly in alcohol problems.

■ VARIATIONS ON A THEME: STRAIN AND CONFLICT, SHAME AND FEAR, DEPRESSION, AND THE PARADOX OF MASCULINITY

The Paradox of Masculinity

Traditional male-role attitudes and masculine gender-role stress are actually not very far apart; in some aspects, they are correlated (McCreary, Newcomb, & Sadave, 1999; Sharpe & Heppner, 1991). Their correlation reveals the contradictory nature of masculinity (Pleck, 1981). Reflecting upon the contradictory nature of the male role, researchers in the field of men's studies have articulated the paradox of masculinity, or the paradox of men's power, as follows: men are powerful and powerless (Pleck, 1989; Kaufman, 1994; Kimmel, 1994; Capraro, 1995).

What is the resolution of the apparent contradiction that constitutes the paradox? How can men be both powerful and powerless? Men's studies observe two aspects of men's lives. First, in objective social analysis, men as a group have power over women as a group: but, in their subjective experience of the world, men as individuals do not feel powerful. In fact, they feel powerless. As at first articulated, and then later resolved by men's studies, the concept of a paradox of men's power offers an important insight into men's lives, one that seems to capture and to explain many of the contradictory claims made by and about men.

Ironically, it is men themselves who make the "rules of manhood" by which men as individuals are "disempowered" (Kimmel, 1994, p. 183). Kaufman (1994) aptly concludes that men's power is actually the cause of men's pain: "men's social power is the source of individual power and privilege. it is also the source of the individual experience of pain and alienation" (Kaufman, 1994, p. 142–143).

The paradoxical nature of masculinity is further illuminated in other men's studies research on at least three critical psychosocial aspects of masculinity: gender-role conflict and strain, shame and fear, and depression. Interestingly, those same aspects of masculinity are themselves important possible connections between men and alcohol. Consequently, the concept of the paradox of men's power draws us to an important conceptual understanding of some men's connections to alcohol.

Conflict and Strain

O'Neil (1990) provides a useful series of interlocking definitions that locate gender-role conflict and strain in relation to the gender role itself. Gender roles are "behaviors, expectations, and values defined by society as masculine or feminine," or "as appropriate behavior for men and women." Gender-role conflict is "a psychological state in which gender roles have negative consequences on the individual or others" through the restriction, devaluation, or violation of oneself or others. Gender-role strain is "physical or psychological tension experienced as an outcome of gender-role conflict." At the bottom of gender-role strain is a "discrepancy between the real self and the gender role" (p. 24, 25). Strain can follow from both conformity and nonconformity to the male role.

In his writings on strain, Pleck (1981, 1995) provides additional insight into the relation between the masculine gender role and conflict or strain. Pleck (1981) maintains that the masculine gender role itself is "dysfunctional," (p. 147) fraught with contradictions and negative consequences. Even when men live up to the role, they suffer well-documented adverse consequences. But, very often, men do not live up to the role. In fact, conflict and strain are inherent in the role, and they are actually the best rubrics under which to understand most men's identity and experience.

In Pleck's (1981) role-strain paradigm, social approval and situational adaptation replace innate psychological need as the social and psychological mechanisms by which men achieve manhood. Violating gender roles (norms and stereotypes) results in social condemnation, a negative consequence experienced as sex-role strain and anxiety, a negative psychological consequence (p. 145, 146). At least one study has connected role conflict and alcohol use. Blazina and Watkins (1996) found that masculine gender-role conflict, in particular the factor cluster of "success, power, and competition," were significantly related to college men's reported use of alcohol.

Shame and Fear

Krugman (1995), reflecting on Pleck's foundational work on gender-role strain, characterizes male-role strain, with its grounding in feelings of inadequacy and inferiority, as a shame-based experience. "Role strain generates shame affect as males fail to live up to the cultural and peer group standards they have internalized" (Krugman, 1995, p. 95). The essence of shame for Krugman is "painful self-awareness" or "a judgment against the self" (p. 99). He advises that shame is active in both male gender-role strain and normal male socialization.

Recent research suggests that normative male socialization employs shame to shape boys' and men's behaviors and attitudes (Krugman, 1995; Pollack, 1999). In common and nonpathological forms, shame becomes integrated into the self and transformed into a cue that tells us when to modify our behaviors and feelings in response to shame's messages about their appropriateness. But although shame may be the powerful leverage to enforce boys' and men's conformity to the male role, men are less likely than women to transform shame because they find shame to be repugnant to their masculinity. Consequently, for Krugman (1995), boys and men internalize male gender roles to avoid shame; but they also learn that dependency needs, for example, are shameful, especially under the gaze of their peer group.

Shame is related to fear (Tomkins, 1991). Shame can magnify fear by linking similar episodes of fear into what Tomkins refer to as a family of episodes, creating a behavioral template in which fear can be anticipated and become more pervasive. In adversarial cultures, and I would include our own society generally in that category, fear and shame are conjoined, resulting in the mutually reinforcing "fear of shame" and "shame of fear" (Tomkins, 1991, p. 538).

Kimmel (1994) places fear and shame at the very center of the social construction of men's identity. For him, men "fear that other men will unmask us, emasculate us, reveal to us and the world that we do not measure up, that we are not real men. Fear makes us ashamed" (p. 131). To avoid shame, Kimmel writes, men distance themselves from the feminine and all associations with it, including mothers, the world of feelings, nurturing, intimacy, and vulnerability.

Without the transformation of shame, men learn to manage shame in other ways. Alcohol is one of the significant ways men manage shame: drinking is a "maladaptive male solution to the pressure of undischarged shame" (Krugman, 1995, p. 120). Speaking metaphorically, Krugman observes that alcohol "dissolves acute shame" (p. 94). Referring to Lansky's study of shame in families, Krugman reports that alcohol, as a disinhibitor, is used by some men "to handle vulnerable and exposed states that generate shameful feelings." Krugman, citing M. Horowitz, advises that alcohol "softens ego criticism" and "facilitates interpersonal connections and self-disclosures" (p. 120). Drinking may also reduce fear (Tomkins, 1991). It seems to me that shame may also be the mechanism that leads men directly to alcohol, which is used to instill conformity to the dictates of traditional masculinity that encourage men to drink.

Depression

In addition to anxiety and shame, male gender-role strain and conflict make themselves known in the lives of men in depression. Depression is significantly related to all four aspects of gender-role conflict: (a) success, power, and competition; (b) restrictive emotionality; (c) restrictive affectionate behavior between men; and (d) conflicts between work and family relations (Sharpe & Heppner, 1991; Good & Mintz, 1990). Traditional masculinity insidiously puts men at risk for depression and also masks the depression, should it actually develop (Lynch & Kilmartin, 1999; Real, 1997).

Whereas Kaufman (1994) uses a discourse of power to explain men's unacknowledged emotions, Lynch and Kilmartin (1999) offer an alternative approach to the pitfalls of masculinity drawn from the point of view of social relations. Men's socialization encourages them to disconnect, or dissociate, from their feelings. An emotionally restrictive masculinity permits men to show their feelings only "in disguised form," and so they become "mostly unrecognized, unexpressed, and misunderstood by self and others" (p. 45). Men, instead, express their feelings in indirect ways, often through behavior that is destructive to themselves or others. Dissociation from feelings and destructive behavior are the two major characteristics of what Lynch and Kilmartin (1999) refer to as "masculine depression" (p. 9, 10).

Heavy drinking, or binge drinking, is one of the ways some depressed men may act out, or manifest, their depression (Berkowitz & Perkins, 1987). Lynch and Kilmartin (1999) cite research indicating that depression is a strong risk factor for substance abuse problems. Krugman (1995) notes a study showing strong correlations between alcohol abuse and major depression, especially among men. Although they do not cite empirical evidence for it, Blazina and Watkins (1996) speculate that traditional men may "self-medicate their pain and depression with alcohol" (p. 461). Although research findings suggest only a possible correlation between alcohol use or abuse and depression, perhaps alcohol use or abuse may actually precede depression. Alcohol and depression are certainly connected in the lives of some men.

Alcohol and the Paradox of Men's Power

Men in our society are supposed to be powerful (1976). According to the empirical findings of McClelland et al. (1972), when men are not powerful, they may often compensate for their lack of power or seek an "alternative to obtaining social power" with alcohol. Stated most dramatically by McClelland, drinking is "part of a cluster of actions which is a principal manifestation of the need for power" (p. 119). For this research, feeling powerful means "feeling that one is vigorous and can [have] an impact on others" (p. 84). But men's power motivation can be personalized (i.e., for "the greater glory or influence of the individual") or socialized for "the good of others" (p. 137).

According to McClelland (1972), a few drinks will stimulate socialized power thoughts for most men, and that is one of the reasons they like to drink. Higher levels of drinking tend to decrease inhibitions and stimulate personalized power thoughts. Heavy drinking in men is uniquely associated with personalized power, McClelland says. Heavy drinking makes men feel strong and assertive and, I would argue, the way they are supposed to feel.

Drinking may be related to men's power in a more profound and paradoxical way. In the aggregate, the connection between some men and heavy or problem drinking appears to be of two sorts: (a) that which follows from simple, apparently uncomplicated, conformity to traditional masculinity—drinking simply because men are supposed to drink; and (b) that which is informed by complex, perceived inadequacy as men, either from men's own point of view, or from that of society. If they do not feel inadequate, then at least they experience a kind of doubt, or a sense of falling short of the cultural ideal of manhood—drinking because of gender-role conflicts.

This distinction may be, after all, only a conceptual, or theoretical,

distinction; in practice, the two sorts of connection co-occur. I wonder if traditional masculinity does not contain within it, socially constructed over time in the course of men's history, the use of alcohol to accommodate gender-role conflict. Given the way traditional masculinity has been constructed, is not gender-role conflict of the sort described by Pleck (1981) and O'Neil (1990) and documented in the lives of the men studied by Tomkins (1991), Krugman (1996), Lynch and Kilmartin (1999), Real (1997), and Kimmel (1994) inherent in most men's lives? Have not men as historical agents, therefore, made provision for taking care of their own? If so, traditional masculine drinking would encompass conflicted drinking; certainly, in the culture of manhood, it does.

If heavy and problem drinking is associated with conformity, overconformity, or conflicted or strained resistance to the imperatives of traditional masculinity, why should this be the case? It would appear that drinking is a kind of fatally flawed defense mechanism, or compensatory behavior. It protects men's objective power as a group, even as it reveals men's subjective powerlessness as individuals and results in a diminution of men's power, particularly through the loss of control of emotions, health, and a variety of other negative consequences.

If this is the case, then drinking would have much in common with other documented psychological defense mechanisms that correlate with male gender-role conflict. And gender-role conflict, following from either conformity or nonconformity, might itself be seen as a defense mechanism that "protects a man's sense of well-being" (Mahalik, Cournoyer, DeFran, Cherry, & Napolitano, 1998, p. 253). Like men's silence (Sattel, 1983), men's drinking turns out to be in the interest of men's power, even as it disempowers individual men. And alcohol, in my view, is the paradoxical drug that is a part of the larger whole, a trope, of a paradoxical masculinity.

As I ponder this material, then, it seems to me that a significant part of men's drinking, like male gender-role stress and strain, men's shame, and masculine depression themselves, is a reflection of both men's power and men's powerlessness about men's privilege and men's pain. Heavy and problem drinking join other aspects of masculinity as they, too, come to be seen as manifestations of the paradox of masculinity. Drinking thus falls into a line of masculine icons, including body building, sexual assault, and pornography, that reveal the paradoxical nature of masculinity itself (Fussell, 1991; Berkowitz, Burkhart, & Bourg, 1994; Brod, 1990; Kimmel, 1990). As I review those icons, it strikes me that at those times men appear most powerful socially, they feel most powerless personally.

■ COLLEGE AND MASCULINITY

College Drinking

What happens when we look at college men? College students, mostly men, are among the heavy drinkers in Rorabaugh's (1981) history of drinking in early American society. Contemporary college men drink more than they did in high school and more heavily than their non-college counterparts, and the gap is widening (Perkins, 1992; Maddox, 1970; Bacon & Strauss, 1953; Johnston, Bachman, & O'Malley, 1996). Men have been the primary public purveyors of alcohol to the college campus. All of the differences in drinking behavior for men and women generally hold true for college men and women (Perkins, 1992; Berkowitz & Perkins, 1987).

Given today's college students' preference for alcohol, one could not really imagine most colleges void of alcohol (Levine & Cureton, 1998). However, given the great variety of colleges and universities, the diversity of today's student populations, and the sweeping nature of the concerns I express in this chapter, most of what follows must necessarily speak primarily to an ideal type, represented for me by the relatively small, residential liberal arts college, occupied by a mostly traditionally aged student population (*Daedalus,* 1999). In the following pages, I shall discuss critical aspects of college that seem to define college men's experience and help explain much of the presence of alcohol on college campuses: adventure, adult development, and permissiveness.

College as Adventure

Green (1993) conceptualizes adventure as a domain of transgression. For Green, adventure takes shape around the themes of "eros" and "potestas"—love and power. Following Bataille, Green asks us to think about civil society "as based on the purposes and values of work, which means the denial of all activities hostile to work, such as both the ecstasies of eroticism and those of violence." Adventure lies in the conceptual space where heroes, "men acting with power," break free of ordinary restraints and "sample the repressed pleasures of sex and violence" (Adams & Nagoshi, 1999, p. 17).

Although Green (1993) makes no reference to drinking in his essays on adventure, we can easily recognize that the terrain of adventure is the same terrain as that of alcohol: "a boy's first drink, first prolonged drinking experience, and first intoxication tend to occur with other boys away from home" (Lemle & Mishkind, 1989, p. 214). Sports and the military are contexts for both adventure and drinking. Drinking games "are an important factor in the socialization of new students into heavy use," particularly for men (Adams & Nagoshi, 1999, p. 105). Drinking, in general, can be an adventure, insofar as it takes men through a "breach" of the social contract and into the realms of violence, sex, and other adventure motifs.

In what way might college be conceptualized as an adventure? College is not literally, or predominantly, a scene of eros and potestas. It is, however, a time and place of an imaginative assertion of manhood outside of civil society, away from home and family, where a kind of heroism is possible. By analogy, we can observe that student life in 19th-century American colleges developed outside of the civil society represented by the faculty and administration in what I would regard as the realm of adventure. Horowitz (1987) argues that what we think of as student life was actually "born in revolt" (p. 23) against the faculty and administration. It is a "world made by the undergraduates," she says (p. 3).

Levine and Cureton (1998) find that colleges today are occupied by a transitional generation that reflects the changing demographics of contemporary American society. Horowitz's history, however, employs a simple tripartite typology of college students that is still largely applicable as a model for understanding students on many campuses in more recent times. That typology deeply resonates with my own many years of experience in student affairs: (a) college men—affluent men in revolt against the faculty and administration who created campus life as "the culture of the college man" (p. 32); (b) outsiders—hardworking men who identify with the faculty (p. 14); and (c) rebels—creative, modernist, and expressive men who conform neither to campus life nor to the faculty (p. 15). Horowitz (1987) observes that these three student types were distinctly male when they first made their appearance, but their female counterparts eventually found their place alongside the men.

Nuwer (1999) argues that there are historical links between traditional male undergraduate life and danger, a key adventure motif. Social interactions initiating students into various campus communities have continuously subjected college men to high risk. Acceptance by their peers is granted in exchange for successfully undertaking the risk involved. A variety of college rituals and traditions often mix danger and alcohol (Nuwer, 1999). Alcohol, itself, is associated with risk in men's lives (Lemle & Mishkind, 1989). Seen this way, college and campus life become an adventure-scape, where young men (college men) imagine their manhood in a developmental moment that is socially dominated by alcohol.

Green (1993) identifies a number of arenas or institutions of adventure: manhood before marriage, hunting, battle, travel, sports, and politics, to name a few. Although there may be feminine variants, Green links adventure to masculinity because society gives men the freedom to "apply force to the world to assert power and identity." Adventure is an act of assertion by which men "imagine themselves" in "a breach of the social contract" (p. 19).

Colleges as a Male Developmental Moment

Beyond seeing the sociology of college and student life organized as adventure, we must also consider the role of individual developmental psychology in the college environment. Paradoxically, just at the moment the great adventure begins, college men feel the most vulnerable. Rotundo (1993) observes that in the 19th-century, "male youth culture" made its appearance in men's development as the vehicle for the transition from

boyhood to manhood. Boys' principal developmental task was disengagement from home, which created conflict between the imperatives of worldly ambition and young men's psychological needs for attachment. Young men of Rotundo's period gathered in business districts and colleges. Wherever they gathered, a "special culture" developed to support them in a time of need (p. 56–62).

Lyman (1987) carries us forward from Rotundo's (1993) historical analysis to the present. In his essay on male bonding in fraternities, he locates college as a developmental time and place between the authority of home and family (in the high school years), and that of work and family (after graduation). He identifies college men's anger, their "latent anger about the discipline that middle-class male roles impose upon them, both marriage rules and work rules" (p. 157). Their great fear is loss of control and powerlessness. Lyman concludes that joking relationships (banter, sexual humor, etc.) among men allow a needed connection without being self-disclosive or emotionally intimate, that is, with little vulnerability. Recent research on first-year college men has characterized their transition to college as often involving separation anxiety and loss, followed by grieving. Among the significant responses that may manifest some college men's grief, we find self-destructive behaviors, including alcohol use (Gold, Neururer, & Miller, 2000).

Shame theory advises that to avoid shame, boys need to distance themselves from their mothers because of the "considerable discomfort with dependency needs at the level of the peer group" (Krugman, 1995, p. 107). College men in groups, such as Lyman's fraternity men, perceive homosexuality and intimate emotional relationships with women to be a threat to their homosocial world. Thus, men are encouraged to treat women as sexual objects, which confirms their heterosexuality, but prevents true intimacy with women.

Alcohol plays a role in men's emotional management under these conditions. Drinking remains a "socially acceptable way for men to satisfy their dependency needs while they maintain a social image of independence" (Burda, Tushup, & Hackman, 1992, p. 187) even as it masks those needs. For example, recent research on drinking games suggests they are actually an environmental context for drinking where a variety of students' social and psychological needs come into play (Johnson, Hamilton, & Sheets, 1999). When men (and women) give reasons for playing drinking games, they are likely to be "tapping into more general motives for drinking" (p. 286). Alcohol may be an effective way to cope in the short term, but it is ultimately "self-destructive" (Burda, Tushup, & Hackman, 1992, p. 191).

For Nuwer (1999), as was true for Horowitz (1987), fraternities are the quintessential emblems of traditional college life. They provide a "feeling of belonging" for students who "crave relationships and acceptance" in their college years (p. 38). They are also the riskiest environments for heavy and problem drinking (Berkowitz & Perkins, 1987). Nationally, just over 80% of fraternity residents binge drink, whereas just over 40% of all college students binge (Wechsler, Dowdall, Maener, Gledhill-Hoyt, & Lee, 1998). Drinking in fraternities is perhaps best understood as an extreme on a continuum of college men's drinking, dramatizing what may be going on to a lesser extent in traditional student life among a range of men. From the point of view of men's needs assessments, we have much to learn from the psychology of brotherhood.

Permissiveness — Real and Imagined

Alcohol is "one of the oldest traditions in the American college," and alcohol-related problems have also been a benchmark of campus life. Until very recently, though, college administrations have been permissive about alcohol, voicing "official condemnation tempered by tacit toleration" (Hoekema, 1994, p. 81–83). Myers (1990) provides a model for "institutional (organizational) denial" of the presence (or extent) of alcohol abuse that could easily apply to college campuses nationally (p. 43). In 1995, Wechsler was explicit about the widespread denial about alcohol on college campuses.

With the increase in the drinking age from 18 to 21 years and increased awareness of the dangers of alcohol abuse, colleges now "typically have policies which promote responsible drinking" and attempt the "management of student drinking and its consequences"

(Hoekema, 1994, p. 84–88). My own informal observations are that liability case law, awareness of the negative impact of alcohol on the achievement of educational mission, and enrollment management concerns for retention have also encouraged colleges to be more vigilant about the role of alcohol in campus cultures.

But among students, permissiveness persists, both in drinking behavior and in attitudes toward drinking. Permissiveness itself is, in part, the result of students' own misperceptions of campus norms for alcohol behavior and attitudes (Rorabaugh, 1981; Perkins, 1991). With reference to the consumption of alcohol and the acceptability of intoxication, students generally perceive themselves to be in a permissive environment. In reality, the environment is not as permissive as they think. Misperceiving the norm leads students who are inclined to drink to consume more alcohol than they otherwise would drink were they to perceive the norm correctly (Perkins & Wechsler, 1996). This social norms research indicates that correcting the misperception through public information campaigns can reduce both problem drinking and binge drinking on college campuses (Fabiano, McKinney, Hyun, Mertz, Rhoads, & Lifestyles, 1998; Haines, 1993).

How well do social norms approaches work with college men who are heavy drinkers? How are masculinity, permissive attitudes about drinking, and misperceptions of the norm related? How accurately do college men perceive their campus norms? For social norms theory and research, the heaviest drinking results from the interaction of the most permissive personal attitudes toward alcohol and the greatest misperception of the norm as more permissive than it actually is. Men as a group are the heaviest drinkers on campus. We might conclude that the heaviest drinking men have the most permissive attitudes about drinking and that they misperceive the norm at the greatest rates. But, theoretically, they should also be most susceptible to the benefits of social norms approaches.

However, in one study, the heaviest drinking college men proved to be the least susceptible to social norms interventions. From 1995 to 1998 Western Washington University implemented a campus-wide social norms approach. Although most students on the campus changed their patterns of drinking in positive ways, the "students reporting they had seven or more drinks on peak occasions [the most consumed at one time in the past month] remained virtually unchanged [at about 35%]." The most recalcitrant students at Western Washington were underage men: "nearly two thirds of the underage men still reported having seven or more drinks on a peak occasion. Only one third of the underage women reporting the same" (Fabiano, McKinney, Hyun, Mertz, Rhoads, & Lifestyles, 1998, p. 3) level of consumption.

In view of the significance of personal attitudes toward alcohol (Perkins & Wechsler, 1996), permissive personal attitudes about alcohol in the group of recalcitrant underage men might have been so robust that they simply overwhelmed any other perceptions of the environment. Prentice and Miller (1993) found that men and women in their study did respond differently to corrections of misperceptions. Perhaps, in the case of at least some college men, personal attitudes about drinking and misperception of the campus norm are so inextricably linked that research and prevention work that addresses the one (personal attitudes) must necessarily be done in conjunction with the same kind of work on the other (misperception of the norm).

Perkins (1992) once characterized "the perceived male stereotype of heavy use as a misperception to which males do not need to conform" (p. 6). Some college men's misperceptions of their campus alcohol norms may be "contained" in their personal attitudes about drinking. Baer found that differences in the perception of campus drinking norms among students in different housing situations on one campus "*already existed prior to college enrollment*" (Adams & Nagoshi, 1999, p. 98) [emphasis mine]. Certainly, if "the impact of public behavior and conversation" on campus can generate misperceptions of the norm (Perkins, 1991, p. 17) a lifetime of powerful messages about the connection between alcohol and manhood would produce great distortions of its own.

Social norms theory, research, and strategies would be enhanced by a closer look at gender in the creation of drinking attitudes and behaviors, in possible differences in the misperception of norms, and in the social mechanisms that lie behind the actual norms. Social norms research surveys should include measures of traditional masculine role strain and should look for correlations between attitudes and perceptions of the norm and actual drinking behavior.

In addition, surveys should replace the generic "college student" with "male student" or "female student" when asking college students about how much students are drinking and asking about their attitudes toward drinking. So, for example, we should ask, "How many drinks does a male [or female] student typically have at a party on this campus?" instead of "do students typically have" or "Is it acceptable for men [or women] to drink with occasional intoxication as long as it does not interfere with other responsibilities?" (Perkins, 1991, p. 15)

The results would have implications for norms-based prevention programs. It would make sense if, in fact, masculinity were found to predispose men to misperceive the norm because assumptions and attitudes about drinking and how drinking relates to manhood are built into masculinity. It would also make sense that the actual and perceived social norms be gender specific.

■ WHAT IS TO BE DONE?

Concrete Responses

Men, alcohol, and college are connected by the paradoxical nature of men's power. What can we do about college men's frequent, heavy, and problem drinking?

Following from the model that has been developed in this essay, nothing short of radical reconstruction of masculinity and a reimagining of the college experience are likely to bring about significant change in college men's drinking. The same paradox that characterizes college men's drinking also provides a pedagogy for change. This is because, while the paradox acknowledges men's pain and powerlessness, it also discourages men from seeing themselves simply as victims, and it insists that men take responsibility for their actions. Colleges, in collaboration with high schools and community agencies, should integrate gender awareness into alcohol education, prevention, and risk-reduction programs. For men, I recommend a comprehensive educational program that addresses four central themes in men's lives: friendship, health, life/work/family, and sexual ethics [see also, Good and Mintz (1990, p. 20)].

As in the case of effective rape prevention education workshops for men, the pedagogy should be workshops that are all male, small group, interactive, and peer facilitated. Such programs have been shown to change some men's attitudes and values that are associated with the perpetration of rape (Berkowitz, 1994). It may be that the rape prevention workshops are changing attitudes because they correct men's misperceived norm of other men's attitudes about women, or vice versa (Berkowitz, 1999).

Attitudes and values associated with problem drinking could be similarly changed. Developing what Lynch and Kilmartin (1999) refer to as "healthy masculinity" that connects men in healthy relationships with other men, family, and intimate partners would be a succinct statement of the goal of such programming. The transition to college is a critical juncture in the consumption of alcohol (Berkowitz & Perkins, 1987). Programming should therefore begin early in the first year and continue well beyond orientation week. Broad-based, fully integrated, social norms educational programs, interventions, and public information initiatives should be implemented (Perkins & Wechsler, 1996). I would add that such programs should be gender informed along the lines I have suggested in this chapter. College men should understand how the paradoxical masculinity I have discussed may orient them to alcohol use and abuse.

College students should be strongly encouraged to get involved in clubs and organizations on campus, to run for office, and to be involved in sports as ways of meeting power orientation needs in socially responsible ways (McClelland, Davis, Kalin, & Wanner, 1972). Those activities themselves must have alcohol education components; otherwise, involvement could have the ironic consequence of promoting heavier drinking (Perkins, 1992). Associations between men and beer in campus media should be discouraged (Postman, Nystrom, Strate, & Weingartner, n.d.; Courtenay, In Press). Given their powerful influence over men's drinking in the first year (Horowitz, 1987), the hazards of drinking games should be especially discussed in educational programming.

In general, college as adventure is a theme that should be discouraged. A "boys will be boys" permissiveness should be rejected. Recognizing and affirming that alcohol does harm, colleges must assert themselves as "moral communities" and move from permissive to restrictive stances on alcohol by first articulating what the harm is, then establishing policies to prevent college community members from harming themselves or others (Hoekema, 1994, p. 150–159). Wechsler and associates (2000) recommend a comprehensive approach to alcohol use on college campuses, including scrutiny of alcohol marketing, more alcohol-free events and activities, and more restrictive policies that control the flow of alcohol on campus. Their recommendation would benefit from more deeply gendered approaches to the problem because the problem, itself, is deeply gendered.

In addition to promoting social norms approaches, preventive education, and risk-reduction education, college administrators should require that frequent violators of alcohol policy seek treatment or seek their education elsewhere. Although critics of treatment may say it addresses the symptoms and not the real problem, which is the campus culture itself, colleges must offer treatment as part of a comprehensive program for renewed campus life. Treatment should seamlessly integrate men's health studies approaches (Levant & Pollack, 1995; Mahalik, 1999). Unfortunately, some college men will be untouched and untouchable by education or treatment, and they must lose the privilege of attending their chosen college and be asked to leave.

Conceptual Responses

Speaking most globally about solving the problem of college men's drinking and solving the problem of the connections between alcohol and masculinity, I would paraphrase what I have previously written about the problem of rape: Our understanding of the specific act of drinking should be embedded in our understanding of masculinity. Drinking is not an isolated behavior; it is a behavior linked to larger systems of attitudes, values, and modalities of conduct in men's lives that constitute masculinity and men's social position relative to women. In this model, alcohol prevention work with men begins with them as men, and with men's questioning of prevailing assumptions about masculinity and what it means to be a man. I am extremely skeptical of any alcohol prevention work that proposes solutions to the problem of drinking that leave masculinity, as we know it, largely intact (Capraro, 1994, p. 22).

The educational challenge, which is really the psychological and political resistance to this solution, lies in the fact that alcohol benefits men as a group, even as it injures men as individuals. Men are likely to resist this global approach because we fear losing the benefits of masculinity conferred upon the group. The path to a reconstructed masculinity or alternatives to the dominant masculinity that includes more variety of men's identities and experiences may look something like Helms's (1995) stage-development model for a positive racial-cultural identity for minority groups. It will not be easy getting there.

In the meantime, in our work with college men who drink, we must look to the bottom of their glasses and find the men inside. For when college men drink, they are simply being men at college, or what they perceive men at college to be. By this I mean that the most useful way to interpret their behavior is not so much in its content, but in its context—first, the imperatives of manhood, then the psychosocial particulars of college life, both of which put men at risk for drinking. Basically, at the bottom of heavy and problematic drinking among college men are the paradoxical nature of masculinity and the corresponding paradoxical nature of alcohol in men's lives. Once we know college men as men, we will know more about why they drink and what we can do about it.

REFERENCES

Adams, C. E, Nagoshi, C. T. Changes over one semester in drinking game playing and alcohol use and problems in a college sample. *Substance Abuse.* 1999;20(2):97–106.

Apollinaire G. Zone. In: *Selected Writings of Guillaume Apollinaire* (trans. Roger Shattuck). New York: New Directions; 1971.

Bacon, S. D, Strauss, R. *Drinking in College.* New Haven: Yale University Press; 1953.

Berkowitz, A. D. A model acquaintance rape prevention program for men. In: Berkowitz,

A. D., ed. *Men and Rape: Theory, Research, and Prevention Education in Higher Education.* San Francisco: Jossey-Bass; 1994.

Berkowitz, A. D. From reactive to proactive prevention: Promoting an ecology of health on campus. In: Rivers, P. C., Shore ER, eds. *Substance Abuse on Campus: A Handbook for College and University Personnel.* Wesport, CT: Greenwood Press; 1997.

Berkowitz, A. D., Burkhart, B. R., Bourg, S. E. *Research on College Research and Prevention Education in Higher Education.* San Francisco: Jossey-Bass; 1994.

Berkowitz, A. D., Perkins, H. W. Recent research on gender differences in collegiate alcohol use. *Journal of American College Health.* 1987;36:123–129.

Berkowitz, A. D. Applications of social norms theory to other health and social justice issues. Paper presented at: Annual Social Norms Conference. July 28–30, 1999; Big Sky, Mont.

Blazina, C., Watkins, C. E. Masculine gender role conflict: Effects on college men's psychological well-being, chemical substance usage, and attitudes toward help-seeking. *Journal of Counseling Psychology.* 1996;43(4):461–465.

Brod, H. The case for men's studies. In: Brod, H, ed. *The Making of Masculinities: The New Men's Studies.* Boston: Allen Unwin; 1987.

Brod, H. Pornography and the alienation of male sexuality. In: Hearn, J., Morgan, D., eds. *Men, Masculinities and Social Theory.* London: Unwin Hyman; 1990.

Burda, P. C., Tushup, R. J., Hackman, P. S. Masculinity and social support in alcoholic men. *Journal of Men's Studies.* 1992;1(2): 187–193.

Capraro, R. L. Review of Theorizing Masculinities. Brod H, Kaufman M, eds. Sage; 1994. *Journal of Men's Studies.* 1995;4(2): 169–172.

Capraro, R. L. Disconnected lives: Men, masculinity, and rape prevention. In: Berkowitz, A. D., ed. *Men and Rape: Theory, Research, and Prevention Programs in Higher Education.* San Francisco: Jossey-Bass; 1994.

Courtenay, W. H. Engendering health: A social constructionist examination of men's health beliefs and behaviors. *Psychology of Men and Masculinity.* In press.

Courtenay, W. H. Behavioral factors associated with disease, injury, and death among men: Evidence and implications for prevention. *Journal of Men's Studies.* In press.

Daedalus. Distinctively American: The residential liberal arts colleges. Winter 1999.

David, D. S., Brannon, R., eds. *The Forty-Nine Percent Majority: The Male Sex Role.* New York: Random House; 1976.

Fabiano, P. M., McKinney, G. R., Hyun, Y-R., Mertz, H. K., Rhoads, K. Lifestyles, 1998: Patterns of alcohol and drug consumption and consequences among Western Washington University students—An extended executive study. *Focus: A Research Summary.* 1999;4(3):1–8.

Fingarette, H. *Heavy Drinking: The Myth of Alcoholism as a Disease.* Berkeley, CA: University of California Press; 1989.

Fussell, S. W. *Muscle: Confessions of an Unlikely Body-builder.* New York: Avon Books; 1991.

Good, G. E., Mintz, L. Gender role conflict and depression in college men: Evidence for compounded risk. *Journal of Counseling and Development.* 1990;69 (September/October): 17–21.

Gold, J., Neururer, J., Miller, M. Disenfranchised grief among first-semester male university students: Implications for systemic and individual interventions. *Journal of the First Year Experience.* 2000;12(1):7–27.

Green, M. The *Adventurous Male: Chapters in the History of the White Male Mind.* University Park, PA: The Pennsylvania State University Press; 1993.

Haines, M. *A Social Norms Approach to Preventing Binge Drinking at Colleges and Universities.* Newton, MA: The Higher Education Center for Alcohol and Other Drug Prevention; 1998.

Helms, J. An Update of Helms' White and People of Color Racial Identity Models. In: Ponterretto, J., et al. *Handbook of Multicultural Counseling.* Newbury Park, CA: Sage; 1995.

Hoekema, D. A. *Campus Rules and Moral Community: In Place of In Loco Parentis.* Lanham, MD: Rowman & Littlefield; 1994.

Horowitz, H. L. *Campus Life: Undergraduate Cultures from the End of the Eighteenth Century to the Present.* Chicago: University of Chicago Press; 1987.

Johnson, A. G. *The Gender Knot: Unraveling Our Patriarchal Legacy.* Philadelphia: Temple University Press; 1997.

Johnson, T. J., Hamilton, S., Sheets, V. L. College students' self-reported reasons for playing drinking games. *Addictive Behavior.* 1999;24(2):279–286.

Johnston, L., Bachman, J. G., O'Malley, P. M. *Monitoring the Future.* Health and Human Services Dept, US Public Health Service, National Institutes of Health, National Institute of Drug Abuse; 1996.

Kaufman, M. Men, feminism, and men's contradictory experiences of power. In: Brod, H., Kaufman, M., eds. *Theorizing Masculinities*. Newbury Park, CA: Sage; 1994.

Kimmel, M. S. Masculinity as homophobia: Fear, shame, and silence in the construction of gender identity. In: Brod, H., Kaufman, M., eds. *Theorizing Masculinities*. Newbury Park, CA: Sage; 1994.

Kimmel, M. S. *Men Confront Pornography*. New York: Crown; 1990.

Krugman, S. Male development and the transformation of shame. In: Levant, R. F., Pollack, W. S., eds. *A New Psychology of Men*. New York: Basic; 1995.

Lemle, R., Mishkind, M. E. Alcohol and masculinity. *Journal of Substance Abuse Treatment*. 1989;6:213–222.

Levant, R. F., Pollack, W. S., eds. *A New Psychology of Men*. New York: Basic; 1995.

Levine, A., Cureton, J. S. *When Hope and Fear Collide: A Portrait of Today's College Student*. San Francisco: Jossey-Bass; 1998.

Lyman, P. The fraternal bond as a joking relationship. In: Kimmel. M. S., ed. *Changing Men: New Directions in Research on Men and Masculinity*. Newbury Park, CA: Sage; 1987.

Lynch. J., Kilmartin, C. *The Pain Behind the Mask: Overcoming Masculine Depression*. New York: Haworth; 1999.

Maddox. G. L., ed. *The Domesticated Drug: Drinking Among Collegians*. New Haven, CT: College and University Press; 1970.

Mahalik, J. R. Incorporating a gender role strain perspective in assessing and treating men's cognitive distortions. *Professional Psychology: Research and Practice*. 1999;30(4): 333–340.

Mahalik, J. R., Cournoyer, R. J., DeFran, W., Cherry, M., Napolitano, J. M. Men's gender role conflict in relation to their use of psychological defenses. *Journal of Counseling Psychology*. 1998;45(3):247–255.

McClelland, D. C., Davis, W. N., Kalin, R., Wanner, E. *The Drinking Man*. New York: The Free Press; 1972.

McCreary, D. R., Newcomb, M. D., Sadave, S. The male role, alcohol use, and alcohol problems. *Journal of Counseling Psychology*. 1999;46(1):109–124.

Moore, D., Leafgren, F., eds. *Problem Solving Strategies and Intervention for Men in Conflict*. Alexandria, VA: American Association for Counseling and Development; 1990.

Myers, P. L. Sources and configurations of institutional denial. *Employee Assistance Quarterly*. 1990;5(3):43–53.

Nuwer, H. *Wrongs of Passage: Fraternities, Sororities, Hazing, and Binge Drinking*. Bloomington, IN: Indiana University Press; 1999.

O'Neil, J. Assessing men's gender role conflict. In: Moore. D., Leafgren, F., eds. *Problem Solving Strategies and Interventions for Men in Conflict*. Alexandria, VA: American Association for Counseling and Development; 1990.

Perkins, H. W. Confronting misperceptions of peer drug use norms among college students: An alternative approach for alcohol and other drug education programs. In: *The Higher Education Leaders/Peer Network Peer Prevention Resource Manual*. US Dept of Education, FIPSE Drug Prevention Program; 1991.

Perkins, H. W. Gender patterns in consequences of collegiate alcohol abuse: A

10-year study of trends in an undergraduate population. *Journal of Studies on Alcohol.* 1992;September:458–462.

Perkins, H. W., Wechsler, H. Variation in perceived college drinking norms and its impact on alcohol abuse: A nationwide study. *Journal of Drug Issues.* 1996;26(4):961–974.

Pleck, J. H. *The Myth of Masculinity.* Cambridge, MA: The MIT Press; 1981.

Pleck, J. Men's power with women, other men, and society: A men's movement analysis. In: Kimmel, M. S., Messner, M. A., eds. *Men's Lives.* New York: Macmillan; 1989.

Pleck, J. The gender role strain paradigm: An update. In: Levant, R. L., Pollack, W. S., eds. *A New Psychology of Men.* New York: Basic; 1995.

Pollack, W. *Real Boys.* New York: Henry Holt; 1999.

Postman, N., Nystrom, C., Strate, L., Weingartner, C. *Myths, Men, and Beer: An Analysis of Beer Commercials on Broadcast Television, 1987.* Washington, DC: AAA Foundation for Traffic Safety; undated.

Prentice, D. A., Miller, D. T. Pluralistic ignorance and alcohol use on campus: Some consequences of misperceiving the social norms. *Journal of Personality and Social Psychology.* 1993;65:243–256.

Real, T. *I Don't Want to Talk About It.* New York: Simon & Schuster; 1997.

Rorabaugh, W. J. *The Alcoholic Republic: An American Tradition.* New York: Oxford University Press; 1981.

Rotundo, E. A. *American Manhood: Transformations in Masculinity from the Revolution to the Modern Era.* New York: HarperCollins; 1993.

Sabo, D., Gordon, D. F. Rethinking men's health and illness. In: Sabo, D., Gordon, D. F., eds. *Men's Health and Illness: Gender, Power, and the Body.* Thousand Oaks, CA: Sage; 1995.

Sattel, J. W. Men, inexpressiveness, and power. In: Thorne, K. H. *Language, Gender and Society.* Newbury House; 1983.

Scher, M., Stevens, M., Good, G., Eichenfield, G. A. *Handbook of Counseling and Psychotherapy with Men.* Newbury Park, CA: Sage; 1987.

Sharpe, M. J., Heppner, P. P. Gender role, gender-role conflict, and psychological well-being in men. *Journal of Counseling Psychology.* 1991;38(3):323–330.

Tomkins, S. *Affect, Imagery, Consciousness. Vol. 3, 1962–1992.* New York: Springer; 1991.

Wechsler, H., Deutsch, C., Dowdell, G. Too many colleges are still in denial about alcohol abuse. (1995) http://www.hsph.harvard.edu/cas/test/articles/chronicle2.shtm/.

Wechsler, H., Dowdall, G. W., Maener, G., Gledhill-Hoyt, J., Lee, H. Changes in binge drinking and related problems among American college students between 1993 and 1997. *Journal of American College Health.* 1998;47:57–68.

Wechsler, H., Kelley, K., Weitzman, E. R., San Giovanni, J. P., Seebring, M. What colleges are doing about student binge drinking: A survey of college administrators. (March 2000) http://www.hsph.harvard.edu/cas/test/alcohol/surveyrpt.shtm/.

CHAPTER 14

Whales Tales, Dog Piles, and Beer Goggles

An Ethnographic Case Study of Fraternity Life

Robert A. Rhoads

*A*round a table in the corner of the basement party room sit ten fraternity brothers. In the middle of the table is a large pitcher of beer, and in front of the brothers are glasses filled with varying amounts of beer. Nine pairs of eyes fixate on one of the brothers, who appears to be telling some sort of story. The brothers lean forward to hear more clearly, as do the 12 or so onlookers, who encircle the ten brothers seated around the table. The onlookers are mostly women, whose wrinkled brows, squinting eyes, and half-hearted smiles reveal both their confusion and amusement.

The storyteller speaks quickly, and at first he sounds as if he is talking in some strange or foreign dialect. After a while, however, it becomes clear that the language spoken is indeed common English, but with an unusual tone and cadence. He looks directly at the brothers, one by one, in no particular order. Quickly he turns his head to the other side of the table as if to fake the brothers. Out of nowhere he stops, and

another brother begins to fashion his own narrative.

At one point, all the brothers except one sit back and laugh, while at the same time pointing with their elbows at another brother, who then fills his glass from the pitcher of beer and chugs the entire contents. Evidently, the storyteller at some point in his tale mentions a code word or nickname that represents another brother sitting at the table. When this occurs, the brother whose name is mentioned must pick up the tale where the previous storyteller left off and begin elaborating his own version. If a brother fails to hear his name or is hesitant in continuing the story, he must chug a full glass of beer.

Something else occurs during this drinking game called *Whales Tales*. At one point the storyteller stops, and the brothers once again laugh and point with their elbows; they target one particular brother who seems unamused by their jests. This brother begins to argue, and although his precise words are not altogether audible, the gist of *his claim is that the proper signal was not given or that some sort of protocol was violated and therefore he will not drink. While this brother argues his case, the other brothers stand up around the table and mockingly grab their shirts with both hands, chest high, with their pointer fingers and thumbs, and pull them in an outward direction to signify imaginary breasts. Then all the brothers, except for the accused, sing a song directed at the apparent transgressor. The song is brief and basically consists of the phrase "you're a woman" repeated several times over to some tune known only to the brothers. While the brothers sing their mocking song about their dishonored companion becoming a woman, the onlookers smile and laugh at the brothers and their amusing game.*

The drinking game Whales Tales was a ritual that I observed at a fraternity house on the campus of Clement University, a pseudonym for a large research university. I use the drinking game to introduce this chapter because it highlights two separate representations of women in fraternity settings. First, women appear as big-busted images offered by men as part of a mocking gesture intended to degrade a male fraternity member. Clearly, to be a woman is to be something less than a man. Second, women appear as passive bystanders observing the brothers in action and, in a sense, condoning their own marginalization. Thus, the game of Whales Tales highlights two significant patterns that I observed throughout my research of fraternity life: (1) the promotion of hostile representations of women and (2) the positioning of women as passive participants. These two patterns

relate to a third issue uncovered in my research: That brothers tend to adopt a narrow conception of masculinity, which fosters oppression of both women and gay men.

In this chapter, I rely on critical views of culture and power to highlight aspects of fraternity life that contribute to the ongoing marginalization and, in some cases the victimization, of women. By critical views, I refer to theories deriving from postmodernism, critical theory, and feminist theory. The chapter is based on an ethnographic case study of a fraternity referred to throughout this chapter as Alpha Beta, a pseudonym.

■ SIGNIFICANCE OF THE PROBLEM

I select fraternity life as an object of inquiry because of the serious problems that fraternities pose to women in particular and society in general. Heys (1988) reports that at least 75 cases of campus gang rapes have occurred over recent years. Bryan (1987) points out that 70 percent of all reported gang rapes occur at fraternity parties. In a 1990 national study conducted at Towson State University, researchers note that approximately half of all reported acquaintance rapes were committed by fraternity members and athletes (Bausell et al. 1991). Another 1990 study, conducted at the University of Illinois at Urbana-Champaign, maintains that 34 of the 54 reported sexual assaults were committed by fraternity members (Johnson 1991).

Martin and Hummer (1989) frame a study of the abusive social contexts for women created by fraternity environments based on a gang rape at Florida State University in which an unconscious woman was raped by several men at one fraternity and then dumped in the hallway of a neighboring fraternity house. The victim was found in a comatose state with crude words and a fraternity symbol written on her thighs. This example highlights only one of the reported incidents; the true magnitude of the problem is unrealized as yet, since fear of being doubly victimized prevents many women from reporting incidents (Johnson 1991).

Consistent throughout most of the reported fraternity assaults is a pattern whereby fraternity members view women in subordinate terms and as sexual objects; women are seen to be unworthy of human dignity and undeserving of normal human rights. The fraternity, in turn, is frequently discussed as an organization that provides a haven for members' negative conceptions of women, and ultimately, reinforces these harmful images (Ehrhart and Sandler 1985; Martin and Hummer 1989; Sanday 1990).

Perhaps the most in-depth research on fraternity culture is the work of Sanday (1990), who documents a number of fraternity rituals and practices that contribute to the marginalization and victimization of women. Her concern is unraveling the extent to which organizational structures contribute to fraternity victimization of women. A central point of her work is the role that the pledge process plays in bringing about a transformation of consciousness so that group identity and attitudes become personalized. She explains that victimization of women begins with new members, who through the pledge process adopt values and attitudes that encourage the oppression of women; and that the covenant between the pledges and the fraternity promises a sense of masculinity and superior power. Sanday goes on to argue that the pledge takes on a new self "complete with a set of goals, values, concerns, visions, and ready-made discourses that are designed to help him negotiate the academic, social, and sexual contexts of undergraduate life from a position of power and status" (1990:135–136).

The findings I present in this chapter support many of Sanday's conclusions about the role fraternity rituals play in reproducing an oppressive environment for women with one important exception. Although Sanday sees the pledge process as central to the reproduction of a group sense of identity and the continuation of a culture of oppression, I suggest in this chapter an alternative conclusion—that the pledge process is largely irrelevant for the continuation and promotion of oppressive fraternity climates for women. I make this claim based on the fact that I observed many of the types of behaviors and rituals Sanday describes, but at a fraternity that has eliminated the pledge process. I return to this issue later in the chapter. For now, I discuss the theoretical and methodological points relevant to this study.

Culture and Power

Jelinek et al. describe culture as a "sort of interpretive paradigm. another word for social reality. both product and process, the shaper of human interaction and the outcome of it, continually created and recreated by people's ongoing interactions" (1983:331). Along a similar line, Geertz writes, "Believing, with Max Weber, that man is an animal suspended in webs of significance he himself has spun, I take culture to be those webs, and the analysis of it to be therefore not an experimental science in search of law but an interpretive one in search of meaning" (1973:5). The notion of culture as "webs of significance" that evolve from social interaction and in turn structure interaction is adopted throughout this chapter. In examining aspects of fraternity life at Alpha Beta, I will attempt to unravel various social practices that both reveal aspects of fraternity culture and, in turn, serve to create the culture.

From a critical perspective, culture is never value-free, nor are dominant cultural patterns uncontested (Benhabib 1986). Different social groups compete to legitimize their versions of reality, their values and beliefs, their ideologies, and ultimately, their own vision of the social world (Gergen 1991). Indeed, the culture of a given social organization is shaped through the enactment of power by dominant groups within that social collectivity. This is true of both societies and organizations (Smircich 1983). Giroux elaborates: "Culture is constituted by the relations between different classes and groups bounded by structural forces and material conditions and informed by a range of experiences mediated, in part, by the power exercised by a dominant society" (1983:163). For Giroux, power is not seen as one directional but instead is something to which all groups have access, albeit to varying degrees.

Giroux highlights the relational aspect of power. Giddens also discusses a relational conception of power when he notes that "[p]ower relations. are always two-way, even if the power of one actor or party in a social relation is minimal compared to another" (1979:93). Along a similar line of thought, Foucault describes power as "a machine in which everyone is caught, those who exercise power just as much as those over whom it is exercised" (1980:156). Burbules (1986), in building upon the work of Foucault and Giddens, elaborates two key points of this relational conception of power. First, he states that "[p]ower is a relation that is not simply chosen (or avoided) but made more or less necessary by the circumstances under which persons come together" (Burbules 1986:97). A second point is that within all power relations a tension exists between compliance and resistance. Burbules notes that, although one agent may be successful in proscribing actions of another, the advantaged agent's alternatives are also constrained by the relation in working to preserve it. "So long as the tension of resistance and compliance remains, it is accurate to say both that X has power over Y and that Y empowers X" (Burbules 1986:97)

Power is often embodied in one group's ability to gain legitimacy and control over facets of society. Oftentimes, one group's power over another is exercised not so much in an organized strategy but is subtly evident in the way various aspects of their culture become legitimated by already established institutions (Bourdieu 1977). In examining fraternity culture from a critical perspective, the focus must be on structures that reinforce positions of inequality in which fraternity members maintain power over others—in the case of this study, over women. A critical perspective therefore stresses the examination of social structures and patterns that render certain groups voiceless (Fraser and Nicholson 1990; hooks 1984, 1992). The questions that must be asked in studying fraternity culture not only relate to who is rendered voiceless but also concern how power is utilized to produce marginalization and in what forms does marginalization appear.

A critical view of culture suggests that it is continuously defined and redefined through social interactions framed by power relations. As "a complex of traditions, institutions, and formations situated within a social sphere of contestation and struggle" (Giroux 1983:164), culture is neither predictive nor easily measured. Researchers, in examining cultural contexts, have adopted methods that provide high levels of sensitivity and flexibility. The goal is not necessarily to test hypotheses but instead to gain understanding of people lives within specific cultural contexts. Such a process is not, as Geertz (1973) reminds us, an experimental science in search of lawlike principles but instead is an interpretive process in search of meaning.

THE STUDY

Methodologically, I build upon the work of Sanday (1990) and Leemon (1972). While Sanday relied primarily on secondhand accounts of fraternity experiences as reported to her by male and female students, Leemon observed fraternity life firsthand. Leemon provides "thick description" of a fraternity's pledge process, but he does not offer the critical analysis that Sanday provides. In my study, I try to draw upon the strengths of each of these works: the firsthand observations that Leemon emphasizes and the critical analyses that Sanday brings to her work.

In the works of both Sanday and Leemon, the significance of fraternity culture is evident. New members are fully accepted when they have demonstrated their adoption of the values, beliefs, and practices that epitomize the fraternity. Fraternity culture should not be seen as monolithic or static, however, since interactions among fraternity members also serve to reshape the organization's culture.

The general method used to conduct this study may be termed an ethnographic case study of organizational culture, a method made popular most notably by Van Maanen (1979). In recent years, ethnographic techniques have become quite useful in exploring educational settings (Eckert 1989; Holland and

Eisenhart 1990; McLaren 1986; Rhoads 1994; Tierney 1988).

Ideally, in conducting cultural research the ethnographer lives and works in the community for six months to a year or more learning the language and seeing patterns of behavior over time. I have worked as a student affairs professional for more than 11 years in the following areas of student life: residence life, student activities, academic and career advising, judicial affairs, student volunteerism and service learning, and athletics. From these experiences, I have worked with numerous student groups, including Greek organizations. Because of my previous involvement in student life and my work with various student groups, I was able to participate in fraternity activities right away without experiencing any communication difficulties.

In conducting my study, I called on a number of research tools used by ethnographers, including formal structured interviews, informal interviews, participant observation, and discussions with several key informants. Twelve formal structured interviews were conducted, which lasted anywhere from one to two hours. The work of Spradley (1979) was used to guide the formal interview process. These interviews were tape-recorded and transcribed verbatim. Copies of the transcripts were given to research participants, who were asked to provide additional comments or clarify any points made during the interview. Only one student returned his interview transcript with any additional comments. Eighteen less formal interviews also were

conducted. Hand notes were used to record these interviews. Informal interviews typically lasted less than an hour. Since Alpha Beta has fewer than 60 members, this means that roughly half of the fraternity was involved in either formal or informal interviews.

In addition to the formal and informal interviews, I was allowed to participate in a number of fraternity activities. These activities ranged from fraternity parties open to a wide range of Clement University students, to more private activities and rituals open only to a few outsiders. During the course of this study (the data-collection phase lasted one semester), I conducted ongoing discussions with several key informants, who explained the significance of various fraternity practices. Finally, numerous documents were examined including the Clement University Greek handbook, minutes from chapter meetings, class papers written by Alpha Beta members that described some of their fraternity experiences, and the fraternity liability policy, just to name a few.

The analysis of data involved reading and rereading pages of text. I focused specifically on textual material either involving fraternity members and women or comments directed at or concerning women. Several of the formal interview questions related specifically to women and their role in the fraternity. Consequently, I was able to develop a number of conceptual categories related to fraternity members' interactions and discussions of women. The emergence of these conceptual categories falls in line with Patton's (1980) discussion of inductive categorization of qualitative data, in which emphasis is placed on themes and categories derived from the data as opposed to predetermined classifications.

Methodologically, this study poses some interesting dilemmas. For example, how does a qualitative researcher who has been given permission by a fraternity to conduct a case study go on then to produce a paper that in effect presents the organization in a negative light? There was a presumption going into the study that my findings most likely would be positive, since Alpha Beta was selected because of its progressiveness. But what struck me throughout my research was that, despite some progressive positions (such as eliminating the pledge process), Alpha Beta nonetheless evidenced many of the oppressive qualities described by Sanday (1990). In the end, I was faced with one of those ethical decisions that ethnographic and qualitative researchers rarely seem to discuss: Should I out of obligation to my research participants ignore the serious implications of their interactions with women and focus on other cultural issues (and there were many), or should I put a concern for advancing understanding of fraternity exploitation of women first? The choice was difficult, but I chose to do the latter.

Upon reading my study, some of the Alpha Beta brothers objected and tried to have my findings censored. The issue was debated for almost a year at Clement University, and because the study had been reviewed and approved by the Institutional Review Board at Clement,

they became involved in the process. After much discussion and debate, I was given approval to publish my findings. Obviously, there is much here that could be explored in terms of academic freedom, research ethics, and the rights of researchers and subjects. I present these circumstances as background information for understanding the methodological issues raised by this study. These issues are significant, and I may explore them in a future paper. But for now, I return to the issue at hand and offer some background information about Alpha Beta.

Organizational Background

Alpha Beta has nearly 60 active members. They are a relatively new chapter at Clement University, having been colonized during the 1980s, and are noted for having ended the traditional pledge process. By the traditional pledge process, I refer to those practices typically associated with the subordination of prospective members, referred to as "pledges." The intent frequently has been to subject pledges to a variety of challenges and situations, sometimes described as "hazing" (Nuwer 1990), so that the brothers can evaluate the pledges' willingness to submit themselves to the organization. By granting recruits immediate full-member status, Alpha Beta's new-member process has successfully eliminated many of the traditional abuses, which largely resulted from an unequal distribution of power between a pledge and a brother.

In eliminating the traditional pledge process, Alpha Beta has demonstrated a willingness to take the lead in adopting fraternity reform. They also were one of the first fraternities to adopt a "bring your own bottle" (BYOB) party policy in an attempt to limit underage drinking as well as abusive drinking. Alpha Beta has made fraternity reform an issue, and many brothers see their progressive stance as an opportunity to be seen as leaders within the Greek system at Clement. Because of their awareness and concern for fraternity reform, Alpha Beta ranks as one of the more progressive fraternities at the university. I make this statement based not only on my own observations but also on other key sources. One source is the campus newspaper, which highlighted some of Alpha Beta's positive stances. Other sources include student affairs administrators, who generally described Alpha Beta as one of the more socially and politically aware fraternities. As one administrator stated, "[Alpha Beta] is one of our more enlightened fraternities. They've taken positive steps in dealing with important fraternity issues. For example, they had someone from Women's Studies speak at a program concerning date rape." It was this progressive quality that led me to select Alpha Beta, since I knew it would take an open-minded group to allow someone to study them.

Although some members of Alpha Beta expressed a sincere concern about important issues faced by fraternities and college students in general, others saw Alpha Beta's progressive stances as a means to establishing a better reputation and thus increasing their social status. In my discussions with members of Alpha Beta it became apparent that a fraternity social ladder existed at Clement University and that a fraternity's social standing was of major concern. I asked a number of Alpha Beta members where they would place their own fraternity on the social ladder and received a near consensus as to where Alpha Beta ranked—at or near the bottom. One member commented, "If you called up any top fraternity and asked them what do you think of [Alpha Beta], they would say we have somewhat of a dorky reputation. In my opinion the campus does think of us kind of low or, as Neal [a pseudonym] said, 'as a no name.' The house has a lot to do with it, where you rank. The house and the kind of parties you throw."

The significance of the fraternity social ladder cannot be understated. As one brother explained, "Fraternity social status ultimately relates to the attractiveness and prestige of the sorority women that a house can attract and additionally the desirability by students to be members." Various brothers indicated that several factors go into the relative status of a fraternity, some of which include the quality and location of the fraternity house, the fraternity's ability to attract desirable sororities to social functions, and the type and scale of parties and social events successfully carried out.

■ FINDINGS

Based on the analysis of data, three categories of findings relating to fraternity members' interactions with women emerged: (1) the promotion of hostile representations of women, (2) the positioning of women as passive participants, and (3) issues related to gender perceptions.

Hostile Representations of Women

Women were frequently characterized in ways that depicted them as something less than human beings—as objects worthy of manipulation or disdain. They were discussed as "tools" or "whores" and were frequently seen as targets for sexual manipulation. For example, one brother alluded to an ongoing debate the fraternity was having over the possible adoption of a little-sister program. He believed that little sisters were merely a tool used to attract new fraternity members: "It's really just a rush [the process of recruiting new members] tool." Having a little-sister program, however, does not guarantee attracting new fraternity members. A concern has to be exhibited for the "attractiveness" of the women. As this brother added, "If you have a bunch of undesirable-looking creatures or a bunch of people wearing your letters that you know you wouldn't normally hang around with, that's bad." In this brother's statement, women who the brothers define as unattractive are seen as something less than human—as "creatures." Women were frequently spoken of in derogatory ways if they had, or allegedly had, slept with more than one of the brothers. This thought was confirmed by one brother, who described a woman who supposedly had slept with several brothers as a whore who if she had sex with one more brother would get a free fraternity hat. Terms such as "hogger" or "two-bagger" were also used to describe women who were not seen as attractive by the Alpha Beta brothers. There were a couple of women that the brothers placed in the "hogger" category who hung out regularly at the fraternity house. According to a number of the brothers, these women only hung around so that they could sleep with the brothers. Supposedly a number of different Alpha Beta brothers had slept with them, but interestingly enough, none of the brothers I spoke with ever stated that they had in fact slept with any of the women—it was always someone else who had.

Along a related line, the brothers had a phrase for the behavior of a fellow member who might be drunk enough at a party to pursue a woman whom the brothers classified as a hogger. This was referred to as "beer goggling" or "wearing your beer goggles." "It's when you're drunk, and you hit on anything that moves. It's up to your brothers to help you out when you're this drunk and make sure you don't do anything you'll regret later—like sleep with some hogger." Underlying all of this is, of course, patriarchy—systematic and structural conditions in which men have higher status and privilege than women. As Connell notes, "Though not all men oppress all women, it is still true that there is a general oppression of women by men. This is precisely the defining point of patriarchy. All women live and act in conditions shaped by the structural fact of men's supremacy" (1983:44).

Some of the Alpha Beta brothers were aware of the patriarchal attitudes that some brothers held. As an example, some of the brothers planned an educational program with a local sorority designed to encourage discussions of relationships between men and women. In attempting to shed light on the problematic relations between college men and women, one Alpha Beta brother noted the following:

> College men tend to objectify women—not just fraternity men but independents too. In fact, it may be an even bigger problem with independents since we at least offer educational programs on sexual awareness. There's a problem with women too though. The women at this university—and you hear this as an excuse for rape which is wrong—but if they allow themselves to be treated in a particular manner, then they're just as much at fault as we are. And I think that's why it's important to have joint education. So that the women stand up and look you in the eye and say, "Hey, I don't like it when you do this." I think that's very important and that's why a lot of the assault programs are done between a fraternity and a sorority. I think there's more and more pressure being placed on fraternities to become accountable in their actions toward women.

But once again, even when supposedly enlightened voices are heard, an attitude of "we are not the problem" surfaces. In the preceding passage, although the brother admits that a serious problem exists between college men and women, he fails to acknowledge the specific problems connected with fraternities and ultimately resorts to blaming the victim. This type of attitude toward women was not uncommon.

Even more startling than blaming women for their own victimization was a notion that they were not really victimized to begin with. This attitude was expressed in the following comment: "You have to remember one thing—that girls can just say 'I was raped' and then they were raped. You know what I mean? Girls have that power. Women have that power." Here, we get an image of women as "liars" who have power over men because of their potential to create stories about being raped.

Evidenced by the comments in this section is the tendency for Alpha Beta brothers to view women as objects for sexual manipulation. Such a tendency dehumanizes women and places them in subordinate positions to their male counterparts, who are seen to have a variety of significant and positive qualities. Even when brothers attempted to be sensitive to the oppressive nature of fraternity relations with women, a finger invariably was pointed once again at the victim—in this case, women.

Positioning of Women as Passive Participants

Although women were frequently permitted to participate in Alpha Beta functions, their participation was limited and defined by the fraternity members. A typical scene involved the brothers participating in some type of recreational activity or game, such as intramural football, while the women observed from the sidelines. This was the case at several social events that I attended as well. But there was one specific event in which women were accepted, in fact, encouraged to participate. It was a drinking game that involved playing cards (a different game than Whales Tales), in which the loser was often required to chug a glass of beer. Martin and Hummer (1989) note that the encouragement of women to participate in drinking activities fits in with fraternity members' use of alcohol as a weapon against sexual reluctance.

One specific ritual highlights the passive role that was frequently defined for women. It relates to a dating ritual that many fraternities practice—the ritual of lavaliering. Lavaliering, as one brother explained, "is a ritual that we have with a brother and his girlfriend. It's pretty serious; so you only do this if you're really involved with someone. It's an engagement type of thing." I spoke with a woman who had recently participated in the lavaliering ceremony. Secrecy prohibited her from describing the ritual in detail, but she did offer the following description:

> Several brothers came to my dorm room and blindfolded me. They told me that they couldn't tell me where or what was going on—although I had my suspicions. I was taken to a room in the basement of Alpha Beta, where rituals and ceremonies are normally performed. My blindfold was eventually removed, and I could see that the room was filled

with brothers all wearing their robes used for fraternity rituals. The only light was from lit candles spread around the room. At first I was a bit nervous, but then I saw my boyfriend and I knew everything was alright.

Alpha Beta's ritual of lavaliering casts a frightening shadow when the social conditions are deconstructed. A woman is blindfolded by several men and taken to a dark basement in a fraternity house. The basement room is lit only by candles and is filled with men in ceremonial robes. The event is supposed to be a surprise. In the scenario described to me, the woman was very excited about her participation in the ritual. Despite her willingness and enthusiasm to participate in an apparently harmless activity, she was placed in a position of powerlessness. Although she may not have been in danger during this ritual, I am left to ponder the long-term implications of women being placed in positions in which fraternity members have complete control and women are left with only blind faith. Sanday (1990) suggests that some women who participate in fraternity activities do so to gain acceptance among the brothers, who occupy a privileged position on campus. Fraternities are seen as a source of social affirmation. As a result, many women are often placed in dangerous and compromising situations in which exploitation and victimization at the hands of brothers is likely. For the woman I spoke with about lavaliering, the ritual was the first and only chance she had to participate in a fraternity secret ceremony.

She was excited and proud to have the opportunity. In essence, it was an opportunity for acceptance.

Attempts to involve women more actively in fraternity life were frequently discussed and debated by the Alpha Beta brothers. Discussions usually involved a heated debate over the introduction of a little-sisters program. Little sisters are college women who become officially associated with a fraternity; they participate in activities with the brothers but do not have full membership. Sometimes, little sisters are expected to plan and carry out programs where in effect they become the "servants" of the brothers—such as organizing a party and performing the role of servers. Sanday (1990) criticizes these types of programs for the dangerous dynamics that they establish, whereby women are placed in positions of subordination to fraternity members. In a discussion related to little sisters, one brother commented, "We should have little sisters. I know if we get them it raises our insurance. I have no idea why. Probably because national [Alpha Beta's national organization] doesn't want them. Every time something arises around here, it's a political issue." I asked this brother what he thought of the negative connotations associated with little-sister programs. He commented:

Right. They end up being 'ho's [whores] and hanging around and doing all that kind of thing. We have them now. They don't need to be under a separate name because they're here now. There's girls who just come out to the fraternity to have someone to sleep with that night. You know? There's a girl who lives over there [pointing to his left] who we joke about. After ten [guys] she gets a free hat. She only needs one more. It's that kind of thing. It's kind of disgusting if you ask me.

The comments in this section highlight the concern that for the most part women's participation in Alpha Beta activities occurred under the jurisdiction and control of the brothers. As a result, women frequently became passive participants in various fraternity rituals and activities. The result is that women are placed in positions of limited power where they may become unsuspecting victims of fraternity abuse.

Perceptions of Gender

There is perhaps a strong link between the Alpha Beta brothers' relations with and attitudes toward women and their views of masculinity and gender. To highlight this point, I note the brothers' attitudes toward gay men as well as actions and beliefs depicting a machismo vision of masculinity.

To support the claim that brothers condone a macho conception of manhood, I describe an Alpha Beta ritual, which is also found at other fraternities. At one party I attended a brother discussed an activity that he referred to as "stair diving." He described it in the following manner: "Basically stair diving is just what it says—stair diving. We stand at the top of the stairs and dive down headfirst. The goal is to see who can land the furthest down the steps. I'm the stair-diving champion right now." This brother was very proud of his title as stair-diving champion, and it seemed to confirm his own notion of physical ability and ultimately his place in the fraternity. He also bragged about being the top football player in the fraternity and told a story of the first time he played with the brothers and how none of them could tackle him. Throughout discussions with many of the brothers I was aware of a heavy emphasis on physical qualities, namely, athleticism and attractiveness. But a few Alpha Beta members spoke openly about their disdain for the emphasis upon physical appearance among their own fraternity and fraternities in general. One of these brothers noted, "You can go to some of the top fraternities on this campus, and it'll look like they cloned their members. All well-built and attractive. The sororities are the same way too."

Another frequent fraternity behavior that provided some insights was a ritual known as a "wedgie"—which involved the forced removal of another brother's underwear while he was wearing them and without taking off his pants. Several brothers wrestle the victim to the ground and then reach inside his pants and grab the elastic portion of the underwear and pull until they are ripped off the victim. A brother described the process as a very painful experience and added, "When I go to a party, I either don't wear any underwear or I wear an old pair that would be easily ripped off. They did it to me once in front of a date I brought,

and it was embarrassing. She thought we were real immature."

Performing wedgies involves close physical contact among several brothers and not only can be interpreted for the violent event that it is but additionally can be seen as an activity that permits physical contact between men. A similar ritual the brothers practiced from time to time was "dog piling"—which like the wedgie ritual involved a great deal of close physical contact. Dog piles involve several brothers jumping on or "piling" on top of another brother and roughing him up, so to speak. They may mess up his hair or rustle his clothes; the activity is meant to be fun and seems to develop a sense of bonding among the brothers involved. Being selected for a dog pile appeared to be some type of honor or at least a sort of recognition that one belongs to the group. As is the case with the wedgie ritual, dog piling provides the brothers with an outlet for acceptable physical contact. Among a group whose culture stresses a very macho conception of manhood, other types of physical contact are seen as objectionable, especially contact involving sensitivity or caring between males.

The strong emphasis upon physical qualities, such as strength, fearlessness, and aggressiveness, represents a narrow conception of manhood. This leads some Alpha Beta brothers to participate in dangerous activities such as stair diving. The emphasis on the machismo is also reflected in a strong disdain for gay students, whom the brothers tend to see as lacking in masculinity. Here, the brothers exhibit what some social theorists term sexual inversion theory—a belief that gay men are really more like women than they are like men (Tyler 1991). Because the brothers see women as inferior and since gay men are viewed to be more like women than men, oppressing gay men is carried out in the defense of maleness. For example, several of the brothers expressed an outright contempt for gay men. One told a story of an acquaintance who had joined a fraternity and later, in this brother's sarcastic tone, "discovered his sexuality." He commented on how Alpha Beta brothers might respond to such a scenario:

> With nothing to base it on, if we were to have a gay brother—and it's entirely possible that we do—we just don't know it. [Long pause.] The attitude here would be to tar and feather him and hang him from the highest rooftop. And that saddens me. But knowing that that's the case and every brother knowing that that's the case, most likely a brother would not admit anything to this group. Which is sad. But that's something that would take a long time to change, and it would only change when society's ideals change. I think that fraternities are very conservative when it comes to reflecting the ideals of society.

Although the preceding brother commented on the hypothetical, another described an actual event that depicts some members' fear and animosity toward gay men. During coming out week at Clement University—a week in which lesbian, gay, and bisexual students are

encouraged to come out of the closet and become more open about their sexual orientation—several of the brothers tied pairs of underwear to a traffic pole in front of the Alpha Beta house. They then set the underwear on fire to highlight their dislike of "flaming homosexuals." This activity was described by one of the brothers as the "flaming wedgie ritual."

The findings in this section suggest that some of the oppressive behaviors exhibited by Alpha Beta members may reflect in part their efforts to affirm a sense of masculinity. In acting out oppressive behaviors toward gay men as well as participating in fraternity rituals such as wedgies and dog piles, the Alpha Beta brothers may be protecting their own narrow sense of masculinity while at the same time meeting a basic need for physical contact. My findings support those of Sanday, who argues that fraternity members also may be masking "a deep fear, hatred and fascination with homosexuality" (1990:122). Unfortunately, fraternity members adopt a very narrow conception of masculinity, a macho conception (Ehrhart and Sandler 1985; Martin and Hummer 1989).

A narrow and stereotypical conception of masculinity and a "fear, hatred, and fascination" with homosexuality may also contribute greatly to the oppressive nature of female–male relations. Confusion regarding their own sexual identity may contribute to many brothers' perceptions of women. That is, when manhood is defined as machismo and demonstrated in the ways described in this chapter—such as gay bashing, dog piling, and performing wedgies, as well as other aggressive behaviors—the likelihood that brothers will have mature perceptions of womanhood seems small.

■ DISCUSSION

Alpha Beta displays many of the rituals, practices, and behaviors that Sanday describes in her analysis of fraternity culture. But as I note earlier in this chapter, Sanday sees the pledge process as a crucial structure for promoting the victimization of women among fraternity members. What do we make of her conclusion, in light of the fact that Alpha Beta ended their pledge process over three years ago, and thus only the current seniors went through such a process?

I offer two alternative explanations. First, the pledge process is often described as a rite of passage to fraternity membership (Leemon 1972). Sanday adopts such a view in her analysis. A focus on the pledge process tends to view fraternity socialization as an either/or proposition—one is either a member or one is not. Of course, surviving the pledge process serves to move one from nonmember status to a full member of the brotherhood. But if we view organizational culture as a dynamic force that both shapes and is shaped by social interactions, then we must also recognize that socialization must necessarily be ongoing. Since the culture of an organization is in essence never complete, then socialization to that same culture must also be incomplete. Here I

borrow from Van Maanen's (1976, 1983) work on organizational socialization and argue that fraternity socialization is an ongoing process and that pledging only serves as an initial phase of such a process. From such a perspective, even if the pledge process is eliminated, other structural mechanisms exist to socialize recruits to the values, attitudes, and beliefs of the organization. In the case of Alpha Beta, chapter meetings, fraternity parties, secret ceremonies, and rituals all contribute to a brother's sense of identity within the fraternity and his sense of brotherhood. This view helps to explain why the brothers of Alpha Beta continue to exhibit many of the oppressive attitudes and behaviors described in Sanday's work despite the fact that they have eliminated the pledge process.

Another explanation exists. Here I borrow from Scott (1965), who points out that new fraternity members may bring a common set of unified values to the fraternity; some of these values may already reflect oppressive attitudes toward women. From this perspective, the fraternity takes on a group sense of identity not so much because of the trials and tribulations members pass through together, but because the brotherhood is held together by the common values, beliefs, and attitudes brought to the organization. Self-selection thus plays a preeminent role in fostering a sense of group identity. The fraternity in turn merely provides a vehicle for enacting dispositions that are already held.

Both of these explanations offer some understanding as to why the culture of Alpha Beta continues to marginalize women. It seems logical then to consider that both may contribute to the lasting influence of patriarchy within the Alpha Beta fraternity. In other words, new members bring certain dispositions about women with them when they join the fraternity. In turn, these dispositions are not only reinforced, but additional hostile conceptions of women are ingrained through interactions with other brothers. In this way, the brothers' attitudes and beliefs about women shape the culture of Alpha Beta, while at the same time the culture frames their interactions. The result is an organizational culture that continues to situate women's lives on the margins.

■ CONCLUSION

As male-dominated societies, fraternities represent many of the traditions of patriarchy. The notion of patriarchy relates to the delineation and separation of men and women as social categories in which men are elevated to higher status and privilege. Fraternities, by excluding women or including them only under certain conditions, reflect patriarchal notions and ultimately promote the marginalization and even the victimization of women.

The brothers of Alpha Beta contributed to the oppression of women through machismo behavior, objectification of women, and the subordination of feminine traits, while enacting roles of power and domination disguised in dimly lit ceremonies and ritualized garb. Even

those brothers most concerned with reconstructing a fraternal organization in which oppression is nonexistent were in the end guilty of patriarchal practices and beliefs. Although women do not gain formal membership within Alpha Beta, they nevertheless participate to a significant degree in the fraternity experience. Because their participation is under almost complete control of the brothers of Alpha Beta, women become marginalized and face possible victimization.

REFERENCES

Bausell, R. B., C. R. Bausell, and D. G. Siegel 1991 *The Links among Drugs, Alcohol, and Campus Crime*. Silver Spring, MD: Business Publishers.

Benhabib, Seyla 1986 *Critique, Norm, and Utopia*. New York: Columbia University Press.

Bourdieu, Pierre 1977 *Outline of a Theory of Practice*. R. Nice, trans. Cambridge, UK: Cambridge University Press.

Bryan, William. A. 1987 Contemporary Fraternity and Sorority Issues. In *Fraternities and Sororities on the Contemporary College Campus*. R. B. Winston Jr. and W. R. Nettles III, eds. Pp. 37–56. New Directions for Student Services, 40. San Francisco: Jossey-Bass.

Burbules, Nicholas C. 1986 A Theory of Power in Education. *Educational Theory* *36*(2):95–114.

Connell, Robert W. 1983 *Which Way Is Up?: Essays on Sex, Class, and Culture*. Sydney: George Allen & Unwin.

Eckert, Penelope 1989 *Jocks and Burnouts: Social Categories and Identity in the High School.* New York: Teachers College Press.

Ehrhart, Julie K., and Bernice B. Sandler 1985 *Campus Gang Rape: Party Games?* (Research Report). Washington, DC: American Association of Colleges.

Foucault, Michel 1980 *Power and Knowledge: Selected Interviews and Other Writings.* New York: Pantheon.

Fraser, Nancy, and Linda J. Nicholson 1990 Social Criticism without Philosophy: An Encounter between Feminism and Postmodernism. In *Feminism/Postmodernism.* L. J. Nicholson, ed. Pp. 19–38. New York: Routledge.

Geertz, Clifford 1973 *The Interpretation of Cultures.* New York: Basic Books.

Gergen, Kenneth J. 1991 *The Saturated Self: Dilemmas of Identity in Contemporary Life.* New York: Basic Books.

Giddens, Anthony 1979 *Central Problems in Social Theory.* Berkeley: University of California Press.

Giroux, Henry A. 1983 *Theory and Resistance in Education: A Pedagogy for the Opposition.* South Hadley, MA: Bergin & Garvey Publishers.

Heys, S. 1988 In Gang Rape, the Mob Rules as "Men Rape for Other Men." *Atlanta Constitution,* June 7:14.

Holland, Dorothy C., and Margaret A. Eisenhart. 1990 *Educated in Romance: Women, Achievement, and College.* Chicago: University of Chicago Press.

hooks, bell. 1984 *Feminist Theory from Margin to Center.* Boston: South End Press.

hooks, bell. 1992 *Black Looks: Race and Representation.* Boston: South End Press.

Jelinek, Mariann, Linda Smircich, and Paul Hirsch 1983 Introduction: A Code of Many Colors. *Administrative Science Quarterly 28*(3): 331–338.

Johnson, Constance 1991 When Sex Is the Issue. *U.S. News and World Report,* October 7:34–36.

Leemon, Thomas A. 1972 *The Rites of Passage in a Student Culture.* New York: Teachers College Press.

Martin, Patricia Yancey, and Robert A. Hummer 1989 Fraternities and Rape on Campus. *Gender & Society 3*(4): 457–473.

McLaren, Peter 1986 *Schooling as a Ritual Performance.* London: Routledge & Kegan Paul.

Nuwer, Hank 1990 *Broken Pledges: The Deadly Rite of Hazing.* Atlanta: Longstreet.

Patton, Michael Q. 1980 *Qualitative Evaluation Methods.* Newbury Park, CA: Sage.

Rhoads, Robert A. 1994 *Coming Out in College: The Struggle for a Queer Identity.* Westport, CT: Bergin & Garvey.

Sanday, Peggy R. 1990 *Fraternity Gang Rape: Sex, Brotherhood, and Privilege on Campus.* New York: New York University Press.

Scott, William A. 1965 *Values and Organizations: A Study of Fraternities and Sororities.* Chicago: Rand McNally & Company.

Smircich, Linda 1983 Concepts of Culture and Organizational Analysis. *Administrative Science Quarterly 28:* 339–358.

Spradley, James P. 1979 *The Ethnographic Interview.* Fort Worth, TX: Holt, Rinehart and Winston.

Tierney, William G. 1988 *The Web of Leadership: The Presidency in Higher Education.* Greenwich, CT: JAI Press.

Tyler, Carole-Anne 1991 Boys Will Be Girls: The Politics of Gay Drag. In *Inside/Out: Lesbian Theories, Gay Theories*. D. Fuss, ed. Pp. 32–70. New York: Routledge.

Van Maanen, John 1976 Breaking In: Socialization to Work. In *Handbook of Work, Organization, and Society*. R. Dubin, ed. Pp. 67–130. Chicago: Rand McNally College Publishing.

Van Maanen, John 1979 The Fact of Fiction in Organization Ethnography. *Administrative Science Quarterly 24*: 539–550.

Van Maanen, John 1983 Doing New Things in Old Ways: The Chains of Socialization. In *College and University Organization: Insights from the Behavioral Sciences*. J. L. Bess, ed. Pp. 211–247. New York: New York University Press.

CHAPTER 15

Toward a Transformed Approach to Prevention

Breaking the Link between Masculinity and Violence

Luoluo Hong

Boys and men are most often the perpetrators of interpersonal violence (Courtenay, in press; Miedzian, 1991), including homicide (Healthy People, 1991; Health, United States, 1999; Poe-Yamagata, 1997), physical assaults (Douglas, Collins,, Warren, et al., 1997; Centers for Disease Control, 1991, 1992; Valois, Vincent, McKeown, Garrison, & Kirby, 1993), sexual assaults (Koss, Gidycz, & Wisniewski, 1987; Rapaport & Burkhart, 1984; Muehlenhard & Linton, 1987; Struckman-Johnson & Struckman-Johnson, 1994), domestic abuse (Walker, 1979; Campaign Against Family Violence, 1991; Uniform Crime Reports, 1992), and bias-related crimes (Levin, 1993), according to a review of the literature. Similarly, men and boys are three to five times more likely than women and girls to bear weapons (Valois, Vincent, McKeown, Garrison, & Kirby,

1993; Miller, Hemenway, & Wechlser, 1999), thus increasing their risks for homicide and suicide (Kellermann, Rivara, Rushforth, et al., 1993; Kellermann, Rivara, Somes, et al., 1992). In addition, boys and men are a significant proportion of the victims of violence (Courtenay, in press), including physical assaults (Sourcebook of Criminal Justice Statistics, 1994; Kivel, 1992; Finkelhor & Wolak, 1995) and sexual assaults (Isely, 1996).

In the face of such evidence, a growing number of researchers and writers argue that the predominant male socialization process in the United States inculcates in boys and men a hegemonic and limiting code of masculinity that intimately links traditional male gender roles with violence and, therefore, may predispose men to be perpetrators and victims of violence (Berkowitz, 1992; Courtenay, 1998; Katz, 1995; Kimmel &

Clarence, 1993; Marshall, 1993; Messner, 1992; Messner & Sabo, 1994; Pollack, 1998; Weinberg, 1998; Good, Hepper, Hillenbrand-Gunn, & Wang, 1995). Although violence has historically been discussed in gender-neutral terms, Courtenay (1999), as well as Katz and Jhally (1999) believe that specialists in violence prevention must recognize the gender-related nature of violence.

Nevertheless, the vast majority of institutions of higher education fail to target college men meaningfully in primary prevention efforts (i.e., specific measures that stop or reduce the possibility of violent behavior in the first place) (Modesto, 1996; Roth & Moore, 1995). Nor do colleges and universities address the entire continuum of campus interpersonal violence described by Roark (1993). Instead, most institutions focus solely or primarily on sexual assault and rely on a menu of traditional approaches, including (a) risk-reduction and self-defense workshops designed for women; (b) environmental changes to make the campus safer or to reduce the availability of alcohol and other drugs used to facilitate sexual assault; (c) victim-advocacy programs and augmentation of campus judicial proceedings; and (d) single-sex or coeducational workshops that use the health belief model (Rosenstock, Strecher, & Becker, 1988) to correct misperceived sexual cues (Abbey, 1982, 1991; Abbey, Cozzarelli, McLaughlin, & Harnish, 1987; Abbey & Melby, 1986), debunk rape myths (Burt, 1991; Foubert, 2000), and describe how to obtain positive consent (Berkowitz, 1994).

None of the first three of these approaches is a true form of prevention; labeling them as such is a misnomer. The first two approaches fail to address the agency of the sexual assault perpetrator, and the third approach intervenes after the sexual assault incident has already occurred. The fourth approach, although it forms the foundation of effective sexual assault prevention, does not fundamentally change the broader sociocultural determinants of behavior that may supersede individual attitudes, beliefs, and intentions.

By contrast, a transformed approach to violence prevention would continue to address sexual assault and would also address other prevalent forms of campus violence, including physical assaults and hate crimes. In acknowledging the gender-related nature of violence, a transformed approach would also strive to open what Allen (1993) refers to as the man box and expand the definitions of what is appropriately masculine, thus alleviating both perceived and real peer pressure that may motivate men to engage in physical and sexual aggression to affirm their masculinity. Such an approach would necessarily disassociate the heretofore "masculine" traits of agency and action from violence (Pollack, 1998) in all of our social institutions, including the family, school, church, workplace, and media. Finally, a transformed approach would involve and engage students—particularly men—in meaningful ways that emphasize ownership for activism and social change and would do so within the context of long-term and sustained prevention initiatives.

■ MEN AGAINST VIOLENCE: A MODEL FOR A TRANSFORMED PREVENTION APPROACH

The student organization Men Against Violence (MAV) is the first of its kind and scope in the United States and represents an operational embodiment of a transformed approach to campus violence prevention. MAV focuses on changing cultural and peer reference group norms, rather than on individual and interpersonal variables. The organization provides a male peer-support network that alleviates the stress and anxiety of dating relationships and everyday living, not by reinforcing narrow conceptions of masculinity (Schwartz & DeKeseredy, 1997), but by generating shared norms of nonviolence and communication. It expands notions of gender-role expectations on an ongoing, long-term basis in a peer group setting through two venues: (a) an explicit examination and critical analysis of hegemonic masculinity, which refers to predominant social concepts of appropriate attitudes and behaviors for men and traditional male socialization processes, and its relationship to violence; and (b) an implicit learning process, in which peer education and service learning activities serve as the conduit for developing a close-knit community of men whose guiding values represent broader, nonlimiting ideas of what is appropriate, acceptable behavior for "real men."

Through both formal (e.g., guided by the advisor) and informal (e.g.,

spontaneous socializing) interactions, members of MAV are creating a male peer culture, albeit a loose one, that supports a new masculinity—a masculinity that is inherently nonviolent. MAV challenges college men at a time in their development when gender and sexual identities are salient (Berkowitz, 1992; Chickering, 1969). It urges them to approach male-female relationships in an equitable manner, resolve conflicts effectively, overcome homophobia, develop meaningful friendships with other men, and express and manage anger or fear appropriately.

Developing the Peer Support Network

Motivated by concern about violence on campus, 15 charter members representing a cross-section of male students at Louisiana State University (LSU) came together and formulated the idea for a service organization dedicated to combating stalking, domestic violence, fighting, hate crimes, hazing, rape, and vandalism. MAV was founded in February 1995 and the group received official recognition as a student organization at LSU in April 1995. "Brother" chapters of MAV in various stages of organization have been chartered at Eastern Washington University, Idaho State University, Southern University, Southwest Texas State University, the University of Florida at Gainesville, and the University of Wyoming at Laramie.

MAV is sponsored by the student health center on campus and its advisor is a health education professional from the center. Its structure and underlying philosophy are similar to the community action model of peer education described by Fabiano (1994) in the *Journal of American College Health*. An executive board of 8 officers is elected each year in April and convenes weekly to provide leadership and engage in strategic planning for MAV. An advisory board consisting of 14 faculty, staff, and alumni meet on a monthly basis to provide guidance and support to the executive board. The meetings consist of a business portion followed by an educational rap session. General meetings occur roughly six times each semester and are open to all MAV members and the general campus community.

MAV training conferences each semester allow members to develop relevant skills before they engage in peer education. In addition, a leadership development workshop occurs each year in early April to facilitate a smooth transition between the outgoing and incoming executive boards. As a nonprofit organization, MA subsidizes its own efforts by fund raising, collecting membership dues, selling T-shirts, and soliciting corporate and individual sponsorships.

Membership Criteria

Membership is open to all full-time undergraduate and graduate students; staff, faculty, and graduates may join as alumni members. As of September 1998, each of the Greek-letter social fraternities for men is mandated to have three liaison members who participate in MAV. Other students who join of their own accord represent a wide variety of academic standings, ethnic/racial backgrounds, personal interests, and student affiliations [including intercollegiate athletic teams and Reserve Officer Training Corps (ROTC) units], making MAV indisputably the most diverse student organization on LSU's campus. Because research indicates that men are more effective in educating their male peers about violence in single-sex settings (Kivel, 1992; Berkowitz, 1994; Earle, 1996), only men are eligible to serve on the executive board. Even though women can and do join MAV, 97% of the current members are men.

MAV's purpose, as outlined in the March 1995 constitution, is "to reduce the frequency and severity of violent acts among the students, faculty, and staff of Louisiana State University" and to emphasize the special responsibility that men have in doing so. Members of MAV engage in four activity areas that form the acronym ACES:

- Awareness includes media efforts to increase campus and community understanding of violence and the violence culture; publication each semester of a newsletter, *Noenum Violentus,* for campus-wide distribution; and new-member recruitment.
- Community Action entails volunteer service projects, policy revision, and political activism; programming for other students in the areas of sexism, racism, and homophobia; rethinking masculinity; sexual, physical, and

psychological violence; anger management and conflict resolution; firearm safety; "group think" and hazing; and the connections between violence and substance abuse.

- Education includes efforts aimed at academic classes, fraternity houses, residence halls, local K-12 schools, and regional and national conferences.
- Support urges MAV members to provide support and intervention for both victims and perpetrators of violence. The offices of the dean of students and the department of residential life both mandate educational interventions through MAV for those students who are on disciplinary probation for violent or aggressive behavior.

■ METHOD

During the 1997/98 academic year, I conducted a case study of Men Against Violence for my doctoral dissertation. Participants in the study, selected through purposeful, intensity sampling (Patton, 1990), were the 8 men who were the MAV executive board officers that year. Five of the study participants were White, 3 (including the president of MAV) were African American. They ranged in age from 19 to 28 years. All but 2 of the officers were born and raised in Louisiana. Of the others, 1 was an international student from the Netherlands; the other, although born in Houston, Texas, had spent a considerable part of his life traveling in the United States and overseas. Two of the men were majoring

in international trade and finance, 2 in business, and 1 each in marketing, sociology, psychology, and political science-sociology (a double-major). The median length of membership in MAV was three semesters.

In making my analyses, I was guided by a feminist framework (Harding, 1987; hooks, 1984) and adhered to ethnographic principles established by Spradley (1980). The qualitative methodology included (a) more than 250 hours of participant observations (including a memorable 4-day trip to San Marcos to attend the regional peer education conference at Southwest Texas State University); (b) eight ethnographic interviews, varying from 90 minutes to 4 hours, with each MAV officer; and (c) document analyses of meeting minutes, letters, and newsletter articles. To protect the interests and well-being of study participants, I followed ethical guidelines outlined by Spradley (1979). Triangulation in data collection assured greater validity in the results (Patton, 1990). After collecting the data, I conducted a cultural themes analysis in the manner described by Lincoln and Guba (1985) and created an ethnographic record in the spirit and style of MacLeod (1995). The data and conclusions in this paper represent only one portion of the dissertation research project.

Brannon and David's (1976) four metaphors ("No sissy stuff"; "Be a big wheel"; "Be a study oak"; "Give 'em hell") for traditional, hegemonic masculinity served as a conceptual framework for the study. It is important to note that these metaphors do not describe the actual lives of the vast majority of men in the United States; instead, they define a social construct referred to as real men and suggest how such men ought to behave. Although men exhibit a multitude of masculinities (Connell, 1987; Laberge & Albert, 1999), one ideal of masculinity becomes dominant and marginalizes other definitions. This hegemony is reinforced by such societal institutions as political power, mass media, and corporate culture.

With Connell's (1987) point in mind, one must recognize two situations in which hypermasculinity—men's overcompensation for an insecure gender identity, with a commensurate increase in aggression and violent behavior—may occur. First, men who are denied full access to typical male privileges and status because of their stigmatized race, class, or sexual orientation are likely to adhere to stricter, more extreme conceptions of traditional masculinity (Kimmel & Clarence, 1993; Green, 1987; Staples, 1982; Courtenay, 2000). Denied access through traditional routes for establishing economic and political hegemonic masculinity, these men instead "prove" their manhood by exhibiting it in extreme forms that some writers have labeled the "cool pose" in analyzing media representations of African American men (Gray, 1994; Majors & Billson, 1992).

Second, the literature indicates that men whose primary cohabitation or social affiliation is with other men tend to display exaggerated conformity to traditional male role norms. Examples of such groups of men include campus fraternities

(Martin & Hummer, 1989; O'Sullivan, 1993; Sanday, 1990); intercollegiate and professional team sports, primarily the high contact sports such as football, basketball, lacrosse, and ice hockey (Messner, 1992; Benedict, 1998; Crosset & McDonald, 1995; Nelson, 1994); and military combat units, especially in times of war (Brownmiller, 1975; O'Sullivan, 1992; Pope, 1993). Not surprisingly, most gang rapes that occur on campus are perpetrated by men who are active in one of these groups (O'Sullivan, 1991).

Given MAV's goal of preventing violence both directly (violence as undesirable behavior) and indirectly (violence as an expression of hegemonic masculinity), one would expect some changes in the 8 study participants' conceptions of masculinity as a result of their involvement in the organization. In addition, one might anticipate some parallel changes in views toward violence. The study participants did, indeed, exhibit measurable and meaningful changes in attitudes, beliefs, and behaviors relative to normative gender expectations. These changes and their relation to hegemonic masculinity, for discussion purposes, can be loosely categorized in the same manner that Gerschick and Miller (1995) did in their study: (a) rejection, in which a participant renounces dominant norms for male behavior, creates his own code of manhood, or completely denies masculinity as important in his life; (b) reformulation, in which an individual redefines traditional conceptions of masculinity in his own terms; and (c) reliance, whereby an individual remains sensitive or hypersensitive to particular aspects of prevailing gender stereotypes. This pattern is comparable to Connell's (1995) triad of transforming, resisting, and reproducing hegemonic masculinity.

■ NO SISSY STUFF: REJECTION, REFORMULATION, RELIANCE

The first of Brannon and David's (1976) tenets, "No sissy stuff," teaches men to avoid behaving in any manner that can be even vaguely labeled or perceived as feminine. Indeed, Connell (1987, 1995) argues that hegemonic masculinity by necessity must be defined as nonfeminine. In childhood, boys who cry are admonished with, "Stop being like your baby sister." If a boy falls or injures himself, he might be told, "Take it like a little man." Coaches frequently use epithets like "sissy," "girlie," or "wuss" to degrade poor performance by male athletes. Boys who engage in women's sports are labeled as "queers" or "fags" (Laberge & Albert, 1999). And because being gay has stereotypically and erroneously been equated with being "feminine," fear of femininity is also exhibited as homophobia. That is, real boys and men are threatened by men who willingly choose, as Dworkin (1981) suggests, to fulfill roles that are traditionally reserved for women (being the receptive sexual partner). Observes Kimmel (1993):

> Homophobia (which I understand as more than fear of homosexual men; it's

also fear of other men) keeps men acting like men, keeps men exaggerating their adherence to traditional norms, so that no other men will get the idea that we might really be that most dreaded person: the sissy. (p. 127)

If men are fearful of being perceived or labeled as "gay," then they may overcompensate to prove that they are "straight" (Kivel, 1992) Compulsory heterosexuality (Connell, 1995; Frye, 1980; Rich, 1980)—the pressure to have female sexual partners and to have sex more often—becomes a route to confirming one's manhood (Kimmel & Clarence, 1993). In fact, says Weinberg (1998), "The motivation for all male violence is related to males attempting to reinforce and render incontestable their heterosexual masculinity" (p. 16).

The testimony of the MAV officers in this study indicated that their fathers, mothers, and peers had socialized all of them into stereotypical norms of masculinity; many indicated that homophobia ensured that they adhered to this stereotypical code. Almost all of the officers reported that their involvement in an organization like MAV aroused suspicion about their sexual orientation among their peers on campus, as if only feminine men would care about violence—which historically has been framed as a "women's issue." TB, a former LSU football player, said many of his erstwhile teammates said, "Well, [MAV] is a good organization, but I'm too macho for this organization." As a result, each of the officers underwent a personal

struggle to reject or reformulate hegemonic masculinity to accommodate his
involvement in MAV.

The resulting defensiveness regarding their masculinity prompted a bitter
struggle between the officers and me
about allowing women on the executive
board. As a man, Schultz (1995)
observed that "it's easier to be a guy with
other guys when there's a chick around.
It gives you all something in common to
relate to." Although I could understand
the MAV officers' desire to have women
on the executive board, my past experience demonstrated that the presence of
women in peer education organizations
allowed men to shift the responsibility
for caring and serving onto the shoulders
of the women. Consequently, the
number of men involved inevitably
dwindles, leaving only the women. After
allowing one young woman to fill an
interim position of secretary on the
board, the officers finally understood my
concerns. At their behest, the members
of MAV passed an amendment to their
constitution in April 1998 that mandated
an all-male executive board. Said CH of
their decision:

> It never occurred to me until the
> [American College Health Association]
> conference in New Orleans. I saw
> a lot of women. And when we
> went to San Marcos [for the peer
> education conference] . . . it was very
> rare that you saw a guy. And so I'm
> thinkin' . . . I definitely see how [in]
> other organizations, if women start to
> take a role, then they'll take [another]

job. And they'll take another one. After
awhile, the guys will get less interested
and less focused on it. And we'll all
drop out and that's probably what
would'a happened.

Clearly, the struggle to overcome
homophobia and reclaim those areas of
emotion and response that are typically
outside of the man box is difficult. In
recalling fights from his childhood and
adolescence, TB said, "If you got hurt
or whatever, you went home crying
to your momma and you was a sissy.
[But] if you took the pain and you stood
out and you fought with everyone else,
you were a man." In the following
statement, MB recognizes the subtle, yet
palpable, boundaries that are placed on
his behavior and thoughts by traditional
norms of masculinity:

> You can witness it in every [peer ed-
> ucation] program: there's always that
> one guy that thinks he's more manly
> than the other ones by his attitudes, not
> his actions. I sometimes slip—not con-
> sciously, ya know, but unconsciously. I'm
> not thinking the things they think. Like
> if a girl asks me, do I think a guy looks
> good, I'll say, "Yeah, he's cute." Guys
> take that as me being effeminate.

Yet, through interactions with positive adult male role models (e.g., advisory
board members or guest speakers), some
of the MAV officers began to see the
importance of adopting a broader definition of masculinity, a definition that included some behaviors that may even be

regarded as feminine, thus reformulating and contesting hegemonic masculinity. In response to a guest speaker at one of the general meetings, LS said,

> Coach Baldwin professes you need to be in touch with your feminine side. It's a very gentle point from a man who teaches violence [laugh]. I mean, he's a football coach . . . I mean, football is war; you can look at it that way . . . and men like that—that is, a manly male . . . For me, [being a man is] to be in touch with your feminine side, your feelings . . . also, to be open-minded and tolerant.

LS's construction of open-mindedness and tolerance as feminine qualities is interesting, given MAV's consistent history of racial diversity among its membership.

Nevertheless, the traditional mandate of no sissy stuff continued to be a source of tension and anxiety for the MAV officers. They eagerly and passionately took up the cause against racism, becomingly actively involved in campus activities and events in support of racial harmony, including participation in and speaking out at the Martin Luther King, Jr., commemorative marches. Nevertheless, they continued to engage in homophobic behavior—derogatory language about gay me, belief in stereotypes about "what makes people become gay," and expressions of disgust at male homosexuality. They were also concerned about their public image as a potentially gay organization, a concern that was fueled when one officer returned from a peer education program and reported that a fraternity member had called the officers a "bunch of fairies."

Although they verbally espoused the civil rights of and tolerance for gays and lesbians, many of the officers demonstrated a reliance on hegemonic masculinity and an accompanying need to reassure themselves and others outside of MAV. "But, we're not gay," they said. Their homophobia was sufficiently palpable that the few gay and bisexual men who chose to join MAV and disclosed their sexual orientation to me, unbeknownst to the officers, eventually left the organization because of their discomfort.

In addition, whereas they verbalized their belief that women were their equals, several of the officers, particularly the African Americans (consistent with Staples's (1982) and Kimmel's (1993) observations about hypermasculinity among men of color) still engaged in the sexual objectification of women. Some of the officers frequented strip joints. Other officers still adhered to the "virgin-whore" double standard view about women's sexuality. It was rare for any gathering of the officers not to generate some references to women's body parts or vivid descriptions of personal sexual exploits. Although I recognized that some of the officers' comments were merely normal, harmless expressions of sexual interest appropriate to this stage in their lives, I also felt that such reliance on hegemonic masculinity (i.e., compulsory heterosexuality) was a way to alleviate their homophobic anxieties. In response to his fellow executive board members' bragging about their sexual exploits with women, JG said,

> Some people are exaggerating...I don't think they [have] women flocking to them as much as they say they do. I mean, come on now, I'm not stupid. And I know that they stretch it a bit more than what it probably really is. To tell you the truth, a lot of guys do that.

■ BE A BIG WHEEL: REJECTION, REFORMULATION, RELIANCE

Brannon and David's (1976) second tenet of hegemonic masculinity, "Be a big wheel," urges men to strive for dominance, power, wealth, and success. Real men are expected to compete to be the biggest wheel, whether in the workplace or on the playing field. In fact, sports are among the primary arenas in which men battle each other to determine who is bigger, stronger, faster, or more skilled. In this battle, winning—not simply placing—is the only option for the truly "big man on campus" (Messner, 1992; Laberge & Albert, 1999). It is also through sports, according to Messner (1992), that boys become men:

> For my male peers and for me, athletic competition was an unambiguously male world. It was this world of athletic competition that provided us with the major social context in which we developed

relationships with each other, and in which we shaped our own identities and self-images. (p. 1)

However, this all-male world also has direct implications for violence. Nelson (1994) notes that:

> By creating a world where masculinity is equated with violence, where male bonding is based on the illusion of male supremacy, and where all of the visible women are cheerleaders, manly sports set the stage for violence against women. (p. 7)

Similarly, Keen (1991) declares that men historically assert power through violence as part of their "warrior psyche." An extension of this premise is the stereotypical expectation that truly masculine men ought to have deep voices, big muscles, and an intimidating presence. At a minimum, they ought to be physically superior to women (Connell, 1987; Courtenay, 2000; Gerschick & Miller, 1995). In fact, predominant conceptions of American masculinity assign men the role of "aggressor" and women the role of "gatekeeper" in sexual situations. Contrary to women's experiences, most men are taught to regard sexuality as a realm of danger and to view sexual intercourse as an act of conquest (Kimmel & Clarence, 1993; Box, 1983).

MAV officers also perceived pressure to compete and to win as a way of meeting normative expectations of manhood. Said JH of his socialization experiences,

Father, he was always, like, you better never come home [after getting] your ass kicked. If you do, you're going to get your ass kicked by me. [With my] peers, it was basically the same kind of philosophy as my dad . . . I played football. I played baseball. This was [the way] with all the athletes . . . if you got into a fight, you better win, or you better have a good showing—and that other person better be hurt pretty well.

However, as a result of his involvement with MAV, CH, another of the officers, came to a reformulation of traditional masculinity:

You may not necessarily be a coward . . . but sometimes you may have to look like one . . . so it seems like you gotta be confident in yourself a little bit more. Like if somebody's about to fight, you just gotta walk off.

JG, who struggled with managing his own anger, talked about anger's relationship to violence:

We're always talking about date rape and domestic violence and everything like that. I think a lot of it has to do with the tempers of men . . . I think that's the root of a lot of the [violence] . . . . It seems like at the drop of the hat, it's like, somebody's ready to kill somebody. I mean, like in bars and stuff; alcohol does contribute to some degree, but I think also it's [poor] anger management.

Essentially, JG is rejecting norms of male combativeness as an acceptable

expression of anger. Similarly, LM recognizes that there are other ways to resolve conflict besides violence: "MAV has helped me to believe that being a man is about finding a way to resolve conflicts without hurting yourself or other people." Again, this represents a reformulation of traditional male gender role expectations. TB remarks:

I don't feel the same way I felt when I was growing up—that I had to fight these guys to prove that I was a man, ya know? That I had to drink this much alcohol to prove that I could fit in and be like everyone else.

The newfound desire to separate beliefs about masculinity and aggression is echoed in this statement:

Just 'cuz you're able to fight, lift more or do stuff like that, I don't think that makes you a man. Knowing when to walk away . . . from like, a bad situation [like a fight or something], is [what makes you a man].

Like his peers, LS also sought an alternative to the big wheel man; at the same time, he recognized the difficulty in following such a path:

I brought up a scenario [with my fraternity brothers]; I'm walking to class and [some members of a rival fraternity] decide to attack me. What would I do? Some people would be like, "Oh, I'd fight back" or whatever, and I was saying I would let them beat me up, 'cuz to me that puts them in the wrong and

[me] in the right...I mean, you can't go wrong—you did nothing. I guess it was passive resistance. But I think most people won't—[they] aren't going to believe you're Gandhi.

Finally, if collaboration is the alternative to competition, then JH also reformulated the big-wheel expectation of traditional masculinity in another way. He observed,

> When I first joined, it seemed like two people ran the whole organization...And then this year...each one of us has a distinct role. If JG has an opinion, it gets involved. If MB has his opinion, it gets involved in the organization. I think that with all of us, we make [MAV] a lot better by using everyone's opinion instead of just a select few.

The pressure to be a big wheel also generated some cognitive dissonance and inconsistent behavior. The MAV officers recognized the need to work collaboratively if they were to make the organization succeed, yet I distinctly perceived a competitive undercurrent in many of the interactions between the officers. They would compete over who was the most dedicated officer, who had done the most peer education programs, who was the most popular among the general membership, and who had recruited the greatest number of new members—all concerns that represented a reliance on a male gender stereotype that celebrates winning.

Reliance on a masculine norm of physical dominance—a belief that men are supposed to be bigger and stronger than women—also emerged. When asked by a fellow ROTC air force pilot if he would trust a woman to take him into battle, LM truthfully replied,

> I guess that question sort of brought out feelings that were in myself, and to wonder how I really felt about women [and equal rights]. Because, man, I have to be honest. When he asked me, I was like, some of 'em I would, but some of 'em I would not. There was this lady I knew [from the base]...and she flew aircraft...that lady—I mean, excuse the term—she acted like a man. And I would have no problems with her. But...I met [this] female pilot and she was...just an inch thick, fingernails painted, and wore dresses...and I [just don't know if I] would feel comfortable with my life in her hands.

■ BE A STURDY OAK: REJECTION, REFORMULATION, RELIANCE

"Be a sturdy oak," Brannon and David's (1976) third tenet of hegemonic masculinity, expects real men to be independent, controlled, and unemotional, as well as to reveal no vulnerabilities. In the tradition of John Wayne and the Marlboro Man, men who are sturdy oaks exude a manly air of toughness, aloofness, and rugged individualism. These men take care of their wives and children by "bringing home the bacon"; their families depend on them, but, conversely, they do not rely on others. Caring emotionally for the family and building intimate connections are tasks that are stereotypically allocated to women (Belenky, Clinchy, Goldberger, & Tarule, 1986; Gilligan, 1982). A large body of research consistently indicates that men do, indeed, have fewer friendships and smaller social networks than women do (Courtenay, in press). Thus, they spend less time practicing the skills needed to build those connections. The term "pussy-whipped" is frequently used as an insult for men who are perceived as letting their female partners "control" them or "have the upper hand." Given that seeking help or advice for pain symptoms or mental distress is regarded as a sign of weakness for real men, it is not surprising that men are extremely reluctant to seek medical attention or visit a counselor (Courtenay, 1998). Weinberg (1999) sums up the spirit of "Be a sturdy oak" as follows:

> Leading, doing, building, destroying— these are the work of Real Men who don't do "lady" things like feeling, listening, nurturing, caring. Emotional intimacy is something many males would like to achieve, but don't yet have the vocabulary, experience, or practice necessary to succeed. The vulnerability necessary for emotional intimacy scares most males. (p. 5)

In rejecting or reformulating the dominant male norm to be a sturdy oak,

the officers of MAV developed many new insights about relationships and friendships—the traditionally "feminine" realm of connection and intimacy. Said LS, speaking of his father, "we never talked about anything, like, personal. I can talk about personal things with my mom, and even then it's kind of a struggle." This training in self-isolation is an important barrier to overcome in reformulating conceptions of masculinity. Remarked JG, "I think every guy basically keeps a lot of stuff to himself—part of it because of male pride.... It's also male stupidity." His sentiment was echoed by JH, who observed,

> Men have walls, big time, I think. And that's something that I thought was weird. In MAV, yeah, everybody's gonna have their own little walls, but...for the most part, we've pretty much opened up to each other about almost anything.

JH was not the only individual for whom MAV afforded the first opportunity in his life to develop caring, meaningful friendships with other men. For the officers who were also members of social fraternities, their friendships in MAV were comparable to fraternal ties, but they felt that the emotional bonds were more significant than those found in a social fraternity. One of those officers, LS, said,

> Men should be able to talk. I've always talked openly about all kinds of different things. But a lot of men, [they] don't talk openly about certain things. With my friends [outside of MAV]...I can

talk to them about anything, but it's [as if they're complete strangers]. The dialogue [we're] having in [MAV] meetings and amongst ourselves is very open and revealing.... You're going to realize...that probably if you go outside of MAV and you're open with another man like that, they might be open, but then if they're not, they may be like, well, oaky, this is someone I can talk to. So, you've kind of started a chain reaction.

Nevertheless, this growing intimacy among men was not an easy bond for these MAV officers to forge, given their training in hegemonic masculinity and the power of homophobia to keep men acting like men. Of his friendships with the other MAV officers, CH observed:

> It's gone beyond, "This is my boy," or "This is my partner" and stuff like that. It's more [like] we got legitimate feelings for another guy. Ya know, I'm not saying you're attracted to him [but if] something happens to this guy, it's almost like something just happened to your brother. [Men have friends and all], but you're not supposed to be close to any guys unless you could be gay or something like that. Nowadays, you know, I got a couple of friends like that, that...I'd do anything for 'em if I could.

By sharing with each other, men learn that the stereotypical expectation of be a sturdy oak can be rejected and simultaneously can correct a misperceived social norm. Listen to LM:

I used to think that, ya know, you couldn't really sit down with a bunch of guys and talk about [laughs]...fear: don't let anybody know you're scared. Don't let anybody know you have weaknesses anyway...But I guess I found out that a lot of guys have the same problems I have...fear of women [laughs]...some guys actually admitted that they were afraid to walk up to a woman.... They're afraid of fighting.... In relationships, most guys won't admit that they're in love, that they really care for somebody. [In high school, I was mostly friends with women], but with my association with MAV...I notice I'm having more and more male friends, like, [we] just sit down and chill.

Even MB, who grew up with a very emotionally distant father and still struggles with issues related to domestic violence (his father hit his mother), says, "I've learned that communication is very important. That's one thing that I've learned [from MAV] and applied."

I also observed the officers beginning to reformulate conceptions of be a sturdy oak by acknowledging their vulnerability and their need for others. This is JH's insight after conducting numerous peer education programs for coeducational audiences:

> Men and women are so different in what we think each other wants that we don't even realize that basically what we want ends up bein' almost the same thing. We want somebody that's trusting,

somebody that we can care for and enjoy bein' with.

He goes on to acknowledge:

> Most times, men are seen as the person
> who's supposed to go work and stuff and
> go make the money and come home
> and just sit there and do his little thing.
> I think that [MAV] promotes men to be
> active, and if we have kids, to be active
> and raise them properly. It's to be ac-
> tive in your community and help other
> people instead of just being a worker.

Whereas parenting and community involvement are traditionally viewed as
more appropriate and natural roles for
women, JH, in his reformulation, was
seeing fatherhood and citizenship as
essential aspects of being a man. TB
expressed fond memories of volunteer-
ing at a local elementary school, during
which he had one of his first opportunities to serve as an adult male model for
young children:

> I can remember one statement that I
> made during the program—it was when
> I told the kids that I loved them. And
> they didn't understand why a stranger
> would stand up there saying, "I love
> you," "I want you to succeed and grad-
> uate," and "Do good things in life, take
> care of your family and community"
> and everything like that. And the prin-
> cipal reiterated what I said by asking,
> "Did y'all hear what he said? He said
> he loves you, and he didn't even know
> you!" And the kids were like, "Yeah!"
> They were like, "We love you, too!"

In fact, all of the MAV officers voiced
a desire to help others and to adopt the
ethic that embraces the community service that was central to MAV's mission.
This sentiment was especially salient
for the three African American officers,
each of whom was keenly aware of the
lower life expectancy odds facing Black
men as a result of their higher rates of
homicide (Health, United States, 1999).

I also witnessed rejection and reformulation of the myth of being a sturdy
oak in another context. During the
course of the study, one of the officers,
LM, was being battered by his girlfriend.
It took a lot of courage for him to talk
about it with his fellow officers, and he
came to me first to express his embarrassment and shame about the situation.
LM was simultaneously afraid that the
others in the group would see him as less
than a man because he was the "victim"
in this case. He feared that they might
attribute some responsibility for the bat-
tery to him and therefore consider him
unworthy to be in MAV:

> It worried me how [the officers]
> felt about [her punching me] and
> how they would feel about me being
> part of the organization after that. I
> guess I didn't really consider myself as
> fighting, because...I never threw a
> punch—actually, I didn't even defend
> myself...I don't know why. I had tried
> to justify [her hitting me] by saying,
> "Well, her father was abusive, so it's
> natural for it to be passed down." But
> then I guess I convinced myself that was
> no excuse.

It is rare that we witness a man revealing his vulnerability in such an honest manner.

As with the first two tenets of hegemonic masculinity, reliance on being a sturdy oak surfaced, as well. The officers found it difficult to abandon their self-perceived roles as protector-defender. Although the men in this study acquired new insights about gender equality and grew to recognize the ways that men's violence toward women is supported by institutionalized power dynamics, their desire to prevent such violence was still guided more by what I would call a chivalric, paternalistic view of women (e.g., women are the weaker sex, so they need our protection) and less by a desire to make fundamental changes in that power system.

■ GIVE 'EM HELL: REJECTION, REFORMULATION, RELIANCE

"Give 'em hell" is Brannon and David's (1976) fourth and final tenet of hegemonic masculinity and is directly correlated with violence. Real men are asked to be risk-takers, to be daring, and to be aggressive. A real man does not "stand down" if his dignity or manhood has been disrespected, and certainly no real man could allow any insult to his girlfriend or mother to go unchecked. Research indicates that twice as many boys as girls report believing that physical fighting is an appropriate response when

someone insults you, steals from you, or flirts with someone you like, whereas more than three-and-a-half times more boys than girls believe fighting is an appropriate response when someone cuts in line (National Adolescent Student Health Survey, 1989). Interestingly, White college men from the South are most likely to start a fight if they believe that their "most valued possessions, namely [their] reputation for strength and toughness," are threatened (Nisbett & Cohen, 1996).

Furthermore, college men who ascribe to more traditional beliefs about masculinity report higher rates of unprotected sexual activity, binge drinking, and motor vehicle accidents than their less traditional male peers (Courtenay, 1998). These expectations of traditional manhood also explain why boys are more likely to carry a weapon to school or to pick a fight. The give 'em hell gender role norm is poignantly and succinctly reflected in a recent television commercial by Wrangler, which touts men's jeans that come in boys' two favorite colors: black and blue.

So many of the MAV officers had been raised with the idea that real men had to raise hell. Commented TB:

> When I was living in the projects . . . we did everything for money . . . everything was competition. And everything was macho. Everything was you gotta be a man . . . ya know, drink some of this and put some hair on your chest and all that craziness . . . . As far as the violence issue, it was always macho to carry a gun. It was always macho to be able

to drink a certain amount of drink, ya know? And if you can beat up so many different people . . . you were like a god [laughing]!

Like TB, another officer, CH, had grown up picking fights with peers, even if it was only because "somebody looked at [him] funny." However, in October 1997, that old way of resolving conflicts was tested and rejected. CH had gone on a date with the ex-girlfriend of another MAV member and ended up spending a platonic night sleeping on the couch at her apartment. The other MAV member found CH at the apartment. In a fit of jealousy, he called CH out and incited him to fight by shoving him and yelling curse words at him. Because of his involvement with MAV, CH made a conscious choice to walk away that night. He said,

> I couldn't tell if I was more mad because he hit me or more mad because of who he was [an MAV member] and he hit me. I haven't been that mad in a very long time . . . [but] I told him I didn't wanna mess up the [MAV] image for him.

In this next statement, TB explicitly talked about rejecting the connection between taking risks and masculinity:

> MAV has helped me to get rid of those old demons and realize that I can be a man without having the alcohol, without having the drugs, without having all the macho things that was installed in me by my brothers to make me out

as a man. I'm a man without all those things.

On a similar note, MB reformulated maturity as it relates to manhood; he essentially implies that the give 'em hell mentality of risk-taking is a sign of immaturity, and that real men do not have to resort to those things:

> In MAV, I think it's odd [but] we deal with boys: it's one of the problems. I believe if you were a man, there wouldn't be any need for MAV. Real men wouldn't get angry. Real men would know when to say "when" if they were drinking. Real men wouldn't, ya know, beat up their wives, or wouldn't sexually assault or rape.

Male gender is the best predictor of carrying weapons, which, in turn, is correlated with higher rates of accidental injury and death (Health, United States, 1999). JH's reaction when he saw a fellow officer pull out a butterfly knife therefore also represented a desire to reject risk-taking behavior:

> Just to have a butterfly knife in your pocket . . . I mean, that right there is opening yourself up for a . . . violent act to happen. If you have a gun on you, you have a chance to have a violent act [happen], because you could shoot somebody. You might not intentionally mean to, but it could still happen.

Reliance on give 'em hell surfaced in a manner that I had not anticipated.

Several of the MAV officers had apparently been challenged on various occasions by some of their peers with the question, "Since you're in MAV, does that mean I can hit you right now, and you won't fight back?" Thus, the issue of violence versus self-defense became an important delineation that the officers felt they needed to make. As one past officer said, "MAV isn't against self-defense; we're against violence." This continuing need to make a distinction between violence and self-defense (with the key differentiating factor being who instigated the fight) is firmly espoused by JH, who said, "You gotta defend yourself. I mean, that's just a fact of life. I mean, you can't just let someone beat you up." For JH, being beaten up was inconsistent with his beliefs about manhood—he would be letting someone disrespect him.

In general, the concept of diffusing a conflict before it escalated to physical violence was a difficult concept for almost all of the MAV officers to accept, and in this area, all of the officers except one relied on stereotypical norms of male bravado. In fact, LS described a hierarchy of violence in which fighting was less serious than rape, perhaps succumbing to the old adage that "boys will be boys." He said,

> I think date rape is a worse sin than fighting. I would say rape, especially date rape—someone you know—is a great evil. Fighting though, probably because [it's] more common . . . I would describe it as a lesser evil.

■ CONCLUSIONS

Although many theorists have identified a relationship between hegemonic masculinity and an increased likelihood for both perpetrating and experiencing violence among men in the United States, this study is one of the few that assesses the impact of an educational intervention designed to break that link. As was true in the research conducted by Connell (1995), Laberge and Albert (1999), and Gerschick and Miller (1995), the participants in this study continued to reproduce and to rely on some aspects of hegemonic masculinity.

They did so even as they reformulated and contested many of the same aspects of masculinity, indicating that the process of constructing masculinity is dynamic and complex. Given the long-term and ongoing nature of this educational intervention, there is every reason to believe that many of these changes will be lasting—particularly if these men find similar male peer support networks when they leave the university.

This study demonstrates and documents meaningful, significant changes in the attitudes, beliefs, and behaviors of a tight-knit group of college men in relation to violence and to traditional conceptions of manhood. These data also lend credence to Kivel's (1992) observation that "if we [men] have learned to be violent, we can unlearn it. And since this learning came from men, the most powerful way to learn other, gentler ways is also from men" (p. 96). Although the study results cannot be generalized to other universities and programs, a student organization like MAV undoubtedly provides a viable model of how higher education professionals can work toward implementing a transformed approach to preventing violence. MAV, which was developed in the pattern described by Kuh et al. (1994), is a program to foster student learning and student development that has been student-defined as much as it has been carefully crafted by a health professional.

If we are truly concerned about ending violence against women, then it is imperative that we begin working with men to prevent it. If we recognize that violence against women is part of a greater cycle of hurt and pain that encompasses violence against men, we then will labor equally to eliminate all forms of violence. If we value our male students as much as our female students, we then will abhor violence among men as intensely as we abhor violence against women.

As long as colleges and universities continue to provide only date rape seminars that focus on the individual and interpersonal variables of sexual violence without reconstructing hegemonic masculinity, as long as they care only about violence against women and attack only the correlates (e.g., firearms, alcohol) but not causes of violence, the effectiveness of such interventions is very dubious. Our ultimate goal in higher education ought to be to have a positive and meaningful impact on student learning and student wellbeing (Burns, 1999).) We must, therefore, move toward a transformative approach to preventing campus violence.

REFERENCES

Abbey A. Sex differences in attributions for friendly behavior: Do males misperceive females' friendliness? *J Pers Soc Psychol.* 1982; 42:830–838.

Abbey A. Misperception as an antecedent of acquaintance rape: A consequence of ambiguity in communication between men and women. In: Parrot A, Bechhofer L, eds. *Acquaintance Rape: The Hidden Crime.* New York: John Wiley & Sons; 1991.

Abbey A, Cozzarelli C, McLaughlin K, Harnish R. The effects of clothing and dyad sex composition on perception of sexual intent: Do women and men evaluate these cues differently? *J Appl Soc Psychol.* 1987; 17:108–126.

Abbey A, Melby C. The effects of nonverbal cues on gender differences in perceptions of sexual intent. *Sex Roles.* 1986;15:283–298.

Allen M. *Angry Men, Passive Men: Understanding the Roots of Men's Anger and How to Move Beyond It.* New York: Fawcett Columbine; 1993.

Belenky M, Clinchy B, Goldberger N, Tarule J. *Women's Ways of Knowing: The Development of Self, Voice and Mind.* New York: Basic; 1986.

Benedict J. *Athletes and Acquaintance Rape.* Sage Series on Violence Against Women, Vol 8. Thousand Oaks, CA: Sage; 1998.

Berkowitz A. College men as perpetrators of acquaintance rape and sexual assault: A review of recent research. *J Am Coll Health.* 1992;40:175–181.

Berkowitz A. From reactive to proactive prevention: Promoting an ecology of health on campus. In: Rivers P, Shore E, eds. *Substance Abuse on Campus: A Handbook for College and University Personnel.* Westport, CT: Greenwood; 1997.

Berkowitz A. *Men and Rape: Theory, Research and Prevention Programs in Higher Education.* San Francisco: Jossey-Bass; 1994.

Box S. *Power, Crime and Mystification.* London: Tavistock; 1983:147.

Brannon R, David D. *The Forty-Nine Percent Majority: The Male Sex Role.* Reading, MA: Addison-Wesley; 1976.

Brownmiller S. *Against Our Will: Men, Women and Rape.* New York: Simon & Schuster; 1975.

Burt M. Rape myths and acquaintance rape. In: Parrot A, Bechhofer L, eds. *Acquaintance Rape: The Hidden Crime.* New York: John Wiley; 1991.

Burns W. *Learning for Our Common Health: How an Academic Focus on HIV/AIDS Will Improve Campaign Against Family Violence.* Chicago: American Medical Association; 1991.

Centers for Disease Control. *Behaviors related to unintentional and intentional injuries among high school students—United States, 1991.* MMWR. 1992;41:760–772.

Centers for Disease Control. *Physical fighting among high school students—United States, 1990.* MMWR. 1992;41:91–94.

Chickering A. *Education and Identity.* San Francisco: Jossey-Bass; 1969.

Connell R. *Gender and Power.* Stanford, CA: Stanford University Press; 1987:184.

Connell R. *Masculinities.* Berkeley: University of California Press; 1995:139.

Courtenay W. Behavioral factors associated with disease, injury, and death among men: Evidence and implications for prevention. *Journal of Mens Studies.* In press.

Courtenay W. College men's health: An overview and a call to action. *J Am Coll Health.* 1998;46:279–290.

Courtenay W. Constructions of masculinity and their influence on men's well-being: A theory of gender and health. *Soc Sci Med.* 2000;50:69–85.

Courtenay W. Youth violence? Let's call it what it is. *J Am Coll Health.* 1999;48: 141–142.

Crosset T, McDonald M. Male student athletes reported for sexual assault: A survey of campus police departments and judicial affairs offices. *Journal of Sports and Social Issues.* 1995.

Douglas K, Collins J, Warren C, et al. Results from the 1995 national college health risk behavior survey. *J Am Coll Health.* 1997;46:55–66.

Dworkin A. *Pornography: Men Possessing Women.* New York: Dutton; 1981.

Earle J. Acquaintance rape workshops: Their effectiveness in changing the attitudes of first-year college men. *Journal of Student Affairs Administration, Research and Practice.* 1996; 34:2–18.

Education and Health. Washington, DC: Association of American Colleges and Universities; 1999.

Fabiano P. From personal health into community action: Another step forward in peer health education. *J Am Coll Health.* 1994; 43:115–121.

Finkelhor D, Wolak J. Nonsexual assaults to the genitals in the youth population. *JAMA.* 1995;274:1692–1697.

Foubert J. The longitudinal effects of a rape-prevention program on fraternity men's attitudes, behavioral intent, and behavior. *J Am Coll Health.* 2000;48:158–163.

Frye M. *The Politics of Reality: Essays in Feminist Theory.* Freedom, CA: The Crossing Press; 1983.

Gerschick T, Miller A. Coming to terms: Masculinity and physical disability. In: Sabo D, Gordon D, eds. *Men's Health and Illness: Gender, Power, and the Body.* Thousand Oaks, CA: Sage; 1995: 187.

Gilligan C. *In a Different Voice: Psychological Theory and Women's Development.* Cambridge, MA: Harvard University Press; 1982.

Good G, Hepper M, Hillenbrand-Gunn T, Wang L. Sexual and psychological violence: An exploratory study of predictors in college men. *Journal of Mens Studies.* 1995;4: 59–71.

Gray H. *Black Male: Representations of Masculinity in Contemporary American Art* [exhibition catalogue]. New York: Whitney Museum of American Art; 1994.

Green R. *The "Sissy Boy Syndrome" and the Development of Homosexuality.* New Haven, CT: Yale University Press; 1987.

Harding S. Introduction: Is there a feminist method? In: *Feminism and Methodology.* Bloomington: Indiana University Press; 1987.

Health, United States, 1999 With Health and Aging Chartbook. Hyattsville, MD: National Center for Health Statistics, DHHS Publication No PHS 99–1232; 1999.

Healthy People 2000: National Health Promotion & Disease Prevention Objectives. Washington, DC: US Dept of Health and Human Services. DHHS Publication No 91–50212, US Government Printing Office; 1991.

hooks b. Feminism: A movement to end sexist oppression. In: *Feminist Theory: From Margin to Center.* Boston: South End Press; 1984.

Isely P. Sexual assault of college men: College-age victims. *Journal of Student Affairs Administrations, Resources, and Practice.* 1996;34:2–18; 1998;35:305–317.

Katz J. Reconstructing masculinity in the locker room: The Mentors in Violence Prevention Project. *Harvard Educational Review.* 1995;65:163–174.

Katz J, Jhally S. The national conversation in the wake of Littleton is missing the mark. *The Boston Globe.* 1999;May 2:E1.

Keen S. *Fire in the Belly: On Being a Man.* New York: Bantam; 1991.

Kellermann A, Rivara F, Rushforth N, et al. Gun ownership as a risk factor for homicide in the home. *N Engl J Med.* 1993;329: 1084–1091.

Kellermann A, Rivara F, Somes G, et al. Suicide in the home in relation to gun ownership. *N Engl J Med.* 1992;327:467–472.

Kimmel M, Clarence W. Iron Mike, Tailhook, Senator Packwood, Spur Posse, Magic—and us. In: Buchwald E, Fletcher P, Roth M, eds. *Transforming a Rape Culture.* Minneapolis: Milkweed; 1993.

Kivel P. *Men's Work: How to Stop the Violence That Tears Our Lives Apart.* Center City, MN: Hazelden; 1992.

Koss M, Gidycz C, Wisniewski N. The scope of rape: Incidence and prevalence of sexual aggression and victimization in a national sample of higher education students. *J Consult Clin Psychol.* 1987;55:162–170.

Kuh G, Douglas K, Lund J, Ramin-Gyurnek J. *Student Learning Outside the*

Classroom: Transcending Artificial Boundaries. ASHE-ERIC Higher Education Reports, Vol 23 (8). Washington, DC: The George Washington University, Graduate School of Education and Human Development; 1994.

Laberge S, Albert M. Conceptions of masculinity and of gender transgressions in sport among adolescent boys. Men and Masculinities. 1999;1:243–267.

Levin B. A dream deferred: The social and legal implications of hate crimes in the 1990s. Journal of Intergroup Relations. 1993:9.

Lincoln Y, Guba E. Naturalistic Inquiry. Beverly Hills, CA: Sage; 1985.

MacLeod J. Ain't No Makin' It: Aspirations and Attainment in a Low-Income Neighborhood. Boulder, CO: Westview; 1995.

Majors R, Billson J. Cool Pose: The Dilemmas of Black Manhood in America. New York: Lexington; 1992.

Marshall D. Violence and the male gender role. Journal of College Student Psychotherapy. 1993;8:203–218.

Martin P, Hummer R. Fraternities and rape on campus. Gender and Society. 1989;3:457–473.

Messner M. Power at Play: Sports and the Problem of Masculinity. Boston: Beacon; 1992.

Messner M, Sabo D. Sex, Violence and Power in Sports: Rethinking Masculinity. Freedom, CA: Crossing Press; 1994.

Miedzian M. Boys Will Be Boys: Breaking the Link Between Masculinity and Violence. New York: Doubleday; 1991.

Miller M, Hemenway D, Wechsler H. Guns at college. J Am Coll Health. 1999;48:7–12.

Modesto N. Dictionary of Public Health and Education Terms and Concepts. Thousand Oaks, CA: Sage; 1996.

Muehlenhard C, Linton M. Date rape and sexual aggression in dating situations: Incidence and risk factors. Journal of Counseling Psychology. 1987;34:186–196.

National Adolescent Student Health Survey: A Report on America's Youth. Oakland, CA: American School Health Association, Association for the Advancement of Health Education, Society for Public Health Education; Third Party; 1989.

Nelson M. The Stronger Women Get, the More Men Love Football: Sexism and the American Culture of Sports. New York: Avon Books; 1994.

Nisbett R, Cohen D. Culture of Honor: The Psychology of Violence in the South. Boulder, CO: Westview; 1996.

O'Sullivan C. Acquaintance gang rape on campus. In: Parrot A, Bechhofer L, eds. Acquaintance Rape: The Hidden Crime. New York: John Wiley & Sons; 1991.

O'Sullivan C. Fraternities and rape culture. In: Buchwald E, Fletcher P, Roth M, eds. Transforming a Rape Culture. Minneapolis: Milkweed; 1993.

O'Sullivan C. Navy resembles a fraternity in its sexism [letter to the editor]. The New York Times. 1992; August 10.

Patton M. Qualitative Evaluation and Research Methods. 2nd ed. Newbury Park, CA: Sage; 1990.

Poe-Yamagata E. Known Juvenile Homicide Offenders by Sex, 1980–1995. Washington, DC: Office of Juvenile Justice and Delinquency Prevention; 1997.

Pollack W. Real Boys: Rescuing Our Sons From the Myths of Boyhood. New York: Henry Holt; 1998.

Pope B. In the wake of Tailhook: A new order for the Navy. In: Buchwald E, Fletcher P,

Roth M, eds. *Transforming a Rape Culture.* Minneapolis: Milkweed; 1993.

Rapaport K, Burkhart B. Personality and attitudinal characteristics of sexually coercive college males. *J Abnorm Psychol.* 1984;93: 216–221.

Rich A. Compulsory heterosexuality and lesbian existence. *Signs.* 1980:5.

Roark M. Conceptualizing campus violence: Definitions, underlying factors, and effects. *Journal of College Student Psychotherapy.* 1993;8:1–27.

Rosenstock I, Strecher V, Becker M. Social learning theory and the health belief model. *Health Education Quarterly.* 1988;15:175–183.

Roth J, Moore M. Reducing violent crimes and intentional injuries. In: *National Institute of Justice Research in Action.* Washington, DC: US Department of Justice, October 1995.

Sanday P. *Fraternity Gang Rape: Sex, Brotherhood, and Privilege on Campus.* New York: New York University Press; 1990.

Sandler B, Ehrhart J. *Campus Gang Rape: Party Games?* Washington, DC: Project on the Status and Education of Women, Association of American College and Universities; 1985.

Schultz J. Getting off on feminism. In: Walker R, ed. *To Be Real: Telling the Truth and Changing the Face of Feminism.* New York: Anchor; 1995.

Schwartz M, DeKeseredy W. *Sexual Assault on the College Campus: The Role of Male Peer Support.* Thousand Oaks, CA: Sage; 1997.

Sourcebook of Criminal Justice Statistics—1993. Washington, DC: US Department of Justice. Publication No NCJ-148211, US Government Printing Office; 1994.

Spradley J. *Participant Observation.* Orlando, FL: Harcourt Brace Jovanovich; 1980.

Spradley J. *The Ethnographic Interview.* Orlando, FL: Harcourt Brace Jovanovich; 1979.

Staples R. *Black Masculinity: The Black Male's Role in American Society.* San Francisco: Black Scholar Press; 1982.

Struckman-Johnson C, Struckman-Johnson D. Men pressured and forced into sexual experience. *Arch Sex Behav.* 1994;32:93–114.

Uniform Crime Reports. Washington, DC: Federal Bureau of Investigation, US Government Printing Office; 1992.

Valois R, Vincent M, McKeown R, Garrison C, Kirby S. Adolescent risk behaviors and the potential for violence: A look at what's coming to campus. *J Am Coll Health.* 1993;41:141–147.

Walker L. *The Battered Woman.* New York: Harper Perennial; 1979.

Weinberg J. How boys become men: Deciphering the messages of enigmatic fathers. *Teaching Sexual Ethics Newsletter.* 1998;2: 2–10.

Weinberg J. How boys become men, part II: Growing up alone. *Teaching Sexual Ethics Newsletter.* 1999;1:2–12.

Weinberg J. How homophobia affects all boys and men. *Teaching Sexual Ethics Newsletter.* 1998; 2:10–17.

College Men Behaving Badly

Implications for Educational Practice

W hat should educators and administrators do to decrease the number of men who are cited for violating campus judicial policies and eliminate destructive episodes involving men on their campuses? As the chapters in Part Three suggest, traditional approaches (e.g., risk reduction; self-defense classes) for addressing destructive behaviors on college campuses rarely bring about measurable changes. This is so because the link between these behaviors and the social construction of masculinities is often overlooked. Here we offer practical implications and suggestions for developing comprehensive approaches to addressing destructive behaviors. We believe men must be held accountable for violations of campus policies. At the same time, we find it equally important to support men in managing gender role conflicts that motivate them to violate campus policy in the first place.

The notion that men value meaningful interpersonal relationships and opportunities to connect socially with other men is implied throughout the chapters in Part Three. However, pursuing these types of interactions in the absence of alcohol, sports, or action-oriented activities is contradictory to social constructions of masculinities that emphasize independence and restricted emotionality for men. Rocco L. Capraro maintains in Chapter 13 that college men often seek out these interactions with other men during their transition from home to a new campus environment where feelings of powerlessness and vulnerability are intensified. Therefore, men will be well-served by having structured opportunities to establish healthy relationships with other men that do not prioritize destructive attitudes and behaviors. Student organizations and productive activities that attract men provide good starting points for getting men to work collaboratively in ways and facilitate the interpersonal connections they desire. For example, on campuses where health and fitness are important interests for men, forming a committee of men to plan an intramural sports tournament may be a good way to engage men. Similarly, educators who oversee male residence halls should consider convening a group to plan and develop service projects for students in the hall as a way to encourage men to build healthy relationships. Educators who use student data to determine what activities would best capture the interests of the men on their campuses are likely to be more effective than those who do not. It is also important to take the steps necessary to ensure that these groups and programs do not become contexts where destructive behaviors are reinforced.

Higher education and student affairs researchers attribute a disproportionate amount of the hazing incidents (Nuwer, 2004), sexual assaults (Foubert & Newberry, 2006), and binge drinking (Elkins, Helms, & Pierson, 2003; Kuh & Arnold, 1993; Wechsler, 1996) occurring on college campuses to the activities that take place in fraternities. Chapter 14 by Robert A. Rhoads illustrates quite clearly the ways in which fraternity cultures harbor destructive male gender behavior, notably sexism and homophobia. By no means are we suggesting that fraternities do not make positive contributions to campus communities. Nor are we arguing that these groups do not help men achieve desirable student outcomes. However, it is imperative that student affairs educators find ways to work with chapter leaders and advisors to address problematic behaviors within their respective chapters. Proactive strategies, as opposed to relying exclusively on reactive responses to critical incidents, are likely to yield the results that educators are seeking in this regard. For example, educators may consider hosting forums at which reports of gender-related misbehavior (e.g., violence, alcohol-related incidents, sexual assault and harassment) can be shared and discussed. One key outcome of these forums should be an action plan that can be implemented at the chapter level to address these issues. Campuses should also hold chapters responsible for quantitative decreases in the number of incidents involving their members on an annual basis. The point we emphasize is that if fraternities are not considered in this effort, patterns of destructive male behavior will almost certainly persist. Similar approaches need to be employed within men's sports teams as well (which we discuss in Part Six).

Addressing psychological conflicts among college men also seems warranted in campus-based efforts to reduce destructive behavior. Mental health services are typically underutilized by college men because men are socialized to believe that seeking help is an admission of weakness. Nevertheless, the four chapters in Part Three unequivocally state that destructive male behavior is directly linked to gender role conflict among men. Therefore, it is very important that educators find ways to connect men, especially those who are struggling emotionally, with mental health professionals before they become depressed, violent, and dangerous to themselves and others. Given men's negative attitudes and perceptions of therapy, educators will need to be very strategic in designing and presenting these interventions to men. For instance, rather than hosting a support group for men in the campus counseling center, consider secure spaces that men find welcoming and comfortable. Similarly, educators may find that online support groups or therapy sessions are more effective than traditional face-to-face sessions in getting men to initially seek counseling.

Men may also benefit from ongoing interactions with adult men who can offer ongoing mentoring and role modeling. In Chapter 15, Hong attributes the transformation she observed among her participants to the connections they had with "positive" adult male role models who helped the men conceptualize masculinities more broadly. This is not to suggest that women cannot teach men how to be good men. But when men see for themselves what "good masculinity" looks like, especially from men with whom they identify based on shared backgrounds or experiences, they may more readily embrace these behaviors and incorporate them into their own gender performance. Thus, student affairs educators who work with men should consider reaching out to faculty members, campus administrators, and graduate students who consistently model ways to express masculinities without relying on destructive strategies to do so to support undergraduate men. Educators may also find it necessary to reach out to local alumni and community members who may be able to serve in this capacity. Although a formal mentoring program need not be established, structured opportunities to interact periodically should be considered.

Lastly, Capraro asserts that men feel most vulnerable and powerless during periods of transition and consequently may be more compelled to act out in an aggressive manner during these times. This may help explain why younger students, particularly those who are enrolled in their first or second year of college, are cited more often for judicial offenses than third- or fourth-year students. For many students, college marks the first time they have lived away from home. The absence of parental supervision provides men with new opportunities to assert their independence and express themselves as men in ways they may not have before, such as through drinking and risky sex. Transitioning to college may also entail establishing new friendships with other men and may bring on more pressure for men to assert themselves by acting out in destructive ways. For these reasons, it seems that first-year and perhaps transfer students should be targeted more purposefully for outreach and interventions to reduce destructive behaviors.

REFERENCES

Elkins, B., Helms, L. B., & Pierson, C. T. (2003). Greek letter organizations, alcohol, and the courts: A risky mix? *Journal of College Student Development 44*(1), 67–80.

Foubert, J. D., & Newberry, J. T. (2006). Effects of two versions of an empathy-based rape prevention program on fraternity men's survivor empathy, attitudes, and behavioral intent to commit rape or sexual assault. *Journal of College Student Development, 47*(2), 133–148.

Kuh, G. D., & Arnold, J. C. (1993). Liquid bonding: A cultural analysis of the role of alcohol in fraternity pledgeship. *Journal of College Student Development, 34*, 327–334.

Nuwer, H. (Ed.). (2004). *The hazing reader*. Bloomington, IN: Indiana University Press.

Wechsler, H. (1996). Alcohol and the American college campus: A report from the Harvard School of Public Health. *Change, 28*, 20–25.

COLLEGE MEN'S HEALTH AND WELLNESS: INTRODUCTION

Part Four begins with an exceptional contribution authored by Will H. Courtenay (Chapter 16), a noted psychologist and leading men's health expert, in which he reports the following: "Men in the United States suffer more severe chronic conditions, have higher death rates for all 15 leading causes of death, and die nearly seven years younger than women." Some of the contributing factors that eventually lead to these illnesses begin in college and persist into latter stages of adulthood. Take for instance poor dietary choices. Among the luxuries afforded to undergraduates is the freedom of meal choices; they can eat as much pizza as they'd like, as there is usually no one around to monitor their diets. Then there is the infamous "freshmen 15"—the 15 pounds that many gain during the first college year. In the absence of parental supervision, students can also drink lots of beer, sleep as little as their bodies will allow, and develop destructive addictions to drugs, alcohol, sex, pornography, gambling, or the Internet. Infrequent versus daily check-ins with family members enable many college students to hide the mental health, self-esteem, and body image issues with which they struggle. Health choices made during this developmental period have longer-term implications for personal quality of life.

Although male and female undergraduates alike make poor healthy choices, men are more likely to engage in extremism. Binge drinking is more common among them, their propensity to fight and commit acts of violence against each other is higher, and they smoke more cigarettes, experiment with hard drugs (for example, cocaine and methamphetamines) more often, beat each other more viciously when pledging Greek-letter organizations, and engage in unprotected sex more often and with more partners. Despite exercising more frequently and for longer periods, college men aren't nearly as concerned as are their female peers with dieting and consuming healthy foods. Moreover, a male collegian is usually less inclined to seek counseling or psychological help for his personal problems; he discusses health issues less often with his friends; and upon the onset of sickness, he waits longer before seeing a physician. Most alarming is that suicide is the second-leading cause of death (after automobile accidents) among college students; male students commit suicide four times more often than do women. These trends beg the following important question: "What's up with guys, why do they so routinely put themselves in harm's way?"

In Chapter 16, Courtenay proposes a theory of men's health that offers enormously powerful insights into this problem. Using feminist and social constructionist perspectives, Courtenay links health behaviors and choices with the social structuring of gender and power. Specifically, he suggests that the presumed invincibility and toughness of men are tied to their masculinities and are used to negotiate power and status among each other as well as superiority over women. Concerning the latter, weakness is commonly viewed as a sign of femininity. One praiseworthy feature of Courtenay's chapter is his examination of the effects of ethnicity, socioeconomic status, educational level, sexual orientation, and social context on the construction of masculinities and health outcomes among men in the United States. Moreover, he explains how institutional and social structures (for example, the government, military, health care systems, schools, and colleges) help sustain and reproduce men's health risks via widely disseminated caricatures of men as the stronger sex.

Health-related gender stereotypes are also considered by Ida Jodette Hatoum and Deborah Belle in Chapter 17. They challenge the common misperception that only women are concerned with body image. Their study of 89 college men explored the nexus between media consumption (magazines, movies, and television) and body concerns. Those who read male-directed magazines (*Men's Fitness, Details, FHM, Maxim,* and 18 others) were likely to have low self-esteem about their own physiques. In fact, over three-fourths of the men indicated, "I would like to have more upper body muscle." Participants were least satisfied with the appearance of their stomachs and abdominal muscles. Magazine depictions of the hypermuscular male body also shaped these students' concerns about general fitness, their beauty product use, and their willingness to take dietary supplements to build muscle. Moreover, Hatoum and Belle found that the more men read these magazines and watched movies, the more they preferred thin women. However, watching television and movies was not significantly associated with concerns these men had about their own bodies. The authors further note that advertisements directed toward men often sell sex.

In Chapter 18, Joseph LaBrie and his colleagues write about their study of over 1,500 sexual encounters among 93 heterosexual college men (that's an average of 16 encounters per student). Perhaps their most troubling yet unsurprising finding is that drinking alcohol decreases men's condom use. Those who believed their drunkenness would negatively affect their sexual performance were likely to forego protection. The authors also report differences in quantities of alcohol consumed and sexual choice making by three partner types: new (a young woman he meets for the first time at a bar and then has sex with her the same night), casual (someone he occasionally sleeps with but not exclusively), and regular (his girlfriend). Theirs is an important contribution to this book, as it illuminates the role of alcohol in men's assumption of sexual risk.

Heterosexual college men, because of their age and sexual orientation, are often-times ignored in conversations about HIV and other sexually transmitted infections. This is a point that Scott D. Rhodes and his colleagues make in Chapter 19. They studied the sexual behaviors of over 1,000 heterosexual and gay college men. After controlling for a number of variables, the authors found that gay men reported using condoms less frequently, had sex under the influence of illicit drugs more often, and were more likely to have sex with multiple partners in a given month than were the heterosexual respondents to the survey. But notwithstanding these findings, anyone (gay or straight) who has 16 sexual encounters—some with different partners while drunk and without using condoms—assumes risk of infection.

Taken together, the chapters in Part Four explain the social undercurrents of men's health dilemmas, offer data on body image and sexual health trends, and, most important, include practical suggestions for decreasing the rate at which male students harm themselves and those who care about them.

CHAPTER 16

Constructions of Masculinity and their Influence on Men's Well-Being

A Theory of Gender and Health

Will H. Courtenay

en in the United States, on average, die nearly 7 years younger than women and have higher death rates for all 15 leading causes of death (Department of Health and Human Services [DHHS], 1996). Men's age-adjusted death rate for heart disease, for example, is 2 times higher than women's, and men's cancer death rate is $1\frac{1}{2}$ times higher (DHHS, 1996). The incidence of 7 out of 10 of the most common infectious diseases is higher among men than women (CDC, 1997). Men are also more likely than women to suffer severe chronic conditions and fatal diseases (Verbrugge and Wingard, 1987), and to suffer them at an earlier age. Nearly three out of four persons who die from heart attacks before age 65 are men (American Heart Association, 1995). Furthermore, men's health shows few signs of improving—their cancer death rates

have increased more than 20% over the past 35 years; the rates for women have remained unchanged during the same period (American Cancer Society, 1994).

A variety of factors influence and are associated with health and longevity, including economic status, ethnicity and access to care (Laveist, 1993; Pappas et al., 1993; Doyal, 1995). However, these factors cannot explain gender differences in health and longevity. For instance, while lack of adequate health care, poor nutrition and substandard housing all contribute to the health problems of African Americans (Gibbs, 1988), they cannot account for cancer death rates that are 2 times higher among African American men than among African American women (National Institutes of Health [NIH], 1992). Health behaviours, however, do help to explain gender differences in health and longevity. Many health

307

scientists contend that health behaviours are among the most important factors influencing health, and that modifying health behaviours is "the most effective way" to prevent disease (Woolf et al., 1996, p. xxxvii). Although not all health professionals and scholars would agree, the evidence supporting this belief is compelling. According to a former U.S. surgeon general, a wealth of scientific data have "confirmed the importance . . . of health behaviours in preventing disease" and "suggest that efforts directed at improving these behaviours are more likely to reduce morbidity and mortality in the United States than anything else we do" (Koop, 1996, p. viii). An independent scientific panel established by the U.S. government that has evaluated thousands of research studies recently estimated that half of all deaths in the United States could be prevented through changes in personal health practices (U.S. Preventive Services Task Force [USPSTF], 1996). Similar conclusions have been reached by other health experts reviewing hundreds of studies (Woolf et al., 1996). These findings provide strong evidence of risk reduction through preventive practice; they are among the factors that have recently revolutionised the U.S. health care system, a system that increasingly emphasises interventions that can effectively contain health care costs through disease prevention (USPSTF, 1996). These findings also recently led the U.S. assistant secretary for health to claim that "it is particularly pertinent to highlight the health consequences of behaviour" (Lee, 1996, p. v).

Many sociocultural factors are associated with and influence health-related behaviour. Gender is one of the most important of these factors. Women engage in far more health-promoting behaviours than men and have more healthy lifestyle patterns (Walker et al., 1988; Kandrack et al., 1991; Lonnquist et al., 1992; Rossi, 1992; Courtenay, 1998a, 1998b, in press a). Being a woman may, in fact, be the strongest predictor of preventive and health-promoting behaviour (Mechanic and Cleary, 1980; Brown and McCreedy, 1986; Ratner et al., 1994). Government health surveillance systems are providing increasing evidence of gender differences in specific behaviours associated with risk among nationally representative samples. Data from one such system indicate that the prevalence of risk behaviours among adults is more common among men than women for all but 3 of 14 (nonsex-specific) behaviours, including smoking, drinking and driving, using safety belts, getting health screenings, and awareness of medical conditions (Powell-Griner et al., 1997). Compared to men, women nationally are making the most beneficial changes in their exercise habits (Caspersen and Merritt, 1995), are less likely to be overweight (Powell-Griner et al., 1997; National Institutes of Health, 1998), and are more likely to consume vitamin and mineral supplements (Slesinski et al., 1996). Among adults in South Carolina, women are more likely than men to practice a cluster of healthy behaviours (Shi, 1998). Among California college students, men are more likely than women to engage in 20 of 26 specific high-risk behaviours (Patrick et al., 1997). A recent, extensive review of large studies, national data, and metanalyses summarises evidence of sex differences in behaviours that significantly influence health and longevity (Courtenay, in press a). This review systematically demonstrates that males of all ages are more likely than females to engage in over 30 behaviours that increase the risk of disease, injury and death.

Findings are generally similar for health care visits. Although gender differences in utilisation generally begin to disappear when the health problem is more serious (Verbrugge, 1985; Waldron, 1988; Mor et al., 1990), adult men make far fewer health care visits than women do, independent of reproductive health care visits (Verbrugge, (1985, 1988); Kandrack et al., 1991). According to the U.S. Department of Health and Human Services (1998), among persons *with health problems,* men are significantly more likely than women to have had no recent physician contacts, regardless of income or ethnicity; poor men are twice as likely as poor women to have had no recent contact, and high-income men are $2^{1}/_{2}$ times as likely.

Despite their enormous health effects, few researchers or theorists have offered explanations for these gender differences in behaviour, or for their implications for men's health (Verbrugge, 1985; Sabo and Gordon, 1995; Courtenay, 1998a). Early feminist scholars were among the first to engender health, noting, for example, the absence of women as subjects in health research and the use

of males as the standard for health. The result, however, has been an exclusive emphasis on women, and "gender and health" has become synonymous with "women's health" (e.g. Bayne-Smith, 1996). Although health science of this century has frequently used males as study subjects, research typically neglects to examine men and the health risks associated with men's gender. Little is known about *why* men engage in less healthy lifestyles and adopt fewer health-promoting beliefs and behaviours. The health risks associated with men's gender or masculinity have remained largely unproblematic and taken for granted. The consistent, underlying presumption in medical literature is that what it means to be a man in America has no bearing on how men work, drink, drive, fight, or take risks. Even in studies that address health risks more common to men than women, the discussion of men's greater risks and of the influence of men's gender is often conspicuously absent. Instead, the "gender" that is associated with greater risk remains unnamed (e.g., Donnermeyer and Park, 1995). Left unquestioned, men's shorter life span is often presumed to be natural and inevitable.

This paper proposes a relational theory of men's health from a social constructionist and feminist perspective. It provides an introduction to social constructionist perspectives on gender and a brief critique of gender role theory before illustrating how health beliefs and behaviour are used in constructing gender in North America, and how masculinity and health are constructed within a relational context. It further examines how men construct various forms of masculinity— or masculinities—and how these different enactments of gender, as well as differing social structural influences, contribute to differential health risks among men in the United States.

■ HEALTH AND THE SOCIAL CONSTRUCTION OF GENDER

Constructionism and Theories of Gender

Previous explanations of masculinity and men's health have focused primarily on the hazardous influences of "*the* male sex role" (Goldberg, 1976; Nathanson, 1977; Harrison, 1978; Verbrugge, 1985; Harrison et al., 1992). These explanations relied on theories of gender socialisation that have since been widely criticised (Deaux, 1984; Gerson and Peiss, 1985; Kimmel, 1986; Pleck, 1987; West and Zimmerman 1987; Epstein, 1988; Messerschmidt, 1993; Connell, 1995). The sex role theory of socialisation, still commonly employed in analyses of gender, has been criticised for implying that gender represents "two fixed, static and mutually exclusive role containers" (Kimmel, 1986, p. 521) and for assuming that women and men have innate psychological needs for gender-stereotypic traits (Pleck, 1987). Sex role theory also fosters the notion of a singular female

or male personality, a notion that has been effectively disputed, and obscures the various forms of femininity and masculinity that women and men can and do demonstrate (Connell, 1995).

From a constructionist perspective, women and men think and act in the ways that they do not because of their role identities or psychological traits, but because of concepts about femininity and masculinity that they adopt from their culture (Pleck et al., 1994a). Gender is not two static categories, but rather "a set of socially constructed relationships which are produced and reproduced through people's actions" (Gerson and Peiss, 1985, p. 327); it is constructed by dynamic, dialectic relationships (Connell, 1995). Gender is "something that one does, and *does* recurrently, in interaction with others" (West and Zimmerman, 1987, p. 140; italics theirs); it is achieved or demonstrated and is better understood as a verb than as a noun (Kaschak, 1992; Bohan, 1993; Crawford, 1995). Most importantly, gender does not reside in the person, but rather in social transactions defined as gendered (Bohan, 1993; Crawford, 1995). From this perspective, gender is viewed as a dynamic, social structure.

Gender Stereotypes

Gender is constructed from cultural and subjective meanings that constantly shift and vary, depending on the time and place (Kimmel, 1995). Gender stereotypes are among the meanings used by society in the construction of gender, and are characteristics that are generally believed to be typical either of women or of men. There is very high agreement in our society about what are considered to be typically feminine and typically masculine characteristics (Williams and Best, 1990; Golombok and Fivush, 1994; Street et al., 1995). These stereotypes provide collective, organised—and dichotomous—meanings of gender and often become widely shared beliefs about who women and men innately *are* (Pleck, 1987). People are encouraged to conform to stereotypic beliefs and behaviours, and commonly do conform to and adopt dominant norms of femininity and masculinity (Eagly, 1983; Deaux, 1984; Bohan, 1993). Conforming to what is expected of them further reinforces self-fulfilling prophecies of such behaviour (Geis, 1993; Crawford, 1995).

Research indicates that men and boys experience comparatively greater social pressure than women and girls to endorse gendered societal prescriptions—such as the strongly endorsed *health-related* beliefs that men are independent, self-reliant, strong, robust and tough (Williams and Best, 1990; Golombok and Fivush, 1994; Martin, 1995). It is, therefore, not surprising that their behaviour and their beliefs about gender are more stereotypic than those of women and girls (Katz and Ksansnak, 1994; Rice and Coates, 1995; Street et al., 1995; Levant and Majors, 1998). From a social constructionist perspective, however, men and boys are not passive victims of a socially prescribed role, nor are they simply conditioned or socialised by their cultures. Men and boys are active agents in constructing and reconstructing dominant norms of masculinity. This concept of agency—the part individuals play in exerting power and producing effects in their lives—is central to constructionism (Courtenay, 1999a).

Health Beliefs and Behaviours: Resources for Constructing Gender

The activities that men and women engage in, and their gendered cognitions, are a form of currency in transactions that are continually enacted in the demonstration of gender. Previous authors have examined how a variety of activities are used as resources in constructing and reconstructing gender; these activities include language (Perry et al., 1992; Crawford, 1995); work (Connell, 1995); sports (Connell, 1992; Messner and Sabo, 1994); crime (Messerschmidt, 1993); and sex (Vance, 1995). The very manner in which women and men do these activities contributes both to the defining of one's self as gendered and to social conventions of gender.

Health-related beliefs and behaviours can similarly be understood as a means of constructing or demonstrating gender. In this way, the health behaviours and beliefs that people adopt simultaneously define and enact representations of gender. Health beliefs and behaviours, like language, can be understood as "a set of strategies for negotiating the social landscape" (Crawford, 1995, p. 17), or tools for constructing gender. Like crime, health behaviour "may be invoked as a practice through which masculinities (and men and women) are differentiated from one another" (Messerschmidt, 1993, p. 85). The findings from one small study examining gender differences and health led the author to conclude that "the doing of health is a form of doing gender" (Saltonstall, 1993, p. 12). In this regard, "health actions are social acts" and "can be seen as a form of practice which constructs...'the person' in the same way that other social and cultural activities do" (Saltonstall, 1993, p. 12).

The social experiences of women and men provide a template that guides their beliefs and behaviour (Kimmel, 1995). The various social transactions, institutional structures and contexts that women and men encounter elicit different demonstrations of health beliefs and behaviours, and provide different opportunities to conduct this particular form of demonstrating gender. If these social experiences and demonstrated beliefs or behaviours had no bearing on the health of women and men, they would be of no relevance here. This, however, is not the case. The social practices required for demonstrating femininity and masculinity are associated with very different health advantages and risks (Courtenay, 1998a, in press b). Unlike the presumably innocent effects of wearing lipstick or wearing a tie, the use of health-related beliefs and behaviours to define oneself as a woman or a man has a profound impact on one's health and longevity.

■ THEORISING MASCULINITY IN THE CONTEXT OF HEALTH

As Messerschmidt (1993, p. 62) notes in regard to the study of gender and crime, a comprehensive feminist theory of health must similarly include men "not by treating men as the normal subjects, but by articulating the gendered content of men's behaviour". The following sections provide a relational analysis of men's gendered health behaviour based on constructionist and feminist theories, and examine how cultural dictates, everyday interactions and social and institutional structures help to sustain and reproduce men's health risks.

Gender, Power and the Social Construction of the "Stronger" Sex

A discussion of power and social inequality is necessary to understand the broader context of men's adoption of unhealthy behaviour—as well as to address the social structures that both foster unhealthy behaviour among men and undermine men's attempts to adopt healthier habits. Gender is negotiated in part through relationships of power. Microlevel power practices (Pyke, 1996) contribute to structuring the social transactions of everyday life, transactions that help to sustain and reproduce broader structures of power and inequality. These power relationships are located in and constituted in, among other practices, the practice of health behaviour. The systematic subordination of women and lower-status men—or patriarchy—is made possible, in part, through these gendered demonstrations of health and health behaviour. In this way, males use health beliefs and behaviours to demonstrate dominant—and hegemonic—masculine ideals that clearly establish them as men. Hegemonic masculinity is the idealised form of masculinity at a given place and time (Connell, 1995). It is the socially dominant gender construction that subordinates femininities as well as other forms of masculinity, and reflects and shapes men's social relationships with women and other men; it represents power and authority. Today in the United States, hegemonic masculinity is embodied in heterosexual, highly educated, European American men of upper-class economic status.

The fact that there are a variety of health risks associated with being a man, in no way implies that men do not hold power. Indeed, it is in the pursuit of power and privilege that men are often led to harm themselves (Clatterbaugh, 1997). The social practices that undermine men's health are often the instruments men use in the structuring and acquisition of power. Men's acquisition of power requires, for example, that men suppress their needs and refuse to admit to or acknowledge their pain (Kaufman, 1994). Additional health-related beliefs and behaviours that can be used in the demonstration of hegemonic masculinity include the denial of weakness or vulnerability, emotional and physical control, the appearance of being strong and robust, dismissal of any need for help,

a ceaseless interest in sex, the display of aggressive behaviour and physical dominance. These health-related demonstrations of gender and power represent forms of microlevel power practices, practices that are "part of a system that affirms and (re)constitutes broader relations of inequality" (Pyke, 1996, p. 546). In exhibiting or enacting hegemonic ideals with health behaviours, men reinforce strongly held cultural beliefs that men are more powerful and less vulnerable than women; that men's bodies are structurally more efficient than and superior to women's bodies; that asking for help and caring for one's health are feminine; and that the most powerful men among men are those for whom health and safety are irrelevant.

It has been demonstrated elsewhere (Courtenay, 1998a, 1999a,b) that the resources available in the United States for constructing masculinities are largely unhealthy. Men and boys often use these resources and reject healthy beliefs and behaviours in order to demonstrate and achieve manhood. By dismissing their health care needs, men are constructing gender. When a man brags, "I haven't been to a doctor in years," he is simultaneously describing a health practice and situating himself in a masculine arena. Similarly, men are demonstrating dominant norms of masculinity when they refuse to take sick leave from work, when they insist that they need little sleep, and when they boast that drinking does not impair their driving. Men also construct masculinities by embracing risk. A man may define the degree of his masculinity, for example, by driving dangerously or performing risky sports—and displaying these behaviours like badges of honor. In these ways, masculinities are defined *against* positive health behaviours and beliefs.

To carry out any one positive health behaviour, a man may need to reject multiple constructions of masculinity. For example, the application of sunscreen to prevent skin cancer—the most rapidly increasing cancer in the United States (CDC, 1995a)—may require the rejection of a variety of social constructions: masculine men are unconcerned about health matters; masculine men are invulnerable to disease; the application of lotions to the body is a feminine pastime; masculine men don't "pamper" or "fuss" over their bodies; and "rugged good looks" are produced with a tan. In *not* applying sunscreen, a man may be simultaneously demonstrating gender and an unhealthy practice. The facts that 1½ times more men than women nationally believe that one looks better with a tan (American Academy of Dermatology, 1997), that men are significantly less likely to use sunscreen (Mermelstein and Riesenberg, 1992; Courtenay, 1998a,b), and that the skin cancer death rate is twice as high for men as for women (CDC, 1995b), may be a testament to the level of support among men for endorsing these constructions.

When a man does experience an illness or disability, the gender ramifications are often great. Illness "can reduce a man's status in masculine hierarchies, shift his power relations with women, and raise his self-doubts about masculinity" (Charmaz, 1995, p. 268). The friend of a U.S. senator recently cautioned him against publicly discussing his diagnosis of prostate cancer, contending that "some men might see [his] willingness to go public with his private struggle as a sign of weakness" (Jaffe, 1997, p. 134). In efforts to preserve their masculinity, one researcher found that men with chronic illnesses often worked diligently to hide their disabilities: a man with diabetes, unable to maneuver both his wheelchair and a cafeteria tray, would skip lunch and risk a coma rather than request assistance; a middle-aged man declined offers of easier jobs to prove that he was still capable of strenuous work; an executive concealed dialysis treatments by telling others that he was away attending meetings (Charmaz, 1995).

Femininities and Men's Health

It is not only the endorsement of hegemonic ideals but also the rejection of feminine ideals that contributes to the construction of masculinities and to the systematic oppression of women and less powerful men. Rejecting what is constructed as feminine is essential for demonstrating hegemonic masculinity in a sexist and gender-dichotomous society. Men and boys who attempt to engage in social action that demonstrates feminine norms of gender risk being relegated to the subordinated masculinity of "wimp" or "sissy". A gay man who grew up on Indiana farms said he would have been ridiculed as a "sissy" had he done the (risk-free) tasks of cooking, baking, and sewing that he preferred: "My uncle would have started it and it would have spread out from there. Even my grandfather would say, 'Oh, you don't want to do that. That's girl stuff'" (Fellows, 1996, p. 12). Health care utilization and positive health beliefs or behaviours are also socially constructed as forms of idealised femininity (Courtenay, 1999a,b). They are, therefore, potentially feminising influences that men must oppose with varying degrees of force, depending on what other resources are accessible or are being utilised in the construction of masculinities. Forgoing health care is a means of rejecting "girl stuff."

Men's denial and disregard of physical discomfort, risk and health care needs are all means of demonstrating difference from women, who are presumed to embody these "feminine" characteristics. These behaviours serve both as proof of men's superiority over women and as proof of their ranking among "real" men. A man's success in adopting (socially feminised) health-promoting behaviour, like his failure to engage in (socially masculinised) physically risky behaviour, can undermine his ranking among men and relegate him to a subordinated status. That men and boys construct masculinities in opposition to the healthy beliefs and behaviours of women—and less masculine (i.e., "feminised") men and boys—is clearly apparent in their discourse, as evidenced by the remarks of one firefighter: "When you go out to fires, you will work yourself into the ground. Just so nobody else thinks you're a puss" (Delsohn, 1996, p. 95). Similarly, one

author, the chief editor of a major publishing company, recently revealed his concern about disclosing his pain to others after a radical prostatectomy: "I was reluctant to complain further [to hospital staff], for fear of being thought a sissy" (Korda, 1996, p. 148). In prison, men criticise fellow prisoners who "complain too much" about sickness or pain or make frequent health care visits, as displaying signs of "softness" (Courtenay and Sabo, in press).

Differences Among Men

Contemporary feminist theorists are as concerned about differences among men (and among women) as they are about differences between women and men. As (Messerschmidt, 1993, p. 87) notes, "'Boys will be boys' differently, depending upon their position in social structures and, therefore, upon their access to power and resources". Although men may endorse similar masculine ideals, different men may enact these ideals in different ways. For example, although most young men in the United States may agree that a man should be "tough" (Courtenay, 1998a), *how* each man demonstrates being tough—and how demonstrating toughness affects him physically—will be influenced by his age, ethnicity, social class and sexuality. Depending upon these factors, a man may use a gun, his fists, his sexuality, a mountain bike, physical labor, a car or the relentless pursuit of financial strength to construct this particular aspect of masculinity.

Social class positioning "both constrains and enables certain forms of gendered social action" (Messerschmidt, 1993, p. 94) and influences which unhealthy behaviours are used to demonstrate masculinity. Demonstrating masculinities with fearless, high-risk behaviours may entail skydiving for an upper-class man, mountain climbing for a middle-class man, racing hot rods for a working-class man and street fighting for a poor urban man. Many working-class masculinities that are constructed as exemplary—as in the case of firemen—require the dismissal of fear, and feats of physical endurance and strength, that often put these men at risk of injury and death. The avoidance of health care is another form of social action that allows some men to maintain their status and to avoid being relegated to a subordinated position in relation to physicians and health professionals, as well as other men. For an upper-middle-class business executive, refusing to see a physician can be a means of maintaining his position of power. Prisoners can similarly maintain their status by disregarding their health care needs: "When you got stabbed you usually bandaged yourself up . . . To go to the doctor would appear that you are soft" (Courtenay and Sabo, in press).

The construction of health and gender does not occur in isolation from other forms of social action that demonstrate differences among men. Health practices may be used simultaneously to enact multiple social constructions, such as ethnicity, social class and sexuality. The use of health beliefs and behaviours to construct the interacting social structures of masculinity and ethnicity is illustrated in this passage by a Chicano novelist:

A macho doesn't show weakness. Grit your teeth, take the pain, bear it alone. Be tough. You feel like letting it out? Well, then let's get drunk with our *compadres* . . . Drinking buddies who have a contest to see who can consume the most beer, or the most shots of tequila, are trying to prove their maleness (Anaya, 1996, p. 63).

Too often, factors such as ethnicity, economic status and sexuality are simply treated by health scientists as variables to be controlled for in statistical analyses. However, the social structuring of ethnicity, sexuality and economic status is intimately and systematically related to the social structuring of gender and power. These various social structures are constructed concurrently and are intertwined. When European American working-class boys speed recklessly through a poor African American neighborhood, not wearing safety belts and yelling epithets out their windows, they are using health risk behaviours—among other behaviours—in the simultaneous construction of gender, power, class and ethnicity; when they continue these behaviours in a nearby gay neighborhood, they are further reproducing gender, power and normative heterosexuality. Similarly, poor health beliefs and behaviours are used by men and boys to construct masculinities in conjunction with the use of other behaviours such as crime (Messerschmidt, 1993), work (Pyke, 1996) and being "cool" (Majors and Billson, 1992). Committing criminal acts may be insufficient to win a young man inclusion in a street gang; he may also be required to prove his manhood by demonstrating his willingness to ignore pain or to engage in physical fighting.

Making a Difference: The Negotiation of Power and Status

Just as men exercise varying degrees of power over women, so they exercise varying degrees of power among themselves. "Masculinities are configurations of social practices produced not only in relation to femininities but also in relation to one another" (Pyke, 1996, p. 531). Dominant masculinities subordinate lower-status, marginalised masculinities—such as those of gay, rural or lower-class men. As Connell (1995, p. 76) notes, "To recognise more than one kind of masculinity is only a first step"; "we must also recognise the relations between the different kinds of masculinity: relations of alliance, dominance and subordination. These relationships are constructed through practices that exclude and include, that intimidate, exploit, and so on" (Connell, 1995, p. 37). In negotiating this perilous landscape of masculinities, the male body is often used as a vehicle. The comments of one man in prison illustrate how the male body can be used in structuring gender and power:

> I have been shot and stabbed. Each time I wore bandages like a badge of honor . . . Each situation made me feel a little more tougher than the next guy . . . Being that I had survived, these things made me feel bigger because I could imagine that the average person couldn't go through a shoot out or a

knife fight, survive and get right back into the action like it was nothing. The perception that I had constructed in my mind was that most people were discouraged after almost facing death, but the really bad ones could look death in the eye with little or no compunction (Courtenay and Sabo, in press).

Physical dominance and violence are easily accessible resources for structuring, negotiating and sustaining masculinities, particularly among men who because of their social positioning lack less dangerous means.

The health risks associated with any form of masculinity will differ depending on whether a man is enacting a hegemonic, subordinated, marginalised, complicit or resistant form. When men and boys are denied access to the social power and resources necessary for constructing hegemonic masculinity, they must seek other resources for constructing gender that validate their masculinity (Messerschmidt, 1993). Disadvantages resulting from such factors as ethnicity, economic status, educational level and sexual orientation marginalise certain men and augment the relevance of enacting other forms of masculinity. Rejecting health behaviours that are socially constructed as feminine, embracing risk and demonstrating fearlessness are readily accessible means of enacting masculinity. Messerschmidt (1993, p. 110) notes that "participation in street violence, a more frequent practice when other hegemonic masculine ideals are unavailable (e.g., a job in the paid-labor market), demonstrates to closest friends that one is 'a man'"—or as one young man reported, "If somebody picks on you or something, and you don't fight back, they'll call you a chicken. But . . . if you fight back . . . you're cool" (Majors and Billson, 1992, p. 26). Among some African American men and boys, "toughness, violence and disregard of death and danger become the hallmark of survival in a world that does not respond to reasonable efforts to belong and achieve" (Majors and Billson, 1992, p. 34). The results of one small study suggest that toughness and aggression are indeed means for young inner-city African American men to gain status in communities where few other means of doing so are available: "If a young man is a 'tough guy,' peers respect him . . . The highest value is placed on individuals who defend themselves swiftly, even if by doing so they place themselves in danger" (Rich and Stone, 1996, p. 81). Gay and bisexual men or boys may also attempt to compensate by endangering themselves or by adopting physically dominant behaviours rather than being relegated to a lower-status position. As one man put it, "I really hated football, but I tried to play because it would make me more of a man" (Fellows, 1996, p. 40). Gay men may also refuse to engage in behaviour that reduces the risk of contracting AIDS when that behaviour contradicts dominant norms of masculinity: "Real men ignore precautions for AIDS risk reduction, seek many sexual partners, and reject depleasuring the penis. Abstinence, safer sex, and safer drug use compromise manhood" (Levine, 1998; pp. 146–147).

Marginalised men may also attempt to compensate for their subordinated status by defying hegemonic masculinity and constructing alternative forms of masculinity. As Pyke (1996, p. 531) explains, men "with their masculine identity and self-esteem undermined by their subordinate order-taking position in relation to higher-status males" can and do use other resources to "reconstruct their position as embodying *true* masculinity" (emphasis added). Other authors have variously referred to these alternative enactments of gender as *oppositional* (Messerschmidt, 1993), *compulsive* (Majors and Billson, 1992), *compensatory* (Pyke, 1996), or *protest* (Connell, 1995) masculinities. These "hypermasculine" constructions are frequently dangerous or self-destructive (Meinecke, 1981). Majors and Billson (1992, p. 34) suggest that compulsive masculinity can "lead toward smoking, drug and alcohol abuse, fighting, sexual conquests, dominance and crime". Pyke (1996, p. 538) describes lower-class men who "ostentatiously pursued drugs, alcohol and sexual carousing . . . [to compensate] for their subordinated status in the hierarchy of their everyday work worlds". Similarly, working-class men can and do "use the physical endurance and tolerance of discomfort required of their manual labor as signifying true masculinity, [as] an alternative to the hegemonic form" (Pyke, 1996, p. 531). When the demonstration of the (dominant) heterosexist ideal is not an option—as among gay men—dismissing the risks associated with high numbers of sexual partners or unprotected anal intercourse can serve for some men as a means of demonstrating a protest masculinity. In describing coming out gay, one young man said, "Rage, rage, rage! Let's do everything you've denied yourself for 25 years. Let's get into it and have a good time sexually" (Connell, 1995, p. 153).

It is important to note that although these hypermasculinities may aspire to or be complicit in the reconstruction of an idealised form of masculinity, they are not hegemonic. The fact that some inner-city African American men are successful in being "tough" or "cool," and that some gay men refuse to have protected sex, does not mean that these men are enacting hegemonic masculinity. On the contrary, for marginalised men, "the claim to power that is central in hegemonic masculinity is constantly negated" (Connell, 1995, p. 116).

Like unhealthy behaviours, dominant or idealized beliefs about manhood also provide the means for demonstrating gender. These signifiers of "true" masculinity are readily accessible to men who may otherwise have limited social resources for constructing masculinity. In fact, among young men nationally, lower educational level, lower family income and African American ethnicity are all associated with traditional, dominant norms of masculinity (Courtenay, 1998a). The stronger endorsement of traditional masculine ideology among African American men than among nonAfrican American men is a consistent finding

(Pleck et al., 1994b; Levant and Majors, 1998; Levant et al., 1998). Among African American men, the endorsement of dominant norms of masculinity is stronger for both younger and nonprofessional men than it is for older, professional men (Hunter and Davis, 1992; Harris et al., 1994).

Gay and bisexual men may also adopt culturally sanctioned beliefs about masculinity to compensate for their subordinated and less privileged social position. National data indicate that young men in the United States who are not exclusively heterosexual hold more traditional or dominant beliefs about masculinity than young men who are exclusively heterosexual (Courtenay, 1998a). Although this finding may at first glance appear counterintuitive, it is consistent with a constructionist and relational theory of men's health. The endorsement of hypermasculine beliefs can be understood as a means for gay and bisexual men to prove to others that, despite their sexual preferences, they are still "real" men. Diaz (1998) also maintains that gay Latino men are more compelled to demonstrate dominant norms of masculinity than nongay Latino men.

A growing body of research provides evidence that men who endorse dominant norms of masculinity engage in poorer health behaviours and have greater health risks than their peers with less traditional beliefs (Neff et al., 1991; Pleck et al., 1994a; Eisler, 1995; O'Neil et al., 1995). One recent longitudinal study of 1676 young men in the United States, aged 15 to 23 years, is among the few nationally representative studies to examine the influence of masculinity on health behaviour over time. When a variety of psychosocial factors were controlled for, beliefs about masculinity emerged as the strongest predictor of risk-taking behaviour $2\frac{1}{2}$ years later. Dominant norms of masculinity—the most traditional beliefs about manhood adopted by young men—predicted the highest level of risk taking and of involvement in behaviours such as cigarette smoking, high-risk sexual activity and use of alcohol and other drugs.

This feminist structural framework for understanding men's health may help to explain the many health differences found among men, based on their ethnicity, socioeconomic status and education (DHHS, 1998). It may help to explain, for example, why men with the least education are twice as likely to smoke cigarettes as the most highly educated men, and nearly 3 times more likely to report frequent heavy alcohol use; and why their death rate for injuries is nearly $3\frac{1}{2}$ times higher and (among those 25 to 44 years of age) their death rate for homicide is 7 times higher (DHHS, 1998).

Rethinking Compulsive, Oppositional, Compensatory and Protest Masculinities

The terms *compulsive, oppositional, compensatory* and *protest* masculinities can be somewhat misleading. *Most* men are compulsive in demonstrating masculinity, which, as Connell (1995) notes, is continually contested. Furthermore, *most* masculinities that men demonstrate in the United States are oppositional or compensatory; relatively few men construct the hegemonic masculine ideal. This is not to suggest, however, that hegemonic masculinity is not profoundly influential. On the contrary, hegemonic masculinity is a ubiquitous aspect of North American life. Most men necessarily demonstrate alternative masculinities in relation to hegemonic masculinity that variously aspire to, conspire with or attempt to resist, diminish or otherwise undermine hegemonic masculinity. They do this not only in relation to other men perceived to embody hegemonic ideals, but also in relation to institutionalised, hegemonic social structures—including the government and media, the judicial system, corporate and technological industries and academia. However, to suggest that only certain men are compulsive in demonstrating dominant norms of masculinity is to risk further marginalising the subordinated masculinities of lower-class, non-European American, nonheterosexual men. Masculinity *requires* compulsive practice, because it can be contested and undermined at any moment.

Whichever term one chooses to use to describe masculinities that resist (or undermine) hegemonic masculinity, it is critical to distinguish among various forms of resistant masculinity. In terms of men's health, the risks associated with enacting gender can differ greatly among different forms of resistant masculinity. Gay men who identify as *radical fairies* (Rose, 1997) and pacifists provide two examples of men who actively undermine hegemonic masculinity. These men are enacting very different resistant masculinities than those enacted by inner-city gang members, who are constructing an alternate *yet still authoritative and dominant* form of masculinity. Indeed, when lower-class men who lack access to cultural or economic resources attempt to demonstrate power and authority through the use of physical violence, it could be argued that they are not enacting a "compensatory" form of masculinity, but rather a form of *situational or interpersonal hegemony*. Furthermore, the resistant masculinities demonstrated by pacifists, radical fairies and inner-city gang members lead to very different levels and categories of health risk; the masculinities enacted by radical fairies and pacifists may in fact reduce their risks, unlike those forms requiring the use of physical dominance or violence.

Further Contextualising Men's Health

As Messerschmidt (1993, p. 83) notes, "Although men attempt to express hegemonic masculinity through speech, dress, physical appearance, activities and relations with others, these social signs of masculinity are associated with the specific context of one's actions and are self-regulated within that context." Because masculinity is continually contested, it must be renegotiated in each context that a man encounters. A man or boy will enact gender and health differently in different contexts. On the football field, a college student may use exposure to injury and denial of pain to demonstrate masculinity, while at parties he may use excessive drinking to achieve the same end. A man may consider the expression of emotional

or physical pain to be unacceptable with other men, but acceptable with a spouse or girlfriend. In some contexts, such as a prison setting (Courtenay and Sabo, in press), the hierarchies of masculinities are unique to that particular context.

Farm life provides a context within which to examine the negotiation of one form of rural masculinity. Growing up on a farm, much of what boys learn to do to demonstrate hegemonic masculinity requires them to adopt risky or unhealthy behaviours, such as operating heavy equipment before they are old enough to do so safely. As two rural men said, "if you're over ten, you'd better be out doing men's work, driving a tractor and that kind of thing" (Fellows, 1996, p. 173); and, "my brother Tony and I started driving the pickup on the farm at age six, as soon as we could reach the pedals. We also learned how to drive a tractor" (Fellows, 1996, p. 305). Another rural man describes similar expectations: "if you were a guy . . . you were born to be a total, typical, straight male—to play sports, to hunt, to do everything a guy was supposed to do" (Fellows, 1996, p. 307). The ways to enact masculinity are dictated in part by cultural norms, such as the belief held by most Pennsylvanians that "farmers *embody* the virtues of independence and self-sufficiency" (Willits et al., 1990, p. 572; emphasis added). Farmers who attempt to demonstrate this cultural ideal of masculinity undermine their health—and there are many such farmers. Among Wisconsin residents who had suffered agricultural injuries—most of whom were men—farmers were the most likely to delay seeking health care; half of them waited for over 2 hours and one in four waited 24 hours (Stueland et al., 1995). Long (1993) described a farmer who caught his finger in equipment while harvesting his wheat field; he pulled his finger out—severing it—wrapped his hand in a handkerchief, and finished his work for the day before seeking medical care.

It has been emphasised elsewhere (Courtenay and Sabo, in press; Rich and Stone, 1996) that the negotiation of masculinity in certain contexts can present men with unique health paradoxes, particularly in regard to physical dominance and the use of violence. The perception both among some men in prison (Courtenay and Sabo, in press) and some inner city African American men Rich and Stone (1996) is that failing to fight back makes a man vulnerable to even more extreme victimisation than does retaliating. This health paradox is reflected in the "protective, though violent, posture" described by Rich and Stone (1996, p. 81): "If you appear weak, others will try to victimize you . . . if you show yourself to be strong (by retaliating), then you are perceived as strong and you will be safe" (pp. 80–81). Although these men may neither actively resist nor embrace hegemonic masculinity, they are complicit in its reconstruction.

Institutional Structures, Masculinities and Men's Health

The institutionalised social structures that men encounter elicit different demonstrations of health-related beliefs and behaviours, and provide different opportunities to conduct this particular means of demonstrating gender. These structures—including the government and the military, corporations, technological industries, the judicial system, academia, health care system and the media—help to sustain gendered health risks by cultivating stereotypic forms of gender enactments and by providing different resources for demonstrating gender to women than they provide to men. Institutional structures, by and large, foster unhealthy beliefs and behaviours among men, and undermine men's attempts to adopt healthier habits (Courtenay, 1998a, in press a).

The workforce is one such structure. The work that men do is the most dangerous work. Mining, construction, timber cutting and fishing have the highest injury death rates in the United States, while the largest number of total injury deaths occur in construction, transportation, agriculture, farming, foresting and fishing—all of which are jobs held primarily by men (Bureau of Labor Statistics, 1993; National Institute for Occupational Safety and Health [NIOSH], 1993). Consequently, although they comprise only half (56%) of the U.S. workforce, men account for nearly all (94%) fatal injuries on the job (NIOSH, 1993). Furthermore, as one small study found, positive health-related activities often conflict with the work activities expected of men—and work is typically given precedence, as evidenced by one man's comments: "I'd do more [to be healthy], but I can't with my job hours. My boss at the lab would kill me" (Saltonstall, 1993,

p. 11). When a corporate law firm requires its employees to work 12- to 14-hour days, it is limiting access to health care for its (primarily male) attorneys.

Although they have a profound influence on men's health, institutional structures are not simply imposed on men any more than a prescribed male sex role is simply imposed on men. "Social structures do not exist autonomously from humans; rather... as we engage in social action, we simultaneously help create the social structures that facilitate/limit social practice" (Messerschmidt, 1993, p. 62). Men are agents of social practice. When men demonstrate gender "correctly," in the ways that are socially prescribed, they "simultaneously sustain, reproduce and render legitimate the institutional arrangements that are based on sex category" (West and Zimmerman, 1987, p. 146). In a continuous cycle, definitions of gender influence social structures, which guide human interactions and social action, which in turn reinforce gendered social structures. This ongoing process results in a gender division and a differential exposure that inhibits both women and men from learning behaviours, skills and capacities considered characteristic of the "opposite" gender (West and Zimmerman, 1987; Epstein, 1988). Men sustain and reproduce institutional structures in part for the privileges that they derive from preserving existing power structures. The businessman who works tirelessly, denies his stress, and dismisses his physical needs for sleep and a healthy diet often does so because he expects to be rewarded with money, power,

position and prestige. Thus, although they are increasing their health risks, men who achieve these hegemonic ideals are compensated with social acceptance; with diminished anxiety about their manhood; and with the rewards that such normative, masculine demonstrations provide in a patriarchal society.

In these regards, men also contribute to the construction of a health care system that ignores their gendered health concerns. Indeed, they are often the very researchers and scientists who have ignored men's gendered health risks. As Assistant Surgeon General Susan Blumenthal, who directs the Office on Women's Health at the U.S. Public Health Service, noted recently, "Men need to become advocates and speak passionately about their health, but they may be concerned that speaking out will reveal weakness, not strength" (Jaffe, 1997, p. 136). As Coward (1984, p. 229) notes, men have kept their bodies from being the subjects of analysis: "Men's bodies and sexuality are taken for granted, exempted from scrutiny, whereas women's are extensively defined and overexposed. Sexual and social meanings are imposed on women's bodies, not men's... men have left themselves out of the picture because a body defined is a body controlled".

The Medical Institution and Its Constructions of Gender and Health

Connell (1993) identifies three institutions that are particularly relevant in the contemporary organization of gender:

the state, the workplace/labor market and the family. The health care system and its allied health fields represent a particularly important structural influence in the construction of gender and health. In the case of cardiovascular disease, for example, it is often noted that the fact that women are less likely than men to be routinely tested or treated for symptoms can foster unrealistic perceptions of risk among women (Steingart et al., 1991; Wenger, 1994). Rarely, however, have the ways in which health care contributes to social constructions of men's health been examined. Recently, it has been argued that sociologists, medical researchers and other health professionals have all contributed to cultural portrayals of men as healthy and women as the "sicker" gender (Gijsbers van Wijk et al., 1991); to strongly held beliefs that men's bodies are structurally more efficient than and superior to women's bodies (Courtenay, 1998a); and to the "invisibility" of men's poor health status (Annandale and Clark, 1996).

As Nathanson (1977, p. 148) noted two decades ago, sex differences in health and health-related behavior arise "out of a medical model that has singled out women for special professional attention"; "women are encouraged and trained to define their life problems in medical terms and to seek professional help for them" (p. 149). While the personal practice of participating in health care is constructed as feminine, the institutional practice of conducting, researching or providing health care is constructed as masculine and defined as a domain of masculine

power. Physicians, who are primarily men, maintain power and control over the bodies of men who are not physicians and the bodies of women, as well as over male and female health professionals in lesser positions of power, such as nurses and orderlies. In these ways, the health care system does not simply adapt to men's "natural" masculinity; rather, it actively constructs gendered health behaviour and negotiates among various forms of masculinity. Medical, sociological and feminist approaches to addressing gender and health have all contributed to the devaluing of women's bodies and to the privileging of men's bodies, as two feminist authors have noted recently (Annandale and Clark, 1996).

Historically, women but not men in the United States have been encouraged to pay attention to their health (Nathanson, 1977; Lonnquist et al., 1992; Signorielli, 1993; Oakley, 1994; Annandale and Clark, 1996; Reagan, 1997). According to Reagan (1997), who recently analysed decades of cancer education in the United States, these educational efforts have been directed primarily at women. Although many counseling and psychological interventions with men have been recommended in the past two decades (Courtenay, in press c), very rarely are these interventions designed to reduce men's health risks (Courtenay, 1998c). Men also receive significantly less physician time in their health visits than women do (Blanchard et al., 1983; Waitzkin, 1984; Weisman and Teitelbaum, 1989), and generally receive fewer services and dispositions than women (Verbrugge and

Steiner, 1985). Men are provided with fewer and briefer explanations—both simple and technical—in medical encounters (Waitzkin, 1984; Hall et al., 1988; Weisman and Teitelbaum, 1989). During checkups, they receive less advice from physicians about changing risk factors for disease than women do (Friedman et al., 1994). Only 29% of physicians routinely provide age-appropriate instruction on performing self-examinations for testicular cancer, compared to the 86% who provide instruction to women on performing breast examinations (Misener and Fuller, 1995). A recent review revealed that no study has ever found that women received less information from physicians than men, which led the authors to conclude that the findings "may reflect sexism in medical encounters, but this may act to the advantage of female patients, who have a more informative and positive experience than is typical for male patients" (Roter and Hall, 1997, p. 44).

A variety of scientific methodologic factors and research methods—developed and conducted primarily by men—have also contributed to the model of deficient women's bodies (Courtenay, 1998a, in press b). For example, the use of behavioural indices of health—such as bed rest and health care utilization—both pathologises women's health and underestimates the significance of men's health problems. These indices confound our understanding of morbidity, because they actually represent how men and women cope with illness rather than representing their true health status (Gijsbers van Wijk et al., 1991); thus they obscure

what may be greater illness among men (Verbrugge, 1988; Kandrack et al., 1991). The assumption underlying these and other indices of health is that male behaviour is the normative or hidden referent; consequently, researchers and theorists alike presume that women are in poorer health because women get more bed rest than men do and see physicians more often. The terms applied to these behaviours—behaviours that can be considered health promoting—further pathologise women's health: women's excess bed rest and women's overutilisation of health services. These terms simultaneously transform curative actions into indicators of illness, make women's health problematic, and reinforce men's position in providing the standard of health or health behaviour.

Given that women are unquestionably less susceptible to serious illness and live longer than men, it would seem that women should provide the standard against which men's health and men's health behaviour are measured. If this were the case, we would be compelled instead to confront men's *inadequate* bed rest and men's *under*utilisation of health care. However, the social forces that maintain women's health as problematic are strong. When morbidity statistics and women's greater propensity for illness are challenged as an artifact of research, for example, the conventional reading of this challenge further pathologises women's health by suggesting that women "aren't really ill at all, they're only inventing it" (Oakley, 1994, p. 431). In contrast, the interpretation that men really *are* ill and they are simply denying it is rarely proposed. It was recently argued that a cultural perception of men's health problems as nonexistent is required both to construct women's bodies as deficient and to reinforce women's disadvantaged social position (Annandale and Clark, 1996). To maintain this construction, "women 'cannot' be well and...men cannot be ill; they are 'needed' to be well to construe women as sick" (Annandale and Clark, 1996, p. 32). By dismissing their health needs and taking physical risks, men are legitimising themselves as the "stronger" sex.

Despite countless examples in research, literature and daily life, the poor health beliefs and behaviours that men use to demonstrate gender remain largely invisible—a testament to the potency of the social construction of men's resiliency and health. Medical and epidemiologic examinations of health and health behaviour consistently fail to take into account gender, apart from biologic sex. For example, while men's greater use of substances is well known, the reasons why men are more likely to use substances are poorly understood and rarely addressed. Similarly, although injury and death due to recreation, risk taking and violence are always associated with being male, epidemiologic and medical findings are consistently presented as if gender were of no particular relevance (Courtenay, 1999b). Few health scientists, sociologists and theorists identify masculinities—and rarely even male sex as a risk factor; fewer still have attempted to identify what it is about men, exactly, that leads them

to engage in behaviours that seriously threaten their health. Instead, men's risk taking and violence are taken for granted.

The failure of medical and epidemiologic researchers to study and explain men's risk taking and violence perpetuates the false, yet widespread, cultural assumption that risk-taking and violent behaviours are natural to, or inherent in, men. Similarly, cultural assumptions that men simply don't (read inherently) seek help pre- vent society from defining men's underutilisation of health services as a problem. Although it too is taken for granted, there is nothing natural about the fact that men make fewer health visits than women. Early in their lives, most adolescent girls in the United States are *taught* the importance of regular physical exams and are introduced to them as a part of being a woman; adolescent boys are not taught that physical exams are part of being a man. Furthermore, for many men, it is their wives, girlfriends and mothers who monitor their health and schedule any medical appointments that they have. Men who want to take greater responsibility for their health will need not only to cross gendered boundaries, but also to learn new skills. Gendered health perspectives that address social structural issues and masculinity are similarly absent from health science research and literature. Such perspectives could, for example, utilise a gendered approach to examining men's work and their far greater exposure to industrial carcinogens as a possible explanation for their greater risk of cancer as compared to women.

The Social Construction of Disease

Depression provides one example of how the health care system contributes to the social construction of disease. Despite suicide rates that are 4 to 12 times higher for men than for women (DHHS, 1994), according to Warren (1983), early documentation on the prevalence of depression among women based on self-reporting has resulted in an emphasis on treating women for depression and suggested an immunity to depression among men. Although young men account for nearly seven of eight suicides among those 15 to 24 year old (DHHS, 1996), an age group in which suicide is the third leading cause of death, a recent large study based exclusively on self-report data concluded that depression is a "more critical" health problem for college women than for college men (Sax, 1997, p. 261). This study fails to take into account men's suicides in this age group. It also disregards decades of research that have consistently found a lack of significant sex differences in *diagnosable* depression among college students (Nolen-Hoeksema, 1987; Courtenay, 1998b).

Treatment rates are also used as indicators of morbidity. However, because depressed men have been found to be more likely than depressed women to not seek help (Chino and Funabiki, 1984; O'Neil et al., 1985), treatment rates are likewise an inaccurate measure of depression. Gender-biased diagnostic decisions of mental health clinicians also contribute to inaccuracies in morbidity statistics (Waisberg and Page, 1988; Ford and Widiger, 1989; Fernbach et al., 1989; Adler et al., 1990). One recent large and well-constructed study found that clinicians were less likely to identify the presence of depression in men than in women, and that they failed to diagnose nearly two thirds of the depressed men (Potts et al., 1991).

Although the failure among clinicians to diagnose depression in men contributes to men's low treatment rates, men's own unwillingness to seek help contributes to the social construction of their invulnerability to depression. Indeed, in response to depression, men are more likely than women to rely on themselves, to withdraw socially, to try to talk themselves out of depression, or to convince themselves that depression is "stupid" (Warren, 1983; Chino and Funabiki, 1984; O'Neil et al., 1985). Nearly half of men over age 49 nationally who reported experiencing an extended depression did not discuss it with anyone (American Medical Association, 1991). Instead, men tend to engage in private activities, including drinking and drug use, designed to distract themselves or to alleviate their depression (Chino and Funabiki, 1984; Nolen-Hoeksema, 1987). Denial of depression is one of the means men use to demonstrate masculinities and to avoid assignment to a lower-status position relative to women and other men. As Warren (1983, p. 151) notes, "The linkage between depression and femininity may provide men with the strongest motivation to hide their depression from others," and, "Because depression is frequently accompanied by feelings of powerlessness and diminished control, men may construe depression as a sign of failure".

■ CONCLUSION

Research consistently demonstrates that women in the United States adopt healthier beliefs and personal health practices than men. A wealth of scientific data suggests that this distinction accounts in no small part for the fact that women suffer less severe chronic conditions and live nearly 7 years longer than men. From a social constructionist perspective, this distinction can be understood as being among the many differences that women and men are expected to demonstrate.

If men want to demonstrate dominant ideals of manhood as defined in North American society, they must adhere to cultural definitions of masculine beliefs and behaviours and actively reject what is feminine. The resources available in the United States for constructing masculinities—and the signifiers of "true" masculinity—are largely unhealthy. Men and boys do indeed use these resources and adopt unhealthy beliefs and behaviours in order to demonstrate manhood. Although nothing strictly prohibits a man from demonstrating masculinities differently, to do so would require that he cross over socially constructed gender boundaries, and risk reproach and sometimes physical danger for failing to demonstrate gender correctly. By successfully using unhealthy beliefs and behaviours to demonstrate idealised forms of masculinity, men are

able to assume positions of power—relative to women and less powerful men—in a patriarchal society that rewards this accomplishment. By dismissing their health needs and taking risks, men legitimize themselves as the "stronger" sex. In this way, men's use of unhealthy beliefs and behaviours helps to sustain and reproduce social inequality and the social structures that, in turn, reinforce and reward men's poor health habits.

It should be noted that some men do defy social prescriptions of masculinity and adopt healthy behaviours, such as getting annual physicals and eating healthy foods. But although these men are constructing a form of masculinity, it is not among the dominant forms that are encouraged in men, nor is it among the forms adopted by most men. It should also be noted that women can and do adopt unhealthy beliefs and behaviours to demonstrate femininities, as in the case of unhealthy dieting to attain a culturally defined body ideal of slimness. However, as has been demonstrated elsewhere (Courtenay, 1998a, in press b), the striving for cultural standards of femininity leads women to engage primarily in healthy, not unhealthy, behaviours.

This relational theory of gender and men's health will undoubtedly meet with resistance from many quarters. As a society, we all work diligently at maintaining constructions of women's health as deficient, of the female body as inferior, of men's health as ideal, and of the male body as structurally efficient and superior. From a feminist perspective, these constructions can be viewed as preserving existing power structures and the many privileges enjoyed by men in the United States. Naming and confronting men's poor health status and unhealthy beliefs and behaviours may well improve their physical well-being, but it will necessarily undermine men's privileged position and threaten their power and authority in relation to women.

REFERENCES

Adler, D. A., Drake, R. E., Teague, G. B., 1990. Clinicians' practices in personality assessment: does gender influence the use of DSM-III axis II? *Comprehensive Psychiatry* *31*(2), 125–133.

American Academy of Dermatology, 1997. *"It Can't Happen to Me": Americans Not As Safe From the Sun As They Think They Are*. American Academy of Dermatology, Schaumburg, IL.

American Heart Association, 1995. *Heart and Stroke Facts: 1995 Statistical Supplement*. American Heart Association, Dallas, TX.

American Medical Association, 1991, October. Results of 9/91 Gallup survey on older men's health perceptions and behaviours (News Release). American Medical Association, Chicago, IL.

Anaya, R., 1996. "I'm the king": the macho image. In: Gonzales, R. (Ed.), *Muy Macho*. Doubleday, New York, pp. 57–73.

Annandale, E., Clark, J., 1996. What is gender? Feminist theory and the sociology of human reproduction. *Sociology of Health and Illness 18*(1), 17–44.

Bayne-Smith, M. (Ed.), 1996. *Race, Gender, and Health*. Sage Publications, Thousand Oaks, CA.

Blanchard, C. G., Ruckdeschel, J. C., Blanchard, E. B., Arena, J. G., Saunders, N. L., Malloy, E. D., 1983. Interactions between oncologists and patients during rounds. *Annals of Internal Medicine 99*, 694–699.

Bohan, J. S., 1993. Regarding gender: essentialism, constructionism and feminist psychology. *Psychology of Women Quarterly 17*, 5–21.

Brown, J.S., McCreedy, M., 1986. The Hale elderly: health behaviour and its correlates. *Research in Nursing and Health 9*, 317–329.

Bureau of Labor Statistics, 1993. *National Census of Fatal Occupational Injuries, 1993*. Bureau of Labor Statistics, Washington, DC.

Caspersen, C.J., Merritt, R.K., 1995. Physical activity trends among 26 states, 1986–1990. *Medicine and Science in Sports and Exercise 27*(5), 713–720.

Centers for Disease Control, 1995a. *Skin Cancer Prevention and Early Detection: At-a-Glance*. Centers for Disease Control, Atlanta, GA.

Centers for Disease Control, 1995b. Deaths from melanoma—United States, 1973–1992. *Morbidity and Mortality Weekly Report, 44*(44), 337, 343–347.

Centers for Disease Control, 1997. Demographic differences in noticeable infectious disease morbidity—United States, 1992–1994. *Morbidity and Mortality Weekly Report, 46*(28), 637–641.

Charmaz, K., 1995. Identity dilemmas of chronically ill men. In: Sabo, D., Gordon, D.F. (Eds.), *Men's Health and Illness: Gender, Power and the Body*. Sage Publications, Thousand Oaks, CA, pp. 266–291.

Chino, A.F., Funabiki, D., 1984. A cross-validation of sex differences in the expression of depression. *Sex Roles 11*, 175–187.

Clatterbaugh, K., 1997. *Contemporary Perspectives on Masculinity: Men, Women and Politics in Modern Society,* 2nd ed. Westview Press, Boulder, CO.

Connell, R.W., 1992. *Masculinity, violence and war.* In: Kimmel, M.S., Messner, M.A. (Eds.), *Men's Lives,* 2nd ed. Macmillan, New York, pp. 176–183.

Connell, R.W., 1993. The big picture: masculinities in recent world history. *Theory and Society 22*, 597–623.

Connell, R.W., 1995. *Masculinities.* University of California Press, Berkeley, CA.

Courtenay, W. H., 1998a. Better to die than cry? A longitudinal and constructionist study of masculinity and the health risk behaviour of young American men. (University of California at Berkeley). Dissertation Abstracts International, 59(08A), (Publication number 9902042).

Courtenay, W. H., 1998b. College men's health: an overview and a call to action. *Journal of American College Health 46*(6), 279–290.

Courtenay, W. H., 1998c. Communication strategies for improving men's health: the 6-point HEALTH plan. *Wellness Management, 14*(1), 1, 3–4.

Courtenay, W. H., 1999a. *Situating men's health in the negotiation of masculinities.* The Society for the Psychological Study of Men and Masculinity Bulletin (The American Psychological Association) 4(2), 10–12.

Courtenay, W. H., 1999b. Youth violence? Let's call it what it is. *Journal of American College Health 48*(3), 141–142.

Courtenay, W. H. Behavioural factors associated with disease, injury, and death among men: evidence and implications for prevention. *Journal of Men's Studies* (in press a).

Courtenay, W. H. Engendering health: a social constructionist examination of men's health beliefs and behaviours. *Psychology of Men and Masculinity* (in press b).

Courtenay, W. H. Social work, counseling, and psychotherapeutic interventions with men and boys: a bibliography. *Men and Masculinities* (in press c).

Courtenay, W. H., Sabo, D. Preventive health strategies for men in prison. In: Sabo, D., Kupers, T., and London, W. (Eds.), *Confronting Prison Masculinities: The Gendered Politics of Punishment.* Temple University Press, Philadelphia, PA (in press).

Coward, R., 1984. *Female Desire: Women's Sexuality Today.* Paladin Publishing, London.

Crawford, M., 1995. *Talking Difference: On Gender and Language.* Sage Publications, Thousand Oaks, CA.

Deaux, K., 1984. From individual differences to social categories: an analysis of a decade's research on gender. *American Psychologist 39*(2), 105–116.

Delsohn, S., 1996. *The Fire Inside: Firefighters Talk About Their Lives.* HarperCollins Publishers, New York.

Department of Health and Human Services, 1994. *Mortality, Part A. In: Vital Statistics of the United States, 1990, vol. II.* Public Health Service, Hyattsville, MD.

Department of Health and Human Services, 1996. Report of final mortality statistics, 1994. *Monthly Vital Statistics Report, 45*(3, Supplement). Public Health Service, Hyattsville, MD.

Department of Health and Human Services, 1998. *Health, United States, 1998: Socioeconomic Status and Health Chartbook*. National Center for Health Statistics, Hyattsville, MD.

Diaz, R.M., 1998. *Latino Gay Men and HIV: Culture, Sexuality and Risk Behaviour*. Routledge, New York.

Donnermeyer, J.J., Park, D.S., 1995. Alcohol use among rural adolescents: predictive and situational factors. *International Journal of the Addictions 30*(4), 459–479.

Doyal, L., 1995. *What Makes Women Sick: Gender and the Political Economy of Health*. Rutgers University Press, New Brunswick, NJ.

Eagly, A.H., 1983. Gender and social influence: a social psychological analysis. *American Psychologist 38*, 971–981.

Eisler, R.M., 1995. The relationship between Masculine Gender Role Stress and men's health risk: the validation of a construct. In: Levant, R.F., Pollack, W.S. (Eds.), *A New Psychology of Men*. Basic Books, New York, pp. 207–225.

Epstein, C.F., 1988. *Deceptive Distinctions: Sex, Gender and the Social Order*. Yale University Press, New Haven, CT.

Fellows, W., 1996. *Farm Boys: Lives of Gay Men from the Rural Midwest*. University of Wisconsin Press, Madison, WI.

Fernbach, B.E., Winstead, B.A., Derlega, V.J., 1989. Sex differences in diagnosis and treatment recommendations for antisocial personality and somatisation disorders. *Journal of Social and Clinical Psychology 8*, 238–255.

Ford, M.R., Widiger, T.A., 1989. Sex bias in the diagnosis of histrionic and antisocial personality disorders. *Journal of Consulting and Clinical Psychology 57*, 301–305.

Friedman, C., Brownson, R.C., Peterson, D.E., Wilkerson, J.C., 1994. Physician advice to reduce chronic disease risk factors. *American Journal of Preventive Medicine 10*(6), 367–371.

Geis, F.L., 1993. Self-fulfilling prophecies: a social psychological view of gender. In: Beall, A.E., Sternberg, R.J. (Eds.), *The Psychology of Gender*. Guilford Press, New York, pp. 9–54.

Gerson, J.M., Peiss, K., 1985. Boundaries, negotiation, consciousness: reconceptualising gender relations. *Social Problems 32*(4), 317–331.

Gibbs, J.T., 1988. Health and mental health of young black males. In: Gibbs, J.T. (Ed.), Young, *Black and Male in America: An Endangered Species*. Auburn House, New York, pp. 219–257.

Gijsbers van Wijk, C.M.T., Vliet van, K.P., Kolk, K.P., Everaerd, W.T., 1991. Symptom sensitivity and sex differences in physical morbidity: a review of health surveys in the United States and the Netherlands. *Women and Health 17*, 91–124.

Goldberg, H., 1976. *The Hazards of Being Male: Surviving the Myth of Masculine Privilege*. Nash Publishing, Plainview, NY.

Golombok, S., Fivush, R., 1994. *Gender Development*. Cambridge University Press, Cambridge, MA.

Hall, J.A., Roter, D.L., Katz, N.R., 1988. Meta-analysis of correlates of provider behaviour in medical encounters. *Medical Care 26*, 657–675.

Harris, I., Torres, J.B., Allender, D., 1994. The responses of African American men to dominant norms of masculinity within the United States. *Sex Roles 31*, 703–719.

Harrison, J., 1978. Warning: the male sex role may be dangerous to your health. *Journal of Social Issues 34*(1), 65–86.

Harrison, J., Chin, J., Ficarroto, T., 1992. Warning: the male sex role may be dangerous to your health. In: Kimmel, M.S., Messner, M.A. (Eds.), *Men's Lives,* 2nd ed., Boston: Allyn & Bacon, pp. 271–285.

Hunter, A.G., Davis, J.E., 1992. Constructing gender: an exploration of Afro-American men's conceptualisation of manhood. *Gender and Society 6*, 464–479.

Jaffe, H., 1997. Dying for dollars. *Men's Health, 12*, 132–137, 186–187.

Kandrack, M., Grant, K.R., Segall, A., 1991. Gender differences in health related behaviour: some unanswered questions. *Social Science and Medicine 32*(5), 579–590.

Kaschak, E., 1992. *Engendered Lives: A New Psychology of Women's Experience.* Basic Books, New York.

Katz, P.A., Ksansnak, K.R., 1994. Developmental aspects of gender role flexibility and traditionality in middle childhood and adolescence. *Developmental Psychology 30*(2), 272–282.

Kaufman, M., 1994. Men, feminism, and men's contradictory experiences of power. In: Brod, H., Kaufman, M. (Eds.), *Theorising Masculinities.* Sage Publications, Thousand Oaks, CA, pp. 142–163.

Kimmel, M.S., 1986. Introduction: toward men's studies. *American Behavioural Scientist 29*(5), 517–529.

Kimmel, M., 1995. *Manhood in America: A Cultural History.* Free Press, New York.

Koop, C.E., 1996. Foreword. In: Woolf, S.H., Jonas, S., Lawrence, R.S. (Eds.), *Health Promotion and Disease Prevention in Clinical Practice.* Williams and Wilkins, Baltimore, MD, pp. 7–9.

Korda, M., 1996. *Man to Man: Surviving Prostate Cancer.* Random House, New York.

Laveist, T.A., 1993. Segregation, poverty and empowerment: health consequences for African Americans. *Milbank Quarterly 71*(1), 41–64.

Lee, P.R., 1996. Foreword . In: *U.S. Preventive Services Task Force, Guide to Clinical Preventive Services,* 2nd ed. Williams and Wilkins, Baltimore, MD, p. 5.

Levant, R.F., Majors, R.G., 1998. Masculinity ideology among African American and European American college women and men. *Journal of Gender, Culture and Health 2*(1), 33–43.

Levant, R.F., Majors, R.G., Kelley, M.L., 1998. Masculinity ideology among young African American and European American women and men in different regions of the United States. *Cultural Diversity and Ethnic Minority Psychology 4*(3), 227–236.

Levine, M., 1998. *Gay Macho: The Life and Death of the Homosexual Clone.* New York University Press, New York.

Long, K.A., 1993. The concept of health: rural perspectives. *Nursing Clinics of North America 28*(1), 123–130.

Lonnquist, L.E., Weiss, G.L., Larsen, D.L., 1992. Health value and gender in predicting health protective behaviour. *Women and Health 19*(2/3), 69–85.

Majors, R., Billson, J.M., 1992. *Cool Pose: The Dilemmas of Black Manhood in America.* Touchstone, New York.

Martin, C.L., 1995. Stereotypes about children with traditional and nontraditional gender roles. *Sex Roles 33*(11/12), 727–751.

Mechanic, D., Cleary, P.D., 1980. Factors associated with the maintenance of positive health behaviour. *Preventive Medicine 9*, 805–814.

Meinecke, C.E., 1981. Socialised to die younger? Hypermasculinity and men's health. *The Personnel and Guidance Journal 60*, 241–245.

Mermelstein, R.J., Riesenberg, L.A., 1992. Changing knowledge and attitudes about skin cancer risk factors in adolescents. *Health Psychology 11*(6), 371–376.

Messerschmidt, J.W., 1993. *Masculinities and Crime: Critique and Reconceptualisation of Theory*. Rowman and Littlefield Publishers, Lanham, MD.

Messner, M.A., Sabo, D.F., 1994. *Sex, Violence and Power in Sports: Rethinking Masculinity*. The Crossing Press, Freedom, CA.

Misener, T.R., Fuller, S.G., 1995. Testicular versus breast and colorectal cancer screen: early detection practices of primary care physicians. *Cancer Practice 3*(5), 310–316.

Mor, V., Masterson-Allen, S., Goldberg, R., Guadagnoli, E., Wool, M.S., 1990. Prediagnostic symptom recognition and help seeking among cancer patients. *Journal of Community Health 15*(4), 253–261.

Nathanson, C., 1977. Sex roles as variables in preventive health behaviour. *Journal of Community Health 3*(2), 142–155.

National Institute for Occupational Safety and Health, 1993. *Fatal injuries to workers in the United States, 1980–1989: a decade of surveillance*. National Institute for Occupational Safety and Health, Cincinnati, OH (DHHS [NIOSH] No. 93–108).

National Institutes of Health, 1992. *Cancer statistics review: 1973–1989*. U.S. Government Printing Office, Washington, DC (NIH Publication No. 92–2789).

National Institutes of Health, 1998. *Clinical Guidelines on the Identification, Evaluation and Treatment of Overweight and Obesity in Adults*. National Heart, Lung and Blood Institute, Rockville, MD.

Neff, J.A., Prihoda, T.J., Hoppe, S.K., 1991. "Machismo," self-esteem, education and high maximum drinking among Anglo, Black and Mexican-American male drinkers. *Journal of Studies on Alcohol 52*, 458–463.

Nolen-Hoeksema, S., 1987. Sex differences in unipolar depression: evidence and theory. *Psychological Bulletin 101*(2), 259–282.

Oakley, A., 1994. Who cares for health? Social relations, gender and the public health. *Journal of Epidemiology and Community Health 48*, 427–434.

O'Neil, J.M., Good, G.E., Holmes, S., 1995. Fifteen years of theory and research on men's gender role conflict: new paradigms for empirical research. In: Levant, R.F., Pollack, W.S. (Eds.), *A New Psychology of Men*. Basic Books, New York, pp. 164–206.

O'Neil, M.K., Lancee, W.J., Freeman, J.J., 1985. Sex differences in depressed university students. *Social Psychiatry 20*, 186–190.

Pappas, G., Queen, S., Hadden, W., Fisher, G., 1993. The increasing disparity in mortality between socioeconomic groups in the United States, 1960 and 1986. *New England Journal of Medicine 239*(2), 103–109.

Patrick, M.S., Covin, J.R., Fulop, M., Calfas, K., Lovato, C., 1997. Health risk behaviours among California college students. *Journal of American College Health 45*, 265–272.

Perry, L.A., Turner, L.H., Sterk, H.M. (Eds.), 1992. *Constructing and Reconstructing*

Gender: The Links Among Communication, Language and Gender. State University of New York Press, Albany, NY.

Pleck, J.H., 1987. *The Myth of Masculinity,* 3rd ed. M.I.T. Press, Cambridge, MA.

Pleck, J.H., Sonenstein, F.L., Ku, L.C., 1994a. Problem behaviours and masculinity ideology in adolescent males. In: Ketterlinus, R.D., Lamb, M.E. (Eds.), *Adolescent Problem Behaviours: Issues and Research.* Lawrence Erlbaum, Hillsdale, NJ, pp. 165–186.

Pleck, J.H., Sonenstein, F.L., Ku, L.C., 1994b. Attitudes toward male roles among adolescent males: a discriminant validity analysis. *Sex Roles 30*(7/8), 481–501.

Potts, M.K., Burnam, M.A., Wells, K.B., 1991. Gender differences in depression detection: a comparison of clinician diagnosis and standardised assessment. *Psychological Assessment 3*, 609–615.

Powell-Griner, E., Anderson, J.E., Murphy, W., 1997. State-and sex-specific prevalence of selected characteristics—behavioural risk factor surveillance system, 1994 and 1995. *Morbidity and Mortality Weekly Report,* Centers for Disease Control, Surveillance Summaries, *46*(3) 1–31.

Pyke, K.D., 1996. Class-based masculinities: the interdependence of gender, class and interpersonal power. *Gender and Society 10*, 527–549.

Ratner, P.A., Bottorff, J.L., Johnson, J.L., Hayduk, L.A., 1994. The interaction effects of gender within the health promotion model. *Research in Nursing and Health 17*, 341–350.

Reagan, L.J., 1997. Engendering the dread disease: women, men and cancer. *American Journal of Public Health 87*(11), 1779–1187.

Rice, T.W., Coates, D.L., 1995. Gender role attitudes in the southern United States. *Gender and Society 9*(6), 744–756.

Rich, J.A., Stone, D.A., 1996. The experience of violent injury for young African-American men: the meaning of being a "sucker". *Journal of General Internal Medicine 11*, 77–82.

Rose, B. (Ed.), 1997. *A Radical Fairy's Seedbed: The Collected Series.* Nomenus, San Francisco.

Rossi, J.S., 1992, March. Stages of change for 15 health risk behaviours in an HMO population. Paper presented at the 13th annual scientific sessions of the Society of Behavioural Medicine, New York.

Roter, D.L., Hall, J.A., 1997. *Doctors Talking with Patients/Patients Talking with Doctors: Improving Communication in Medical Visits.* Auburn House, Westport, CT.

Sabo, D., Gordon, D.F.(Eds.), 1995. *Men's Health and Illness: Gender, Power and the Body.* Sage Publications, Thousand Oaks, CA.

Saltonstall, R., 1993. Healthy bodies, social bodies: men's and women's concepts and practices of health in everyday life. *Social Science and Medicine 36*(1), 7–14.

Sax, L., 1997. Health trends among college freshmen. *Journal of American College Health 45*(6), 252–262.

Slesinski, M.J., Subar, A.F., Kahle, L.L., 1996. Dietary intake of fat, fiber and other nutrients is related to the use of vitamin and mineral supplements in the United States: the 1992 National Health Interview Survey. *Journal of Nutrition 126*(12), 3001–3008.

Shi, L., 1998. Sociodemographic characteristics and individual health behaviours. *Southern Medical Journal 91*(10), 933–941.

Signorielli, N., 1993. *Mass Media Images and Impact on Health: A Sourcebook.* Greenwood Press, Westport, CT.

Steingart, R.M., Packer, M., Hamm, P., Coglianese, M.E., Gersh, B., Geltman, E.M., Sollano, J., Katz, S., Moye, L., Basta, L.L., Lewis, S.J., Gottlieb, S.S., Bernstein, V., McEwan, P., Jacobson, K., Brown, E.J., Kukin, M.L., Kantrowitz, N.E., Pfeffer, M.A., 1991. Sex differences in the management of coronary artery disease. *New England Journal of Medicine 325*(4), 226–230.

Street, S., Kimmel, E.B., Kromrey, J.D., 1995. Revisiting university student gender role perceptions. *Sex Roles 33*(3/4), 183–201.

Stueland, D., Mickel, S.H., Cleveland, D.A., Rothfusz, R.R., Zoch, T., Stamas, P., 1995. The relationship of farm residency status to demographic and service characteristics of agricultural injury victims in central Wisconsin. *The Journal of Rural Health 11*(2), 98–105.

U.S. Preventive Services Task Force, 1996. *Guide to Clinical Preventive Services,* 2nd ed. Williams and Wilkins, Baltimore, MD.

Vance, C.S., 1995. Social construction theory and sexuality. In: Berger, M., Wallis, B., Watson, S. (Eds.), *Constructing Masculinity.* Routledge, New York, pp. 37–48.

Verbrugge, L.M., 1985. Gender and health: an update on hypotheses and evidence. *Journal of Health and Social Behaviour 26*, 156–182.

Verbrugge, L.M., 1988. Unveiling higher morbidity for men: the story. In: Riley, M.W. (Ed.), *Social Structures and Human Lives.* Sage Publications, Thousand Oaks, CA, pp. 138–160.

Verbrugge, L.M., Steiner, R.P., 1985. Prescribing drugs to men and women. *Health Psychology 4*(1), 79–98.

Verbrugge, L.M., Wingard, D.L., 1987. Sex differentials in health and mortality. *Women and Health 12*(2), 103–145.

Waisberg, J., Page, S., 1988. Gender role nonconformity and perception of mental illness. *Women and Health 14*, 3–16.

Waitzkin, H., 1984. Doctor-patient communication: clinical implications of social scientific research. *Journal of the American Medical Association 252*, 2441–2446.

Waldron, I., 1988. Gender and health-related behaviour. In: Gochman, D.S. (Ed.), *Health Behaviour: Emerging Research Perspectives.* Plenum, New York, pp. 193–208.

Walker, S.N., Volkan, K., Sechrist, K.R., Pender, N.J., 1988. Health promoting lifestyles of older adults: comparisons with young and middle-aged adults, correlates and patterns. *Advances in Nursing Science 11*, 76–90.

Warren, L.W., 1983. Male intolerance of depression: a review with implications for psychotherapy. *Clinical Psychology Review 3*, 147–156.

Wenger, N.K., 1994. Coronary heart disease in women: gender differences in diagnostic evaluation. *Journal of the American Medical Women's Association 49*, 181–185.

Weisman, C.S., Teitelbaum, M.A., 1989. Women and health care communication. *Patient Education and Counseling, 13*, 183–199.

West, C., Zimmerman, D.H., 1987. Doing gender. *Gender and Society 1*(2), 125–151.

Williams, J.E., Best, D.L., 1990. *Measuring Sex Stereotypes: A Multination Study*. Sage Publications, Thousand Oaks, CA.

Willits, F.K., Bealer, R.C., Timbers, V.L., 1990. Popular images of 'rurality': data from a Pennsylvania survey. *Rural Sociology 55*(4), 559–578.

Woolf, S.H., Jonas, S., Lawrence, R.S. (Eds.), 1996. *Health Promotion and Disease Prevention in Clinical Practice*. Williams and Wilkins, Baltimore, MD.

CHAPTER 17

Mags and Abs

Media Consumption and Bodily Concerns in Men

Ida Jodette Hatoum and Deborah Belle

Men's concerns with their bodies have been understudied over the past several decades (Mishkind, Rodin, Silberstein, & Striegel-Moore, 1986; Nemeroff, Stein, Diehl, & Smilack, 1994), especially in comparison to women's bodily concerns, which have received extensive research attention. It has been shown that women often experience body dissatisfaction, particularly the desire to be thinner (Brumberg, 1997; Cohn & Adler, 1992; Fallon & Rozin, 1985; Harrison, 2000; Harrison & Cantor, 1997; Mintz & Betz, 1986; Monteath & McCabe, 1997; Posavac, Posavac, & Posavac, 1998; Rand & Wright, 2001; Wegner, Hartmann, & Geist, 2000; Wilcox & Laird, 2000) and that this dissatisfaction is associated with dangerous eating disorders (Brumberg, 1997; Stice & Shaw, 1994; Striegel-Moore, Silberstein, & Rodin, 1986). As a result, it has become normative to assess thinness related bodily preoccupations in both women and men. However, in simply comparing the two genders in their desire for thinness, men's unique concerns, particularly about being underweight or undermuscular, have not often been examined, nor have the potentially dangerous attitudes and behaviors associated with these concerns.

When these issues are explicitly addressed, it is found that men do, in fact, experience their own specific types of bodily concerns and that *under*weight men have some of the problems typical of *over*weight women. Harmatz, Gronendyke, and Thomas (1985) found that on questions pertaining to self-image and interpersonal status, the scores from underweight men and overweight women were indistinguishable. The underweight men (as compared to "normal" weight men) viewed themselves as less desirable and less good-natured, and they viewed their dating partners as less desirable, less intelligent, and less assertive. Furthermore, the underweight men dated

337

less, felt more likely to be rejected, and were more lonely.

As early as the 1960s, researchers found that boys frequently desired larger chests, wrists, shoulders, forearms, and especially biceps (Huenemann, Shapiro, Hampton, & Mitchell, 1966). The researchers speculated that the boys who expressed the desire to be larger were concerned with becoming more muscular, not merely with gaining weight in pounds. Other studies conducted around this time further supported the finding that men and boys preferred a muscular physique, regardless of their own current stature (Dibiase & Hjelle, 1968; Staffieri, 1967). Furthermore, muscular body types have been assigned positive attributes for men, both by adults (Dibiase & Hjelle, 1968) and by children as young as 6 years old (Staffieri, 1967).

Similarly, percentage of body fat has been recognized as a critical component of a man's perception of himself. Huddy, Nieman, and Johnson (1993) found an inverse relationship between percent body fat and body satisfaction, which indicates that muscularity and the degree to which one is "dense" are crucial factors in predicting body satisfaction among men. Muscularity plays such a central role in a man's perception of himself that Pope, Katz, and Hudson (1993) went so far as to suggest that some men suffer from a syndrome comparable to anorexia. They termed this syndrome "reverse anorexia," defined as a condition in which normal to overweight men perceive themselves as too small and go to extreme lengths, such as intense body building and the use of steroids, in order to "bulk up."

In recent years, cultural standards have shifted so that increasingly large male bodies are now the most admired physiques. Leit, Pope, and Gray (2001) examined the changing standard of what is considered the ideal male physique in a study that parallels Garner, Garfinkel, Schwartz, and Thompson's research (Garner, Garfinkel, Schwartz, and Thompson, 1980) showing that *Playboy* magazine centerfolds have become thinner and thinner over the years. Leit et al. documented the increasing "denseness," or concentration of muscularity, of the male centerfolds of *Playgirl* magazine. They found that the physiques presented are so large and muscular that at times they suggest the use of anabolic steroids. Just as the culturally approved female body is becoming thinner, the cultural ideal for masculinity demands increasing muscularity.

Many different cultural icons represent the physical ideal for women. Perhaps the consummate unattainable feminine ideal is the popular doll Barbie, whose busty figure and slim waist have always been physically impossible for a real-life woman to attain. In contrast, action figures once accurately represented the physiques of strong, healthy men. However, an analysis of the evolution of the physiques of the top male action toys (GI Joe and characters from *Star Wars*) over a period from 1964 until 1998, found that modern male action figures are larger and more muscular than previous versions of the same characters. These current action figures are so large, in fact, that some are more muscular than humanly possible, even with the help of substances such as anabolic steroids (Pope, Olivardia, Gruber, & Borowiecki, 1999).

As the cultural ideal is shifting to become ever more muscular, men are becoming increasingly preoccupied with attaining that male body ideal (Mishkind et al., 1986; Nemeroff et al., 1994). Research suggests that there are negative psychological effects of striving for impossible physical ideals (Pope et al., 1993; Mishkind et al., 1986), although these effects have been studied more often among women than among men. Social comparison processes, particularly the tendency to make upward social comparisons with those who have more beautiful and socially admired bodies, can lead to dissatisfaction and demoralization (Collins, 1996). Although beauty magazines can provide useful tools for improving one's appearance, media exposure to unrealistically thin images has been shown to lead to dissatisfaction with appearance in both adolescent girls (Levine, Smolak, & Hayden, 1994) and adult women (Wilcox & Laird, 2000). Exposure to "ideal" female bodies via media is correlated with weight concern (Harrison & Cantor, 1997; Posavac et al., 1998), body dissatisfaction (Becker, Burwell, Gilman, Herzog, & Hamburg, 2002; Harrison & Cantor, 1997; Wegner et al., 2000), reduced self-esteem (Wilcox & Laird, 2000), and disordered eating (Becker et al., 2002; Harrison & Cantor, 1997; Vaughan & Fouts, 2003) among women and girls.

In fact, Anderson and DiDomenico (1992) found a dose-response relationship between the number of dieting messages sent to women and men via magazines and the corresponding prevalence of eating disorders. When they analyzed the content of the 10 most popular men's and women's magazines, they found a 10:1 ratio of diet promoting content in women's magazines compared to men's magazines. This is precisely the ratio of eating disorders found in women and men.

It is important to note that the 10:1 ratio cited by Anderson and DiDomenico refers to eating disorders, the extreme behaviors of restricting food intake or binging and purging. Body dissatisfaction is recognized as a precursor to the behaviors that are symptoms of eating disorders (Brumberg, 1997; Stice & Shaw, 1994; Striegel-Moore et al., 1986). However, whereas most women who are dissatisfied with their bodies want to be thinner, dissatisfied men often desire to be bulkier (Drewnowski & Yee, 1987; Mintz & Betz, 1986). Therefore, it is unlikely that most men who are dissatisfied with their bodies would be classified as having eating disorders.

Furthermore, Anderson and Di-Domenico conducted their research using data available from 1989, before the introduction into the American market of magazines such as *Maxim, Stuff,* and *FHM*. These magazines have virtually revolutionized the media messages to which men are exposed, emphasizing the importance of a highly muscular and expensively groomed body. Since Anderson and DiDomenico's research, there has been a congruent rise in popularity of magazines that appeal to men's vanity and health such as *Men's Health, Men's Journal,* and *Men's Fitness,* as well as the continuing appeal of older magazines such as *GQ* and *Esquire* ("Mediamark," 2001).

Not only are men exposed to increasingly unrealistic images of male bodies, but now a man's exposure to the barely clothed "ideal" female figure is no longer limited to explicitly pornographic magazines, the swimsuit issue of *Sports Illustrated,* or the occasional racy spread in mainstream media. A large portion of the content of many popular men's magazines is dedicated to thin women—who usually have large breasts—wearing nothing but skimpy bikinis (and often even less—a common pose for a model is to be naked with just her arm or a strategically placed shadow to cover part of her breasts). Because men are more likely than women to judge potential partners on the basis of physical attractiveness (Mazur, 1986), there is added pressure for women to achieve the cultural ideal of physical beauty. It has been shown that as early as the ninth grade, boys rate physical attractiveness as the most important quality for a woman to have (Mazur, 1986). Women are not oblivious to this fact, and they perceive that society values, and men prefer, a female figure that is extremely thin (Cohn & Adler, 1992; Fallon & Rozin, 1985; Mintz & Betz, 1986).

Among men, the extent of media consumption (specifically television) is associated with higher standards of physical beauty for women (Harrison & Cantor, 1997). Furthermore, Kenrick and Gutierres (1980) found that men who had watched an episode of the popular television show *Charlie's Angels* rated an average woman as less attractive than did men who had not watched the program. In another study (Cash, Cash, & Butters, 1983), both men and women rated photographs of women of average attractiveness that were placed among photographs of other women who were either very attractive or unattractive. The average women were deemed more attractive when judged among the unattractive photographs and less attractive when judged against the very attractive women. These data demonstrate that exposure to images of particularly attractive women led to higher beauty standards for women.

The aim of this study was to investigate the association between men's media exposure and their attitudes toward the ideal male body, the ideal female body, and behaviors undertaken to improve the body, such as weight lifting and dieting. It was hypothesized that men who had high levels of media exposure would report beliefs and behaviors indicative of dissatisfaction with their own bodies and would also endorse higher standards for acceptable female bodies, particularly thinness.

■ METHOD

Participants

The participants were 89 male students recruited at a dormitory in a large northeastern university. Their mean age was 19.46 years, with a range of 18 years to 23 years. The racial/ethnic breakdown was as follows: 73.0% European American, 9.0% Asian, 6.7% Hispanic, 2.2% African American, 2.2% Indian, and 2.2% "Other"; 4.1% of the sample chose not to answer the race/ethnicity item. These percentages are similar to the university's racial breakdown, as reported on the website (59% European-American, 11.4% Asian, 4.7% Hispanic, 2.5% African American, and 22.4% unknown). The students represented 31 different majors, and they had completed a mean level of 1.5 years of college.

Measures

Swansea Muscularity Attitudes Questionnaire (SMAQ)

This measure was developed by Edwards and Launder (2000) in order to investigate and assess men's muscularity concerns. The 20-item scale has two components: Drive for Muscularity (DFM), which examines a person's desire to obtain greater muscularity, and Positive Attributes of Muscularity (PAM), which examines the perceived social benefits of being muscular. Edwards and Launder reported Cronbach's alphas of .94 for PAM and .91 for DFM.

Our pilot study of the SMAQ with a small sample of men ($n = 9$) revealed unanimous frustration with the repetitive nature of the questions. We developed a revised version of the SMAQ, which consisted of one-half the original questionnaire (a total of 10 questions), five of which assessed DFM and five

of which assessed PAM. Scoring of the revised SMAQ differed from the original method used by Edwards and Lauder in that each item was scored on a scale from 1 (*strongly disagree*) to 5 (*strongly agree*) as opposed to a 1–7 scale. The scoring system was changed in the current study to match the scoring of other questions within the questionnaire in order to avoid confusion. In this study, Cronbach alpha scores were .97 for PAM and .97 for DFM. Evidence for the construct validity of the revised scales was found in the significant and positive correlations between the revised PAM score and men's responses to the following items: "I spend a lot of time thinking about how muscular I am," $r = .65$, $p < .001$; "I would like to have more upper body muscle," $r = .48$, $p < .001$; "I would like to have more muscular legs," $r = .40$, $p < .001$; and "I feel guilty if I do not exercise," $r = .56$, $p < .001$. Construct validity for the revised DFM was found in the significant and positive correlations between the revised DFM score and men's total amount of time spent exercising per week, $r = .27$, $p < .05$, their membership in a gym, $r = .40$, $p < .001$, as well as their responses to "I lift weights to build muscle," $r = .73$, $p < .001$, and "I take dietary supplements to build muscle," $r = .39$, $p < .001$.

Men's Endorsement of Thinness and Dieting for Women Scale

This scale was developed by Harrison and Cantor (1997) to evaluate a man's desire that a woman be thin. It assesses the importance of various aspects of a woman's physical appearance by asking for the man's personal opinion as well as his perception of the opinion of his friends. Six items assess whether a man believes that a woman must be thin to be beautiful, the importance of thinness when choosing a woman to date, his perception of his friends' opinions as to whether a woman must be thin to be beautiful, his perceptions of his friends' opinions as to the importance of thinness when choosing a woman to date, his personal disappointment if a blind date were not thin, and his rating of the importance of thinness in someone he is dating. Each item is scored on a scale from 1 (*not at all important/strongly disagree*) to 5 (*very important/strongly agree*), and scores are added together to form a composite variable. Harrison and Cantor reported a Cronbach's alpha of .81. In this study, the Cronbach's alpha was .74, after the removal of the blind date question, which had lowered the alpha to an unacceptable level.

Self-Esteem

The Rosenberg Self-Esteem Inventory (Rosenberg, 1965) is a widely used 10-item scale that measures global self-esteem. Self-esteem is recognized as a stable trait that describes a person's positive or negative attitude toward the self. The reproducibility score in Rosenberg's original study was .93, and the Cronbach's alpha for this study was .62. Responses were scored using Rosenberg's original scoring method, yielding a possible range of 0 (*high self-esteem*) to 6 (*low self-esteem*).

Media Exposure

Participants were asked to report the number of hours per week they spent watching television, watching movies, watching music videos, and reading magazines. In addition, they were given a list of 22 male-directed magazines[1] and asked to indicate which of those magazines they had at least skimmed through in the past month. These magazines were chosen to represent a comprehensive list of available magazines identified by magazine publishers and/or distributors as being from the "men's magazine" genre. This list includes all men's magazines having a high circulation focused specifically on men's fitness and/or lifestyles ("Mediamark," 2001), as well as other lower circulation magazines of the same genre distributed by Publisher's Clearing House.

Body Improvement Behaviors and Concerns

Questions were added to investigate the specific concerns men had about their bodies and actual behaviors undertaken to improve their bodies, such as dieting, exercise, and the use of beauty products.[2] In separate sections of the questionnaire men were asked to report their height, current weight, and ideal weight. A score was computed to reflect the difference between ideal and actual weight; a positive score indicates the desire to gain weight, and a negative score indicates the desire to lose weight. Furthermore, Body Mass Index (BMI) was calculated from the information on actual height and weight. BMIs less than 18.5 are considered underweight, between 18.5 and 24.9 are considered normal weight, between 25 and 29.9 are considered overweight, and greater than 30 are considered obese.

Procedure

All participants were recruited at a large dormitory, outside a large dining hall, during a period in which both students who lived in the dormitory as well as others just passing through were available. A table was set up in a central location with a large, bright sign that read "Men Needed for Study; Please Help!" Students passed by the table to get to their dormitory rooms, regardless of whether or not they intended to eat in the dining hall. Participants were told that the confidential survey would take about 10–15 min to complete, and they were offered candy as thanks for participation. Participants were given a consent form, and after signing it, were then handed the questionnaire. Upon completion, the participants were thanked and given a debriefing form.

■ RESULTS

Descriptive Data

The average Body Mass Index (BMI) of the participants was 23.9, a value that is at the upper end of the normal range. BMI scores for the participants ranged from 18.0 to 37.2, with a standard deviation of 3.8. On the basis of their BMI scores, 4.7% of the participants were categorized as underweight, 65.1% were of normal weight, 24.4% were

overweight, and 5.8% of the participants were obese. The sample was divided as to whether they wanted to gain or lose weight. Men who wanted to lose weight (30.3%, $n = 27$) were fewer than those who wanted to gain weight (50.6%, $n = 45$); 19.1% ($n = 17$) wanted neither to gain nor lose any weight. Of those who were underweight, 25% wanted to lose weight, 50% wanted to gain weight, and 25% wanted to stay at their current weight. Of those who were of normal weight, 17.9% wanted to lose weight, 64.3% wanted to gain weight, and 17.9% wanted to stay their current weight. Of those who were overweight, 66.7% wanted to lose weight, 14.3% wanted to gain weight, and 19.1% wanted to stay their current weight. Finally, of those who were obese, 80% wanted to lose weight, 0% wanted to gain weight, and 20% wanted to stay their current weight. Those who wanted to lose weight wanted to lose an average of 18.7 lbs (range = 1–60 lbs), and those who wanted to gain weight wanted to gain an average of 15.2 lbs (range = 1–75 lbs).

Of the men in our sample, 29.2% of the men had been on at least one diet in the past 5 years (range = 0–25 diets, $M = 1.10$, $SD = 3.34$), and 68.5% of the men were members of a gym. The participants spent an average of 5.8 hr exercising per week (range = 0–28 hr, $SD = 6.40$). Self-esteem scores ranged from 0 to 5, with a mean score of .34 ($SD = 1.31$), which indicates that this sample had relatively high self-esteem. According to Rosenberg's convention, scores of 0 to 1 indicate high self-esteem, and scores of 1.5 to 2.5 indicate medium self-esteem. A higher score on the self-esteem measure denotes a lower level of self-esteem (Rosenberg, 1965).

When asked in open-ended questions about their bodily concerns, respondents were most focused on and/or dissatisfied with the abdomen, arms, and upper body (see Table 17.1). Furthermore, when asked to rate their level of agreement or disagreement with a series of statements about their attitudes and behaviors, respondents displayed high levels of concern about their bodies (see Table 17.2). In our sample 30.3% of the men surveyed had taken dietary supplements to build muscle, 14.6% had taken dietary supplements to burn fat, and 32.6% would skip a meal if they had not exercised on a particular day (see Table 17.3). The men used an average of two beauty products per month including cologne, hair gel, body waxing, and manicures (range = 0–6 products, $SD =$ 1.33). The participants reported watching an average of 4.00 hr of television (range = 0–23, $SD =$ 5.63), 2.87 hr of movies (range = 0–12, $SD =$ 2.61), and 0.39 hr of music videos (range = 0–4, $SD =$ .80) in the preceding week. They reported spending an average of 1.89 hr reading magazines (range = 0–10,

Table 17.1.   Respondents' Attention to Different Areas of the Body

Part of Body Noticed First when Looking at a Picture of a Male Model	($n = 77$)
Abdominal muscles/stomach	32.5%
Chest/upper body	28.6%
Arms	16.9%
Face	13.0%
Shoulders	6.5%
Frame/stature	3.9%
Other	13.0%

Part of Own Body with which Respondent was most Dissatisfied	($n = 65$)
Abdominal muscles/stomach	38.5%
Arms	21.5%
Chest/upper body	18.5%
Legs	10.8%
Weight	10.8%
Health	9.2%
Back/back muscles	7.7%
Gluteus	6.2%
Face	3.1%

Note: Percentages can sum to more than 100% because participants could choose more than one body part. The two questions were asked in an open-ended format.

Table 17.2. Percentage of Respondents Who Agreed or Strongly Agreed with Each Statement

I would like to have more upper body muscle.	77.5%
It is important to me that I exercise regularly.	74.2%
I feel guilty if I do not exercise.	58.4%
I lift weights to build muscle.	56.2%
I would like to have more muscular legs.	55.1%
If I gain weight, females will not find me attractive.	27.0%
I spend a lot of time thinking about how muscular I am.	23.6%
I spend a lot of time thinking about how much I weigh.	18.0%

Table 17.3. Percentage of Respondents Who Sometimes, Often, or Always Engaged in Each Behavior

If I do not exercise on a particular day, I will skip a meal or restrict food intake.	32.6%
I take dietary supplements to build muscle.	30.3%
I take dietary supplements to burn fat.	14.6%

$SD = 2.10$), and indicated that they had skimmed an average of 2.10 male-directed magazines within the past month (range = 0–8, $SD = 2.00$).

Media Exposure, Self-Esteem, and Bodily Concerns

In order to be sure that the relationships among media consumption, self-esteem, bodily concerns, and endorsement of thinness in women are not merely a function of men's current body size, we controlled for BMI. Table 17.4 shows the statistical correlations among exposure to different forms of media, self-esteem, bodily concerns, and endorsement of thinness in women after controlling for current BMI. As can be seen in the table, the form of media that is most strongly associated with bodily concern is male-directed magazines.

Although the number of magazines skimmed did not correlate with weight concerns, it did correlate with every measure of muscularity concern, as well as with most measures of general fitness concern. Number of hours spent watching music videos was strongly associated with consumption of dietary supplements to build muscle, but not with other muscularity, weight, or general fitness concerns. Hours spent reading magazines, watching television, and watching movies did not correlate significantly with any measure of men's concerns about their own bodies. After we controlled for BMI, low self-esteem was correlated with every measure of weight concern and the number of beauty products used within the month (see Table 17.4), but not with muscularity or general fitness concerns. Low self-esteem was not correlated with any measure of media exposure.

Media Exposure, Bodily Concerns, and Beauty Standards for Women

Endorsement of thinness in women was associated with the number of male-directed magazines skimmed within the

Table 17.4. Partial Correlations Among Media Consumption, Bodily Concerns, Self-Esteem, and Endorsement of Thinness for Women, Controlling for Body Mass Index

	Number of Male-directed Magazines Skimmed	Hours with Magazines	Hours with Television	Hours with Movies	Hours with Music Videos	Self-esteem	Endorsement of Thinness for Women
Weight concerns							
Number of diets undertaken within the past 5 years	0.12	0.09	−0.14	0.01	0.01	0.22*¤	0.22*
"I spend a lot of time thinking about how much I weigh"	0.15	−0.09	−0.04	−0.03	−0.08	0.30**	0.18
"If I gain weight, females will not find me attractive"	−0.09	0.12	0.05	0.06	0.09	0.22*	0.24
"If I do not exercise on a particular day, I will skip a meal"	0.07	0.07	−0.05	0.03	−0.01	0.29**	0.29**
"I take dietary supplements to burn fat"	0.02	0.24	0.02	0.12	0.10	0.14*	0.20
Muscularity concerns							
Positive Attributes of Muscularity	0.39***	−0.09	0.10	0.10	0.09	0.16	0.36**
Drive for Muscularity	0.40***	−0.02	0.08	0.06	0.16	−0.08	0.40***
"I spend a lot of time thinking about how muscular I am"	0.41***	−0.11	−0.03	−0.05	0.10	0.13	0.27**

"I would like to have more upper body muscle"	0.31**	0.07	0.05	0.11	0.14	−0.07	0.24*
"I would like to have more muscular legs"	0.17*	0.17	0.02	0.13	0.19	−0.03	0.27*
"I lift weights to build muscle"	0.39***	0.04	−0.01	−0.14	0.21	−0.05	0.24**
"I take dietary supplements to build muscle"	0.28**	0.01	−0.07	−0.11	0.28	−0.13	0.25*
General fitness concerns							
Hours spent exercising per week	0.24*	−0.01	0.09	0.06	−0.02	−0.10	0.30**
Number of beauty products used within a month	0.26*	−0.13	−0.08	0.02	0.01	0.28**	0.24*
Holder of a gym membership (yes/no)	0.28**	−0.01	−0.02	0.00	0.15	0.05	0.17
"I feel guilty if I do not exercise"	0.17	0.10	−0.05	−0.03	0.02	0.14	0.25*
"It is important to me that I exercise regularly"	0.18	0.08	−0.03	−0.16	0.15	0.01	0.17
Endorsement of thinness for women	0.27**	0.17	0.16	0.40***	0.10	−0.01	

*p < .05, **p < .01, ***p < .001

month and hours spent watching movies (see Table 17.4). Men who more strongly endorsed thinness in women were also more concerned with their own bodies. Various weight concerns, muscularity concerns, and general fitness and appearance concerns were all significantly related to stronger endorsement of thinness for women.

■ DISCUSSION

Participants in the study demonstrated considerable dissatisfaction with their own bodies. Despite the fact that 65.1% of the men in the sample were within their normal weight for height range (BMI), 80.9% desired to be a weight different than their own. Because men were divided (50.6% wanted to gain an average of 15.2 lbs, and 30.3% wanted to lose an average of 18.7 lbs), averaging the data would have indicated that men's ideal weight was very close to their actual weight and that men simply wanted to gain an average of 2.1 lbs.

Closer analysis reveals that the majority of those who were underweight and of normal weight desired to gain weight, whereas the majority of those who were overweight or obese desired to lose weight. Many men in this study desired more muscular upper bodies and more muscular legs, and they spent a lot of time thinking about how much they weighed and how muscular they were. Their attitudes, as well as their behaviors, attested to the high levels of concern that these men had about their

bodies. One-third of the men skipped a meal when they had not exercised, and one-seventh had taken dietary supplements to burn fat. It is striking that one-third of the sample had taken dietary supplements to build muscle.

The hypothesis that higher levels of male-directed magazine readership would be associated with higher levels of desire to improve one's body, particularly one's muscularity, was supported. Those who had skimmed through more male-directed magazines in the previous month clearly demonstrated elevated concern about every aspect of muscularity and also aspects of general fitness. Men who read more male-directed magazines also used more beauty products, took more dietary supplements to build muscle, spent more time exercising, were more likely to hold a gym membership, more frequently endorsed the positive attributes of muscularity, had a higher personal drive for muscularity, and endorsed other attitudes and behaviors related to muscularity and fitness.

Similarly, time spent watching music videos was associated with the use of dietary supplements to build muscle. However, neither the time a man spent watching television and movies, nor the time he spent reading magazines from other genres, was related to any measure of concern about his own body.

It is important to note that the number of male-directed magazines skimmed through within the previous month was not significantly correlated with the total number of hours spent reading magazines. One of the reasons for this may be a problem with the method of recall: time estimates may have been quite imprecise. Another possibility is that the two variables are, in fact, examining different things. Number of magazines skimmed specifically examined the number of male-directed magazines, whereas time spent reading magazines concerned magazine readership in general, including business and news magazines. Male-directed magazines provide a much greater concentration of messages about the need for a muscular, attractive body.

Most of the research currently available on the relationship between self-esteem and bodily concerns is focused on women. This study expands those findings and shows that low self-esteem is very clearly linked to both attitudes and behaviors indicative of weight concerns among men, including dieting and the use of dietary supplements to burn fat.

In contrast to the association between self-esteem and weight concerns among men, concerns with muscularity were not associated with low levels of self-esteem among men after Body Mass Index was controlled. Although this study lacks the statistical power necessary to demonstrate that those who are within the "normal" and "overweight" weight ranges have stable self-esteem, whereas those who are "underweight" or "obese" have lower levels of self-esteem, the data suggest this trend, and it would be interesting for future researchers to examine this possibility.

Because the current study is correlational, it is entirely possible that reading male-directed magazines does not increase concern with one's body. Instead, men who are already highly concerned with their bodies may choose to read male-directed magazines. At this point, correlational studies are necessary to determine relationships among variables that have not been comprehensively studied. Longitudinal and controlled experimental research is necessary to disentangle the direction of these effects and determine the causal sequence. Whether magazines induce or contribute to bodily dissatisfaction, bodily dissatisfaction causes people to purchase magazines, or both factors contribute to a vicious spiral, it is important to track what, if any, cultural shifts are occurring in the general climate of bodily concern among men. It has been found through longitudinal research with adolescent girls that an increase in magazine readership leads to an increase in eating disorder symptomatology (Vaughan & Fouts, 2003). Further research into this relatively new area of men's body image may reveal what is already documented for women: that certain forms of media exposure increase the level of concern with one's body.

Men's media exposure was not only associated with their concerns about their own bodies, but was also strongly associated with their concerns about the bodies of women. Furthermore, men who had more weight, muscularity, and general fitness concerns about themselves also had higher thinness standards for women. The more male-directed magazines a man had skimmed and the more movies he had seen, the more he endorsed thinness in women. That movie exposure was so strongly associated with endorsement of thinness in women is particularly interesting because men's movie exposure was completely unrelated to their concerns about their own bodies. Images of women found within the pages of male-directed magazines and in many movies certainly border on, or even enter, the realm of pornography. Exposure to pornography has been linked to increased violence against women, to desensitization, and to the objectification of women (Brooks, 1995; Zillmann, 1989). A component of the objectification of women is the increased demand for bodily perfection. Thus, men's media exposure may well be a problem for women, contributing to an environment in which men come to seek increasingly thin women, and women become overly concerned with their bodies because they fear losing the attention of men if they are not extremely thin.

One of the most noticeable limitations of this study is the homogeneous nature of the sample population. Although relatively representative of the racial composition at the university where the study was conducted, the sample population is mostly White, which means that the results are most representative of White college men, not all men in general. In addition, the recruitment method resulted in a self-selected sample. Perhaps those who are most obsessed with their own personal appearance chose not to take the time to stop and help with the study. Another limitation of this study is that the questionnaire, especially the section on thinness in women, assumed heterosexuality. No question was asked about the sexual preference of the participant, and future researchers should examine and distinguish between the qualities that are important to men with different sexual orientations. Furthermore, many men who participated in this study suggested that there are other aspects of men's body image beyond weight and muscularity that are important to examine, such as body hair, freckles, and penis size. This study included only one measure of self-concept and mental health. In future research it would be beneficial to examine other aspects of mental health in addition to self-esteem, such as depression or anxiety. Another method future researchers should embrace is a more reliable method of measuring media exposure. Self-report, as used in this study, is notoriously unreliable, and future researchers should have participants more accurately judge their media consumption, for example, by tracking their media exposure in a daily diary. In the current study, the reliability of the self-esteem scale was low; a more reliable measure might have yielded more significant associations.

It would also be beneficial to study younger men to see exactly when certain beliefs about muscularity form and also when men begin to internalize the norms presented in society. From a public health standpoint, it is critical to understand the development of body dissatisfaction in order to prevent and treat harmful cognitions that can lead to harmful behaviors. Intervention at a point when attitudes are forming would most benefit those men who do begin to internalize harmful societal ideals.

Longitudinal research is needed to track the increasing readership of male-directed magazines, as well as concomitant changes in men's attitudes about their bodies. In addition it will be important to track changes over time in the usage of dietary supplements to build muscle (one-third of the men in this study had used them), as well as other potentially harmful behaviors that men engage in as a result of bodily dissatisfaction.

New men's magazines have recently been introduced into the market, and images that depict the ideal male physique are becoming increasingly acceptable and prevalent as a method of advertising. Billboards, newspapers, magazines, graphics on public transportation and in taxis, the Internet, and a variety of different forms of television offer many advertising options. A primary goal of advertising is to make a population dissatisfied with the status quo so that they will purchase the new product. Sex appeal and the female body have long been used to sell everything from perfume to cars to alcohol to food. Now advertisers are beginning to sell products via male sexuality. As noted by Kilbourne (1999), if advertising didn't work, then businesses wouldn't be spending billions of dollars on it.

The men's magazine industry is currently thriving and expanding. In 2002 Stephen Colvin, president of Dennis Publishing (which produces the men's magazines *Maxim* and *Stuff*) was named

Adweek's Executive of the Year for his part in creating a market for these magazines (Cash, 2002). Tony Cash (2002) of *Adweek* magazine explained, "it was long assumed that young men didn't give a flip about magazines. Then along came *Maxim, FHM,* and *Stuff,* titles that instantaneously captured the attention of the elusive young male audience." *Maxim* is currently the fastest-growing men's magazine in the United States. As noted by Verne Gay (2000) of *Brandweek* magazine, "*Maxim* has grown into a money-making monster—the biggest, baddest monster out there."

Now that there is a market for this type of magazine, publishers have begun to capitalize on it. Just as adolescent girls have long had magazines such as *Seventeen, Teen,* and *YM,* adolescent boys will now have *MH-18* (from the publishers of *Men's Health*) that promises information on "fitness, sports, girls, gear, and life." The cover of the May 2002 issue announced articles titled "Build Monster Biceps," "32 Cool Things You Need Now," and "Eat Junk, Lose Fat." The pages inside have male models demonstrating how to do certain weight-lifting techniques. Who are these models showing boys how to lift weights? They are grown men with bulging biceps, pectorals, and legs. *MH-18* was introduced at the end of 2001, so demographics of actual readership are not yet available. However, if the demographics parallel those of adolescent girls' magazines, then content and advertisement could be targeted to an audience of boys as young as 12 years of age. This has potential to be disastrous for the health and development of these boys. Excessive bodily concern may lead boys and young men to damage their bodies through inappropriate exercise behavior or unhealthy nutritional practices such as skipping meals, using anabolic steroids, and taking dietary supplements. However, adolescents are the fastest growing market (they spent 153 billion dollars in 1999; Youth Markets Alert, 2000) and as the common advertising sentiment is, "hook 'em while they're young," advertising to early adolescent boys is likely only to increase.

In this study, media exposure, especially to male-directed magazines, did in fact relate to positive beliefs about muscularity and to behaviors such as dieting, exercising, and the use of beauty products. With the increasing audience for male-directed magazines and other media, it becomes increasingly important to understand how bodily concerns are engendered so that we can help both men and women confront current body concerns and prevent future ones.

NOTES

1. Male-Directed Magazines: *Achilles Heel, ALTHEIA, Barracuda Magazine, Breaka Interactive, Chap Magazine, Details, Esquire, FHM, Fire Engine, Gear Magazine, The Guy Code, Loaded, Maxim, Men's Fitness, Men's Health, Men's Journal, Men's Voices, Razor Magazine, Sexbuzz Magazine, Stuff, Swung Magazine,* and *Varla.*

2. Beauty Products: body waxing, brow waxing/tweezing, cologne, facials, hair coloring, hair gel, manicures, massage, moisturizer, tanning, and tooth whitener.

REFERENCES

Anderson, A. E., & DiDomenico, L. (1992). Diet vs. shape content of popular male and female magazines: A dose-response relationship to the incidence of eating disorders? *International Journal of Eating Disorders, 11,* 283–287.

Becker, A. E., Burwell, R. A., Gilman, S. E., Herzog, D. B., & Hamburg, P. (2002). Eating behaviours and attitudes following prolonged exposure to television among ethnic Fijian adolescent girls. *The British Journal of Psychiatry, 180,* 509–514.

Brooks, G. R. (1995). *The centerfold syndrome: How men can overcome objectification and achieve intimacy with women.* San Francisco: Jossey Bass.

Brumberg, J. J. (1997). *The body project: An intimate history of American girls.* New York: Random House.

Cash, T. (2002, March 4). Overview—Triumph of the niche. *Adweek,* 4–8.

Cash, T. F., Cash, D. W., & Butters, J. W. (1983). "Mirror, Mirror, on the wall . . . ?": Contrast effects and self-evaluations of physical attractiveness. *Personality and Social Psychology Bulletin, 9,* 351–358.

Cohn, L. D., & Adler, N. E. (1992). Female and male perceptions of ideal body shapes: Distorted views among Caucasian college students. *Psychology of Women Quarterly, 16,* 69–79.

Collins, R. L. (1996). For better or worse: The impact of upward social comparison on self evaluations. *Psychological Bulletin, 119,* 51–69.

Dibiase, W. J., & Hjelle, L. A. (1968). Body-image stereotypes and body-type preferences among male college students. *Perceptual and Motor Skills, 27,* 1143–1146.

Drewnowski, A., & Yee, D. K. (1987). Men and body image: Are males satisfied with their body weight? *Psychosomatic Medicine, 49,* 626–634.

Edwards, S., & Launder, C. (2000). Investigating muscularity concerns in male body image: Development of the Swansea Muscularity Attitudes Questionnaire. *International Journal of Eating Disorders, 28,* 120–124.

Fallon, A. E., & Rozin, P. (1985). Sex differences in perceptions of desirable body shape. *Journal of Abnormal Psychology, 94,* 102–105.

Garner, D. M., Garfinkel, P. E., Schwartz, D., & Thompson, M. (1980). Cultural expectations of thinness in women. *Psychological Reports, 47,* 483–491.

Gay, V. (2000, October 23). Newsstand seductress. *Brandweek, 41,* 80–81.

Harmatz, M. G., Gronendyke, J., & Thomas, T. (1985). The underweight male: The unrecognized problem group of body image research. *Journal of Obesity and Weight Regulation, 4,* 258–267.

Harrison, K. (2000). The body electric: Thin-ideal media and eating disorders in adolescents. *Journal of Communication, 54,* 119–143.

Harrison, K., & Cantor, J. (1997). The relationship between media consumption and eating disorders. *Journal of Communication, 47,* 40–67.

Huddy, D. C., Nieman, D. C., & Johnson, R. L. (1993). Relationship between body image and percent body fat among college male varsity athletes and nonathletes. *Perceptual and Motor Skills, 77,* 851–857.

Huenemann, R. L., Shapiro, M. S., Hampton, M. C., & Mitchell, B. W. (1966). A longitudinal study of gross body composition and body conformation and their association with food and activity in a teen-age population. *American Journal of Clinical Nutrition, 18,* 325–338.

Kenrick, D. T., & Gutierres, S. E. (1980). Contrast effects and judgments of physical attractiveness: When beauty becomes a social problem. *Journal of Personality and Social Psychology, 38,* 131–140.

Kilbourne, J. (1999). *Can't buy my love: How advertising changes the way we think and feel.* New York: Simon & Schuster.

Leit, R. A., Pope, H. G. , & Gray, J. J. (2001). Cultural expectations of muscularity in men: The evolution of Playgirl centerfolds. *International Journal of Eating Disorders, 29,* 90–93.

Levine, M. P., Smolak, L., & Hayden, H. (1994). The relation of sociocultural factors to eating attitudes and behaviors among middle school girls. *Journal of Early Adolescence, 14,* 471–490.

Mazur, A. (1986). U.S. trends in feminine beauty and overadaptation. *Journal of Sex Research, 22,* 281–303.

Mediamark Research Incorporated study of media and markets. (2001). New York: Mediamark Research.

Mintz, L. B., & Betz, N. E. (1986). Sex differences in the nature, realism, and correlates of body image. *Sex Roles, 15,* 185–195.

Mishkind, M. E., Rodin, J., Silberstein, L. R., & Striegel-Moore, R. H. (1986). The embodiment of masculinity: Cultural, psychological, and behavioral dimensions. *American Behavioral Scientist, 29*, 545–562.

Monteath, S. A., & McCabe, M. P. (1997). The influence of societal factors on female body image. *Journal of Social Psychology, 137*, 708–727.

Nemeroff, C. J., Stein, R. I., Diehl, N. S., & Smilack, K. M. (1994). From the Cleavers to the Clintons: Role choices and body orientation as reflected in magazine article content. *International Journal of Eating Disorders, 16*, 167–176.

Pope, H. G., Katz, D. L., & Hudson, J. I. (1993). Anorexia nervosa and "reverse anorexia" among 108 male bodybuilders. *Comprehensive Psychiatry, 34*, 406–409.

Pope, H. G., Olivardia, R., Gruber, A., & Borowiecki, J. (1999). Evolving ideals of male body image as seen through action toys. *International Journal of Eating Disorders, 26*, 65–72.

Posavac, H., Posavac, S., & Posavac, E. (1998). Exposure to media images of female attractiveness and concern with body weight among young women. *Sex Roles, 38*, 187–201.

Rand, C. S., & Wright, B. (2001). Thinner females and heavier males: Who says? A comparison of female to male ideal body sizes across a wide age span. *International Journal of Eating Disorders, 29*, 45–50.

Rosenberg, M. (1965). *Society and the adolescent self-image.* Princeton, NJ: Princeton University Press.

Staffieri, J. R. (1967). A study of social stereotype of body image in children. *Journal of Personality and Social Psychology, 7*, 101–104.

Stice, E., & Shaw, H. E. (1994). Adverse effects of the media portrayed thin-ideal on women and linkages to bulimic symptomatology. *Journal of Social and Clinical Psychology, 13*, 288–308.

Striegel-Moore, R. H., Silberstein, L. R., & Rodin, J. (1986). Toward an understanding of risk factors for bulimia. *American Psychologist, 41*, 246–263.

Vaughan, K. K., & Fouts, G. T. (2003). Changes in television and magazine exposure and eating disorder symptomatology. *Sex Roles, 49*, 313–320.

Wegner, B. S., Hartmann, A. M., & Geist, C. R. (2000). Effect of exposure to photographs of thin models on self-consciousness in female college students. *Psychological Reports, 86*, 1149–1154.

Wilcox, K., & Laird, J. D. (2000). The impact of media images of super-slender women on women's self-esteem: Identification, social comparison, and self-perception. *Journal of Research in Personality, 34*, 278–286.

Youth Markets Alert. (2000). *Teen spending increased in 1999.* New York: EPM Communications.

Zillman, D. (1989). *Effects of prolonged consumption of pornography.* Hillsdale, NJ: Erlbaum.

CHAPTER 18

Effects of Alcohol, Expectancies, and Partner Type on Condom Use in College Males

Event-Level Analyses

Joseph LaBrie, Mitch Earleywine, Jason Schiffman,
Eric Pedersen, and Charles Marriot

Ninety percent of college students are sexually active, with many reporting multiple partners. In a survey of 5,514 first-year undergraduates, 54% of men and 37% of women already had five or more sexual partners, and 29% of men and 12% of women had 10 sexual partners (MacDonald et al., 1990). Young people also drink alcohol in large amounts. Nationally, 80–90% of all underage college students' drink (Haines & Spear, 1996), and 44% of college students binge drink (drinking five or more drinks in one sitting for men or four or more for women), and 20% binge drink three or more times during a two- week period (Wechsler, Lee, Kuo, & Lee, 2000). The notion that alcohol consumption in college students results in problematic behavior is well-entrenched. From missed class to

death, from vandalism to sexual assault, problematic drinking leaves its mark (Hingson, Heeren, Zakoes, Kopstein, & Wechsler, 2002).

Risky sex (e.g., sex without a condom) is a problematic behavior that may covary with drinking. Research indicates that the prevalence of condom use is increasing, yet approximately 82% of college men and 87% of college women continue to report sex with multiple partners while failing to use condoms consistently (Seidman & Reider, 1994). The consequences of risky sex include increased risk for HIV and other STDs. Approximately 42,000 new HIV infections occurred in the United States during 2002, an increase from the previous year by almost 1.000 newly infected people (Centers for Disease Control and Prevention [CDC], 2002).

355

The CDC further reports that two thirds of all non–HIV STDs occur among those under the age of 25. The large number of college students who report not using condoms consistently with multiple partners, paired with the high prevalence of student drinking, has led researchers and educators to suggest that alcohol use may increase the likelihood of HIV and other STDs by decreasing the likelihood of condom use during sex. Dingle and Oei (1997) labeled this proposed effect of drinking the "transmission hypothesis," where individuals transmit HIV and other STDs among their partners during unprotected sex while intoxicated. Public AIDS prevention campaigns have directly targeted the proposed relationship between drinking and risky sex.

Untangling the proposed relationship between alcohol and risky sex has proven to be an elusive task. The first studies examining this link were global association studies, which correlated quantity and frequency measures for alcohol use with various measures of sexual risk. These studies typically found that heavy drinkers were more likely to engage in high-risk sexual behavior, such as less consistent condom use (Hingson, Strunin, Berlin, & Heeren, 1990; McEwan, McCallum, Bhopal, & Madhok, 1992; Shillington, Cottier, Compton, & Sptiznagel, 1995) and more sexual partners (Graves, 1995). A similar association, however, was absent in other studies (e.g., Gold & Skinner, 1993; Leigh, Temple, & Trocki, 1994). Despite the generally positive findings, data from global association studies do not allow researchers to disentangle the relation between drinking and risky sexual behavior. It is not possible to determine if revealed relations are direct and causal. Since these studies do not look at specific situations involving sex and drinking, they also fail to determine whether drinking and sexual activity occur at the same time.

The next level of studies were situational association studies, which examined the relationship between risky sex and alcohol use during sexual activity. Correlations in these studies revealed that the frequency with which alcohol is consumed prior to sex is generally related to the frequency of risky sex (Bagnall, Plant, & Warwick. 1990; Buchanan, Poppen, & Reisen, 1996; Stall et al., 1986). Other studies found that not all individuals who use alcohol during sex are more likely to engage in high-risk sexual behavior (e.g., Leigh, 1990). Situational association studies are limited as well, because revealed associations may be an artifact of the relations between the total amount of sex and the total amount of risky behavior (Leigh, 2002). Also, it is not possible to determine if the occasions that included both drinking and sex were the same occasions where risky sex occurred.

Event-level studies look at particular dynamics in sexual or drinking events. In an event-level study, participants describe behavior during a particular event or several events from their lives rather than report general trends or averages of behavior. Studies involving event-level analysis have produced mixed results and vary as a function of level of analysis. Some studies report that drinking prior to first sexual events with a new partner significantly reduces the likelihood of condom use (e.g. Cooper, Pierce, Huselid, 1994; Robertson & Plant, 1988). Other studies report no difference in condom use between sex involving drinking and sex without drinking (e.g. Bailey, Camlin, & Ennett, 1998; Testa & Collins, 1997), while another found no association between drinking and unsafe sexual practices (Temple, Leigh, & Schafer, 1993). Failing to find consistent results in a meta-analysis of event-level studies, Leigh (2002) suggested that the relations between alcohol use and risky sex might depend on the type of partner involved and the context of the sexual event. The mixed results from the first event-level studies have led researchers to focus on potential mediators and moderators of the drinking and risky sex relationship, such as expectancies, the amount of alcohol consumed, and partner type (new, casual, or regular).

■ ALCOHOL EXPECTANCIES

Alcohol expectancies are beliefs and ideas about the positive and negative effects that alcohol has on an individual's behavior. Positive expectancies include beliefs that the use of alcohol increases sociability and reduces stress and tension. Negative expectancies include beliefs that drinking impairs motor and cognitive abilities.

Most research on alcohol expectancies has shown that positive expectancies are related to heavier patterns of drinking (e.g. Marlatt & Gordon, 1985). Yet a recent review of expectancy studies reported that interpersonal and intersituational alcohol expectancies can affect post-drinking behavior (Vogel-Sprott & Fillmore, 1999). Sex-related alcohol expectancies, which include beliefs that alcohol facilitates sexual encounters, increases arousal, disinhibits sexual behavior, and makes people less likely to use condoms during sex, might influence post-drinking sexual behavior.

Two studies (Corbin & Fromme, 2002; LaBrie, Schiffman, & Earleywine, 2002) identified a link between alcohol expectancies toward sex and subsequent risky sexual behavior. LaBrie et al. reported that expectancies specific to alcohol's impact on condom use mediated the relation between drinking and risky sex intentions, accounting for a significant part of the link between drinking and risky sex. Corbin and Fromme found that in first sexual events with regular partners and first sexual events with casual partners, the amount of alcohol consumed correlated with lower condom use *only* for participants with strong sex-related alcohol expectancies, revealing an *Alcohol x Expectancy* interaction. For the most recent sex event with a regular partner, however, neither alcohol use nor the interaction of alcohol use and expectancies were associated with condom use. Thus, the mediation of alcohol expectancies may be further moderated by partner type or event context.

PARTNER TYPE

Distinctions between new, casual, and regular partners are important because partner type may moderate a relationship between drinking and risky sex. Corbin and Fromme (2002) only assessed people having sex with a new partner and a regular partner (both first and last events). These represent opposite ends of the spectrum, losing potentially valuable information from individuals in the middle of the continuum and potentially masking important results when looking for main effects. It is important to examine sexual events with casual partners in addition to events with new and regular partners. Casual partners can be defined as people who have had fewer than five sexual events together and who have known each other for less than one month (Weinhart et al., 1998). Casual partners fall between new and regular partners; completely new partners are novel and may be hypersensitive to the possibility of their new partner's disease potential, whereas regular partners know each other well and may have regular patterns of sexual behavior in place. Moreover, with regular partners, perceived vulnerability to STD transmission may decrease, shifting the function of condom use from protection against STDs to prevention of pregnancy. For these participants, drinking and alcohol expectancies may have little impact on condom use since the partners will most likely have negotiated a stable pattern of sexual behavior. In contrast, casual partners most likely have not know each other long enough to have established a regular pattern of sexual activity together, and yet have reduced sensitivity to sexual risk since they have had sex together before. These casual partner events may more likely be influenced by alcohol use and expectancies.

AMOUNT OF ALCOHOL

The amount of alcohol consumed prior to the sexual event is important to examine as well. Weinhardt and Carey (2000) suggested that there is a distinction between consuming alcohol before the sexual event (i.e., having only one or two drinks) and actually being intoxicated proximal to the event (i.e., binge drinking), and that this distinction might prove important. It may be that alcohol only impacts sexual risk-taking at certain levels of intoxication.

In an extensive review of the literature, Weinhardt and Carey (2000) suggested that large-scale survey studies using event-level assessments are necessary to determine if and in what contexts drinking impacts sexual risk-taking. Multiple-event assessment and within-subject analysis have been used in only three studies examining the alcohol-risky sex hypothesis. Larger, more detailed studies could produce evidence for such an association. Furthermore, large event-level studies with multiple sex events for each participant will make it possible to look at individual sex events involving and not involving alcohol, partners of varying levels of relationship status, and amount of alcohol consumed prior to sex.

HYPOTHESES

This study investigated the influence of alcohol consumption (number of drinks consumed prior to sex event/binge drinking prior to the sexual event) on the decision to use a condom in over 1,500 sex events in a high-risk sample of male college students. We examined the influence of partner type (new partner, casual partner, regular partner) and sex-related alcohol expectancies (low, medium, and high) as likely moderators of condom use in sex events involving alcohol consumption. We predicted that drinking prior to a sexual event would significantly decrease condom use. We further predicted that this would be moderated by type of partner; participants would use condoms more with casual partners than with regular partners, but less than with new partners. Also, we expected that alcohol would decrease condom use significantly in sex events with casual partners and that participant's expectancies about alcohol's sex-related effects would alter the frequency of condom use during sex involving prior drinking. An interaction between alcohol consumption and expectancy would be consistent with these ideas, with increased alcohol consumption leading to decreased condom use, particularly among people with strong expectancies about alcohol. Therefore, we predicted an *Alcohol x Expectancy* interaction.

METHOD

Participants

Male college students ($N = 315$) responded by phone to on-campus fliers, classroom announcements, and advertisements in the student daily newspaper seeking research participants for a study on attitudes and behaviors toward sex and drinking. Those who drank more than twice a week and who had two or more sexual partners in the previous two months were invited to participate. These criteria created a participant pool of 96 male students that could be considered high-risk with respect to drinking and sexual behavior. These students participated in the study and received a $25 stipend for their participation.

Almost all ($n = 93$) of these students had sex only with women. These 93 heterosexual male college students formed the sample for subsequent analyses. They averaged 20.58 ($SD = 2.45$) years of age, and their ethnic self-identification was representative of the institution's student body. Sixty-nine percent were Caucasian, 18% were Hispanic, 10% were Asian American, and 3% were African American. Participants drank an average of 3.41 ($SD = 2.45$) times per week and consumed an average of 6.25 ($SD = 2.72$) drinks per drinking occasion. Participants also averaged 3.23 ($SD = 1.80$) sexual partners within the past three months and had a mean condom use of 59% ($SD = 33.08$) when engaging in sexual intercourse.

Procedure

An independent human subjects review board approved all procedures used in the study. Participants completed a questionnaire of basic demographic information as well as attitudinal and behavioral measures. After they completed the questionnaire, a doctoral-level psychologist certified in Motivational Interviewing interviewed each participant using the Timeline Followback Interview: Sexual Behavior and Substance Use (TLFB-SS) protocol.

Measures

Timeline Followback Interview: Sexual Behavior and Substance Use

Each participant performed the Timeline Followback Interview: Sexual Behavior and Substance Use (TLFB-SS) (Weinhardt et al., 1998; used with permission from Michael Carey). The TLFB-SS is a structured, calendar-aided interview adapted from the TLFB protocol for alcohol and drug use (Sobell & Sobell, 1992). The TLFB-SS yields a detailed assessment of sex and drinking while providing information about the behaviors and their occurrence on the event level. Each behavior in the TLFB-SS (sex and alcohol) is assessed separately over a 3-month period, with participants reporting on every sexual and drinking event over that period. A sex event, for the purposes of this study, was any sexual experience that included either vaginal or anal penetration or both. For each sexual event, participants described their sexual partner and reported on whether they used a condom. According to the TLFB-SS, persons with whom a participant had sex for the first time are New Partners, partners known for less than a month and with whom the participant has had sex less than five times are Casual Partners, and partners a participant knew longer than one month or with whom the participant had sex with five or more times are Regular Partners. For each drinking event, participants reported the time of day they drank and the number of standard drinks they consumed (a standard drink is equivalent to one 12-ounce beer, one 4-ounce glass of wine, or 1 ounce of hard liquor). When drinking and sex occurred on the same day, participants reported on whether and how much of the drinking took place within two hours of the sexual event.

Sex-Related Alcohol Expectancies

Derman and Cooper (1994) developed a scale to assess sex-related alcohol expectancies. The scale's 3-factor structure has good statistical properties. The factors are sexual enhancement (Factor 1), increased sexual risk-taking (Factor 2), and disinhibition of sexual behavior (Factor 3). Each participant in the current study determined his level of agreement on a 7-point Likert scale for each of the items. Factors 2 and 3 reflect the extent to which alcohol impacts potential risky behaviors and, therefore, they are more conceptually appropriate and sensitive to expectancy effects on alcohol-related risky behavior than Factor 1. Therefore, only scores from these two factors were used in the analyses of alcohol expectancies.

The sexual risk-taking factor measures items such as "I am less likely to take precautions before sex." "I am less likely to use a condom," and "I am less likely to talk with a new sexual partner." Items on the disinhibition factor include "I have sex with people I wouldn't have sex with if I were sober," "I am more likely to do sexual things I wouldn't do when sober." and "I find it harder to say no to sexual advances."

RESULTS

Descriptive Data

The 93 participants reported 1,538 sexual events; 207 (14%) occurred with a new partner (first-time sexual event with that partner). 171 (11%) occurred with a casual partner (known less than a month or fewer than 5 sex events together), while 1.160 (75%) occurred with a regular partner (known more than a month or more than 5 sex events). Condoms were used in 764 (49%) sexual events.

Analyses Across All Sex Events

Partner Type Predicting Alcohol Consumption

For each sex event, partner type (new. casual, or regular) was entered as a fixed factor, with Amount of Alcohol Consumed (number of drinks consumed) entered as the dependent measure in a one-way ANOVA. There were significant differences of alcohol

consumption between partner types, $F(2.1535) = 32.754$, $p < .001$. Post hoc comparisons also revealed significant differences in alcohol consumption between all partner types (all two-way comparisons were significant at $p < .01$). Greatest alcohol consumption occurred within two hours before sex between new partners ($M = 4.8$ drinks, $SD = 5.2$), followed by sex with casual partners ($M = 3.2$ drinks, $SD = 5.0$) and sex with regular partners ($M = 2.3$ drinks, $SD = 3.8$).

Partner Type Predicting Condom Use

The relationship between partner type (new, casual, or regular) and condom use (yes or no) was examined, revealing significant differences in condom use across partner types, $\chi^2(2, N = 1,538) = 29.67$, $p < .0001$. Sixty percent of new partner sex events and 63% of the casual partner sex events involved condom use. However, condoms were only used in 45% of the regular-partner sexual encounters. As expected, participants used condoms more often with new or casual partners than they did with regular partners.

Alcohol Consumption Predicting Condom Use

Out of 630 sex events in which participants drank alcohol, 45% (285) involved a condom and 55% (345) did not. Out of 908 sex events in which participants *did not* drink, 53% (479) involved condoms and 47% (429) did not. There was a significant relationship between whether or not drinking occurred prior to sex and condom use. $\chi^2(1, 1, 538) = 6.603$, $p < .01$. revealing that drinking before the sexual event was significantly related to decreased condom use across all events, regardless of partner type. Thus, over all sex events, drinking prior to sex is associated with reduced condom use, and drinking occurs more in new and casual partner sex events when compared to regular partner events.

Within-Subject Analyses of Alcohol Consumption on Condom Use

Within-subjects analyses of whether or not drinking occurred prior to sex and condom use were conducted using paired samples t-tests. Participants' means for condom use when drinking were compared to means for condom use when not drinking for each partner type. Only those participants with less than 100% condom use were used in these analyses since these participants engaged in risky sex at least some of the time, and thus. drinking may influence their condom use. There were no significant differences between participants' mean percentage of condom use when drinking compared to not drinking in sexual events with new partners ($M = 65\%$, $SD = 46.4$ vs. $M = 66\%$, $SD = 46.2$) and regular partners ($M = 43\%$, $SD = 42.7$ vs. $M = 50\%$, $SD = 41.8$). However, in sexual events with casual partners (not the first event), drinking did negatively influence condom use, $t(35) = 2.30, p < .05$. In these events, the mean percentage condom use when drinking occurred prior to sex was 56% ($SD = 47.2$), while the mean when not drinking was 72% ($SD = 38.7$). Mean percentages of condom use by partner type with and without drinking are shown in Figure 18.1.

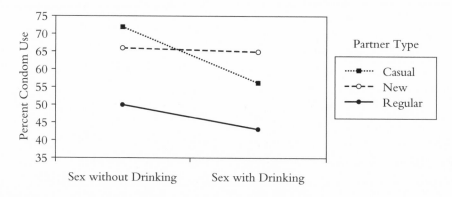

Figure 18.1. Participants' Mean Condom Use Percentage by Partner Type and Alcohol Use.

Note. This figure shows an *Alcohol x Partner Type* interaction on condom use. A significant difference was found between percent condom use of casual partner sex events without alcohol consumption and percent condom use of casual partner sex events with alcohol consumption regardless of amount consumed ($t[35] = -2.30, p < .05$).

Between-Subjects Analyses on the Role of Alcohol Expectancies

Scores from the Sex-Related Alcohol Expectancies questionnaire were used to create three levels of composite expectancies: low ($n = 21$), medium ($n = 41$), and high ($n = 31$). Based on median splits of the disinhibition and sexual risk-taking factors, participants who scored above the median on both factors were placed into the high expectancy group, those who scored above the median on one factor while scoring below the median on the other were placed into the medium group, and participants who scored below the median on both factors were placed into the low group. Those classified in the high expectancy group bad expectancies that drinking would disinhibit them sexually and interfere with their ability to practice safer sex. Participants in the low expectancy group did not believe that alcohol disinhibited them sexually or interfered with safer-sex practices. We created these expectancy groups to determine if prior expectancies impacted condom use when drinking.

Composite expectancy (low, medium, and high) was entered as a fixed factor with participants' mean percentage condom use with drink and condom use with binge drink entered as the dependent measures in separate one-way ANOVAs. For events involving drinking at any level, there was a significant interaction effect for expectancy group on condom use. $F(2, 82) = 4.23$, $p < .05$. Post hoc comparisons (LSD) revealed significant differences in mean condom use percentage between participants in the low expectancy group ($M = 65\%$, $SD = 36.03$) and the high expectancy group ($M = 35\%$, $SD = 36.49$), as well as between medium ($M = 58\%$, $SD = 39.45$) and big expectants (see Figure 18.2).

There also was a significant interaction between expectancy group and binge drinking before sex on mean condom use percentage ($F[1, 39] = 7.08$, $p < .01$). Again, post hoc comparisons revealed significant differences in mean condom use percentage when binge drinking occurred prior to sex between the high expectancy group ($M = 31\%$, $SD = 35.32$) and the low expectancy group ($M = 62\%$, $SD = 38.35$), as well as between the medium expectancy group ($M = 61\%$, $SD = 40.22$) and the high expectancy group.

To determine if the interaction between expectancy group and drinking was influenced by amount of alcohol consumed, we analyzed sex events in which drinking occurred and in which participants drank fewer than five drinks (non-binge drinking). For those sex events that did not involve binge drinking prior to sex, there was no significant interaction between expectancy group and drinking on condom use. Participants' mean condom percentage for non-binge drinking sex events was 52% ($SD = 44.18$). Thus, it appears that the revealed differences between groups when drinking and when binge drinking are most directly related to the binge drinking incidents. Amount consumed and expectancy group interact to reduce condom use for those who drink more

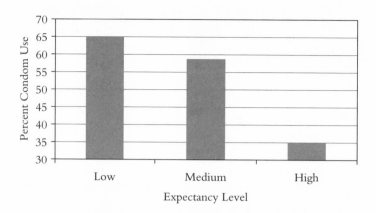

Figure 18.2. Impact of Sex-Related Alcohol Expectancies on Condom Use When Drinking.

Note. Values represent participants' mean percent condom use in sex events involving alcohol consumption. There was a significant drop in percent condom use for participants in the high expectancy group as compared to the low ($p < .05$) and medium expectancy ($p < .05$) groups. Those in the high sex-related alcohol expectancy group had higher expectancies that drinking would disinhibit them sexually and interfere with their ability to practice safer sex relative to the other two groups.

than five drinks and who expect drinking to increase their risk-taking.

Further Analysis of Expectancies

For each partner type, the risk-taking and disinhibition factors of the sex-related alcohol expectancies of participants were each entered as a fixed factor, with condom use percentage with drink entered as the dependent measures, in separate one-way ANOVAs. Disinhibition expectancies were related to percent condom use with drink for casual partners, $F(1, 32) = 8.31$, $p < .01$, and percent condom use with drink for all sex events. $F(1, 83) = 7.5$, $p < .01$. Results were not significant for risk-taking expectancies, revealing that expectancies participants hold about alcohol's effects on their inhibitions may be more influential

in the decision to use a condom relative to expectancies about alcohol's effects on risk-taking.

We compared means in an effort to clarify the disinhibition expectancies' influence on condom use percentage when alcohol is consumed proximal to the sex event versus when no drinking occurs before sex. Again, participants who always used a condom were excluded from the analysis based on the rationale that they are not at risk for problems associated with risky sex. Also, participants were divided into low and high disinhibition groups based on a median split of that sex-expectancy factor.

In sex events involving alcohol, participants in the low disinhibition expectancy group used a condom significantly more ($M = 66.13\%$, $SD = 36.74$) than participants in the high disinhibition expectancy group ($M = 42.70\%$. $SD = 38.35$), $F(1, 83) = 8.03$, $p < .01$. There was no significant difference in mean condom percentage for low versus high disinhibition groups in sex events that did not involve alcohol use. The mean scores revealed that participants who maintained low expectancies yet drank before sex had higher mean condom use percentage than high disinhibition participants who did not drink ($M = 51.96$, $SD = 38.89$). Thus, alcohol's influence on condom use may be moderated by sex related disinhibition expectancies. These expectancies appear to interact with alcohol use to reduce the likelihood of condom use.

■ DISCUSSION

Few studies have examined multiple individual events in an effort to establish a link between alcohol consumption and risky sex (Weinhardt & Carey, 2000). The present study, a multiple-event assessment which included within-subjects analyses, addressed several key issues while examining over 1,500 sex events across a three-month period in 93 male college students at high risk for problems associated with drinking and risky sex.

The type of partner, alcohol consumption, alcohol expectancies, and condom use all covary. The participants consumed more alcohol the less they knew the partner, but they were more likely to use condoms with new partners. Condom use declined with alcohol consumption, particularly for individuals

who saw alcohol as a sexual disinhibitor. Alcohol also decreased condom use with a casual partner. This combination of casual partner and alcohol seems particularly detrimental to safer sex. While 72% of casual partner sex events where no drinking occurred involved condom use, only 56% of similar events after drinking involved condom use. Also, a few previous sexual experiences with a partner seem to create a false sense of security against STDs. This can lead to more alcohol consumption with a casual partner than with a regular partner and less condom use with a casual partner than with a new partner. Increasing awareness about the potential for STD transmission with casual partners could have tremendous impact on safer-sex behaviors.

These data support the idea that alcohol consumption decreases safer sex, but only in specific situations, thus providing partial support for the transmission hypothesis (that individuals transmit HIV and other STDs by having unprotected sex while intoxicated). Although alcohol clearly decreases condom use, certain situations may override the effect, including sex with a new partner. Encouraging men to treat casual partners as new partners may promote safer-sex behaviors. If participants are capable of using a condom after drinking with a new partner, the same skills should apply with a casual partner.

Individual differences also contribute to the link between alcohol and safer sex, including expectancies that alcohol acts as a sexual disinhibitor. LaBrie et al. (2002) suggested that past alcohol consumption impacts expectancies for condom use. The presence of alcohol may cause activation of specific expectancies in memory related to condom use, thereby impacting actual condom use. Countering these expectancies through various challenges could prove particularly helpful. Alcohol expectancies for safe sex likely develop iteratively: each sexual encounter that follows drinking contributes to expectancies about the next. These expectancies may respond to the standard cognitive interventions that alter other drug-related beliefs, such as re-framing or examining evidence (Beck, Wright, Newman, & Liese, 1993). In addition, expectancy challenges, which surreptitiously administer placebos to drinkers and then reveal that any behavioral effects are self-generated, have altered drinking behaviors (Darkes & Goldman, 1993). Comparable challenges might assess sexual disinhibition in people who believe that they have consumed alcohol. If persons receiving placebo report heightened sexual disinhibition, they may realize that the effect is not pharmacological after they learn that they have consumed a placebo.

The role of monogamy and variation is clearly important to these findings. The participants each had more than two sexual partners in over two months. Surprisingly, participants almost universally categorized a partner as monogamous (over 90% of partners were classified as monogamous), even if they had several partners in the same week or within a few weeks. This result suggests that traditional notions of monogamy (being sexual only with one person to whom one is committed in a long-term relationship) are not operational among these college men. It is unclear if their partners considered them monogamous. Thus, thinking of sex with a monogamous partner as safe can prove dangerous. This is particularly true given the current findings in casual partner sex events. College males may have multiple casual sex partners while thinking they are monogamous and that alcohol negatively impacts condom use with these partners, thus putting them at greater risk for STD transmission. Based on the non-traditional understanding of monogamy among this age group, researchers and health professionals can no longer rely on self-reports of monogamy to infer minimized risk for HIV and other STD transmission. Regular partners may need to be emphasized as partners in which only strong, trustful, traditionally monogamous relationships are established. Even in these relationships, however, condom use should still be encouraged.

Several improvements could enhance future event-level research. There was no difference in condom use between expectancy groups when non-binge drinking occurred. However, after binge drinking, the participants with strong disinhibition and risk-taking expectancies (high expectancy group) averaged 31% condom use, compared to 62% in the low expectancy group. Although this finding is important, accounting for the level of intoxication instead of the amount of alcohol consumed is an important distinction that future research could pursue. Including each participant's height and weight, allowing for more accurate estimates of the level of intoxication, might better explain the relationship of actual intoxication level during the sexual event with condom usage.

Similarly, since the only substance assessed was alcohol, it is unknown whether sex occurred in concert with alcohol alone. Other drugs could have contributed to sexual risk-taking, used alone or in combination with alcohol. Future studies examining multi-drug and alcohol use with sexual behavior would provide additional information regarding how, in what circumstances, and in what combinations substance use is related to risky sexual behavior.

Further, with only 93 heterosexual male participants from a college sample, the generalizability of results may be limited. Further research is needed examining multiple events overtime using larger and more representative samples of the overall population. The present college male participants represent a high-risk population due to their predilection for high alcohol consumption and sexual frequency.

Many students begin drinking heavily once college begins, and increased opportunity for sexual encounters with new and casual partners may emerge. Examining samples that include gay or bisexual men, women, and people who vary more in age, education, and health status could help present a clearer picture of the mediators and moderators between alcohol consumption and risky sexual behaviors. The role of alternative forms of birth control as potential deterrents to condom use may be particularly important in studies of women.

Nonetheless, the high-risk male college students examined in this study are an important population to understand, both for reducing negative effects of drinking and stemming the growing rate of HIV and other STDs among young adults. By choosing a high-risk sample, this study found a drinking and risky sex relationship in one of the worst strategic groups on college campuses. These young men drink frequently and have sex with multiple partners over a short period of time. Thus, it may be that male students who average 15 sexual events over a three-month period, who engage in sexual activity with more than one partner, and who drink regularly may form an STD core group on many college campuses. These "high risk" students are engaging in risky sexual behavior and their condom use appears to be reduced depending on the amount of alcohol consumed before sex, sex-related alcohol expectancies, and type of partner.

These data establish that alcohol consumption and alcohol expectancies contribute to risky sex behavior and that sexual encounters with casual partners that involve drinking can prove particularly risky for failing to use a condom. Enlightening students about the risks of sex with casual partners and challenging their expectancies about alcohol as a sexual disinhibitor might help decrease the spread of HIV and other STDs in the college population.

REFERENCES

Bagnall, G., Plani, M. & Warwick. W. (1990). Alcohol. drugs, and AIDS-related risks: Results from a prospective study. *AIDS Care, 2*, 309–317.

Bailey, S. L., Camlin, C. S. & Ennet, S. T. (1998). Substance use and risky sexual behavior among homeless and runaway youth. *Adolescent Health, 23*, 378–388.

Beck, A.T., Wright, F. D. Newman, C. K. & Liese. B. S. (1993). *Cognitive Therapy of Substance Abuse.* New York: Guilford.

Buchanan, D. R., Poppen, P. J. & Reisen, C. A. (1996). The nature of partner relationship and AIDS sexual risk-taking in gay men. *Psychology and Health, 11*(4), 54–555.

Centers for Disease Control and Prevention. (2002). *HIV/AIDS Surveillance Report, 14*, 1–40.

Cooper, M. L. Pierce, R. S. & Huselid, R. K. (1994). Substance use and sexual risk taking among black adolescents and white adolescents. *Health Psychology, 13*, 251–262.

Corbin, W. R. & Fromme, K. (2002). Alcohol use and serial monogamy as risks for sexually transmitted diseases in young adults. *Health Psychology, 21*, 229–236.

Darkes, J. & Goldman, M. S. (1993). Expectancy challenge and drinking reduction: Experimental evidence for a mediational process. *Journal of Consulting and Clinical Psychology. 61*, 344–353.

Derman, K., & Cooper, M. (1994). Sex-related alcohol expectancies among adolescents: I. Scale Development. *Psychology of Addictive Behaviors, 8*, 152–160.

Dingle, G. A., & Oei, T, P. S. (1997). Is alcohol a cofactor of HIV/AIDS? Evidence from immunological and behavioral studies. *Psychological Bulletin, 122*, 56–71.

Gold, R. S. & Skinner, M. J. (1993). Desire for unprotected intercourse preceding its occurrence: The case of young gay men with an anonymous partner. *International Journal of STDs and AIDS, 4*, 326–329.

Graves, K. (1995). Risky sexual behavior and alcohol use among young adults: Results from a national survey. *American Journal of Health Promotion, 10*, 27–36.

Haines, M. & Spear, S. F. (1996). Changing the perception of the norm: A strategy to decrease binge drinking among college students. *Journal of American College Heath, 45*, 134–40.

Hingson, R. W., Heeren, T., Zakoes, R. C., Kopstein, A., & Wechsler, H. (2002). Magnitude of alcohol-related mortality and morbidity among U. S. college students ages 18–24, *Journal of Studies on Alcohol, 63*, 136–144.

Hingson, R. W., Strunin, L., Berlin, B. M. & Heeren, T. (1990). Beliefs about AIDS, use of alcohol and drugs, and unprotected sex among Massachusetts adolescents. *American Journal of Public Health, 80*, 295–299.

LaBrie, J. W., Schiffman, J. & Earleywine. M. (2002). Expectancies specific to condom use mediate the alcohol and sexual risk relationship. *The Journal of Sex Research, 39*, 145–152.

Leigh, B. C. (1990). Alcohol and unsafe sex: An overview of the research and theory. In D. Seminara, D. R. Watson, & A. Pawlowski, (Eds.). *Alcohol, Immunomodulation, and AIDS.* New York: Alan R. Liss.

Leigh, B. C. (2002). Alcohol and condom use: A meta-analysis of event-level studies. *Sexually Transmitted Diseases, 29*, 476–482.

Leigh, B., Temple, M. & Trocki, K. (1994). The relationship of alcohol use to sexual activity in a U. S. national sample. *Social Science and Medicine, 39*, 1527–1535.

MacDonald, N. H., Welts, G. A., Fisher, W. A., Warren, W. K., King, M. A., Doherty, J. A., et al. (1990). High-risk STD/HIV behavior among college students. *Journal of the American Medical Association, 263*, 3155–3159.

Marlatt, G. A. & Gordon, J. R. (Eds.). (1985). *Relapse prevention: Maintenance strategies in the treatment of addictive behaviors.* New York: Guilford Press.

McEwan, R. T., McCallum, A., Bhopal, R. S., & Madhok, R. (1992). Sex and the risk of HIV infection: The role of alcohol. *British Journal of Addiction, 87*, 577–584.

Robertson, J. A. & Plant, M. A. (1988). Alcohol, sex, and risks of HIV infection. *Drug and Alcohol Dependence, 221*, 75–78.

Seidman, S. N. & Reider, R. O. (1994). A review of sexual behavior in the United States. *American Journal of Psychiatry, 151*, 330–341.

Shillington, A. M., Cottier, L. B., Compton, W. M. & Spitznagel, E. L. (1995). Is there a relationship between "heavy drinking" and HIV high-risk sexual behaviors among general population subjects? *International Journal of Addictions, 30*, 1453–1478.

Sobell, L. C. & Sobell, M. B. (1992). Timeline Follow-back: A technique for assessing self reported alcohol consumption. In R. Lilten & J. Allen (Eds.), *Measuring alcohol consumption: Psychosocial and biochemical methods.* Totowa, NJ: Humans Press.

Stall, R., McKusick, L., Wiley, J., Coates, T. J. & Ostrowe, D. G. (1986). Alcohol and drug use during sexual activity and compliance with safer-sex guidelines for AIDS: The AIDS behavioral research project. *Health Education Quarterly, 13*, 359–371.

Temple, M. T., Leigh, B. C., & Schafer, J. (1993). Unsafe sexual behavior and alcohol use at the event level; Results of a national survey. *Journal of Acquired Immune Deficiency Syndromes, 6*, 393–401.

Testa, M., & Collins, R. L. (1997). Alcohol and risky sexual behavior: Event-based analyses among a sample of high-risk women. *Psychology of Addictive Behaviors, 11*, 190–201.

Vogel-Sprott, M. & Fillmore, M. T. (1999). Expectancy and behavioral effects for socially used drugs. In I. Kirsch (Ed.), *How Expectancies Shape Experience* (pp. 233–262). Washington. D.C.: American Psychological Association.

Wechsler, H., Lee, J., Kuo, M., & Lee, H. (2000). College binge drinking in the 1990s: Results of a national survey. *Journal of American College Health, 48*, 199–210.

Weinhardt, L. S. & Carey, M. P. (2000). Does alcohol lead to sexual risk behavior? Findings from event-level research. *Annual Review of Sex Research, II*, 125–157.

CHAPTER 19

Exploring the Health Behavior Disparities of Gay Men in the United States

Comparing Gay Male University Students to Their Heterosexual Peers

Scott D. Rhodes, Thomas McCoy, Kenneth C. Hergenrather, Morrow R. Omli, and Robert H. DuRant

Public health dialogue in the United States (U.S.) currently is occurring around health disparities that exist by biological sex and race and ethnicity (Amaro & de la Torre, 2002; Courtenay, 2000; Treadwell & Ro, 2003). Less discussion has focused on health disparities that exist by sexual orientation. Of course, any discussion of the tremendously disproportionate HIV infection rates by race and ethnicity inherently includes sexual orientation.

Gay men are disproportionately affected by some health outcomes such as infectious diseases, e.g., HIV (Catania et al., 2001) and types of viral hepatitis (Atkins & Nolan, 2005), and by some noncommunicable diseases, e.g., lung cancer resulting from increased rates of smoking (Greenwood et al., 2005) and AIDS-related malignancies (Catania et al., 2001). However, the data that identify health outcomes and their associated behaviors by sexual orientation are extremely limited and inexact. In most behavioral and epidemiologic studies, including those studies that are population based, measures of sexual orientation are not included (Gay and Lesbian Medical Association, 2001; Greenwood et al., 2005; Rhodes & Yee, 2005; Sell & Becker, 2001). Without data on sexual orientation, assessing the health of gay men is difficult. Thus, little is known about the health of gay men as compared to their heterosexual peers (Rhodes & Yee, 2005). Furthermore, we are aware of no studies that explore health behaviors of gay college students as compared to their heterosexual peers.

Because many of the behaviors that contribute to health outcomes are initiated in adolescence and early adulthood, we sought to compare the health-compromising behaviors of self-identifying gay male university students to their self-identifying heterosexual peers.

■ METHODS

In the fall of 2004, a stratified random cross-sectional sample of undergraduate college students attending 10 universities (8 public and 2 private) in North Carolina (NC) were invited to complete an online Internet-based assessment of high-risk behaviors. Marketing this study included 3 steps. First, posters were placed in common areas on campus (e.g., residence halls and dorms, student unions, and cafeterias) encouraging students to check their electronic-mail (e-mail) accounts for an invitation to participate in the study. The poster also indicated that (a) students would receive $10.00 via PayPal™, a method to send and receive money online, for completing the assessment, and (b) two students from each university who completed the assessment would be chosen at random to receive $100.00. Then, students from each campus were randomly selected and sent postcards asking them to check their e-mail accounts for an invitation to complete the online Internet-based assessment. These same randomly selected students were sent messages by e-mail describing the study and encouraging them to complete the online Internet-based assessment. The e-mail messages contained a link to a secure Uniform Resource Locator (URL) where the student completed the assessment.

Assessment Instrument

Assessment items, based on self-report, used predefined response options with binary, categorical, or Likert-scale response options to facilitate readability and administration. The assessment took between 17 and 24 minutes to complete, depending on the skip patterns of each participant.

Items measured included demographic characteristics, such as age, gender and sex, sexual orientation, ethnicity and race, and marital status. Each participant was asked his current academic classification ("freshman," "sophomore," "junior," and "senior") and whether part- or full-time student status.

Sexual orientation was assessed using the item: "How would you describe your sexuality?" Response options included: "Bisexual"; "Gay or Homosexual"; "Heterosexual or Straight"; "Transgender"; and "Other." Each participant who selected transgender was asked whether "female to male" or "male to female."

Involvement in on- and off-campus activities were assessed through a variety of items that measured participant involvement in (a) fraternities/sororities,

(b) student government, (c) political organizations, (d) athletic teams (both intercollegiate and club level), (e) academic clubs, (f) honor societies, (g) performing arts, (h) student government, (i) religious groups, and (j) campus media organizations. Employment status and volunteer activities also were assessed.

Each participant was asked his current living arrangement (e.g., single-sex residence hall/dorm, co-ed residence hall/dorm, on-campus fraternity/sorority housing, and off-campus housing); religious service attendance; grade point average; and parental educational attainment.

Health behaviors measured included sexual behavior, such as number of partners in the past 30 days, gender and sex of sexual partners, substance use during sexual activity, condom use frequency ("never," "rarely," "sometimes," and "always"), and drinking behaviors including user or non-user and times drunk in a typical week. For men in this study, binge drinking was defined as consuming 5 drinks within 2 hours, a commonly used, although debated, definition of binge drinking (DeJong, 2003). Each participant also was asked to describe his current use of alcohol ("abstainer," "abstainer/former drinker," "light drinker," "moderate drinker," "heavy drinker," "problem drinker").

Other substance use was assessed. Cigarette use, smokeless tobacco use, marijuana use, and other drug use (including cocaine, methamphetamines, diet pills, hallucinogens [e.g., acid, LSD,

PCP], and ecstasy) were assessed, including lifetime history of use and during the past 30 days.

History of intimate partner violence including victimization and perpetration was assessed using 2 items: (a) "Has a date or boyfriend or girlfriend, ever started a physical fight with you?" and (b) "Have you ever started a physical fight with a date or boyfriend or girlfriend?" Response options for each items included: "Yes" and "No."

Prior to administration, the assessment was pre-tested and revised twice with university students from a non-study university for attention, comprehension, personal relevance, credibility, and acceptability.

Statistical Analyses

The objective of the statistical analyses was to estimate the differences in health-compromising behaviors between gay and heterosexual men and explore and adjust for demographic and academic characteristics. Descriptive analyses were performed to examine overall prevalence, group prevalence, and distribution shape. Demographic and behavioral data were then analyzed in bivariate analyses using chi-square and Fisher's exact tests for categorical variables, and t-tests and Wilcox on rank-sum tests for continuous variables, comparing gay men to heterosexual men. Unadjusted odds ratios (OR) were calculated for behaviors from the bivariate analysis and exact confidence intervals estimated using Thomas' method (Thomas, 1971).

Behaviors found to be significantly different by sexual orientation in the bivariate analyses were analyzed in a multi-variable logistic regression model using a generalized linear mixed-modeling approach (GLMM; Wolfinger & O'Connell, 1993) that adjusted for the within-university clustering of health behaviors with demographic and academic characteristics as covariates. For the GLMM modeling, campus was considered a random effect with students nested within campus. The purpose for the GLMM approach was twofold: (a) to adjust for campus differences in student characteristics and health behaviors, and (b) to account for the fact that students from the same campus may be more alike than students from different campuses. Diagnostics and potential influential observations were investigated for the adequacy of the model fit and assumption checking. From this modeling, adjusted odds ratios (AOR) were calculated for behaviors and confidence intervals estimated. All analyses were performed in SAS v8.2 (SAS Institute, Cary, NC) and also using the SAS GLIMMIX macro. Significance was considered to be resulting in a p-value < 0.05.

RESULTS

Of a total of 2,645 participants who completed the assessment, 1,014 participants self-identified as male and as "gay or homosexual" or "heterosexual or straight." All 10 campuses were represented with 84 to 182 participants from each campus depending on the campus population size. Mean age of these men was 20 years (± 2.5; range 17–30). Of the 1,014 men, 43 (4.2%) self identified as gay/homosexual and 971 (95.8%) self identified as heterosexual/straight. The demographic characteristics of the men by sexual orientation are presented in Table 19.1. No significant differences were found on the demographic characteristics between those students in the sample who identified as gay and those who identified as heterosexual, except on academic classification. Gay men were more likely to report higher academic classification.

Table 19.2 presents health behavior comparisons by sexual orientation. When compared to their heterosexual peers, gay men were more likely to report inconsistent condom use ($p < .03$); having multiple sexual partners in the past 30 days ($p < .01$); and a lifetime history of illicit drug use ($p < .02$). Gay men also were more likely to report ever having started a physical fight with a date (gay men with a male date and heterosexual men with a female date; $p < .02$). No differences were found between the groups for all other health-compromising behaviors including current and past alcohol use and cigarette smoking.

When adjusting for the variables listed in Table 19.1, including age, race, academic classification, residence type, and university clustering, 3 significant differences between gay and heterosexual men remained. When compared to their heterosexual peers, gay men had 2.05

Table 19.1. Comparison of Gay and Heterosexual Male Students on Selected Demographic and Academic Characteristics

Characteristic	Gay Men[a] (n = 43)	Heterosexual Men[a] (n = 971)	p[b]
Age in years	21.3 ± 3.3	20.3 ± 2.5	.08
Race		791 (83)	.64
White	36 (84)	52 (5)	
Black/African-American	4 (9)	63 (7)	
American Indian or Pacific Islander	2 (5)	23 (2)	
Multiracial	1 (2)		
Hispanic Ethnicity	2 (5)	27 (3)	.35
Academic Classification		217 (23)	.03
Freshman	6 (14)	329 (34)	
Sophomore	14 (33)	191 (20)	
Junior	7 (16)	200 (21)	
Senior	12 (28)	18 (2)	
Undergraduate, 5th yr.	4 (9)		
Residence		586 (61)	.32
On-campus	23 (53)	374 (39)	
Off-campus	20 (47)		

Notes:

[a]Mean ± SD or n (%), as appropriate.

[b]For categorical variables, chi-square or Fisher's exact tests were used. For continuous variables, t-tests or Wilcoxon rank-sum tests were used.

times higher odds of reporting inconsistent condom use (95% confidence interval [CI] = 1.02–4.12; $p = .04$). Gay men had 3.32 times higher odds of reporting multiple partners within the past 30 days (95% CI = 1.34–8.20; $p = .009$). Gay men reported an average of 1.46 ($SD = 0.76$) sexual partners while their heterosexual peers reported a mean of 1.25 ($SD = 0.73$) ($p < .05$).

Although gay men were not significantly more likely to report using illicit drugs in the past 30 days than their heterosexual peers, they did have 2.09 higher odds of reporting a lifetime history of illicit drug use (95% CI = 1.09–4.03; $p = .03$).

These adjusted OR and 95% confidence intervals are presented in Table 19.3.

■ DISCUSSION

Several findings deserve discussion. First, gay men reported having a higher academic classification than their heterosexual peers. This finding could be a result of gay students feeling comfortable and coming "out" over the course of their university experience. Coming or being "out" describes the internal acceptance and external expression or voluntary public announcement of one's sexual

Table 19.2. Differences Between Gay and Heterosexual Male Students on Selected Behaviors, Unadjusted Bivariate Analysis

Behavior	Gay Men n (%)	Heterosexual Men[a] n (%)	OR	95% CI	P
Inconsistent condom use	21 (58)	271 (41)	2.05	1.04–4.05	.03
Multiple partners in past 30 days	9 (35)	67 (15)	3.09	1.16–7.67	.01
Any binge drinking, past 30 days	23 (53)	484 (50)	1.14	0.62–2.10	.69
Moderate/heavy/problem alcohol use	16 (37)	399 (42)	0.84	0.44–1.57	.58
Drank in high school	24 (56)	535 (56)	1.01	0.54–1.86	.99
Smoked cigarettes, past 30 days	17 (40)	279 (29)	1.59	0.85–2.98	.14
Smoked marijuana, past 30 days	12 (28)	228 (24)	1.24	0.63–2.45	.54
Used amphetamines, past 30 days	3 (7)	27 (3)	2.59	0.48–8.96	.13
Used any form of cocaine, past 30 days	2 (5)	36 (4)	1.25	0.14–5.15	.68
Used Rohypnol, GHB, or Liquid X, past 30 days	1 (2)	3 (<1)	7.56	0.77–74.3	.16
Other illicit drug use, past 30 days	6 (14)	77 (8)	1.85	0.62–4.62	.16
Lifetime history of illicit drug use	18 (42)	243 (25)	2.11	1.13–3.94	.02
Date ever started a physical fight	4 (9)	56 (6)	1.65	0.41–4.82	.32
Ever started a physical fight with a date	3 (7)	12 (1)	5.91	1.03–23.0	.02

Notes:
[a]Referent group for the calculation of the OR.
OR = Odds ratio; 95% CI = 95% confidence interval.

Table 19.3. Increased Odds of Reporting Risk Behaviors Among Gay Male Students Compared to Their Heterosexual Peers, Clustered Multivariable Logistic Regression Analysis

Behavior	Adjusted Odds Ratio (AOR)[a]	95% CI	P
Inconsistent condom use	2.05	1.02–4.12	.04
Multiple partners in past 30 days	3.32	1.34–8.20	.009
Lifetime history of illicit drug use	2.09	1.09–4.03	.03

[a]Using Generalized Linear Mixed Modeling to adjust for the within-university clustering of behaviors and demographic and academic characteristics provided in Table 19.1.

orientation as a gay individual (Rhodes & Yee, 2006). Because identifying as gay was not associated with age, however, academic classification may be a proxy for feeling more comfortable about self identifying as gay that may increase as one increases time (or years) within a university community.

Gay men also were more likely to report inconsistent condom use during sexual intercourse than their heterosexual peers. After adjusting for age, race, academic classification, residence type, and university clustering, gay men had twice the odds of reporting inconsistent condom use when compared to their heterosexual peers. This finding is especially important because same-sex sexual behavior among men continues to be a primary mode of HIV transmission in the U.S. Although there had been a decline in the prevalence and incidence of HIV infection among gay men in the U.S. during the last 10–15 years, data suggest that self-identifying and non-self-identifying gay men still account for a significant proportion of all new infections (Karon, Fleming, Steketee, & De Cock, 2001) and a majority of all new AIDS diagnoses (Centers for Disease Control and Prevention [CDC], 2005). Recent reports suggest that the rates of new infections among gay men, after this period of decline, may be on the rise, especially among younger gay men (CDC, 2001; Kellogg, McFarland, & Katz, 1999), and epidemiological data in NC indicates that among some subgroups of gay university students, HIV incidence and prevalence may be as high as 14% and

32%, respectively (Anonymous, 2004; Miller et al., 2002). Recent studies also have observed increasing incidence rates of STDs among gay men in the U.S. (CDC, 1999, 2001; Fox et al., 2001; Williams et al., 1999).

Furthermore, among heterosexual couples, condoms compete with other forms of birth control. Thus, because heterosexual couples may choose other forms of birth control as opposed to condoms, which for gay men is solely a form of disease prevention, it is particularly noteworthy that heterosexual men still report using condoms more consistently during sexual intercourse than their gay peers. Understanding why this may occur requires further research. Perhaps condom use messages targeting university students are reaching and resonating with heterosexual students but not reaching or resonating with gay students.

Furthermore, primary prevention efforts (e.g., social marketing campaigns targeting heterosexual university students and one-on-one counseling and testing provided by student health services) currently may be geared towards heterosexual students. Increasing targeted and tailored approaches to meet the prevention needs of gay men in college may be warranted.

Because some students may feel uncomfortable about disclosing their risks to others including campus officials or student health center providers (Rhodes & Hergenrather, 2002), campus-based primary prevention strategies also may benefit from increasing the potential for risk disclosure through the creation of environments conducive to risk disclosure and the delivery of and attention to targeted and tailored intervention strategies. For example, an interactive software program on computers placed in student health centers may allow users to progress along a continuum to act on their information and prevention needs through electronic "cues to action" that encourage gay men to discuss their risks with a provider (Rhodes, DiClemente, Yee, & Hergenrather, 2001; Yee & Rhodes, 2002).

Just as has been found within racial ethnic disparity research (Institute of Medicine, 2003), providers may not recognize manifestations of prejudice and negative effect. Providers may need comprehensive training in (a) maintaining non-homophobic assumptions and attitudes; (b) distinguishing a patient's sexual behavior from identity; (c) communicating clearly and sensitively; (d) using gender-neutral terms; and (e) recognizing how personal provider attitudes affect clinical judgments (Harrison & Silenzio, 1996; Wallick, Cambre, & Townsend, 1992). Although previous research has identified distrust for providers as a barrier to risk disclosure and thus appropriate screening and care for gay men (Rhodes & DiClemente, 2003; Rhodes & Hergenrather, 2002), further research is necessary to explore provider receptivity to working with gay men and how their feelings about homosexuality affect their provision of services.

This study also found that gay men were significantly more likely to report multiple sexual partners during the past 30 days. It has been hypothesized that socially-constructed and stereotypically rigid notions of masculinity may contribute to risk behavior among males (Courtenay, 2000; Hong, 2000; Moynihan, 1998; Rhodes et al., in press). Masculinity often implies that men must prove their manhood through their actions which can be most efficiently communicated to others through being aggressive, not expressing emotion, not seeking health care, and engaging in risk behavior. Rigid and stereotypical notions of masculinity may yield intensified outcomes for gay men who do not meet these standards by virtue of their orientation (Halkitis & Parsons, 2003). Gay men may feel as though they cannot meet gender role expectations because of their orientation and thus may pursue other means of asserting their manhood, such as having multiple partners and engaging in other sexual risk behaviors (Rhodes & Yee, 2006).

The stress and depression resulting from this conflict between what it means to be a man and one's gay identity also may contribute not only to the increased rates of sexual intercourse with multiple partners but also to substance use and abuse. In this sample, gay men were more likely to report a history of illicit drug use. However, they were not more likely to report using illicit drugs during the past 30 days. This finding could be the result of the low frequency of gay men who reported drug use during the past 30 days which affected precision to estimate these differences. Larger sample sizes may yield significant differences.

It is important to note that other risk behaviors such as binge drinking, alcohol use, and smoking cigarettes were not significantly different when comparing gay men to their heterosexual peers. This lack of significance may be due to the current wide use of these substances on university campuses. Further studies are necessary to explore substance use trends comparing gay and heterosexual men.

Limitations

The current study is not without limitations. First, the observed associations are based on cross-sectional data. Additional studies using a prospective-cohort design will be necessary to evaluate the significance and stability of these findings over time. Furthermore, although a self-administered format was utilized that may minimize response bias, and included techniques found to increase validity of self-reported behavior (Fishbein & Pequegnat, 2000), including the use of the Internet (Rhodes, Bowie, & Hergenrather, 2003), these results remain based on self-reported data with their potential limitations (Pequegnat et al., 2000).

Although the total sample was large with 1,014 self-identifying as male, 43 (4.2%) self-identified as gay which limited the potential to see differences between the groups. However, this study does provide preliminary quantitative comparison data for a population about which little is known. To our knowledge, no other published study has compared self-identifying gay and self-identifying heterosexual men on such a broad variety of health behaviors or during a stage within the life course in which most of the behaviors that contribute to negative health outcomes are initiated.

Unfortunately, accurate response rates were un-calculable due to the unknown number of potential participants who received and read their e-mail. Although studies have indicated that e-mail can be an efficient method to recruit large numbers of university students (Kypri, Gallagher, & Cashell-Smith, 2004), this study found that many students used multiple e-mail accounts and did not use their university e-mail accounts with frequency. Some students relied on other e-mail accounts associated with other e-mail hosting services, and some e-mail systems filtered messages, assuming that these recruitment communications were "spam" mail (i.e., electronic junk mail) and rejected the message before the students received the message.

Also, this sample was not ethnically or racially diverse; however, post hoc analyses confirmed that this sample reflected the ethnic and racial composition of the 10 campuses.

Finally, how participants who completed the assessment compared to their peers on campus is unclear. Because the use of electronic technology such as e-mail for data collection is a relatively recent occurrence, understanding how differential motivations to participate affect participation rates is not well understood. Although electronic data collection has been promoted (Rhodes et al., 2003), careful attention to the process of data collection must be maintained to ensure the correct interpretation of findings. Further research is needed to understand electronic data collection and its limitations in both theory and practice.

CONCLUSIONS

Because our most severe and costly health and social problems are caused, in a large part, by many of the behaviors that begin in adolescence and early adulthood, research that identifies how behaviors differ by sexual orientation is imperative in order to develop meaningful interventions to affect health outcomes. Unfortunately only recently, have some population-based studies attempted to incorporate measures (both direct or, more often, proxy measures) of sexual orientation among study participants (Cochran & Mays, 2000; Gilman et al., 2001). This is an important step as prevention science addresses health ecologically, recognizing the individual within multiple influencing contexts.

This analysis examined health behavior disparities based on self-identification of sexual orientation. No doubt many differences exist between men who self identify as gay and those men who do not self identify as gay but still engage in same-sex sexual behavior with other men (e.g., bisexual men and men who have sex with men [MSM]). Subsequent research should include (a) efforts to understand and distinguish sexual orientation in terms of identify, desire, and behavior throughout the life course; (b) more comprehensive surveillance and data collection to identify and understand disparities in health-compromising behavior and disease outcomes among gay, bisexual, and heterosexual men and MSM of all ages; and (c) the development, implementation, and evaluation of creative yet scientifically-sound interventions to reach a variety of men to prevent a variety of health-compromising behaviors and promote men's health.

REFERENCES

Amaro, H., & de la Torre, A. (2002). Future health needs of women of color. Public health needs and scientific opportunities in research on Latinas. *American Journal of Public Health*, 92, 525–529.

Anonymous. (2004). HIV increasing among black college males HIV transmission among black college student and non-student men who have sex with men–North Carolina, 2003. *AIDS Patient Care and STDS*, 18, 371.

Atkins, M., & Nolan, M. (2005). Sexual transmission of hepatitis B. *Current Opinion in Infectious Diseases*, 18, 67–72.

Catania, J. A., Osmond, D., Stall, R. D., Pollack, L., Paul, J. P., Blower, S. et al. (2001). The continuing HIV epidemic among men who have sex with men. *American Journal of Public Health*, 91, 907–914.

Centers for Disease Control and Prevention. (1999). Increases in unsafe sex and rectal gonorrhea among men who have sex with men–San Francisco, California: 1994–1997. *MMWR Morbidity and Mortality Weekly Report*, 48, 45–48.

Centers for Disease Control and Prevention. (2001). HIV incidence among young men who have sex with men–seven U.S. Cities, 1994–2000. *MMWR Morbidity and Mortality Weekly Report,* 50, 440–444.

Centers for Disease Control and Prevention. (2005). *HIV/AIDS surveillance report, 2003* (No. 15). Atlanta, GA. US Department of Health and Human Services.

Cochran, S. D., & Mays, V. M. (2000). Lifetime prevalence of suicide symptoms and affective disorders among men reporting same-sex sexual partners: Results from NHANES III. *American Journal of Public Health,* 90, 573–578.

Courtenay, W. H. (2000). Constructions of masculinity and their influence on men's well-being: *A theory of gender and health. Social Science and Medicine,* 50, 1385–1401.

DeJong, W. (2003). Definitions of binge drinking. *JAMA Journal of the American Medical Association,* 289, 1635 .

Fishbein, M., & Pequegnat, W. (2000). Evaluating AIDS prevention interventions using behavioral and biological outcome measures. *Sexually Transmitted Diseases,* 27, 101–110.

Fox, K. K., del Rio, C., Holmes, K. K., Hook, E. W., 3rd, Judson, F. N., Knapp, J. S. et al. (2001). Gonorrhea in the HIV era: A reversal in trends among men who have sex with men. *American Journal of Public Health,* 91, 959–964.

Gay and Lesbian Medical Association. (2001). *Healthy people 2010: Companion document for lesbian, gay, bisexual, and transgender (LGBT) health.* San Francisco, CA. Gay and Lesbian Medical Association.

Gilman, S. E., Cochran, S. D., Mays, V. M., Hughes, M., Ostrow, D., & Kessler, R. C. (2001). Risk of psychiatric disorders among individuals reporting same-sex sexual partners in the national comorbidity survey. *American Journal of Public Health,* 91, 933–939.

Greenwood, G. L., Paul, J. P., Pollack, L. M., Binson, D., Catania, J. A., Chang, J. et al. (2005). Tobacco use and cessation among a household-based sample of US urban men who have sex with men. *American Journal of Public Health,* 95, 145–151.

Halkitis, P. N., & Parsons, J. T. (2003). Intentional unsafe sex (barebacking) among HIV-positive gay men who seek sexual partners on the internet. *AIDS Care,* 15, 367–378.

Harrison, A. E., & Silenzio, V. M. (1996). Comprehensive care of lesbian and gay patients and families. *Primary Care,* 23, 31–46.

Hong, L. (2000). Toward a transformed approach to prevention: Breaking the link between masculinity and violence. *Journal of American College Health,* 48, 269–279.

Institute of Medicine. (2003). *Unequal treatment: Confronting racial and ethnic disparities in health care.* Washington, DC. National Academy Press.

Karon, J. M., Fleming, P. L., Steketee, R. W., & De Cock, K. M. (2001). HIV in the United States at the turn of the century: An epidemic in transition. *American Journal of Public Health,* 91, 1060–1068.

Kellogg, T., McFarland, W., & Katz, M. (1999). Recent increases in HIV seroconversion among repeat anonymous testers in San Francisco. *AIDS,* 13, 2303–2304.

Kypri, K., Gallagher, S. J., & Cashell-Smith, M. L. (2004). An internet-based survey method for college student drinking research. *Drug and Alcohol Dependence,* 76, 45–53.

Miller, C. L., Spittal, P. M., LaLiberte, N., Li, K., Tyndall, M. W., O'Shaughnessy, M. V.

et al. (2002). Females experiencing sexual and drug vulnerabilities are at elevated risk for HIV infection among youth who use injection drugs. *Journal of Acquired Immune Deficiency Syndromes, 30*, 335–341.

Moynihan, C. (1998). Theories in health care and research: Theories of masculinity. *British Medical Journal, 317*, 1072–1075.

Pequegnat, W., Fishbein, M., Celentano, D., Ehrhardt, A., Garnett, G., Holtgrave, D. et al. (2000). NIMH/APPC workgroup on behavioral and biological outcomes in HIV/STD prevention studies: A position statement. *Sexually Transmitted Diseases, 27*, 127–132.

Rhodes, S. D., Bowie, D. A., & Hergenrather, K. C. (2003). Collecting behavioural data using the world wide web: Considerations for researchers. *Journal of Epidemiology and Community Health, 57*, 68–73.

Rhodes, S. D., & DiClemente, R. J. (2003). Psychosocial predictors of hepatitis B vaccination among young African-American gay men in the Deep South. *Sexually Transmitted Diseases, 30*, 449–454.

Rhodes, S. D., DiClemente, R. J., Yee, L. J., & Hergenrather, K. C. (2001). Correlates of hepatitis B vaccination in a high-risk population: An internet sample. *American Journal of Medicine, 110*, 628–632.

Rhodes, S. D., Eng, E., Hergenrather, K. C., Remnitz, I. M., Arceo, R., Montaño, J., & Alegría Ortega, J. Exploring Latino men's HIV risk using community-based participatory research. *American Journal of Health Behavior*, in press.

Rhodes, S. D., & Hergenrather, K. C. (2002). Exploring hepatitis B vaccination acceptance among young men who have sex with men: Facilitators and barriers. *Preventive Medicine, 35*, 128–134.

Rhodes, S. D., & Yee, L. J. (2006). Public health and gay and bisexual men: A primer for practitioners, clinicians, and researchers. In M. Shankle (Ed.), *The handbook of lesbian, gay, bisexual, and transgender public health: A practitioner's guide to service: Haworth*, 119–144.

Sell, R. L., & Becker, J. B. (2001). Sexual orientation data collection and progress toward Healthy People 2010. *American Journal of Public Health, 91*, 876–882.

Thomas, D. G. (1971). Algorithm as-36. Exact confidence limits for the odds ratio in a 2 × 2 table. *Applied Statistics, 20*, 105–110.

Treadwell, H. M., & Ro, M. (2003). Poverty, race, and the invisible men. *American Journal of Public Health, 93*, 705–707.

Wallick, M. M., Cambre, K. M., & Townsend, M. H. (1992). How the topic of homosexuality is taught at U.S. Medical schools. *Academic Medicine, 67*, 601–603.

Williams, L. A., Klausner, J. D., Whittington, W. L., Handsfield, H. H., Celum, C., & Holmes, K. K. (1999). Elimination and reintroduction of primary and secondary syphilis. *American Journal of Public Health, 89*, 1093–1097.

Wolfinger, R., & O'Connell, M. (1993). Generalized linear mixed models: A pseudo-likelihood approach. *Journal of Statistical Computation and Simulation, 48*, 233–243.

Yee, L. J., & Rhodes, S. D. (2002). Understanding correlates of hepatitis B virus vaccination in men who have sex with men: What have we learned? *Sexually Transmitted Infections, 78*, 374–377.

College Men's Health and Wellness

Implications for Educational Practice

As the chapters in Part Four make clear, college men will literally kill themselves if educators do not intervene—this extends beyond their higher rates of suicide to include a range of other destructive acts that put their lives at risk. But few comprehensive initiatives exist on college and university campuses to promote healthy life choices among male undergraduates; many institutions offer no gender-specific programming of this sort. Thus, we recommend the introduction of a men's health campaign that promotes every dimension of wellness—diet, fitness, good sexual judgment, freedom from addictions, and mental health. This campaign could be co-sponsored by the health center, the residence life department, campus dining services, the LGBT center, the Office of Sorority and Fraternity Affairs, athletics, and the counseling center. The team that works on the health campaign should include professionals from these offices. Faculty from gender studies, counseling and educational psychology, and departments where courses on kinesiology and nutrition are taught should also be invited to participate in the design, marketing, and implementation of this campaign. Most important, an institution that aspires to launch a successful health campaign must include undergraduate men on its team.

As has been our approach in other portions of the book, we want to carefully avoid being too prescriptive here. Undoubtedly, a campus team such as the one we are recommending in Part Four would be considerably more familiar with its local context than are we. Therefore, we think it best to not spell out for an institution the exact activities that should be associated with its health campaign. What might appeal to men at the University of Pennsylvania or prove effective for those enrolled at San Diego State are unlikely to work everywhere else. Notwithstanding our reluctance, we do offer *some* guidance for campuses that wish to assemble teams to strategically improve men's health outcomes in college.

What we are recommending here is a year-long, multipronged, and well-coordinated set of initiatives—not a men's health week or a fragmented set of activities tucked away in isolated corners of campus. It would behoove stakeholders involved in the launch of this campaign to first pursue a better understanding of men's health-related attitudes and behaviors. This should occur through surveys, individual interviews and focus groups, and informal conversations with male students on the campus. And of course student members of the team could also offer particularly instructive insights on what would be likely to appeal to their same-sex peers. Data derived through these means will minimize the risk of introducing a men's health campaign that either responds to the wrong issues or is not reflective of the male students who are enrolled at that particular institution. Moreover, identifying in advance the barriers to good health would better enable the team to proactively craft strategic responses.

Also essential is an awareness of the effects of hegemonic masculinities on men's health behaviors. Team members should read Courtenay's chapter in this book as well as other publications that help explain why male students perceive themselves to be immune to negative health consequences, and how erroneous assumptions regarding their invincibility manufactures a multitude of physically, emotionally, and psychologically harmful behaviors. It is important to know why a guy feels compelled to drink his buddies under the table or get himself into a rowdy fistfight with another dude who unapologetically steps on his shoe at the bar. Or why after having unprotected sex with a prostitute he does not feel an urgent need to be tested for sexually transmitted infections. Those who endeavor to reach men who are visibly troubled will stand a better chance of doing so if they read Michael Kimmel's book *Guyland* and other publications that offer theoretical insights on men and masculinities.

Once the team has sufficient understanding and data to guide its efforts, the design of the campaign should begin with an emphasis on responding effectively to health issues and risks encountered by every male student on campus—heterosexuals, men's volleyball team members, lower-income men without health insurance who have never been to a physician, gay men, and fraternity men, to name a few. Again, attempting to do this without first knowing who these men are and which specific health-related risks they most often encounter will probably lead to a failed initiative. Although some resources and activities should be directed toward specific male subgroups, the majority will lend themselves to wider participation. For example, group therapy sessions that focus on body image issues could be marketed to all men on campus. Or some effort designed to increase men's awareness of the life-threatening aspects of hazing could include student-athletes, men in the marching band (a group whose underground hazing often goes unexposed), and of course freshmen and others who are considering pledging fraternities.

Garnering student enthusiasm and support for the health campaign will be challenging but is nonetheless essential. In addition to including students on the planning and implementation team, it would also be advantageous to partner with resident assistants, student leaders in men's organizations (including fraternity chapter presidents), captains of men's sports teams, and others to promote the initiative and ignite interest among other men with whom they interact. These students are best positioned to convince their peers that being a healthy man is cool. Perhaps their photographs could be used on the campaign website, flyers, posters, and other promotional materials. It also seems sensible to suggest featuring these men in a prominent manner at assorted activities associated with the campaign. For example, having the star basketball player, the most popular fraternity man on campus, the president or highest-ranking officer in the LGBT student organization, and well-known others publicly commit themselves to being first in line during a "Men Get Tested for HIV" event will inspire many others to do the same.

The team, of course, should solicit student feedback on each component of the campaign. The focus of these assessments should extend beyond merely counting how many men attend an event. Instead, emphasis should be placed on exploring students' perceptions of educational worth and relevance, as well as on determining the effects of participation on their attitudes and behaviors. One major goal of any health initiative should be to help men figure out productive ways to resolve identity conflicts, as healthy masculinities are directly linked to a plethora of other positive health outcomes. It is important to determine the extent to which this has occurred for men on campus as a result of their engagement in health campaign-related efforts. We definitely advocate doing some assessment immediately following individual events; however, more useful will be data collected from men who participated in the weeks, months, and semesters that follow.

In *The Gender Gap in College,* Linda Sax reports that undergraduate men exercise more than do their female counterparts, a finding that is consistent with Cuyjet's (1997) research. But Sax also notes that male students diet less, consume alcohol more frequently, and smoke more cigarettes than do women. The campaign we are recommending here must challenge men to recognize that good health extends beyond lifting weights and playing basketball. A significant portion of it ought to be educational. We have not yet seen evidence to suggest that young men are fully aware of their vulnerabilities or the wide spectrum of health risks they assume. What we do know is that men are less likely than are women to seek help for their problems.

Elizabeth Saewyc and her colleagues found trivial gender differences in their 2009 study of college and university students who had been exposed to violence (including romantic relationship abuse). For the most part, men were just as likely as were the women they surveyed to report having recently been on the receiving end of a violent act. The study was based on students who visited health clinics on five campuses. An alarming fraction of male undergraduates never go to the health center or take advantage of counseling services on campus, but they do have emotional issues associated with the violence Saewyc et al. (2009) report, as well as other mental problems that go unaddressed. Men need to know they need help, the importance of seeking it, where to find it, and the enduring health benefits conferred to those who get it. In our view, this should be at the center of a men's health campaign.

Given the tumultuous developmental period in which college men commonly find themselves (Kimmel, 2008), it is obvious to us that more attention should be placed on deliberately raising consciousness among them and responding more systematically to their health needs. Men typically do not graduate from college one day and immediately abandon bad habits to transition to healthier lifestyles the next. Hence, educators and administrators must work collaboratively and comprehensively to help students recognize as early as possible the long-term value in taking better care of themselves. The men's health campaign we have advocated here is one way to achieve these aims.

REFERENCES

Cuyjet, M. J. (1997). African American men on college campuses: Their needs and their perceptions. In M. J. Cuyjet (Ed.), *Helping African American men succeed in college.* New Directions for Student Services (No. 80, pp. 5–16). San Francisco: Jossey-Bass.

Kimmel, M. S. (2008). *Guyland: The perilous world where boys become men.* New York: HarperCollins.

Sax, L. J. (2008). *The gender gap in college: Maximizing the developmental potential of women and men.* San Francisco: Jossey-Bass.

Saewyc, E. M., Brown, D., Plane, M., Mundt, M. P. et al. (2009). Gender differences in violence exposure among university students attending campus health clinics in the United States and Canada. *Journal of Adolescent Health, 45*(1), 1–8.

PART FIVE

COLLEGE MEN OF COLOR: INTRODUCTION

I don't see color. With the election of President Barack Obama, we now live in a post-racial America. Therefore, I don't understand why we continue to acknowledge racial differences. Focusing more on our similarities will help minority males better understand that we're more alike than dissimilar. I'm not racist, but I am having a hard time figuring out why they need their own fraternities and organizations—why can't they just join ours? Why are they so separate—how can we get them to integrate more with us? This book is supposed to be about all men, so why is there a special section on Blacks, Latinos, and Asians? And why is there no chapter devoted exclusively to White male collegians. Are we not men too?

Eduardo Bonilla-Silva's book, *Racism Without Racists: Color-Blind Racism and the Persistence of Racial Inequality in the United States,* furnishes answers to many of these questions. Bonilla-Silva dispels the myth of color blindness and offers numerous examples that contradict claims of a post-racial America. His main argument is that racism does not perpetuate itself—there are people who do racist things and maintain systems (sometimes unknowingly) that persistently manufacture racial injustice. This perspective begs the question of how outcomes disparities between students of color and their White peers are sustained if there is no racism in educational environments and institutional structures. Like Bonilla-Silva, Critical Race Theorists critique the myths of color blindness and meritocracy. Those who claim they don't see color are in essence denying students' racial identities and rendering unbelievable their lived experiences with race in predominantly White contexts.

In Chapter 20 Juan R. Guardia and Nancy J. Evans write about Latino fraternity members. Indeed, there would be no need for these Greek-letter organizations if there were equitable access to predominantly White fraternities and if the cultural norms of Interfraternity Council (IFC) chapters were more inclusive of students from diverse backgrounds. But several studies confirm this is usually not the case (see Chang & DeAngelo, 2002; De Los Reyes & Rich, 2003), despite longstanding critiques of racial hegemony and exclusionary practices in IFC groups (Horowitz, 1951; Lee, 1955). Using Urie Bronfenbrenner's bioecological theory of human development as a conceptual framework, Guardia and Evans show how membership in a predominantly Latino fraternity enhanced one important outcome—ethnic identity development—among the men they interviewed. Although their study was conducted at an institution where 54.2 percent of the students were Latino, findings Guardia and Evans report signify the importance of providing Latino men a racially familiar space in which to find support, Spanish-speaking peers, cultural affirmation, and opportunities to develop a healthy sense of self.

As is the case in the IFC fraternity chapters, White men have set the hegemonic masculine rules by which all others are expected to abide on campus. As such, William M. Liu asserts the following in Chapter 21: "Racism adds to the confusion of being a minority man in America." His psychological study investigated the role of racism and prejudicial treatment on Asian American male undergraduates. For many of these students, internalized conflict ensued as they attempted to reconcile their recognition of stereotypes about Asian men as effeminate with the social expectations of manhood. As indicated in other parts of this book, gender role conflict is experienced by many men and is therefore not isolated to a single racial or ethnic group. However, the confusion and conflict that Liu writes about is a burden that most White male students are not forced to carry. They can focus on academic and social endeavors without the distraction of racist caricatures of themselves. At no fault of their own, Asian American men are dually disadvantaged by the model minority and the model gender majority myths we described in Chapter 1 of this book.

As Shaun R. Harper illustrates in Chapter 22, Black male collegians have also been harmed by negative misperceptions about their racial and gender group. One way this occurs is through the internalization of negative stereotypes that White people hold about African Americans. As Harper explains, internalized racism occurs when socially stigmatized groups accept and recycle negative messages regarding their aptitude, abilities, and societal place, thus resulting in self-devaluation and the invalidation of others within the group. In the context of schooling, this has often been explored using Signithia Fordham and John Ogbu's (1986) "Acting White" hypothesis, which contends that peers of academically successful Black students often accuse them of acting like their White peers. Based on a study of Black male college achievers, Harper's chapter furnishes evidence that contradicts such claims. He reveals how the men he studied negotiated support from their same-race peers. In Chapter 23, Michael Herndon describes how Black male collegians also rely on churches and other religious institutions for support and discusses ways in which spirituality increases resilience among these men as they navigate a predominantly White institution. One participant in Herndon's study confessed: "Spirituality helps me cope with White people."

Regarding the last two chapters in Part Five, there would be no transference and internalization of racist stereotypes among Blacks if they were not first manufactured by Whites. Explained in Chapter 22 are ways in which Black male student leaders negotiated achievement alongside acceptance, popularity, and peer support. These energies could have been more productively reappropriated if there didn't exist an oppressive social script that disassociates Black males from academic achievement. Likewise, these students wouldn't need to develop resilience in predominantly White contexts or search so desperately for spiritual support in external venues (i.e., church) if their interactions with White peers and faculty were less oppressive and if more support were available on their campuses. If we, in fact, lived in a post-racial America masculine norms would be equitably reconstructed by men from all racial and ethnic backgrounds, Whites would stop oppressing people of color with racist stereotypes and antics to maintain their superiority, and male students of color would feel as welcome as others on predominantly White campuses.

REFERENCES

Bonilla-Silva, E. (2006). *Racism without racists: Color-blind racism and the persistence of racial inequality in the United States* (2nd ed). Lanham, MD: Rowman & Littlefield.

Chang, M. J., & DeAngelo, L. (2002). Going Greek: The effects of racial composition on White students' participation patterns. *Journal of College Student Development, 43*(6), 809–823.

De Los Reyes, G., & Rich, P. (2003). Housing students: Fraternities and residential colleges. *The Annals of the Academy of Political and Social Science, 585*(1), 118–123.

Fordham, S., & Ogbu, J. U. (1986). Black students' school success: Coping with the "burden of 'acting White'". *Urban Review, 18*(3), 176–206.

Horowitz, H. W. (1952). Discriminatory fraternities at state universities: A violation of the Fourteenth Amendment? *Southern California Law Review, 25*(3), 289–296.

Lee, A. M. (1955). *Fraternities without brotherhood: A study of prejudice on the American campus.* Boston: Beacon.

CHAPTER 20

Factors Influencing the Ethnic Identity Development of Latino Fraternity Members at a Hispanic Serving Institution

Juan R. Guardia and Nancy J. Evans

I n 2003, the United States (U.S.) Census Bureau announced that Hispanics are the nation's largest minority group. As of July 2004, the Hispanic population constituted 41.3 million people—14% of the nation's population (U.S. Census Bureau, 2005). In 2000, Hispanics represented 22% of 18-to-24-year-olds enrolled in colleges and universities, up from 16% in 1980 (Llagas & Snyder, 2003). Llagas and Snyder noted, "The increase in Hispanic enrollment is being driven by both population growth and by increasing proportions of the [Hispanic] population enrolling in colleges and universities" (p. 96). With such increases of Hispanics in higher education, Hispanic Serving Institutions (HSIs) have become an important option for Hispanic students entering higher education. According to Santiago (2007), almost half of all Latino

undergraduate students were concentrated in the 6% of institutions identified as HSIs in the United States. Latino college students at HSIs (and at all colleges) are involved on campuses in a variety of ways. One way in which Latino college students become involved is by participation in Greek life, specifically Latino Greek letter organizations (LGLOs).

The purpose of this phenomenological study was to understand how membership in a Latino fraternity at an HSI enhances members' ethnic identity development. Minimal research has been done on Latino college students' participation in LGLOs. The research that has been done on LGLOs has focused on the history of such organizations (Johnson, 1972; Kimbrough, 2003; Mejia, 1994; Rodriguez, 1995), their growth (Castro, 2004; Kimbrough, 2002), and how they empower and provide academic and social support (Adam, 1999; Helem, 2004; Reyes, 1997). Only one study has focused on the impact of participation in a LGLO on ethnic identity. Nuñez (2004) found that members gained a heightened sense of ethnic identity through their participation in a Latina-based sorority at a predominantly White university in the Midwest. Several participants in Nuñez's study indicated that they were not active with Latino/a student organizations prior to joining the sorority. After becoming members, the women found that the sorority served as a support system with regard to ethnicity and ethnic identity and encouraged them to become involved in other Latino/a and minority student organizations and programs. As a result, their sense of themselves as Latina women was heightened.

This research study was focused on a Latino fraternity at an HSI located in the Southeast. No previous research was found that addressed how participation in a Latino fraternity at an HSI influenced members' ethnic identity development. This study is important because it focused on a combination of contexts with regard to Latino college students: a Latino fraternity nested within an HSI. Thus, through the voices of members of a Latino fraternity at an HSI, this study examined the following questions:

1. How is ethnic identity defined within the Latino fraternity?

2. In what ways does membership in a Latino fraternity at an HSI enhance members' ethnic identity development?

3. In what ways does attending an HIS enhance the ethnic identity development of Latino fraternity members beyond the contributions made by membership in the Latino fraternity?

■ ETHNIC IDENTITY DEVELOPMENT

Ethnic, cultural, and racial identity development have been explored by various researchers (Atkinson, Morten, & Sue, 1983; Cross, 1978; Helms, 1990; Kim, 1981). Although a variety of ethnic identity development models, including Phinney's (1993) model of ethnic identity formation and Torres's (1999) bicultural orientation model (BOM), have been applied to Latino/a college students, we used Ferdman and Gallegos's (2001) racial identity orientation model in this study. The model is composed of six different orientations, varying from White-identified to Latino-integrated (see Table 20.1). Although there are six different orientations, they "do not exhaust the possibilities nor do they address the complex issues involved in ethnic and cultural identity" (Ferdman & Gallegos, p. 50). As Ferdman and Gallegos noted, because Latinos/as originate from a variety of different countries and have different cultures and social classes, they "are treated as an ethnic and cultural category more than a racial one" (p. 44); however, we deemed this model to be most appropriate for this study because it is broader than Torres's (1999) and not linear in

Table 20.1. Ferdman and Gallegos (2001) Latino/a Racial Identity Orientations Model (p. 49)

Orientation	Lens	Identify As/Prefer	Latinos Are Seen	Whites Are Seen	Framing of Race
Latino-Integrated	Wide	Individuals in a group context	Positively	Complex	Dynamic, contextual, socially constructed
Latino-Identified (Racial/Raza)	Broad	Latinos	Very Positively	Distinct; could be barriers or allies	Latino/not Latino
Subgroup-Identified	Narrow	Own subgroup	My group OK, others maybe	Not central (could be barriers or blockers)	Not clear or central; secondary to nationality, ethnicity, culture
Latinos as Other	External	Not White	Generically, fuzzily	Negatively	White/not White
Undifferentiated/Denial	Closed	People	"Who are Latinos?"	Supposed color-blind (accept dominant norms)	Denial, irrelevant invisible
White-Identified	Tinted	Whites	Negatively	Very positively	White/Black, either/or, one-drop or "mejorar la raza" (i.e., improve the race)

fashion as is Phinney's. In addition, the variety of orientations that this model offers allowed Latino fraternity members the option to identify which orientations they chose in the specific microsystems (Latino fraternity, family, and the HSI campus) that were relevant in this study.

Ultimately, as Evans, Forney, and Guido-Dibrito (1998) described, "ethnic identity develops from the shared culture, religion, geography, and language of individuals who are often connected by strong loyalty and kinship" (pp. 79–80). All of these factors play important roles in the ethnic identity development of Latino/a college students.

■ LATINO FRATERNITIES

For many Latino/a college students, membership in fraternities and sororities is a way of being involved on campus, a factor that Astin (1984) found to be important in student learning and personal development. The literature has highlighted how fraternity membership leads to self-reported growth in leadership abilities (Astin 1993), the development of career-related skills (Pascarella & Terenzini, 2005), openness to diversity by members who are students of color (Pascarella, Edison, Nora, Hagedorn, & Terenzini, 1996), and the extrinsic value members attach to education (Pascarella & Terenzini). Fraternities and sororities also fulfill cultural and academic needs for many college students (Whipple & Sullivan, 1998).

Latino fraternities began in the late 1800s as secret societies whose members were elite and wealthy students from various Latin American countries attending prestigious colleges and universities in the United States (Mejia, 1994; Rodriguez, 1995). These secret societies "evolved into alliances or loose-knit fraternities of Latinos who shared the same social background" (Rodriguez, p. 26). The Union Hispano Americana was a secret society founded in 1898 at Rensselaer Polytechnic Institute (Fine, 2003) and eventually merged with Phi Lambda Alpha fraternity (founded in 1919 at the University of California, Berkeley) in 1921 (Anson & Marchesani, 1991). Phi Lambda Alpha later merged with Sigma Iota (originally founded in 1904 as the Sociedad Hispano-Americana, which in 1912 became the first Latino fraternity at Louisiana State University) and formed Phi Iota Alpha Fraternity on December 26, 1931 (Baily, 1949; Johnson, 1972; Kimbrough, 2003; Torbenson, 2005),

making it the oldest existing Latino fraternity in the United States.

Since the founding of Phi Iota Alpha, the number of LGLOs has grown substantially. The 1980s and 1990s was a time of remarkable growth for Latino fraternities and Latina sororities. Although many Latino/a college students sought membership in historically white fraternities and sororities, they found that "they did not fit the mold of the traditional, already-established, nationally recognized fraternities and sororities" (Miranda & Martin de Figueroa, 2000, p. 7). As Miranda and Martin de Figueroa observed, "The desire to be part of mainstream culture, yet preserve one's own heritage, gave birth to the Latino/Latina fraternities and sororities" (p. 7).

■ THEORETICAL PERSPECTIVE

Although various researchers have addressed the ethnic identity of Latino college students (Phinney & Alipuria, 1990; Schneider & Ward, 2003; Torres, 2003; Torres & Baxter Magolda, 2004), we found no studies that were focused on the ethnic identity development of Latino fraternity members and the relation of identity development to the campus environment. Using Bronfenbrenner's (2005a) bioecological theory of human development as the guiding framework, we proposed a theoretical model that focuses on the Latino fraternity members and the HSI campus environment. Bronfenbrenner (2005b) defined the bioecological theory of human development as:

> The scientific study of the progressive, mutual accommodation, throughout the life course, between an active, growing human being and the changing properties of the immediate settings in which the developing person lives, as this process is affected by the relations between these settings, and by the larger contexts in which the settings are embedded. (p. 107)

Bronfenbrenner's (2005a) bioecological theory of human development consists of five systems (levels) that describe the interactions between human beings and their environment: the *microsystem, mesosystem, exosystem, macrosystem,* and *chronosystem*. Using Bronfenbrenner's theory in her study of mixed-race college students' identities, Renn (2003) described how through each of the first four levels, an "individual receives messages about identity, developmental forces and challenges, and resources for addressing those challenges" (p. 388). The following are descriptions of the five systems and how they provide a framework for this study.

The microsystem "is a pattern of activities, roles, and interpersonal relations experienced by the developing person in a given face-to-face setting with particular physical and material features and containing other persons with distinctive characteristics of temperament, personality, and systems of belief" (Bronfenbrenner, 2005b, p. 148). The mesosystem "comprises the linkages and processes taking place between two or more settings containing the developing person . . . in other words, a mesosystem is a system of microsystems" (Bronfenbrenner, 2005a, p. 148). Using the microsystems identified in this study, mesosystem interrelations include the Latino fraternity and the HSI campus environment and the Latino fraternity and the families of fraternity members. Renn (2003) provided an example with regard to Latino ethnic identity:

> The messages a student receives about what it means to be "really Latino" in one microsystem (a friendship group of other Latinos) may be supported or challenged by messages from another microsystem (the professor of his class on the cultures of Latin America). (p. 389)

Renn went on to describe how other messages may come from family or fraternity brothers.

Exosystems are settings in which the individual does not actively participate but in which events occur that influence an individual's development. Renn (2003) described the following exosystems that had the potential to impact the identities of the mixed-race college students in her study: academic major, financial aid awarded, and parents' income.

The subculture and culture of which the individual is a part is the macrosystem. Bronfenbrenner (2005a) defined the macrosystem as consisting of:

> The overarching pattern of micro, meso, and exosystems characteristic of a given

culture, subculture, or other broader social context, with particular reference to the developmentally instigative belief systems, resources, hazards, lifestyles, opportunity structures, life course options, and patterns of social interchange that are embedded in each of these systems. The macrosystem may be thought of as a societal blueprint for a particular culture, subculture, or other broader social context. (pp. 149–150)

Bronfenbrenner's examples are applicable to this study on how membership in a Latino fraternity at an HSI enhances members' ethnic identity development.

The chronosystem is the final system in Bronfenbrenner's (1995) bioecological theory of human development. As he described it:

> The individual's own developmental life course is seen as embedded in and powerfully shaped by conditions and events occurring during the historical period through which the person lives.... A major factor influencing the course and outcome of human development is the timing of biological and social transitions as they relate to the culturally defined age, role expectations, and opportunities occurring throughout the life course. (p. 641)

In the chronosystem, changes over time may influence the development of individuals and the previous systems (micro-, exo-, and mesosystems) in which they are embedded. Because Latino fraternity members shared past experiences and events that had influenced their ethnic identity development, the chronosystem was considered in this study.

■ FRAMEWORK

For the purposes of this study, we chose a basic interpretative qualitative approach. In basic Interpretive research "the researcher is interested in understanding how participants make meaning of a situation or phenomenon, this meaning is mediated through the researcher as instrument, the strategy is inductive, and the outcome is descriptive" (Merriam & Associates, 2002, p. 6).

The goal of this study was to make meaning of how membership in a Latino fraternity at an HSI enhances ethnic identity development. The philosophical assumption underlying this study is constructionsim. Crotty (1998) defined *constructionsim* as "the view that all knowledge, and therefore all meaningful reality as such, is contingent upon human practices, being constructed in and out of interaction between human beings and their world, and developed and transmitted within an essentially social context" (p. 42). Constructionism was appropriate for this study so we could understand, through dialogue with the participants, how they made meaning of their membership in a Latino fraternity at an HSI.

To understand the participants' meaningmaking, phenomenology was chosen as the qualitative research approach. According to Merriam and

Associates (2002), "a phenomenological study focuses on the essence or structure of an experience" (p. 7). Phenomenology "involves a return to experience in order to obtain comprehensive descriptions that provide the basis for reflective structural analysis that portrays the essence of the experience" (Moustakas, 1994, p. 13).

METHODS

Participants

At an HSI located in the Southeastern United States, 7 members of a Latino fraternity (to which we assigned the pseudonym Omega Beta) participated in this study. For the purpose of this study, the HSI was referred to as Latino University. The entire chapter membership of Omega Beta was asked to participate in this study. A few months previous to the study, a letter of introduction was e-mailed to the president of the fraternity describing the proposed study, when it would take place, the reason their organization was chosen, and why we specifically chose their institution. I, Juan R. Guardia, met with the president and another member of the fraternity on October 15, 2005. The meeting served an important purpose: for the fraternity members to meet me personally and ask any questions they had regarding the study. During the meeting, the members expressed that they were very intrigued and interested in the study. At the end of the meeting, they verbally agreed to participate in the study. No incentives were offered to the participants other than the satisfaction of telling their stories as Latino fraternity members. Out of the 9 members, 7 participated in this study. Based on a demographic questionnaire that participants completed, Table 20.2 shows the responses provided by the 7 participants and their level of participation in the study. All of the participants in the study are referred to by their self-selected pseudonym.

In 2004, Latino University enrolled 35,061 students (website citation withheld for confidentiality). The racial/ethnic breakdown was: 54.2% Hispanic, 12.7% African American, 3.6% Asian, 0.1% Native American, and 19.2% White. Non-reported and other students who chose not to identify accounted for 9.8%. At the time of the study, Latino University had 11 fraternities on campus; 10 are historically White and 1 was Latino. Since then, an additional Latino fraternity has been added. The dominant ethnic background of members of all 12 fraternities is Hispanic/Latino.

Procedure

In addition to the demographic questionnaire, data collection procedures included three semistructured interviews and one focus group; observation of the participants on and off campus; document collection; and journaling. Juan R. Guardia completed all data collection and analysis; thus, first person singular references below refer to Guardia.

I conducted semistructured interviews with all participants to engage them in open discussions of their experiences

Table 20.2. Demographic Information of the Omega Beta Study Participants

Pseudonym	Age	Class Year	Self-Identified	Time Lived in the U.S.	Primary Language	Level of Participation
Bart	19	Freshman	Guatemalan	Born in Guatemala; U. S. since 1990	Spanish	Interviews 1–3; Participant Observation; Focus Group
Bob	23	Senior	Honduran & Latino	Born in U.S.	Spanish	Interviews 1–3; Participant Observation; Focus Group
David	24	Senior	Latino & Colombian-American	Born in U.S.	English	Interviews 1–3; Participant Observation; Focus Group
Joe	24	Senior	Trinirican (Trinidadian & Puerto Rican)	Born in U.S.	English	Interviews 1–3; Participant Observation; Focus Group
Rodrigo	20	Junior	Latino	Born in U.S.; moved to Honduras for 5 years then moved back to U.S.	Spanish	Interviews 1–3; Participant Observation; Focus Group
Siebel	22	Senior	Cuban & Latino	Born in U.S.	English & Spanish	Interviews 1–3; Participant Observation
Tony	19	Freshman	Cuban	Born in U.S.	Spanish	Interviews 1–3; Participant Observation; Focus Group

"and to allow interviewees to express their opinions and ideas in their own words" (Esterberg, 2002, p. 87). This format allowed me to "listen carefully to the participant's responses and to follow his . . . lead" (Esterberg, p. 87). I used the three interview series designed by Dolbeare and Schuman (as cited in Seidman, 1998, p. 11) when interviewing members of the Latino fraternity.

During Interview 1, I collected data on the participants' life stories. Using a set of open-ended questions that were prepared in advance, I gathered information that set up the context for each individual interview. All the participants were asked the same questions, including:

1. Tell me about your home background and family.

2. Please talk about when you first realized your own ethnicity. How old
   were you? Who or what event introduced you to thinking about it?

3. What is it like to be a college student at Latino University? A Latino
   at Latino University?

4. Why did you choose to become a
   member of a Latino fraternity?

These questions allowed me to establish a
rapport and trust with the participants.

Interview 2 specifically focused on
the research questions and their experiences as members of the Latino
fraternity. Participants provided in-depth
information and shared experiences that
enhanced their ethnic identities as members of a Latino fraternity at an HSI. In
Interview 3, I provided the participants
with some emerging themes and asked
them to reflect on their previously reported experiences. In addition, they provided member checks with regard to
the previous data collected. I used a
90-minute format for interviews conducted in this series.

An additional method for data collection was a focus group. This method
allowed me to produce data and gather
insights from Latino fraternity members
that would have been "less accessible without the interaction found in [the] group"
(Morgan, 1997, p. 2). I conducted one focus group, which lasted 75 minutes, in a
conference room in the student union. Six
of the 7 fraternity members participated.
Through the focus group I established a
connection with all of the fraternity members and observed their interactions with

one another. In addition, due to the limited time I was able to be at Latino University, the small group interview format
allowed me to collect a large amount of
data in a short period of time, which generated "a rich understanding of participants' experiences and beliefs" (Morgan,
1997, p. 11).

I observed the participants in a variety of settings. It was my goal to range
between a non-participant to a complete
participant, depending on the situation.
For example, during the study I acted as
a non-participant when recording observational notes of the activities that took
place at chapter meetings. On the other
hand, I was a complete participant when
I attended a Black Greek letter step show
at a neighboring college with the participants. A step show is characterized "by
synchronized hand and foot movements,
along with singing, dancing, chanting,
and acting" (Kimbrough, 2003. p. 197).
At this activity, the participants and I
discussed Latino fraternities, among other things. My notes included data about
the time, place, physical setting, and
fraternity members present, but most
importantly, the behaviors I observed.
These observational notes were critical as
they described and made meaning of the
Latino fraternity members' experiences
and how they played a role in their
ethnic identity development.

Throughout the study, I collected
documents that pertained to the Latino
fraternity members' ethnic identity
development. Lincoln and Guba (1985)
noted that documents "are a rich source
of information, contextually relevant and

grounded in the contexts they represent" (p. 277). Participants provided me with a variety of documents that outlined the history of the chapter at Latino University and the organization nationally, including a fraternity pamphlet, chapter website, and a flyer describing Omega Beta, which included a national map highlighting where chapters of Omega Beta are located. In addition, I reviewed the fraternity's history book for background information on the organization.

Lincoln and Guba (1985) suggested the use of a reflexive journal in which the researcher records information about self and the method being used. Throughout the study, I took notes of personal reflections on the interviews and all aspects of the study so that I was able to capture all my experiences in the field. Such reflections assisted me in understanding my perceptions of students' interpretations of their experiences and the context in which those experiences were described.

A key aspect in qualitative research is the concept of trustworthiness. The issues of credibility, transferability, dependability, and confirmability (Lincoln & Guba, 1985) were addressed throughout the study. Credibility was maximized through prolonged engagement in the field, member checks, and peer debriefing. I was at the study site for the entire month of February 2006, which allowed me to develop an in-depth understanding of the Latino fraternity members' experiences. In addition, I used member checks, which provided participants the opportunity to comment on my interpretation of the data (Lincoln & Guba, 1985; Merriam & Associates, 2002). Moreover, two colleagues served as peer debriefers, questioning me and commenting on the study. Transferability was enhanced via rich, thick description of the data collected (Creswell, 2003). Triangulation of data from one-on-one interviews, the focus group, participant observation, and document analysis aided in ensuring the dependability of this study (Marshall & Rossman, 1995). A major technique in establishing confirmability is the confirmability audit, or audit trail (Lincoln & Guba, 1985). Using a three-ring binder, I created an audit trail, which included all raw data, including tape recordings and field notes from the interviews, focus group, and observations. An additional aspect of confirmability is reflexivity on the part of the researcher. As such, I kept a journal that included personal notes and reflections.

Personally, I must acknowledge my insider/outsider status as a researcher for this study. I am a member of the Latino/a community, specifically Cuban. I was raised in the Southeastern United States and attended an HIS community college. I am also a member of a Latino fraternity, Phi Iota Alpha Fraternity, Inc. It is important to note that the Latino fraternity that I studied is not the same organization to which I belong. I acknowledge that would be a conflict of interest. My insider status as a member of the Latino/a and Latino fraternity communities provided me with opportunities to which a non-Latino/a or non-Latino fraternity researcher may not have had access.

Although being a member of a LGLO increased my insider status, I could possibly have been seen as an outsider as well, which could have decreased my ability to gain the trust of the participants. My goal was to let members of Omega Beta know that although I am a member of Phi Iota Alpha, our commonality as members of Latino fraternities was most important. In addition, I stressed to them the importance of this study as no one has yet explored how membership in a Latino fraternity affects members' ethnic identity development.

Data Analysis

Moustakas's (1994) method of organizing phenomenological data assisted me in coding and analyzing the data I collected about Latino fraternity members' experiences. I began data analysis after my first set of interviews and continued after I completed my last interviews. Throughout the interviews, focus group, and observations, I reflected on my own experience and the interactions between the participants and me. I began transcribing the audiotaped interviews and focus group while on-site and completed this work once I returned home. After I completed transcribing, I began open coding, "working intensively with the data, line by line" (Esterberg, 2002, p. 158), developed tentative ideas, and placed them into "invariant meaning units and themes" (Moustakas, p. 122). Specifically, I made notes in the margins of my transcripts and used different colored highlighters; each color represented an emerging theme. Through inductive data

analysis, notes were grouped into themes that led to interpretations and findings (Whitt, 1991).

◼ FINDINGS AND DISCUSSION

The findings derived through phenomenological data analysis (Moustakas, 1994) yielded six different themes related to the three primary research questions guiding this study: family, the HSI campus, other Greeks and Greek Affairs policies, gender, language, and involvement. Figure 20.1 provides a visual representation of identified themes as viewed through the lens of Bronfenbrenner's bioecological theory of human development (2005).

For purposes of this study, each theme is presented in the context of the five systems within the theoretical model that guided this study: microsystems (home family, Latino fraternity, and HSI campus); mesosytems (language and involvement); exosystem (Other Greeks and Greek Affairs policies); macrosystem (gender); and chronosystem (past events).

Microsystems

The significance of family was described by participants throughout the three interviews and the focus group. Participants provided a variety of rich examples that highlighted the importance family played in their ethnic identity development. The theme of family is divided into two subcategories: home family and

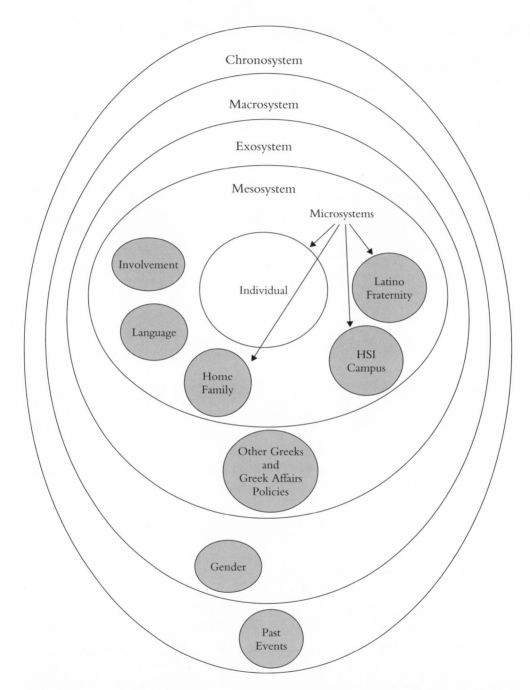

Figure 20.1.   Visual Representation of Identified Themes as Viewed Through the Lens of Bronfenbrenner's Bioecological Theory of Human Development (2005).

the fraternity *hermandad* (brotherhood). An additional microsystem is the HSI campus environment.

Home Family

Home family played an important role in members' ethnic identity development as described by various participants. Siebel, who chose both Latino-identified and Subgroup-identified racial identity orientations, stated, "Well pretty much my ethnic identity development I owe to my family because they're the ones that brought me up the way they did." In addition, his family has helped him see himself as a "Latino, and not just Cuban." Rodrigo added that his family "always instilled in me to be prideful of where I came from . . . and remember my roots," which supports his Latino-identified racial identity orientation. *Familismo* refers to "the importance of the extended family as a reference group and as providers of social support" (Tatum, 1997, p. 137). One example that highlights *familismo* was Tony's upbringing without his father around and how the extended family provided him with male role models. In addition, he mentioned that he views his cousins more like brothers and sisters. Further, Tony credits his family as the reason he identifies as Cuban, which also influenced him in identifying with the Latino-integrated orientation.

Fraternity Hermandad

Miranda and Martin de Figueroa (2000) explained that LGLOs provide a family atmosphere on college and university campuses. In his dissertation study, Reyes (1997) described how an ethnic fraternity provided his participants with a sense of family. Moreover, LGLOs serve as a home away from home for students and provide on-campus camaraderie and support networks that are important to the academic, social, and cultural lives of Latino/a college students (Jerez, 2004; Mejia, 1994; Puente, 1992). The Latino fraternity also played an important part in members' ethnic identity development in this study. Siebel stated, "The thing of the fraternity, they helped me see a lot more of who I am . . . the brothers have helped me see myself as a Latino." Participants also defined ethnic identity within the fraternity as "diverse" and "multicultural" within a Latino context, suggesting that "it's the [Latino] culture that defines us."

The fraternity *hermandad* also played a strong role in how members' identified ethnically. Castro (2004) noted that membership in multicultural Greek organizations "provide[s] support as well as cultural education to individuals who are still defining the many aspects of their identity" (p. 1). For Bart, Siebel, and David, the Omega Beta *hermandad* has assisted them in identifying outside of their respective Latino/a nationalities with the greater Latino/a community, thus providing them with affirming messages regarding their ethnic identities. Joe's racial identity orientations ranged from Latino-identified to White-identified. He mentioned that the brothers of Omega Beta have assisted him in exploring the Latino side of his ethnic identity: They "helped me be more

Latino." In addition, identifying with the greater Latino/a community allowed these men to embrace a Pan-American view of Latinos/as as they discussed the economic, political, and social issues affecting the Latin American nations.

Several participants mentioned that the educational process Omega Beta members go through enhanced their ethnic identity development. Through the educational process, members learned more about the organization and about themselves. Joe noted, "I would say that our educational process kind of helps you bring out the Latino in you, I guess that's the best way to say it." Bart added, "You prove a lot to yourself pretty much [during the educational process]. You learn a lot about yourself."

HSI Campus

Finally, the HSI campus also contributed to members' ethnic identity development. Latino University's campus environment embraces and promotes the Latino/a culture in a variety of ways, including providing Latino-style fast food and nightly salsa dancing classes. In addition, many faculty and staff at Latino University identify as Hispanic/Latino/a and speak Spanish. Bart said, "I'm surrounded by nothing but Hispanics and that's a good feeling." In addition, participants mentioned that they are in a comfortable environment where a majority of the students look like them and speak Spanish. As Bob eloquently stated, "You know this campus has actually made me realize that there's a lot more pride in actually being Hispanic . . . [it]

basically just boosted [my ethnic identity] up." Rodrigo summed it up: "We're at [Latino University] and everyone's just Latino . . . you really don't ever feel out of place here. Nothing reminds you more of it."

Mesosystems

Language emerged from the interrelation between participants' home families and the Latino fraternity; involvement emerged from the interrelation between the Latino fraternity and HSI campus. As such, language and involvement were two themes from the mesosystem described by participants as having an influence on their ethnic identity development.

Language

Language was an important part of participants' ethnic identity development. Most of the 7 men spoke Spanish; others spoke English and some Spanglish. *Spanglish* is a combination of English and Spanish and is spoken by most second- and third-generation Hispanics living in the United States. It emerges when one switches from Spanish to English (and vice versa) within the same sentence. Padilla (1997) described how Latino/as "have created an everyday language by transforming the language of the dominant culture—almost ridiculing standard English—into a vernacular speech intelligible only to us" (p. 27). Bart's racial identity orientations were both Latino-integrated and Latino-identified, and he described how important it is for him to continue speaking his native language:

"Growing up here [in the United States], my parents made sure I knew how to speak Spanish. Even though I don't speak it perfect because I learned it from them, but as long as I maintain [it] is what matters the most. And I think that's every Hispanic's goal when they move here is to maintain the language." However, David's first language was English because his mother wanted him to assimilate into the larger dominant White society. However, David knew Spanglish and using it was his form of cultural resistance. For David, speaking Spanglish defies "the dominant culture, a moment of liberation" (Padilla, p. 26). For Bart, David, and the other participants, speaking Spanish and Spanglish keeps them connected to their culture and enhances their ethnic identity.

Various participants discussed the interrelation of language between participants' home families and Omega Beta. Siebel noted that speaking Spanish with fraternity brothers is an extension of speaking Spanish with family. Through the fraternity, he felt that "I have this thing [connection] to a certain group." Rodrigo, a native Spanish speaker at home, mentioned that he enjoys speaking his native tongue with his fraternity brothers. Thus, speaking Spanish with family is reinforced and supported by his fraternity brothers. The fraternity also increased participants' knowledge of Spanish. For example, Bob stressed that knowing Spanish is an essential aspect of the Omega Beta educational process: "I would say mostly through our educational process. We encounter certain parts where

we actually obviously have to speak in Spanish to understand what you're saying in Spanish." David elaborated,

> We have certain information and education that's in Spanish. At one level you have to be able to speak some words in Spanish and know what they mean and regardless of people who aren't Latino and join [Omega Beta]; they end up learning something out of it.

Participants explained how knowing Spanish enhanced their ethnic identity development. Bart noted that "[Spanish] helps me so I don't forget from where I come from." David added, "When we're together [as a fraternity] we speak Spanish and Spanish is kind of like our family language."

Involvement

The participants stressed that being involved is an important part of their fraternity and collegiate experience at Latino University. Siebel reflected, "If it wasn't for the fraternity I probably wouldn't be involved in any extracurricular activities here [at Latino University]." Joe noted that after joining the Latino fraternity "you want to just start being involved . . . and so it starts snowballing and stuff." Other participants mentioned that their involvement in Omega Beta led to their becoming involved in other campus organizations, including, for example, the Hispanic Heritage Month Committee, which aided in their ethnic identity development, and the Student Programming Council. Through their involvement in Omega Beta and other clubs and organizations on campus, participants' collegiate experience and ethnic identity were enhanced.

Exosystem

Participants shared strong feelings during individual interviews and the focus group about other Greeks and Greek Affairs policies at Latino University, both of which can be considered aspects of the exosystem that indirectly influence identity development. Members of Omega Beta mentioned how they are well received by other minority Greeks and the Black Greek letter organizations, but are perceived differently by mainstream fraternities and sororities. Bob elaborated on how the mainstream Greeks view them, specifically because they were the only Latino fraternity at Latino University: "It's the thug-looking guys, those bad boys, the Latin boys; we're labeled as that because [we're] in a Latino fraternity."

Participants also discussed how Greek Affairs policies inhibit their culture and ethnic identity development. The Latino fraternity is a member of the Interfraternity Council, which consists of all the mainstream fraternities. David shared his thoughts:

> I myself don't really care much for IFC. They talk about mainly issues that have nothing really to do with us. We talk about rush [enrollment membership for mainstream fraternities] for an hour or two and we're sitting there like, "We

don't rush, so there's nothing for us to even discuss."

His statement reflects that although David identified with the Latino-integrated orientation, he views Whites as distinct, either as barriers or allies, from the Latino-identified orientation. Bob explained that they would rather have a multicultural Greek council to serve their needs.

> If we did have...a Multicultural Greek Council...I think we would be able to do more events as a whole...[and] more people, Hispanic people [would] really actually want to join what would be a multicultural organization whether it be Latino or multicultural, but it gives them more of an option.

Having a multicultural Greek council would enhance members' ethnic identity development as they would be supported by a variety of other Latino and multicultural Greek organizations.

Macrosystem

The macrosystem includes aspects of the larger societal culture that affect individuals. Some participants discussed how the macrosystem of gender played a role in their ethnic identity development. Bart shared how becoming a member of the fraternity also helped him with his gender identity:

> [The] thing I value the most is earning the [Greek] letters because it was one of the hardest things [to do] but

it represented a lot more than just the letters. It represented a step towards becoming a man and towards taking responsibility.

Joe elaborated: "I think Latino men got to have a lot more pride as far as like [being] protective, like don't mess with my family." Santiago Rivera (2003) stated that an aspect of *machismo* behavior is the Latino male displaying a protective attitude toward members of his family. Gonzalez (1996) pointed out that "Latino men have been more hesitant in reevaluating their gender roles than White males" (p. xv). How the intersection of gender and ethnic identity was viewed and defined by members of Omega Beta Latino fraternity was an important aspect of this study as all participants were Latino males.

Chronosystem

The past experiences participants shared, such as where they grew up, how they were raised by their families, and their experiences in and out of school, helped to shape who they are as Latinos and how they choose to identify with regard to their ethnic identities. Members of Omega Beta described past events and experiences that contributed to their ethnic identity development. Bob, who chose the Latino–integrated orientation, mentioned how his family influenced his ethnic identity:

Since I was raised by my grandparents ...having that type of Hispanic influence is major, even though [I was]

born in the United States, you have to accustom yourself to American ways, but at the same time try not to forget your Latin roots. I was always [taught] that.

Joe mentioned that because his father is from Trinidad and his mother is from Puerto Rico, his dual ethnicity allowed him to create his own ethnic identity:

I [identify as] Trinirican...Because at first I used to be like, "Oh, yeah I'm Spanish and Trinidadian." Latino people aren't always the same, it's like you have to be more specific. So it kind of evolved into Trinirican after a while.

Throughout this study, participants were allowed to self-identify and choose the term that best described their ethnic identity. Most members of Omega Beta identified with their families' country of origin as opposed to Hispanic or Latino, terms often associated with members of the Latino/a community. In addition, participants selected the racial identity orientation(s) from Ferdman and Gallegos's (2001) model that best described them. We found no research that had previously applied Ferdman and Gallegos's model to Latino/a college students or at an HSI. Although Ferdman and Gallegos's model uses the label, racial identity orientation, it was suitable for Latino fraternity members when selecting an orientation that described their ethnic identity. For example, Siebel chose the Latino-identified and Subgroup-identified orientations because his ethnic identity revolves around his Cuban nationality within the context of the broader Latino/a community. As such, the model proved to be beneficial to describe the Latino population within this HSI institutional context.

■ CONCLUSIONS

Data collected were compared with the theoretical model guiding this study, which resonated with the experiences participants shared regarding the six major themes that emerged: family, the HSI campus, other Greeks and Greek Affairs policies, gender, language, and involvement. When presented collectively, these themes provide an understanding of how membership in a Latino fraternity at an HSI enhances members' ethnic identity development. Responses to the three research questions that guided this study were specifically addressed during the analysis. The first question asked how ethnic identity is defined within the Latino fraternity. Members of Omega Beta Latino fraternity defined ethnic identity within the Latino fraternity as "diverse," "multicultural," and "a big pot of jambalaya mixed ethnicities." Siebel stated, "It's the culture that defines us." Although Omega Beta is historically a Latino fraternity, many members, including some members at Latino University, were not Latino. As such, participants felt that "diverse" and "multicultural" best captured how ethnic identity is defined by Omega Beta Latino fraternity.

The second question was focused on ways that membership in a Latino fraternity at a Hispanic-Serving Institution enhances members' ethnic identity development. Omega Beta Latino fraternity provided members with various opportunities that enhance their ethnic identity. The *hermandad* provided members with a familial atmosphere and Latino unity. Participants noted that there was an "instant love" between brothers and that being a member allowed them to explore their identity outside their respective nationalities and identify with the broader Latino/a community. In addition, many participants pointed out that they are able to speak and comprehend Spanish as a result of their fraternity involvement. Omega Beta members mentioned how the fraternity provided some members the opportunity to learn Spanish and others the opportunity to practice speaking Spanish more often. Whether it was through the educational process, during chapter meetings and activities, or performing their greeting, speaking Spanish enhanced members' awareness of their ethnic identity.

The final question regarded ways in which attending an HSI enhances the ethnic identity development of Latino fraternity members beyond the contributions made by membership in the Latino fraternity. Participants constantly discussed ways in which attending an HIS enhanced their ethnic identities, including interactions with Hispanic/Latino/a faculty and staff and the many ways in which the university catered to the Latino/a community. Moreover, attending a University where 54.2% of the population identified as Hispanic also contributed to their ethnic identity development.

■ IMPLICATIONS

Findings from this study highlight how membership in a Latino fraternity at an HIS enhances members' ethnic identity development. These findings suggest implications that student affairs and higher education administrators, such as deans of students, Greek affairs coordinators, and campus diversity professionals should consider as they advise and/or work with Latino fraternities, both at HSIs and at non-HSI campuses.

This study illustrated how a Latino fraternity enhances members' ethnic identity development. Similar to the findings of other researchers (Jerez, 2004; Mejia, 1994; Miranda & Martin de Figueroa, 2000; Puente, 1992; Wingett, 2004), participants explained that they joined Omega Beta Latino fraternity because they sought an organization that embraced the Latino culture and provided them with a familial (*hermandad*) atmosphere on campus. Members also described how speaking Spanish was reinforced and supported by fraternity brothers. These findings suggest that membership in a Latino fraternity enhances members' ethnic identity. Student affairs and higher education administrators should take note that members of Latino fraternities seek out such organizations because the LGLOs embrace the Latino/a culture and provide a familial atmosphere, which

in some cases may not be found in the general campus environment. Promoting Latino/a fraternities and sororities, as well as other Latino/a organizations, can be a way of supporting Latino/a students and enriching their college experience.

The HSI campus environment also encourages members' ethnic identity development. As Bob and David stated, the campus enhanced their pride as Latinos. The campus environment is filled with elements of the Latino/a culture, including language, cultural traditions, and food. In addition, most faculty and staff are Latino/a, which also played an important part in members' ethnic identity development. Other studies have indicated that HSI campuses support the development of the Latino/a culture and understand the needs of their Latino/a students. Dayton, Gonzalez-Vasquez, Martinez, and Plum (2004) found that students described HSIs as institutional environments that comforted them and where faculty and staff supported them. Non-HSIs should consider hiring bilingual Latino/a faculty and staff who can contribute to the campus's Latino/a culture and support this student population.

Participants suggested that a Multicultural Greek Council would further enhance members' ethnic identity development. Such councils provide students the opportunity to be around other Greeks who have similar racial and ethnic backgrounds, which can encourage all members' ethnic (and possibly racial) identity development. Greek affairs professionals who have multicultural Greek councils on their respective campuses understand that the needs of multicultural Greeks are very different from those of traditional mainstream Greek organizations. Some examples of the differences between traditional Greek councils (such as Interfraternity and Panhellenic councils) and Multicultural Greek councils include the governance structure, recruitment of prospective members, the membership intake/educational process for initiates, and commitment to the unification of organizations whose purpose is to promote diversity and inclusion in the campus community. As such, Greek affairs and student affairs professionals who do not have multicultural Greek councils on their campuses may want to consider establishing such a council.

Implications for Future Research

No previous research had been conducted on how membership in a Latino fraternity at an HSI enhances members' ethnic identity development. As such, this study opens the door for more research focusing on ethnic identity development of Latino/a college students and on Latino/a fraternities and sororities.

Throughout my time at Latino University, I discovered that a majority of Latino/a students at Latino University are members of mainstream fraternities and sororities. Does membership in mainstream fraternities and sororities (and possibly Black Greek letter organizations) also enhance members' ethnic identity development? If so, in what way? These questions merit further investigation.

Research should also be conducted on the ethnic identity development of Latino/a college students not affiliated with LGLOs. For example, a study on the ethnic identity development of Latino/a college students involved in cultural clubs and organizations is warranted. In addition, what influence does membership in non–Latino/a cultural clubs and organizations have on Latino/a college students' ethnic identity development?

Torres (2003) suggested that Latino/a college student ethnic identity development should be investigated in different contexts and social environments. Previous research on Latino/a college student ethnic identity development has taken place mostly at predominantly White institutions and community colleges (Nuñez, 2004; Schneider & Ward, 2003; Torres, 1999, 2003; Torres & Baxter Magolda, 2004). Although the current study adds information about ethnic identity development at an HSI, research on the ethnic identity development of Latino/a college students attending historically Black colleges and universities and tribal colleges warrants consideration.

Future research studies should also consider the ethnic identity development of Latino/a graduate students who become members of LGLOs. Another avenue to explore would be to compare the experiences of graduate students who are members or are considering becoming members of LGLOs, to the experiences of undergraduates, and what, if any, influence membership has on their ethnic identity development.

Limitations of the Study

There were several limitations in this study, including that the study took place at only one HSI and only one Latino fraternity was asked to participate. Because this study focused on the experiences and accounts of Latino fraternity members at an HSI located in the Southeast, the results from this study cannot be generalized to all Latino fraternities at HSIs, let alone all HSIs. In addition, the ethnic identity development of Latino university men outside of the fraternity at the HSI was not addressed.

I was further limited by the 4-week time period of my on-site visit at Latino University. However, I was familiar with Latino University through several friends who attended and work at the institution. In addition, I visited the campus previously during my "contact visit" (Seidman, 1998), which allowed me to get a better understanding of the campus environment. Moreover, during the contact visit I met with two members of Omega Beta, and we established a rapport even before I arrived at Latino University in Spring 2006.

Second, my "insider status" as a member of the Latino/a community and of a Latino fraternity allowed me greater access to the participants. Marin and VanOss-Marin (1991) suggested that "same-ethnicity data collectors should be employed in research projects where

personal contact is involved" (p. 53). Specifically, they "can enhance rapport, [the] willingness to disclose, and the validity and reliability of the data provided" (Marin & VanOss-Marin, p. 53). Participants in the study were very candid and forthcoming with their responses, and I strongly believe that being a member of both the Latino/a and Latino Greek communities enhanced and validated the data collected.

REFERENCES

Adam, M. (1999, February 26). Greeks empowering Hispanics. *Hispanic Outlook in Higher Education, 12*, 17–19.

Anson, J. L., & Marchesani, R. F. (Eds.). (1991). *Baird's manual of American college fraternities* (20th ed). Indianapolis, IN: Baird's Manual Foundation.

Astin, A. W. (1984). Student involvement: A developmental theory. *Journal of College Student Personnel, 25*, 297–308.

Astin, A. W. (1993). *What matters in college: Four critical years revisited*. San Francisco: Jossey-Bass.

Atkinson, D. R., Morten, G., & Sue, D. W. (1983). *Counseling American minorities*. Dubuque, IA: Brown.

Baily, H. J. (Ed.). (1949). *Baird's manual of American college fraternities* (15th ed). Menasha, WI: Banta.

Bronfenbrenner, U. (1995). Developmental ecology through space and time: A future perspective. In P. Moen & G. H. Elder, Jr. (Eds.), *Examining lives in context: Perspectives* on the ecology of human development (pp. 619–647). Washington, DC: American Psychological Association.

Bronfenbrenner, U. (Ed.). (2005a). *Making human beings human: Bioecological perspectives on human development*. Thousand Oaks, CA: Sage.

Bronfenbrenner, U. (2005b). Ecological systems theory. In U. Bronfenbrenner (Ed.), *Making human beings human: Bioecological perspectives on human development* (pp. 106–173). Thousand Oaks, CA: Sage.

Castro, M. M. (2004, April). The growth of multicultural organizations. Retrieved October 4, 2005 from http://www.fraternity advisors.org/pdf/prof_dev/2005_04_PD.pdf

Creswell, J. W. (2003). *Research design: Qualitative, quantitative, and mixed methods approaches* (2nd ed). Thousand Oaks, CA: Sage.

Cross, W. (1978). The Thomas and Cross models of psychological nigrescence: A literature review. *Journal of Black Psychology*, 4, 13–31.

Crotty, M. (1998). *The foundations of social research*. Thousand Oaks, CA: Sage.

Dayton, B., Gonzalez-Vasquez, N., Martinez, C., & Plum, C. (2004). Hispanic-serving institutions through the eyes of students and administrators. In A. M. Ortiz (Ed.), *Addressing the unique needs of Latino American students* (New Directions for Student Services, No. 105, pp. 29–40). San Francisco: Jossey-Bass.

Esterberg, K. G. (2002). *Qualitative methods in social research*. Boston: McGraw Hill.

Evans, N. J., Forney, D. S., & Guido-Dibrito, F. (1998). *Student development in college: Theory, research, and practice*. San Francisco: Jossey-Bass.

Ferdman, B. M., & Gallegos, P. I. (2001). Racial identity development and Latinos in the United States. In C. L. Wijeyesinghe & B. W. Jackson III (Eds.), *New perspectives on racial identity development: A theoretical and practical anthology* (pp. 32–66). New York: New York University Press.

Fine, E. C. (2003). *Soulstepping: African American step shows*. Chicago: University of Illinois Press.

Gonzalez, R. (Ed.). (1996). *Muy macho: Latino men confront their manhood*. New York: Random House.

Helem, L. (2004). Greeks go Latin—or vice versa. Retrieved November 4, 2005 from http://www.msnbc.msn.com/id/6314738/site/newsweek/

Helms, J. (1990). *Black and White racial identity: Theory, research, and practice*. New York: Greenwood.

Jerez, Y. (2004, September/October). It's all Greek to me. *iCarambaU. College Magazine*, 12 .

Johnson, C. S. (1972). *Fraternities in our colleges*. New York: National Interfraternity Foundation.

Kim, J. (1981). *The process of Asian-American identity development: A study of Japanese American women's perception of their struggle to achieve positive identities*. Doctoral dissertation, University of Massachusetts, Amherst.

Kimbrough, W. M. (2002, January 22). *Guess who's coming to campus: The growth of Black, Latin and Asian fraternal organizations*. Retrieved October 4, 2005 from http://www.naspa.org/membership/mem/nr/article.cfm?id = 563

Kimbrough, W. M. (2003). *Black Greek 101*. Madison, NJ: Fairleigh Dickinson University Press.

Lincoln, Y. S., & Guba, E. G. (1985). *Naturalistic inquiry*. Newbury Park, CA: Sage.

Llagas, C., & Snyder, T. D. (2003). *Status and trends in the education of Hispanics* (NCES 2003–008). Washington, DC: U.S. Department of Education, National Center for Education Statistics.

Marin, G., & VanOss-Marin, B. (1991). *Research with Hispanic populations* (Applied Social Science Research Methods Series, Vol. 23). Newbury Park, CA: Sage.

Marshall, C., & Rossman, G. B. (1995). *Designing qualitative research* (2nd ed). Thousand Oaks, CA: Sage.

Mejia, A. (1994, October). Hispanics go Greek. *Hispanic, 7*, 34.

Merriam, S. B., & Associates. (2002). *Qualitative research in practice*. San Francisco: Jossey-Bass.

Miranda, M. L., & Martin de Figueroa, M. (2000, Summer). *Adelante hacia el futuro!* (Forward to the future) Latino/Latina students: Past, present, and future. *Perspectives*, 6–8.

Morgan, D. L. (1997). *Focus groups as qualitative research*. Thousand Oaks, CA: Sage.

Moustakas, C. (1994). *Phenomenological research methods*. Thousand Oaks, CA: Sage.

Nuñez, J. G. (2004). *The empowerment of Latina university students: A phenomenological study of ethnic identity development through involvement in a Latina-based sorority*. Unpublished master's thesis, Iowa State University, Ames.

Padilla, F. M. (1997). *The struggle of Latino/Latina university students: In search of a liberating education*. New York: Routledge.

Pascarella, E., Edison, M., Nora, A., Hagedorn, L., & Terenzini, P. (1996). Influences on students' openness to diversity and challenge in the first year of college. *Journal of Higher Education, 67*, 174–195.

Pascarella, E. T., & Terenzini, P. T. (2005). *How college affects students (Vol. 2)*: A third decade of research. San Francisco: Jossey-Bass.

Phinney, J. S. (1993). A three-stage model of ethnic identity development in adolescence. In M. E. Bernal & G. P. Knight (Eds.), *Ethnic identity: Formation and transmission among Hispanics and other minorities* (pp. 61–79). New York: State University of New York Press.

Phinney, J. S., & Alipuria, L. L. (1990). Ethnic identity in college students from four ethnic groups. *Journal of Adolescence, 13*, 171–183.

Puente, T. (1992, March). Special report: Hispanics on campus—Getting organized. *Hispanic*, 31–32.

Renn, K. (2003). Understanding the identities of mixed-race college students through a developmental ecology lens. *Journal of College Student Development, 44*, 383–403.

Reyes, G. (1997). *Does participation in an ethnic fraternity enable persistence in college?* Unpublished doctoral dissertation, University of Southern California.

Rodriguez, R. (1995). *Hermandades* on campus: Elite Latino secret societies and fraternities of the past give way to today's brotherhoods and sisterhoods. *Black Issues in Higher Education, 12,* 26–29.

Santiago, D. A. (2007). Choosing Hispanic-serving institutions (HSIs): A closer look at Latino students' college choices. *Excelencia in Education*: Washington, D.C.

Santiago-Rivera, A. (2003). Latinos values and family transitions: Practical considerations for counseling. *Counseling and Human Development, 35,* 1–20.

Schneider, M. E., & Ward, D. J. (2003). The role of ethnic identification and perceived social support in Latinos' adjustment to college. *Hispanic Journal of Behavioral Sciences, 25,* 539–553.

Seidman, I. (1998). *Interviewing as qualitative research.* New York: Teachers College Press.

Tatum, B. D. (1997). *Why are all the Black kids sitting together in the cafeteria?* New York: Basic Books.

Torbenson, C. L. (2005). The origin and evolution of college fraternities and sororities. In T. Brown, G. S. Parks, & C. M. Phillips (Eds.), *African American fraternities and sororities: The legacy and the vision* (pp. 37–66). Kentucky: University Press of Kentucky.

Torres, V. (1999). Validation of a bicultural orientation model for Hispanic college students. *Journal of College Student Development, 40,* 285–298.

Torres, V. (2003). Influences on ethnic identity development of Latino college students in the first two years of college. *Journal of College Student Development, 44,* 532–547.

Torres, V., & Baxter Magolda, M. (2004). Reconstructing Latino identity: The influence of cognitive development on the ethnic identity process of Latino students. *Journal of College Student Development, 45,* 333–347.

U.S. Census Bureau. (2005, September 8). *Hispanic heritage month: September 15–October 15.* Retrieved October 5, 2005 from http://www.census.gov/Press-Release/ www/releases/archives/facts_for_features_ special_editions/005338.html

Whipple, E. G., & Sullivan, E. G. (1998). Greek letter organizations: Communities of learners? In E. G. Whipple (Ed.), *New challenges for Greek letter organizations: Transforming fraternities and sororities into learning communities* (New Directions for Student Services, No. 81, pp. 19–27). San Francisco: Jossey-Bass.

Whitt, E. J. (1991). Artful science: A primer on qualitative research methods. *Journal of College Student Development, 32,* 406–415.

Wingett, Y. (2004, September 30). *Minorities going Greek: Find connection in ethnic fraternities, sororities.* Retrieved October 4, 2005, from http://www.azcentral.com/ families/education/articles/0930latinoblack frats.html

CHAPTER 21

Exploring the Lives of Asian American Men

Racial Identity, Male Role Norms, Gender Role Conflict, and Prejudicial Attitudes

William M. Liu

As the body of masculinity literature grows, understanding masculinity among men of color (i.e., racial and ethnic minority men) remains limited. This limitation is potentially problematic for masculinity research and clinical applications because race and racism are salient issues among people of color (Helms, 1995). Specifically, it is unclear how men of color navigate expectations of masculinity set forth by the dominant White society that marginalizes men of color. The research limitations seem especially pertinent for Asian American men because socioculturally, they have been racially stereotyped as effeminate and nonmasculine (Chua & Fujino, 1999; Mok, 1998). Although a few research studies exist (e.g., Chua & Fujino, 1999; Kim, O'Neil, & Owen, 1996; Levant, Wu, & Fischer, 1996), the relationship between racism and masculinity among Asian American men specifically has been left virtually unexamined. Thus, to fully understand Asian American masculinity, psychologists need to appreciate the complexity of Asian American masculine experiences as a product of masculine and racial intersections. The focus of this study was to explore the relationship between racism, prejudicial attitudes, and masculinity.

■ ASIAN AMERICAN MEN'S HISTORY AND CULTURE

History

To begin understanding the cultural and racial issues Asian American men negotiate, it is important to grasp their history and current situation. Asian Americans, in general, represent a broad group of ethnic backgrounds that have been "racialized" into a homogenous racial group

415

in the United States (J. W. Chan, 1998; Omi & Winant, 1994). From Orientals, to Yellow and Brown people, to Asian Americans, to Asian Pacific Americans, and, finally, to Asian American and Pacific Islanders (Federal Register, 1997; Uba, 1994), racial malleability has been part of the struggle for self-definition. However, along with racial and ethnic self-determinism, Asian American men have also struggled to break stereotypes and redefine themselves as men in the United States (J. W. Chan, 1998; Mok, 1998).

From the early 1800s as the United States ventured into Asia seeking trade and territory, Asia and its inhabitants have been gendered as feminine to facilitate American and European colonialism (Takaki, 1990). Asia and its people became quintessential feminine beings to the West's masculinity. Consequently, Asian women became prototypical women while Asian men were "emasculated," "feminized," and marginalized (J. W. Chan, 1998; Leupp, 1995; Mok, 1998). Early Asian male settlers in the United States, many of whom were seeking work, were considered to be cheap, non-masculine labor that was exploited by American industry. Working on the railroads, sugar cane plantations of Hawaii, ore mining, factories, and on farms, many Chinese, Asian Indian, Japanese, Filipinos, and Korean migrants found themselves subjected to racism, lynching, job exclusion, denial of citizenship and land ownership, anti-miscegenation laws (laws against racial intermixing), and, eventually, immigration exclusion (S. Chan, 1991; Takaki, 1990). These hostilities did not

end in the early 1900s, but continued as Vietnamese and South Asians (e.g., Cambodians and Laotians) were also targeted as the United States participated in various conflicts from the 1950s through the 1970s. To this day, Asian Americans are still singled out for racism and experience marginalization.

Culture

Some Asian American men are brought up under stringent gender role expectations such as a focus on group harmony and filial piety, carrying on their family name and conforming to the expectations of the parents (S. J. Lee, 1996). Often, pleasing parents and parental pressure to succeed lead to academic stress, poor self-image and performance, and interpersonal dysfunction. Depending on age and acculturation, though, cultural and masculinity issues may vary. For example, among older Asian American men, especially fathers, threats to their patriarchal position (i.e., a loss of masculinity, stress and frustration, and inability to be the breadwinner) within the family may result in a reassertion of control over the family through physical abuse (Lum, 1998; Rimonte, 1991). For some men, domestic violence is justified or minimized as a culturally congruent means to reinforce cultural and patriarchal structures (Rimonte, 1991).

Among Southeast Asians (e.g., Vietnamese, Cambodians, and Laotians) who fled turmoil in their homelands and found themselves unprepared for a new culture and life as expatriates (K. Chin,

1996; Kibria, 1993; Long, 1996; Zhou & Bankston, 1998), isolation and alienation sometimes created hostile family conditions. Many men lost their families, jobs and earning ability, status and authority, community, and loved ones upon arriving in the United States. Women working was also perceived to further dissolve men's patriarchal position. Japanese American men also experienced a similar condition during and following their internment (Nagata, 1998). For Southeast Asian men, because a sense of powerlessness and depression often follows migration changes, efforts to regain their masculinity were often brutally fraught with domestic violence and jealous outbursts that centered on the "American" man's (i.e. White) money and sexual prowess (Kibria, 1993). The end result drove away loved ones and further magnified their marginal status as men in America.

Contemporary Asian American Masculinity Problems

Racism adds to the confusion of being a minority man in America. For instance, even though the model minority image (e.g., educationally and economically successful) is supposedly positive, Asian American men are still denigrated as asexual overachievers (J. W. Chan, 1998; Mok, 1998). Chan postulated that Asian American men are faced with a choice when confronted with the White masculine norm. For many Asian American men it is either copy the dominant White male or "accept the fact we are

not men" (J. W. Chan, 1998, p. 94). This middle ground is a difficult position for Asian American men because they may need to simultaneously accept and repudiate the White masculine norm in search of alternative definitions of masculinity (J. W. Chan, 1998).

However, it is unclear how Asian American men negotiate issues of masculinity because much of the research has not focused on the lives of men of color (Cazenare, 1984; Lazur & Majors, 1995). When research has focused on Asian American men, they are typically compared with "normative" White masculinity. For example, Chua and Fujino (1999) found that Asian American men did not see their masculinity in opposition to femininity. Instead, Asian American masculinity was usually tied to being polite, obedient, and a willingness to do domestic tasks, whereas White men endorsed a more traditional notion of masculinity that avoided those attributes listed by Asian American men (Chua & Fujino, 1999). This study, though, is limited because no measures of racism or masculinity were used and the focus was on comparing Asian American masculinity to White masculinity. Additionally, it is unclear how Asian American men understand or cope with gender role conflicts and expectations or racism.

Kim et al. (1996) studied gender role conflict among 125 Asian Americans. Along with the Gender-Role Conflict Scale (GRCS; O'Neil, Helms, Gable, David, & Wrightsman, 1986), she gave the participants the Suinn-Lew Asian Self-Identity Acculturation Scale

(SL-ASIA; Suinn, Ahuna, & Khoo, 1992). Results generally showed no differences in acculturation scores along four patterns of gender role conflict (Kim et al., 1996). In a canonical correlation, the gender role conflict domains corresponding with higher acculturation scores were success, power, and competition and acculturation was related to lower scores on restrictive emotionality (Kim et al., 1996). The authors contended that restricting emotions is one of the costs that Asian American must deal with in their success. Acculturation was another important variable because the Asian American men may have felt freer to display their emotions as American society generally has a more liberal notion on the expression of affect than in typical Asian societies (Kim et al., 1996). The problem with this study is in the use of an acculturation instrument rather than a racial identity instrument that could explicitly address the effects of race and racism. Kohatsu (1992) has shown that acculturation tends not to provide any significant explanatory power over racial identity, and that research wanting to investigate the issue of "race" in the lives of Asian Americans should use the racial identity scale.

Racial Identity

Racial identity theory is one way to understand how Asian American men experience racism (Helms, 1995). The theory has five statuses from which people think about, feel, and act toward racism in their lives. In the first status of Conformity, the person idealizes the values, beliefs, and culture of the White dominant society and denigrates his or her own race and culture (Helms, 1995). In the second status of Dissonance, the person struggles with conflicting attitudes toward the White and minority groups. The previously held beliefs (i.e., stereotypes) of minorities are questioned as well as their affiliation toward the White dominant group. The third status is Resistance and Immersion, which posits that minorities attempt to fully plumb the effects of racism in his or her life. Consequently, the reaction typically exemplified in this status is anger and hostility toward those of the White group. Guilt, anger, and shame are salient effects in this status. In an effort to purge "Whiteness" and racism from his or her life, the cognitive stance usually positions anything connected to Whiteness as evil and bad, while anything of the minority culture is good and true. The final status is Internalization (Helms, 1995), wherein the person works against racism. At this point, the individual is supposed to have a better sense of self and no need to denigrate any group, individual, or culture.

Ideally, the multicultural person is reflected in this status. In one study on racial identity, Kohatsu (1992) used the Cultural Identity Attitudes Scale (Helms & Carter, 1990) among 267 Asian American college students and found that Asian American men tended to be more aware of racism than women. In post hoc analyses of ethnic groups, Kohatsu discovered that Vietnamese men, specifically, were more aware of racism than Korean, Chinese, and Japanese women.

Prejudicial Attitudes

Prejudicial attitudes are another way of understanding oppressive attitudes. This is an important dimension because Asian American men can possibly cope and defend against racism, but still harbor other prejudicial or sexist attitudes and beliefs. These sexist attitudes and beliefs may be congruent with dominant sexist attitudes against women and may potentially offer Asian American men a way of connecting with dominant masculinity. In one study that tested this hypothesis among 289 Asian American college students, researchers found that different levels of prejudicial beliefs, as assessed by the Quick Discrimination Index (QDI; Ponterotto et al., 1995), varied according to gender and acculturation. Contrary to their initial hypothesis that acculturation into the dominant society would be related to higher prejudicial attitudes, results showed that Asian American college students who were highly acculturated tended to have lower prejudicial attitudes. Another significant finding was that men tended to have higher prejudicial attitudes than women, regardless of the level of acculturation. Results point to the possibility that Asian American men have many issues that they have to contend with other than their racial identification or cultural affiliation.

■ THE PRESENT STUDY

This exploratory study posited three hypotheses. First, there would be significant relationships between the GRCS

(O'Neil et al., 1986) subscales, total score, and the Male Role Norms Inventory (MRNI; Levant & Fischer, 1998) subscales scores and between the MRNI Traditional Attitudes Toward Masculinity total score, the People of Color Racial Identity Attitude Scale (POCRIAS; Helms, 1995), and prejudicial attitudes. Second, POCRIAS and prejudicial attitude scores will significantly predict total score. Third, POCRIAS and prejudicial attitude scores will significantly predict MRNI subscription.

■ METHOD

Participants

Out of 500 surveys distributed, 336 surveys were returned and 323 surveys were usable. Seven surveys were not filled in correctly, and women filled in the other six surveys. The overall return rate for this study was 65%. The participants were recruited from four different higher educational institutions. Participants were from a large East Coast public university ($n = 167$), a small West Coast community college ($n = 21$), a medium-sized West Coast public university ($n = 120$), and a medium-sized West Coast private university ($n = 15$). Participants were recruited from introductory psychology courses (West Coast), Asian American studies courses (East Coast), fraternity meetings (West Coast), and a fraternity alumni e-mail list.

The sample for this study had a mean age of 21.07 years ($SD = 4.09$). Of the participants, 86 were freshmen,

73 sophomores, 69 juniors, 47 seniors, 15 graduate students, 24 were college graduates, and 9 did not report any status. In an effort to collapse the ethnicity data to make meaningful categories for analyses, census guidelines developed by the Office of Management and Budget's Revisions to the Standards for the Classification of Federal Data on Race and Ethnicity (Federal Register, 1997) were used. From these standards, seven categories were formed: Chinese ($n = 118$), Korean ($n = 75$), Japanese ($n = 26$), Filipino ($n = 34$), South Asian ($n = 15$), Southeast Asian ($n = 23$), and biracial and biethnic ($n = 25$). Seven individuals reported they were racially Asian American, but reported no ethnicity data.

Instruments

People of Color Racial Identity Attitude Scale (Helms, 1995)

The POCRIAS is a 50-item inventory that measures four statuses from Helms's racial identity theory. The four statuses measured are as follows: conformity, dissonance, immersion and resistance, and internalization. A Likert scale with responses ranging from 1 (*strongly disagree*) to 5 (*strongly agree*) is used. Kohatsu's (1992) study among Asian Americans had the following Cronbach's alphas: .71 for conformity, .76 for dissonance, .74 for immersion and resistance, and .67 for integrative awareness (i.e., internalization). In this study, the Cronbach alphas were the following: .80 for the full scale, .78 for conformity, .72 for

dissonance, .75 for immersion and resistance, and .86 for internalization.

Gender-Role Conflict Scale (O'Neil et al., 1986)

The GRCS is a 37-item instrument designed to assess four dimensions of gender role conflict with the following subscales: Success, Power, and Competition (SPC); Restrictive Emotionality (RE); Restrictive Affectionate Behavior Between Men—Homophobia (RABBM); and Conflict Between Work and Family Relations (CBWFR). A 6-point Likert scale with responses ranging from 1 (*strongly disagree*) to 6 (*strongly agree*) is used. The instrument had adequate internal consistency from .80 to .87 (Good et al., 1995). In Good et al. (1995), the coefficient alphas were .92 for the total scale score, .88 for SPC, .89 for RE, .92 for RABBM, and .79 for CBWFR. For this study, the reliabilities were for the full scale .90, for SPC .84, for RE .82, for RABBM .81, and for CBWFR .77.

The Male Role Norms Inventory (Levant & Fischer, 1998)

The MRNI is a measure designed to assess the degree to which men endorse to culturally sanctioned norms for male behavior (e.g., traditional male behavior). The instrument is a 57-item measure that consists of eight subscales. Participants respond to a 7-point Likert scale with responses ranging from 1 (*strongly disagree*) to 7 (*strongly agree*). The MRNI subscales are as follows: Avoidance of

Femininity (AF), Rejection of Homosexuals (RH), Self-Reliance (SR), Aggression (AGG), Achievement/Status (Ach/Stat), Attitudes Toward Sex (Att-Sex), Restrictive Emotionality (ReEm), Non-Traditional Attitudes Toward Masculinity (Non-Trad), and Traditional Attitudes Toward Masculinity (Trad). Studies using the MRNI have shown adequate reliability for the instrument. For instance, Levant et al. (1996) compared 399 Americans with 394 Chinese from the People's Republic of China and found the following Cronbach alphas: .82 (AF), .58 (RH), .51 (SR), .65 (AGG), .69 (Ach/Stat), .81 (Att-Sex), .81 (ReEm), .56 (Non-Trad), and .88 for the total scale. Cronbach alphas for the current study were the following: .89 for the MRNI full scale, .69 (AF), .45 (RH), .73 (SR), .65 (AGG), .66 (Ach/Stat), .69 (Att-Sex), .63 (ReEm), .59 (Non-Trad), and .91 (Trad).

The Quick Discrimination Index (Ponterotto et al., 1995)

The QDI was designed to measure subtle racist and sexist attitudes. The instrument has 30 items that are answered on a 5-point Likert scale with responses ranging from 1 (strongly disagree) and 5 (strongly agree). Low scores are indicative of low sensitivity to race and gender issues and reflect higher prejudicial attitudes; high scores are indicative of greater sensitivity to race and gender issues and reflect low prejudicial attitudes. Ponterotto et al. reported a Cronbach alpha of .88 for the full scale. In a previous study of 289 Asian American college students, Liu, Pope-Davis, Nevitt, and Toporek (1999) reported a Cronbach alpha of .82. For this study, the reliability for the QDI was .69.

Procedure

Participants who were solicited in the introductory psychology and Asian American studies courses were given extra credit for filling out the packet. The principal investigator, an Asian American man, served as the survey proctor.

■ RESULTS

Analysis for Ethnic Group Differences

A one-way multivariate analysis of variance (MANOVA) was conducted to examine the differences between the independent variable—ethnic group—and the dependent variables—racial identity, GRCS, and MRNI. The results indicated a nonsignificant omnibus effect of ethnic groups on the combined dependent variables (Wilks's Lambda = .31), $F(19, 323) = 1.05$, $p > .05$. Because there were no significant differences on the racial identity, GRCS, and MRNI subscales, the ethnic groups were collapsed into seven categories. Furthermore, because no significant differences were found, ethnicity was not controlled for in the regression analyses.

Relationship Among Racial Identity, Prejudicial Attitudes, Gender Role Conflict, and Male Role Norms

A Pearson product–moment correlation was conducted on GRCS total and sub-scale scores with the MRNI subscales and total score (Table 21.1). Because this was an exploratory study, all subscales were used in the MRNI, despite low-reliability coefficients. Significant relationships were found. The GRCS total score was significantly positively associated with MRNI: AF ($r = .37, p < .01$), RH ($r = .28, p < .01$), SR ($r = .46, p < .01$), AGG ($r = .36, p < .01$), Ach/Stat ($r = .39, p < .01$), Att-Sex ($r = .19, p < .01$), ReEm ($r = .34, p < .01$), Non-Trad ($r = .20, p < .01$), and Trad ($r = .46, p < .01$). Results appear to suggest that participants who endorsed MRNI sub-scales tend to subscribe to masculine gender expectations, such as self-reliance and traditional masculine attitudes, and were also likely to experience feelings of conflict. In other words, if men were to behave according to masculine gender norms, they also had a related experience of conflict. GRCS total score was also significantly correlated with dissonance ($r = .20, p < .01$), immersion and resistance ($r = .19, p < .01$), and internalization ($r = .27, p < .01$). These results suggest that gender role conflict is salient throughout various statuses of racial identity.

The SPC subscale of the GRCS was also significantly associated with all of the MRNI subscales. The SPC subscale was significantly and positively related to AF ($r = .34, p < .01$), RH ($r = .24, p < .01$), SR ($r = .56, p < .01$), AGG ($r = .45, p < .01$), Ach/Stat ($r = .40, p < .01$), Att-Sex ($r = .11, p < .01$), ReEm ($r = .27, p < .01$), Non-Trad ($r = .27, p < .01$), and Trad ($r = .44, p < .01$). Internalization was also associated with this GRCS subscale ($r = 43, p < .01$). Results suggest those who endorsed success, power, and competition as a masculine attitude, or who believed that power and control over others and accomplishments were a measure of self-worth, were also likely to endorse certain masculine attitudes congruent with male role norms. The results suggest avoidance of feminine things, rejection of homosexuals, self-reliance, aggression, being goal oriented and status seeking, having traditional masculine attitudes toward sex, restricting emotional expression, and having both traditional and nontraditional masculine attitudes were related to the participants' feeling of being successful and powerful over others. Additionally, results suggest that as Asian American men have fewer attitudes toward denigrating racial others, control revolving around gender remains pertinent.

The RE subscale of the GRCS was significantly and positively associated with several MRNI subscales. The results showed that RE was positively related to AF ($r = .25, p < .01$), RH ($r = .15, p < .01$), SR ($r = .16, p < .01$), AGG ($r = .13, p < .05$), Ach/Stat ($r = .22, p < .01$), Att-Sex ($r = .17, p < .01$), ReEm ($r = .29, p < .01$), and Trad ($r = .27, p < .01$). Conformity ($r = .17, p < .01$), dissonance ($r = .24, p < .01$), and immersion and resistance ($r = .18,$

Table 21.1. Correlation Between Racial Identity, GRCS, MRNI, and QDI

Variable	1	2	3	4	5	6	7	8	9	10	11	12	13	14	15	16	17	18	19
GRCS																			
1. TOTAL	—																		
2. SPC	.80**	—																	
3. ReEM	.73**	.33**	—																
4. RABBM	.70**	.37**	.56**	—															
5. CBWFR	.62**	.48**	.30**	.25**	—														
MRNI																			
6. AF	.37**	.34**	.25**	.32**	.16**	—													
7. RH	.28**	.24**	.15**	.33**	.14**	.56**	—												
8. SR	.46**	.56**	.16**	.24**	.32**	.45**	.37**	—											
9. AGG	.36**	.45**	.13**	.16**	.26**	.55**	.40**	.68**	—										
10. Ach/Stat	.39**	.40**	.22**	.28**	.22**	.63**	.56**	.53**	.56**	—									
11. Att-Sex	.19**	.11*	.17**	.20**	.07*	.56**	.49**	.23**	.33**	.59**	—								
12. Re	.34**	.27**	.29**	.31**	.13*	.54**	.50**	.50**	.41**	.55**	.57**	—							
13. Non-Trad	.20**	.27**	.07	.05	.23**	.06	-.03	.36**	.35**	.10	-.05	-.01	—						
14. Trad	.46**	.44**	.27**	.35**	.24**	.82**	.71**	.71**	.72**	.84**	.73**	.77**	.15**	—					
POCRIAS																			
15. Conf	.05	.07	-.17**	.06	.08	.04	-.03	-.10	-.04	-.00	.03	.01	-.10	-02	—				
16. Diss	.20**	.08	.24**	.14**	.18**	.10	.10	.06	.08	.13*	.14*	.09	.10	.14*	.20**	—			
17. Imm/Res	.19**	.05	.18**	.23**	.19**	.16**	.16**	.01	.07	.13*	.21**	.15**	.02	.15**	.19**	.33**	—		
18. Intern	.27**	.43**	-.04	.04	.25**	.20**	.10	.48**	.41**	.19**	-.01	.08	.38**	.27**	.27**	-.01	-.07	—	
19. QDI Total	.05	03	-.03	.01	.11*	-.14*	-.10	.10	.09	-.18**	-.17**	-.09	.21**	-.10	.05	-.07	-.04	.22**	—

Note. GRCS = Gender-Role Conflict Scale; SPC = Success, Power, and Competition; ReEM = Restrictive Emotionality; RABBM = Restrictive Affectionate Behavior Between Men — Homophobia; CBWFR = Conflict Between Work and Family Relations; MRNI = Masculine Role Norms Inventory; AF = Avoidance of Femininity; RH = Rejection of Homosexuals; SR = Self-Reliance; AGG = Aggression; Ach/Stat = Achievement/Status; Att-Sex = Attitude-Toward Sex; Re = Restrictive Emotionality; Non-Trad = Non-Traditional Attitudes Toward Masculinity; Trad = Traditional Attitudes Toward Masculinity; POCRIAS = People of Color Racial Identity Attitude Scale; Conf = Conformity; Diss = Dissonance; Imm/Res = Immersion and Resistance; Intern = Internalization; QDI = Quick Discrimination Index.

*p < .05.

**p < .01.

$p < .01$) were also correlated with RE. Results suggest that participants who restricted their emotions were likely to endorse masculine role expectations of avoiding feminine things, rejecting homosexuals, being self-reliant, aggressive, goal-oriented and status seeking, having traditional masculine attitudes toward sex, and harboring traditional masculine attitudes. Racially, it seems that Asian American men's restriction of emotions are also related to statuses of racial identity that reflect conformity to dominant cultural ideals, struggle over racial self-definition, and ethnocentrism.

The RABBM subscale of the GRCS was positively associated with AF ($r = .32, p < .01$), RH ($r = .33, p < .01$), SR ($r = .24, p < .01$), AGG ($r = .16, p < .01$), Ach/Stat ($r = .28, p < .01$), Att-Sex ($r = .20, p < .01$), ReEm ($r = .31, p < .01$), and Trad ($r = .35, p < .01$). Dissonance ($r = .14, p < .01$) and immersion and resistance ($r = .23, p < .01$) were also correlated. Endorsing the subscales of the MRNI (e.g., RH and Att-Sex), except Non-Trad, was congruent with the inability of these men to express intimacy, sexuality, and affection for men and women in healthy ways. RABBM and racial identity correlations also suggest that Asian American men's emotional separation from other men is related to a feeling of marginalization from dominant and Asian

American Men and Increasing Ethnocentrism

The CBWFR subscale of the GRCS was significantly and positively related with AF ($r = .16, p < .01$), RH ($r = .14,$

$p < .01$), SR ($r = .32, p < .01$), AGG ($r = .26, p < .01$), Ach/Stat ($r = .22, p < .01$), ReEm ($r = .13, p < .05$), Non-Trad ($r = .23, p < .01$), and Trad ($r = .24, p < .01$). Dissonance ($r = .18, p < . 01$), immersion and resistance ($r = .19, p < .01$), internalization ($r = .25, p < .01$), and prejudicial attitudes ($r = .11, p < .01$) were significantly correlated with this GRCS subscale. Results suggest that men who experienced difficulty balancing the demands of work, family, and home were likely to support certain notions of male role norms. Additionally, Asian American men's conflict in work and leisure was positively related to racial struggles, ethnocentrism, and racial awareness, as well as fewer prejudicial attitudes.

The AF subscale of the MRNI was associated with immersion and resistance ($r = .16, p < .01$), internalization ($r = .20, p < .01$), and prejudicial attitudes ($r = -.14, p < .05$). RH was correlated with immersion and resistance ($r = .16, p < .01$); SR was associated with internalization ($r = .48, p < .01$); AGG was correlated with internalization ($r = .41, p < .01$); Ach/Stat was associated with dissonance ($r = .13, p < .01$), immersion and resistance ($r = .13, p < .01$), internalization ($r = .19, p < .01$), and prejudicial attitudes ($r = -.18, p < .01$); Att-Sex was correlated with dissonance ($r = .14, p < .01$), immersion and resistance ($r = .21, p < .01$), and prejudicial attitudes ($r = -.17, p < .01$); ReEm was associated with immersion and resistance ($r = .15, p < .01$); Non-Trad was correlated with internalization ($r = .38, p < .01$) and prejudicial attitudes ($r =$

Table 21.2. Summary of Hierarchial Multiple Regression Analyses With Multicultural Education Controlled for, Racial Identity Statuses and Prejudicial Attitudes as Predictors, and Gender-Role Conflict Scale Total Score as the Criterion

Step and Predictor Variable	R	R^2 Adj.	R^2	ΔR^2	ΔF	Sig. F	β	Sig.
Step 1	.03	−.00	.00	.00	.27	.60		
Multicultural education							.03	.60
Step 2	.37	.12	.14	.14	9.67	.00**		
Multicultural education							−.04	.49
Conformity							.05	.46
Dissonance							.13	.04*
Immersion and resistance							.17	.01**
Internalization							.30	.00***
Quick Discrimination Index							.01	.87

Note. Adj. = adjusted; Sig. = significance.
*$p < .05$.
**$p < .01$.
***$p < .001$.

.21, $p < .01$); and Trad was correlated with dissonance ($r = .14, p < .01$), immersion and resistance ($r = .15, p < .01$), and internalization ($r = .27, p < .01$). Results seem to suggest that Asian American men's racial and prejudicial attitudes vary according to specific male role norms. However, overall, nontraditional masculine attitudes were related to higher scores on fighting against racism and more openness to diversity. Conversely, traditional male role norms were associated with racial group marginalization, ethnocentrism, and fighting against racism.

Predicting Gender Role Conflict with Racial Identity and Prejudicial Attitudes

A hierarchical regression analysis examined the relationships between POCRIAS subscale scores, prejudicial attitudes, and GRCS subscale scores (Table 21.2). Because many of the students were enrolled in Asian American studies courses, their exposure to this material was controlled for in the analysis by entering in their exposure to multicultural topics. Predictor variables were racial identity and prejudicial attitudes scores, and the criterion variable was gender role conflict total score.

To control for multicultural education, it was entered in the first step of the hierarchical regression analysis. Step 1 was not significantly different from zero ($R^2 = .00$), $F(1, 313) = 0.27, p = .60$. The second step of the hierarchical regression was significantly different from zero when the POCRIAS subscale scores and prejudicial attitude scores were entered ($R^2 = .14, R^2$ Adj. $= .12$), $F(5, 308) = 9.67, p = .00$ ($R^2 \Delta = .14, F\Delta = 9.67$, Sig. $F\Delta = .00$). Racial identity and prejudicial attitudes accounted for 14% of

Table 21.3. Summary of Hierarchial Multiple Regression Analyses with Multicultural Education Controlled for, Racial Identity Statuses and Prejudicial Attitudes as Predictors, and Masculine Role Norms Inventory Traditional Total Score as the Criterion

Step and Predictor Variable	R	R^2 Adj.	R^2	ΔR^2	ΔF	Sig. F	β	Sig.
Step 1	.00	−.00	.00	.00	.00	.96		
Multicultural education							.00	.96
Step 2	.36	.11	.13	.13	9.12	.00★★		
Multicultural education							−.02	.69
Conformity							.05	.44
Dissonance							.10	.11
Immersion and resistance							.14	.01★
Internalization							.30	.00★★★
Quick Discrimination Index							.16	.01★

Note. Adj. = adjusted; Sig. = significance.
★$p < .05$.
★★$p < .01$.
★★★$p < .001$.

the variance in gender role conflict. The two nonsignificant predictors were conformity ($\beta = .05$, $T = 0.75$, $p = .46$) and prejudicial attitudes scores ($\beta = .01$, $T = .17$, $p = .87$). There were three significant predictors in this model: dissonance ($\beta = .13$, $T = 2.08$, $p = .04$), immersion and resistance ($\beta = .16$, $T = 2.76$, $p = .01$), and internalization ($\beta = .30$, $T = 5.15$, $p = .00$). Hence, the more one endorsed racial identity attitudes of racial confusion, ethnocentrism, and integration, the more one was likely to experience gender role conflict.

Predicting Male Role Norms with Racial Identity and Prejudicial Attitudes

A hierarchical regression analysis was conducted to investigate the relationships among POCRIAS subscale scores, prejudicial attitudes, and the MRNI Traditional Masculinity total score (Table 21.3). Because many of the students were enrolled in Asian American studies courses, their exposure to this material was controlled for in the analysis by entering in their exposure to multicultural topics. The predictor variables were the POCRIAS subscale scores and prejudicial attitudes scores, and the criterion variable was the MRNI total score.

To control for multicultural education, it was entered in the first step of the hierarchical regression analysis. Step 1 was not significantly different from zero ($R^2 = .00$), $F(1, 313) = .00$, $p = .97$. When racial identity and prejudicial attitudes were entered on the second step of the hierarchical regression analysis, the model was significantly different from zero ($R^2 = .13$, R^2 Adj. $= .11$, $F(5, 308) = 9.12$, $p = .00$ ($R^2\Delta = .13$,

$F\Delta = 9.12$, Sig. $F\Delta = .00$). The four POCRIAS subscales and the prejudicial attitudes score accounted for 13% of the variance in MRNI Trad scores. Thus, there was support for Hypothesis 5. The two nonsignificant predictors were conformity (ß $= -.05$, $T = -0.77$, $p = .44$) and dissonance (ß $= .10$, $T = 1.62$, $p = .11$). There were three positive predictors of traditional masculine attitudes. The first two significant predictors were immersion and resistance scores (ß $= .14$, $T = 2.48$, $p = .01$) and internalization scores (ß $= .30$, $T = 5.10$, $p = .00$). The direction of the beta weights appears to suggest that the endorsement of traditional masculine attitudes was positively related to endorsement of immersion and resistance or internalization attitudes.

The third significant predictor was prejudicial attitudes. Prejudicial attitudes was a significant predictor of traditional masculine attitudes (ß $=-.16$, $T = -2.78$, $p = .01$). The beta weight suggests that this predictor, while significant, was not a strong predictor of traditional masculine attitudes. Thus, the direction of the beta weights appears to moderately suggest that, as one becomes open to diversity and others who are different, one is also not likely to endorse traditional masculine attitudes.

■ DISCUSSION

Support was found for the hypotheses in this study. Results are discussed in terms of GRCS and POCRIAS, MRNI and POCRIAS, and then the regression results. To begin, the GRCS SPC sub scale was correlated with all of the MRNI subscales. Thus, an endorsement of SPC attitudes may also mean an endorsement of traditional male role norms. However, SPC shared the most variance with MRNI SR, AGG, and Trad subscales (31%, 20%, and 19% of the variance shared, respectively). That is, to be a successful man means subscribing to certain routes of success such as being self-reliant, aggressive, and having traditional masculine attitudes. The conflict around success may reflect what the individual believes are the acceptable behaviors within his peer group at a particular time. Additionally, internalization racial attitudes shared 18% of the variance with this subscale, suggesting racial identity integration does not necessarily mean the absence of a need for success, power, and competition, but rather that they may work together as dual processes among Asian American men.

On the GRCS RE and RABBM subscales, all MRNI subscales were significantly correlated, except for the Non-Trad subscale. On the RE subscale, the Asian American man may be unable, and to some extent, unwilling to express emotions, and he disallows others the same experience. Likewise, if Asian American men find it difficult to express and articulate their feelings, they also may be unsure of why they feel uncomfortable around other men. Consequently, Asian American men may endorse the rejection of homosexuals as a behavior to help make sense of their feelings. While some of the difficulty that Asian

American men experience in expressing affect can be attributed to subscription to dominant male role norms, subscription to male role norms accounted for only 2% to 8% of the shared variance on the RE subscale. Moreover, racial identity statuses of conformity, dissonance, and immersion and resistance shared only 2%, 5%, and 3%, respectively, of the variance on this subscale. Hence, other variables may be contributing to the Asian American man's difficulty in expressing affect. For instance, Asian cultural values of affective restraint (Sue, 1989) could be playing a role in restricting Asian American men's affect.

On the RABBM subscale, it seems that endorsing traditional masculinity ideology is related to difficulty with intimate relationships with other men. This sample of men may associate femininity and homosexuality as part of expressing affect between men. This is congruent with previous research findings (e.g., Levant & Fischer, 1998) and may be explained as a man's need to avoid and reject behaviors that are perceived as unmasculine (i.e., feminine). However, because the variance accounted for between GRCS, POCRIAS, and the MRNI ranged from 2% to 12%, much of the variance is not explained. Thus, Asian cultural values of homophobia (Leupp, 1995), among other variables, are also possibly working to restrict affective expression, and the measures used in my study did not assess for the role of Asian cultural values in Asian American men's lives.

Asian American men also experience conflicts over a man's ability to balance the demands of work and home. The highest relationship with MRNI subscales was with SR (10% of the variance shared), which could result from focusing on self-efficacy and sufficiency in work such that they are unable, or do not know how to, allow themselves to relax. The other domains of male role norms (i.e., avoidance of femininity, rejection of homosexuals, aggression, achievement/status, restrictive emotionality, and nontraditional and traditional masculine attitudes), while statistically significant, did not contribute much to explaining the conflicts that this sample experienced between work and leisure. Racial identity also did not appear to contribute much to explaining the variance (3% to 6%). Perhaps, the conflict between work, leisure, and family that Asian American men may be experiencing may also be related to cultural expectations of being successful (Uba, 1994). Because the sample is mostly college-aged students, success may revolve around the Asian value of academic success (Uba, 1994). Additionally, because Asian American students may aspire toward graduate or professional schools (Liu & Sedlacek, 1999), they may be focused on their career goals at the expense of their leisure activities or personal time. Thus, apart from gender role conflict and masculine role norms, Asian cultural values, rather than experiences with racism, may be contributing toward conflicts that Asian American men experience around work and leisure.

Relationships between POCRIAS and MRNI suggest that dissonant racial attitudes were related to achievement and status orientation, attitudes toward sex, and overall traditional male role norms; ethnocentric racial attitudes were associated with avoidance of things feminine, rejection of homosexuals, achievement and status orientation, attitudes toward sex, restrictive emotionality, and overall traditional male role norms; and internalization attitudes were related to avoiding things feminine, aggression, achievement and status orientation, and nontraditional and traditional male role norms. Higher prejudicial attitudes were related to avoidance of things feminine, achievement and status orientation, and attitudes toward sex. Openness toward diversity was related to nontraditional masculine attitudes. While there were several significant relationships, the variance accounted for in these relationships varied from 2% to 17%. Results also seem to suggest that Asian American men's racial attitudes are not highly related to their attitudes around male role norms. This may be a consequence of sampling men from introductory Asian American studies courses and Asian American fraternities, wherein issues of race are just coming to awareness and gender role conflict is not particularly salient in a homogenous gender group.

In the regression, racial identity and prejudicial attitudes accounted for 14% of the variance. In predicting gender role conflict attitudes in this study, the three statuses that were significant

predictors—dissonance, immersion and resistance, and internalization—all have the common element of questioning previously held beliefs. As such, it may be possible that, as Asian American men start to question their racial beliefs, they may also start questioning their beliefs about gender. Thus, because the GRCS is a measure of distress related to a person's gender role behaviors, the racial identity statuses of dissonance, immersion and resistance, and internalization may also be assessing other aspects of distress revolving around racial attitudes.

The hypothesis that racial identity and prejudicial attitudes would predict traditional male role norms was partially supported. Racial identity and prejudicial attitudes accounted for 13% of the variance in male role norms. The three significant predictors were immersion and resistance, internalization, and prejudicial attitudes. The significant racial identity predictors focus on achieving an internalized sense of self (i.e., away from an ascribed identity). However, in achieving an internalized racial identity, Asian American men must also negotiate what it means to be a man of color in a White dominant society.

In the regression analyses, results suggest that those who endorsed immersion and resistance and internalization attitudes were also likely to endorse male role norms (i.e., Trad score). In immersion and resistance, the Asian American man attempts to find stability in his racial identity and seeks to define himself as an Asian American outside dominant White society's influences. He eschews all dominant notions of race and culture and endorses mainly to an Asian orientation. This reorientation toward Asian culture allows the Asian American man to justify his behaviors and attitudes as congruent with Asian cultural values. This idealizing of Asian culture also translates to how the Asian American man relates to himself as a man (i.e., in traditional ways). Thus, many of the traditional male roles may be congruent with being a traditional Asian man, but the Asian American man is unaware that he may be endorsing both dominant and Asian notions of masculinity.

However, in internalization, the achievement of an internalized racial sense of self may also infer an acceptance of other aspects of oneself. That is, rather than feeling conflicted over having traditional masculine roles, the Asian American man in internalization comes to accept the positive and negative aspects of traditional male role norms. In coming to accept the positive and negative aspects of Asian and White culture, the Asian American man also is internalizing the positive and negative aspects of masculinity that each culture expects from men. In this status, aspects of traditional masculinity may not be completely negative, but instead, may be useful for the Asian American man in negotiating issues of racism.

Prejudicial attitudes were also a significant negative predictor of traditional masculine attitudes. This inverse relationship, in which low scores on the QDI indicate high prejudicial attitudes

and high scores indicate low prejudicial attitudes, can be interpreted in the following way: Those who had low scores were likely to endorse traditional masculine attitudes, whereas those who had high scores were less likely to endorse traditional masculine attitudes. These findings appear to suggest that traditional masculine attitudes encompass various prejudicial attitudes and behaviors such as rejection of femininity and homosexuals. As a result, endorsement of these attitudes may also imply support for sexist attitudes. It may be possible that sexist attitudes are a necessary aspect of having traditional masculine attitudes because these attitudes help one to rationalize the supposed role of men. Moreover, having certain prejudicial attitudes, such as sexism, may facilitate a subscription to traditional male role norms.

RESEARCH LIMITATIONS AND IMPLICATIONS FOR FUTURE RESEARCH

Limitations to this study are as follows: First, the population sampled was convenience sampling and may not be representative of the general population of Asian American men. Second, the Asian American men may reflect a limited racial identity range because they are participating in Asian American groups and courses. Additionally, this study was correlational in design and, therefore, causality could not be determined from the results. Finally, there were some low Cronbach alphas among some of the

MRNI subscales. Because of these low reliabilities, some of the findings are tentative because of the amount of error possible.

The results suggest that racism did play a modest role among the members of this Asian American male sample. The low variance accounted for in the two hierarchical multiple regression analyses (14% and 13%) seem to suggest that other variables, aside from racial identity, may be useful in explaining the masculinity issues among Asian American men. Even though Asian American men do experience gender conflict commensurate with non–Asian American men, experiences with racism did not account for much of the variance. Hence, what is not clear is the role that Asian cultural values may play in masculinity. Because Asian American men may already have grown up in an environment that values restricting affective expression, and the dominant culture only reinforces these values, it may be difficult for clinicians to distill apart the role of dominant and Asian culture in masculinity. Consequently, Asian American men may be struggling with dual pressures to restrict emotions for self and others. Clinicians' awareness that Asian American men may come into counseling with some affective reticence may alleviate counselors' frustration when emotions are not forthcoming.

For research, it may be necessary to investigate different ways Asian American men cope with racism and how they relate to others around them through their cultural values. While much has been written about Asian cultural values, it may be interesting to examine how this constellation of values (e.g., harmony in relationships, filial piety) may be configured differently according to gender. Examination of the relationship of ethnic and racial identity is an area of research that could be expanded (Alvarez, Kohatsu, Liu, & Yeh, 1996). In this study, I used only the racial identity theory and measurement, but theoretically, ethnic and racial identity may play concomitant and salient roles in the lives of Asian Americans. Perhaps if larger samples for each ethnic group were recruited, differences between the ethnic groups could be studied. Future research could focus on investigating the intragroup differences (i.e., ethnic) among this community and the validity of current masculinity theories in explaining minority men's experiences.

REFERENCES

Alvarez, A., Kohatsu, E., Liu, W., & Yeh, L. (1996, February). Rethinking Asian Pacific American racial identity: Distinctions between racial and ethnic identity. Paper presented at the meeting of the Winter Roundtable on Cross-Cultural Counseling and Psychotherapy, New York.

Cazenare, N. A. (1984). Race, socioeconomic status, and age: The social context of American masculinity. *Sex Roles, 11*, 639–656.

Chan, J. W. (1998). Contemporary Asian American men's issues. In L. R. Hirabayashi (Ed.), *Teaching Asian America: Diversity and the problem of community issues* (pp. 93–102).

Lanham, MD: Rowman and Littlefield Publishers.

Chan, S. (1991). *Asian Americans: An interpretive history*. Boston: Twayne Publishers.

Chin, J. L. (1998). Mental health services and treatment. In L. C. Lee & N.W.S. Zane (Eds.), *Handbook of Asian American psychology* (pp. 485–504). Thousand Oaks, CA: Sage.

Chin, K. (1996). *Chinatown gangs: Extortion, enterprise, and ethnicity*. New York: Oxford University Press.

Chua, P., & Fujino, D. C. (1999). Negotiating new Asian-American masculinities: Attitudes and gender expectations. *The Journal of Men's Studies, 7*, 391–413. Federal Register (1997, October 30). Office of management and budget: Revisions to the standards for the classification of federal data on race and ethnicity (Notices, Vol. 62, No. 210). Washington, DC: Author.

Good, G. E., Robertson, J. M., O'Neil, J. M., Fitzgerald, L. F., Stevens, M., Debord, K.A., et al. (1995). Male gender role conflict: Psychometric issues and relations to psychological distress. *Journal of Counseling Psychology, 42*, 3–10.

Helms, J. E. (1995). An update of Helms' White and People of Color racial identity models. In J. G. Ponterotto, J. M. Casas, L. A. Suzuki, & C. M. Alexander (Eds.), *Handbook of multicultural counseling* (pp. 181–198). Thousand Oaks, CA: Sage.

Helms, J. E., & Carter, R. (1990). *A preliminary overview of the Cultural Identity Attitude scale*. Unpublished manuscript.

Helms, J. E., & Cook, D. A. (1999). *Using race and culture in counseling and psychotherapy: Theory and process*. Needham Heights, MA: Allyn & Bacon.

Kibria, N. (1993). *Family tightrope: The changing lives of Vietnamese Americans*. Princeton, NJ: Princeton University Press.

Kim, E. J., O'Neil, J. M., & Owen, S. V. (1996). Asian-American men's acculturation and gender-role conflict. *Psychological Reports, 79*, 95–104.

Kohatsu, E. (1992). The effects of racial identity and acculturation on anxiety, assertiveness, and ascribed identity among Asian American college students (Doctoral dissertation, University of Maryland, College Park, 1992). *Dissertation Abstracts International, 54*(2), 1102B.

Lazur, R. F., & Majors, R. (1995). Men of color: Ethnocultural variations of male gender role strain. In R. F. Levant & W. S. Pollack (Eds.), *A new psychology of men* (pp. 337–358). New York: Basic Books.

Lee, S. J. (1996). Perceptions of panethnicity among Asian American high school students. *Amerasia Journal, 22*(2), 109–125.

Leupp, G. P. (1995). *Male colors: The construction of homosexuality in Tokugawa Japan*. Berkeley: University of California Press.

Levant, R. F., & Fischer, J. (1998). The Male Role Norms Inventory. In C. M. Davis, W. H. Yarber, R. Bauserman, G. Schreer, & S. L. Davis (Eds.), *Sexuality-related measures: A compendium* (2nd ed, pp. 469–472). Thousand Oaks, CA: Sage.

Levant, R. F., Wu, R., & Fischer, J. (1996). Masculine ideology: A comparison between U.S. and Chinese young men and women. *Journal of Gender, Culture, & Health, 1*, 207–220.

Liu, W. M., Pope-Davis, D. B., Nevitt, N., & Toporek, R. L. (1999). Understanding the function of acculturation and prejudicial attitudes among Asian Americans. *Cultural Diversity and Ethnic Minority Psychology,* 5, 317–328.

Liu, W. M., & Sedlacek, W. E. (1999). Differences in leadership and co-curricular perception among entering male and female Asian Pacific American college students. *Journal of the First-Year Experience,* 11(2), 93–114.

Long, P.D.P. (1996). *The dream shattered: Vietnamese gangs in America.* Boston: Northeastern University Press.

Lum, J. L. (1998). Family violence. In C. C. Lee & N.W.S. Zane (Eds.), *Handbook of Asian American psychology* (pp. 505–526). Thousand Oaks, CA: Sage.

Mok, T. A. (1998). Getting the message: Media images and stereotypes and their effect on Asian Americans. *Cultural Diversity and Mental Health,* 4, 185–202.

Nagata, D. K. (1998). Internment and intergenerational relations. In C. C. Lee & N.W.S. Zane (Eds.), *Handbook of Asian American psychology* (pp. 433–456). Thousand Oaks, CA: Sage.

Omi, M., & Winant, H. (1994). *Racial formation in the United States: From the 1960s to the 1990s.* New York: Routledge.

O'Neil, J. M., Helms, B. J., Gable, R. K., David, L., & Wrightsman, L. S. (1986). Gender-Role Conflict Scale: College men's fear of femininity. *Sex Roles,* 14, 335–350.

Ponterotto, J. G., Burkard, A., Rieger, B. P., Grieger, I., D'Onofrio, A., Dubuisson, A., et al. (1995). Development and initial validation of the Quick Discrimination Index (QDI). *Educational and Psychological Measurement,* 55, 1016–1031.

Rimonte, N. (1991). A question of culture: Cultural approval of violence against women in the Pacific-Asian community. *Stanford Law Review,* 43, 1311–1362.

Sue, D. W. (1989). Ethnic identity: The impact of two cultures on the psychological development of Asians in America. In D. R. Atkinson, G. Morten, & D. W. Sue (Eds.), *Counseling American minorities: A cross cultural perspective* (pp. 103–115). Dubuque, IA: William C. Brown.

Suinn, R. M., Ahuna, C., & Khoo, G. (1992). The Suinn-Lew Asian Self-Identity Acculturation Scale: Concurrent and factorial validation. *Educational and Psychological Measurement,* 52, 1041–1046.

Takaki, R. (1990). *Iron cages: Race and culture in 19th-century America.* New York: Oxford University Press.

Uba, L. (1994). *Asian Americans: Personality patterns, identity, and mental health.* New York: Guilford Press.

Zhou, M., & Bankston, C. L., III. (1998). *Growing up American: How Vietnamese children adapt to life in the United States.* New York: Russell Sage Foundation.

CHAPTER 22

Peer Support for African American Male College Achievement

Beyond Internalized Racism and the Burden of "Acting White"

Shaun R. Harper

More than any other group of men in our society, Black males are perceived as lacking in intellectual skills. Stereotyped via racism and sexism as being more body than mind, Black males are far more likely to be affirmed for appearing to be dumb . . . well-educated Black men have learned to act as if they know nothing in a world where a smart Black man risks punishment (hooks, 2004, p. 33).

In her book, *We Real Cool: Black Men and Masculinity,* author and activist bell hooks (2004) discusses the deleterious effects of mass media images, within–race disempowerment, and class-based education on African American male socialization. Accordingly, young African American men are groomed to devalue educational achievement, as due to societal messages that are internalized and reinforced by Black families and peers. She notes that in some Black households the boy who likes to read is suspected to be at risk for developing feminine or "sissy" characteristics—the same perceptions held among Black male peer groups in schools are often juxtaposed with low teacher expectations for Black male school success. Consequently, few receive the support needed to overcome longstanding educational inequities and societal disadvantages. While White teachers, school administrators, and educational structures that maintain White supremacy are largely responsible for African American male underachievement, equally troublesome is the internalization and validation of these messages within Black communities.

Internalized racism (or internalized oppression) occurs when socially stigmatized groups (e.g., Black males) accept and recycle negative messages regarding their aptitude, abilities, and societal place, which results in self-devaluation and the invalidation of others within the group (Essed, 1991; Jones, 2000; Lipsky, 1987; Pheterson, 1990; Pyke & Dang, 2003). That is, the oppressed begin to believe in their own inferiority, both individually and collectively (Baker, 1983). In turn, members of the group consciously or unknowingly endorse the ideologies of the oppressor by communicating counterproductive and racist messages to other group members. Ultimately, within-group socialization toward negative and what is perceived as racially normative codes of conduct often ensues. Lipsky (1987) makes clear that this tendency is not a source of racism but instead an internalized reaction to externally imposed oppression.

Lipsky (1987) also partially attributes failed attempts at Black collectivism and liberation as well as the leadership decline within Black communities to internalized racism. Specifically, she asserts that internalized oppression compels African Americans to criticize, attack, or have unrealistic expectations of those who willingly step forward to assume leadership responsibilities. Thus, Lipsky maintains, the support needed for effective Black leadership is rarely extended, which causes burnout among African American leaders. Patricia Hill Collins (2004) contends that Black male elected officials, business leaders, executives, and academicians are thought to be "intellectual sissies" who

align themselves too closely with White culture:

> Staying in school and studying hard moves them closer to images of Bill Cosby selling Jello or Michael Jordan talking to Bugs Bunny or Tiger Woods refusing to claim Blackness at all. If the "academic sidekick" or "intellectual sissy" becomes seen by African American boys and young men as the price they have to pay for racial integration, it should not be surprising that increasing numbers of Black men reject this route to success. (p. 177)

As a result, few low-income and working-class African American males aspire to careers in leadership or pursue the educational credentials requisite for assuming such positions; those who do rarely receive support and validation from their same race peers.

Internalized racism erodes individual enthusiasm, makes certain attitudes and behaviors normative, and undermines collaborative action for racial uplift (Jones, 2000). For example, instead of collectively striving to dispel faulty stereotypes regarding African Americans, many will endorse those misperceptions by encouraging Black male athleticism over intellectualism, as one example. Paulo Freire (1970) discussed the "self-deprecation" phenomenon, which he characterized as a sense of self-hatred and low self-esteem among the oppressed. "So often do [the oppressed] hear that they are good for nothing, know nothing, and are incapable of learning anything—that they are sick, lazy, and unproductive—that in the end they become convinced of their own unfitness" (p. 94). For African American males, nowhere is this oppression more commonplace than in schools, the context in which an achiever is supposedly accused by his same-race peers of "acting White."

The anti-college-going messages articulated in rapper Kanye West's (2004) debut album, *The College Dropout*, blatantly suggest postsecondary education is overrated and degree attainment is culturally worthless. Several skits on the album feature a fictitious African American male collegian who speaks in a voice that would be characterized by most as White. Marketed primarily to Black listeners, these lyrics were consumed by millions, which offers an example of the commercialization and mass production of internalized racism. Although college attendance is likened to Whiteness in West's album, most conceptual, theoretical, and empirical considerations of internalized racism within the context of schooling have focused on African American students in K–12 settings. Thus, little is known about peer attitudes and support tendencies among African American college students. Even less attention has been devoted to considering dynamics among African American male undergraduates, the population that is least retained among both sexes and all racial/ethnic groups in higher education (Harper, 2006a; NCES, 2005). The purpose of this study is to explore the role of peers in the postsecondary educational experiences of African American male high-achievers at predominantly White universities. The emphasis placed on peers in this chapter is important, as Astin (1993) contends, peers are most influential in the experiences of undergraduate students.

■ LITERATURE REVIEW

Few researchers have examined the experiences of academically talented African American college students in general (Fries-Britt, 1998, 2002, 2004; Fries-Britt & Turner, 2001, 2002; Griffin, 2006), and male high-achievers specifically (Bonner, 2001; Fries-Britt, 1997; Harper, 2004, 2005a, 2005b, 2006b). Therefore, the use of literature from the K-12 school studies was necessary to provide a context for this study.

African American Peers and Early Schooling Experiences

Studies regarding the experiences of gifted and academically talented African American youth are fraught with descriptions of negative peer interactions. Reportedly, these students are forced to contend with complex social and emotional adjustment issues in school, including the development of healthy self-concepts and feelings of belongingness (Baldwin, 1991; Ford, 1996; Lindstrom & Van Sant, 1986). Moreover, high-achievers often encounter difficulty integrating their social, racial, and academic identities (Cooley, Cornell, & Lee, 1991; Ford & Harris, 1997). The title of Kunjufu's (1988) book, *To Be Popular or Smart: The Black Peer Group,* captures the essence of this struggle. Ford (1996) suggests many academically talented African American students purposely underachieve in school and hide their intellectual competence in order to negotiate cultural entrée into Black peer groups. Fordham and Ogbu (1986) refer to this as "camouflaging," while Horvat and Lewis (2003) report that such acts are part of managing academic success. "When caught in this psychological and social-emotional tug-of-war, some Black students attempt to sabotage their achievement [by] procrastinating, failing to do assignments, and refusing to be in gifted education and advanced-level classes"(Grantham & Ford, 2003, p. 22).

In their study of gender differences among African American students, Ford and Harris (1995) found that more than 40 percent of the participants in the sample were underachieving, a disproportionate number of whom were men. Furthermore, female students in the sample also had significantly higher grade point averages than their male counterparts. At least a portion of these achievement differences is explained by hegemonic conceptions of masculinity among African American boys and teens. According to James Earl Davis (2003), African American males tend to set the standards for popularity at school mostly through hip-hop culture and athleticism, and there is often little room for negotiation within peer groups. The African American male middle school students in Davis's (2001) study developed a strict masculine code of conduct in their school that was characterized by various socially constructed attitudinal and behavioral norms that were in conflict with academic achievement. Examples include pursuing romantic relationships (but not friendships) with female students and being perceived as "cool." Davis found that those who failed to adhere to the masculine code were victimized by their peers and "usually expelled from the confines and benefits of boy networks at the school" (p. 178).

While the focus of this chapter is on peers, it should be noted that the subtractive and invalidating ethos of predominantly White K–12 school environments often lead African American students to assume that academic achievement is incongruent with their cultural interests and values (Gay, 2000; Hollins & Spencer, 1990; Irvine, 1990; Ladson-Billings, 1995), which in turn leads to the perpetuation of internalized racism. Grantham and Ford (2003) argue that too few efforts are employed to improve Black student achievement in school and educators need to focus on helping academically talented students develop healthy racial identities and affirming relationships with their same-race peers.

The "Acting White" Hypothesis

Signithia Fordham and John Ogbu's (1986) study illuminates many of the aforementioned elements of internalized racism. Specifically, they contend that academically successful African American students must cope with the burden of being constantly accused of "acting White" by their peers.

> Black students' academic efforts are hampered by both external factors and within-group factors . . . schooling is perceived by Blacks, especially by Black adolescents, as learning to act White, or as trying to cross cultural boundaries. And, importantly, school learning is viewed as a subtractive process. In our view, then, the academic learning and performance problems of Black children arise not only from a limited opportunity structure and Black people's responses to it, but also from the way Black people attempt to cope with the "burden of 'acting White.'"(p. 201)

Fordham and Ogbu purport that this burden plays itself out in predominantly Black and racially integrated school settings. Furthermore, they say social ostracism, exclusion from Black activities inside and outside of school, labeling, and even physical assault are among the challenges with which academic achievers must contend. Others have referred to this phenomenon as "oppositional peer culture" (Ainsworth-Darnell & Downey, 1998; Ferguson, 2001). Fordham (1988) adds that some high-achieving African American students embrace "racelessness"—meaning they distance themselves from Black culture as a response to the lack of same-race peer support they receive at school.

According to Ogbu and Simons (1998), African American students are usually supportive of their same-race peers when they earn good grades, but it is the embracing of perceivably White attitudes and behaviors used to earn those grades that are deemed problematic. In addition to the ramifications noted earlier, Ogbu (2004) asserts that the burden of "acting White" includes accusations of being an "Uncle Tom" or "sellout," perceived disloyalty to the Black community, personal embarrassment and public humiliation, and a loss of Black friends. He suggests that mentors can serve as mediators against peer pressure and self-doubt but indicates that mentorship is typically not extended to Black achievers. Ogbu also posits that academically talented students feel compelled to conduct, either formally or informally, a "social cost-benefit analysis" of school success, and they then act accordingly.

Fordham and Ogbu's hypothesis has been the center of contention in subsequent studies of Black student achievement (see Ainsworth-Darnell & Downey, 1998; Cook & Ludwig, 1998; Ferguson, 2001; Spencer, Noll, Stolzfus, & Harpalani, 2001). These researchers have consistently found that African American students do not value education or school achievement any less than do their White peers from similar socioeconomic or familial backgrounds, and that many high-achievers have positive self-esteem, high goal orientations, and strong Black identities. In their study of Black female students in urban high schools, Horvat and Lewis (2003) found that Black peer groups affirmed, embraced, and celebrated the participants' academic achievements. It should be noted that the women in the Horvat and Lewis study were also actively involved in a range of out-of-class activities at their high schools, which their peers reportedly sanctioned and supported.

Ferguson (2001) contends that achievement is more negotiable among African American students than Fordham and Ogbu's work suggests. He argues that those who are interested in school success must invest effort into academic endeavors while signifying an authentic sense of racial solidarity with their African American peers. Ferguson rejects the "acting White" hypothesis and offers an alternative perspective on oppositional culture that he characterizes as uniquely African American:

> Among its essential features is the drive to maintain a shared sense of African American identity that is distinct from (that is, in opposition to) the Other . . . the Other is not White people, especially as individuals. Instead, the Other is the cultural system of White superiority within which negative racial stigma is kept alive and out of which insinuations of Black inferiority and marginality emanate. Black racial solidarity serves as a mechanism of mutual validation and a shield . . . any apparent attempt by a Black person to escape the stigma of race by joining the Other—by speaking and behaving in ways that appear to seek an exemption from the stigma while leaving it unchallenged—may meet the accusation of acting White. (pp. 377–378)

Peer Influences of African American College Achievement

Limited insight has been offered into the role of peers in African American college achievement. Fries-Britt (1998) found that many academically talented students entered college with few or no relationships with other high-achieving African American students. These students came from primary and secondary schools where most of their time was spent in gifted programs with few of their same-race peers. As with their early schooling experiences, many of the participants were primarily enrolled in classes with White students in the honors college at their university. Consequently, they had few opportunities to interact with other African Americans and relied heavily upon a special program for minority achievers to meet other students from their race. Because of limited interactions with their same-race peers, Fries-Britt (2002) posits that high-achievers become aware that they belong to an underrepresented group and accustomed to not expecting other African Americans to do well.

Fries-Britt and Turner (2002) assert that some African American students purposely assimilate into White culture, which does not necessarily mean they know less about Black culture or have weaker racial identities. Instead, they "have learned to become bicultural, developing a repertoire of expressions and behaviors from both the White and Black community and switching between them as appropriate" (p. 320). The participants in Fries-Britt's (1998) study reflected on the uneasy exchanges they had with other African American students who were not in the program for academically talented collegians. On the one hand, they valued the affiliation with a program that facilitated interactions with other academically talented African Americans, but on the other, the participants longed for opportunities to be connected to the larger African American community on campus. Some students admitted to camouflaging their academic talents and concealing their connection to the program in order to fit in with other African American students at their university. Fries-Britt (1997) specifically addresses the needs of and issues faced by high-achieving African American undergraduate men. She notes that pressure to fit in with and earn the respect of their male peers is a considerable source of stress for male high-achievers. Athletic ability, instead of academic talent, is one characteristic that garnered peer recognition within Black male peer groups.

Though not based on high-achievers, Davis's (1994) and (1999) comparative studies of African American undergraduate men at historically Black colleges and universities (HBCUs) and predominantly White institutions (PWIs) show that students at both institutional types report comparable levels of peer support. Bonner (2001) examined two high-achieving African American male students' perceptions of the impact of peer relationships on their academic success in college; one participant attended an HBCU, and the other was enrolled at a PWI. Both participants acknowledged the academic and social support they received from peers that led to increased confidence in their abilities. Interestingly, the HBCU student believed his campus environment nurtured and encouraged high achievement; thus, he comfortably displayed confidence in his academic abilities. The PWI student, on the other hand, "maintained that he did not wear his academic talent on his sleeve, but preferred to be more subtle and unassuming regarding his scholastic achievements" (p. 11). Bonner concluded that the predominantly White campus environment contributed to this student's discomfort with flaunting his giftedness. Neither Davis nor Bonner disclose the outlets through which peer support was derived or the strategies the African American male participants in their studies undertook to leverage same-race peer support.

Limited empirical exploration of the "acting White" hypothesis within the context of higher education, as well as the inconclusiveness and lack of specificity in the existing published research regarding same-race peer support for African American male college achievement, call into question the following: (1) What roles do African American peers play in the experiences of high-achieving African American male undergraduates at PWIs, (2) through what outlets is peer support derived, (3) how is same-race peer support garnered and negotiated among African American male achievers at predominantly White universities, and (4) what support is there for the "acting White" hypothesis and internalized racism among African American male collegians? These questions were investigated in this study.

METHOD

This chapter is based on a larger qualitative data set regarding the experiences of high-achieving African American undergraduate men. Data used here were extracted from a more comprehensive project. The phenomenological study sought to understand what it is like to be a high-achieving African American male college student at a large, predominantly White university and included questions regarding relationships with and support derived from others. The phenomenology tradition in qualitative research focuses on understanding and describing the "lived experiences" of the participants involved in the study (Denzin & Lincoln, 2000). A phenomenological account gets inside the common experience of a group of people and describes what the participants have experienced, how they have experienced it, and the meanings they make of their shared experience (Moustakas, 1994). Polkinghorne (1989) suggests that the researcher and readers of a phenomenological research study should be able to say, "I understand better what it is like for someone to experience that" (p. 46). This type of qualitative study usually provides full, detailed descriptions of the phenomenon under study (Miles & Huberman, 1994). The aim of the present study was to

capture, in the high-achievers' words, perceptions of same-race peer support for college achievement and strategies through which peer relationships were negotiated.

Sites

This study was conducted at six large, public research universities in the Midwest: the University of Illinois, Indiana University, the University of Michigan, Michigan State University, The Ohio State University, and Purdue University. These six institutions are similar in terms of size, age, reputation, and selectivity. Collectively enrolling more than 189,000 undergraduates, these six institutions were all classified as Doctoral/Research Universities-Extensive by the Carnegie Foundation for the Advancement of Teaching (2000). On average, 6.3 percent of the students at the institutions were African American during the time at which data were collected, with African American undergraduate enrollments ranging from 3.1 percent to 8.8 percent. The mean six-year graduation rate for African American male undergraduates at these institutions was 50.7 percent, compared to 74.2 percent for White males and 58.8 percent for African American females. Consistent with national trends (Harper, 2006a), African American men had the lowest graduation rates among both sexes and all racial/ethnic groups across the six universities. At the time of data collection, 33.8 percent of the African American students at these universities were male.

Sample

Key administrators on the six campuses (i.e., deans, vice presidents, and directors of campus programs) were asked to identify high-achieving African American male student leaders who had earned cumulative grade point averages above 3.0 on a 4.0 scale, established lengthy records of leadership and involvement in multiple campus organizations, earned the admiration of their peers (as determined by peer elections to campus leadership positions), developed meaningful relationships with faculty and high-ranking campus administrators, participated in enriching educational experiences (e.g., study abroad programs, internships, learning communities, and summer research programs), and earned numerous awards and honors for their college achievements. Using these criteria, 32 African American undergraduate men at the six universities were identified and selected for participation in this study.

The sample included four sophomores, 12 juniors, and 16 seniors, representing a wide variety of academic majors. The mean GPA for the sample was 3.32. All of the participants were between the ages of 18 and 22 and single with no dependents. Twelve participants grew up in single-parent homes, and the remaining 20 were from homes with two parents. Regarding the educational levels of their parents, the participants reported the following: both parents attended college (n = 9); one parent attended college (n = 10); and neither parent attended college (n = 13). Collectively, the 32 participants had been awarded more than $489,000 in merit-based scholarships, awards, and prizes for their college achievements. The participants expressed high educational and career aspirations, with 72 percent indicating the intent to someday earn a doctoral degree. The remaining 28 percent planned to pursue master's degrees, mostly MBAs from top business schools. None of the participants in this study were college student-athletes. Nominators reported that these 32 high-achievers were the only African American male undergraduates on the six campuses who satisfied the previously noted criteria established for participation in this study.

Data Collection Procedures

Each of the 32 African American men was asked to participate in a two-to-three hour face-to-face interview and at least two follow-up interviews via telephone. I visited each campus at least once to conduct the first round of individual interviews; four campuses were visited twice. A semi-structured interview technique was used in the face-to-face interview sessions, which simultaneously permitted data collection and authentic participant reflection (Holstein & Gubrium, 1995). Although standard questions and interview protocol were used in the interviews, discussions often became conversational, thus allowing the participants to reflect on the experiences they deemed most significant. Full transcripts from all sessions were sent to each participant for confirmation within eight weeks following his interviews.

Data Analysis

Step-by-step techniques prescribed by Moustakas (1994) were used to analyze the data collected from interviews with the participants. I first bracketed my initial impressions and assumptions as I read each line of the participants' transcripts. The margins of the transcripts were marked with reflective comments regarding my own suppositions and preliminary judgments about the data. After bracketing, the transcripts were sorted and key phases were linearly arranged under tentative headings using the NVivo® Qualitative Research Software Package. This process resulted in the identification of 36 invariant constituents (Moustakas, 1994), which were subthemes that consistently held true for at least 84.4 percent of the sample. The invariant constituents were helpful in understanding the participants' shared experiences and were later clustered into thematic categories.

Before the categories were solidified, a textural summary (what the high-achiever experienced) and a structural summary (how he experienced the phenomenon of being an actively engaged student leader at a PWI) were written for each participant. Seven thematic categories were identified that captured the essence of the participants' shared experiences, two of which related directly to the role of peers in the high-achievers' experiences and success

on predominantly White university campuses. Only findings from those two themes are reported in this chapter.

Trustworthiness and Quality Assurance

Several steps were taken to ensure quality and trustworthiness in this study. Lincoln and Guba (1986) offered four measures for evaluating methodological rigor and accuracy in qualitative research: credibility, transferability, dependability, and confirmability. These four measures "replace the usual positivist criteria of internal and external validity, reliability, and objectivity" used to ensure quality in quantitative studies (Denzin & Lincoln, 2000, p. 21). Credibility was addressed through member checks, follow-up interviews via telephone, and referential adequacy (the storage and accessibility of cassette tapes from the interviews, full transcripts and confidential documents, etc.). An informant team consisting of at least two participants from each institution was established for member checks. This team, representing more than 25 percent of the sample, read and provided feedback on my written interpretations of their collective experiences.

To ensure credibility, feedback was solicited from six peer debriefers who are experienced qualitative researchers and are familiar with African American men's issues. Debriefers were given raw transcripts as well as the individual textural and structural descriptions I wrote for the study participants. Debriefers and I engaged in a series of ongoing discussions regarding the tentative meanings I made of the high-achievers' experiences throughout the data analysis phase of the study. Transferability is ensured by the earlier description of sites from which data were collected. Findings from this study will likely transfer agreeably to large predominantly White public research universities. Last, to ensure dependability and confirmability, audits were conducted by members of the aforementioned peer debriefing team, a diverse team of four senior faculty colleagues, and one additional qualitative research methodologist.

Limitations

Despite efforts to ensure trustworthiness, two methodological and analytical shortcomings are readily apparent. The most glaring limitation of this study is the reliance on self-reported data of peer perceptions. Interviews were only conducted with the 32 high-achieving African American undergraduate men, not their peers. Although the participants believed their same-race peers held certain views of them, other African American students on the six campuses may have reported something different. A second major shortcoming pertains to the limited transferability of the findings from this study. High-achieving African American male students at single-sex institutions, HBCUs, small liberal arts colleges, and other institutional types might report peer interactions and experiences that differ from those of the 32 participants who attended the six large PWIs in the present study.

■ FINDINGS

From the interviews with the 32 high-achievers emerged three categories of findings regarding their experiences with other African American college students. Reported below are descriptions of peer support, the outlets through which this support was accessed, and the ways in which the high-achievers negotiated and leveraged support among their same-race peers on the six university campuses.

Self-Reports of Peer Support

Peers played a significant role in the high-achievers' collegiate successes. Reportedly, male and female students alike extended tremendous support to the African American men in the sample. No participant reported social ostracism or feelings of alienation from other African American students. Instead, they all described how peer support significantly enhanced the quality of their experiences as high-achievers in predominantly White learning environments. "There is no way I would have been nearly as successful at Ohio State were it not for the support of other African American students here. They have applauded everything I have done so far," Cullen noted. Other participants indicated that they would have accomplished less without the support of other African Americans. When asked to whom they would attribute their college achievements, the high-achievers consistently replied: (1) God, (2) themselves, (3) their parents, and (4) their peers—almost always in that order.

Although the participants had fostered meaningful relationships with students outside the African American race, they repeatedly reported that their African American peers had been most encouraging and validating. "The Black community is happy to see someone doing something positive, so that's why they've been so supportive," one high-achiever claimed. Several participants attributed this provision of peer support to the underrepresentation of African American male students on their campuses (recall that they comprised only one-third of the African American undergraduates at the six universities). Furthermore, the shortage of African American male student leaders on campus seemingly worked to their advantage in terms of garnering peer recognition for their leadership efforts and academic achievement.

Bryant noted:

> They know how it is to be the only African American student in all of your classes and they know that most Black organizations on campus are led by African American women, not the brothas'. So, when they see a brotha' who is involved and stepping up to be a leader in class or outside of the classroom, they are especially proud and supportive.

Jibreel added that because African American male achievers and leaders were "few and far between," he was easily noticed by his same-race peers, and they were generally inclined to encourage his success.

It is especially important to acknowledge the participants' perceptions of support from other African American male students on campus. "I think 99.9 percent of the African American men have accepted me, even though I wasn't necessarily looking for their acceptance. They respect me; they don't look at me as some type of sellout," Michael shared. Most of the high-achievers' same-race male peers were considerably disengaged, did not pursue involvement opportunities or leadership positions on campus, struggled academically in their classes, and devoted their out-of-class time to playing video games, pursuing romantic endeavors with women, and participating in sports and fitness activities. Despite differences in the expenditure of their time, the high-achievers maintained that their disengaged male peers supported them, recognized their efforts and contributions, and never questioned their masculinities. Alric's comments illuminate this shared perspective: "Even though they aren't leaders and could probably care less about being involved themselves, they always support and uplift me nonetheless." No participant reported that he had ever been accused of "acting White" because he chose to do well in his classes or devote his out-of-class time to educationally purposeful activities. In fact, it appears that the exact opposite occurred—their African American male and female peers applauded their achievements and helped the participants make the most of their college experiences.

Outlets for Same-Race Peer Support

In addition to describing the affirmation extended by their African American peers, the participants also discussed the processes and venues through which they accessed peer support. First, several students noted that peers aided in their successful adjustment to college. Arnold, a senior at Indiana University, offered the following reflection of his experience in the Pharaoh's Club, a support group for African American males (typically first-year students) at IU:

> I felt really connected to the guys in that group, so I really connected with the university from the start. Since then, I was like, "Okay, this was a good experience." I mean, I didn't feel alone on campus because I had that group of guys that I was always going back to for support. We were all taking the same classes and experiencing the same things as freshmen. So I learned that organizations and friends in those organizations could really help in that transition from high school to college. Those friends in the Pharaoh's Club really helped me.

Edwin expressed similar views regarding the relationship between involvement in student organizations and peer support:

> The University of Michigan is a huge place. You're talking about 35,000 people. If you're not involved, I don't understand how you have friends.

Joining these clubs and getting in leadership roles is how I have met a lot of my Black friends and supporters.

Without exception, each participant mentioned clubs and activities, especially predominantly Black student organizations, as the venues through which he initially accessed same-race peer support for his college achievements and leadership.

As they became increasingly engaged in student organizations, the high-achievers noted that peer support for their pursuit of leadership also escalated. Because their involvement and leadership were overwhelmingly (but not exclusively) situated in predominantly Black student organizations, the participants relied heavily on African American students to support their agendas and quests for advancement.

Paul, a student at the University of Illinois, provided the following reflection:

> In becoming a student leader, other students motivated me with their words and their affirmations of the things I was doing. Just saying, "Paul, you know, you're doing such a great job; I really hope that you continue to be involved in this, and we have a meeting for this on Monday... I hope you'll come and run for this position." People just motivated me and they thought more positively of me than I was thinking of myself at times.

Paul served as president of the National Association for the Advancement of Colored People (NAACP) chapter at the University of Illinois; president of Iota Phi Theta (a predominantly Black fraternity); coordinator and treasurer of the African American Advisory Board Peer Recruitment Program; treasurer of the Black Student Union; and a member of the Association of Black Cultural Centers national conference committee. This level of participation in elected and appointed positions confirms the high regard in which his African American peers held his leadership. Otherwise, they would not have elected him to all these positions in predominantly Black student organizations, Paul believed.

The high-achievers also suggested their African American peers supported them simply because they were African American. This was critical for those who were involved in mainstream and predominantly White student organizations. "They don't really know what the organization does, but because they feel this camaraderie with another African American student who's running for a particular leadership position, they're going to vote for that student because he or she is Black." Keely Stewart suspected he was elected Student Representative to the Board of Trustees at the University of Illinois in part because of the support he received from African American students who had no clue who he was but knew he was African American. Similarly, Christopher, who served as vice president of the student government on his campus, said many African American students did not know him personally, "but they at least knew I was Black, some

were aware that I'm in Kappa Alpha Psi [a predominantly Black fraternity], and maybe a few had caught a glimpse of my leadership in previous roles." Therefore, they cast their votes in Christopher's favor during the student government election.

Forty-one percent of the participants held membership in one of the five national historically Black fraternities on their campuses. It should be made clear that fraternity affiliation is not requisite for African American male achievement or the acquisition of peer support at PWIs, as more than half of the participants in this study were unaffiliated. However, the 13 fraternity men in the sample acknowledged the organizations as an additional outlet for peer support and affirmation. They spoke at length about the value of having a close-knit group of African American male peers for whom achievement was important. Ted, then president of the Alpha Phi Alpha fraternity chapter at Purdue, noted that fellow members consistently encouraged academic achievement and were proud when he and the others did well. Ted also described various achievement incentives and recognition initiatives within the fraternity. Brian added, "Kappa Alpha Psi's fundamental purpose is achievement. Everyone in the chapter works to uphold this principle, and we support each other and hold each other accountable." All the fraternity men recalled the support their fellow chapter members extended as they sought major campus leadership positions as well as when they faced academic hardships and reached academic milestones.

In addition to fraternity brothers, the high-achievers also described the positive relationships they had formed with other African American male student leaders on campus. Many intentionally chose to surround themselves with guys who were "going somewhere," doing positive things on campus, and staying clear of trouble. This was the case both in high school and in college. On every campus I visited, each participant knew and had relationships with the other high-achieving African American male students I was interviewing. "The ironic thing is that I probably know every single person on the list that you're interviewing here at Purdue. We all know each other because we all support each other," David commented. As one participant walked out of the room and another entered, it was obvious that they knew each other well. It was not uncommon for two participants to shake hands, engage in the characteristically masculine "half hug," or strike up a brief conversation between the interviews.

The participants also had no problem admitting that some of the other participants in this study helped pave the way for them. For instance, Indiana University student Marshawn noted:

> Christopher Smith [another participant] was an orientation leader the summer before I was an orientation leader; he was a Union Board Director the year before I became a Union Board Director; and he was in IUSA the year before I was in IUSA. Primarily, I have followed him.

Although they were members of different fraternities, Christopher served as a peer mentor for Marshawn and encouraged his achievement through role modeling, advice giving, and public affirmation of his capabilities. Similarly, five of the six participants from the University of Michigan were members of H.E.A.D.S., an organization for African American male intellectuals on campus. They all described how supported they felt by fellow H.E.A.D.S. members and how African American men in the organization introduced each other to various institutional resources for academic support and leadership opportunities.

The high-achievers' interactions with and support for each other sometimes extended beyond their campuses. For instance, Ohio State student Cullen Buie and Purdue student Landon Lockhart were close friends in high school and continued to encourage each other throughout the college years. Three participants from three different campuses met during an eight-week summer internship program at Procter & Gamble in Cincinnati and remained connected for support upon returning to their respective universities. Also, Marshawn, Landon, Arnold, and Ted, all members of Alpha Phi Alpha, knew each other from district fraternity meetings and leadership conferences. A senior at Michigan State acknowledged another participant at the University of Illinois whom he had met at a leadership retreat his sophomore year; reportedly, the two regularly kept in touch and exchanged advice on winning campus elections.

Clarence attended a national conference for African American student leaders in Virginia the previous year. "I thank God for that trip. It was so refreshing to meet other Black student leaders and achievers. Keeping in touch with them has been a source of inspiration for me to continually strive toward greatness here at Michigan State," he added. Each high-achiever cited African American peers on his campus and beyond who supported, encouraged, and uplifted him.

Leveraging Peer Support

> The Bible says that if you let your light shine, people will recognize you. I'm a Christian, and I try to live my life for the Lord by treating people like I want to be treated. My peers support me because they know my efforts to advance the African American community here at Michigan State are genuine; it's not an act and I'm not a fake.

Robert's reflections are characteristic of the many explanations given by the 32 high-achievers articulating the volume of support extended by same-race peers. Each participant perceived himself as personable, indicating that he led by example and served as a role model for others. These personal characteristics garnered peer support for the African American men in this study. They also thought their peers deemed them credible because they had demonstrated excellence in prior leadership roles on their campuses. "I am known to get the job done and give

it my all," DeJuan contended. "That's why people respect and support me." Regarding their reputations as student leaders, Clarence said he was known to "put up or shut up," while Amondo indicated that he was a trustworthy innovator who effectively conveyed the needs of African American students to administrators at his university.

As previously mentioned, the participants were primarily involved in predominantly Black student organizations on their campuses. Their demonstrated dedication to Black and minority causes was one way same-race peer support was earned. Michael asked, "How can I be a sellout when the bulk of my waking energy is devoted to Black activities and clubs? No one has ever accused me of such because my contributions and my Blackness speak for themselves." In addition to serving as advocates for African American student interests, the participants also discussed their outreach efforts to other African American men. A participant at Ohio State commented:

> I have earned the respect of several brothas' on this campus because I am the one who is always pulling on their coattails saying, "Come on, get involved in this Black club, or come out to this Black event." Even though they don't always accept the invitation, they know how committed I am to uplifting our race.

Regarding leadership in Black student organizations, Michael added that "someone's gotta do it. They support me because I am one of the few African American males who helps get it done."

Raymond similarly also elaborated on the nexus between his leadership and the support he received from other African American students, especially men, at the University of Michigan.

> Brothas' understand that I am not just doing it for myself, but for other brothas' and sistas.' Because of that, I have a lot of respect from everyone on campus...even the Black male student-athletes know what I am doing, and they respect me so much.

Because they were visible spokespeople for the African American communities on their campuses, the high-achievers thought their peers saw them as leaders with whom they could identify. "Because I am one of their main ambassadors here at Purdue, Black students are proud of me when I excel, and they can identify with me as a charismatic Black male leader," David claimed. Clarence offered similar remarks: "I treat other African Americans as if they are my sisters and brothers, more than just acquaintances and constituents. Most of them know me, and they identify with me, even though they may make different choices." In sum, their demonstration of character and their reputations for being role models, reliable student leaders, and champions of African American student issues are the ways in which the 32 high-achievers were able to garner same-race peer support for their leadership and college achievements.

■ DISCUSSION AND IMPLICATIONS

Kunjufu (1988) posits that African American boys in primary and secondary schools are forced by their peers to choose between being popular and being smart. The participants in this study have successfully negotiated being both. Fordham and Ogbu (1986) claim these social pressures are often rooted in the belief that school achievement is characteristic of White students, not African Americans. As such, high-achieving African American students are often accused of "acting White." The participants in the present study reported dissimilar interactions with their same-race peers. Instead of accusing them of "acting White," other African Americans on the six campuses (including uninvolved male students) encouraged the high-achievers, supported their leadership, and applauded their successes. In fact, the participants unanimously cited support from their African American peers as essential to their success in college. Thus, the results of this study do not support Fordham and Ogbu's "acting White" hypothesis. Instead, findings here confirm previous assertions that African American students value their own and their peers' educational achievement. Furthermore, many high-achievers have positive self-esteem, high goal orientations, and strong

Black identities (Ainsworth-Darnell & Downey, 1998; Cook & Ludwig, 1998; Ferguson, 2001; Spencer, Noll, Stolzfus, & Harpalani, 2001).

It appears that the high-achiever's active involvement in initiatives to advance the African American community on his campus and to ensure that Black concerns were heard by the administration helped protect him from any possible peer perceptions of White-likeness. To "act White" yet hold major leadership positions in predominantly Black student organizations is illogical. Likewise, "acting White" suggests a weak racial identity and a lack of familiarity with issues affecting the African American community. Reportedly, other African American students on the six campuses were well aware of the high-achievers' efforts to address Black issues through involvement in organizations and participation on major campus committees. The breadth of the participants' achievements as well as their visibility on campus seemed to have shaped their peers' perceptions. If they were solely academic achievers instead of well-rounded student leaders who achieved both inside and outside the classroom, perhaps their peers would have rendered a different verdict on their Blackness. This conjecture deserves empirical exploration.

High-achieving students in Fries-Britt's (1995) study relied heavily on a race specific program for academically talented students to meet and interact with other African Americans. Although many of the high-achievers in the present study participated in special academic success programs for racial/ethnic minority students (e.g., the Minority Achievers Program at Indiana University), serving as members of Black fraternities and leaders of other Black student organizations were the primary ways through which they were afforded opportunities to interact with other African Americans. Fries-Britt (1997) maintains, "Establishing peer group connections for gifted Black students can be difficult as they seek to find other students who share their interest and level of ambition" (p. 3). Again, engagement in student organizations provided the high-achievers a chance to interact with African American students who were committed to similar causes and had common interests. Beyond serving as venues for meeting other highly involved students, leadership in Black student organizations also enabled the participants to establish connections with uninvolved African American students whose social needs were met and voices were represented through those organizations.

Several researchers have found that high-achieving African American students in K–12 schools "camouflage" their academic talent in order to fit in with their same-race peers (Ford, 1996; Fordham & Ogbu, 1986; Grantham & Ford, 2003; Horvat & Lewis, 2003). Clearly, that was not the case in the present study. Because the participants were viewed as role models by other African American students on campus, they were expected to do well in their classes and to continually represent excellence in their out-of-class endeavors. Therefore, they did not hide their talents or keep secret their accomplishments. It appears that the more their same-race peers became familiar with their contributions and achievements, the more they supported the high-achievers. Furthermore, the participants in the present study did not embrace "racelessness" as Fordham (1988) suggested, nor did they assimilate into White culture as Fries-Britt and Turner (2002) say many high-achieving African American students do. Instead, they were engaged in an array of activities on their campuses and devoted a significant portion of their energies and efforts to Black causes.

Contextual differences also seem to account for differences in same-sex peer reactions to engagement in activities other than those that characterize what Harper, Harris, and Mmeje (2005) call "context-bound gendered social norms"—prescriptive and locally agreed-upon masculine attitudes and behaviors. Like the participants in Davis's (2003) study, African American men on the six university campuses had developed masculine codes of conduct that were primarily characterized by athleticism and physical activity, the pursuit of romantic relationships with female students, being perceived as "cool," and various attitudinal and behavioral norms that did not focus on academic achievement. However, participants in the present study indicated that there were opportunities for negotiation, which is different from Davis's findings. Davis (2001) reported that those who fail to adhere to the masculine code are victimized

by their peers and expelled from boy networks at school. Although the decisions they made regarding the expenditure of their out-of-class time were far from normative, the high-achievers felt extremely supported by their same-race male peers. This shift in African American male peer support for activities beyond "the masculine code" from middle school to college should be explored more deeply.

Four practical implications for college and university administrators can be derived from this study. First, support (financial and otherwise) for predominantly Black clubs and minority student groups is imperative, as those organizations serve as the primary venues through which Black leadership is developed and achievement is embraced. Second, given the role of the five historically Black fraternities in offering social support and academic encouragement to African American male undergraduates, attempts should be made to sustain these organizations and increase African American male interest in membership. Third, because they afford opportunities for the cultivation of meaningful relationships with others who share similar values, goals, and experiences, administrators should commit financial resources for African American students to attend conferences and participate in leadership retreats. This is especially important because student leaders may find peer connections, validation, and support in these external venues that may not be available locally. Last, programming (e.g., a conversation series) that brings together members of different

African American student subgroups to discuss the importance of peer support and confront internalized racism is necessary.

In light of the findings that emerged in this study, two lingering questions are worthy of acknowledgment: (1) Is immunity from internalized racism and accusations of "acting White" extended to those who are not interested in becoming student leaders or being actively involved in predominantly Black student organizations, and (2) given the apparent strength of the participants' Black identities, would African American achievers whose racial identities are not as well-developed or as widely publicized also receive support from their same-race peers for their college achievements? While leadership and active engagement served as negotiation tools for the high-achievers, there is insufficient evidence to suggest that they would have been treated differently were they not as involved. In fact, the participants indicated that basic character traits (being dependable, approachable, fair, hard-working, etc.) also garnered same-race peer support. As noted previously, few researchers have explored the "acting White" hypothesis and internalized racism within the context of higher education. Additional effort should be devoted to investigating these concepts among various subgroups of African American collegians: uninvolved high academic achievers versus academically successful student leaders, those with strong Black identities versus students who embrace "racelessness,"

and African American women versus their same-race male counterparts.

■ CONCLUSION

There was no evidence of internalized racism—at least in the domains of academic achievement and Black male leadership—on the six campuses where data were collected for this study. Though different from the majority of their same-race male peers, the participants' achievements were not deemed abnormal or characteristically White. While there may possibly be limited encouragement for actually attending college (which was not explored in this study), it is clear that support and validation exist on university campuses once African American men enroll. For those who wish to make the most of their experiences both inside and outside the classroom, same-race peer support and opportunities for meaningful engagement with other African American students are both possible and likely. After listening to Kanye West's (2004) *The College Dropout*, one may erroneously conclude that college attendance, let alone college achievement, is extremely unpopular among African Americans. The experiences of the 32 African American men in this study confirm otherwise.

REFERENCES

Ainsworth-Darnell, J. W., & Downey, D. B. (1998). Assessing the oppositional culture explanation for racial/ethnic differences in school performance. *American Sociological Review*, 63(4), 536–553.

Astin, A. W. (1993). *What matters in college? Four critical years revisited*. San Francisco: Jossey-Bass.

Baker, D. G. (1983). *Race, ethnicity and power: A comparative study*. Boston: Routledge.

Baldwin, A. Y. (1991). Gifted Black adolescents: Beyond racism to pride. In M. Bireley & J. Genshaft (Eds.), *Understanding the gifted adolescent: Educational, developmental and multicultural issues* (pp. 231–239). New York: Teachers College Press.

Bonner II, F. A. (2001). *Gifted African American male college students: A phenomenological study*. Storrs, CT: The National Research Center on the Gifted and Talented.

Carnegie Foundation for the Advancement of Teaching. (2000). *The Carnegie classification of institutions of higher education*. Stanford, CA: Author.

Cook, P. J., & Ludwig, J. (1998). The burden of "acting White": Do Black adolescents disparage academic achievement? In C. Jencks & M. Phillips (Eds.), *The Black White test score gap* (pp. 375–400). Washington, DC: Brookings Institution Press.

Cooley, M. R., Cornell, D. G., & Lee, C. (1991). Peer acceptance and self-concept of Black students in a summer gifted program. *Journal for Education of the Gifted, 14,* 166–177.

Davis, J. E. (1994). College in black and white: Campus environment and academic achievement of African American males. *Journal of Negro Education,* 63(4), 620–633.

Davis, J. E. (1999). What does gender have to do with the experiences of African American college men? In V. C. Polite & J. E. Davis (Eds.), *African American males in school and society: Practices and policies for effective education* (pp. 134–148). New York: Teachers College Press.

Davis, J. E. (2001). Black boys at school: Negotiating masculinities and race. In R. Majors (Ed.), *Educating our Black children: New directions and radical approaches* (pp. 169–182). New York: RoutledgeFalmer.

Davis, J. E. (2003). Early schooling and academic achievement of African American males. *Urban Education,* 38(5), 515–533.

Denzin, N., & Lincoln, Y. (2000). Introduction: The discipline and practice of qualitative research. In N. Denzin & Y. Lincoln (Eds.), *Handbook of qualitative research* (2nd ed., pp. 1–28). Thousand Oaks, CA: Sage.

Essed, P. (1991). *Understanding everyday racism*. London: Sage.

Ferguson, R. F. (2001). A diagnostic analysis of Black-White GPA disparities in Shaker Heights, Ohio. *Brookings Papers on Education Policy,* 2001, 347–414.

Ford, D. Y. (1996). *Reversing underachievement among gifted Black students: Promising practices and programs*. New York: Teachers College Press.

Ford, D. Y., & Harris III, J. J. (1995). Underachievement among gifted African American students: Implications for school counselors. *School Counselor,* 42(3), 196–203.

Ford, D. Y., & Harris III, J. J. (1997). A study of the racial identity and achievement of Black males and females. *Roeper Review,* 20(2), 105–110.

Fordham, S. (1988). Racelessness as a strategy in Black students' school success: Pragmatic strategy or pyrrhic victory? *Harvard Educational Review,* 58(1), 54–84.

Fordham, S., & Ogbu, J. U. (1986). Black students' school success: Coping with the "burden of 'acting White.'" *Urban Review,* 18(3), 176–206.

Freire, P. (1970). *Pedagogy of the oppressed.* New York: Continuum.

Fries-Britt, S. L. (1997). Identifying and supporting gifted African American men. In M. J. Cuyjet (Ed.), *Helping African American men succeed in college. New directions for student services* (No. 80, pp. 65–78). San Francisco: Jossey-Bass.

Fries-Britt, S. L. (1998). Moving beyond Black achiever isolation: Experiences of gifted Black collegians. *Journal of Higher Education,* 69(5), 556–576.

Fries-Britt, S. L. (2002). High-achieving Black collegians. *About Campus,* 7(3), 2–8.

Fries-Britt, S. L. (2004). The challenges and needs of high-achieving Black college students. In M. C. Brown II & K. Freeman (Eds.), *Black colleges: New perspectives on policy and practice* (pp. 161–176). Westport, CT: Praeger.

Fries-Britt, S. L., & Turner, B. (2001). Facing stereotypes: A case study of Black students on a White campus. *Journal of College Student Development,* 42(5), 420–429.

Fries-Britt, S. L., & Turner, B. (2002). Uneven stories: Successful Black collegians at a Black and a White campus. *The Review of Higher Education,* 25(3), 315–330.

Gay, G. (2000). *Culturally responsive teaching.* New York: Teachers College Press.

Grantham, T. C., & Ford, D. Y. (2003). Beyond self-concept and self-esteem: Racial identity and gifted African American students. *The High School Journal,* 87(1), 18–29.

Griffin, K. (2006). Striving for success: A qualitative exploration of competing theories of high-achieving Black college students' academic motivation. *Journal of College Student Development,* 47(4), 384–400.

Harper, S. R. (2004). The measure of a man: Conceptualizations of masculinity among high-achieving African American male college students. *Berkeley Journal of Sociology,* 48(1), 89–107.

Harper, S. R. (2005a). Leading the way: Inside the experiences of high-achieving African American male students. *About Campus,* 10(1), 8–15.

Harper, S. R. (2005b, November). High-achieving African American men's behavioral responses to stereotypes at predominantly White universities. Paper presented at the annual meeting of the Association for the Study of Higher Education, Philadelphia, PA.

Harper, S. R. (2006a). *Black male students at public flagship universities in the U.S.: Status, trends, and implications for policy and practice.* Washington, DC: Joint Center for Political and Economic Studies.

Harper, S. R. (2006b). Enhancing African American male student outcomes through leadership and active involvement. In M. J. Cuyjet (Ed.), *African American men in college* (pp. 68–94). San Francisco: Jossey-Bass.

Harper, S. R., Harris III, F., & Mmeje, K. C. (2005). A theoretical model to explain the overrepresentation of college men among campus judicial offenders: Implications for campus administrators. *NASPA Journal,* 42(4), 565–588.

Hill Collins, P. (2004). *Black sexual politics: African Americans, gender, and the new racism.* New York: Routledge.

Hollins, E. R., & Spencer K. (1990). Restructuring schools for cultural inclusion: Changing the schooling process for African American youngsters. *Journal of Education,* 172, 89–100.

Holstein, J. A., & Gubrium, J. F (1995). The active interview. *Qualitative research method series* (No. 37). Thousand Oaks, CA: Sage.

hooks, b. (2004). *We real cool: Black men and masculinity.* New York: Routledge.

Horvat, E. M., & Lewis, K. S. (2003). Reassessing the "burden of 'acting White'": The importance of peer groups in managing academic success. *Sociology of Education,* 76(4), 265–280.

Irvine, J. J. (1990). *Black students and school failure.* Westport, CT: Greenwood Press.

Jones, C. P. (2000). Levels of racism: A theoretical framework and a gardener's tale. *American Journal of Public Health,* 90(8), 1212–1215.

Kunjufu, J. (1988). *To be popular or smart: The Black peer group.* Chicago: African American Images.

Ladson-Billings, G. J. (1995). Toward a theory of culturally relevant pedagogy. *American Education Research Journal,* 35, 465–491.

Lindstrom, R. R., & Van Sant, S. (1986). Special issues in working with gifted minority adolescents. *Journal of Counseling and Development,* 64, 583–586.

Lipsky, S. (1987). *Internalized racism.* Seattle: Rational Island Publishers.

Miles, M. B., & Huberman, A. M. (1994). *Qualitative data analysis: An expanded sourcebook* (2nd ed). Thousand Oaks, CA: Sage.

Moustakas, C. (1994). *Phenomenological research methods.* Thousand Oaks, CA: Sage.

National Center for Education Statistics. (2005). Integrated postsecondary education data system. Washington, DC: U.S. Department of Education, Institute of Education Sciences.

Ogbu, J. U. (2004). Collective identity and the burden of "acting White" in Black history, community, and education. *The Urban Review,* 36(1), 1–35.

Ogbu, J. U., & Simons, H. D. (1998). Voluntary and involuntary minorities: A cultural-ecological theory of school performance with some implications for education. *Anthropology and Education Quarterly,* 29(2), 155–188.

Pheterson, G. (1990). Alliances between women: Overcoming internalized oppression and internalized domination. In L. Albrecht & R. Brewer (Eds.), Bridges of power: Women's multicultural alliances (pp. 34–48). Philadelphia, PA: New Society.

Polkinghorne, D. E. (1989). Phenomenological research methods. In R. S. Valle & S. Halling (Eds.), *Existential-phenomenological perspectives in psychology* (pp. 41–60). New York: Plenum.

Pyke, K., & Dang, T. (2003). "FOB" and "Whitewashed": Identity and internalized racism among second generation Asian Americans. *Qualitative Sociology,* 26(2), 147–172.

Spencer, M. B., Noll, E., Stolzfus, J., & Harpalani, V. (2001). Identity and school adjustment: Revisiting the "acting White" assumption. *Educational Psychologist,* 36(1), 21–30.

West, K. (2004). *The college dropout* [CD]. New York: Roc-a-Fella Records.

CHAPTER 23

Expressions of Spirituality Among African American College Males

Michael K. Herndon

I n the past three decades, scholars have examined the role of spirituality and religious participation in the lives of African Americans. Considerable attention in this body of scholarly inquiry has been devoted to the sustaining effects of spirituality and religious practices in the family (Billingsley, 1968; Hill, 1972; Taylor, Chatters, Jayakody, & Levin, 1996). Few studies have viewed spirituality and religious practices in the arena of the academy. The purpose of this chapter is to examine spirituality among African American college males.

■ SPIRITUALITY AND RELIGION DEFINED

Researchers have defined spirituality in various ways. For example, Jagers and Smith (1996) suggested that spirituality is a worldview that is central to the cultural expressions found in the African Diaspora. On the other hand, Love and Talbot (1999) maintained that spirituality is a process that involves the pursuit for discovering direction, meaning, and purpose in one's life. Still other scholars, such as Mattis (2000), argued that spirituality is complex and includes belief in a supernatural dimension of life, a personal relationship with God; living according to God's will, and holding intrinsic beliefs and values. Some researchers maintain that there is a vast difference between spirituality and religion. Religion is typically associated with organized, institutional activities. It involves the practices and rituals of attendance in worship services, the reading of sacred texts, and affiliation with an organized church, mosque, or synagogue (Mattis, 2000).

■ AFRICAN AMERICANS, SPIRITUALITY, AND RELIGION

African Americans tend to have a strong religious orientation (Cone, 1990). That is, African Americans typically embrace the value of religion, its liberating power, the reliance on a higher power, and the practical application of spiritual principles in life (McAdoo, 1993). European Americans tend to view religion from a theoretical perspective (Thistlethwaite & Engel, 1990). European Americans do not necessarily place less value on spiritual matters, but may be more inclined to view spirituality from an intellectual, abstract, and highly conceptual perspective. The differences in theological perspectives between African Americans and Whites may be attributed to race, class, and social conditions (Taylor & Chatters, 1991). African Americans may also more heavily embrace spirituality as a coping mechanism to deal with stress.

Mundane extreme environmental stress (M.E.E.S.) is a conceptual framework Carroll (1998) developed to explain issues surrounding emotional support and African American college students enrolled at predominantly White institutions (PWIs). The stress that African American students experience on White campuses is mundane. That is to say, this kind of stress is so prevalent in the daily experiences of African Americans, that in many cases, it is considered a part of routine activities. This kind of stress is viewed as extreme. It has the potential to negatively affect African American students' emotional well-being, perceptions of self, and manner of thinking, feeling, and acting (Carroll, 1998).

The type of stress that Carroll (1998) has described is environmental. This is to suggest that the stress some African American students experience at majority institutions is produced, fostered, and embedded within the fabric of the campus environment. All of these factors—mundane, extreme, and environmental—work to create stress (Carroll, 1998). As a result of these environmental conditions, some African American students may turn to spirituality as a coping mechanism. Institutions of higher education may provide various forms of support to African American male students (Allen, 1992; Carroll, 1998). One form of support is academic. Academic support may be manifested in tutoring services, contact with faculty, and peer mentoring programs. Academic support is also provided through campus facilities like libraries and computer laboratories that support student learning (Allen, 1987; Tinto, 1993).

African American men at PWIs also need emotional support. Emotional support may be viewed as the form of support individuals received during life's stresses and strains. This support can take the form of providing assistance with coping or serving as a buffer in times of crisis (Cohen & Willis, 1985). Students may receive this kind of support formally from services provided by campus counseling centers. Others may seek emotional support informally from faculty, staff, or peers in the campus community.

Still another form of assistance beneficial to African American men on college campuses is social support (Mallinckrodt & Leong, 1992). In the context of the college environment, social support relates to the friendship and social networks formed by students. Student clubs and organizations are examples of social support networks. Participation in collegiate athletics and intramural sports provides social support for some students. Still other students receive social support from interactions in living and learning communities in residence halls (Mallinckrodt & Leong, 1992).

A fourth form of support for African American men is financial support (St. John & Noell, 1989). Students may receive financial support from multiple sources. One form of financial support is present in the various federal and state need-based programs. For instance, students may be awarded Pell grants or guaranteed student loans through the federal government. Students may also benefit from financial support programs offered through their state government. Financial support also may be provided from institutional resources. For example, some students may qualify for grants, loans, or scholarships directly from the institution of enrollment (St. John & Noell, 1989).

These forms of support (academic, emotional, social, and financial) are needed for all students, regardless of race or gender. However, some campuses have made special efforts to provide support for African American students. Administrative units in higher education provide varying forms of institutional support for African American students (Tinto, 1993). Support efforts range from the construction of cultural centers on predominately White campuses (Tomlinson, 1992) to the role faculty and administrators play in retaining African American students (Schneider, 1992).

While these forms of institutional support are critical to African American male college student success, there may be one additional component African American students need. Despite the efforts of administrators on predominantly White campuses, many African American males seek support from resources beyond those provided by the campus community, particularly in the form of spirituality and religious practices. African American students at predominately White institutions report higher levels of spirituality and religiosity than White students at predominantly White campuses (Walker & Dixon, 2002). Therefore, it would seem that opportunities to practice one's religion or engage in acts of spirituality are beneficial for African American students attending majority institutions. In general, the literature has overlooked the role of spirituality in the daily lives of African American students.

The studies have particularly ignored the relationship between spirituality and academic performance among members of this group (Walker & Dixon, 2002).

■ PURPOSE OF THE STUDY

The purpose of this study was to explore the role of spirituality in the life of African American college males. The study was specifically designed to examine spirituality as a factor related to African American college males' ability to remain in school. Thus, the research question for the study was: How does spirituality among African American male college students affect their ability to stay in school?

■ METHODOLOGY AND INSTRUMENTATION

To collect data, the researcher conducted two sample selections. First, the researcher selected a rural predominantly White institution. Second, African American male students who were enrolled at the selected rural PWI at the time of the study were invited to participate in this study based upon the referral of student participants.

The researcher developed an interview protocol. The protocol consisted of two sections. The first section sought demographic information about the participants, including age and years of completed education. The second section gathered data about the research question.

Description of the Sample

Thirteen African American male students participated in this study. The students ranged in age from 19 to 26 years of age. Participants in the study were pursuing degrees in the fields of architecture, business, chemistry, education, engineering, and mathematics at a comprehensive research university in the Mid-Atlantic United States. Ten participants identified with the tradition of Christianity, one participant was affiliated with the religion of Islam, and two considered themselves as "other."

Authenticity and Trustworthiness

Authenticity in qualitative research relates to whether the technique employed in the study is designed to elicit data relevant to the questions posed in the study (Denzin & Lincoln, 1994). One step was taken to enhance authenticity in the present study. The researcher asked seven experts to examine the interview protocols and verify that the researcher posed questions likely to elicit data relevant to the research question.

Trustworthiness, in qualitative research, relates to the credibility and objectivity in the collection, reporting, and analysis of data (Ely, Anzul, Friedman, Garner, & Steinmetz, 1991). To enhance trustworthiness in the study, the researcher took two steps. First, the researcher summarized at the end of each interview what he believed were the key points the individual respondent made. Participants were invited to add, delete, or change major points if they so desired. This step ensured that the researcher would accurately report data elicited from each participant.

Second, the researcher provided transcripts of each interview to the respective participant and asked participants to review, edit, add, or change their comments as appropriate. This step was taken to ensure that participants were confident that the transcripts accurately reflected their opinions. Such participant review is a typical method of enhancing trustworthiness in qualitative research (Bryman & Burgess, 1994).

Data Analysis Procedures

The researcher employed the grounded theory method for data collection. The grounded theory method is a qualitative research technique that is widely used (Strauss & Corbin, 1990) and allows for data collection and analysis to occur simultaneously. This approach allows for continuous change in data collection and analysis and affords researchers the opportunity to make decisions related to analyses based upon personal perceptions. This procedure is known as the constant comparative method. Using this approach, the researcher allows the data to generate theory (Strauss & Corbin, 1990).

Analysis occurred by open and axial coding. Open coding is the examination and breaking down of collected data. These data are grouped in categories for theme identification as themes emerge. Axial coding involves the process of sorting themes into groupings and categories

while analyzing the meanings and interrelationships among categories (Strauss & Corbin, 1990).

■ FINDINGS

African American college males described the role of spirituality and their ability to remain in school. After analyzing all the data of the individual interviews and reviewing field notes, three themes emerged: (1) spirituality bolsters resilience; (2) spirituality provides a sense of purpose; and (3) spiritual support is provided by African American religious institutions. In the following sections, the researcher describes each theme. Quotes from the transcripts are used to present themes.

Spirituality Bolsters Resilience

The first theme revealed in the findings related to spirituality as a bolster for resilience. Participants maintained that their abiding acts of spirituality contributed to their ability to remain in school. These acts of spirituality included prayers, church attendance, and reading scriptures or inspirational writings. Participants reported that these behaviors served as coping mechanisms. Further, respondents believed that these acts assisted in shouldering the stresses and strains of life and caused them to excel in the face of academic and social adversities. One student commented: "Spirituality helps me to push more often to get ahead. It helps me accept there will be pitfalls, challenges, and shortcomings and that it is key to get up more times than one falls down." Another participant stated: [Spirituality] helps me cope with White people. Sometimes I find it difficult to interact with them." Still another student reported: "Spirituality in academics is very important because during the bad times, I'm encouraged to push on." One participant stated that spirituality assisted him with resilience in a White environment:

It is very frustrating attending school at a predominantly White college. However, I constantly remind myself that I cannot and will not allow myself to be defeated by the obstacles that have been placed before me. My spirit helps me to stay strong and never give up. My spirit also tells me that, once I give up, I am defeated. If I allow this to happen, I am of no use to anyone.

Spirituality Provides a Sense of Purpose

In the second theme, research participants described spirituality as providing a sense of purpose, direction, and focus in life. Participants referred to purpose in terms of current and future tasks that should be accomplished. The following quotes are illustrative of this theme. One respondent related: "Keeping in touch with my spirit allows me to have peace of mind and helps me to stay focused. No matter how hard times may get, I am always in touch with my spirit." Yet another student stated: "Spirituality remains the structure of my inner core.

Without it, I would have no focus or sense of purpose in life. I feel that it is something that must be developed and appreciated over time." One participant remarked:

The role of spirituality has shown its face more and more. It propelled me to go back to school to have a degree with a purpose. It gave me purpose in doing well and having a certain amount of scholarly excellence. Spirituality shined even brighter for me. I faced academic challenges that I was a stranger to. Even though I face grim circumstances, spirituality allows me to maintain focus and faith. It's helped me to refine my mission and how it relates to my academic goals. What seem to be dark circumstances, I turn around. It has been my guide, comforter, shield, and a source of energy. Spirituality plays the most important role in my life. Without spirituality, my life will be empty and have a lot of uncertainty.

Another respondent claimed, "Spirituality is my sole purpose of existence. The things that I am, that I strive to do, and all that I look forward to in the future are based upon my spirituality."

Spiritual Support Provided by African American Religious Institutions

The findings of this study suggest that African American religious institutions have a responsibility to support African American males. Local congregations are pivotal, as they allow college students a formal venue to continue exploring their spirituality. The following quotes demonstrate the tenor of this theme. One respondent exclaimed:

> It [the church] is essential to my survival as a student. I couldn't have accomplished my academic goals without a place to go. It's only a building, a testament to God, but still a building. The people are the true testament. It is through them that God manifests His beauty. They have encouraged me to stay in school and to do well and to put God first. They have also encouraged me to choose my battles wisely and to allocate my time wisely so as to not be overly burdened by this system of things.

Another participant explained: "They [church members] have connected me to [local institution]/they have become my extended family and support network." Last, an additional student reported:

> I attend several local churches in the area and find that upon doing my homework, getting in my devotional time, and meditating on the Word I read through the week, I receive an extra boost of encouragement to keep me in check.

■ DISCUSSION AND LIMITATIONS

Spirituality was viewed as an anchor and source of comfort, as reported by most of the respondents. Prayer, participation in religious services, and private devotions were valued among participants in this study. In general, it is reasonable to conclude that African American males who have a faith in God and who receive spiritual support from families and others are more likely to succeed in college. The results of this study offer some important implications for several interest groups. These include not only African American college males and their families, but also individuals who work to recruit African American males to higher education and those who develop student success programs. In addition, African American clergy and laypersons may be well served by the implications of this study. For example, African American parents need to establish spiritual expectations, values, and beliefs that will help their students succeed. It is the responsibility of parents to be sure that their students are developing spiritually prior to their arrival at communities of higher education. The findings of the study suggest that such spiritual development and formation will assist students to persevere and endure through adverse situations as they matriculate through higher education.

Students may reflect upon the relationship between their own spirituality and academic pursuits. Such reflection may help students to assign meaning to broad political, social, and ethical issues. This form of introspection may enhance the formation of one's worldview and may be a critical factor in students' decision-making abilities. Moreover, developing one's spirituality appears to foster a sense of intestinal fortitude. In several instances, participants described their spirituality as "my spirit." The researcher interpreted this phraseology as an internal locus of control and guiding force, empowering one to remain centered and focused in challenging conditions.

The results of this study also hold implications for administrators who develop programs for African American males in out-of-class experiences. For example, student affairs staff can play a critical role in coordinating programs related to spirituality in the residence halls and assisting students in identifying campus ministries and local congregations. In addition to the role of family members and campus administrators, local centers of worship are essential to the continued spiritual development of college students. For instance, members of African American churches and mosques located in vicinities surrounding institutions of higher education can help students to continue in their faith. Local congregations of believers may assist students with outreach programs that may include the weekly study of sacred texts, preparing meals for students during specified study breaks, and providing transportation to weekly worship services. Local congregations and college students may also mutually benefit when one worship service in each month is devoted to the interests and needs of students. Such activities may allow students to develop resources and fictive kin relationships away from home.

Clearly, there were limitations to this study. The first was the nature of its design. This study used qualitative research methods and, as with all qualitative studies, the results are generalizable only to the particular samples within this study. Other limitations also relate to the qualitative nature of the study. For example, it was possible that the interview protocol did not include questions that would lead participants to talk about other elements related to the role of spirituality as it relates to one's success in higher education. If this occurred, the results might have been influenced. Likewise, it is possible that participants interpreted questions differently than the researcher intended. If so, this might have influenced their responses and hence influenced the results of the study.

Finally, but perhaps most important, it is possible that the researcher's own biases influenced the data collection or data analysis process. The researcher is African American. Since his race was evident to participants, it is possible that respondents provided information that was less than candid or that reflected what they thought the researcher was seeking. Being African American was beneficial in gaining access to the participants. On the other hand, respondents might have assumed that the researcher knew all about the complexities of being African American and may not have been as forthcoming in providing data. It was also possible that the researcher's own life experiences influenced the way he perceived the findings. If either of these eventualities occurred, the results would likely have been influenced. Despite these limitations, however, the study provided some important information about African American college students and their sense of spirituality and confidence on a majority White campus.

■ CONCLUSIONS

This study identified three themes that explain the role of spirituality among African American male college students. These factors enhance student persistence. If African American males embrace and maximize their spirituality, the findings suggest that they will persist in college. Likewise, developing relationships with believers affiliated with a local assembly appears to enhance students' sense of spirituality. The cultural dynamics of spiritual applications are different for African Americans than for their White counterparts. Defining, involving, and maintaining spiritual practices while in college appears to be different for African Americans. More research is needed to examine the complexities of ethnicity, spirituality, and participation in higher education.

REFERENCES

Allen, W. A. (1987). Black colleges vs. White colleges: The fork in the road for African American students. *Change,* 19, 28–34.

Allen, W. A. (1992). The color of success: African American college student outcomes at predominantly White and historically African American public colleges and universities. *Harvard Educational Review,* 62, 26–44.

Billingsley, A. (1968). *Black families in White America.* Englewood Cliffs, NJ: Prentice Hall.

Bryman, A., & Burgess, R. G. (Eds.). (1994). *Analyzing qualitative data.* New York: Routledge.

Carroll, G. (1998). *Environmental stress and African Americans: The other side of the moon.* Westport, CT: Praeger Publishers.

Cohen, S., & Wills, T. (1985). Stress, social support, and the buffering hypothesis. *Psychological Bulletin,* 98, 310–357.

Cone, J. H. (1990). God is black. In S. B. Thistlethwaite & M. P. Engel (Eds.), *Lift every voice: Constructing Christian theologies from the underside* (pp. 81–94). San Francisco: HarperCollins Publishers.

Denzin, N. K., & Lincoln, Y. S. (Eds.). (1994). *Handbook of qualitative research.* Thousand Oaks, CA: Sage Publications.

Dressler, W. (1987). Household structure in a southern African American community. *American Anthropologist,* 87, 853–862.

Ely, M., Anzul, M., Friedman, T., Garner, D., & Steinmetz, A. (1991). *Doing qualitative research: Cycles within circles.* New York: The Palmer Press.

Hill, R. (1972). *Strengths of Black families.* New York: National Urban League.

Jagers, R. J., & Smith, P. (1996). Further examination of the spirituality scale. *Journal of Black Psychology,* 22, 429–442.

Love, P., & Talbot, D. (1999). Defining spiritual development: A missing consideration for student affairs. *NASAP Journal, 37*, 361–375.

Mallinckrodt, B., & Leong, F. (1992). Social support in academic programs and family environments: Sex differences and role conflicts for graduate students. *Journal of Counseling and Development, 70*, 716–723.

Mattis, J. S. (2000). African American women's definitions of spirituality and religiosity. *Journal of Black Psychology, 26*, 101–122.

McAdoo, H. P. (Ed.). (1993). *Family ethnicity: Strength in diversity*. Newbury Park, CA: Sage Publications.

St. John, E. P., & Noell, J. (1989). The effects of student financial aid on access to higher education: An analysis of progress with special consideration of minority enrollment. In C. Turner, M. Garcia, A. Nora, & L. Rendon (Eds.), *Racial and ethnic diversity in higher education* (pp. 563–580). Needham Heights, MA: ASHE Reader Series, Simon and Schuster.

Schneider, A. J. (1992). African American student retention: The role of African American faculty and administrators at traditionally White institutions. In M. Lang & C. Ford (Eds.), *Strategies for retaining minority students in higher education* (pp. 125–132). Springfield, IL: Charles C. Thomas Publishing.

Strauss, A. L., & Corbin, J. (1990). *Basics of qualitative research: Grounded theory procedures and techniques*. Newbury Park, CA: Sage Publications.

Taylor, R. J., & Chatters, L. M. (1991). Religious life. In J.S. Jackson (Ed.), *Life in African American America* (pp. 105–123). Newbury Park, CA: Sage Publications.

Taylor, R. J., Chatters, L. M., Jayakody, R., & Levin, J. S. (1996). Black and White differences in religious participation: A multisample comparison. *Journal for the Scientific Study of Religion, 35*, 403–410.

Thistlethwaite, S. B., & Engel, M. P. (1990). *Lift every voice: Constructing Christian theologies from the underside*. San Francisco: HarperCollins Publishers.

Tinto, V. (1993). *Leaving college: Rethinking the causes and cures of student attrition*. Chicago: University of Chicago Press.

Tomlinson, L. M. (1992). A qualitative investigation of administrators' assessment of cultural centers on predominantly White campuses. In M. Lang & C. Ford (Eds.), *Strategies for retaining minority students in higher education* (pp. 85–94). Springfield, IL: Charles C. Thomas Publishing.

Walker, K. L., & Dixon, V. (2002). Spirituality and academic performance among African American college students. *Journal of Black Psychology, 28*, 107–121.

College Men of Color
Implications for Educational Practice

C hapters in Part Five reveal much about the experiential complexities of male students of color on college and university campuses. Their interactions with predominantly White environments, in particular, are quite different from their same-sex peers who comprise the majority. Urgently necessary are institutional responses to the realities of race for college men of color. Recommendations offered here are framed around statements and questions from the Introduction to Part Five regarding the myth of a post-racial America.

■ I DON'T SEE COLOR

Anyone who attempts to eradicate outcomes disparities between racial minority males and their White counterparts must first acknowledge that such differences are attributable, at least in part, to structural racism. As such, men's gendered experiences are colored by the inequitable distribution of power, privilege, and voice in shaping prevailing masculine scripts on campus. It is therefore necessary to critically challenge one's own colorblind ideologies as well as those of colleagues who work with students. As we mentioned earlier, claiming to not see color is an offensive way of denying the racialized experiences of men of color—those who make diversity possible through their presence and cultural contributions to college environments yet are simultaneously oppressed by people and structural norms that render them subordinate. Although color blindness is most often embraced by those who mean well and seek to thwart the amplification of racial differences, college men of color need the exact opposite. They are better served by advocates who see them for who they are (note that we didn't say "see them as different") and make widely known to colleagues and White students how the experiential realities of men of color help explain persistent gender gaps in engagement and achievement. We recommend removing racial blinders that obstruct the view of how differently men of color interact with predominantly White spaces in which hegemonic masculinities were constructed and are constantly reinforced without their participation.

■ WHY CAN'T THEY JUST JOIN OUR FRATERNITIES?

As mentioned in the Introduction to this section, men of color have long been excluded from predominantly White fraternities; at many institutions, those who seek membership are often met with resistance. Likewise, the occasional few who are granted the privilege of participation are expected to assimilate into a culture that belongs to the White majority, where color blindness supposedly renders their ethnic backgrounds unimportant. Thus, advisors to the Interfraternity Council (IFC) and chapters populated primarily (or exclusively) by White male undergraduates should engage these members in critical dialogue that awakens their consciousness about why segregation persists in most Greek systems; how little effort they actually exert to recruit members of color; and what needs to be done to make the culture of a predominantly White fraternity more welcoming to and inclusive of racially diverse members. Furthermore, advisors to IFC fraternities should also work to help members understand the value-added nature of ethnic fraternities—how they offer Latino men, for example, a culturally affirming space that is almost always missing from predominantly White fraternities they had no involvement in creating.

■ ETHNIC STUDENT ORGANIZATIONS: WHY ARE THEY SO SEPARATE?

Educators and administrators should rely on Chapters 20, 22, and 23 of this book to justify the continued need for ethnic student organizations. Juan Guardia, Nancy Evans, and Shaun Harper offer what we view as compelling insights into the value of clubs, organizations, and activities that are specifically geared toward racial minority students. No, we are not separatists. However, chapters in Part Five expose the psychoemotical exhaustion that routinely ensues when one is the only student of color in each of his courses, on his entire residence hall floor, on the golf team, on the student senate executive board, and in campus spaces he occupies throughout the day. His desperate need for cultural familiarity, comfort, and validation is therefore understandable, at least to us. Moreover, minority student organizations are often the only place on campus where a student of color might find supportive others to sustain his persistence toward baccalaureate degree attainment—participants described by Michael Herndon in Chapter 23 had to go off campus (church, to be exact) to find the encouragement they needed. Hence, minority males need advocates who defend the significance of population-specific student organizations. These educators must help administrators and campus activity fee allocation boards (which are usually composed almost exclusively of White students) recognize the necessity of committing institutional resources (fiscal, advisory, and spatial) to ethnic organizations and activities for students of color.

■ WHY IS THERE NOTHING DEVOTED TO WHITE MALES?

Much of this book is in fact about White undergraduate men and the hegemonic masculinities they consistently reinforce on college and university campuses. Those who work with White students have a responsibility to help them recognize their privilege as well as the meaningful roles they can play in the elusive quest for racial justice. A good teacher will be able to effectively awaken consciousness of how institutional structures are overwhelmingly reflective of the social, cultural, political, and economic interests of White students. One way to do this is through a dialogue group for White and minority men, in which a skilled facilitator enables students to talk through who really benefits from the disproportionate share of institutional resources, whose perspectives on masculinities are most pervasive, and what is needed to help all men feel equally included, affirmed, and important on campus. In the absence of a structured conversation venue such as this, many White men will understandably perceive an emphasis on men of color as disregard for their needs and issues. These topics can also be addressed through programming offered in residence halls, in a dialogue series jointly sponsored by the IFC and the minority Greek council, and in classroom discussions.

■ FOCUS MORE ON OUR SIMILARITIES

Persons who declare color blindness often advance this recommendation. If done properly, it is something with which we actually agree (although we have made painstakingly clear that we both see color and are certain that racism still exists).

We believe it to be educationally beneficial and worthwhile to bring together men from all racial and ethnic backgrounds to talk about themselves as men and to work collaboratively on the accomplishment of a certain goal. For example, a service learning opportunity would be an ideal occasion to have men work together on something meaningful and process their shared experience. The educator who supervises the experience can help men understand how they were similarly affected by it and what common benefits were conferred to all who participated. Moreover, this professional should also point out how the men behaved. An example of a question that might be posed is, "Seth, you appeared uncomfortable sharing the leadership of this activity with Kwame; why was that?" And another is, "You were supposed to work collaboratively, so why were all the White guys working together on this one dimension of the project and all the Asian Americans on another?" Processing service learning or any other type of collaborative experience in this way will help male students become more thoughtful about how they interact with other men, especially those from different backgrounds.

THE ELECTION OF PRESIDENT OBAMA

The last dimension of the opening statements from which we wish to offer practical implications is the erroneous misconception that racism went to its final resting place on January 20, 2009. Given that Harper and Hurtado's study of campus racial climates was published in 2007, just two years prior, it is possible (though highly unlikely) that racial disadvantage miraculously disappeared from the structural fabric of American higher education. But this is not an assumption under which educators and administrators should perform their work. Instead, they ought to engage in ongoing assessments to determine how men and women from different racial backgrounds perceive, respond to, and are affected by the campus climate. Surveys, focus groups with specific populations, and informal conversations with multiple students (not just a single spokesperson for an entire racial group) are some options for garnering these insights.

Also, President Obama is biracial; he has intersecting identities. We believe it important for educators and administrators to address more conscientiously the multiple dimensions of men's identities—some are Vietnamese and low income, others are Black and gay or Native American and White. Professionals who endeavor to respond effectively to the needs of male students of color cannot treat them as a monolithic group and should offer programs, services, and resources that enable their identities to productively intersect. Lastly, to become the first man of color to be elected President of the United States is undeniably a significant marker of achievement. Insights into his journey toward success in politics and fatherhood are vividly disclosed in Obama's (2006) autobiography, *The Audacity of Hope*. In this same way, postsecondary educators should seek out male students of color who thrive in college, despite the odds stacked against them. Much can be learned from men who earn good grades, are actively engaged and assume leadership positions on campus, and resist the internalization of debilitating racial and gender stereotypes about them. As we suggested in Chapter 1, more programming models and interventions should be based on what is learned from male achievers.

REFERENCES

Harper, S. R., & Hurtado, S. (2007). Nine themes in campus racial climates and implications for institutional transformation. In S. R. Harper, & L. D. Patton (Eds.), *Responding to the realities of race on campus*. New Directions for Student Services (No. 120, pp. 7–24). San Francisco: Jossey-Bass.

Obama, B. (2006). *The audacity of hope: Thoughts on reclaiming the American dream*. New York: Vintage.

PART SIX

COLLEGE MEN AND SPORTS: INTRODUCTION

Sports play a prominent role in the gender socialization of adolescent boys. In our own research, nearly every male student we have interviewed has somehow referenced his participation in youth sports. Very few of these men continue their participation in organized sports after high school. Yet these experiences have long-lasting effects on their beliefs and assumptions about gender and masculinities. We have also found that even though a small number of college men participate in intercollegiate athletics, the prominence and visibility of men's sports teams influence male campus norms and gender dynamics in observable ways. These were some of the reasons that compelled us to dedicate some space in this volume to college men and sports. Part Six will also bring much-needed attention to student-athletes in the published higher education and student affairs literature on gender and masculinities. The five chapters in Part Six cover a range of sports-related issues that

473

impact men's experiences on college campuses, notably gender equity, gender role conflict, and the stratification of masculinities in sports, to name a few.

The masculine conceptualizations of men who have permanent physical limitations have gone largely unaddressed in the recent discourse on college men and masculinities. Recall the phenomenon of male gender role conflict that was presented and discussed in Part One. This phenomenon describes the psychological stress and anxiety that manifest when men are unable to express masculinities according to culturally defined expectations. Because men's bodies weigh heavily in their gender performance, we suspect that men with physical disabilities experience some internalized conflict that can be attributed to this aspect of their identities. Our assertion raises the questions: "Do men with physical disabilities experience gender role conflict related to this aspect of their identities?" and if so, "What strategies do they rely upon to manage gender role conflict?" These questions were considered in a study by Diane E. Taub, Elaine M. Blinde, Kimberly R. Greer presented in Chapter 24. The authors explore how participation in physical activities and sports can challenge stigmas and stereotypes that construct men who are disabled as weak and physically incompetent. Through a series of in-depth interviews with college men who were active in sports and a range of physical activities despite having some physical disabilities, Taub and her colleagues discovered that participation in sports and physical activities does, in fact, facilitate physical competence for men with physical disabilities and counter negative stereotypes of this group. Taub and her colleagues also make an important link to participation in sports and the social construction of masculinities. They found that the participants valued their participation in sports because it provided opportunities for them to demonstrate competitiveness, dominance, independence, and physical prowess—characteristics that are culturally defined as masculine—despite their physical limitations.

Less than half of Black male college student-athletes are awarded a college degree within six years of their enrollment. In comparison, 60% of their White male counterparts earn a college degree in six years. These data are troubling and have led some to conclude that Black male student-athletes are "pimped" or "exploited" by institutions that benefit financially from their physical talents but take no interest in their academic success. Two chapters in this section focus on the educational gains and outcomes (or lack thereof) of Black male college student-athletes.

In Chapter 25, Shaun R. Harper uses the critical race concept of "interests convergence" to argue why the transfer success of Black male student-athletes should be an institutional priority for community college administrators, faculty, and coaches. Harper contends that the interests of Black male student-athletes and the community colleges for which they compete "converge" around one key outcome variable, "transfer to a four-year institution." The essence of Harper's argument is as follows: When compared to men of other racial/ethnic backgrounds, Black male student-athletes have higher expectations for pursuing professional athletic careers. Four-year college and university athletic programs offer a critical pathway to professional sports. Therefore, a critical mass of Black male community college student-athletes desire to transfer to a four-year institution and ultimately compete professionally in their respective sports. Likewise, student transfer to four-year institutions is an area of accountability for which community college leaders are being held more responsible. Based on the convergence of these interests, Harper offers four compelling reasons for why community college leaders should be more serious and strategic in ensuring the transfer success of Black male student-athletes.

In Chapter 26 Krystal K. Beamon challenges the widely held assumption that participation in athletics provides Black men from underprivileged backgrounds opportunities for educational advancement they would not have been afforded otherwise. Based on findings from a study of Black men who formerly competed in Division I football and basketball, Beamon offers compelling evidence that shows how athletic participation can be disadvantageous for Black men's academic and long-term career success. For example, nearly all of Beamon's participants had earned college degrees but because of their institutions' preoccupation with eligibility for student-athletes rather than academic excellence or success believed their academic development was compromised. Another compelling, yet very unfortunate, finding is that most of the participants felt as though they had been "used" or "exploited" by their institutions. This perception was informed, in part, by the huge disparities between what the former student-athletes had been given by the institutions as compensation for their participation in athletics and the money the institutions generated from their sports through television contracts, ticket sales, merchandising, and other sources of revenue.

In Chapter 27, Michael A. Messner and Nancy M. Solomon offer a critical analysis of the public debate surrounding gender equity and Title IX legislation in college athletics. Title IX, as it relates to college sports, mandates that institutions have proportionality in the number of women and men who participate in athletics. To meet this mandate, some athletics departments have eliminated multiple minor men's sports teams (cross-country, swimming, gymnastics, golf, tennis, and wrestling), thereby reducing the number of male student-athletes. This practice is very prevalent at institutions with football programs because fielding these teams requires a large number of male student-athletes to participate and consumes a large chunk of department resources to pay for coach's salaries, travel costs, equipment, and scholarships. The result is a backlash against women's sports and claims of discrimination against men. Some critics believe that efforts to achieve gender equity in sports are irrational because, unlike women, men are "biologically programmed" to participate in sports. Despite evidence of the contrary, which shows that women's interests in sports actually increases when there are more opportunities to participate, the assumption here is that gender equity is a pointless goal because women will never have the level of interest in sports as men.

Of central concern for Messner and Solomon is where men in minor sports teams, who face the threat of elimination, position themselves in the Title IX debate. More often than not, these men side with critics of Title IX even though they would be better-served if institutions distributed resources more equitably across men's sports. Messner and Solomon offer several examples of how a fraction of the money that is allocated to one football program could be used to fund an entire nonrevenue team while still meeting Title IX mandates. This discussion sheds light on several key issues related to patriarchy and male privilege in college sports. Because sports are viewed by many as a privileged space for men, efforts to provide opportunities for women to participate in this domain are met with fierce resistance by men. In addition, this discussion illuminates some of the ways in which masculinities are stratified in college sports programs. Messner and Solomon posit that men who participate in team sports that require aggression or violent contact (e.g., football and men's basketball) are assumed to be more masculine than men who participate in noncontact or individual sports. This hierarchy often guides decision making in college athletics regarding the distribution of resources. On many campuses, resources are distributed disproportionately in favor of football and men's basketball.

In Chapter 28, Jackson Katz discusses the Mentors in Violence Prevention (MVP) program. MVP uses sport as a context to challenge hegemonic masculinities, to engage college men in efforts to stop men's violence against women, and to promote healthier gender-related beliefs, attitudes, and behaviors among men. Katz maintains that since the overwhelming majority of violence against women is committed by men, it's critical that men assume leadership and take action to stop it. In contrast, violence against women has always been viewed by society as a women's issue—as evidenced by the number of prevention efforts directed toward women on college campuses (e.g., self-defense courses, sexual assault prevention) and the relatively few programs and interventions that involve men.

MVP targets male "bystanders"—men who observe other men, often peers, act in violent or sexist ways toward women but do not challenge their behavior. Katz maintains that these men represent a "silent majority" who, with proper training, would be willing to challenge their peers when they see violence and abuse taking place. Male athletes, particularly those in high-profile sports, are also targeted for involvement in MVP because their participation and success in sports affords them some respect and credibility among peers and younger men. Thus, according to Katz, these men are well-positioned to take leadership in ending men's violence against women.

Much like the Men Against Violence initiative described by Hong in Part Three of this volume, MVP is another example of how college men can be provided structured opportunities to reflect and dialogue with other men about masculinities. In fact, Katz contends that this is the "single most important" feature of the program. Given its success in college and professional sports, where some of the most intensely masculine cultures and ideas are fostered, it seems reasonable to conclude that the MVP model can be employed successfully with many different groups of men on college campuses, including student leaders, residence hall advisors, fraternity members, first-year students, and men of color as examples.

Taken together, several key issues related to masculinities in college sports resonate across these chapters. We see very clearly how sport is a context that rewards men, particularly those who perform masculinities in very traditional ways. Consequently, women and men who lack certain physical capabilities or athletic prowess are subordinated or denied opportunities to participate in this domain. We also see how the competitive ethos of college sports is not restricted to the courts or playing fields. The "win at all costs" ethic is quite pervasive and often threatens student access for women and student success for men of color. On a more positive note, some potentially promising examples of how sports can be used to promote and facilitate student learning and development in college are also offered in these chapters.

CHAPTER 24

Stigma Management Through Participation in Sport and Physical Activity

Experiences of Male College Students with Physical Disabilities

Diane E. Taub, Elaine M. Blinde, and Kimberly R. Greer

As a critical component of one's social identity, the body influences social interactions and perceptions of others (Cash, 1990; Shontz, 1990). Especially in Western cultures that promote ableism and beautyism, bodily configurations and physical attributes represent central defining dimensions of an individual (Cash, 1990; Hahn, 1984, 1988). An emphasis on physical prowess and "the body beautiful" can over shadow other personal attributes (Cash, 1990; Hahn, 1984).

Physical disability constitutes one of several socially defined categories of stigma, an attribute that is deeply discrediting (Goffman, 1963; Susman, 1994; Wang, 1992). Individuals with a physical disability fall outside the range of what is considered normative or ordinary, thus spoiling their social identity and complicating interactions with able-bodied persons (Goffman, 1963). When a physical disability becomes the defining feature of an individual, others often focus on the disability to the exclusion of relevant personal characteristics (Asch, 1984; Levitin, 1975). Even with increased mainstreaming and political lobbying, individuals with physical disabilities frequently experience various forms of devaluation and discrimination (Groch, 1994).

When disabilities are physical in nature, the body represents the mechanism through which the disability is manifest. Regardless of the context, type, or degree of physical disability, the disabled body is the focus of attention and the source that evokes a negative reaction (Gerschick & Miller, 1994, 1995; Shontz, 1990). Because this body is considered inferior, passive, and weak, it is viewed as atypical

(Fine & Asch, 1988; Gerschick & Miller, 1994, 1995; Goffman, 1963). Assumed properties of a disabled body elicit a stigmatized response and illustrate a societal perception of "negative difference" (Susman, 1994, p. 15).

Qualities of a disabled body are thought to challenge notions of physical competence and to violate appearance norms (Hahn, 1988; Schur, 1984; Susman, 1994). Concerning physical competence, a disabled body is stigmatized because of its assumed lack of individual autonomy (Hahn, 1988) and condition of helplessness, passivity, and dependency (Elliott, Ziegler, Altman, & Scott, 1990; Fine & Asch, 1988; Gerschick & Miller, 1994, 1995). Everyday skills and competencies of individuals with physical disabilities also are questioned routinely (Higgins, 1980). Internalization of these assumptions by able-bodied others impairs social interactions and leads to a questioning of the legitimacy of the stigmatized (Elliott et al., 1990).

Along with challenging beliefs about physical competence, a disabled body violates conventional standards related to body build, physical attractiveness, and bodily expression (Hahn, 1988; Kaiser, Freeman, & Wingate, 1990; Shontz, 1990; Wendell, 1989). Such aspects of bodily appearance represent salient social stimuli that affect interactions (Cash, 1990; Shontz, 1990). Those individuals who depart from normative images of human physique and "fail to meet prescribed standards of physical attractiveness" are devalued and stigmatized (Hahn, 1988, p. 41). For people with

physical disabilities, an atypical bodily appearance may reduce opportunities "that are open to others without hesitation" (Shontz, 1990, p. 157). Individuals with physical disabilities who also possess aspects of the prevailing standards of beauty are a source of ambivalence for the able-bodied community (Kaiser et al., 1990).

As the disabled body is the focal point of negative difference, the stigma of individuals with physical disabilities is often immediately perceivable. Possessing observable and devalued attributes, these individuals engender discredited stigma (Goffman, 1963). The particular form of stigma management utilized by persons with a discredited stigma consists of their attempts to control tension during social interactions. For example, one strategy to manage the stigmatizing effects associated with a physical disability is to compensate for the discrediting attribute (Elliott et al., 1990; Goffman, 1963). Compensation involves stigmatized individuals gaining proficiency in activities in which they are usually not included or expected to perform well (Elliott et al., 1990; Goffman, 1963).

One possible means to alter the image of a disabled body is through involvement in sport and physical activity (Pfuhl & Henry, 1993; Warren, 1980). For other stigmatized groups including Black men and gay men, such participation may yield wider societal acceptance. In the Black subculture, athletic prowess for Black men elevates social status (Eitzen & Sage, 1993), whereas for gay men, sport involvement can lessen the stereotype of gay men as effeminate (Coakley, 1994). Sport and physical activity participation also may demonstrate that individuals with physical disabilities are more able and similar to able-bodied peers than stereotypes suggest (Nixon, 1984). This involvement can reaffirm ability rather than disability and serve as a means to affirm one's bodily competence (Asken, 1991).

The current study represents one aspect of a larger research project examining the sport and physical activity experiences of individuals with physical and sensory disabilities. Sport and physical activity is conceptualized as encompassing a broad spectrum, ranging from competitive and structured events (e.g., wheelchair basketball, road racing) to informal and unstructured physical fitness contexts (e.g., exercising, weight lifting, swimming). These activities include team and individual sports, as well as sport and physical activity that is done informally with friends or alone.

For this study, in-depth interviews were conducted with male college students with physical disabilities; responses related to managing a stigmatized identity emerged from discussions regarding positive and negative experiences associated with sport and physical activity. Given that a disabled body is assumed to violate norms of physical competence and bodily appearance, the purpose of this paper is to investigate how participation in this context may be one technique of stigma management for individuals with physical disabilities. The uniqueness of this research is that it explores how benefits of sport and physical activity

involvement may be used as a means of compensating for a discrediting attribute.

■ METHODS

Sampling Characteristics

Male college students with physical disabilities were recruited from both personal contacts and the Office of Disability Support Services (DSS) at a large Midwestern university in the U.S. Informational sign-up sheets posted at the DSS office were the primary recruiting device. Such convenience sampling is considered feasible when particular groups of people are difficult to access or when certain types of individuals are uncommon in the population (Maxwell, 1996).

The focus of this study was on permanent physical conditions that restrict movement and substantially limit one or more of the major life activities of an individual (Mayerson, 1991). Although people with physical disabilities differ in terms of their movement capabilities, they nevertheless are members of a group stigmatized because of their physical attributes. The sample included 24 male college students with a variety of physical disabilities, including paraplegia ($n = 8$), quadriplegia ($n = 4$), cerebral palsy ($n = 4$), partial paralysis ($n = 3$), back injury ($n = 1$), spina bifida ($n = 1$), knee injury ($n = 1$), ankylosing spondylitis ($n = 1$), and osteogenesis imperfecta ($n = 1$). Nine individuals were born with a physical disability, whereas the other 15 students had acquired their disability. The length of time having an acquired disability averaged 11 years, ranging from 3 to 18 years.

Ages of respondents ranged from 20 to 51 years, with a mean age of 29. The sample was composed of 21 Whites and three African-Americans. In addition, respondents had diverse participation patterns in sport and physical activity, ranging from limited (e.g., occasionally lifting weights) to frequent involvement (e.g., being a member of the university wheelchair basketball team). Their participation in sport and physical activity at the time of the study averaged two times per week. With the exclusion of wheelchair sports, involvement for these individuals primarily occurred in an integrated setting with the able-bodied.

Interview Protocol

As the focus of this research concerned the perceptions and lived experiences of male college students with physical disabilities, the interview method was selected as an appropriate data collection tool. Interview questions were derived from a review of the literature in the areas of stigma, physical disability, and sport, as well as from the responses of five pilot interviews conducted with male college students with physical disabilities. A variety of issues were addressed in the final interview schedule, including the life history of individuals' physical disability, relative importance of sport and physical activity in respondents' lives, degree of past and current involvement in sport and physical activity (e.g., type of activity, duration, frequency) as compared to other activities, personal outcomes of sport and physical activity, and self-perceptions of physical capabilities and body image.

Respondents also were asked about such issues as what they personally gain or lose from participation, how sport and physical activity makes them feel and what this involvement means to them, what they learn about themselves from this activity, and ways in which sport and physical activity might assist or hinder their interactions in other contexts. Other questions centered on how they view their bodies when engaged in sport and physical activity, and whether this perception differs from participation in nonphysical activities (e.g., attending classes, working on a computer, and driving a vehicle). Individuals were asked how others react to their involvement in sport and physical activity, and how these reactions affect self-perceptions of their bodies. Physical, psychological, and social outcomes realized from their participation in sport and physical activity were examined.

To encourage individuals to fully discuss topics most salient to their lived experiences, interview questions were open-ended and techniques were utilized to promote clarification and elaboration of responses. For example, probes used by the interviewer included "please explain," "could you provide an example," "why do you think this," and "how did this make you feel." To facilitate fluid, uninterrupted discussions and accurate data gathering, interviews were tape-recorded. The interviews lasted between 60 and 90 minutes. Code numbers and pseudonyms were employed to ensure that responses were confidential.

Two graduate students individually conducted the interviews in a private campus office that was reserved for this research. Both interviewers had received extensive methodological training; each individual completed doctoral level methodology courses and was mentored in qualitative methods, including participation in pilot interviews, under the direction of the principal investigators.

Data Analysis

Verbatim transcriptions of the tape-recorded interviews were completed and examined for accuracy. Procedures for analyzing this data were modeled after those outlined by Bogdan and Biklen (1992). The investigators independently performed content analysis on the transcribed interviews to identify common themes, patterns, and concepts. Overall, this examination produced consistency among the researchers. Upon completion of content analysis, mutually agreed-upon coding categories were identified. Coding categories were generated based on regularities in the data and reflected an array of responses. Two primary themes related to sport and physical activity as a form of stigma management were physical competence and enhanced bodily appearance. Secondary themes included physical skill, fit healthy body, muscular body, and liberated body. Summary sheets were developed for each secondary theme with relevant comments from the interviews transferred to their respective summary sheet. Because this research had a relatively small sample size, subgroup comparisons involving factors such as ethnicity, age, length of disability, participation patterns, and type of disability could not be examined in-depth.

■ RESULTS

As the purpose of this paper is to explore how sport and physical activity lessens the devaluation of men with physical disabilities, the data analysis centered on the role of such participation in managing the stigma associated with a disabled body. Our focus was on the reasons individuals with physical disabilities believe sport and physical activity compensates for a discredited physical difference. Although involvement was generally viewed as positive, a few respondents did mention negative or disempowering aspects of their sport and physical activity. For example, trivialization of participation by onlookers, dependence on others to assist with their equipment, and awareness of physical limitations could detract from the overall benefits of involvement.

However, such peripheral outcomes did not negate the principal findings that the vast majority of respondents perceived participation in sport and physical activity as a positive experience and as an effective avenue to manage the stigma concerning a disabled body.

From interview responses, two primary themes emerged that illustrate how sport and physical activity may compensate for a disabled body or exceed expectations associated with a physical disability. Responses from male college students with physical disabilities indicated that they believed such participation can facilitate (a) physical competence, and (b) enhanced bodily appearance.

Physical Competence

Individuals with physical disabilities are often stigmatized because of their presumed lack of physical competence. The able-bodied community frequently assumes that the bodies of individuals with physical disabilities are disabling and weak rather than enabling and healthy (Fine & Asch, 1988; Gerschick & Miller, 1994, 1995; Goffman, 1963). Two general areas of physical competence acquired through sport and physical activity were identified in the comments of respondents: (a) demonstration of physical skill, and (b) demonstration of a fit healthy body.

Demonstration of Physical Skill

One aspect of physical competence noted in the responses was the ability of sport and physical activity to provide opportunities for demonstrating a variety of physical skills. By displaying the body in an active manner, these individuals with physical disabilities believed they were countering stereotypes of their physical incompetence.

Throughout the interviews, it was evident respondents thought the able-bodied community doubted their physical capabilities and skills. Nearly all of these students mentioned that others assumed sport and physical activity was outside the physical domain of individuals with physical disabilities. For example, a respondent with cerebral palsy who has participated in bowling and volleyball commented, "the perception is that people who are handicapped can't do anything. There is a definite perception that people who are handicapped can't play sports because they are not physically fit enough." One individual with partial paralysis indicated that his goal for sport participation was to do "some thing they [able-bodied individuals] thought I could not do to show that I as a handicapped person can do anything that a regular person can."

An individual with quadriplegia who plays basketball and tennis added that "people who have no knowledge of people with disabilities expect them to just kinda sit around." Another respondent who participates in tennis and plays on a wheelchair basketball team indicated that he likes to show the world that able-bodied persons are not the only ones who can participate in sport or who can say "well, I've got a game, I gotta go."

Although nearly all respondents believed others doubted their physical ability, they thought sport and physical activity enhanced their movement capabilities. When asked what involvement in sport meant to him, an individual with congenital partial paralysis who swims and jet skis remarked:

I think being engaged in some aspect of your body that you have control over, and where you can set new goals, new expectations for your body. counting up what your body can do I think is incredibly important for people with disabilities, because I think the whole society thing is well, since your body is different, you can't do it [sport].

Or, as another respondent who plays wheelchair basketball stated when asked how he views his body when engaged in sport, "the body just needs a little helping around, but it is still getting the job done." Commenting on attitudes of able-bodied individuals after they observed his participation in football and floor hockey, a student with osteogenesis imperfecta indicated that others "think I would be more limited than I am. They are more astounded that you can do it [sport]."

Approximately half of the respondents reported that individuals were amazed when they were able to demonstrate proficiency in sport skills. For example, one student who plays wheelchair basketball indicated that spectators are "in awe" of his participation, while an individual with congenital partial paralysis stated he "frequently amazed everyone else" with his involvement in scuba diving and swimming. Moreover, one respondent with paraplegia who has participated in snow skiing added that able-bodied observers are "surprised" at what he can do. While discussing his sport abilities, another individual with paraplegia remarked that he can catch a football better than people who are able-bodied. He further indicate d that "I can be better than some people [in sport]

regardless of whether I am in the chair or not."

Demonstration of a Fit Healthy Body

A second dimension of physical competence discussed in the interviews related to how respondents believed sport and physical activity facilitated development of a body that is healthy and physically fit. Through their participation, these individuals with physical disabilities felt they were challenging stereotypes of a disabled body as being sick and weak.

Comments of respondents indicated that nearly all of them were cognizant of negative attributes regarding health and fitness aspects of disabled bodies. For example, an individual with cerebral palsy stated, "a lot of people consider disability kind of synonymous with disease. By presenting ourselves as active, healthy, living, and contributing members of the society, we allow ourselves to break that stereotype." When asked what factors influence how he views his body, a respondent with paraplegia remarked:

A lot of people still tend to look at you as somehow frail or injured or helpless, things like this. I think that is really unfortunate because they [labels] may affect people and cause them to feel that way about themselves, and that is really sad.

Approximately half of these individuals mentioned that participation in sport and physical activity compensated for stereotypes associated with a disabled body by making their bodies appear healthier. Comments such as "basketball made me much more healthier," "I'm a lot more healthier when I participate in sports," and "it [sport] is a way to stay healthy" were frequently given when discussing the effect of sport and physical activity. A 24-year-old respondent who had acquired quadriplegia 6 years ago stated that through his involvement in basketball and tennis, "[my body] looks much better than it did before [the disability]... much more healthy than I was before, definitely. I thought I looked frail before and I look much healthier." One individual with paraplegia who has participated in wheelchair basketball indicated, "if you have a healthy body in society, you are gonna get around better especially if you are in a chair. Sports is the big boost that makes me wanna better myself."

A benefit mentioned by approximately half of the respondents when discussing their involvement in sport and physical activity was fitness. Although commonly assumed to be outside the domain of individuals with physical disabilities (Coakley, 1994; Nixon, 1984), being in shape or being in good physical condition were often identified as desired outcomes of participation in sport and physical activity. Various components of physical fitness, including "endurance," "flexibility," "energy," and "strength" were noted in responses. For example, benefits such as "builds up my cardio-vascular system," "keeps myself in good shape," and "gets my physical conditioning up" were frequently mentioned. One individual with paraplegia who has played

basketball and softball stated, "I think I'm in a lot better shape than I would have if I wasn't participating in sports. I would be a couch potato."

By being healthy and physically fit through sport and physical activity, nearly all respondents believed they were able to influence the attitudes of others toward them. For example, an individual with paraplegia described how he felt about the positive responses received from able-bodied spectators for his involvement in various sport activities. "[This reaction] makes me feel pretty good; I'm just showing them what I do. I'm doing something good for my body and I think that they see that." Moreover, during a discussion of how he thought his participation in activities such as scuba diving affected the perceptions of others, a student who had acquired partial paralysis revealed:

> Especially since I'm so badly handi-
> capped, I'm not supposed to be able
> to do any of these sporting activities.
> But I've got to keep myself in excellent
> shape, and I've got to be able to change
> everyone's opinions about the handicap
> view.

In summary, sport and physical activity furnished a context in which respondents believed they could defy or minimize stereotypes of their body as lacking physical skill and being physically unfit and unhealthy. This environment provided a unique opportunity for these individuals with physical disabilities to focus on their body and its capabilities.

Involvement in sport and physical activity by individuals with physical disabilities may compensate for the negative physical difference associated with a disabled body. Respondents perceived that accentuating their physical competence can result in a disabled body that is less stigmatized and devalued.

Enhanced Bodily Appearance

The second theme emanating from interview comments related to how respondents thought sport and physical activity compensates for negative perceptions about the appearance of the disabled body. Individuals with physical disabilities are assumed to deviate from conventional standards of body build, physical attractiveness, and bodily expression (Hahn, 1988; Kaiser et al., 1990; Shontz, 1990; Wendell, 1989). Two aspects of appearance transformed through sport and physical activity were noted in the remarks of respondents: (a) demonstration of a muscular body, and (b) demonstration of a liberated body.

Demonstration of a Muscular Body

A disabled body may be viewed as a typical because of its physique and outward appearance. Respondents believed that as a result of assumed inactivity, the bodies of individuals with physical disabilities are commonly thought to lack muscularity and physical development. One bodily domain influenced by sport and physical activity related to the development of muscle definition.

Approximately half of the respondents voiced pride in "building up muscles," "becoming bigger," and "building myself up" through sport and physical activity. One individual with congenital partial paralysis reported that as a result of lifting weights, he was able to increase from a 36- to a 42-inch chest. Expressing pleasure at this improvement in his upper body, he commented that "I was building up areas of my body that I've never addressed before in that way, shape, or form." Another individual indicated that through wheelchair basketball, "I've like noticed changes in my body, like my arms are getting more shape and more definition in them."

Participation in sport and physical activity enabled respondents to develop a physique they thought compensated for stereotypical assumptions about a disabled body. Individuals, especially those who use wheelchairs, discussed how able-bodied others were surprised at the muscular development of their bodies. For example, one respondent with paraplegia indicated that weight lifting helped his "body become more defined [and] more acceptable to people. [Others] want to see a nice, built body, and they'll say, 'he's strong, he's massive, he must work out all the time.'"

Demonstration of a Liberated Body

Respondents indicated another common assumption about individuals with physical disabilities is that their bodies depart from conventional standards of attractiveness and bodily expression. Sport and physical activity was perceived by these participants as one way to challenge the notion that their bodies are unattractive and unable to engage in movement of an expressive nature.

One dimension of a liberated body discussed by a few respondents was related to the issue of weight. While indicating awareness of a societal emphasis on an attractive bodily appearance, individuals often mentioned weight as one aspect of their bodies they felt they could transform. For example, when asked why they were involved in sport and physical activity, respondents frequently cited factors such as "want to lose weight" or "get thinner." While discussing his reason for sport participation, an individual with partial paralysis remarked:

> I feel I am too fat, too out of shape, getting flabby. I think that I am fat and out of shape. When I weight lift, I get thinner and I start to lose weight. When I lay off the weights, I see myself getting out of shape.

The topic of weight also was discussed when asked how sport and physical activity affected views of their bodies. For example, one individual with paraplegia who described himself as overweight thought that physical activity could help him achieve a socially desirable weight. Believing the appearance of his body was within his control, he described displeasure with being overweight: "[I am] a little angry because I know I can work on my weight [through weight lifting]." Another

individual with paraplegia discussed how perception of his body is influenced by sport participation:

> I want to be able to roll outside with a tank top on and not have my stomach sticking out. If I was not doing sports I would probably be a lot heavier and I would not have the gumption to really want to lose weight. If I was not doing sports, I would be a fat tub of goo right now.

Further, through sport and physical activity, a few respondents thought that weight loss could affect impressions of able-bodied others about the physical attractiveness of individuals with physical disabilities. As a student with paraplegia stated, "[I] need to lose some weight and it's just all cosmetic. I feel that I'll look better, therefore people will like me more."

Sport and physical activity also provided these individuals with physical disabilities a context for demonstrating a liberated body by using their body in an unrestrained manner. Such participation can recast notions that a disabled body is unable to engage in expressive forms of movement. Through sport and physical activity, respondents found they could experience their bodies in a creative and graceful manner.

Nearly all individuals initiated discussions regarding the qualitative dimensions of their involvement in sport and physical activity. For one participant, wheelchair basketball was "a way to express myself," while another enjoyed the sensation of swimming because "when I'm in the water, I'm free of the wheelchair." Such experiences were discussed in reference to sport and physical activity being able to compensate for preconceived notions of a disabled body as rigid and void of refined movement.

Approximately half of the respondents thought the expressiveness of their body while participating in sport and physical activity affected their awareness of a physical self. As one individual commented, involvement in sport "completes the picture [by adding] a sense of the body self to the mind self." In discussing what participation in sport meant to him, a respondent with congenital partial paralysis remarked:

> [Sport] may give them [individuals with physical disabilities] a self, a sense of their physical self as being beautiful and capable and natural. And I do not think many people with disabilities have that opportunity [or] are given that opportunity.

When asked how involvement in a variety of sport activities affected his body image, a student with congenital partial paralysis revealed, "Having engaged in sports has certainly changed my thinking and my body concept. I really do see my body as much more friendly."

In summary, these individuals with physical disabilities believed they experienced and displayed both a muscular and a liberated body through sport and physical activity. In contrast to nonphysical settings, this context provided a unique occasion in which respondents could more readily compensate for their stigma by altering the appearance of their body. Such participation may counter stereotypes of the disabled body as deviating from conventional standards of muscular body build, physical attractiveness, and bodily expression. Presenting the body through the domain of sport and physical activity can be one means by which the stigma of a disabled body may be managed.

■ DISCUSSION

Being a participant in sport and physical activity represents a socially valued role that may allow individuals with physical disabilities to diminish the stigma of a physical disability (Goffman, 1963). Such involvement can serve to compensate for a discredited attribute in that stereotypes underlying the stigma of a disabled body are challenged (Elliott et al., 1990; Goffman, 1963). As participation in sport and physical activity is often unexpected for individuals with physical disabilities, their involvement may create an alternative impression of the disabled body. For example, such participation inverts notions of physical incompetence and negative appearance by highlighting physical skills and a liberated body.

While discussing personal outcomes of their involvement, respondents emphasize the importance of the participation experience itself rather than the type, intensity level, or formal nature of the physical activity. For these individuals, the opportunity to be involved in sport and physical activity is itself rewarding. Sport and physical activity generally is a privileged context for persons who are physically able and competent (Sage, 1990). Compared with nonphysical activity, sport and physical activity for individuals with physical disabilities transpires in a unique environment in which competence and appearance of their body can be altered.

Interview responses suggest that for men with physical disabilities, sport and physical activity is one domain especially conducive for stigma management. This context provides significant socialization for the development and demonstration of masculine characteristics and qualities such as competitiveness, dominance, independence, and physical prowess (Messner, 1989, 1990a, 1992; Sage, 1990). For men with physical disabilities whose bodies are marginalized and stigmatized, attributes related to their manliness are routinely questioned (Gerschick & Miller, 1994, 1995). Being perceived by others as masculine is improbable for these individuals because of the incongruence between the expectations of hegemonic masculinity and the assumed incapabilities associated with physical disability (Gerschick & Miller, 1994, 1995). Compensation may be an especially important strategy for men with physical disabilities in challenging societal perceptions of a disabled body and in asserting claims of masculinity. The socialization of males to value sport involvement might partially explain why these men choose sport and physical activity as a context for stigma management.

Several comments from respondents indicate that individuals with physical disabilities internalize societal norms regarding both physical competence and bodily appearance. For example, acceptance of conventional standards of ableism and beautyism by respondents involves their equating physical skill and attractiveness with social desirability. Such normative internalization is common among members of socially marginalized groups (Miller, 1995; Wolf, 1986). Respondents seem unaware that they strive toward elitist standards of beauty and body image; their efforts are paradoxical as they identify with norms that are oppressive for individuals with physical disabilities.

To fully explore the dynamics of the role of sport and physical activity as a strategy of stigma management, additional research should be conducted. For example, it is important to examine the sport and physical activity experiences of women, and individuals of various age groups, with physical disabilities. Female participants may be doubly stigmatized in that they violate both the normative assumption of sport as a context for males and as a domain for the physically able. As sport is male-dominated and perpetuates notions of masculinity (Messner, 1989, 1990a, b, 1992; Sage, 1990), the outcomes of participation for women with physical disabilities can differ from the experiences of their male counterparts. Because women are not as socialized as men to value sport participation, women with physical disabilities might not readily choose physical activity as an avenue for stigma management.

Further, as this study focuses on young adult to middle-aged individuals, future research should address outcomes of participation in sport and physical activity for both children and older adults with physical disabilities. Such investigations may refine understanding of the relationship between involvement in physical activity and stigma management.

Although self-perceptions of individuals with physical disabilities have real consequences for their personal behavior and social interactions, individuals without physical disabilities should be interviewed to assess their perceptions of respondents' involvement in sport and physical activity. Whereas respondents thought such participation may alter societal stereotypes of the disabled body, obtaining the beliefs of able-bodied others may provide further insights into whether they view individuals with physical disabilities differently following participation in sport and physical activity.

In conclusion, sport and physical activity is a context in which nearly all respondents believe they can manage the stigma associated with a disabled body. Through their involvement, individuals with physical disabilities may compensate or demonstrate an alternative image capable of diminishing the effect of a discrediting attribute. In particular, the assumed negative difference of their physical competence and bodily appearance can be transformed. Such modification does not negate the previously stigmatized self but provides an identity that may be perceived as more favorable. Even though respondents are not elite athletes, participation in activities ordinarily closed to them can provide opportunities to display a less stigmatized self. As sport and physical activity is unexpected among individuals with physical disabilities, compensation as a strategy of stigma management may result in a less spoiled identity.

REFERENCES

Asch, A. The experience of disability: A challenge for psychology. *American Psychologist,* 1984, 39, 529–536.

Asken, M. J. The challenge of the physically challenged: Delivering sport psychology services to physically disabled athletes. *The Sport Psychologist,* 1991, 5, 370–381.

Bogdan, R. C., & Biklen, S. K. *Qualitative research for education* (2nd Ed.). Boston: Allyn and Bacon, 1992.

Cash, T. F. The psychology of physical appearance: Aesthetics, attributes, and images. In T. F. Cash and T. Pruzinsky (Eds.), *Body images: Development, deviance, and change.* New York: The Guilford Press, 1990, pp. 51–79.

Coakley, J. J. *Sport in society: Issues and controversies* (5th Ed). St. Louis: Mosby, 1994.

Eitzen, D. S., & Sage, G. H. *Sociology of North American sport* (5th Ed). Madison, WI: Brown & Benchmark, 1993.

Elliott, G. C., Ziegler, H. L., Altman, B. M., & Scott, D. R. Understanding stigma: Dimensions of deviance and coping. In C. D. Bryant (Ed.), *Deviant behavior.* New York: Hemisphere, 1990, pp. 423–443.

Fine, M., & Asch, A. Disability beyond stigma: Social interaction, discrimination, and activism. *Journal of Social Issues*, 1988, 44, 3–21.

Gerschick, T. J., & Miller, A. S. Gender identities at the crossroads of masculinity and physical disability. *Masculinities,* 1994, 2, 34–55.

Gerschick, T. J., & Miller, A. S. Coming to terms: Masculinity and physical disability. In D. Sabo and D. F. Gordon (Eds.), *Men's health and illness: Gender, power, and the body*. Thousands Oaks, CA: Sage, 1995, pp. 183–204.

Goffman, E. *Stigma: Notes on the management of spoiled identity*. Englewood Cliffs, NJ: Prentice-Hall, 1963.

Groch, S. A. Oppositional consciousness: Its manifestation and development. The case of people with disabilities. *Sociological Inquiry,* 1994, 64, 369–395.

Hahn, H. Sports and the political movement of disabled persons: Examining nondisabled social values. *Arena Review,* 1984, 8, 1–15.

Hahn, H. The politics of physical differences: Disability and discrimination. *Journal of Social Issues,* 1988, 44, 39–47.

Higgins, P. C. Societal reaction and the physically disabled: Bringing the impairment back in. *Symbolic Interaction,* 1980, 3, 139–156.

Kaiser, S. B., Freeman, C. M., & Wingate, S. B. Stigmata and negotiated outcomes: Management of appearance by persons with physical disabilities. In C. D. Bryant (Ed.), *Deviant behavior*. New York: Hemisphere, 1990, pp. 444–464.

Levitin, T. E. Deviants as active participants in the labeling process: The visibly handicapped. *Social Problems,* 1975, 22, 548–557.

Maxwell, J. A. *Qualitative research design: An interactive approach*. Thousand Oaks, CA: Sage, 1996.

Mayerson, A. Title I—Employment provisions of the Americans with disabilities act. *Temple Law Review,* 1991, 64, 499–520.

Messner, M. Masculinities and athletic careers. *Gender & Society,* 1989, 3, 71–88.

Messner, M. Boyhood, organized sports, and the construction of masculinities. *Journal of Contemporary Ethnography,* 1990, 18, 416–444. (a)

Messner, M. A. Men studying masculinity: Some epistemological issues in sport sociology. *Sociology of Sport Journal,* 1990, 7, 136–153. (b)

Messner, M. A. *Power at play: Sports and the problem of masculinity*. Boston: Beacon, 1992.

Miller, J. B. Domination and subordination. In P. S. Rothenberg (Ed.), *Race, class, and gender in the United States: An integrated study* (3rd Ed). New York: St. Martin's, 1995, pp. 57–64.

Nixon, H. L. II. Handicapism and sport: New directions for sport sociology research. In N. Theberge and P. Donnelly (Eds.), *Sport and the sociological imagination*. Fort Worth, TX: Texas Christian University Press, 1984, pp. 162–176.

Pfuhl, E. H., & Henry, S. *The deviance process* (3rd Ed). New York: Aldine de Gruyter, 1993.

Sage, G. H. *Power and ideology in American sport: A critical perspective*. Champaign, IL: Human Kinetics, 1990.

Schur, E. M. *Labeling women deviant: Gender, stigma, and social control*. New York: McGraw-Hill, 1984.

Shontz, F. C. Body image and physical disability. In T. F. Cash and T. Pruzinsky (Eds.), *Body images: Development, deviance, and change*. New York: The Guilford Press, 1990, pp. 149–169.

Susman, J. Disability, stigma and deviance. *Social Science and Medicine,* 1994, 38, 15–22.

Wang, C. Culture, meaning and disability: Injury prevention campaigns and the production of stigma. *Social Science and Medicine,* 1992, 35, 1093–1102.

Warren, C.A.B. Destigmatization of identity: From deviant to charismatic. *Qualitative Sociology,* 1980, 3, 59–72.

Wendell, S. Toward a feminist theory of disability. *Hypatia,* 1989, 4(2), 104–124.

Wolf, C. Legitimation of oppression: Response and reflexivity. *Symbolic Interaction,* 1986, 9, 217–234.

CHAPTER 25

Race, Interest Convergence, and Transfer Outcomes for Black Male Student-Athletes at Community Colleges

Shaun R. Harper

Much has been published about the experiences of student-athletes in higher education. Some researchers have offered important insights into the psychosocial and identity-related challenges these students commonly face (Martin, 2009; Parham, 1993; Pinkerton, Hinz, and Barrow, 1989; Sedlacek and Adams-Gaston, 1992), while others have written about various issues related to career planning, academic motivation, and post-college outcomes (Adler and Adler, 1987; Gaston-Gayles, 2004; Miller and Kerr, 2002; Pascarella and Smart, 1991; Pascarella and others, 1999; Simons, Van Rheenen, and Covington, 1999). A smaller body of literature has focused specifically on black male participation in college sports (Beamon, 2008; Benson, 2000; Donnor, 2005; Martin and Harris, 2006; Messer, 2006; Person and LeNoir, 1997). This research has been almost exclusively concerned with student-athletes at four-year colleges and universities, and mostly at the National Collegiate Athletic Association's (NCAA) Division I competition level. Consequently, much remains to be known about community college student-athletes in general and black male sports participants at those institutions specifically.

The aforementioned studies on black male student-athletes at four-year institutions mostly describe racial differences in educational outcomes between them and their white male teammates. In his analyses of graduation rates data from the NCAA, Harper (2006) found that across four cohorts of college student-athletes, 47 percent of black men graduated within six years, compared to 60 percent of white males and 62 percent of student-athletes overall. The averages across four cohorts of basketball players

494

were 39 percent and 52 percent for black men and white men, respectively. Forty-seven percent of black male football players graduated within six years, compared to 63 percent of their white teammates. Harper's findings led to the following conclusion: "Perhaps nowhere in higher education is the disenfranchisement of black male students more insidious than in college athletics" (p. 6).

In addition to these quantifiable racial gaps in degree attainment, more than 25 years ago Edwards (1984) observed the following about black sports participants: "They must contend, of course, with the connotations and social reverberations of the traditional 'dumb jock' caricature. But Black student-athletes are burdened also with the insidiously racist implications of the myth of 'innate Black athletic superiority,' and the more blatantly racist stereotype of the 'dumb Negro' condemned by racial heritage to intellectual inferiority" (p. 8). More recently, Benson (2000) found that many black males are socialized to prioritize sports over academics when they are in high school, and such messages are sustained (and arguably amplified) once they enroll in college. In an article in the *Chronicle of Higher Education* titled, "Black Athletes and White Professors: A Twilight Zone of Uncertainty," black male student-athletes reported feeling that they were not taken seriously by many of their white professors (Perlmutter, 2003). Related to this, Comeaux and Harrison (2007) found that engagement with faculty, particularly outside the classroom, was essential to academic achievement for black and white male student-athletes alike, but professors devoted significantly more time to academic engagement with white student-athletes.

While much of the existing literature on black male student-athletes in Division I sports programs at four-year institutions explores the social construction of their athletic identities, their lived experiences with racial stereotyping and low expectations, and one specific outcome variable (bachelor's degree completion), these topics remain largely unexplored in the context of community college sports. In fact, Harris and Harper (2008) contend that most of what has been published about male community college students narrowly pertains to how many enroll, earn associate's degrees, and transfer. Little emphasis has been placed on demonstrated institutional commitment to the overall success of black male students, particularly those who play on sports teams at community colleges. Thus, the purpose of this chapter is to consider the mutual benefits that could accrue for these students and the colleges they attend when transfer rates to four-year institutions are strengthened. Although transferring to a four-year college or university is the outcome variable of interest here, I certainly recognize the importance of examining learning and other developmental outcomes; this is something I hope to see in future scholarship on black male community college student-athletes. I later explain why I chose to focus expressly on transferring to the four-year as an outcome. Critical Race Theory, specifically the Interest

Convergence tenet, is introduced in the next section and used for explanatory sensemaking throughout the chapter.

CRITICAL RACE THEORY AND INTEREST CONVERGENCE

Based on scholarly perspectives from law, sociology, history, ethnic studies, and women's studies, Critical Race Theory (CRT) is a conceptual lens used to examine racism, racial (dis)advantages, and the inequitable distribution of power and privilege within institutions and society (Bell, 1987; Delgado and Stefancic, 2001). CRT also challenges misconceptions regarding colorblindness, merit, and racial equity; critiques the presumed innocence of self-proclaimed white liberals; and ignites consciousness that leads to social justice and advances for people of color (Crenshaw, Gotanda, Peller, and Thomas, 1995). According to Donnor (2005), CRT offers an especially useful lens through which "to better recognize and more fully understand the forces that have constructed a system in which African American male athletes are cheered on the field by wealthy alumni and powerful fans while at the same time denied opportunities to earn the degree that could lead to wealth and power of their own" (p. 63).

One major tenet of CRT is Interest Convergence, which, according to Delgado (1995), typically compels white people to advocate for the advancement of people of color only when their own self-interests are better served. Put differently, theorists posit that those in the majority who enact social, political, and economic change on behalf of minorities rarely do so without first identifying the personal costs and gains associated with such actions. This perspective is informed by the Marxist theory that the bourgeoisie will work toward progress for the proletariat only when advances ultimately end up benefitting the bourgeoisie more (Taylor, 2006). While it is certainly not my intent to liken community colleges to "the bourgeoisie," I do argue that many white college faculty, administrators, and coaches will need to be made aware of the overall benefit to the institution (and in some instances, to themselves) before moving forward a serious strategic agenda to improve educational outcomes for black male student-athletes. Hence, Interest Convergence is used in this chapter to help answer the following question: "Why would a community college whose faculty and staff is majority white deliberately engage in efforts to strengthen the rate at which its black male student-athletes transfer to four-year institutions?"

Delgado and Stefancic (2001) argue that prior attempts to eradicate racism and racial differences in social, educational, and economic outcomes have produced minimal results due to the insufficient convergence of interests. "We cannot ignore and should learn from and try to recognize situations when there is a convergence of interests" (Bell, 2000, p. 9). Making clear how transferring more black male student-athletes to four-year institutions will ultimately increase the overall transfer rate for the community college is one example; I say more about this later. Another is pointing out how the prevailing culture of the college would benefit from having black male sports participants—those who are often among the most visible students on campus (Person and LeNoir, 1997)—model for their peers (other student-athletes and non-athletes alike) a serious disposition toward academic achievement.

■ IN THE COMMON INTEREST OF TRANSFERRING

I have identified transferring from community college to a four-year institution as an important intersecting point of interest. For many (but certainly not all) black male student-athletes, the opportunity to play their chosen sports on a bigger and more competitive field or court is appealing. Thus, aspirations of transferring to a four-year college or university are more common than not for this group. These aspirations are in many ways connected to longer-term goals of playing professional sports. Donnor (2005) indicates: "Black males participating in sports are more likely to possess aspirations for pursuing sports professionally than their white counterparts because they believe they will be treated fairly. As a result, African American males will generally interpret their involvement in intercollegiate (and interscholastic) sports as a conduit for achieving their career aspirations" (p. 48).

Rudman (1986) found that blacks were more likely than whites to aspire to careers in professional sports. He suggested this difference in sport orientation is a result of social structures (for example, racism) that limit opportunities for blacks in other professional occupations. According to a 2006 NCAA report, 1.8 percent of college football players are drafted by the National Football League (NFL) and 1.2 percent of men's college basketball players are drafted by the National Basketball Association (NBA). Although these odds are generally well-known, many black male student-athletes, including those at community colleges, exert tremendous effort to render themselves competitive for professional sports drafts. Transferring to a four-year institution makes the actualization of professional sports aspirations considerably more likely; this is something that many black male community college athletes understand and work toward.

Similarly, transferring students to four-year institutions is a publicly stated goal and core function of most community colleges. Transfer readiness and actual transfer rates remain among the most widely studied topics in the community college literature (Pascarella and Terenzini, 2005). However, due to a number of structural, financial, and informational barriers, only a small proportion of community college students who intend to transfer to a four-year institution actually do so (Advisory Committee on Student Financial Assistance, 2008; Long, 2005). Even when students' goals are transfer-oriented, many end up ineligible or insufficiently prepared to transfer (Hagedorn and others, 2006; Laanan, 2003). Previous research has found that transfer rates are especially low among racial/ethnic minorities and low-income students. For example, Hagedorn and others (2006) note, "Students of color and those from low-income backgrounds are disproportionately impacted by the sluggish nature of transfer, because the majority of these students who go to college will begin their postsecondary education in community colleges" (p. 224). Notwithstanding this area of institutional underperformance, transferring more students to four-year institutions remains among the major priorities for community colleges—one for which accountability agents are demanding increased effectiveness, as enrollments are beginning to reach capacity at many public four-year institutions and states are relying more on community colleges to provide the first stage of postsecondary education for students (Long, 2005).

Despite this common goal between student-athletes and community colleges, black men transfer at low rates, especially in comparison to their white male peers. I recently discovered racial disparities in transfer rates among student-athletes at several community colleges. For example, Pima Community College District in Arizona transferred 17 percent of its black male football players, in comparison to 63 percent of their white teammates, to four-year institutions in 2008. Similar trends were found in men's basketball programs at Dixie State College in Utah (25 versus 56 percent), Enterprise-Ozark

Community College in Alabama (25 versus 50 percent), and Gadsden State Community College in Georgia (0 versus 67 percent), to name a few. Data from these four and several other institutions make clear that transfer as a shared outcome of interest among many black male student-athletes and the community colleges they attend has not effectively converged.

■ WHAT'S IN IT FOR THE COLLEGE?

In my view, the Interest Convergence tenet of CRT has at least one noteworthy limitation. It presumes that white persons rarely do anything "out of the goodness of the hearts" that advantages people of color. Accepting this as an absolute truth would be shortsighted. I acknowledge that there are white community college faculty, staff, and coaches who care authentically about minority student success. Indeed, some colleagues are committed for reasons that extend beyond their own selfish profits (educational and otherwise). However, I still find perspectives on Interest Convergence useful, as there are some white community college professionals who will need to clearly see the ultimate value in deliberately constructing educational environments that increase transfer rates specifically for black male student-athletes. Some may not easily recognize how their individual efforts might ultimately benefit the college overall, not just one segment of the student body (black males). Therefore, in this section I offer four ways in which community colleges would benefit from transferring larger numbers of black male student-athletes to four-year institutions.

First, when transfer rates for black male student-athletes increase, so too do overall transfer rates for the college. This is especially true at community colleges where disproportionate numbers of black male students play on sports teams. Given the dismal transfer rates for community college students in general (Laanan, 2003; Long, 2005) and students of color in particular (Hagedorn and others, 2006), every individual black male student who transfers could make a potentially noticeable contribution to an institution's overall rate. In this era of increased transparency and accountability, institutions are expected to furnish evidence on the production of key educational outcomes (U.S. Department of Education, 2006). For community colleges, transferring students to four-year institutions is among the areas in which accountability agents expect to see progress. Thus, closing gaps between black male student-athletes and their white teammates would ultimately fortify the college's efforts to confirm its educational effectiveness.

Increasing the number of black male-student athletes who transfer to four-year institutions would also result in reputational gains for the community college. Harper and Hurtado (2007) found that some institutions garner reputations within minority communities for being racist, which negatively affects student recruitment. Black and Latino participants in the study reported that

family members discouraged their interests in certain predominantly white institutions because they were known to maintain toxic campus racial climates and had long been ineffective in fostering enabling environments for minority student success. As a community college helps more black male student-athletes actualize their goals of transferring to four-year institutions, its reputation for doing so will improve. This could potentially compel talented prospective student-athletes to more strongly consider one particular college over others. For example, if a prospective black male basketball player knows a certain community college does an outstanding job of helping members of the basketball team transfer to four-year institutions with excellent basketball programs, he would likely be more inclined to apply, enroll, and play basketball at that community college. Attracting more student-athletes who choose an institution for this reason could also create a transfer culture on community college sports teams.

Third, coaches who work at community colleges where the president holds educators and administrators uncompromisingly accountable for student success also have much to gain from enacting efforts to increase transfer rates among black male student-athletes. Benson (2000) found that coaches were complicit in the academic underperformance of black male student-athletes. In fact, coaches often conveyed to these students that athletics were more important than academics. Community college leaders must expect athletics departments to furnish evidence of their contribution to the institution's transfer mission. If the compensation and reappointment of coaches were based not only on wins and losses but also on transfer and graduation rates, then those who work most closely with student-athletes would have more incentive to ensure their success. In the absence of accountability from the president, district leaders, and other top administrators, athletics departments will continue to help manufacture racial gaps in transfer rates like those I cited earlier in this chapter. Seventy percent of the former black male student-athletes who participated in Beamon's (2008) study also had careers of varying length in professional sports. These men reported feeling like "used goods" by the colleges and universities at which they had been student-athletes. For sure, such feelings are unlikely to incite these alumni to contribute financially to their alma maters.

Finally, community colleges should recognize that student-athletes who transfer to four-year institutions could eventually be among the 1.2 percent drafted by NBA or the 1.8 percent drafted by the NFL. Once their professional sports careers become lucrative, these black male alumni could be solicited for donations to the college. It is possible that some for whom the community college served as the springboard into sports participation at four-year institutions and subsequently into professional athletics may be easily persuaded to support the college's development endeavors. Long (2005) asserts, "Even as their role increases and their transfer function grows in importance,

community colleges are facing reductions in funding" (p. 2). Given this, community colleges would benefit from expanding their revenue sources to include donations from alumni (Jenkins and Glass, 1999). It is possible that the wealthiest former students may be those who transferred to four-year institutions and later secured multi-million dollar contracts to play on professional sports teams.

■ CONCLUSION

I just offered four examples of how community colleges and their athletics departments and coaches would benefit from increasing transfer rates among black male student-athletes. These reasons were not meant to replace other more altruistic motives such as an authentic commitment to racial equity, improving transfer rates for the sake of mission realization, or investing in the actualization of all students' aspirations and success. I recognize these as most important. However, persistent disparities in transfer rates between black men and their white male counterparts signify to us that few educators, administrators, and coaches are likely to participate in the strategic closing of racialized outcomes gaps if the tangible returns on their personal investments are not made more apparent. Regardless of the impetus, current transfer rates make clear that considerably more effort is required to improve the rate at which black male student-athletes transfer from community colleges to four-year institutions. Necessary and important are increased transparency and accountability, more research expressly focused on race and community college athletics, and the effective convergence of black male student-athletes' interests with those of the community colleges they attend.

REFERENCES

Adler, P., and Adler, P. A. "Role Conflict and Identity Salience: College Athletics and the Academic Role." *Social Science Journal,* 1987, *24*(4), 443–455.

Advisory Committee on Student Financial Assistance. *Transition Matters: Community College to Bachelor's Degree.* Washington, D.C.: Author, 2008.

Beamon, K. K. "Used Goods: Former African American College Student-Athlete's Perception of Exploitation by Division I Universities." *The Journal of Negro Education,* 2008, 77(4), 352–364.

Bell, D. A. *And We Are Not Saved: The Elusive Quest for Racial Justice.* New York: Basic Books, 1987.

Bell, D. A. "*Brown vs. Board of Education:* Forty-five Years After the Fact." *Ohio Northern Law Review,* 2000, *26*, 1–171.

Benson, K. F. "Constructing Academic Inadequacy: African-American Athletes' Stories." *The Journal of Higher Education,* 2000, 71(2), 223–246.

Comeaux, E., and Harrison C. K. "Faculty and Male Student Athletes: Racial Differences in the Environmental Predictors of Academic Achievement." *Race, Ethnicity and Education,* 2007, *10*, 199–214.

Crenshaw, K., Gotanda, N., Peller, G., and Thomas, K. (eds.). *Critical Race Theory: The Key Writings that Formed the Movement.* New York: New Press, 1995.

Delgado, R. *Critical Race Theory: The Cutting Edge.* Philadelphia: Temple University Press, 1995.

Delgado, R., and Stefancic, J. *Critical Race Theory: An Introduction.* New York: New York University Press, 2001.

Donnor, J. K. "Towards an Interest-convergence in the Education of African American Football Student-athletes in Major College Sports." *Race, Ethnicity and Education,* 2005, *8*(1), 45–67.

Edwards, H. "The Black 'Dumb Jock': an American Sports Tragedy." *The College Board Review,* 1984, *131*, 8–13.

Gaston-Gayles, J. "Examining Academic and Athletic Motivation Among Student Athletes at a Division I University." *Journal of College Student Development,* 2004, *45*(1), 75–83.

Hagedorn, L. S., Moon, H. S., Cypers, S., Maxwell, W. E., and Lester, J. "Transfer between Community Colleges and Four-Year Colleges: The All-American Game." *Community College Journal of Research and Practice,* 2006, *30*(3), 223–242.

Harper, S. R. *Black Male Students at Public Universities in the U.S.: Status, Trends and Implications for Policy and Practice.* Washington, D.C.: Joint Center for Political and Economic Studies, 2006.

Harper, S. R., and Hurtado, S. "Nine Themes in Campus Racial Climates and Implications for Institutional Transformation." In S. R. Harper and L. D. Patton (eds.), *Responding to the Realities of Race on Campus.* New Directions for Student Services, no. 120. San Francisco: Jossey-Bass, 2007.

Harris III, F., and Harper, S. R. "Masculinities Go to Community College: Understanding Male Identity Socialization and Gender Role Conflict." In J. Lester (ed.), *Gendered Perspectives in Community Colleges*. New Directions for Community Colleges, no. 142. San Francisco: Jossey-Bass, 2008.

Jenkins, L. W., and Glass, C. J. "Inception, Growth, and Development of a Community College Foundation: Lessons to be Learned." *Community College Journal of Research and Practice*, 1999, *23*(6), 593–612.

Laanan, F. S. "Degree Aspirations of Two-Year College Students." *Community College Journal of Research and Practice*, 2003, *27*(6), 495–518.

Long, B. T. *State Financial Aid: Policies to Enhance Articulation and Transfer*. Boulder, CO: Western Interstate Commission for Higher Education, 2005.

Martin, B. E. "Redefining Championship in College Sports: Enhancing Outcomes and Increasing Student-Athlete Engagement." In S. R. Harper and S. J. Quaye (eds.), *Student Engagement in Higher Education: Theoretical Perspectives and Practical Approaches for Diverse Populations*. New York: Routledge, 2009.

Martin, B. E., and Harris III, F. "Examining Productive Conceptions of Masculinities: Lessons Learned from Academically Driven African American Male Student-Athletes." *Journal of Men's Studies*, 2006, *14*(3), 359–378.

Messer, K. L. "African American Male College Athletes." In M. J. Cuyjet (ed.), *African American Men in College*. San Francisco: Jossey-Bass, 2006.

Miller, P. S., and Kerr, G. "The Athletic Academic and Social Experiences of Intercollegiate Student-Athletes." *Journal of Sport Behavior*, 2002, *25*(4), 346–365.

National Collegiate Athletic Association. *Report on Careers in Professional Sports*. Indianapolis, IN: Author, 2006.

Parham, W. D. "The Intercollegiate Athlete: A 1990s Profile." *The Counseling Psychologist*, 1993, *21*(3), 411–429.

Pascarella, E. T., and Smart, J. C. "Impact of Intercollegiate Athletic Participation for African American and Caucasian Men: Some Further Evidence." *Journal of College Student Development*, 1991, *32*(2), 123–130.

Pascarella, E. T., and Terenzini, P. T. *How College Affects Students, Volume 2: A Third Decade of Research*. San Francisco: Jossey-Bass, 2005.

Pascarella, E. T., Truckenmiller, R., Nora, A., Terenzini, P. T., Edison, M., and Hagedorn, L. S. "Cognitive Impacts of Intercollegiate Athletics Participation: Some Further Evidence." *Journal of Higher Education*, 1999, *70*(1), 1–26.

Perlmutter, D. "Black Athletes and White Professor: A Twilight Zone of Uncertainty." *Chronicle of Higher Education*, 2003, B7–B9.

Person, D. R., and LeNoir, K. M. "Retention Issues and Models for African American Male Athletes." In M. J. Cuyjet (ed.), *Helping African American Men Succeed in College*. New Directions for Student Services, no. 80. San Francisco: Jossey-Bass, 1997.

Pinkerton, R. S., Hinz, L. D., and Barrow, J. C. "The College Student-Athlete: Psychological Considerations and Interventions." *Journal of American College Health*, 1989, *37*(5), 218–225.

Rudman, W. J. "The Sport Mystique in Black Culture." *Sociology of Sport Journal*, 1986, *3*(4), 305–319.

Sedlacek, W. E., and Adams-Gaston, J. "Predicting the Academic Success of Student-Athletes Using SAT and Non-Cognitive Variables." *Journal of Counseling & Development,* 1992, *70*(6), 724–727.

Simons, H. D., Van Rheenen, D., and Covington, M. V. "Academic Motivation and the Student-Athlete." *Journal of College Student Development,* 1999, *40*(2), 151–162.

Taylor, E. "A Critical Race Analysis of the Achievement Gap in the United States: Politics, Reality, and Hope." *Leadership and Policy in Schools,* 2006, *5*(1), 71–87.

U.S. Department of Education. *A Test of Leadership, Charting the Future of U.S. Higher Education: A Report of the Commission Appointed by Secretary of Education Margaret Spellings.* Washington, D.C.: U.S. Department of Education, 2006.

CHAPTER 26

Used Goods

Former African American College Student-Athletes' Perceptions of Exploitation by Division I Universities

Krystal K. Beamon

Sports have become key social institutions in American society that are connected to the economy, education, family, and other spheres of social life. Many scholars have noted that a specific set of difficulties arise for African American males in competitive athletics, especially in high school and collegiate athletics (Benson, 2000; Edwards, 1988, 2000; Harrison, 2000; Hobennan, 2000; Lapchick, 1996; Lomax, 2000; Sellers & Kupenninc, 1997; Siegel, 1996). As a means to upward mobility, educational institutions are thought to prepare students for a future beyond their halls. In terms of African American male student-athletes, there are two opposing perspectives that are employed regarding sports' role in the educational development of the group: (a) athletics may provide educational opportunities to African Americans from underprivileged backgrounds that would

not otherwise be available, and (b) sports have exploited the majority of African American athletes (Sellers, 2000). Although participation in athletics is often considered a golden opportunity for African Americans, compelling evidence to the contrary has been presented for decades (Beamon & Bell, 2006; Edwards, 1983, 1988; Lapchick, 1996). In fact. serious involvement in athletics has hampered the development of African American males in several areas, including academic and occupational achievement (Lomax, 2000).

For decades, Edwards (2000) has researched the nexus between sociology and sports, particularly, how sports have affected the African American family and community. He suggested that the overemphasis on sports participation has drained Black talent away from other areas of economic and cultural success and argues that the push toward athletics as seen within Black families is hindering the social and cognitive growth of African American youth (Edwards, 1983–2000). Furthermore, the mass media constantly deluges society with images glorifying African American men who are successful by employing avenues connected with sports and reinforces the stereotype of African American males as exclusively athletically talented (Hall, 2001).

Collegiate student-athletes, particularly, African American male student-athletes, often have lower career maturity, an impaired aptitude to devise educational and career plans, with self-esteem and an identity based on athletics (Baillie & Danish, 1992; Blann, 1985; Harrison & Lawrence, 2003; Kennedy & Dimick, 1987). African American male student-athletes in football and basketball also have lower academic achievement, stronger expectations for a professional sports career, and are socialized more intensely toward sports than their White counterparts (Beamon & Bell, 2002, 2006; Edwards, 2000; Eitle & Eitle, 2002; Hoberman, 2000; Pascarella, Truckenmiller, Nora, Terenzini, Edison, & Hagedorn, 1999). Pursuing athletic achievement in an obsessive manner and doing so to the detriment of educational and occupational aspirations is described in an Edwards's study as a triple tragedy for African Americans:

> One, the tragedy of thousands upon thousands of black youths in the obsessive pursuit of sports goals that the overwhelming majority of them will never attain. Two, the tragedy of the personal and cultural underdevelopment that afflicts so many successful and unsuccessful black sports aspirants. Three, the tragedy of cultural and institutional underdevelopment throughout black society as a consequence of the drain in talent potential toward sports and away from other vital areas of occupational and career emphasis such as medicine, law, economics, politics, education, and technical fields. (as cited in Harrison, 2000, p. 36)

Due to higher visibility and expectations, these deficiencies are even more pronounced for athletes competing in the revenue-generating sports at Division I institutions. Revenue-generating sports are those that are most likely to yield profits and notoriety. Those sports are defined for the purposes of this study as football and men's basketball. This study uses in-depth ethnographic interviews of former African American Division I student-athletes in order to examine the extent to which they feel that universities emphasized their education as opposed to their athletic performance in order to prepare them for careers off the playing field or court.

■ BACKGROUND

No one would have anticipated that on August 3, 1852, when Harvard and Yale met in the first intercollegiate athletic event, a rowing contest, that such a lasting marriage between the universities and athletics would begin (Lewis, 1970). Today, universities use the commercialization of their sports programs to generate revenue, increase visibility, recruit students, and receive alumni support, which creates a pressure to win (Donnor, 2005; Upthegrove, Roscigno, & Charles, 1999). Due to their ability to raise the university's profile and add to the profitability of a school's athletic programs, exceptional athletes are of great financial value to universities. As a result of overrepresentation of African Americans in revenue-generating sports, it is estimated that these student-athletes have earned more than a quarter of a trillion dollars over a 40-year period; and even if 100% of African American athletes earned degrees, the economic value of those degrees would only be 5% of the total value of their athletic contribution (Watkins study as cited in Salome, 2005). The need for superior athletes to maintain team performance and produce revenue may cause institutions to neglect their educational responsibilities to student athletes by creating contradictory pressures that place the role of student and the role athlete at odds (Edwards, 2000; Hoberman, 2000; Upthegrove, Roscigno, & Charles, 1999). One of the alleged negative consequences of the relationship between the athletic and educational institutions is the exploitation of student-athletes for their athletic ability (Donnor, 2005). Specifically, the exploitation is especially significant to African Americans in revenue-generating sports because they often create "enough revenue to financially underwrite the non-revenue-producing athletic sports such as crew, swimming, tennis and golf that are overwhelmingly populated by white middle and upper class students" (Donnor, 2005, p. 48).

With the clear emphasis placed on the physical capabilities of student-athletes, their academic capacities and role as a student are often overlooked (Eitzen, 2000, 2003; Hawkins, 1999; Litsky, 2003; Maloney & McCormick, 1993). Sack and Stuarowsky (1998) discussed this emphasis by stating, "Universities are far more concerned with exploiting the athletic talent [of student athletes] than with nurturing academic potential" (p. 104).

It has been noted that some student-athletes are academically unprepared for college and a gap exists in the graduation rates of African American student-athletes compared to White student-athletes (Benson, 2000; Edwards, 1983; Lapchick, 1996; Washington & Karen, 2001). In 2006, African American football players graduated from Division I institutions at a rate that was 12% lower than that of their White teammates, 62% for Whites and 49% for African Americans (National Collegiate Athletic Association, NCAA, 2006). White male basketball players at Division I institutions graduate at a rate of 51 %, while African Americans graduate at a rate of 41 % (NCAA, 2006). A more accurate statistic is the graduation success rate which adds in student-athletes who enter mid year or transfer into an institution and subtracts those with allowable exclusion and those who would otherwise be deemed academically ineligible on returning to an institution

(NCAA, 2006). The graduation success rate differentials by race are even more staggering. In football the rate is 77% for Whites and 55% for African Americans and in men's basketball the rate is 76% for Whites and 51% for African Americans (NCAA, 2006). Football and basketball powerhouses are ranked each year by *USA Today;* at eleven of those top twenty football and basketball programs, the graduation differentials between African Americans and Whites were greater than the national average ("African American College Athletes," 2002). While student–athletes often fulfill their obligation to the university by performing athletically and bringing notoriety to the universities, all too often Black students do not see the benefits of their labor by playing professionally or earning a degree. Of those who do graduate, many graduate in less marketable majors "riddled with 'keep 'em eligible' less competitive 'jock courses' of dubious educational value and occupational relevance" (Edwards, 1988, p. 138). Exploitation has been alleged in studies and commentaries (Donnor, 2005; Hawkins, 1999). Meggysey (2000) stated that the NCAA and its member institutions "exploit the talent of Black athletes and deny these same athletes access to a quality education" as well as limiting "employment opportunities of Black athletes after their career ends" (p. 27).

Social Reproduction Theory

The exploitation phenomenon can be examined through the lens of the social reproduction theory, which is based on the concept that social institutions, such as the institution of education, work to reproduce dominant ideology and its structures of knowledge (Giroux, 1983). Proponents of social reproduction theory argue that the function of schools is to recreate the conditions needed to reproduce the social division of labor (Giroux, 1983). According to Giroux, schools impart differing classes and social groups with the skills and knowledge needed to maintain the status quo in the labor force, which is stratified by the variables of class, race, and gender. The interrelationship of the institutions of sport and education has created a situation in which structural components (e.g., the NCAA, athletic departments, economy) and individual actors (e.g. coaches, teammates, family members) work together to reproduce the current stratification seen in the labor force (Singer, 2002). This is certainly the case for African American male student athletes. By aiding, catering, and nurturing the student's athletic role to the detriment of his or her true academic success and occupational development, educational institutions reproduce students with social inequalities. This phenomenon is illustrated in the sports world where there is an overrepresentation of Black athletes, but the decision-making positions of athletic directors, coaches, owners, and managers are still largely held by White males. African American coaches in the NFL and NBA only make up 17% and 10%, respectively, of the total number of head coaches in these leagues that are largely composed of African American players (Lapchick & Matthews, 2001).

Additionally, some universities do little to endorse an academic lifestyle among student athletes (Gerdy, 2000). A clear emphasis on the athletic abilities of student-athletes at the high school and university level, reproduce student-athletes with an educational inequality who are not prepared academically or culturally for the transition into the occupational sector. This is especially true of African American male athletes who have been shown to have higher expectations of "going pro" and have been intensively socialized toward sports and embracing the athletic identity (Beamon & Bell, 2002).

The educational attainment of student-athletes is frequently hindered by athletic training and travel; and student-athletes often find it difficult to balance athletics, academics, and social roles. Athletes have less time available for the educational process that "extends beyond going to class everyday to socializing with research and study groups, participating with student organizations, and attending campus activities apart from athletics" (Hawkins, 1999, p. 8). Additionally, due to psychological and physical fatigue from sports participation, student-athletes have decreased levels of motivation to study and diminished abilities to benefit from institutional assistance, such as tutorial programs and counseling (Beamon & Bell, 2002; Person, Benson-Quaziena, & Rogers, 2001). African American males are seen as particularly vulnerable to these circumstances since

they often enter college with general background disadvantages (e.g., socioeconomic status, academic preparedness) and goal-discrepancy concerning professional sports careers (Roscigno, 1999; Sellers & Kuperminc, 1997).

Student-athletes work under numerous constraints. These constraints include the inability to change majors or drop courses because of eligibility requirements or choose majors that may offer courses during times set aside for sports participation (i.e. majors such as architecture or chemistry with afternoon labs). While students who are not athletes have the freedom to explore courses and majors, spend time on internships, drop and add courses with changing needs and focus on finding a career that suits their abilities, many student-athletes do not share these liberties. In order to remain eligible, student-athletes are often pushed into choosing majors that are most compatible with athletic participation, even if they are uninterested or unprepared for those majors (Adler & Adler, 1987; Cornelius, 1995).

■ PROCEDURE

The current literature raises a few questions such as, do African American male student-athletes perceive themselves to be exploited by universities and how does that perception affect their college experience? These questions could be answered by hearing their voices through qualitative research. Several scholars have noted that African American athletes' voices should be heard to truly understand the obsessive pursuit of sports fame and the academic and occupational shortcomings that exist among them (Adler & Adler 1991; Benson, 2000; Winbush 1988). This study presents the viewpoints of former student-athletes concerning the universities' role in the alleged exploitation of athletes. It is based on a sample of 20 African American men who formerly played football or basketball at a Division I university.

Both purposive (selective) and snowball (rare) sampling were used in this research. The criteria for participation were as follows:

- Must be African American male
- Must be a former student-athlete from a Division I university
- Must have played a revenue-generating sport (football or men's basketball)

African Americans were targeted for participation because of their lower levels of academic success (i.e., lower graduation rates) and higher expectations for professional sports careers. The study was exclusive to Division I universities because of their high visibility and perceived profitability. Males from revenue-generating sports were used because of the racial differences and the graduation rates that are lower than those among women and men in non-revenue generating sports (NCAA, 2006). The twenty participants were from universities all over the country, many of which would be considered "powerhouses." As a former student-athlete and from past

research conducted on student-athletes, some personal connections were used for initial contacts. They were contacted by telephone or in person and given (or read) the description of the study. From there, snowballing led to the identification of additional participants.

In-depth semi-standardized interviews were used as the data collection technique. The interviews ranged from one to five hours, with the average interview lasting about two and one-half hours. Transcription and analysis were performed by this researcher. The questions were open-ended, non-biased, and designed to elicit candid responses. For example, respondents were asked the following questions: "Talk about your college experiences in sports," "Talk about your collegiate experience with academics," and "How did you choose a major"? These questions produced very similar responses from the majority of participants. The findings presented in this study consist of direct quotes offered in the form of rich narratives articulated by the respondents.

Backgrounds of the Participants

The athletes interviewed ranged from ages 22 to 47. Most were in their twenties, with two who were ages 45 and 47. The two of their responses added to the significance of the findings by demonstrating that perceptions seem to remain constant over time, since their responses were similar to the younger participants. Respondents were either playing sports professionally, holding jobs in other professions, training for possible

Table 26.1. Participant Background Information

Participant	Collegiate Sport	Current Age	Current Occupation	Years in Professional Sports	Undergraduate Degree
Adam	Football	27	AFL[a]	6 in AFL	Computer Science
Brad	Football	23	NFL[b]	1 in NFL	Hotel and Restaurant
Calvin	Football	22	Unemployed	0	Hotel and Restaurant
Devin	Football	25	Unemployed	3 in NFL	Business Administration
Eddy	Basketball	34	Business Sales Manager	0	Criminal Justice
Fred	Football	23	Agility Trainer	6 months in NFL	Business
Gavin	Football	22	Unemployed	0	Education
Hubert	Football	26	Mortgage Broker	1 NFLE[c]; 1.5 in NFL	Journalism
Ivan	Football	34	Manager	1 in CFL[d], 1 in NFLE; 7 in AFL	Exercise and Sport Science
Jack	Basketball	31	Advertising and Sales	0	None
Kevin	Football	27	AFL	4 in NFL; 1 in AFL	None
Lenny	Football	31	Firefighter	3 in NFL; 1 in CFL	Sociology
Matt	Football	27	Mortgage Loan Officer	1 in AFL	Fine Arts
Nate	Football	26	College Football Coach	2 in NFLE	Sports Administration
Oliver	Football	26	Police Officer	0	Sociology
Perry	Football	36	Firefighter	Less than 1 in NFL	Social Work
Quinton	Basketball	45	Firefighter/Entrepreneur	Harlem Globetrotters, Europe	Missing Data
Richard	Football	47	Firefighter	2 in NFL	Sociology
Steve	Football	33	Fire Rescuer	0	Accounting
Tevin	Football	33	Firefighter	5 in NFL/NFLE	Criminal Justice

Note
[a] Arena Football League;
[b] National Football League;
[c] National Football League Europe;
[d] Canadian Football League.

on-the-field sports careers, or unemployed. Table 26.1 shows background and demographic information about the participants. Pseudonyms were assigned in order to ensure their confidentiality. According to the table 17 out of the 20 participants hold degrees (with one choosing not to answer the question) and many (13) of the former student-athletes have careers outside of sports, which is not consistent with the expectations of the researcher. This apparent contradiction of the literature could be attributed to snowball sampling in which the first respondent held a degree and identified additional respondents with degrees. Most (17) were football players, this may be due to the sheer numbers of collegiate football players versus basketball players, since football teams average a little more than 100 players and basketball teams have fewer than 20. Their majors were somewhat varied, with the social sciences being the most popular major.

■ FINDINGS

During transcription and coding, several themes found in the literature as well as new ideas became apparent. Except for scholarships, many (18 of 20) of these athletes left the universities feeling as if they had given far more than they had gained and were unprepared for careers away from the playing field or court. The findings were organized according to whether

- The respondents felt that their educational development was emphasized

- The university or student-athletes benefited from collegiate athletic programs, and
- The student-athletes' career preparation was adequate, particularly for choosing a major

Educational Development

Seventeen of the 20 respondents in this study had undergraduate degrees. However, most of them felt that their attainment was not a reflection of the university's emphasis on the academic success of student-athletes, but through their sheer determination. As Calvin stated, "everybody say you a student-athlete, but coaches, they want you to be a athlete first then a student." Several other respondents felt like "athlete-students." Devin discussed the term "student-athlete,"

> They tell you, you a student first and an athlete next, but really you an athlete first and a student second. There is more emphasis on making your practices and meetings. They hit you with the go to class and all that stuff, but they don't care. As long as they get them four years out of you they could care less if you get a degree or not . . . I think they have to (care about athletes getting degrees) cuz they job depends somewhat on it, but personally, I don't think they care.

Other respondents stated that any reference to education was directly related to eligibility. Oliver stated:

> The name of the game is to stay eligible ya know what I'm saying. I guess in the recruitment process, when a coach or

who ever is representing that university is sitting in front of your parents uh, academics is stressed highly. However when you get there, that is not the case.

This sentiment was echoed in Hubert's response:

> I mean they drill on um you going to class and making the grade, but that's only because if you don't go to class and make the grade, then you can't be on the field. Student-athlete, that's not how it is, its athletic-student. It's backwards for college athletics.

Additionally, discussion of graduation or academic achievement was "lip service," as stated by Eddie. Gavin expressed a similar sentiment:

> The coaches I don't think they really care if you do get a degree or not, because ya know they say that but its like they say one thing, but they mean another. They just want you to come and play for them, so ya know you can help their program out.

Adam, who attended a nationally acclaimed football powerhouse, stated that the coaches were very upfront about their emphasis on football over all other priorities, including academics:

> I mean from the time that you get there, they tell ya, "you here for football, you got a scholarship." Its up to you to ya know put yourself in the right classes and to choose the right major . . . Anything else dealing with academics that was up to you. Ya know what I mean. Whereas with football, they took care of all of that, as long as you was playing football, you was treated like a king or whatever.

Benefits

Tevin summarized his perception of exploitation by the university as he rounded out his four years of eligibility this way: "Okay we've used you up now, so goodbye and good luck to ya and don't come back around here no more." Most (14 of 20) of the respondents actually employed phrases with the word "used" such as "used up," "used goods," and "used and abused" to describe the manner in which they felt they were treated by universities. Many (12 of 20) mentioned the labor exploitation of student-athletes, in that the profits generated by successful sports programs are perceived to be enjoyed primarily by the university. The NCAA maintained that student-athletes should be considered amateur athletes driven by education and the physical, mental, and social benefits that are derived from being student-athletes (Netzely, 1997). Most (15 of 20) of these respondents did not feel that college athletes should be considered amateur athletes. They observed the university's contracts with television and radio networks, merchandising companies, and other corporations, in addition to ticket and concession sales, bowl games, and tournaments, and shared that the university was profiting from their labor.

When asked if athletes and universities were benefiting equally from college athletics, 19 of the 20 respondents noted that athletes and universities do not benefit equally. Adam stated:

> The colleges make so much money off of the athletes . . . those athletes are producing those winning records and those winning records are producing millions for that college but the athletes don't see any of that, and they get away with it by saying "well ok we're giving you a free education."

Several respondents also referred to scholarships as a benefit, but not a benefit that could be compared to the profits that universities reap from successful athletic programs. Several respondents discussed scholarships as an unequal benefit for student-athletes. Oliver stated:

> I'd have to say the university will get more out of it because . . . their (the athlete's) school is getting paid for [it], so I guess you could say they reaping the benefit that way, however they're (colleges) gonna reap a whole lot more than I guess what a college education would cost . . . from an overall standpoint, the university will benefit more because, even if you look at bowl games I mean, not even from the financial standpoint of them getting money, but however when they're on television uh they're gonna advertise the university . . . bringing in more students.

Nate also felt that universities benefit more than the athletes:

> You and I both know that there are athletes that spend four or five years at college or university and don't do nothing and the college or university actually just uses them up . . . uh ya know the college athletes are out there working hard ya know they're actually running, ya know getting bumps and bruises things of that nature . . . Okay. And um the university is making millions off of 18–22 year old kids ya know and all the kids are getting is . . . maybe an education out of it.

Kevin echoed those feelings and noted a lack of inability to have his basic necessities met while he was a student-athlete:

> Even though we had a full ride all your academic and everything, books and all that stuff is taken care of but I know when I [was] on campus, I lived on campus in the dorms and that little whatever thirty dollars a month . . . that we got living on campus was nothing especially when you coming from a background, a family background where you can't, ya know I wasn't able to call home and be like ya know 'mom please send me this, send that' you know I had to gut it out with whatever we was getting at the time was like thirty dollars when you were on campus. So I totally agree with how college athletes are not benefiting from all the money we bring to colleges.

Kevin added in another dimension, which is the fact that many student-athletes do not have money to take care of their day-to-day needs because NCAA rules prohibit athletes from working for pay during the season. For that reason, universities offer a very small stipend to student athletes who reside on campus and a larger stipend to those who reside off campus. Both amounts were described by the respondents as largely inadequate. Devin summed it up this way, "they make millions of dollars off of athletes, you get that funky [explicative] scholarship check, you supposed to survive off of that." Matt added that he lived on campus without any financial resources stating that "all I could do is ya know go wash clothes and get a combo meal that's it." Fred agreed that the financial needs of student-athletes were not being met:

> I'm not gone say we should get paid to play, but our monthly income that they give the students is definitely not enough to live. Just because they pay for room and board, if you move off campus that check is really not enough to cover expenses to live especially since they always find reasons to take money out of your check instead of putting money in.

Several respondents, like Brad and Hubert, believed that student-athletes should be paid.

> Brad: I mean they make it hard for guys that are student athletes. I mean you can't have a job...So I mean the

athletes don't win, I mean I believe, myself personally, that student-athletes should be paid...I mean you have no time to make money. I mean you are doing football *24/7,* year-round. I mean, you don't have a summer vacation, you have quote-unquote voluntary practice that you have to be at...So I think they need to set up programs that can help student-athletes to make money where it won't be illegal.

Hubert proposed that student-athletes were not benefiting enough from the monies made by the universities and should be paid for that reason:

> Overall, I see them (universities) benefiting more than we are because of the money that they make off of us. So, your next question would probably be should we get paid? And yes, we should be paid something more than a little scholarship check because if you look at the revenue, that we're bringing in for the university compared to what we get, it is not fair.

Several respondents discussed how other industries profited from student-athletes hard work. This is yet another way in which the athletes are profitable, but do not profit personally from their labor. Lenny's statement was summarized thusly:

> I feel like we were treated unfairly because we didn't get any money for the proceeds that we brought to the university. And uh, I don't know if you

recall, but it was, I think in '92 or '93 was when John Madden first came out with the collegiate Nintendo game or whatever and even had our names and numbers of the players on the jerseys of those players. And we were offended because they were making money with our names . . . . So I felt like on that aspect we were treated unequally or unfairly because they would not share the money that we were making for the universities . . . its totally lopsided. With Nike he (coach) was getting paid a million dollars for us, for the players to wear Nike products, now I feel like it should have been divided a little bit more equally than that . . . And the university was getting money from the ticket proceeds and all the paraphernalia that we were wearing and making popular because we were out there winning . . . we were getting at the time I was playing football, I think we were getting $675 a month stipend and that was supposed to get us meals, wash clothes, pay bills, and man that's just not right. They were making millions of dollars off us in a year so I felt like they coulda divided the money a little bit more toward the athlete who was doing the majority of the workload.

The only equalizing factor mentioned by any respondent was if athletes moved on to play in professional leagues. Matt stated that "the athlete would probably benefit if he knew for sure he was going to the league." Jack went into depth on the subject and his statement summarized the sentiments of several of the respondents:

I think the universities benefit a lot more. I think they use these guys as a meat market and kinda the rules (exploit them) . . . They definitely use the athlete. I think they exploit 'em to a certain degree. They give you the opportunity to get out there and make a name for yourself and you can put yourself up and maybe get drafted into the NBA, but the odds of that are very low.

Career Preparation

One of the major consequences of the overemphasis placed on sports by African American young men is a lack of career maturity. The athletes in this study were socialized by family, the community/neighborhood, and the media toward athletic achievement. Most had very salient athletic identities. Athletics had come first during their college careers and their focus, then, was to stay eligible. The following findings concentrated on the respondent's college preparation for careers after sports, particularly choosing a major.

One of the primary sources of career immaturity among college athletes derives from limitations in choosing a major. They cannot choose majors that have required courses held during times set aside for sports participation. (For example, majors such as architecture or sciences often have afternoon labs.) Several respondents (9 of 20) mentioned these types of constraints limited their choices for majors. Additionally, most (15 of 20) mentioned choosing majors with courses classified as "easy to pass" or departments that were "athlete-friendly." For these reasons and to remain eligible to play their sport, student-athletes often selected more pragmatic educational goals. Devin, a business major, had a desire to become an engineer. He ended up in a major that he was not his first choice:

> My major was something I just kinda wind up getting, I started off wanting to be an engineer, but it's like the labs and stuff would conflict with practice. And cuz I was on scholarship, they figured, uh, my football stuff was more important than going to class or being what I truly wanted to be, so I kinda fell into my degree.

Hubert found himself in the same situation:

> Initially when I first went to college I wanted to major in psychology. But because my um, the classes for my major were going to conflict with football practice. So I was not allowed to choose those classes . . . so instead of psychology I chose journalism.

Perry also had interests that could not be explored due to athletics:

> I had an interest in architecture, but the thing about architecture . . . the school of architecture classes conflicted with football practice. My friend lost his starting position who went through with it and majored in architecture. A few respondents felt as if they were lied to during recruiting concerning what they could major in once they came to campus.

Oliver recounted what he was told on his recruiting visit:

> I wanted to major in criminal justice and when they were recruiting me I was told that I could major in criminal justice but when I got ya know to (college) there wasn't a criminal justice degree. I found out that all the classes were in sociology and that is different that is not criminal justice which is what I wanted to major in.

Perry spoke of how his major was chosen for him. He felt that the university had ulterior motives in pushing student-athletes to chose a major before they had explored any options:

> When I first got there, it was about making the university look good . . . we meet with counselors . . . it was all about making [the university] look good, you know when you watch the football games on Saturday, they put your face up there and it says majoring in whatever. That was the whole purpose of this counseling part, which I later found this out, but basically you get in there and they try to get you to commit to a major because the more people we got in business, makes us look good . . . I committed to business and in that commitment to business, uh I had to then had to get enrolled in classes to head me into that direction. Well those classes were absolutely overwhelming for me . . . so I don't think that they were in our corner as young folks coming to school. I think they were in the corner of [the university] making [the university] look good.

With counseling geared more toward the student-athlete's needs, Perry's interests could have been accommodated with a major in which he could have experienced success and could have led to more fulfilling career options. Instead, Perry majored in an area for which he was inadequately prepared, had no interest, and ultimate had little success. He goes on to state:

> So in order to get off of probation I had to write an appeal letter and get a school to accept me which was social work . . . well I grew up in the system of social work I can relate to this, so I shouldn't have nothing but success in something that I could relate to. This is something a counselor working for me could have found out easy.

Others spoke of academic counselors in the athletic department pushing them toward majors that were not their choice. Matt discusses being talked into a major, and then being unable to change his major back to his first choice:

> Actually it was graphic design and I switched it. Me and my counselor sat down and talked about it, and I told him yeah I want to work with my hands and these different types of things. And he said "you might want to try this [fine arts] and plus you'll graduate faster." So I switched it, then a couple semesters down the road I decided I wanted to switch back to graphic design, because I was kinda looking into it and I found it wasn't nothing in fine arts that really

I could do except . . . work at a museum or something which I didn't want to do. And at that time it was too late, I was already backed up in that major so I was stuck with it.

Fred, who actually wanted to be a meteorologist, was also talked into choosing a major that he was not interested in:

> Um, its funny, cuz I remember how I got in this major because I don't like business. I don't like this major, I don't like the one I got into. And I went in and I said, "I don't know what I want to major in." and they said "well you should go into business cuz . . . it's easy to be successful when you go into this major." I said okay I'll buy it. So when I got into it, and I didn't like it, but I had so many hours toward it, it was no choice but for me to stay into it. I really don't like that.

These athletes' experiences reflect the difficulties they face when choosing a major and, inevitability, these experiences will affect their success in moving out of the world of sports and into the world of work and their ability to identify a career that will be generally rewarding.

■ LIMITATIONS AND IMPLICATIONS OF THE STUDY

The limitations of this research are those typically associated with qualitative research. The first limitation was the generalizability of the findings. This study focused on twenty participants whose responses were consistent with the issues identified in the literature. However, the findings cannot be generalized to describe experiences or perceptions of all African American student athletes in revenue-generating sports. Additionally, this study was limited by gender, focusing exclusively on males. In addition to African American males having lower graduation rates than White males, the differential between White female graduation rates and African American female graduation rates is also significant ("African-American College Athletes," 2002). This suggests that future research should include African American females in order to determine if similar influences affect their collegiate experience. Sampling limitations also existed. Although the sample consisted of men of various ages from universities across the nation, snowballing may have led to respondents with similar experiences. This limitation was addressed by assuring that the five initial contacts were varied by occupation, university, age, and region of the country. Another limitation of the sample is its small size ($N = 20$). However, there are recognized obstacles to gaining research access to members of Division I teams and professional athletes (Benson, 2000; Funk, 1991; Winbush, 1988). Interviewing high-profile athletes involves some of the same difficulties as studying elites; similarly, they are rare, and unlikely to participate (Neuman, 1997). For this reason, although small, any sample adds significantly to the

current body of knowledge This study has implications for institutions of higher education and African American male student-athletes. Universities should foster an atmosphere in which the athletes' roles do not overshadow their roles as students, thus allowing them to choose majors of interest to them that will lead to careers outside of sports.

■ DISCUSSION AND CONCLUSIONS

Sports have opened doors both educationally and economically for African Americans. African American student-athletes graduate at a higher rate than non-athlete African American students ("African-American College Athletes," 2002). Although White athletes also graduate at higher rates than White non-athletes, the financial benefit of athletic scholarships seem to be more advantageous for African Americans ("African-American College Athletes," 2002). In fact, 90% (18 of 20) of the participants in this study revealed that they would not have had the opportunity to attend college without the athletic scholarships they received. Many of the respondents had collegiate experiences that they did not consider to be positive because only (20%) reported having an overall good experience on campus. Although most respondents received a degree, none felt that their educational development was emphasized by the universities they attended or that they fully reaped the benefits of receiving a higher education. Furthermore, 90% noted that universities were reaping far greater benefits, financial and otherwise, than student–athletes. Many lacked career maturity, which stemmed, in part, from their choice of majors because they were limited by time constraints, NCAA rules, and inappropriate counseling. In addition to the lack of emphasis placed on academic achievement and career development, most of the respondents felt taken advantage of, or, as Hubert stated, like "used goods." Therefore, universities that provide opportunities to African American males to attend college through athletic scholarships by emphasizing the importance of the athletic role over the academic one, leaving the student–athletes feeling exploited, failing to prepare for careers, and even hindering their choice of majors, contribute to the reproduction of these inequalities. African American student–athletes who come to college with disadvantages and hardships, hold even stronger aspirations for professional sports careers (Beamon & Bell, 2002; Sellers & Kuperminc, 1997; Upthegrove, Roscigno, & Charles, 1999). Some African American male student–athletes are particularly susceptible to the pressures of winning, which creates contradictory pressures to perform on the field and in the classroom. Student–athletes should demand and take responsibility for a well-rounded education. They should value the educational opportunity as much as they value the athletic opportunity. Additionally, the era of the amateur collegiate athlete may be over. As big-time, commercialized college athletics continue to generate revenue, the pursuit to win likely will result in student–athletes being encouraged to neglect their academic development for the sake of their athletic performance, which further increases the perception of exploitation.

REFERENCES

African-American college athletes: Debunking the myth of the dumb jock. (2002). *The Journal of Blacks in Higher Education,* 35, 36–40.

Adler, P. A., & Adler, P. (1987). Role conflict and identity salience: College athletics and the academic role. *Social Science Journal,* 24, 443–455.

Adler, P. A., & Adler, P. (1991). *Backboards and blackboards: College athletes and role engulfment.* New York: Columbia University Press.

Baillie, P. H., and Danish, S. (1992). Understanding the career transition of athletes. *The Sport Psychologist,* 6, 77–98.

Beamon, K., & Bell, P. (2002). Going pro: The differential effects of high aspirations for a professional sports career on African-American student-athletes and White student-athletes. *Race and Society,* 5, 179–191.

Beamon, K., & Bell, P. (2006). Academics versus athletics: An examination of the effects of background and socialization on African-American male student-athletes. *The Social Science Journal,* 43, 393–403.

Benson, K. F. (2000). Constructing academic inadequacy: African-American athletes' stories of schooling. *Journal of Higher Education,* 71, 223–246.

Blann, F. W. (1985). Intercollegiate athletic competition and student's educational and career paths. *Journal of College Student Personnel,* 26, 115–118.

Cornelius, A. (1995). The relationship between athletic identity, peer and faculty socialization and college student-development. *Journal of College Student Development,* 36, 560–573.

Donnor, J. (2005). Toward an interest-convergence in the education of African-American football student-athletes in major college sports. *Race, Ethnicity, and Education,* 8, 45–67.

Edwards, H. (1983). The exploitation of Black athletes. *AGB (Association of Governing Boards of Universities and Colleges) Reports,* 28, 37–48.

Edwards, H. (1988). The single-minded pursuit of sports fame and fortune is approaching an institutionalized triple tragedy in Black society. *Ebony,* 43, 138–140.

Edwards, H. (2000). Crisis of Black athletes on the eve of the 21st century. *Society,* 37, 9–13.

Eitle, T., & Eitle, D. (2002). Race, cultural capital, and the educational effects of participation in sports. *Sociology of Education,* 75, 123–146.

Eitzen, D. S. (2000). Racism in big-time college sport: Prospects for the Year 2020 and Proposal for Change. In D. Brooks & R. Althouse (Eds.), *Racism in college athletics: The African American athlete's experience* (pp. 293–306). Morgantown, WV: Fitness Information Technology.

Eitzen, D. S. (2003). Sports and fairy tales: Upward mobility through sport. In J. Henslin (Ed.), *Down to earth sociology: Introductory readings* (pp. 405–410). New York: Free Press.

Funk, G. D. (1991). *Major violation: The unbalanced priorities in athletics and academics.* Champaign, IL: Leisure Press.

Gerdy, J. R. (2000). *Sports in school: The future of an institution.* New York: Teachers College Press.

Giroux, H. A. (1983). Theories of reproduction and resistance in the new sociology of education: A critical analysis. *Harvard Educational Review,* 53, 257–293.

Hall, R. (2001). The ball curve: Calculated racism and the stereotype of African-American men. *Journal of Black Studies,* 32, 104–119.

Harris, O. (1994). Race, sport, and social support. *Sociology of Sport Journal,* 11, 40–50.

Harrison, C., & Lawrence, S. (2003). African-American student-athletes' perception of career transition in sport: A qualitative and visual elicitation. *Race, Ethnicity and Education,* 6, 373–394.

Harrison, K. (2000). Black athletes at the millennium. *Society,* 37, 35–39.

Hawkins, B. (1999). Black student athletes at predominantly White, National Collegiate Athletic Association division I institutions and the pattern of oscillating migrant laborers. *Western Journal of Black Studies,* 23, 1–9.

Hoberman, J. (2000). The price of Black dominance. *Society,* 37, 49–56.

Kennedy, S., & Dimick, K. (1987). Career maturity and professional expectations of college football and basketball players. *Journal of College Student Development, 28*, 293–297.

Lapchick, R. (1996). Race and college sports: A long way to go. In R. E. Lapchick (Ed.), *Sport in society* (pp. 5–18). Thousand Oaks, CA: Sage.

Lapchick, R. (2000). Crime and athletes: New radical stereotypes. *Society, 37*, 14–20.

Lapchick, R., & Matthews, K. (2001). *Racial and gender report card*. Boston: Northeastern University, Center for the Study of Sport in Society.

Lewis, G. (1970). The beginning of organized collegiate sport. *American Quarterly, 22*, 222–229.

Litsky, F. (2003, March 25). Study finds top teams failing in the classroom. *New York Times*, p. BI.

Lomax, M. E. (2000). Athletics vs. education: Dilemmas of Black youth. *Society, 37*, 21–23.

Maloney, M., & McConnick, R.E. (1993). An examination of the role that intercollegiate athletic participation plays in academic achievement: Athletes' feats in the classroom. *The Journal of Human Resources, 28*, 555–570.

Meeker, D., Stankovich, C., & Kays, T. (2000). *Positive transitions for student-athletes: Life skills for transitions in sport, college, and career*. Scottsdale, AZ: Holcomb Hathaway.

Meggysey, D. (2000). Athletes in big-time college sport. *Society, 37*, 24–29.

National Collegiate Athletic Association. (2006). *NCAA report on federal graduation rates data Division I*. Retrieved July 15, 2006, from http://web l.ncaa.org/app datal instAggr2006/1_O.pdf

Netzely, D., III. (1997). *Endorsements for student-athletes: A novel approach to a controversial idea. Stetson Law Forum*. Retrieved March 19, 2003, from http://www.law.stetson.edul LawForumlbacklfa1l97 Inetzley.htm.

Neuman, W. L. (1997). *Social research methods: Qualitative and quantitative approaches* (3rd ed). Needham Heights, MA: Allyn and Bacon.

Parker, K. B. (1994). Has-beens and wanna-bes: Transition experiences of former major college football players. *The Sport Psychologist, 8*, 287–304.

Pascarella, E., Truckenmiller, R., Nora, A., Terenzini, P., Edison, M., & Hagedorn, L. (1999). Cognitive impacts of intercollegiate athletic participation: Some further evidence. *The Journal of Higher Education, 70*, 1–26.

Person, D., Benson-Quaziena, M., & Rogers, A. (2001). Female student athletes and student athletes of color. *New Direction for Student Services, 93*, 55–64.

Roscigno, V. J. (1999). The Black-White achievement gap, family-school links and the importance of place. *Sociological Inquiry, 69*, 159–186.

Sack, A., & Stuarowsky, E. (1998). *College athletes for hire: The evolution and legacy of the NCAA's amateur myth*. Westport: Praeger.

Salome, K. (2005). Lost wealth: The economic value of Black male college athletes. *Network Journal, 13*, 32.

Sellers, R. (2000). African-American student-athletes: Opportunity or exploitation. In D. Brooks & R. Althouse (Eds.), *Racism in college athletics: The African-American athlete's experience* (pp. 133–154).

Morgantown, WV: Fitness Information Technology, Inc.

Sellers, R. M., & Kupenninc, G. (1997). Goal discrepancy in African-American male student athletes' unrealistic expectations for careers in professional sports. *Journal of Black Psychology, 23,* 6–23.

Siegel, D. (1996). Higher education and the plight of the Black male athlete. In R. Lapchick (Ed.), *Sport in society* (pp. 19–34). Thousand Oaks, CA: Sage.

Singer, J. N. (2002). "Let Us Make Man": The development of Black male (student) athletes in a big time college sport program. (Doctoral dissertation, The Ohio State University, 2002). *Dissertation Abstracts International, 63,* 1299 .

Upthegrove, T., Roscigno, V., & Charles, C. (1999). Big money collegiate sports: Racial concentration, contradictory pressures, and academic performance. *Social Science Quarterly, 80,* 718–787.

Washington, R. E., & Karen, D. (2001). Sport and society. *Annual Review of Sociology, 27,* 187–212.

Winbush, R. A. (1988). The furious passage of the African-American intercollegiate athlete. *Journal of Sport and Social Issues, 11,* 97–103.

CHAPTER 27

Social Justice and Men's Interests

The Case of Title IX

Michael A. Messner and Nancy M. Solomon

I t is foundational to a sociology of superordinates that groups of people who are differently situated in a system of hierarchies have different interests in social continuity and social change (Goode, 1982; Kimmel & Ferber, 2003). It follows that feminist challenges that push for greater institutional sex equity run counter to men's collective interests. A structural perspective suggests that men's collective interests flow from their shared superordinate positions: "A gender order where men dominate women cannot avoid constituting men as an interest group concerned with defense, and women as an interest group concerned with change" (Connell, 1995, p. 82). Men's collective interests are expressed "through the routine functioning of the institutions in which the dominance of men is embedded—corporations, churches, mass media, legal systems, and governments" (Connell, 2002, p. 144). Through these routine institutional arrangements, men as a group tend to take for granted their right to a "patriarchal dividend," which includes access to a surplus of economic resources, as well as "authority, respect, service, safety, housing, access to institutional power and control over one's life" (Connell, 2002, p. 142).

We would add sport to Connell's (2002) list of institutions through which men have historically reaped a patriarchal dividend. Men have maintained a privileged position and a long-standing sense of entitlement to the majority of athletic resources. However, "The patriarchal dividend is the benefit to men as a group. Individual men may get more of it than others, or less, or none, depending on their location in the social order" (p. 142). So, when women challenge institutional arrangements that have ensured men's access to this privileged position, how do marginalized or subordinated men—those who have enjoyed little or no patriarchal dividend—respond to this challenge?

One way to begin thinking about this question of men's interests is to invoke the now-common observation that in speaking about "men," we may be falsely universalizing a group and oversimplifying the idea of "men's interests." Scholarship on masculinities has long grappled with this dilemma: how to retain the feminist critique of men's global power and privilege over women while appreciating the considerable inequalities and differences among men (e.g., Brod, 1987; Carrigan, Connell, & Lee, 1985). Most analyses of multiple masculinities have invoked the familiar trilogy of social class, race/ethnicity, and sexual orientation. These intersectional theories of power and inequality remind us that "multiple masculinities" are not simply different masculine "styles" but are based on complex group-based relations of power and different—sometimes contradictory—relations to material interests.

A look at sport and recent debates about Title IX suggests that an understanding of additional configurations of masculinities may help us grapple with the intricacies of difference and group interests. Research has demonstrated that, within the gender regime of sport, men construct hierarchies of masculinities based on race, class, and sexual orientation (Anderson, 2002; Carrington, 1998; Messner, 1992). We want to suggest an additional dimension of difference: Hierarchy in men's sport is also based on

different kinds and levels of bodily capital that boys and men develop for different sports. The team sports that require and valorize large, muscled bodies that engage in aggressive contact or violent collision (i.e., basketball and football) occupy the "center" of the U.S. men's sports world and enjoy the lion's share of the privileges and resources. Boys and men in marginal sports often have very different experiences of sport; some of them are overtly insulted—even assaulted—by boys and men in the central sports, being placed into subordinate roles that are coded as feminine (Anderson, 2002). Thus, theoretically, we might expect them to have very different interests in maintaining or challenging the existing hierarchies within sport and between sport and other institutions like schools.

Sport, then, is not patriarchal in a simple, seamlessly binary fashion—males versus females. Sport is male-dominated, but it is also constructed through a hierarchy of masculinities and a very unequal distribution of resources and privilege among boys and men: star athletes over benchwarmers, athletic directors and head coaches over assistant coaches and players, and athletes and coaches in central sports (especially football) over those in marginal "minor" sports (like cross-country, swimming, gymnastics, wrestling, and golf).

But marginal boys' and men's subordinate social location with respect to privileged football and basketball programs does not automatically translate into the participants identifying their interests as aligned with those of girls and women against the gluttony of "major" men's sports programs. As in many other situations, an academic assessment of a group's interests, based simply on identifying the group's social location within a hierarchy of privilege and subordination, is rarely a good predictor of the group's political consciousness or actions. An analysis of "men's interests" cannot simply be reduced to a rational analysis of men's material interests in maintaining their patriarchal privilege. As Bob Pease (2002) argued,

> People do not have objective interests as a result of their location; rather, they formulate . . . their interests, and they do so within the context of the available discourses in situations in which they are located and that they coproduce. (p. 170)

One such "available discourse," as it pertains to school sport, is the 2002 U.S. Department of Education's public hearings about Title IX. These discussions offer an opportunity to examine the ways that the spokespeople for men's sports articulate their interests in a highly politicized forum. In what follows, we will draw from the testimony at the 2002 hearing that we attended in San Diego, California, and at which we both spoke (as pro–Title IX advocates) during the public comments period. We draw from our own notes, taken at the hearing, and from the official public transcripts of the hearing.[1] For our purposes here, we will focus primarily on the various strategies employed by the critics of Title IX, most of whom spoke for groups

and organizations that represented men in "marginal" sports that claimed to have been weakened or threatened by the enforcement of Title IX. We will first provide a brief overview of the significance of the 2002 hearings, in the context of the legal history of Title IX. We will then describe the major patterns in the narratives of the critics of Title IX and analyze these patterns as a way of shedding light on how spokespeople for marginalized groups of men—at least in the context of sport—understand and articulate their interests. We will argue that spokespeople for marginalized boys' and men's sports articulated their interests in a way that supports the interests of dominant groups of men over women and over other men.

■ TITLE IX AND THE 2002 HEARINGS

Title IX of the Education Amendment of 1972 is a one-sentence law barring sex discrimination in all programs of an educational institution that receives federal financial assistance.[2] Since Congress enacted Title IX, girls' and women's involvement in sports has increased exponentially. According to the National Federation of State High School Associations, in 1972 girls were only 7.4% of high school athletes, but by 2003, they were 41.7%. Additionally, the federal General Accounting Office reports that colleges have added nearly 3,800 more women's teams since 1972. Advocates of Title IX argue that this increase in sports participation by females demonstrates that discrimination, and not lack of interest, accounted for the historically low athletic participation rates of women (Acosta & Carpenter, 2002; Carpenter, 2001).

Despite the growth opportunities for women and girls in sports, inequity still exists. Women make up more than half of the undergraduates in college and universities, but they represent just 42% of college varsity athletes nationwide. "In fact, female participation in intercollegiate sports remains below pre-Title IX male participation" (National Women's Law Center, 2002a). Furthermore, although women in Division I colleges make up more than half of the student body, they receive only 43% of athletic scholarship dollars, 32% of recruiting dollars, and 36% of operating budgets (National Women's Law Center, 2002b). Despite the continued lack of opportunities and discrimination against women and girls in sports, a perception exists that the increase in female participation opportunities has resulted in cuts in male sports, and a vigorous backlash against Title IX's athletic regulations persists and has swelled in the past few years.

At the center of the backlash against Title IX has been controversy surrounding the highly publicized cuts of men's sports in various colleges and universities. The advocates of men's sports (especially wrestling and gymnastics programs) have claimed that Title IX has led to a decline in opportunities for men to play certain sports. The "culprit," in their mind, is the "three-part test" outlined in a 1979 Policy Interpretation on Title IX that is used to determine whether a school is providing equal athletic participation opportunities to its students. Schools can comply with this test by satisfying one of three prongs: (a) by having roughly the same proportion of male and female athletes on teams as they have males and females in the student body, known as "substantial proportionality"; (b) by having a "history and continuing practice" of expanding opportunities for the underrepresented sex; or (c) by "fully and effectively accommodating the interests and abilities" of the underrepresented sex.

On June 27, 2002, the U.S. Department of Education established the Commission on Opportunity in Athletics. The purpose and functions of the Commission, according to its charter, was

> to collect information, analyze issues, and obtain broad public input directed at improving the application of current Federal standards for measuring equal opportunity for men and women and boys and girls to participate in athletics under Title IX. The Commission will recommend to the Secretary, in a written report, whether those standards should be revised, and if so, how the standards should be revised.

Between August and December 2002, the 15-person Commission held five "Town Hall meetings" (in Atlanta, Chicago, Colorado Springs, San Diego, and Philadelphia), hearing testimony and gathering information to prepare a January 2003 report for the secretary of education. The formation of the commission set off a firestorm of public debate and an impressive level of mobilization. On one side were spokespeople for men's "minor" sports (especially wrestling, but also tennis and gymnastics) that have declined in number in recent years. On the other side was an array of advocates of girls' and women's sports (including the Women's Sports Foundation, legal advocates, women coaches, and women and girl athletes).

Women's sports advocates viewed the commission as the first step in a Bush administration attempt to weaken or dismantle Title IX's regulations. To support this conclusion, advocates first noted that none of the appointed commissioners represented high schools. The focus was almost entirely on Division 1-A universities with elite, "big-time" athletics programs. By limiting the focus in this manner, the issue of revenue-producing sports was overly emphasized in the testimony and factors considered by the commission (de Verona & Foudy, 2002). Girls' experience in primary and secondary schools was all but ignored. Second, women's sports advocates protested the very assumptions underlying the formation of the commission, which was charged with examining whether current Title IX standards for assessing equal opportunity in athletics are working to promote opportunities for both male and female athletes. Advocates of Title IX saw this inquiry as a "loaded" question because Congress enacted Title IX, an antidiscrimination statute, to ensure equal opportunities for the underrepresented sex. Given the historical discrimination against females in school sports, the underrepresented sex was, and continues to be, female students. Finally, most of the discussion at the hearings focused specifically on the 1979 Policy Interpretation of Title IX, which outlined the three-part test used to determine equity in sports participation opportunities. By limiting the inquiry in this manner, the commission all but ignored other areas of discrimination that relate to the continued inferior treatment and benefits female athletes receive even after they are given the opportunity to participate in sports.

■ THE CRITICS' NARRATIVES

At the San Diego hearing, we identified several common elements in the critics' statements. We will begin to introduce these themes with a somewhat extended excerpt from the statement by Jon Vegosen, a Chicago attorney representing the U.S. Tennis Association, the governing body for tennis in the United States, and the Intercollegiate Tennis Association, the governing body of college tennis:

> We support the tremendous strides that women have made through Title IX, and we want to preserve those gains. We are also concerned about its unintended consequences for both men and women, not only with regard to collegiate tennis programs, but also concerning the adverse impact that Title IX can have on minorities

and grassroots tennis programs . . . . Tennis is truly a gender blind sport. At the college level there are dual meet matches for both men and women varsity players, with an equal number of tournaments and draw sizes . . . . The message is clear, there are no differences between the sexes. There is, however, a profound difference in the gender message at the collegiate level in terms of scholarships and participation. For example, the men's varsity tennis team in a fully-funded Division I school has only 4 1/2 scholarships, the women's team has 8. Most of the men's varsity rosters have a squad limit of 8 players, and the women's roster can have 12 . . . . Another disturbing consequence of Title IX has been the adverse impact on walk-ons. I was a walk-on at Northwestern and became captain my junior and senior year, and I was the first player to be selected at Northwestern to the All Big Ten Team. I experienced valuable life lessons, including goal-setting, time management, teamwork and travel. Today that wouldn't happen . . . . I would be told, "Thanks for your interest, but there's no room for you," and that's what thousands of male athletes in tennis and other sports are told every year. They are turned away, while women's tennis teams struggle to fill their rosters . . . . It is critical to appreciate the long-term impact of the unintended consequences of Title IX for tennis. If these trends continue, men's collegiate tennis will be jeopardized. If that occurs, we will see a devastating effect for minorities and at the grassroots level for girls as well as boys.

Vegosen's statement contained all of the major themes that we heard repeated in various forms by the Title IX critics. The themes are intertwined and can be summarized as follows:

1. We applaud the growth of girls' and women's sports, and we have no intention of trying to turn back the clock on this progress; however, we are critical of Title IX's "unintended consequences."

2. Compliance with the Title IX three-part test is illogical, because it ignores the fact that males have higher levels of interest in playing sports than do females.

3. Cuts in men's sports disproportionately hurt poor and minority males, who often find sports to be their one avenue to college scholarships.

We will next discuss these themes in terms of our main question about how men's interests are articulated.

■ TITLE IX'S "UNINTENDED CONSEQUENCES": MALE VICTIMIZATION BY QUOTAS

Nearly every critic of Title IX began with a statement of support for women's sports and for what they saw to be the original intent of Title IX. They did not want to turn back the clock, they emphasized. They just wanted men to be treated fairly. Critics regularly appropriated conservative language from familiar anti-affirmative action narratives about government-enforced "quota systems" that result in "reverse discrimination." For example, Sam Bell, president of the National Track and Field Coaches Association, criticized the "politically correct roster management" under Title IX as a "quota system" that was set up "in order to satisfy someone's bean counting in Washington." Speaking of the controversial "substantial proportionality" prong of the three-part test, Rick Bay, San Diego State University athletic director, stated,

> It is ironic that while the motivation for the genesis of Title IX was to eliminate discrimination against women, Title IX must now depend on a discriminatory benchmark of its own to validate its desired results . . . whether we'd like to admit it or not, proportionality is a quota system.

Bay's inclusion as an invited speaker was especially illuminating because he is an athletic director who had recently made the decision to cut a men's sport, volleyball (and its $150,000 annual cost), from his budget. Bay said that he did not blame women's sports for this "difficult choice." But, he went on to say, he had made this decision because, faced with a need to cut expenditures from his budget, the "unintended consequences" of Title IX imposed a "quota system" on him that left him no choice but to cut a men's sport. "The by-product of this system," Bay asserted, "is that we have reached a point where women's interest in sports are dictating men's opportunities."

Commissioner Donna De Verona then questioned Bay, stating that she had done "a little research" about the San Diego State University Athletic Department. The previous year they had spent "$4,720 for [football] helmet decals, $40,720 for 600 pairs of Nikes, and $37,796 for hotel rooms and buses on nights before football home games." Faced with Bay's need to trim expenses from the athletic department budget, De Verona observed, "You cut the volleyball team rather than reduce the five million dollar football budget [which was] one million more than the twelve-sport women's sport program budget." Then she asked Bay directly, "Did you consider that maybe you could look at these [football] expenditures and fund volleyball, bring back men's volleyball for next season?" Bay responded to this line of questioning by asserting the dominant logic of big-time college athletic programs:

> Well, football is the one sport . . . that actually generates more money than is spent, and as a result it helps fund all the other sports, including women's sports . . . . Our football budget is pretty modest by competitive standards, and so we're trying to keep our revenue sports relatively strong so that they can generate revenue. So yes, we could have—to answer your question, Donna, I wish we could have sliced $150,000 out of the football budget that you mentioned, but it would have reduced our capability to be competitive in football, which would have in turn reduced our capability to generate revenue to help support all the sports, including the women's programs.

In the San Diego State case, when faced with the option to trim the football budget by 3%, or to eliminate the entire men's sport of volleyball, the internal logic of the athletic department dictated the latter decision. The interests of the football coaches and players are protected by this logic; meanwhile, the interests of men in other sports are put at risk, and then when these men's sports are cut, women's sports are scapegoated. This is precisely how privilege operates—often unmarked and invisible (Kimmel & Ferber, 2003). The problem with this logic, however, is that for the vast majority of schools, "revenue-producing" does not mean "profit-producing." Most football programs—even many of the college football programs that are tied in to the big television dollars—lose money (NCAA, 2000; Zimbalist, 1999). They do not support themselves, let alone other sports teams at their schools. Moreover, the existence of a big-time college football program seems to create conditions that make gender equity less rather than more likely: A study that assessed U.S. colleges' and universities' levels of compliance with Title IX found that, after 25 years of Title IX, institutions with big-time football programs were on average the least likely to be in compliance with gender equity laws (Sabo & Women's Sports Foundation, 1997). Schools with big-time football programs often spend twice as much on football programs as on all women's sports (Eitzen, 1999; Sperber, 2000).

The male-headed football lobby continues to be one of the most powerful groups behind the mobilization against gender equity in U.S. sports. High school and college football programs have successfully labeled themselves as "revenue-generating sports" and have thus created a mostly false image of themselves as geese that lay golden eggs. The successful imposition of an image of the football program as the beneficent supporter of the rest of the athletic department has given the football lobby the leverage it needs to attempt to position itself outside the gender equity debates. In effect, they argue that gender equity calculus should consider three categories of sports: women's sports, men's sports, and football. There have been efforts over the past 30 years to exempt revenue-producing sports from the reach of Title IX's sex equity requirements. However, Congress and the courts have consistently held that the opportunities provided to male athletes on a football or basketball team should not be ignored simply because such sports currently have the ability to generate revenue.

■ MEN'S "NATURAL INTERESTS" AND THE "WALK-ON" AS VICTIM

Though it is usually not directly stated, the idea that males are biologically programmed to be more interested in sport underlies much of the criticism of Title IX's equal participation requirements. After all, if interest in sport is in our nature, then any attempt at gender equity is by definition futile, as schools would be forced to create ever-increasing participation opportunities for females who will never want to play in the same proportion as their male counterparts. One way in which advocates for men's minor sports express this belief is to both laud and then lament the loss of the idealized male "walk-on" participation opportunities that are "tragically" lost to Title IX's equity requirements.

A "walk-on" is a college student who is neither recruited to play sports nor given an athletic scholarship but who shows up and tries out for the team. Chuck Neinas, founding president of the American Football Coaches Association, launched a defense of the supposedly threatened interests of walk-ons as the centerpiece of his presentation to the commission. Roster management under Title IX, he argued, forced men's teams to go smaller and, thus, to turn away walk-ons. "Why is that important?" Neinas asked, "Well, by golly, kids like to try out and be a member of the team." Similarly, Sam Bell, president of the National Track and Field Coaches Association, told several stories of past "walk-on" athletes who had become successful in various ways. He then delivered a passionate defense of the walk-on, as threatened by Title-IX roster management, and concluded, "We will lose a lot of this type of student-athlete if we stay with quotas, with a quota mentality."

The walk-on is a powerful image, we suggest, because it invokes the romantic ideal of the student-athlete as an untarnished amateur who loves the purity of sports. The invocation of this romantic ideal obscures the increasingly negative public image of the scholarship athlete in big-time college sports: He is viewed as spoiled by privilege; he is often in legal or academic trouble; he is not fully deserving as a student; and—crucially—in the public image, he is African American (Cole, 2001). The walk-on, by contrast, is first and foremost a student, who just happens to love sports. He does not seek fame and fortune; he just wants to be on the team. He is also, in the public imagination—like the character in the popular film *Rudy*—an admirably hard-working (albeit athletically limited) White guy. Thus, the critics' foregrounding the image of the walk-on, we suggest, is an accomplishment of political rhetoric: without mentioning race, White males are positioned as "regular kids," victimized by liberal policies gone amuck. The critics' image of the walk-on reveals the "unintended" victimization of White males as irrational, unfair, and un- American. The invocation of the walk-on, then, taps in to and reiterates familiar and highly charged sexist and racist anti-affirmative-action narratives.

The critics' defense of the male walk-on emphasizes these male students' willingness to play under any conditions, impliedly compared to those female athletes who will only play under certain specified conditions. For example, Charles M. Neinas' defense of the walk-on was premised on his assertion that "there are surveys which indicate that males are more anxious to participate in athletics without receiving aid than females." Kimberly Schuld, special assistant to the commissioner at the U.S.

Commission on Civil Rights, and former director of external relations at the conservative Independent Women's Forum, took the issue of differential interest as the centerpiece of her statement to the commission. Like all the critics, Schuld began by asserting that "nobody wants to cut Title IX"; however, the statute "forces schools to artificially manufacture interest" in sports among women:

> We need to take into account that there are differences in interest levels in the aggregate between boys and girls and men and women. Those interest levels are not driven because society tells girls that they can't play sports.... Society is not telling them not to, they simply don't have the interest.... I would argue that it is not the proper role of the government to create interest levels. So I would encourage you to ignore the groupthink and look at the individual.

Schuld's comment revealed how the more overtly conservative opposition to Title IX is part of a larger backlash against liberal government programs that aim to decrease historical inequities. An ideology of extreme individualism is often at the heart of conservative critiques of Title IX and other public attempts to address structural inequities, like affirmative action. "Interest" in playing sports is seen, from this perspective, as an individual attribute (perhaps grounded in biology) that can be measured by social scientific survey methods.

Title IX advocates reject this conservative individualism and the potential elevation of the concept of individual "interest" that might emerge from a historical social science survey data. Instead, they view differential "interest levels" as being grounded in historically shifting structures of discrimination and opportunity. There is a reciprocal relationship between supply and demand for athletic opportunity; when new athletic opportunities for girls and women are provided, participation rates soar (Messner, 2002, pp. 182–183). Static "interest surveys" are likely to tell us as more about the existing structure of opportunity, and attitudes that formed as a result of past discrimination, than about what boys and girls, men and women really "want" (Sabo & Grant, 2005).

To counter the argument that Title IX is creating opportunities disproportionate to actual interest, Title IX advocates raised the issue of women's and men's collective interests in continuity and change. Donna Lopiano, the executive director of the Women's Sports Foundation, directly took on the charge that men's interests were being undermined by Title IX by invoking a schoolyard image that she called "the rule of the sandbox." "It is inevitable," she concluded, "that the previously advantaged class will be unhappy. In all civil rights laws, be it race or gender, the advantaged class perceives a loss when they must give up generations of privilege and advantage." But, Lopiano implied, this does not mean that they are being discriminated against. It means that they must learn to share the sandbox. In this statement, Lopiano neatly described a sociological phenomenon that was described by William Goode in his classic 1982 article, "Why Men Resist." When a superordinate group is even partly nudged from their position of social centrality, they often experience this as a major displacement and respond defensively.

In response to questions about the possible social and historical basis of different gender interest levels in playing sports, Kimberly Schuld revealed the biological essentialism that underlies her perspective: "Participation in those opportunities is driven by interests, and our society does not tell males what they should and shouldn't say about sports. Their biology tells them that." (Schuld's next sentence, which was an offer to "refer the Commission to some very substantial sociological and anthropological studies," was drowned out by audience laughter.)

Every court presented with the argument that one's biology determines interest and justifies disparate treatment has rejected the idea that proportionality is unfair. On the other hand, the organization of sports programs is usually based on the assumption that there are two biological sexes and that sports opportunities are best organized separately for males and females. Thus, unlike in the employment or school admissions arena, sex is a relevant characteristic in allocating athletic participation opportunities. In an attempt to allow schools maximum flexibility to comply with Title IX, the regulations do not require schools to create duplicate athletic opportunities for males and females and allow schools to maintain sex segregated teams. However,

any analysis of sex discrimination in school sports must compare the number of athletic opportunities provided to males with that of females. Accordingly, schools are not precluded from instituting gender-conscious remedies or programs to increase female athletic opportunities. Furthermore, courts have allowed schools faced with limited budgets to reduce athletic opportunities for the overrepresented sex to comply with Title IX. Such flexibility has allowed Title IX to be a dynamic influence in promoting educational equity. The fact that opportunities for females have increased at a greater rate than those for males is not evidence that Title IX results in reverse discrimination but is, rather, an enduring example of the historical disparity in athletic opportunities provided to females.

■ PLAYING THE RACE CARD

We have suggested that "whiteness" was covertly smuggled in to the critics' narratives via the image of the threatened male walk-on. They also wove race overtly into their narratives by claiming that another of Title IX's "unintended consequences" is to reduce athletic (and thus educational) opportunities for underprivileged racial/ethnic minorities. Charles Neinas, for instance, praised college football and basketball for having benefited African Americans and implied that the strict enforcement of Title IX would reduce opportunities for African American males to attend college. Similarly, Jon Vegosen argued that the "unintended consequences of Title IX . . . severely reduce the opportunities for talented young American minorities" to play tennis. The critics' expression of concern that Title IX will harm African American males is the flip-side to a common criticism that the explosion of women's college sports has disproportionately benefited White, middle-class girls and women, while bringing more limited benefits to girls and women of color. For instance, a position paper by the Independent Women's Forum (2003) stated that

> what advocates of Title IX fail to mention is that African-Americans are losing their opportunity to participate in athletics, so that golf, equestrian, crew, and lacrosse can be added for women. But female lacrosse teams, for example, are over 87% White and less than 2% Black. Ultimately, Title IX ends up favoring upper-middle-class Caucasian women—and not helping African-American athletes who truly need financial aid to attend college. (p. 20)

A 2003 Women's Sports Foundation study contradicted these claims. It found that since the passage of Title IX, college women athletes of color have experienced huge increases in athletic opportunities and reaped scholarship assistance at rates greater than their proportion within the athlete population. For example, the report found that increases in participation opportunities

for female athletes generally resulted in a 955% increase in participation opportunities from 1971 to 2000 for female college athletes of color.[3]

Moreover, when it comes to male athletes of color, their representation in NCAA varsity sports compared to their presence in the student body is proportional. When schools have reduced men's sports, more than 85% of the male teams that schools have discontinued are in sports in which males of color are moderately or severely underrepresented (Women's Sports Foundation, 2003). In addition, "more than half of the total participation opportunities added for male athletes were in sports in which male athletes of color were overrepresented" (Women's Sports Foundation, 2003, p. 6). Regardless of this data, in the context of the commission hearings, critics of Title IX strategically deployed the image of the African American male athlete's apparently threatened interests; in effect, the race card was deployed as a wedge against gender equity.

■ MEN'S INTERESTS AND GENDER EQUITY IN SPORTS

This article has been concerned, broadly, with exploring how men's interests are articulated, in the context of challenges to their monopoly over power and resources in a historically male-dominated institution. In the case of public debates over Title IX, we have shown, men's collective interests in retaining a patriarchal dividend are not expressed through an overtly defensive backlash against women's sports. To do so would probably result in political suicide, due to the broad cultural shift in attitudes in favor of girls' and women's sports participation, and due to the mostly positive view that the public holds concerning Title IX. Thus, like a shorter basketball player who hopes to launch a shot against a taller opponent, the critics of Title IX begin with a good "head and shoulder fake" (praising women's sports, and stating support of the "original intent" of Title IX), before attempting to tunnel under the defender for a surprise scoop shot (claims that the unintended consequences of Title IX victimize certain men).

The critics' narratives do not mention the privileges still enjoyed by male athletes and coaches in central sports. Instead, the men in "nonrevenue" marginal sports, and/or individual men who are less athletically talented—especially the "walk-ons"—are the centerpiece of the critics' narrative, and stand in as proxy for men's threatened interests. The invocation of the image of the broken-hearted male wrestler or gymnast whose program has been eliminated is a powerful one, especially because some men's teams have been eliminated in recent years. Over the past 20 years, men's gymnastics and wrestling teams have declined in number. However, the critics of Title IX consistently fail to note that during this same period of time, the number of women's gymnastics and field hockey teams has also declined. Nor do they mention that during a period

in which Title IX was not enforced in school athletic programs because of court rulings limiting the reach of Title IX's antidiscrimination mandate to only those programs that receive directly federal funds, wrestling programs also declined.

On the plus side, whereas many college women's sports have grown in number, men's participation in college sports has increased in football, baseball, crew, lacrosse, squash, track, and volleyball. A 2001 study by the U.S. General Accounting office concluded that over the past decade, most colleges and universities added women's sports without cutting men's sports (Jacobson, 2001). Drawing from a wide range of empirical studies, the National Women's Law Center (2002a) concluded that

> the increase in spending for men's sports has not tapered off in recent years. From 1992–1997, men's athletic operating budgets have increased by 139%. The increase in expenditures for women's sports during this time period, 89%, pales in comparison. The problem is not that Title IX has deprived men of needed athletic resources, but that the lion's share of resources that male athletes receive are inequitably distributed among men's sports.... Of the $1.38 million average increase in expenditures for men's Division 1-A sports programs during the past five years, sixty-three percent of this increase, $872,000, went to football. This increase in Division 1-A football spending during the past five years exceeds the entire average operating budget for all women's sports in 1997 by over $200,000.

Despite these facts, the periodic high-profile cuts of men's programs tend to fuel perceptions that gender equity works against the overall interests of men. In fact, it is only possible to hold this view if one accepts the argument that all men are similarly situated in the "sports hierarchy" and refuses to include football in calculations of sex equity. Football's enormous financial drain on resources—a lion's share of scholarships; skyrocketing salaries for coaches; huge equipment, travel, and recruiting budgets—are often safely hidden behind the nickel-and-diming debates over which "nonrevenue" men's sports should be eliminated to ensure compliance with Title IX proportionality measures. The football lobby shields its own interests by backing the claims that marginal men's sports and male "walk-ons" are being victimized by Title IX.

Minor men's sports advocates participate in this debate by aligning themselves with the football (and often basketball) lobbies, despite the fact that such allegiance may seem to run counter to their apparent interests. Moreover, any claims that football expenditures should be taken seriously within the gender equity equation are likely to evoke exaggerated responses. For instance, a few years ago, the head of the American Football Coaches Association claimed that overzealous advocates of gender equity are "the enemy," who are "out to get" football. Don Sabo (1994) called this defensiveness by the most powerful sport figures "wounded giant sexism." Given their control of resources and their

massive budgets, football programs can hardly claim hardship with a straight face. Rather, they have sought support for the anti-equity cause from the more vulnerable "minor" men's sports. But evidence suggests that the vulnerabilities of men's marginal sports are not due so much to the "unintended consequences" of Title IX. Rather, the vulnerability of marginal men's sports is a routine institutional consequence of the invisible and mostly unquestioned policy of affording football (and often men's basketball) programs a privileged and untouchable status.

So we return to the question of why so many marginal boys and men—and their mostly male coaches—seem to identify with the interests of the football lobby. Why do more of the men in marginalized "nonrevenue sports"—the wrestlers, tennis players, swimmers, gymnasts, cross-country athletes—not identify their interests as consistent with those of women? Nina Eliasoph (1998) argued that people "discover their interests" in every day life, but the process through which they make this discovery "is never a pure rational calculation" (p. 251). This echoes Pease's (2002) argument, introduced earlier, that men's understanding of their interests cannot be explained simply by recognizing their social location. Instead, we need to consider how men formulate their interests through interaction, in institutional contexts (Martin, 2003). In the case of the Title IX hearings, the spokesmen for men's marginal sports have most likely formulated their interests within athletic department contexts, and these contexts are characterized by professional hierarchies headed by men from the central sports of football and basketball.

Football has played a key role in the U.S. gender order over the past half century. In this feminist era, football stands in as a symbolic reference point for a general articulation of "men's interests." As Connell (1995) has pointed out, hegemonic masculinity—the dominant formation of masculinity in any historical moment—is not necessarily something that the vast majority of men fully conform to. Rather, hegemonic masculinity is a collective practice that operates as the ideological center of the current strategy for the continued global subordination of women. So, though a rational assessment of the situation of, say, boys and men who run cross-country; who wrestle, swim, play tennis; or who participate in gymnastics might suggest that their interests run counter to those of big-time football programs, more often than not, these men in marginal sports tend to identify with, and act in complicity with, the dominant discourse of the football lobby. This discourse, as we have seen, tends to invoke a language of male victimization by the state, which is seen as unfairly representing women's interests. The language of bureaucratic victimization of individual men—especially as symbolized by the threatened "walk-on"—may find especially fertile ground among today's young White males, who face a world that has been destabilized by feminism, gay and lesbian liberation, the civil rights movement, and major shifts in the economy. The

resultant articulation of men's interests, then, does not take the form of a direct backlash against women's rights in sports or elsewhere. Instead, it invokes the values of individualism by telling stories of individual men who are victimized by liberal state policies that address group inequalities. And this discourse rests its case on an essentialist foundation: Individual men are just naturally more "interested" in sports than are women.

Given this common reality of marginalized boys and men developing a hegemonic conception of their interests within male-dominated institutions like sport, we wonder how it is possible that some men do develop counter-hegemonic ideas, which they then act on. Many of us are aware of stories of individual men who become overnight equity activists, when they find suddenly that their daughters have been denied access to sport or have been offered substandard playing fields or unqualified coaches. In these cases, individual men clearly see their own interests as intertwined with the interests of their family members. But can this shift in the articulation of men's interests occur at the group level?

At the San Diego conference, attendees were moved by the presentation of Joe Kelly, the executive director of a national advocacy organization called Dads and Daughters. Kelly spoke strongly of the need for fathers to support their daughters to play sports and to take an active role in public issues that effect girls' access to athletic opportunities. Kelly told the commission that gender equity in sports is not only good for girls—it is good for boys and men, too:

> Title IX opens doors for boys, and one of the most important ways it does is when our sons grow up to be fathers. The field of sports has long been fertile ground for strengthening fathers connected with sons, whether or not you play an organized sport, and Title IX now welcomes daughters onto that field . . . . Don't let future fathers and daughters and sons lose this precious field of play. Don't force fathers into the limited world where sons and daughters are valued differently just because of their gender. Fathers need a strongly enforced Title IX.

Kelly's speech—and the existence of his organization—suggests that it is possible for men to understand and articulate their own interests as consistent with those of girls and women, as opposed to the narrowly defined material interests of dominant men. But it takes more than men's experience in sport to allow them to make this kind of dis-identification with privileged men's interests. Boys and men come to understand and articulate their interests within institutional contexts. And it is their daily movement across and within various institutional contexts (e.g., families, workplaces, schools, sport), places that are characterized by very different, sometimes contradictory gender regimes that force boys and men to experience their interests in more complicated ways. In particular, experiences in families—especially as fully involved fathers—encourages some men to identify their own interests as consistent with those of their daughters. As a result, some fathers come to embrace the idea of "sharing the sandbox," due to an emotional grounding in empathy for the situation for their daughters—and by extension, more generally for girls and women.

But fathering is not the only experience that can foster empathy and respect for women. Sometimes, the experience of being subordinated or bullied can lead to a shift in a group's understanding and articulation of their interests. For instance, Eric Anderson (2003) gave a poignant example of how the high school cross-country boys whom he coached were bullied by football players and developed a consciousness that identified their interests as aligned with girls and other marginalized boys on their campus. A concrete outcome was the development of a "gay-straight alliance" that pushed to challenge privileges that high-status male athletes (and their coaches) took for granted. A positive, proactive change would be to create more nonsex- segregated activities for children (including coed sports). Integrated activities can give boys the opportunity to experience girls in ways that build respect for their abilities, and will foster the development of new beliefs about girls' "interest" in sports and possibly their rights to equal opportunities. These kinds of experiences can provide an emotional foundation for a dis-identification with the narrow interests of dominant men and a commitment to take action with girls, women, and other men who are interested in building a more equitable and just world.

NOTES

1. All subsequent quotations from the Title IX hearings are drawn from the transcripts from the San Diego hearing, which can be found on the U.S. Department of Education Web Site at http://www.ed.gov/about/bdscomm/list/athletics/thm.html.

2. Title IX, 20 U.S.C. § 1681 reads, "No person in the United States shall, on the basis of sex, be excluded from participation in, be denied the benefits of or be subjected to discrimination under any education program or activity receiving Federal financial assistance." The law applies to all aspects of an educational institution's programs or activities so long as any part of the institution receives federal financial assistance. See 20 U.S.C. § 1687.

3. This is not to say that school and university administrators should be complacent. Gender equity advocates always stress that sports opportunities and educational resources for athletes from underrepresented groups should be maintained and improved.

REFERENCES

Acosta, R. V., & Carpenter, L. J. (2002). *Women in intercollegiate sport: A longitudinal study—Twenty-five year update.* Brooklyn, NY: Brooklyn College.

Anderson, E. (2002). Openly gay athletes: Contesting hegemonic masculinity in a homophobic environment. *Gender & Society,* 16, 860–877.

Anderson, E. (2003). *Trailblazing: America's first openly gay high school coach.* Fountain Valley, CA: Identity Press.

Brod, H. (Ed.). (1987). *The making of masculinities: The new men's studies.* Boston: Allen & Unwin.

Carpenter, L. J. (2001). Letters home: My life with Title IX. In G. Cohen (Ed.), *Women in sport: Issues and controversies* (2nd ed., pp. 133–154). Oxon Hill, MD: AAHPERD Publications.

Carrigan, T., Connell, R., & Lee, J. (1985). Toward a new sociology of masculinity. *Theory & Society,* 14, 551–604.

Carrington, B. (1998). Sport, masculinity and Black cultural resistance. *Journal of Sport and Social Issues,* 22, 275–298.

Cole, C. L. (2001). Nike's America/America's Michael Jordan. In D. L. Andrews (Ed.), *Michael Jordan, Inc.* (pp. 65–103). Albany: State University of New York Press.

Connell, R. W. (1995). *Masculinities.* Cambridge, UK: Polity.

Connell, R. W. (2002). *Gender.* Cambridge, UK: Polity.

de Verona, D., & Foudy, J. (2002). Minority views on the Report of the Commission on Opportunity in Athletics. *Gender Issues,* 20, 31–56.

Eliasoph, N. (1998). *Avoiding politics: How Americans produce apathy in everyday life.* Cambridge: Cambridge University Press.

Eitzen, D. S. (1999). *Fair and foul: Beyond the myths and paradoxes of sport.* Lanham, MD: Rowman & Littlefield.

Goode, W. J. (1982). Why men resist. In B. Thorne & M. Yalom (Eds.), *Rethinking the family: Some feminist questions* (pp. 131–150). New York: Longman.

Independent Women's Forum. (2003). *Time out for fairness: Women for Title IX reform.* n.p.: Independent Women's Forum.

Jacobson, J. (2001). Among big sports programs, gender equity is No. 1 reason for cutting men's teams, report says. *Chronicle of Higher Education,* March 9.

Kimmel, M. S., & Ferber, A. L. (Eds.). (2003). *Privilege.* Boulder, CO: Westview.

Martin, P. Y. (2003). "Said and done" versus "saying and doing": Gendering practices, practicing gender at work. *Gender & Society,* 17, 342–366.

Messner, M. A. (1992). *Power at play: Sports and the problem of masculinity.* Boston: Beacon.

Messner, M. A. (2002). *Taking the field: Women, men, and sports.* Minneapolis: University of Minnesota Press.

National Women's Law Center. (2002a). *Equal opportunity for women in athletics: A promise yet to be fulfilled.* National Women's Law Center Report, August. Available from http://www.nwlc.org/detail.s.cfm?id=2735&section=athletics

National Women's Law Center. (2002b). *Quick facts on women and girls in athletics.* National Women's Law Center Report, May. Available from http://www.nwlc.org/detail.s.cfm?id=2735&section=athletics

NCAA. (2000). *Revenue and expenses of Division I and II intercollegiate athletics programs: Financial trends and relationships.* Indianapolis, IN: Author.

Pease, B. (2002). (Re)constructing men's interests. *Men and Masculinities, 5,* 165–177.

Sabo, D. F. (1994). Different stakes: Men's support for gender equity in sport. In M. A. Messner & D. F. Sabo (Eds.), *Sex, violence, and power in sports: Rethinking masculinity* (pp. 202–213). Freedom, CA: Crossing Press.

Sabo, D., & Grant, C.H.B. (2005). *Limitations of the Department of Education's online survey method for measuring athletic interest and ability on U.S.A. campuses.* Buffalo, NY: Center for Research on Physical Activity, Sport & Health, D'Youville College.

Sabo, D. F., & The Women's Sports Foundation. (1997). *The Women's Sports Foundation gender equity report card: A survey of athletic participation in American higher education.* East Meadow, NY: Women's Sports Foundation.

Sperber, M. (2000). *Beer and circus: How big-time sports is crippling undergraduate education.* New York: Henry Holt.

Women's Sports Foundation. (2003). *Women's Sports Foundation Report: Title IX and race in intercollegiate sport.* East Meadow, NY: Women's Sports Foundation.

Zimbalist, A. (1999). *Unpaid professionals: Commercialism and conflict in big-time college sports.* Princeton, NJ: Princeton University Press.

CHAPTER 28

Reconstructing Masculinity in the Locker Room

The Mentors in Violence Prevention Project

Jackson Katz

Thirty college football players sit apprehensively in a cramped locker room, waiting to hear what we will say to them about rape, battering, and sexual harassment. Some recount to their younger teammates unpleasant experiences they've had with "date rape" seminars. They're clearly not here voluntarily. Their coach, who attended an orientation session about our program with the entire athletic staff several weeks earlier, has required his players' attendance. He introduces the session and then leaves the room because, as an authority figure, his presence could inhibit the young men's honesty.

I tell the student-athletes that my co-presenter and I are here because the level of men's violence against women in our society is out of control. I tell them it is time we stopped avoiding or denying the problem, and instead started talking about violence against women as a men's issue. Calling this violence a "women's issue," I say, is in fact part of the problem. Why? It sends a signal to guys that it is not our concern: Why would a man concern himself with women's issues? And besides, I continue, don't issues that affect the women and girls that we care about affect us, too?

I ask the young men to raise their hands if they have a sister, girlfriend, mother, grandmother, or female friend. This usually prompts laughter, and some grumbling, but eventually they all put up their hands. The message is clear: it is simplistic and divisive to reduce gender-based violence to a "battle between the sexes" where one side wins at the expense of the other. Men's and women's lives are too interconnected. I remind them that during the course of this presentation, every woman we talk about who has been raped, or abused by her boyfriend, or assaulted by a man in some other way, is somebody's sister, somebody's mother, somebody's daughter. This violence

541

doesn't happen to some abstract category of "women." It happens to women we know and love.

Then I introduce my partner in the Mentors in Violence Prevention (MVP) Project, Byron Hurt, who is in his mid-twenties and a former football quarterback who went through college on a full athletic scholarship. Our different backgrounds—I am Jewish, White, of European descent, and Byron is African American—underscore the fact that sexual harassment of women is a pervasive societal problem that cuts across social distinctions. Byron asks the athletes to close their eyes. "Imagine," he says, "that the woman closest to you—your mother, your girlfriend, your sister—is being assaulted by a man. It's happening at a party, in a residence hall, on the street. Now imagine," he continues, "that there's a man in a position to stop the assault. But he doesn't. He just ignores the situation, or watches."

When the guys open their eyes, Byron asks them how they felt about the assault, and then about the man who stood idly by. They reply that they're upset by the assault, and disgusted that the male bystander didn't intervene. "He's a punk," they offer, a "coward," a "wimp." During the meeting, Byron and I often remind them of how they felt about men who were in a position to prevent or interrupt sexist abuse, but did nothing. This interactive exercise reinforces our point about the need for male leadership on these issues because, of course, no one wants to think of himself as a coward or a wimp.

The exercise also highlights the role of bystanders in reducing incidents of men's violence against women. MVP doesn't address male student-athletes as potential perpetrators; we address them as brothers, friends, teammates, popular students, and, very importantly, as potential mentors for younger kids. We help them see that they are in a position to provide the male leadership necessary to prevent a lot of pain and suffering.

I tell them that's the reason Northeastern University's Center for the Study of Sport in Society created the MVP Project: to inspire male leadership in reducing men's violence against women, an area where up to now there has been precious little male initiative.

■ MVP: CHANGING MASCULINE NORMS

Few violence prevention programs of any kind foreground discussions of masculinity. This is unfortunate, because whether the victim is female or male, males commit more than 90 percent of violent crimes (F.B.I., 1993). When many of these crimes are examined, we can see that attitudes about manhood are often among the critical variables leading to the assault. This is especially obvious in extreme cases of men's violence against women (e.g., rape, battering). Considering this reality, discussing issues of gender, as we do in MVP, should be regarded as a basic component of any violence prevention program.

For men who choose to confront these issues, sexual assault and abuse can involve intensely personal feelings and experiences. Some men are themselves survivors of such abuse. Others have women and girls close to them who have been assaulted. Due to the pervasiveness of these problems in college and high school populations, it is inevitable that some men who participate in anti-rape programs have themselves raped or otherwise abused women.

These factors, in part, explain why all-male workshops help many men "open up." Alan Berkowitz, counseling center director and assistant professor of psychology at Hobart and William Smith College, was an early advocate of focusing on cultural constructions of masculinity in anti-rape work. He has pioneered an all-male anti-rape workshop model. According to Berkowitz (1994), all-male workshops have a number of advantages:

> They allow men to speak openly without fear of judgment or criticism by women, make it less likely that men will be passive or quiet, and avoid the gender-based polarization that may reinforce men's rape-prone attitudes. In addition, a diversity of opinions and viewpoints can be expressed, reflecting men's variety of attitudes and beliefs about appropriate sexual relationships and allowing participants to deconstruct the monolithic image of masculinity the media have presented to them. (p. 36)

This is not to denigrate women's leadership or ability to teach men. However, properly trained men can connect with peers and younger males in a way that is not available even to the best female trainers and teachers. Of course, this is also true in the reverse: male educators, no matter how sensitive or skilled, cannot presume to relate to their female students' experience in the same way as could a woman.

Providing a structured opportunity for men to talk with each other about masculinity—particularly as it relates to men's violence against women—is perhaps the single most important characteristic of the Mentors in Violence Prevention Project. We hold no illusions that a few discussions, however meaningful, will by themselves change deep-seated behaviors. But the sessions accomplish the critical first step of breaking men's silence around these issues.

Many theorists have argued that the socialization of men in the United States encourages a constellation of attitudes and behaviors that predispose them to dominate and abuse women and other men in a variety of ways (Berkowitz, 1992). Because formation of a gendered and sexual identity is one of the important developmental tasks for young adults (Chickering, 1969), adolescent and late-adolescent males and females are particularly susceptible to culturally dominant sex-role assignments.

Severe antisocial aggression, including men's violence against women and gay-bashing, is primarily a learned behavior (Eron, 1987). Eron and others have argued that while genetic and hormonal factors undoubtedly play a role, the learning environment in which the child develops has been viewed as more important. According to Eron, continual and repeated images of violent masculinity in the broadcast media (including sports) reinforce sociocultural norms, which in turn provide standards and values children can use to evaluate the appropriateness of their own behavior and the behavior of others.

One aim of the MVP project is to contribute to a change in the sociocultural construction of masculinity that equates strength in men with dominance over women. Because male athletes, particularly those who are successful in what Mariah Burton Nelson (1994) refers to as the "manly sports" of football, basketball, and hockey, are important masculine role models for many young males, others' perceptions of these athletes' attitudes toward women help to shape the norms of male behavior.

As Berkowitz (1992) reports, recent research suggests that rape is best understood as an extreme on a continuum of sexually assaultive behaviors, and that sexual assault is engaged in by many men and may be somewhat normative. Many studies have examined the frequency of sexual assaults committed by college men. In one study by Rapaport and Burkhart (1984), only 39 percent of males sampled denied coercive involvement, while 28 percent admitted having used a coercive method at least once, and 15 percent admitted to forcing a woman to have intercourse at least once. Koss and others, using data from a large, nationally representative sample of college and university students, found that 25 percent of male respondents had committed some form of sexual assault since age fourteen (Koss, Gidycz, & Wisniewski, 1987, and Koss, 1988, cited in Berkowitz, 1994).

This research also suggests that sexual assault is best understood as occurring in a sociocultural environment that promotes rape-supportive attitudes and socializes men to adhere to them. A key premise of MVP is that the male student-athletes can help to delegitimize "rape-supportive" and "battering-supportive" attitudes by publicly repudiating the sexist, domination-oriented definitions of masculinity that reinforce them.

In more recent work, Berkowitz (1994) also states that there is evidence that many men are uncomfortable with other men's bragging about sexual exploits, dislike men's preoccupation with commenting on women's bodies, and misperceive the extent of other men's sexual activity. These men may belong to a "silent majority" who keep their discomfort to themselves rather than express disagreement or intervene in an environment which they perceive as unsympathetic.

Because of their privileged place within the social hierarchy, successful male athletes have an enhanced level of credibility with their male peers and with younger males. In particular, because these men are seen in many ways as exemplars of traditional masculine success, their attitudes about gender carry weight. With proper guidance and training, they are in a unique position to break the silence of the silent majority.

■ THE MVP PLAYBOOK

The MVP model involves holding three 90-minute sessions each year with each participating college team. A fourth session is scheduled for those student-athletes who wish to be trained further for work with younger students in middle and high schools. The sessions, about half of which are held in locker rooms, usually take place either before or after the team's season, at the rate of roughly once a month. College student-athletes are busy people; one of the biggest challenges we have faced is scheduling.

Before we are ready to schedule any sessions at a college, the MVP team gives a presentation to the entire coaching staff, male and female, at a meeting organized by the athletic director. At this meeting, we introduce the Project much in the same way we do with the student-athletes, and then take the coaches through a typical session, including a demonstration of how we use the MVP Playbook. At the end of the meeting, we begin to schedule individual sessions with various coaches. We usually try to work with the high-profile teams, including football, basketball, hockey, baseball, and lacrosse. Time and resource constraints on our part prevent us from working with every team at a college.

At the first session with the student-athletes, after we have introduced ourselves and conducted the preliminary exercises, we distribute our key teaching tool, the MVP Playbook, which is the focus of the first three sessions. This Playbook, which MVP staff created and designed, consists of a series of party and residence hall scenarios portraying thirteen actual and potential sexual assaults. The scenarios range from sexist comments overheard in the locker room to verbal threats of physical harm, date rape, and gang rape. We make it clear that we see all of these manifestations of sexism as interconnected. We also discuss the relationship between sexism and heterosexism. Playbook scenarios include the harassment of gays and lesbians.

Most of the scenarios focus on bystander behavior, while a few deal with the young men as potential perpetrators. The three MVP sessions facilitated by Byron and myself are highly interactive, as the student-athletes are asked to share experiences they've had in high school or college that are similar to the ones included in the Playbook.

The Playbook scenarios are designed to be as realistic as possible. For example, one called "Slapshot" sets this scene:

> At a party, a teammate pushes and then slaps his girlfriend. People are upset but don't do anything. He's not your close friend, but he is your teammate.

After having someone read the scenario, we have someone else read the "train of thought," which is a type of mental checklist that we suggest men in these situations go through: "If nobody else is stepping in, why should I? . . . It could get ugly. . . . He could turn on me. . . . Am I ready to get into a fight, if it comes to that? . . . What if he has a weapon? . . . " The train of thought is followed on each page by a list of practical and realistic options for intervention: "Nothing—it's none of my business. . . . Get a bunch of people to contain the boyfriend. . . . Talk to the woman and let her know you are willing to help. . . . Report the incident to the coach."

The train of thought concept is adapted from the Habits of Thought model developed by Ronald Slaby of the Harvard Graduate School of Education, who was also an early advisor to the MVP Project. Slaby's model (1994) provides a basis for understanding the behavior of victims, perpetrators, and bystanders. He suggests that behavior is the outcome of social experiences, including personal experiences with violence and those transmitted by the media, interacting with habits of thought (i.e., beliefs, impulsive and reflective tendencies, and problem-solving skills).

The great benefit of implementing this model in working with male student-athletes on the issue of men's violence against women is that rather than focus on the men as actual or potential perpetrators, we focus on them in their role as potential bystanders. This shift in emphasis greatly reduces the participants' defensiveness. It also allows us to emphasize one of our key points: that when men don't speak up or take action in the face of other men's abusive behavior toward women, that constitutes implicit consent of such behavior. When we discuss with the young men their options for intervention in the various scenarios, we are careful not to choose

for them the "best" option; that choice is for each person to make based on a unique set of circumstances. The options we provide are meant to serve as a guide. The list is not comprehensive, but the one option we always include—and strongly discourage—is to do nothing.

Many of the men with whom we work, and men in our society in general, have been socialized to be passive bystanders in the face of sexist abuse and violence. This conditioning is reflected in the oft-heard statement that a situation "between a man and his woman" is "none of my business." When we hear this sentiment articulated in our MVP sessions, we frequently refer back to the initial exercise in which we asked the men how they felt about a fictional man who did nothing when he was in a position to stop violence against a woman they cared about. We remind the men that they all agreed that the bystander was a punk and a coward. In other words, we've positioned the response "it's none of my business" in a new light. It's no longer an acceptable and reasonable attitude held by "one of the guys," but is instead seen as a poor excuse to hide feelings of fear or moral cowardice.

The Playbook and its various scenarios lead to highly interactive discussions about real-life situations that most men have experienced, or at least known about, in their families, circles of friends, teams, home or campus communities. Byron and I share stories from our own lives, and we encourage the young men to do the same. The discussions are typically animated and fast-moving. The discussions can also be intense—with one team, for example, we spent an entire 90-minute session discussing the "Slapshot" scenario.

We then use the personal anecdotes and accounts to raise a number of different issues: Why do men hit women? Does a man establish his manhood by physically controlling a woman? What, then, does it mean to be a man? The specifics vary, but the message advanced in these discussions is consistent: that men have a critical role to play in reducing men's violence against women. We emphasize, furthermore, that violence against women is located on a continuum. It includes not just overt acts of physical abuse, but encompasses the full range of behaviors including sexist comments and jokes, and sexual harassment. We make it clear that we need men to provide leadership to change behavior in all of these areas.

The fourth session is reserved for selected student-athletes who have attended the first three sessions and have expressed an interest in talking to middle and high school boys and girls about men's violence against women. The selection process itself is a key to the success of this stage of the program because we need to be sure that the "mentors" we're training are credible on these issues. Though no fool-proof method exists to ensure selection of effective mentors, we have developed a set of guidelines that the athletic department, in consultation with the counseling center, the health education department, and/or the women's center can use in evaluating potential candidates. We don't necessarily look for young men who have advanced levels of feminist consciousness. The most important requirement is that their reputation and record be consistent with their public commitment to work against sexism.

Our model for preparing college male student-athletes to become mentors for youth does not require extensive knowledge on the part of participants, and at every level we have tried to streamline our message so that we can involve as many student-athletes as possible. We assign several articles for them to read, including the introduction to *Stopping Rape: A Challenge for Men*, by Rus Funk; the introduction to *Power at Play: Sports and the Problem of Masculinity* by Michael Messner; "Men Changing Men" by Robert Allen and Paul Kivel; "What Men Need to Know About Date Rape" by Marybeth Roden; "Male Athletes and Sexual Assault" by Merrill Melnick; "On Becoming Anti-Rapist" by Haki Madhubuti; "Beyond BS and the Drumbeating: Staggering Through Life as a Man" by Frank Pittman; and "The Myth of the Sexual Athlete" by Don Sabo. We also discuss at some length the process of talking both to boys and girls about violence against women, including issues such as what to expect, how to answer difficult questions, and the difference between being a role model and being an expert in the eyes of the adolescents.

We send at least one staff member from the MVP Project out with these student-athletes to meet with both classes and teams of middle and high school students. Our current high school model

548   PART SIX: COLLEGE MEN AND SPORTS

consists of both male and female college student-athlete mentors and MVP staff meeting in single-sex groups with male and female teams or team captains. After these sessions, we schedule a mixed gender meeting and facilitate a joint discussion. The MVP staff then keeps in touch with the student-athlete mentors over the course of the year, and tries to involve them in speaking engagements as often as their schedules permit. We also put student-athlete mentors in touch with local battered women's and rape crisis shelters for possible participation in their youth outreach or other educational programs.

■ PRACTICAL ORIGINS OF THE MVP PROJECT

The Mentors in Violence Prevention Project has its roots in my previous area of study, the social construction of violent masculinity through sports and media imagery. My focus was in the area of sports sociology, specifically male sports culture. Both personal experience and my review of the sports literature confirmed my assumption that there was not a lot being done in the sports culture itself to address the issue of violence, particularly male violence against girls and women. In the past few years, numerous articles in the mainstream media have detailed the involvement of high school, college, and professional athletes in the battering, rape, and gang rape of women. However, few effective college or high school–based prevention programs have specifically

targeted the male athlete population. Athletes for Sexual Responsibility, started by Sandra Caron, is a pioneering and successful program at the University of Maine. Dr. Andrea Parrot, Nina Cummings, and Tim Marchell have developed a comprehensive curriculum to work with male athletes at Cornell University, and Tom Jackson has developed a successful program working with student-athletes at the University of Arkansas. But these and a few others were the rare exceptions. This was clearly an area ripe for educational innovation.

During the spring of 1992, I approached administrators at the Center for the Study of Sport in Society at Northeastern University in Boston, Massachusetts, and presented them with an idea for a new program. The Center already sponsored both a degree-completion program for former Division One college athletes and Project Teamwork, which placed a multiracial and gender-mixed team of former collegiate, Olympic, and professional athletes into middle and high schools to discuss violence prevention as it relates to issues of racial, ethnic, and gender sensitivity. Why not try a similar approach on the issue of men's violence against women? My recent experiences as an educator-activist suggested that this was a promising endeavor. In 1988 I had founded Real Men, an antisexist men's organization based in Boston. Since 1990 I had been travelling around the country on the high school and college lecture circuit talking about my activist work with Real Men, using my background as a former all-star football player and as the first man to earn a minor in Women's Studies at the University of Massachusetts at Amherst to reach men with the message that sexism was our issue. While these types of programs are typically mandatory at the high school or middle school level, programming committees at colleges across the country have historically found it difficult to attract men to programs about men's violence against women, or any programs that foreground a discussion of masculinity.

My proposal to create a program that would inspire other male athletes to provide leadership in the effort to prevent men's violence against women was greeted enthusiastically by executive director Richard Lapchick and associate director and head of programs Art Taylor at the Center for the Sport in Society at Northeastern. Over the next several months, the three of us worked together in developing grant proposals, which culminated in our being awarded a three-year grant from the United States Department of Education's Fund for the Improvement of Postsecondary Education (FIPSE). I was subsequently hired to run the MVP Project, which officially commenced in September 1993.

The FIPSE grant funded the creation of a campus-based program that would use male student-athletes as role models, peer leaders, and mentors to high school students on the issues of battering, rape, and sexual harassment. We also initiated plans to develop a complementary project that was aimed at college female student-athletes. Our commitment was to develop the program at four schools during the first year, two more in the second, and an additional three in the third year. Our goal was to create a model that was replicable and transferable to virtually every college and high school in the country.

We are still in the first couple of years of our project, so it is difficult to measure its potential for long-term success. One evaluative tool we have used is a pre- and post-test survey, which measures attitudes about intervening in incidents involving gender violence. Initial results indicate, not surprisingly, that the most powerful idea we have to counteract in order to be successful is the idea that matters between men and women, including violence, are "private." We also have received a great deal of written and verbal feedback from participating team members suggesting that the MVP sessions are popular with and considered useful by the student-athletes. Many of the men have told us that this was the first time they had ever talked about these issues with other men in a safe space.

We have also developed a three-day training of trainers model that allows MVP staff to travel to colleges and introduce selected male professional staff to the Project's goals and teaching methods. The local staff trainers are typically selected by the Dean of Students and Athletic Departments and may work in residence life, counseling, health education, athletics, or Greek affairs. We strongly recommend that they have some experience with gender issues and good group facilitation skills. Several meetings with teams are included in these training sessions, so the prospective trainers can observe actual MVP sessions.

We plan to develop a comprehensive package of materials, including Playbooks and training manuals and a training video, in order to facilitate the national dissemination of the MVP model. In the spring of 1995 we will pilot a version of the Playbook for female college student-athletes in which women consider a number of alternative bystander responses to scenarios of gender-related violence. In addition, we plan to produce Playbooks for high school boys and girls.

■ CONCLUSION: MOVING BEYOND SILENCE IN SPORTS CULTURE

A great deal of defensiveness has long existed in the sports culture about men's violence against women. Even before the O. J. Simpson case, for example, few people in sport wanted to talk about the rape or abuse of women by male athletes, and how the sexist subculture of the major male team sports (i.e., football, basketball, hockey, baseball) might contribute to the problem. However, recent media attention given to incidents of abusive behavior toward women by high-profile athletes has launched the issue into the national spotlight.

High school and college athletic departments have been particularly sensitive to this heightened focus on athletes' roles in violence against women. Until recently, many athletic administrators in the United States have been wary of

initiating workshops on violence against women, in part due to the belief that offering this type of program acted as a tacit acknowledgement of wrongdoing by athletes within their institution. Such an impression might hurt the public image and the recruiting potential of the athletic department or the school.

Institutional myopia was also responsible for the reluctance of the sports community to confront the issue of men's violence against women. Most high school and college athletic programs are concerned with winning games and building programs, not with "changing the world," as some characterize any form of social awareness education. Some athletic administrators and coaches can see the value in providing alcohol and substance abuse education to their student-athletes; the need for this is self-evident and essentially non-controversial. But the mention of male athletes and rape in the same sentence is often met with stony silence by defensive athletic staffs, if not with angry denials.

A widespread perception exists in our society that male athletes, especially football, basketball, hockey, and baseball players, are disproportionately responsible for sexually assaulting women. This perception has been fed actively since the mid-1980s by a series of newspaper and magazine stories and a handful of surveys that purport to show a link between male team sports and the abuse of women. A recent study of ten Division One schools, completed by researchers at the University of Massachusetts at Amherst and Northeastern University, found that male student-athletes were six times as likely as their non-athlete peers to be reported for sexual assault to campus judicial affairs (Crossett, Benedict, & McDonald, 1995). An ever-growing list of publicized incidents of rape and abuse involving high school, collegiate, and professional athletes has also emerged. There have been enough of these incidents to confirm in the minds of many what the formal statistics have been unable to determine conclusively: that the male team sports culture somehow encourages this sort of behavior.

The MVP Project does not deal directly with whether or not dynamics of the male team sport culture promote sexism and the abuse of women, although we do talk about the public perception of athletes as disproportionately abusive. We focus instead on the social status of male student-athletes and the ways their leadership can make a critical difference in reducing all men's violence toward women. This approach avoids the accusatory rhetoric that often accompanies discussions about whether athletes are more or equally likely as other men to assault women. This strategy is partially born of necessity: if you want to work on violence prevention successfully with athletic departments and student-athletes, it makes sense not to alienate and offend them.

Finally, it is not critical to the success of our project to determine whether or not athletes assault women more often than do non-athletes. While one of our goals is to educate athletes in order to prevent them from committing violence, the overarching objective of our project is to reduce men's violence against women—particularly on college and high school campuses—by inspiring male student-athletes to use their stature among their male peers in the larger student body to promote healthier attitudes and behavior towards women. The rationale is straightforward. If we can convince popular athletes and other exemplars of traditional "masculine" success to model nonsexist behavior, we believe they can contribute to a dramatic shift in male behavior toward women. At the very least, they will help to catalyze a growing intolerance by all men for the abuse of women.

REFERENCES

Allen, R., & Kivel, P. (1994, September-October). Men changing men. *Ms.*, pp. 50–53.

Berkowitz, A. (1992). College men as perpetrators of acquaintance rape and sexual assault: A review of recent research. *Journal of American College Health, 40,* 175–181.

Berkowitz, A. (1994). A model acquaintance rape prevention program for men. *New Directions for Student Services, 65,* 35–42.

Chickering, A. (1969). *Education and identity.* San Francisco: Jossey-Bass.

Crosset, T., Benedict, J., & McDonald, M. (1995). Male student athletes reported for sexual assault: A survey of campus police departments and judicial affairs offices. *Journal of Sports and Social Issues.*

Eron, L. (1987). The development of aggressive behavior from the perspective of a developing behaviorism. *American Psychologist, 5,* 435–442.

Federal Bureau of Investigation. (1993). *Uniform crime reports.* Washington, DC: Author.

Funk, R. E. (1993). *Stopping rape: A challenge for men.* Philadelphia: New Society.

Gilbert, R. (1988). The dynamics of inaction: Psychological factors inhibiting arms control activism. *American Psychologist, 10,* 755–764.

Madhubuti, H. (1993). On becoming anti-rapist. In E. Buchwald, P. R. Fletcher, & M. Roth (Eds.), *Transforming a rape culture.* Minneapolis: Milkweed Editions.

Melnick, M. (1992). Male athletes and sexual assault. *Journal of Physical Education, Recreation, and Dance, 63*(5), 32–35.

Messner, M. (1992). *Power at play: Sports and the problem of masculinity.* Boston: Beacon Press.

Nelson, M. B. (1994). *The stronger women get, the more men love football.* New York: Harcourt Brace.

Rapaport, K., & Burkhart, B. (1984). Personality and attitudinal characteristics of sexually coercive college males. *Journal of Abnormal Psychology, 93,* 216–221.

Roden, M. (1990). *What men need to know about date rape.* Santa Monica, CA: Rape Treatment Center.

Pittman, F. (1992, January–February). Beyond BS and the drumbeating: Staggering through life as a man. *Psychology Today,* pp. 78–84.

Sabo, D. (1989). The myth of the sexual athlete. *Changing Men, 1*(20), 38–39.

Slaby, R. (1994). Development of psychological mediators of violence in urban youth. In J. McCord (Ed.), *Growing up violent: Contributions of inner-city life.* New York: Oxford University Press.

College Men and Sports

Implications for Educational Practice

The key issues and findings that are presented in the section raise several practical implications that warrant the consideration of college educators. One of the most compelling implications is the extent to which sports can be used to encourage healthy lifestyles among men, engage them in educationally purposeful activities, and help men develop healthy relationships with each other. For example, campus recreation programs that engage men in activities that require collaboration, planning, communication, and leadership will allow them to gain practical competencies that will serve them well throughout their professional lives. This effort also entails being purposeful in providing opportunities for men with disabilities to participate in recreational sports programs. Given Taub and her colleagues' findings, programs that facilitate interaction between men with disabilities and those who do not have physical disabilities will likely yield favorable outcomes for both groups of students. Educators should also consider the extent to which campus recreation programs can be used to promote responsible decision making around mental and physical health, nutrition, sex, alcohol, and other health-related issues that challenge men on college campuses. In addition, since men are often more willing to visit the campus recreation center than they are the student health or counseling center, staff from these departments should routinely visit the campus recreation center to reach out to men and share important health information with them.

We realize that coaches are hired to field competitive teams and are evaluated based on this expectation. However, whether they realize it or not, coaches are perhaps most responsible for facilitating their student-athletes' academic success. It is coaches who have the final say on whether or not student-athletes will receive playing time; thus, it is coaches to whom student-athletes believe they are most accountable. If coaches unequivocally communicated to student-athletes

553

that academic excellence is required for playing time, doing well in their courses will be a top priority for student-athletes. We believe that achieving excellence in athletics and academics are not mutually exclusive goals. In fact, a host of practical competences that are necessary for success in sports transfer seamlessly to success in academics, notably discipline, time management, and collaboration. Coaches who help students recognize these competences and see how they are applicable in their academic pursuits will serve their student-athletes well. Along the same lines, coaches should also encourage student-athletes to pursue internships and get involved in student programs and services during the off season to ensure that students are getting a well-rounded educational experience. Understandably, some coaches may be concerned about the time commitment required to participate in these activities. Therefore, it may be necessary for student affairs educators to reach out to coaches and help them recognize how students' involvement in educationally purposeful activities can lead to a host of desirable outcomes.

Like fraternity men, male student-athletes also account for a disproportionate share of misbehavior on college campuses. Sexual assault (Crossett, 2000), binge drinking (Doumas, Turrisi, Coll, & Haralson, 2007; Hill, Burch-Ragan, & Yates, 2001; Trauma Foundation, 1998), and homophobia (Messner & Sabo, 1990) have all been linked by scholars to the heterosexist masculine culture that typifies college athletics. Proactive programming around these issues must be a priority for coaches, athletics administrators, and student affairs educators. The Mentors in Violence Prevention program presented in Chapter 28 of this volume may be an effective model for some campuses. Institutions that require student-athletes to participate in CHAMPS/Life Skills programs could also incorporate gender issues into the curriculum and student learning outcomes of this program. Faculty and campus administrators with expertise in addressing these issues should be consulted or invited as collaborators in these efforts. To the extent possible, team captains should be trained to assume some leadership and responsibility on these issues given the influence they often have in shaping team culture.

Lastly, Krystal K. Beamon's discussion regarding exploitation in college sports raises serious questions regarding the extent to which male student-athletes, particularly Black men who participate in revenue sports, experience the gains and outcomes associated with going to college. Although no one strategy will offset the high-stakes nature of college sports that lead to exploitation, ongoing efforts to support the success of these students is imperative. Institutional leaders must hold coaches and athletics administrators more accountable for ensuring the success of all student-athletes, including men who participate in revenue sports. In addition, senior student affairs administrators should serve on coach hiring and athletics oversight committees to ensure that the decisions that are made by these bodies are in the best interest of students.

REFERENCES

Crosset, T. (2000). Athletic affiliation and violence against women: Toward a structural prevention project. In J. McKay, M. A. Messner, & D. F. Sabo (Eds.), *Masculinities, gender relations and sport* (pp. 147–161). Thousand Oaks, CA: Sage.

Doumas, D. M., Turrisi, R., Coll, K. M., & Haralson, K. (2007). High-risk drinking in college athletes and nonathletes across the academic year. *Journal of College Counseling, 10,* 163–174.

Hill, K., Burch-Ragan, M., & Yates, D. Y. (2001). Current and future issues and trends facing student-athletes and athletic programs. *New Directions for Student Services, 93,* 65–80.

Messner, M. A., & Sabo, D. F. (Eds.). (1990). *Sport, men, and the gender order: Critical feminist perspectives.* Champaign, IL: Human Kinetics.

Trauma Foundation. (1998). *Preventing alcohol-related injury and violence: Resources for action.* San Francisco: Trauma Foundation.

Name Index

Subject Index

Credits

Chapter 2: Kimmel, M. S. (1994). Masculinity as homophobia: Fear, shame, and silence in the construction of gender identity. In H. Brod, & M. Kaufman (Eds.), *Theorizing masculinities* (pp. 119–141). Newbury Park, CA: Sage. Copyright © 1994. Reprinted by permission of the publisher, Sage Publications, Inc., via The Copyright Clearance Center.

Chapter 3: O'Neil, J. M., Helms, B. J., Gable, R. K., David, L., & Wrightsman, L. S. (1986). Gender-role conflict scale: College men's fear of femininity. *Sex Roles*, *14*(5/6), 335–350. Copyright © 1986. Reprinted with kind permission from Springer Science+Business Media.

Chapter 4: Davis, T. L. (2002). Voices of gender role conflict: The social construction of college men's identity. *Journal of College Student Development*, *43*, 508–521. Copyright © 2002. Reprinted by permission of the publisher, Johns Hopkins University Press., via The Copyright Clearance Center.

Chapter 5: Harris III, F., & Harper, S. R. (2008). Masculinities go to community college: Understanding male identity socialization and gender role conflict. In J. Lester (Ed.), *Gendered perspectives on community colleges*. New Directions for Community Colleges, No. 142 (pp. 25–35). San Francisco: Jossey-Bass.

Chapter 6: Mahalik, J. R., Good, G. E., & Englar-Carlson, M. (2003). Masculinity scripts, presenting concerns, and help seeking: Implications for practice and training. *Professional Psychology: Research and Practice*, *34*(2), 123–131. Copyright © 2003 by the American Psychological Association. Reproduced with permission.